W. H. AUDEN
A Commentary

W. H. AUDEN
A Commentary

JOHN FULLER

Princeton University Press
Princeton, New Jersey

Published in the United States of America in 1998
by Princeton University Press,
41 William Street, Princeton, New Jersey 08540

First published in Great Britain in 1998
by Faber and Faber Ltd
3 Queen Square London WCIN 3AU

Photoset by Parker Typesetting Service, Leicester
Printed in England by Clays Ltd, St Ives plc

ISBN 0–691–00419–6

http://pup.princeton.edu

2 4 6 8 10 9 7 5 3 1

Contents

Foreword

1

Auden is a poet who after about 1930 began in an almost programmatic way to turn his back on the obscurity and formal freedom and experimentation of modernism. Indeed, he is nowadays sometimes seen as our first postmodernist poet. This does not mean, however, that he did not continue to be a difficult poet. Poetry is an art which has always exploited and will continue to exploit difficulty and verbal deviousness, and every interested reader is in a sense his or her own commentator who will now and again need a little help.

I published a commissioned *Reader's Guide* to Auden in 1970, at a time when exploration of circumstantial background and detailed attention to explication and allusions had scarcely begun in earnest. The poet was alive, there was very little manuscript material available, and of course I felt it proper to pass over whatever was then rumoured about his domestic life and to respect his own often savagely limited view of the canon of his works. There was, after all, enough work to be done in puzzling over details of interpretation and in tracing for the first time the sources of some of his most celebrated poems. Critics knew about the influence of Anglo-Saxon poetry on the early work, for example, or about his psychosomatic theory of illness, but specific references to lines in Old English poems or to particular ideas and phrases in the work of Groddeck, Lawrence or Rivers had not been made. The extent of his allegorising (for example, in 'The Secret Agent' or in *The Ascent of F6*) was not then realised, and there were many crucial identifications to be made (for example, of Auden's Vision of Agape as expounded in 1964 with the poem 'A Summer Night'). My *Reader's Guide* was written quite quickly, in about eighteen months, with an excited and guilty sense that of the discoveries to be made (discoveries that must be made!) I had time only for a hasty scavenging raid.

The *Reader's Guide* was found to be useful. I had aimed to provide the puzzled reader of Auden with information that would help him or her to read the works with greater understanding. The immense response that I had from the book (not least from those who wanted to enter into debate with me) proved that there had been a need for something systematic of this kind. I had also felt that I was championing a neglected master (in those days still scorned by Leavisites, regretted by English intellectuals as a Lost Leader, and naturally absent from syllabuses).

Now, of course, things are entirely different. The vast range of his unpublished work has not only loomed into view, but has been pretty well mapped and climbed. Papers accumulate in the libraries. Details of his private life are almost too well-known. Scholars have already staked out their Auden specialisms. There is a Society, with its Newsletter. And the poet has in Edward Mendelson one of the most devoted and diligent of executors, editors, bibliographers and critics (surely unique in his multiple role).

Mendelson wrote to me as soon as my *Reader's Guide* appeared, with a list of corrections and suggestions. This was early in his own career, naturally, but welcome evidence of the meticulousness and generosity that has been unfailing for over a quarter of a century. We have exchanged information (and even pupils) ever since. From his labours, and from those of other critics over the ensuing decade, it became clear that my book would soon need updating. At a time when it might have been reprinted I had no wish to see its errors perpetuated, and therefore embarked on its revision.

This *Commentary* is, in a sense, that revision. It is at least twice as long, and contains an abundance of new facts (both new in relation to the earlier volume, and absolutely new). Auden has been revealed as a writer prolific far beyond even the extensive public canon of his lifetime, and I have attempted to say something useful about every original poem, play or libretto of his written in English that has so far reached print (with the exception of most of the juvenilia written before 1927, which are extensively annotated by Katherine Bucknell in her exemplary edition). Sometimes I have found that what I originally wrote might stand. In most cases, however, there are fresh things to be said.

Despite the greater time at my disposal, I still have the sense of having only scraped the surface. And there is much that I have had to leave out. Scholars working in smaller areas of Auden are at this moment turning up material which it will never be possible to incorporate within a volume of this sort (which to be useful must be no larger than it is). There is even more that I may never discover. The responsibility behind the terms I have set myself cannot always be carried through with conviction: there are limits to one man's understanding of such a polymath as Auden.

2

This book is not for reading in the normal way. It is a work of reference. For every separate work by Auden I encapsulate the publishing history, paraphrase difficult passages, explain allusions, point out interesting variants (including material abandoned in drafts), identify sources and influences, look at the verse form and offer critical interpretation. I don't always do all of these things. In particular, I am reticent about the last of them, for reasons of space. I do write up some of the more significant poems with a more leisurely evaluative scope, but it truly intends to be a book that you look things up in, rather than one you read, and for paragraphs at a time it will have the appearance of footnotes.

I have reverted to an arrangement based on the individual collections that Auden himself originally published, with sections on 'uncollected' work interposed. These sections may, of course, contain work subsequently included in the later comprehensive collections, but they contain much fugitive work. I believe that this arrangement is one that the future definitive edition of his poems might well follow, and is one that on the whole gives a more accurate historical sense of his oeuvre.

Poems are treated under their first line. Since Auden's first volumes abandoned titles in favour of numbers, and since he was also for a time in the habit of changing titles, I felt that this was the most reliable procedure. All variant titles are given beneath, with other publishing information, and there is a comprehensive index of titles and first lines which readers consulting the *Commentary* will almost certainly need to use in the first instance, although access to the volume may also be usefully made on occasion through the comprehensive general index.

Acknowledgements

I have tried not to burden the reader with too many references to sources, nor to significant criticism of the work (I have not felt it appropriate to include a bibliography of critical works). Unascribed information will, I trust, be uncontroversial, and will derive either from general detective-work or from papers in the Berg Collection at the New York Public Library. Other sources may be traced through the abbreviations explained below.

In addition to the public labours of Auden scholars I am grateful to many individuals who have supplied me with information, including Richard Davenport-Hines, Tom Deveson, Laurence Heyworth, Bet Inglis, Christopher Lush, David Luke, Bernard O'Donoghue, Heather O'Donoghue, Sally Orrell, Jayanta Padmanabha, Hermann Peschmann, Eleni Ponirakis, Stephen Spender, Saul Touster and Mark Wormald. I owe a great debt to the friendly support and resourceful knowledge of Katherine Bucknell and Nicholas Jenkins. Without the co-operation of Edward Mendelson in giving me access to materials in his possession and permission to make use of discoveries of his own, this book would be a much poorer thing. Indeed, the study itself of Auden cannot be imagined without his benign and stimulating presence.

I am grateful to him also for his permission and that of Auden's Estate to quote from the poet's works, published and unpublished. I am also grateful to Auden's publishers (Faber and Faber; Random House; Princeton University Press) to quote from their Auden editions, and to the libraries listed below in the Abbreviations section to quote from papers in their possession. The unfailing care and courtesy of the curators of these special collections makes a visit a double pleasure.

Abbreviations

This is not a complete list of works referred to in a relatively shortened form, particularly not in the case of works by Auden: many abbreviations in the text are local to the section in which they occur, and the full reference will be found a few pages earlier. Location of MS Notebooks is similarly given in particular sections. Where none is given, the location is the Berg Collection. The 1928–?30 notebook is BL Add MS 52430. Most letters referred to are either in the possession of their recipients (or their heirs) or in the Berg Collection. The letters to Cyril Connolly are in the University of Tulsa Library; the letters to A. E. and E. R. Dodds in the Bodleian Library; the letters to Geoffrey Gorer in the University of Sussex Library; the letters to John Layard in the Library of the University of California at San Diego; the letters to William McElwee in the British Library; the letters to Ursula Niebuhr in the Library of Congress; the letters to Theodore Spencer in the Harvard University Library; the letters to Albert and Angelyn Stevens at the University of Michigan Library.

A Tribute	*W. H. Auden: A Tribute*, ed. Stephen Spender (1975)
Age	*The Age of Anxiety*
AH	*About the House*
AT	*Another Time*
Ansen	Notebooks of Alan Ansen (Berg)
As I Walked Out One Evening	W. H. Auden, *As I Walked Out One Evening: Songs, ballads, lullabies, limericks and other light verse*, ed. Edward Mendelson (1995)
Auden Newsletter	*The W. H. Auden Society Newsletter*
Auden Studies	1: 'The Map of All my Youth': Early Works, friends and influences (1990); 2: 'The Language of Learning and the Language of Love': Uncollected writings; new interpretations (1994); 3: 'In Solitude, for Company': W. H. Auden after 1940 (1995).

	All edited by Katherine Bucknell and Nicholas Jenkins.
BL	Department of MSS, British Library, London
Beach	Joseph Warren Beach, *The Making of the Auden Canon* (1957)
Berg	The Henry W. and Albert A. Berg Collection, New York Public Library (Astor, Lenox and Tilden Foundations)
Bibliography	B. C. Bloomfield and Edward Mendelson, *W. H. Auden: A bibliography 1924–1969*, 2nd edn (1972)
Blair	John G. Blair, *The Poetic Art of W. H. Auden* (1965)
Bodleian	Department of Western MSS, Bodleian Library, Oxford
Britten Letters	Donald Mitchell and Philip Reed, eds, *Letters from a Life: The selected letters and diaries of Benjamin Britten 1913–1976*, 2 vols (1991)
Buffalo	Lockwood Memorial Library, SUNY at Buffalo
Callan	Edward Callan, *Auden: A carnival of intellect* (1983)
Carpenter	Humphrey Carpenter, *W. H. Auden: A biography* (1981)
CP	*Collected Poems*, ed. Edward Mendelson, 2nd edn (1991)
CP45	*The Collected Poetry of W. H. Auden* (1945)
CSP50	*Collected Shorter Poems 1930–1944* (1950)
CSP66	*Collected Shorter Poems 1927–1957* (1966)
Cunningham	V. D. Cunningham, *British Writers of the Thirties* (1988)
CWW	*City Without Walls*
Davenport-Hines	Richard Davenport-Hines, *Auden* (1995)
DM	*The Double Man*
Dog	*The Dog Beneath the Skin*
EA	*The English Auden: Poems, essays and dramatic writings*, ed. Edward Mendelson (1977)
EG	*Epistle to a Godson*

Farnan	Dorothy J. Farnan, *Auden in Love* (1984)
F6	*The Ascent of F6*
FTB	*For the Time Being*
Gorer	Geoffrey Gorer papers at the University of Sussex Library
HC	*Homage to Clio*
'In the year of my youth . . .'	Lucy S. McDiarmid, 'W. H. Auden's "In the year of my youth . . ."', RES n.s. xxix.115 (August 1978)
Juvenilia	*Juvenilia: Poems 1922–28*, ed. Katherine Bucknell (1994)
JW	*Journey to a War*
LI	*Letters from Iceland*
Libretti	*Libretti and Other Dramatic Writings 1939– 1973*, ed. Edward Mendelson (1993)
Lions and Shadows	Christopher Isherwood, *Lions and Shadows: An education in the twenties* (1938)
LS	*Look, Stranger!*
Mendelson	Edward Mendelson, *Early Auden* (1983)
Miller	Charles Miller, *Auden: An American Friendship* (1989)
N	*Nones*
NYL	'New Year Letter'
OED	*The Oxford English Dictionary*
Paid	*Paid on Both Sides*
P28	*Poems* (1928)
P30	*Poems* (1930)
P33	*Poems* (1930, 2nd edn)
Plays	*Plays and Other Dramatic Writings 1928–1938*, ed. Edward Mendelson (1989)
Poets at Work	*Poets at Work: The Paris Review interviews* (1988)
Prose	*Prose and Travel Books in Prose and Verse* (Volume I, 1926–1938), ed. Edward Mendelson (1996)
RES	*The Review of English Studies*
SA	*The Shield of Achilles*
SP58	*Selected Poems* (1958)
SP68	*Selected Poems* (1968)

Spears   Monroe K. Spears, *The Poetry of W. H. Auden:*
                                The disenchanted island (1963)
Texas   The Harry Ransom Humanities Research
                                Centre, University of Texas at Austin
TFG   *Thank You, Fog*
The Prolific and the Devourer W. H. Auden, *The Prolific and the Devourer*, in
                                Antaeus, 41, (Summer, 1981)
Wichita   Rare Books and MSS Collection, University
                                Library, Wichita State University, Kansas

W. H. AUDEN
A Commentary

Poems (1928)

Auden's first collection was mostly hand printed by Stephen Spender during the Long Vacation of 1928 (details in *Bibliography*, pp. 2–3). Auden himself suggested the venture. The difficulties encountered in printing the volume may have led to the omission of several poems in Auden's selection. The volume is dedicated to Christopher Isherwood.

The sprinkler on the lawn

(a) 'The sprinkler on the lawn', ?May 1927; (b) 'Bones wrenched, weak whimper, lids wrinkled, first dazzle known', June 1927; P30, p. 53; (c) 'We saw in Spring', ?August 1926; (d) 'This peace can last no longer than the storm', ?1925; (e) '"Buzzards" I heard you say', ?October 1924; (f) 'Consider if you will how lovers stand', May 1927; 'Extract (for J.B.A.)', *Oxford Poetry*, 1927. The dedicatee was John Bicknell Auden, the poet's brother; (g) 'Amoeba in the running water', ?May 1927; (h) 'Upon the ridge the mill-sails glow', ?May 1927; P28, p. 3; EA, p. 437; *Juvenilia*, p. 205.

An early draft of this designedly heterogeneous sequence was entitled 'The Megalopsych', and was sent to Isherwood in about May 1927, with some comments. A version also exists in a notebook given to Alan Ansen, and now in the Berg Collection. 'The Megalopsych' is prefixed by some lines from Morgenstern's 'Kronprätendenten' in the *Galgenlieder*: 'Im Winkel König Fahrenheit | hat still sein Mus gegessen. | "Ach Gott, sie war doch schön, die Zeit | die man nach mir gemessen!"' This verse was also quoted by Auden in his and Day-Lewis's Preface to *Oxford Poetry 1927*, in a context hostile to 'that acedia and unabashed glorification of the subjective so prominent in the world since the Reformation' (Preface, p. v). As epigraph to 'The Megalopsych', it suggests a nostalgic regret for a lost epoch, perhaps that of childhood before the 'storm' of sexuality. An English version surfaces at the end of the unpublished poem 'There is a danger' (August 1930) and in the Commentary to 'In Time of War' (1939): 'the mirage | Of long dead grandeurs whence the interest has absconded, | As Fahrenheit in an odd corner of great Celsius' kingdom | Might mumble of the summers measured once by him' (lines 186–9).

The nine parts of 'The Megalopsych' are as follows: I 'The sprinkler on the lawn' (with a second stanza, in which on a balcony 'men | Behind cigars anatomize women.' Auden decided to scrap this stanza: 'All I want really is a pianissimo roll on a buggers gong' he wrote to Isherwood); II '"The Megalopsych," says Aristotle'. This part, in a tone of hectic disgust, elaborates Aristotle's definition of the magnanimous man in the *Nichomachean Ethics*, 4.iii.15, as someone who is not a coward, and it confesses, in a style somewhat like an English translation of Catullus ('puella defututa' is from Carmen xli), that the homosexual's confidence is assisted by alcohol and cruising – 'the tirade is about a joy-boy' as he puts it to Isherwood. 'The Reverend Bythesea Bubb' may be a memory of the foolish Bubb whose clothes are stolen at Brighton in 'The One Horse Chay', a poem which Auden included in the *Oxford Book of Light Verse*, p. 405; III '"Buzzards" I heard you say'; IV 'Squatting Euclid drew in sand' (the fastidious-philosopher tone once again, compounded of Huxley and Eliot); V 'The oboe notes' (containing the 'bulb pillow' lines of (c), in an Edward Thomasish setting); VI 'Consider if you will how lovers stand'; VII 'Amoeba in the running water'. This part contains an additional, deprecatory line: 'Dirty thoughts in a green wood', echoing Marvell. About this rather gnomic and perhaps Blakean poem, Auden remarked to Isherwood: 'Does not mean anything but seemed emotive to me and as you like it I suppose communication is adequate. The connection in my mind between "The sword above the valley" and the coming of the Warriors in the Archaic civilisation, with the destruction (worm) of the Miners (penny) need not worry you'; VIII 'Upon the ridge the mill-sails glow'; IX 'I wake with a dry mouth' (a brief and dismissive epilogue).

The sequence as printed in *Poems* could not obviously be read as being about Aristotle's ethical hero (μεγᾰλόψῦχοσ, the great-souled man, with his fully justifiable claim to distinction) unless the note of erotic strain and search for equilibrium suggests a dry-run for the enviable poise of the Truly Strong Man. This poise could only be ironically assumed, as is clear from Auden's letter to William McElwee of summer 1927, referring to his visit with Day-Lewis to Appletreewick: 'Cecil and I had a megalopsych journey culminating in my asking the station master at Skipton "Do you know the geography of the station?"' The megalopsych is contrasted with Christ in *The Dyer's Hand*, p. 135: 'For Christ is not a model to be imitated, like Hector, or Aristotle's megalopsych, but the Way to be followed. If a man thinks that the megalopsych is a desirable model, all he has to do is to read up how the megalopsych behaves and imitate him, e.g., he will be careful, when walking, not to swing his arms.' The megalopsych in a sense defines the Greek tragic hero, since hubris is particularly what the megalopsych cannot be accused of.

The 1928 sequence celebrates calm after intoxication, a calm which is nonetheless illusory, for these emotions will recur: 'This peace can last no longer than the storm | Which started it' (d) and 'if, though we | Have ligatured the ends of a farewell, | Sporadic heartburn show in evidence | Of love uneconomically slain' (f). The sequence begins by bidding farewell to the homoerotic romanticism of school, and there are suggestions of a particular relationship in (c) and (e), the affair's occasions and excuses symbolised (curiously) by a buzzard. The last line of (e) owes something to Yeats's 'The Folly of Being Comforted'. From the moment of birth, the mind and body are divorced (b), and thus love cannot be entered upon freely, though the sexual pressures are cyclical in (g) and (h) with Chaucer's Chanticleer, symbol of propagation, questioning the value of complete knowledge in the cycle of planetary movement. Auden sounds disingenuous in his historical explanation of (g) with its ideas perhaps drawn from W. J. Perry's *The Growth of Civilization* (1924). Surely the contextual point is more forcibly that the phallic life (Worm) has only this rather extraneous power over the social life (Penny)? The result, as one grows older, is the sentimentalism or shrivelled pedantry of (f): 'An evening like a coloured photograph, | A music stultified across the water'. Notions of duty obstruct the loved one's yielding: 'Ought passes through points fair plotted, and you conform, | Seen yes or no. Too just for weeping argument.' (b) – a wonderful conclusion to a hopelessly clotted unrhymed sonnet in sprung-rhythm, imitating Hopkins. Auden cancelled some lines, including the Hopkinsian image of 'flesh dough', from an earlier draft. For 'Eyes, unwashed jewels', cf. *King Lear*, 1.i.271–7 ('The jewels of our father, with washed eyes | Cordelia leaves you': the allusion perhaps suggests a younger sibling's unenlightened exile from misjudging parents). In his unpublished D.Phil. thesis on Day-Lewis, David Pascoe argues that 'Day' is an allusion to the poet, the poem being about sexual frustration during the Appletreewick holiday. Auden was once heard to remark: 'Hopkins ought to be kept on a special shelf like a dirty book, and only allowed to readers who won't be ruined by him' (John Lehmann, *The Whispering Gallery*, 1953, p. 329). Soon after the brilliant parody Ode II in *The Orators*, Auden managed to expunge unadulterated Hopkins from his work (there are some exceptions, such as the opening of 'Me, March, you do with your movements master and rock', *New Country*, 1933, p. 214). The sonnet was omitted from the 1933 edition of *Poems* (1930). (b) derives from earlier and longer drafts (there is an eighteen-line version once belonging to John Pudney entitled 'Aware', with an epigraph from Marston's Sophonisba: 'Happiness makes us base'). In (h), Gargantua pisses against the sun in allusion to Rabelais, I, ch. xi, where his babyhood is spent in excretion and the performance of proverbially vain acts (pissing at the sun was prohibited by Pythagoras. See Browne's *Vulgar Errors*). The reference in (f) to Solomon and Sheba, 'wrong for years', is probably to Yeats's poem 'Solomon to Sheba', where the pair spend all day long in arguing that love is a larger subject than their understanding of it, despite Solomon's proverbial wisdom. The 'study of stones' refers to the fact that its dedicatee was a geologist. Auden clearly felt that his emotional and instinctual life was at the mercy of his intellectual reputation, and it is hard to avoid reading the clinical diction as half-ironically intended.

I chose this lean country

?June 1927; P28, p. 8; EA, p. 439; *Juvenilia*, p. 210.

When sending E. R. Dodds his copy of *Poems*, Auden wrote that this poem was 'now completely rewritten as it is too Yeatsian at present'. The rewriting eventually seems to have involved taking lines 4–13 and the last line and a half, together with lines 12–13, 15 and 22–30 of 'The weeks of blizzard over' (a poem at one time considered for *Poems*, 1928) to make a new poem, 'Missing' (see p. 71). In 'I chose this lean country', the poet is talking with a poet friend (Cecil Day-Lewis, to whom the poem, originally called 'Appletreewick', was at first dedicated, and with whom he was holidaying in Wharfedale in the Long Vacation of 1927, looking over contributions for *Oxford Poetry*). They move from critical gossip of friends (Margaret Marshall, a doctor later to marry John Auden, is 'brazen'; Christopher Isherwood is 'severe') to an awed realisation that love is, subjectively, after all a serious business. This is reinforced by the defiant and scolding bird, symbol of natural forces that are bound to reassert themselves over man's works (the deserted mine, the waterlogged quarry), and by the writer's own confessional dreams. In the dream, the probably homosexual 'professional listener' was in an earlier draft a hare-lipped philosopher who took a salacious and dismissive view of the poet's erotic questionings and 'spluttered "Is that all?," | And winked a lecher's eye, | "Puella defututa" | And laughed himself away.' The phrase is from Catullus (Carmen xli.1) and Auden was fond of quoting it at the time. The cynicism was too strong for the poem as printed, which soon enlarges its scope to become an effort to accommodate the inevitability of the grave (the 'mildewed dormitory') by means of the prophetic imagination ('my corpse | Already wept'). Only the Yeatsian trimeters and the sour diction save the poem from the sentimentality of this notion. Auden's early judgement that it was specifically 'too Yeatsian' is no doubt based on the realisation that its 'choosing', 'climbing', its declaration about visions and universal death, even its image of birds dropping twigs, all derive from part III of Yeats's 'The Tower' (1926).

No trenchant parting this

August 1927; P28, p. 12; P30, p. 74; EA, p. 21; *Juvenilia*, p. 215.

Auden travelled with his father in Yugoslavia during the Long Vacation of 1927. This poem, written in Dubrovnik, continues the interrogation and argument of 'I chose this lean country', and like it is in Yeatsian trimeters. Once more the poet is poised between erotic encounters: the analysis of a vividly remembered love is dispelled by the sight of the physically disciplined diver. In each case, the 'eye' is the agent of evasive or critical qualification of the direct appeal that the erotic symbol of 'idol' or 'diver' makes. The phrase 'The diver's brilliant bow' turns up again in 'A School Song' (*Auden Studies* 2, p. 32) and in 'As I walked out one evening'. The poem was omitted from the 1933 edition of *Poems* (1930).

Suppose they met, the inevitable procedure

September 1927; P28, p. 14; P30, p. 72; EA, p. 22; *Juvenilia*, p. 220.

This poem was written on a reading-party at Carr Bridge near Inverness, a context clearly enough reflected in the poem where the potential lovers sleep apart, though the doors are unlocked. Love is seen as a new heroism, comparable to the more traditional kinds in stanza 3. The energies of the mother giving birth, the fisherman beaching his boat or the soldier making a last defensive stand are not subject to moral scruple. These are contrasted with the hopelessly self-conscious, those who, like Satan and the rebel angels, were cast out of Heaven (the last line is an allusion to the Old English Genesis). Writing to Isherwood in September 1927, Auden pointed out 'the influence of the Virgin Wolf, the proper place as I think for such technique'. *To the Lighthouse* had been published in May: its second section,

'Time Passes', contains similar epic though understated births and deaths (e.g. Prue Ramsay's death in childbirth, and Andrew's in the war in France). Of the third stanza, he remarked in a later letter to Isherwood: 'Womb: – epic birth – Fisherman: the epic life – Bayonets: the epic death, a vision of the life cycle, outside the two pathics [homosexuals], who consider themselves living the free, the true life.' The poem was omitted from the 1933 edition of *Poems* (1930).

On the frontier at dawn getting down

July 1927; P28, p. 15; EA, p. 440; *Juvenilia*, p. 214.

This sonnet, written in Yugoslavia when on holiday with his father, establishes within topographical and descriptive images appropriate to holiday jottings a mood of numbness and stasis. Some details ('Dog Days' and 'the cooled brain in an irreverent hour') appear in a letter to Isherwood written from the Elephant Hotel, Ljubljana, Croatia. 'The cooled brain' may be compared to the 'cool brain' of the Doctor's diagnosis of the shot Spy in *Paid on Both Sides*, a brain that 'appears normal except under emotion'. The repression of emotion here is reflected in the quasi-narrative details ('she ran | Indoors to read her letter'; 'He . . . stiffens to a tower') which distance the poet's mood in both tense and pronoun, as if love were simply a subject for contemplation. Material used here (perhaps from a lost holiday diary) reappears in *The Orators* (EA, p. 65) and in *The Dog Beneath the Skin* (*Plays*, p. 228).

Who stands, the crux left of the watershed

August 1927; P28, p. 16; P30, p. 51; 'The Watershed', CP, p. 41; EA, p. 22; *Juvenilia*, p. 218.

Written in Harborne at his parental home, this poem is descriptive of Auden's sacred landscape among the lead mines of Alston Moor. Auden begins the poem with a compound relative that sets up a general proposition ('Who[ever] stands . . . sees', with echoes of Kipling's 'Who stands if freedom fall' in 'For all we have and are') in a context essentially topographical. This sense of 'who' as 'whoever' is more than a mere grammatical sleight, however, since it sets up a ghostly protagonist in the poem of far greater weight than a hypothesis. This character is and is not the poet. The basis of the tone is, no doubt, that of the wise local chronicler of *The Return of the Native* ('Had a looker-on been posted in the immediate vicinity of the barrow, he would have learned . . .') or perhaps more pertinently that of Thomas Sopwith, *An Account of the Mining Districts of Alston Moor* (1833). The exact location of the features of the landscape is perhaps in doubt: Callan (p. 53) suggests that the crux is Cross Fell ('the precise centre of the ore fields of the Lead Dales'), while the original draft title referred to by Auden when sending the poem to Isherwood is 'Rookhope', from which Cross Fell is not visible. Perhaps the solution is that the crux is the Killhope Cross: keeping it to your left while standing on the A689 'between the chafing grass', you do indeed look down towards the scars of the lead-mining process above Nenthead. Compare Sopwith, p. 179: 'The traveller now descends steeply over wastes of barren and dreary aspect to the mining village of Nent Head . . . Here is a market-house with a clock tower, a Methodist chapel, a good inn, and very extensive washing-floors, where excellent arrangements are made for carrying on the various processes of washing the ore' (in the washing-floors the crushed rock was sieved to extract the galena, or lead sulphide).

Metaphorical interpretations of 'left' in politicised readings of the poem are compelled to ignore the admittedly odd syntax of this opening. Reminders that Auden had driven for the TUC during the General Strike of the previous year may be salutary, but Auden had been nostalgic about the heroic lives of lead miners from about 1924 or 1925 (compare in particular 'Lead's the Best', *Juvenilia*, p. 127, a poem with very much the same scenery as this one). The last mine closed at Nenthead in 1919.

The poem is a self-addressed warning that this kind of life may be observed but not really understood. It can in no sense become an integral part of the experience or well-being ('accessory content') of a young middle-class poet. In 'Lead's the Best' a similar feeling is expressed in the Wordsworthian village gossip and Edward Thomasish folk antiquarianism, and in the final lines, in which the 'bleak philosophy of Northern ridges | Harsh afterglow of an old country's greatness' becomes merely 'Themes for a poet's pretty sunset thoughts'. But if the idea is similar, it has immeasurably matured in perception in the later poem (the earliest, incidentally, to be admitted by Auden into the canon after 1933). Innocent delight in the achievements of the miners has been replaced by a more pervasive sense of symbolic portent in the pathos of their forgotten lives. The details are documentary. Auden wrote a poem about the revived pumping engine at Cashwell in 1924 (*Juvenilia*, p. 75). There is information about this machine in A. Raistrick and B. Jennings, *A History of Lead Mining in the Pennines* (1965), p. 211. The one who 'died | During a storm' was probably the man who caught pneumonia in Allenheads and had to be taken to the doctor in Nenthead. The story is still remembered that after his death he lay two weeks unburied, and was eventually taken back to Allenheads, a distance of about eight miles, at least partly through the mining levels because of the bad weather.

If Hardy presides over the visionary distance of this poem, it is Eliot who has contributed to its diction. The possibly Hardyesque 'frustrate' curiously belonged for Auden in an unwittingly comic context in *The Dynasts* (see *Poets at Work*, p. 294). The industrial landscape is perceived in Eliotic terms: it is 'dismantled', 'comatose', 'ramshackle'. The MS that Auden sent to Isherwood reveals some of this process. An earlier version of lines 4–5 was 'Snatches of tramline banked up from the stream, | The signs of a declining industry', flat as a magazine caption, as Isherwood objected. The substituted medical image in 'comatose' is analogous to Eliot's etherised evening, but going beyond it to implications of general social analysis. The substitution of 'running to the wood' for 'banked up from the stream' works not least because the macabre wood is the right symbol for inchoate breakdown and the reassertion of nature: the new direction of the tramline is implicative, the industry wilfully encountering its own ruin. The wilfulness, the blithe and suicidal innocence, is assisted by 'snatches', a word normally used of fragments of song.

Also Eliotic is the biblical colouring of much of the diction. The land is 'cut off' in the sense of Genesis xli.36, i.e. in the period of the General Strike England has not been protected against seven years of famine. A further allusion to Israel in Egypt is found in the 'stranger' proud of his young 'stock' (see Leviticus xxv.47). Being proud of your 'young stock' is paradoxical (someone whose ancestors came over with the Conqueror could be proud of his old stock), emphasising that in this social context the poet sees himself as a parvenu. Mining in the mother earth is symbolically presented as a male activity in very early Auden, so that the abandoned workings can be seen as a dereliction of fatherhood (strangers and the fatherless are commonly associated in Deuteronomy, Psalms and Jeremiah). The alienation of the Captivity is a difficult concept to import into the poem, but it suits Auden's prophetic response to his troubled relationship with the landscape and with a society in bondage. The poet is not even allowed now to indulge in nostalgia, but is warned away as if from a present danger. And in the brilliant image of the startled hare in the last lines, this danger is shown to work both ways: there are two worlds here, in imminent collision.

Nor was that final, for about that time

October 1927; P28, p. 18; P30, p. 50; EA, p. 24; *Juvenilia*, p. 224.

In the Ansen notebook in the Berg Collection, Auden points out a by no means obvious allusion in the first stanza to *The Wanderer*, lines 45–7. Line 4 is a translation of line 13 of *The Dream of the Rood*, and with other echoes from that poem following. Line 9 alludes to *Antony and Cleopatra*, IV.xv.65 ('Young boys and girls are level now with men'): Auden thought that Shakespeare had written 'equal' and tried to change it. Line 10 alludes to Ezekiel xxxvii.3 (recently used by Eliot in 'Salutation'). Eliot's 'Whispers of Immortality' is echoed in line 3, while the deliberately Eliotic 'daffodil and saxophone' in the final stanza replaced the 'crocuses and walzes' of a draft sent to Isherwood. This Harborne poem is interesting in its defiance of notions of sin and Christian redemption, but it does not easily survive its contrived allusiveness. It was omitted from the 1933 edition of *Poems* (1930).

The crowing of the cock

September 1927; P28, p. 19; P30, p. 48; EA, p. 23; *Juvenilia*, p. 221.

This wonderfully atmospheric reworking of themes from Frazer's *The Golden Bough* was no doubt considered too Yeatsian (and no doubt too ostentatiously allusive) to survive into the 1933 edition of *Poems* (1930). The opening apparently derives from the beginning of the second hymn of Prudentius' *Liber Cathemerinon* ('Nox et tenebrae et nubila, | confusa mundi et turbida, | lux intrat, albescit polus, | Christus venit, discedite'), according to Auden's MS note (Berg). Prudentius was mentioned approvingly in Auden's 1966 article 'The Fall of Rome' (text printed in *Auden Studies* 3, pp. 120ff). Line 12 is borrowed from Spenser ('Not perceable with power of any starr', *The Faerie Queene*, I.i.7). For 'psychogogue' (line 31) see Mann, *Death in Venice*, penultimate paragraph ('Summoner': the word is analogous to 'psychopompos'' as used of Hermes in 'New Year Letter', line 306). For θαλασσα (line 42) see Xenophon's *Anabasis*. For 'the doors being shut' (line 45) see John xx.19 ('the doors were shut where the disciples were, for fear of the Jews'). Auden glossed lines 41–2 as 'asymptotic [EA, p. 418 misreads 'a symptomatic'] movement towards emotional satisfaction' and lines 43–4 as 'The result of repression. The divided self. Puritan right and wrong' in a letter to Naomi Mitchison of 28 October 1930.

Because sap fell away

November 1927; P28, p. 22; EA, p. 441; *Juvenilia*, p. 227.

In one MS Auden dedicates this Oxford poem 'For G. C.', i.e. Gabriel Carritt, the 'snub-nosed winner' of line 10 (lines 9–10 were reused in 'Between attention and attention'). The image of frosted growth leads to a sense of alienation from one's real self ('Honours on pegs, cast humours' suggests that changing out of one's clothes, the badges of rank and character, leads not to love but simply to an inauthentic and distanced consciousness of stale sex). The rhetorical intensity of the second part of the poem is a response to despair (its first three lines were reused in *The Orators*, EA, p. 68). The 'frozen dam' was probably Burke's Dam at Sedbergh (there is a very full discussion of the Sedbergh background to this poem in *Juvenilia*). The 'indolent ulcer' was to be described in Auden's 1929 journal as the personal result of travelling abroad with his family, and it puts in an appearance as late as *The Age of Anxiety* (CP, p. 361).

The mind to body spoke the whole night through

November 1927; P28, p. 23; EA, p. 441; *Juvenilia*, p. 229.

An alternative version (published in *Oxford Poetry*, Spring 1984, p. 91) supplies an additional opening stanza, and the direction 'This is the address of the lost soul to the lost body.' Already, as in 'Because sap fell away', the dualism of mind and body is producing a dramatised and failed heroism, and looks forward to the world of *Paid on Both Sides*. The Dark Tower and tolling bell are from Browning's '"Childe Roland to the Dark Tower Came"' and there are echoes in the final stanza of the Old English 'The Soul's Address to the Body'.

From the very first coming down

December 1927; P28, p. 25; P30, p. 44; 'The Love Letter', CP45, p. 44; 'The Letter', CP, p. 39; EA, p. 25; *Juvenilia*, p. 231.

The new valley is a new love, the season spring, the sun unaccustomed, making the poet frown. But already the year has passed, and he finds himself sheltering behind a sheep-pen during a storm, reflecting on love's restlessness, its endless cycle of erotic desire. The poet and his loved-one have seen spring and autumn, and these will be seen again, but for them the future is not assured. Waiting for the poet when he returns is his loved-one's letter, which makes him frown again ('to interrupt the homely brow'), disturbing his peace of mind, which had warmed 'through and through' as his body had done after the rain-storm. 'Speaking of much but not to come' means either that the loved-one is merely analysing the past with no thought of a future relationship, or that he is full of other thoughts and will not now be joining him. The break in the poem, in the middle of a couplet, seems to represent the break in the relationship that the letter occasions.

In the last lines the poet pretends to accept the situation because of its familiarity: it seems appropriate to him to change as the seasons change. The line 'The stone smile of a garden god' occurs in an early poem 'Spring, a toy trumpet at her lips'. The perhaps less priapic 'country god' shows his approval with a rueful nod and smile: the reticence means that romantic protestation is superfluous if you accept that love is a natural seasonal process. The god might be Pan, traditional protector of flocks, living in mountains, caves and lonely places, for this is appropriate to the Lake District setting of the poem. 'Love's worn circuit' in line 9, really an image from electricity, also suggests the idea of love as a chase as on Keats's urn, and thus brings the consolation of art to the lover who can't run fast enough (Pan and Syrinx). The stone smile is undeniably chilly. The poet accepts the letter's message, but this does not make him brood ('Nor speech is close': the MS reading 'Teeth are not locked' was perhaps too sexually suggestive). There is an undeniable protest lurking in the wry understatement that love 'not seldom' receives an unjust answer, and we note that the nod and the smile contain a fear of making any commitment: perhaps, we feel, some greater commitment should be made, although the addressee of the poem, William McElwee, was heterosexual and did not return Auden's advances.

The four sat on in the bare room

December 1927; P28, p. 27; used in first version of *Paid* (*Plays*, p. 8); *Juvenilia*, p. 232.

It is tempting to see this poem as the earliest in which Auden uses something like the quadripartite psychological allegory of *The Age of Anxiety* (see p. 369). The mind's division into its faculties of Intuition, Feeling, Thought and Sensation would seem in fact to have been suggested by Jung's

Modern Man in Search of a Soul (1933), p. 107, and I argue that the climbing party in *The Ascent of F6* (1936) is based upon such symbolism (see p. 197). If an earlier use here is correct, however, then the 'bare room' would be the skull, and the four speakers would represent the four faculties of the poet in the sequence given above (compare the 'still museum' in *The Age of Anxiety*, CP, p. 383). Lines 3–4 were used in the unpublished 'The blossoms burgeon sumptuously' and also turn up, oddly enough, in what appears to be the first parody of Auden ('Rotation' by Mystan Baudom, *The Oxford University Review*, 25 November 1926, p. 210). Line 6 was reused in 'Between attention and attention'. Lines 7–8 were self-parodied in a letter to William McElwee of 7 December 1927: 'All kinds of sciofacias are now either obsolete or extremely rare' (the joke would be something to do with vouching for his academic ability). The whole poem was used as the chorus immediately following the engagement of John and Anne in the first version of *Paid on Both Sides*. The sense of doom and the unlit fire receive some kind of resolution in 'Taller to-day, we remember similar evenings' (compare the sofa hiding the grate), where the awaited 'enemy' (perhaps the first use of this concept in Auden) has become the 'Adversary' whose too easy questions the lovers have managed for a time to avoid. The overtly heterosexual terms of this poem are unusual, though appropriate to the setting in the charade.

Tonight, when a full storm surrounds the house

January 1928; P28, p. 28; used in both versions of *Paid* (*Plays*, pp. 10, 30); *Juvenilia*, p. 235.

For commentary, see p. 33.

Light strives with darkness, right with wrong

January 1928; P28, p. 29 (misprinted 'Night . . .'); used in both versions of *Paid* (*Plays*, pp. 13, 33); *Juvenilia*, p. 238.

For commentary, see p. 34.

Control of the Passes was, he saw, the key

January 1928; P28, p. 30; P30, p. 54; 'The Secret Agent', CP, p. 41; EA, p. 25; *Juvenilia*, p. 239.

Although an unrhymed sonnet, it was a ten-line version of this Oxford poem that Auden originally sent to Isherwood (omitting the second quatrain, and with a different version of lines 9–10). In another MS, 'street music' replaces the deleted 'street singer'. The sestet in general explains the erotic context of the poem. The last line is taken from the Old English poem 'Wulf and Eadwacer', which is the monologue of a captive woman addressed to her outlawed lover (she is on one island, he on another). The line is: 'þæt mon eaþe tosliteð þætte næfre gesomnad wæs' ('They can easily part that which was never joined together'). Thus the situation is one of unconsummated love. The spy represents the individual's emotional urge to make contact with another human being ('this new district'). It has been pointed out that in August 1927 Mussolini had closed the Alpine passes from Italy into France and Switzerland. Such a political model for isolationism does not, of course, necessarily give the poem a central political meaning. Love is forced to act as a secret agent because the individual does not consciously recognise his desire (the spy) and represses it. 'They', who ignore his wires, and eventually shoot him, represent the conscious will, the Censor, which represses the individual's emotional desires. Like John Nower in *Paid on Both Sides*, 'they' shoot the spy because they are unwilling to face the truth about the situation which he reveals. A later sonnet, 'Meiosis' (see p. 174), works by a very similar allegory, and acts as a useful gloss on the unbuilt bridges (sexual contact). The trouble is not entirely 'their' fault, of course. The spy is betrayed by his own 'side', but also walks into a trap. The 'old tricks' which seduce him are, I think, the limiting social conventions external to the divided individual, but hardly less responsible for his inability to make human contact.

Taller to-day, we remember similar evenings

March 1928; P28, p. 31; P30, p. 73; 'As Well as Can Be Expected', CP45, p. 113; 'Taller To-day', CP, p. 39; EA, p. 26; *Juvenilia*, p. 240.

Auden told Caroline Newton that this Oxford poem was written for 'Saul A'. The 'Adversary' of line 13 may be compared with the 'supreme Antagonist' of 'Consider' (see p. 74). Like the Hopkinsian address to God as 'Sir' in 'Petition' (see p. 76), this oblique reference to the Devil (cf. Job i.6) implies a respectful reappraisal of the Christian terms appropriate to a poem whose symbolism allows a temporary Edenic peace in an orchard. Time works confusingly in the poem to allow memory to conflate meetings over which the speaker has only hypothetical control ('See him turn to the window' is reminiscent of the stage-management of Eliot's 'La Figlia che Piange'). In its imagery and conclusions it is a kind of companion piece to 'The Letter'. The first was a poem of separation, while the second is a poem of union, however precarious. The pair are 'no nearer each other', but together they are happy: their emotional bond is deeper than on the 'similar evenings' of boyhood. Now they are alert to all that threatens love. They are like the fruit of the orchard irrigated by a brook whose source is a glacier: its coldness and remoteness lie on one side, while on the other are the windy headlands with the buried dead (an echo perhaps of the blown purgatory of Eliot's 'Gerontion'). 'Happy we' (changed in *Poems*, 1930) is an echo of the doomed idyll in Handel's *Acis and Galatea*, the Adversary acting as Polyphemus. Those who have not correctly answered his questions 'howl' like the ancestors of the protagonists in *Paid on Both Sides* (EA, p. 15) and like the damned in Yeats's 'All Souls' Night', a poem of summoned ghosts that lies behind much of Auden's work in 1928. Between the glacier and the headlands (like Bede's sparrow flying through the lighted hall, the Old English symbol of human life) is 'this peace'. It will not last (compare 'This peace can last no longer than the storm | Which started it' of poem 1 (d)), but the mere fact of its existing is important, meaning that the moment (call it love or not, call it 'loved' or merely 'endured') has achieved its fulfilment. Later texts omit stanzas 2 and 3, perhaps because of the obscurity of Captain Ferguson (an ex-army officer on the staff at Sedbergh School, as pointed out by Carpenter, p. 79) and because of Old English material similar to that used extensively in *The Orators*.

The spring will come

Spring 1928; P28, p. 33; used in both versions of *Paid* (*Plays*, pp. 11, 31); *Juvenilia*, p. 241.

For commentary, see p. 33.

The summer quickens grass

April 1928; P28, p. 34; used in both versions of *Paid* (*Plays*, pp. 10, 30); *Juvenilia*, p. 242.

For commentary, see p. 33.

Some say that handsome raider still at large

Spring 1928; P28, p. 35; used in both versions of *Paid* (*Plays*, pp. 9, 29); *Juvenilia*, p. 244.

For commentary, see p. 33.

To throw away the key and walk away

August 1928; P28, p. 36; used in final version of *Paid* (*Plays*, p. 27); *Juvenilia*, p. 246.

For commentary, see p. 32.

Paid on Both Sides

A rudimentary text of *Paid on Both Sides* was in existence in August 1928. The enlarged text was completed by December 1928 in Berlin (for full details, see *Plays*, pp. 525ff.). Mendelson prints both 'versions', but as the differences are largely those of enrichment and completion (in particular, the addition of the central psychodrama) I shall only be concerned with the second. Auden drew on a number of his existing poems for this work, including seven which had been printed that summer in *Poems* (1928): XII 'The four sat on in the bare room' (first text only); XIII 'To-night when a full storm surrounds the house'; XIV 'Light strives with darkness, right with wrong'; XVII 'The spring will come'; XVIII 'The summer quickens grass'; XIX 'Some say that handsome raider still at large'; and XX 'To throw away the key and walk away'. It was, in 1930, the first work of his to appear in a non-student publication: 'I have sent you the new *Criterion*', wrote T. S. Eliot to E. McKnight Kauffer, 'to ask you to read a verse play *Paid on Both Sides*, by a young man I know, which seems to me quite a brilliant piece of work . . . This fellow is about the best poet that I have discovered in several years' (*Bibliography*, pp. 3–4). Interest in Auden's self-styled 'charade' was maintained when it was reprinted in *Poems* (1930), and it earned a respectful analysis from William Empson in *Experiment*, no. 7 (1931). It was reprinted in CSP50, p. 197; CLP, p. 9; CP, p. 1; and EA, p. 1. My page references are to *Plays*.

Paid on Both Sides can be regarded jointly with Eliot's *Sweeney Agonistes* (1927) as a major influence on English poetic drama of the 1930s. However, it owes little to Eliot's play. *Paid*, which derives from English sources like the Mummers' Play and uses dreams in the manner of contemporary German Expressionism, contrasts favourably with the calculated effects of Eliot's Aristophanic Minstrel Show. It is a much more private affair, densely written and furiously driven by its extemporised ritual. Auden hoped that it would be put on at Tapscott, the country home of a younger fellow-undergraduate, William McElwee, for whom he had a passion. In this form, it would perhaps have functioned as an elaborate apologia from a homosexual to a heterosexual, a kind of riddling showpiece to clear the air as well as to make accusations. The opportunity was lost (Auden told Isherwood: 'They refuse to do the play, as they say the village won't stand it'), but the modern reader still gets the feeling that the ideal performance of *Paid* would be by amateurs at a house party as a piece of Christmas Eve therapy, for whatever its private function, the piece is most obviously an enigmatic and mythical evaluation of the middle-class ethos of its day. Auden annotated it in Albert and Angelyn Stevens's copy as 'A parable of English Middle Class (professional) family life 1907–1929'. The *terminus a quo* here is Auden's birth date, but significantly the subject is the family: 'From class insecurity, it [the middle class] has developed the family as a defence like the private bands in the tribal migrations' (1929 journal). The charade works to expose both the individual and his class, both actor and audience. As Auden was later to write: 'Drama began as the act of a whole community. Ideally there would be no spectators. In practice every member of the audience should feel like an understudy' (*Plays*, p. 497).

In view of such Eliotic belief, it is natural that Auden should clothe the high seriousness of the themes of his plays with informality and with a variety of tone in action and situation. Both poets believed in the ultimate compatibility of, say, the vulgarity of the music-hall and the ritual of the Mass because these were both, simply, manifestations of that communal emotion which constitutes dramatic experience. Neither the playfulness nor the obscurity of *Paid* should, therefore, be held against it. The terse style of the poetry was developed here for urgency, and to embody the primitive menace of the Icelandic sagas upon which Auden drew for his account of a feud between two mining families.

'I love the sagas,' Auden wrote in 1937, 'but what a rotten society they describe, a society with only the gangster virtues' (*Letters from Iceland*, p.119). To the conception of entrepreneur lead-miner as gangster saga-hero he added that of saga-hero as public schoolboy, an idea he seems to have derived from Isherwood (*New Verse*, November 1937, p. 5). This idea thrown out by Isherwood found a full response in Auden's fusion, in an atmosphere of dark threats, practical jokes, riddles and deliberate under-statements, of what is common to epic struggle and a school cadet force field-day. Further allusive layers are provided by, for example, the names. The suggestion of a German–Jewish conflict (the Nowers are Kurt, Walter, Zeppel, etc. and Culley is one of the 'boys had' by Auden in Berlin in 1928; the Shaws are Aaron, Seth, etc.; the two parties distinguished by coloured arm-bands) is blurred by the fact that Anne's father is called Red Shaw, indicating that the family's biblical names are more appropriately those of

American hillbillies, invoking the classic feud of the Martins and the Coys. The setting is, however, specifically English. The name 'John Nower' may have been borrowed from John de Nowers (d. ?1386), whose memorial Auden would have seen in the north transept of Christ Church Cathedral (Cunningham, p. 418). 'Nattrass' was a contemporary of Auden's at Christ Church, but see the paragraph below for the geographical symbolism.

Edward Callan has sketched the geographical symmetry of the Nowers' house Lintzgarth and the Shaws' house Nattrass, each approximately six miles distant east and west from the central high point of the Kill Hope Cross in County Durham (Callan, pp. 76ff). This cross is, I suggest, the 'crux' of the important poem 'Who stands, the crux left of the watershed' (see p. 9) and therefore a symbol to Auden of the height and distance necessary to survey a landscape of division and alienation. The *Paid* landscape, suggesting a circle analogous to the centre-and-circumference symbolism of 'The Journal of an Airman' in *The Orators* (see p. 102), also involves a conflict between 'insight' and 'spying'. The awareness of John Nower (Lintgarth, Rookhope, in Weardale, Co. Durham) and of Seth's brother (Nattrass, Garrigill, on Alston Moor, Cumbria) is precisely that 'between circumference and circumference', but suppressed by their enmity. The relevant maps are NY 64/74 and NY 84/94 in the OS 1:25,000 Pathfinder Series. Nattrass (no longer marked) is at 732451, Lintzgarth at 926428. The other identifiable locality in the text is Brandon Walls (949409).

What are the 'sides' of the play (apart from the term's obvious relevance to a 'charade')? The title is effectively a quotation from *Beowulf*, line 1305, where Grendel's mother has returned to Heorot to take vengeance on her son's death: 'Ne waes þaet gewrixle til, | þaet hīe on bā healfa | bicgan scoldon | frēonda fēorum!' ('Nor was that a good exchange, that they on both sides should pay with the lives of friends!'). This allusion is simply to the motif of the vengeful mother. Vengeance at a wedding is also described in Beowulf's premonitions of the renewed feud between the Danes and Heathobards (lines 2017–67, with the key phrase 'on bā healfa' again occurring at line 2063). Never far from Auden's mind in the play is the equivalent human waste of the First World War, where heroism is at the service of reactionary forces. A note in his 1929 journal expresses concisely his application of this national scenario to the individual mind: 'A colonel captures a position, after receiving severe wounds himself and the loss of three-quarters of his regiment, to find that the enemy are his own side. Repression is equally heroic and equally foolish' (EA, p. 300). The key to the play (and to the meaning of the title) lies in seeing the society that

Auden portrays as an allegory also of an individual psyche, sick and irrevocably divided.

In Berlin, Auden became interested in the theory of the moral and spiritual origins of illness put forward by the psychologist Homer Lane. Like D. H. Lawrence, Lane taught that the real desires of men are good and must not be repressed; that there is only one sin, and that is disobedience to the inner law of our own nature. To a great extent this notion shifted the Freudian emphasis on cure as restorative of conventional morality to an emphasis on cure as liberation. Auden thought that Freud was wrong in making pleasure negative: 'For Freud happiness is displeasing to God' (1929 journal). The central episodes of *Paid*, in particular, involve an identification on John Nower's part of the division between the families as a spiritual division in himself. As we shall see, psychological malaise is attributed to the influence of the mother, and the terms are by implication sexual. John nearly breaks the feud by marrying Anne Shaw, but Anne's mother revives it, and John dies. Social unity is thus in a sense a psychiatric objective, the point being that no one side can really win: one side's defeat is the defeat of the other.

The play begins with news of John's father's death in a Shaw ambush (p. 15). 'The Mill' would be the Rookhope Smelt Mill, adjacent to Lintzgarth (it had a 2,548 yard flue, issuing in the chimney on Bolt's Law described in 'New Year Letter', lines 1129–33). John is as yet unborn, but the shock of the bad news brings on his premature birth. The condensed time-scale of these first scenes puts the feud into perspective, but it also gives an opportunity to show how the Nowers have already begun to try to break out of the feud pattern. John's father was ambushed on his way to speak with 'Layard'. This is an important clue to the real meaning of the play, since it was through John Layard that Auden had been introduced to Lane's psychological theories (see *Lions and Shadows*, p. 299), and though the reference seems very private, it can only mean that Nower senior was trying to arrive at a true understanding of his predicament by consulting this disciple of Lane's at the time of his death. By contrast, Joan's following speech, addressed to the body of her dead husband and the baby John, is an oblique and sinister call to arms, hypnotic and insidious after the deliberately breezy clichés of the Doctor ('My God, I'm thirsty after all that. Where can I get a drink?'). This is the kind of transition that the audience, or reader, has to become accustomed to: the effect is finely condensed and propulsive.

From the stage recess, Joan contrasts the living with the dead in the first quatrain of her speech (p.15). There is an interesting ambiguity here, for both husband and son are 'new ghost' and neither is able from a former state to learn anything about his present one: both are novices. This is self-evident, but the repetition and incantation lend Joan's words the wisdom of sensed power. In effect she is saying that the dead are now irrelevant, and that the new spirit (ghost = *Geist*) must be instructed by the 'old termers', those experienced in their quest for life's meaning. In the next quatrain, she says that everyone ('Who's' refers back to the 'new ghost') grows to be resentful of youth ('his latest company'), a resentment that only death can end; the 'new ghost' glosses over the fact of death (its plain unconnected-ness with life mentioned in the first quatrain) by concentrating on the aspects that make it an occasion for grief and regret ('sorrow'). We may imagine her pointing ironically at the corpse as she says 'sorrow is sleeping thus'. The third quatrain develops her hard, realistic view of life and death by reference to the feud. Remembering, or being mindful, is not merely nostalgia ('Unforgetting is not today's forgetting | For yesterday') or the petulance of the old ('not bedrid scorning'), but a determination to preserve the continuity of unyielding resolution ('But a new begetting | An unforgiving morning').

Amidst this appeal in generalized terms to the preservation of a social order, the baby utters a cry which seems to symbolise his virility: Joan, like a latterday Volumnia, relishes the day when John will be old enough to take an active part in the feud. The following chorus (p. 16) seems to respond to Joan's authoritarian challenge by acknowledging that the young desire to succeed and to be approved. They perform for their elders but discover no social cohesion ('We were mistaken, these faces are not ours'). In a plainly Shakespearean image, Auden shows that the body which has performed all these feats is simply not to be trusted by a mind which in the final stanza acknowledges a greater power, a 'watcher in the dark' who arouses the desire to awake to a different order of reality, and who proposes clear standards of morality and humility lacking in the 'old systems which await | The last transgression of the sea' (a pair of lines borrowed from the uncollected poem 'Consequences', see p. 41; since 'transgression' is the technical evidence from marine deposits that the sea had spread over the land, the 'stumps' are probably geological). If this is not God, it is something very like God (i.e. the Hopkinsian 'we feel | Your finger'), more like God than like Layard (but for different versions of this admonitory power see the Spectre in *The Enemies of a Bishop* and the Witnesses in *The Dog Beneath the Skin*). Perhaps Auden is here merely exposing the heroic ethos, where the young are instructed 'to point | To jump before ladies' and, like Coriolanus, 'to show our scars'. If so, then the invocation of the last stanza easily carries the suggestion that what is most naturally opposed to Public School Bloody is Public School Pi: it reads in this context as a pastiche of an Anglican prayer mediated through Sophocles.

Now John is grown up, and the real action of the play begins. Dick proposes to emigrate. It may be that the docks which he proposes to sail from symbolise a specific political commitment, since John later seems to be avoiding such commitment when he talks of 'boy's voice among dishonoured portraits | To dockside barmaid speaking | Sorry through wires, pretended speech' (p. 26); but perhaps he is referring to some purely personal betrayal. Dick's emigration, however, is one obvious way out of the feud, and is not a way that Layard would have approved. Auden may have been thinking of his brother Bernard's emigration to Canada shortly after the war (see Carpenter, p. 22).

Meanwhile John is continuing the feud, and in the following scenes plans to ambush Red Shaw at Brandon Walls, which is just over two miles east along the road from Lintzgarth (echoes here of the Cynewulf and Cyneheard story in the Anglo-Saxon Chronicle for 755). The interlude in the public house (the Horse and Farrier was Auden's local in Threlkeld, when staying at the family cottage) offers an opportunity for the recording of some inane contemporary slang and sporting talk. A 'sidecar' consists of brandy and lemon juice, with a dash of orange liqueur. There are particular references in the play to sporting customs at Sedbergh School, probably gleaned from McElwee. 'Chapman did the lake in eight' (p. 18) refers to Frederick Chapman, who was at the school. Auden may have confused the boys' practice of skating on two small tarns on the Kendal Road with their swimming in pools in the river (before being allowed to do this, they had to be able to swim eight lengths of the swimming pool). Much of the material is also reminiscent of Isherwood's verbatim jottings in the Isle of Wight (see *Lions and Shadows*, p. 244) and might have been borrowed from him. A piece of automatic writing that Isherwood produced in the summer of 1928 oddly refers to one of the characters in this scene who was not in the first version of the play: 'ah yes, ah no, ah, ah, far car, stop that, Trudy, drop it or I shoot' (*Lions and Shadows*, p. 276). Similarly, the name 'Basley' in a later chorus of *Paid* (p. 31) is the name of the boy who takes up with Victor Page at school in Isherwood's *All the Conspirators* (also 1928). The affinity between the work of Auden and Isherwood in these months is evidenced by Isherwood's own school-saga experiment, 'Gems of Belgian Architecture', in *Exhumations*, 1966, p. 176.

Trudy's speech (p. 19) expresses a Shakespearean dissatisfaction with the state of feud. It is full of images of monstrous birth, and 'He's trash, yet if I cut my finger it bleeds like his' is very like Shylock's 'If you prick us, do we not bleed?' Walter's reply has an elegiac tone strongly echoing certain Old English poems. Compare, for instance, 'Often the man, alone shut . . .' with the opening of *The Wanderer*: 'Oft him anhaga . . .' (*Exeter Book*, ed. G. P. Krapp and E. V. K. Dobbie, 1936, p. 134). The mood of this elegy, with its lament for lost friends, is maintained, while the line 'Spring came, urging to ships, a casting off' seems to be suggested by *The Seafarer*, lines 48–51 (*Exeter Book*, p. 144):

> Bearwas blostmum nimað, | byrig faegriað
> wongas wlitigiað, | woruld onetteð;
> ealle þa gemoniað | modes fusne
> sefan to siþe, | þam þe swa þenceð
> on flodwegas | feor gewitan.

(The woods blossom, the towns become fair, fields look more than beautiful, the world revives; all these fire the spirit of the eager-minded man, who therefore decides to travel far on the paths of the ocean.)

The point is, of course, that John has not left, but at that very moment is preparing to ambush Red Shaw at Brandon Walls. The alienation of the elegiac personae of these and other Old English poems was to become a potent mood in later work of Auden's (e.g. 'The Wanderer', see p. 78). The general reliance of the speech on the narrative formulae of Old English heroic poems like *Beowulf* or *The Battle of Maldon* (compare 'Edward fell', etc. with lines 117–8: 'Eadweard anne sloge | swiþe mid his swurde') underlines John's feelings at this point that he must accept the feud and avenge his father's death. Stephen's tipsy behaviour after his successful baptism of fire ('Don't go, darling') is appropriate to the emotional tenor of the heroic *comitatus*: together with the praise of courage and athletic achievement (already expounded in the pub scene) comes mere boyish affection and silliness (Stephen's part is doubled with the Doctor's boy later).

At this point, the Spy (a son of Red Shaw) is found, led out and plainly shot (p. 20). This is the occasion for the central and most important section of the play, added in Berlin, four pages of expressionistic fantasy in which John's state of mind is openly allegorised. On the surface, the reason is easy to see: to have the Spy shot is to perpetuate the feud beyond the immediate purpose of revenge. When John exclaims 'I'll destroy the whole lot of you', it would seem that he is already beyond redemption.

John's soliloquy ('Always the following wind of history', p. 21) recognises this evil, returning to the play's earlier theme of the endless perpetuation of education in the sterile traditions of his class. The initial metaphor is of sailing or gliding: the wind of tradition supports us until we encounter those air-pockets of experience where there is no precedent to rely on and we are thrown on our own resources. The superficial routine of the athletic and imperialist middle classes simply does not allow for the higher ideals of love or philosophy, and therefore stunts their growth ('to gaze longer and delighted on | A face or idea be impossible'). John wants to have lived at an earlier stage in the history of organic life (even to have been inorganic) since evolution has been disastrous ('disaster' sends 'his runners' like a conquering general exploring territory). This is a notion common in early Auden, and survives at least until 'In Sickness and in Health', stanza 12.

The chorus (p. 20) then elaborates upon the traditions in which John finds himself trapped, in a beautifully paced survey of capitalist society. Auden is being ingenious here. 'Spring unsettles sleeping partnerships' because at the end of the financial year the partner with the money but with no active interest in the firm may merely find that he has lost his money; foundries and shops improve and expand. Auden brilliantly suggests in these opening lines that the capitalist process is also a natural one, since spring is traditionally the season of love. Thus marriages ('sleeping partnerships') become unsettled by recurring sexual desire, children are conceived ('Foundries improve their casting process') and new generations born ('shops | Open a further wing'). The irony of these double meanings takes a further point from their contrast with John's previous desire for the landscape to appear 'sterile as moon': by a hideous inversion of values, only capitalism appears to be fruitful.

However, as the chorus continues, it soon becomes apparent that disaster is in store: gears rust, land is forfeited. The chorus breaks into a lament for the whole condition of man, who does not choose to be born ('The body warm but not | By choice') and whose desire is for a happier, more primitive social organisation. Man 'learns, one drawn apart, a secret will | Restore the dead', alluding to Confirmation and the gospel of the Resurrection, but the sensational promise of religion leads nowhere: men die (as in the First World War) in millions. Thus the after-life is a cheat, man's moral vows melt like ice ('the most solid wish he tries to keep | His hands show through') and therefore, considering his suffering, he really had, as John had wished, better be stone ('too deep for shafts', a Wordsworthian echo).

Both of these last speeches indicate the range of ideas and meaning that lies behind John's inherent defeatism and depression, and prepare one for the faster pace and more elusive symbols of the following scenes (pp. 22–6). These scenes are complex and difficult, not only because they rely on some very obscure sources, but because here Auden is trying to get across a psychological theory in terms of grotesque knockabout humour. As a dramatic experiment it is interesting and novel in its intensity, but it has proved a stumbling-block to appreciation of the play.

Homer Lane had spoken out against repression of our real desires. He also pointed out that much of our behaviour stems from our earliest experiences of fear and punishment, that the child's play is often a dramatised rebellion against parental authority. Thus it is that at this point of *Paid* the feud comes to represent just such a pattern of human behaviour, especially inasmuch as it was observed to derive from the profound experience of weaning from the mother's breast. Auden returned again and again in his 1929 journal to the necessity of weaning and the freedom from parental authority which it represented: too much mother-love has alienated him from women ('I am my mother') and too much reliance upon inherited thoughts and emotions has forced him into something like 'the excitement of running away from home' (quotations from 1929 journal). The theme is at the heart of the poem 'It was Easter as I walked in the public gardens' (see pp. 59ff). In the fantasy of John's interrogation of the Spy, it is plain that accuser and accused are to be identified (the Spy is 'really' dead), since it is John's mother who threatens the Spy with a giant feeding-bottle.

Before this interpretation can be pursued, however, it is necessary to look at the form and characters of the scenes. Many of these are taken from the old Mummers' Play, which Auden must have read in R. J. E. Tiddy's *The Mummers' Play* (1923). There is also an account of a performance in Hardy's *The Return of the Native*. Auden included an extract from the Mummers' Play in *The Poet's Tongue* (1935), i.187.

Father Christmas is the traditional Presenter of the Mummers' Play. Bo conceivably might derive from Sambo, also a Mummers' character, though the chime of Bo/Po suggests that the polarity they represent is essentially a child's view of male and female role-playing, with barely differentiated results. The Man-Woman seems to be an imaginative misunderstanding of the phrase used by Tiddy to describe the character in his introduction: 'It has been suggested that the man-woman is the survival of an endeavour to promote fertility by the mere fact of wearing a woman's clothes.' In fact the role was usually a mute one: the character merely came in wielding a broom. Auden turns it into something much more significant.

Finally, the major borrowing from the Mummers' Play is the scene of the Doctor and his Boy (pp. 24–5). A number of parallel extracts from Tiddy may be compared with this scene:

Fool. Five pounds for a doctor.
Another person. Ten pounds to stop away.

(Tiddy, p. 246)

John Finney. Hold him yourself then.
Doctor. What's that, you saucy young rascal?
John Finney. Oh, I hold him, sir, etc.

(Tiddy, pp. 165–6)

Father Christmas. Pray, Doctor, what can you cure?
Doctor. Oh, all sorts of diseases,
Whatever my physick pleases,
If it's the itch, the pitch, the palsy & the gout,
If the devil is in, I can fetch him out.

(Tiddy, p. 162)

Jack brings the implements, consisting of hammer, saw, files, pincers, etc., and throws them to the ground.

(Tiddy, p. 177)

Ladies and gentlemen, all this large wolf's tooth has been growing in this man's head ninety-nine years before his great grandmother was born: if it hadn't been taken out today, he would have died yesterday . . . Rise up, bold fellow, and fight again.

(Tiddy, p.166)

How is it that John and the Spy are to be identified? The Nower–Shaw feud represents a psychic split in one individual. When the Spy groans at the revelations of the Man-Woman, John cannot bear it, and shoots him (p. 24). This suggests, by the evident theme of sexual repression, that John represents the repressive Censor, and the Spy the repressed natural drives – the Ego and the Id respectively. In *The Orators* spying is identified with introversion (EA, p. 74) and perverted lovers are described as 'haters of life . . . who when the saving thought came shot it for a spy' (EA, p. 63).

The trial scene is based, curiously enough, on a dream reported and analysed by the psychiatrist W. H. R. Rivers in his book *Conflict and Dream*

(1923, pp. 22ff). This is the dream of a medical captain who had served in France during the First World War. His experiences (especially those centring on the death of a French prisoner mortally wounded during his escape from the German lines) made him reluctant to return to the practice of his profession. Rivers concludes after a careful analysis: 'The interpretation has shown that the dream was the transformed expression of a wish to commit suicide in order to escape from a conflict which was becoming intolerable' (Rivers, p.28).

In his dream, the Captain finds himself giving a patriotic speech at a London theatre, the Golders Green Empire. As he mounts the stage, his place in the audience is filled by his double, who suffers in agony as he speaks. The Captain feels the strong desire to put him out of his misery by shooting him. As recounted, the dream is a fascinating and dramatic account of mental disturbance. Clearly, Auden used it both to suggest that John envisages the Spy's death as a form of suicide, and also to underline a meaning already introduced in the play, that his state of mind is itself a result of the decline of Western civilisation, represented in this instance by the horrors of the First World War, the war that Auden's generation felt so much guilt about because they were too young to take part in it.

John is the accuser (p. 22), but when called to give evidence can only make a jingoistic speech closely similar in tone and content to the Captain's in his dream: 'We must continue the struggle to the last man. Better let us die than lose our manhood and independence and become the slaves of an alien people . . . I know . . . that we have suffered and are all suffering dreadful agony . . . There must be no surrender. We must not give in' (Rivers). This is simply the automatic response, perpetuating the feud.

The following speech of Bo implies that some break is possible. The first four lines seem imitative of the last section of *The Waste Land*, and the remainder of the speech, continuing the military imagery, elaborates the possibility of a change of heart. Decision, action and conviction are, it seems to say, still possible. But the Spy groans, as the Captain's double groans in the dream. Compare Joan with her feeding-bottle ('Be quiet, or I'll give you a taste of this') with the Canadian (representing the Captain's in-laws) who is standing at the exit of the Golders Green Empire ('Silence there . . . or I'll deal with you . . . I'll give you a taste of this'). In *Paid* it is not a proposed return to the Front which has caused the mental disorder, but the oppressive relationship with the Mother and the sensual deprivation of weaning (see *Lions and Shadows*, p. 193, for a contemporary joke of Auden's about insufficient weaning: 'I must have something to suck'): hence the threat of the feeding-bottle. In his Berlin journal Auden connected the homosexual's interest in the penis with a lack of breast-feeding.

Po's speech (p. 23) produces the alternative to ambiguous action: nostalgic, introverted self-regard. Success finds at last only a furtive hoarded love, a love which is no better than the mother's patient, possessive fidelity to the long-departed son. The implication is that the adventurer on northern ridges in Bo's speech is in fact the same person as the doomed son in the snow-drift of Po's speech, a familiar Auden character who reached fruition as Ransom in *The Ascent of F6*. The nature of the elusive 'honour' is supported by references to *Don Quixote*. The Don returned to his estates and to sanity at the end of the book, and it was Sancho Panza who accepted the long-promised 'island' governorship, albeit as a practical joke (*Don Quixote*, II.42).

The Spy groans again (cf. Rivers: 'the man in my chair . . . groaned aloud in agony') so John produces a revolver, saying that it is better to get it over. Joan's words 'This way for the Angel of Peace' are taken verbatim from the Captain's dream, where they are spoken by a doctor who, like the Canadian, is guarding one of the exits to the theatre, and refer to the solution of suicide. Father Christmas's words are almost exactly paralleled by Rivers, who himself appears in his patient's dream at this point, saying: 'Don't do it . . . the man is ill, but he will get well.'

Here the Man-Woman appears (significantly 'a prisoner of war'), representing the real victim of the feud: love. It is evident that war itself has no place for love, but in terms of the psychic fantasy we are ready for admonitions from the Life Force, speaking in the Owenesque half-rhymes that Auden liked to use for plangent resolution and resignation on this subject (compare not only the choruses 'The Spring unsettles sleeping partnerships', p. 21, and 'To throw away the key and walk away', p. 27, but also 'Since you are going to begin today' in *Poems*, 1930). It is tempting to see the Man-Woman as an ambiguous symbol representing the homosexual predicament (a Cocteauesque *truc* like the hermaphrodite in *Le Sang d'un poete*) and to relate it to a later Auden character, Baba the Turk, Rakewell's bearded wife in *The Rake's Progress*. Auden denied such a reading of this latter work as 'obscene' (*Secondary Worlds*, p. 101), but it is at least clear that the figure in each case represents the hero's repression of natural sexual love: in *Paid*, Oedipal narcissism, experiment, fear, sexual self-consciousness; in the opera, an *acte gratuit*. In Berlin Auden was reading Proust, and finding the first part of *Sodome et Gomorrhe* 'very inadequate'. 'He rightly lays stress on two things,' Auden wrote in his journal. 'The Buggers as the great secret society and "the invert's terrible nerves".' But all his talk about the "man-woman" seems astoundingly superficial and quite meaningless.' Auden was to capitalise on this distinction when he came to write *The Orators*. Proust's term here for homosexuals ('hommes-femmes') seems a distracting coincidence, for the tone of the Man-Woman's speech is a clinical reproof, more like the mumming character with the broom after all. What it represents is a kind of daemon of John's maladjustment, a reminder of causes, a baleful analyst (and therefore, perhaps, the poet's own self-addressed voice, which is why he told Stephen Spender: 'I am the Man-Woman').

Its speech (p. 23) brings John to the pitch of crisis where he has to put the 'spy' out of his misery. It tells him that there is no second chance. He has been educated to believe that love is purely scandal and romance: through his reading ('traffic in memoirs') he takes it that love is achieved by romantic protestation. This futile daydream is continued in the next three lines in a Robin Hood metaphor: John had his 'orders to disband', but 'remained in woods'. His real emotional and sexual needs remained unfulfilled, so that love 'went | Hearing you call for what you did not want'. The remainder of the Man-Woman's speech elaborates the frigid sexual resources that follow from such false attitudes: masturbation and nerve-racked calculated attempts at sexual gratification. The phrase 'mother told you that's what flowers did' appears in the 1929 journal as a comment on getting an erection when sleeping innocently with a friend: part of the problem with the middle classes was their confusion between a need for physical contact and sexual needs. The speech continues by showing how the rationalising Ego has taken over. Love gives the talkative intellectual some justification for preferring the spirit to the body: sex can then come to seem an 'extra' which has somehow to be acted out. This is close to Lawrence's sex in the head. Love can't be followed now, because it belongs where 'all talking is forbidden'.

The shooting is now repeated in the fantasy (p. 24), and the comic Mummers' Play Doctor is called for. The Doctor is more than merely comic, however. He is a Homer Lane figure who is required to resurrect the shot Spy (i.e. the repressed Id) and who actually does succeed. Much of this scene is a simple dramatic borrowing from Tiddy (see p. 27) with additional comic material ('Tickle your arse with a feather' etc. may be a Marlburian joke borrowed from John Betjeman whom Auden knew at Oxford. See *Summoned by Bells*, vii), but the rest is intended to suggest the kind of healing powers the Doctor possesses. He says that he has discovered the origin of life, but makes it plain that he does not refer to mere physical life, for death is an incontrovertible fact to him: he will leave his head for medical analysis at his death, but 'the laugh will be gone and the microbe in command'. John tries to see what the Doctor is doing as he takes the circular saws, bicycle-pumps and so on from his bag, ready to examine the Spy's body, but the Doctor pushes him away. John is a 'war-criminal' and his evidence is valueless: in other words, the Ego is to blame, and is thus powerless to assist in restoring the psychic health of the individual. The Doctor examines the body and blames 'the conscious brain' which, more effectively than the Devil, 'advances and retreats under control and poisons everything round it'. The cure is effected by the traditional withdrawal of a gigantic tooth.

John's anxiety remains, however: he still seeks the Spy like a train he is late for. In the end they are reunited, and plant a tree together (a private allusion, possibly, to the poet's patron saint, St Wystan, who planted a stick which grew into a tree?). Their words here indicate yet again the play's theme that the past is irrevocably lost. John says (p. 26) that they were 'Sametime sharers in the same house', i.e. both the womb and the human organism it houses itself in and therefore also the 'house' of society. 'Now cannot mean to them' suggests that the builders of the 'house' (i.e. both parents and class-ancestors) are fixated in the past. A note in the 1929 journal states that only the 'classic' Few with their organised bravado love the 'here', compared with the romantic Mass with their organised fear who love the 'there'. The middle-class boy's background is both betrayed ('dishonoured portraits') by the actual situation, and a cause of its betrayal ('pretended speech'). The dockside barmaid is evidently a symbol of a social and sexual bravado which actually fails (no doubt Auden really had Berlin bar-boys in mind: he pictured himself in his journal 'as the Baron Charlus. Actually I was a middle-class rabbit'). The Spy's speech, with its imagery of war refugees, underlines the alienation of the split psyche (the rootlessness of the *déclassé* artist, perhaps: 'We stay and are not known'). They are 'attendants on the same machine' (the body) and are yet divided.

The central fantasy of the play ends here, and it ends pretty inconclusively, it might be said. But a dramatic development has taken place, and after the scene in which the emigrating Dick takes his leave (p. 26), John is in a position to examine his predicament rationally.

In his soliloquy (pp. 26–7) he discovers the importance of love, its social and personal healing power. He equates his life with a city. Now, he says, he has an understanding of himself that leaves him 'lighted and clean' instead of dark and dirty like the slum he had previously made of his life. He has

been proud and indifferent: his 'streets' have witnessed the conveniently
arranged 'accidents' of the rich. Now love, 'sent east for peace | From
tunnels', perhaps like the revolutionary Andrei Zhelyabov who assassinated
Alexander II in 1881, 'Feels morning streaming down | Wind from the
snows.' The Russian allusion seems to be maintained in the last stanza: love
is no longer uncommitted ('Nowise withdrawn by doubting flinch'), nor yet
committed to any rigid programme ('belief's firm flange'), but simply
rejoices in the new fruitful life indicated by the Eisensteinian montage of
'The tugged-at teat | The hopper's steady feed, the frothing leat'. These
largely maternal images lead him to contemplate intermarriage with the
Shaws as a way out of both feud and emotional sterility. He asks his servants
to fetch his horse.

The next chorus (p. 27) is perhaps the most important in the play. It had
already appeared as a poem in its own right in *Poems* (1928), no. XX, but in
the new context its meaning is immeasurably opened up. If the Nowers and
the Shaws are essentially alike, the feud exists only on its own terms. In some
kinds of charade both 'sides' act simultaneously, and to the difficulty of
guessing is added the difficulty of finding the chance to act out your
meaning. Auden means to suggest that finding oneself in this psychological
predicament in society is like finding oneself in a kind of game which may
be 'won'. To avoid the inherited state of feud between the sides, one can
emigrate, like Dick, or one can marry, like John and Anne; but to do this is
really to spoil the game and not to solve it. The chorus suggests that to be an
'abrupt exile' in this way is evasive. Somehow one should stay in the charade
and try to guess the answer, i.e. learn through experience. Change must be
not revolutionary (the conspirator's smile during the royal toast, gunpow-
der) but evolutionary (developing gills). Even Freudian 'confession of the
ill' is unnecessary compared with the primacy of the empirical. Katherine
Bucknell suggests the influence of Coué's auto-suggestion here, via Auden's
analyst, Margaret Marshall (*Juvenilia*, p. 247). The historical process must
be respected (compare 'following a line with left and right' with 'But left
and right alternately | Is consonant with History' in *The Double Man*, p. 154)
and the past seen as irrevocably past compared with what is to come:
'although some posts | Are forwarded', 'these [a reading from P28] are still
to tempt; areas not seen . . .' In other words, an existentialist solution is
offered: the future will be arduous, and is described in terms of the
Wanderer following a misleading signpost in a snow-storm. The future is not
predictable, even when its 'guessed-at wonders would be worth alleging',
and the Wanderer will 'receive no normal welcome'. But this is the only way

in which the true meaning of the charade may be discovered, as in a new valley which entirely alters the familiar landscape.

A brief scene (p. 28) shows that the feud is still in full swing. 'The Hangs' is a valley north of Auden's school, Gresham's. The 'Barbon road' is another Sedbergh reference: Barbon is to the south of the school and was used for the Corps Field Day. There follows the announcement of John's engagement to Anne Shaw. The two families mix, but Seth talks about getting a chance for revenge.

The following scene between John and Anne (pp. 29–31), which largely consists of four poems from the 1928 *Poems* (nos XIX, XVIII, XIII and XVII in that order), provides a lyrical and elegiac investigation into the nature of love, and of the old world and the new. John is so conditioned by the school-saga ethos that love seems strange to him, he says. 'Cautley' is a waterfall to the north of Sedbergh, on the route of the ten-mile race (which, *pace* Carpenter, p. 107n, began and ended at the school). The passage 'Some say that handsome raider still at large' elaborates the idea that only the first-hand experience will do: what others tell us is no use to us. The Yeatsian trimeter of 'The summer quickens all' is a common form in *Poems* (1928) and beautifully points the ephemerality of their love: disaster will surely come. At this point Anne tries to persuade John to join Dick abroad, but John says that he has decided to stay. In a speech with a powerful All Souls' Night feel to it, Anne appears to presume that John is being faithful to the memory of the dead. (Morgan's and Cousin Dodds's deaths are reminiscent of the end of Eliot's 'Gerontion': 'against the wind, in the windy straits | Of Belle Isle' and '. . . in the snow . . . driven . . . | To a sleepy corner'). She says that the dead, despite their astonishing deaths, have no moral power over the living: 'The too-loved clays . . . shall not speak | Out of that grave [,] stern on no capital fault.' If John escapes now, he need not have regrets or any desire to make up for committed violence: he will only have 'lightly touched the unworthy thing'. John replies: 'We live still', meaning that their continued good fortune is itself reproached by those who have suffered. Anne says that the dead forget. John's rather elliptic reply suggests, I think, that he feels the failings of the dead to be eternal qualities, recurrent in themselves, 'echoes . . . what dreams or goes masked . . . touches of the old wound' (original sin).

The chorus 'The Spring will come' (p. 31) concurs, or at least implies that the system is hardly likely to change as a result of a single perception of its rottenness: the defeated factory-owner and the wounded outlaw are at the mercy of cyclical change ('Spring' = history), and the individual who has made an advance beyond the present conditions of his society finds only an 'alone success'. The 'good word' of God (see Hebrews vi.5) proves illusory. The Old English Wanderer figure is again introduced through an echo of the 'Hwaer cwom' passage in that poem (lines 92ff). John and Anne go inside, and the chorus asks 'For where are Basley who won the Ten, [the ten mile cross-country race at Sedbergh] | Dickon so tarted by the House, | Thomas who kept a sparrow-hawk?' The implication is that John has lost the friendship of his feud comrades as the Wanderer had lost his 'seledreamas', his joy in the communal life of the hall. The tongue is ashamed, 'deceived by a shake of the hand', because John really regrets the lost fellowship, or was mistaken about the degree of its emotional meaning for him. His predicament has been subtly delineated throughout the play: guilt and division, alternating hope for the future and regret for the past, a feeling that he cannot and should not escape, a search for love, a carrying of old weaknesses. The play now moves swiftly to his death.

At the marriage party, after the departure of the guests ('Quarry Hazel' is a red, occasionally lead-bearing sandstone), Mrs Shaw reproaches Seth for complying with the truce (p. 32) and reminds him of his brother's (the Spy's) death. In a brief soliloquy, remarkably similar in style to some of Isherwood's interior monologues in *All the Conspirators*, Seth thinks of his brother as a blubbing coward, and resolves to be 'a stern self-ruler' and kill John as his mother has instructed. John is killed, and we are led to believe that the feud will continue. In this scene of female influence Auden may have had in mind Hildigunna in Njal's Saga or Thorgerd in the Laxdael Saga persuading their menfolk to vengeance by any available means. There is also a close parallel in the wedding of Ingeld in *Beowulf*, lines 2017–67. These traditional sources seem likelier than more recent verse plays such as Wilfred Gibson's *Kestrel's Edge* (1924), as suggested by Michael Sidnell, in which Naomi Angerton's going off with Robert Ellershaw, the man who shot her husband, and being rebuked by her sons for doing so, would appear to be a precise inversion of the female impulse to revenge in Auden's play.

In the final Sophoclean chorus (P28, XIV: absence of stanzas cancelled in manuscript disguise the fact that it was written in terza rima), Auden suggests that in a society like this 'no man is strong.' Probably his reading of Malinowski and other anthropologists gave him the idea of putting an Oedipal conflict into a matrilineally organised society. John cannot 'bring home a wife' because in a matrilocal marriage he would have to live with the bride's family (i.e. at Nattrass); and, as is emphasised, at the wedding he is only a guest in the Shaw house. To preserve her ascendancy (as well as to perpetuate the feud), Mrs Shaw is obliged to have John killed: 'His mother and her mother won'. The predicament is to reappear in Auden's work, notably in *The Orators, The Ascent of F6* and *The Bassarids.* What it really 'means' is that maternal possessiveness can produce emotional disaster in the son, with the result that he finds himself divided, perpetuating social violence, barely able through conscious effort to achieve a normal love relationship, incurably homosexual. The play, with its fiercely concentrated and alternating images of freezing and release, makes no real decision to face these implications, and it was only in the year following the composition of *Paid* that Auden was able to begin to accept the last of these consequences.

Uncollected Poems 1925–30

Fine evenings always bring their thoughts of her

July 1925; 'The Sunken Lane', *Oxford Magazine* (Commemoration number, 19 June 1926), p. 8; *Juvenilia*, p. 98.

This is a lyric of the 'pre-Eliot' period, using a circuitous syntax to express the embarrassing and barely acknowledged fact that the poet's memories of nature (and of a beauty beyond the human) play a pre-eminent part in his memories of the girl. There is dramatic skill in the zeugma of the lines about kissing her neck, but the relished climax belongs (after a submerged struggle) to the linnet.

The fells sweep upward to drag down the sun

Christmas vacation 1925–6; 'Lead's the Best', *Oxford Outlook*, viii, 38 (May 1926), pp. 119–20; *Juvenilia*, p. 127.

This poem belongs to a tradition stretching from Wordsworth to the Georgians of the poet as an itinerant gatherer of local lore, insistent questioner of the oldest inhabitant, trying to make himself invisible. He is both outside the inn and inside asking the questions that are abbreviated by the closing of the door. The ambiguity reinforces the poet's role as an outsider, ignorant of the lost heroic lives of the lead miners, forced to become merely an officiating intelligence, carried away by the sheer Tennysonian performance of the blank verse in lines 18–33 (though line 20 is from *The Tempest*, 1.ii). Katherine Bucknell has pointed out the similarities in Auden's procedure here to Gordon Bottomley's 'Little-holme', *Georgian Poetry 1918–1919*, pp. 11–13 (*Juvenilia*, p. 129). For 'Threlheld' read 'Threlkeld', the Lake District village close to the Auden family's cottage. 'Cashwell' also appears in 'The Watershed', and 'Green[-h]earth' in 'The Secret Agent'. 'Hodge' (derived from 'Roger') is the traditional name for a rustic, used by many poets, including Hardy. A 'heading' is a mining gallery with access to new ore. The touches of Hardy (clarinets in country churches), Thomas (the two-headed giant in the combe-bottom) and Frost (the opening dialogue) are characteristic of the poetry of 1924–5, though here perhaps as much part of the world that has passed as part of Auden's way of seeing it. 'The bleak philosophy of Northern ridges' is used again in 'Narcissus' (see p. 44) and the whole poem is in an interesting sense a dry-run for Auden's first canonical poem, 'The Watershed' (see p. 8), where the poet moves beyond his role as Georgian outsider and becomes the more radically dislocated 'stranger' common in Auden's mythical landscape.

Stop fingering your tie; walk slower

April–May 1926; 'Chloe to Daphnis in Hyde Park', *Oxford Outlook*, viii, 39 (June 1926), pp. 209–10; *Juvenilia*, p. 134.

This exercise in springtime pastoral is haunted by Elizabethan conventions and allusions, principally to Feste's song, 'O Mistress mine' in *Twelfth Night* ('Trip no further, pretty sweeting; | Journeys end in lovers meeting'). As usual in Auden's poems of this period, the girl's journey is by no means over. Her lover fingers his tie and their coat-sleeves touch. The casual accident is enough to bestow divinity on an animal love (cf. Adela and Ronnie in Forster's *A Passage to India*, chapter 8). The conversation flags; though added together they are still divided. Stanza 5, line 4, alludes to a contemporary popular song. Self-evidently an Easter poem, it ironically sets nature's instinctive understanding of sexual resurrection against the modern self-consciousness of the human lovers (for some other Easter poems of Auden's, see the sonnet 'April is here but when will Easter come?', ?1923; 'Spring, a toy trumpet at her lips', 1927; 'It was Easter as I walked in the public gardens', 1929; and 'Get there if you can and see the land you once were proud to own', 1930). Tellingly, Auden reused the detail of the mower in 'Journal of an Airman' in his description of the suburban heterosexual world of The Hollies (EA, p. 85). According to a transcript made by A. S. T. Fisher which omits stanzas 4–5 and adds a final stanza, the poem was written 'of A. W. P.', i.e. Anthony Wyatt Parker, an Exhibitioner in Natural Sciences at Christ Church who matriculated in 1924, one year before Auden.

Though Time now tears apart

?May 1926; 'At Parting', *Cherwell*, xvi, ns 4 (22 May 1926), p. 130; *Juvenilia*, p. 140.

The trimeter quatrains of this brief poem of parting suggest the influence of Emily Dickinson, particularly in the oblique use of a commonplace image in the first stanza (the screws that are tightened are, I think, those of a metaphorical coffin, the weary ritual burial of a love affair that is the only response to a shattered universe of lovers who have learned to acknowledge boundaries).

The lips so apt for deeds of passion

?May 1926; 'Portrait', *Cherwell*, xvi, ns 4 (22 May 1926), p. 130; *Juvenilia*, p. 141.

The calm ironical and impersonal tone of this rebuke to a world which can create inaccessible beauty successfully disguises its function as a lament for unrequited love: the lover pretends to a rueful and philosophical distance from fate's botched masterpiece – botched only, one gathers, by the subject's imperviousness to wooing. Isherwood refers to this poem ('Some notes on the early poetry', *A Tribute*, p. 77) as an example of Auden's craze for the poetry of Edwin Arlington Robinson.

Six feet from One to One

?Spring 1926; 'Amor Vincit Omnia', *Oxford Outlook*, viii, 39 (June 1926), p. 180; *Juvenilia*, p. 142.

The substance of this complaint about sexual timidity is conceived in the Metaphysical mould (with echoes of Marvell and Carew) but the overall form and manner is, of course, much closer to Emily Dickinson with its abrupt and laconic opening and close, and the suppressed power of its trimester quatrains. Sailing no farther than the 'shores of Occiput' sounds like a friendly cupping of the head.

He reads and finds the meaning plain

Spring 1926; 'The Letter', *Oxford Poetry 1926*, pp. 4–5; *Juvenilia*, p. 132.

This letter that breaks off an affair, though received with an ultimate shrug, has at first a momentous effect that questions the universe. The process of argument is interesting to compare with 'From the very first coming down', also later called 'The Letter' (see p. 12). The gushing of spring and its sudden failure in the poet's case is reduced in the later poem to a 'green | Preliminary shiver'. What was to become a stoical and elliptic acceptance of the cycle of the seasons is here still a bemusement before the 'stablished sequence of the laws', Tennysonian diction perhaps appropriate to the poem's form (doubled-up *In Memoriam* stanzas). There are allusions in stanza 3 to *Othello*, v.ii.345, and 1 Samuel x.11.

Inexorable Rembrandt rays, which stab

May–June 1926; 'Thomas Epilogises', *Oxford Poetry 1926*, pp. 1–3; *Juvenilia*, p. 146.

This ostentatiously allusive and difficult poem shares nine of its lines with 'They are all gone upstairs into the world' (see below) and would appear to be a version of it made unfit for public consumption, or at least a version of the idea behind the title which might impress the readers of *Oxford Poetry*, co-edited by the poet. The setting is the train that is taking 'Thomas' to his holiday cottage; the mood is a nihilistic anti-romanticism appropriate to such a sceptical persona. One is reminded that Auden chose the pseudonym 'Didymus' for his 1942-3 column in the Catholic periodical *Commonweal* (see John Deedy, *Auden as Didymus*, 1993). However, there may be no intention to allude to any particular character. 'Tommy' is a characteristic name for a mother's boy (see Auden's poem 'Tommy did as mother told him', *As I Walked Out One Evening*, p. 12, and 'Caliban to the Audience', CP, p. 435). 'οικαδε, etc.' is from the *Odyssey*, v.219, quoted more fully in the 'Letter to William Coldstream' in *Letters from Iceland*. The line 'Love mutual has reached its first eutectic [melting point]' is often quoted as an example of Auden's clinical diction. For 'sigmoid curve', cf. 'The sigmoid curve of autocatalytic reactions' in the 1928–?30 notebook: Auden remained interested in the idea that desire creates its own death. The dwindling is the result of the autocatalysis of orgasmic 'death'. Eliphaz, Zophar and Bildad are the three friends of Job who come to bring him comfort, described here in Sitwellian terms: they 'creak a wooden sarabande' observed by a winking Silenus (cf. 'The stone smile of a country god' in 'From the very first coming down').

They are all gone upstairs into the world

?May 1926; 'Thomas Prologizes', *Oxford Magazine*, xlvi, 17 (3 May 1928), pp. 467–8; *Juvenilia*, p. 136.

It is not clear why this version of Auden's Thomas poem (which appears to be earlier than 'Inexorable Rembrandt rays, which stab', see above) should have been published two years after Auden sent it to Isherwood and a year and a half after the *Oxford Poetry* version, which had used nine of its lines. Auden wrote in explanation: 'The idea of course is an adolescent, who feels that all his old ideas are breaking up and have taught little but lyric and lechery. Then he thinks "lets get on to something new" and in the usual way of romantic adolescence thinks that he is capable of doing any great and heroic thing though what he isn't quite sure of. The last part of course is obvious "cui bono" '. In this version, Thomas is much more cynical about tradition.

The resurrection theme is handled in an Eliotic manner. There is an allusion to Vaughan (line 1). For lines 20–21, see Frazer, *The Golden Bough*, on Osiris. Line 22 is borrowed from *The Changeling*, v.iii (or more likely Eliot's 1927 essay on Middleton). Some words ('callipygous', 'reins') seem to have been borrowed by Tom Driberg for his poem 'Panorama in Lilliput' (*Oxford Poetry 1927*, p. 13). Further resemblances between Driberg's poems and Auden's in these years are a matter for speculation.

The title refers punningly to Browning's 'Artemis Prologizes', where the goddess recounts the story of Hippolytus, brought to his death by the incestuous love of his stepmother, Phaedra. Auden may have been particularly taken by this theme, and by the original intention of Browning to make his poem a prelude to a Euripidean play about the resurrected Hippolytus. There may be an allusion to the predatory Phaedra in the lines '. . . Isobel who with her leaping breasts | Pursued me through a summer', lines which Auden singled out in 1964 as being the worst he had ever written (*Bibliography*, first edition, p. vii).

The princes rush downward on to the shore

August–September 1926; 'Bank Holiday', *Oxford Outlook*, viii, 40 (November 1926), pp. 242–4; *Juvenilia*, p. 156.

The dramatisation of a plebeian holiday has something of the exotic and daydream fantasy of Edith Sitwell's seaside poems, but the admonitions of the fortune teller, Madame Zana, interleaved with the demotic comments

of the holidaymakers ('Mummy, I want to do big') out-Eliots Eliot in its
social range and in its irony. The memories of love expire dismally in
images from the 'Preludes' (Wind shuffles by [,] that scavenger in rags [,] |
Collecting souls from vacant paper bags').

She said, 'How tiring the lights are!'

Autumn 1926; 'Consequences', *Oxford University Review*, ii, 5 (18 November 1926),
p. 177; *Juvenilia*, p. 162.

It may seem appropriate that a poem of this title should play with the idea of
inconsequentiality. At its most dramatic this is embodied in the idea of the
mature male cut off in his prime (in the epigraph, taken from Owen's
'Futility'), though the disillusionment of the poem itself is predominantly
psychosexual. Psychosexual too, one might say, is the point of the game of
fictional encounters called 'Consequences', and all that is arbitrary in the
game itself (where each element is contributed in ignorance of what has
gone before) is subtly conveyed in the opening of the poem, which recounts
an incident of thwarted passion somewhat in the vein of Eliot's 'Dans le
Restaurant'. The Eliotic tone continues ('Now we have heard conclusion on
this matter'), though a sermon from Auden's prep school days also puts in
an appearance (cf. 'Address for a Prize-Day', EA, p. 61. Isherwood describes
Auden's own imitation of this sermon in *Lions and Shadows*, p. 184). The
point would seem to be the ending rather than the beginning of life. The
'denuded stumps' are probably a geological metaphor for sterility (cf. 'The
houses rolled into the sun', *Oxford Poetry*, Spring 1984, p. 86, and the chorus
'Can speak of trouble', in *Paid*, in which the image is also used). 'Gubber-
tusks' (actually 'Gubber-tushes') are sticking-out teeth.

In Spring we waited. Princes felt

Autumn 1926; 'In Due Season', *Oxford Outlook*, viii, 41 (December 1926), p. 298;
Juvenilia, p. 164.

This love poem is one of the few that somehow make a virtue of the Eliotic
disguise that Auden was wearing for much of 1926. The title (which Auden
used again in August 1968 for a poem collected in *City Without Walls*) is
biblical: 'A word spoken in due season, how good is it!' (Proverbs, xv.23).
The grotesque contrasts (the Princes and the itching lover, the Angel of
God turned into a kind of Grendel, pockets versus hair) maintain their

bizarre coherence in the manner of Eliot's quatrain poems. The poem was reprinted without Auden's permission in *Oxford Poetry 1928*. The pedal-entry in the fugue puts in an appearance in *The Orators*, EA, p. 69.

When Little Claus meets Big Claus in the road

1926; 'Pride', *Yale Review*, lxxi, 1 (Winter 1982); *Juvenilia*, p. 180.

The influence of Eliot is very marked here. The use of the comma in stanzas 2 and 4 may be compared with 'Sweeney Among the Nightingales', stanza 6. The soul of the smugly sublimated persona is 'jostled' rather as the sensitive soul is 'trampled' in 'Preludes', IV. The story of Big Claus and Little Claus is from Hans Andersen, and had also been used in a poem by Wilfred Owen.

Spring, a toy trumpet at her lips

April 1927; 'Easter Monday', *Oxford Poetry Now*, 2 (Michaelmas 1976); *Juvenilia*, p. 183.

This is another street scene or 'holiday excursion' poem in couplet quatrains, with images of a sterile spring in the style of Eliot: the 'eunuch-king' Attis is substituted for the risen Christ. The ingenious idea in lines 1–2 became the opening of a chorus in *Paid on Both Sides* (EA, p. 7, see p. 25). The 'toy trumpet', and the 'umbrellas', are simply spring flowers. The fastidious tone of 'Lady Venus' and the 'κινεμα-star' are reminiscent of the Pound of *Hugh Selwyn Mauberley*.

Four walls are drawn tight round the crew of us

?May 1927; 'Cinders', *Oxford University Review*, i, 8 (3 June 1926), p. 284; *Juvenilia*, p. 143.

The restless allusiveness of this poem is perhaps suitable to its subject, a meditation on the antinomy of spirit and body among undergraduates working late in a library. God is reduced simply to the chief ultimate unit of being ('Arch-Monad', a notion from Leibniz in the disguise of a tutor), while the power of gods has passed to the undergraduates, 'poets almost' until disturbed by lust. Auden interestingly compares himself to Coleridge, who seems to him to be the type of omnivore poet whose sexual affairs were a distraction both from 'lyric' and from 'celestial manoeuvrings' (the allusion is in line 32: compare Lamb's description of Coleridge as 'an

Archangel a little damaged' in a letter to Wordsworth, 26 April 1816).
Chanticleer, symbol of hectic propagation, dispels both religious revelation
(Advent) and scientific knowledge (Platonic year, i.e. the complete cycle of
the movement of heavenly bodies). His questioning was reused in poem 1
(h) of *Poems* (1928).

Out of sight assuredly, not out of mind

June 1927; *Oxford Poetry*, i, 3 (Spring 1984), p. 86; *Juvenilia*, p. 194.

Auden sent a longer version of this poem, which was entitled 'Letter to a
friend upon the week-end visit to his home' and included a section of
debate between the owl and the nightingale, to Isherwood in early June
1927. The intended recipient of the poem was William McElwee. Auden
remarked in an accompanying letter to Isherwood: 'I think you will
probably dislike the enclosed poem; it is partly a deliberate experiment in
the letter as a verse form, with the slight pompousness which should be
associated therewith.' Auden went on to defend the literary convention of
the bird debate, and later sent Isherwood a revision and expansion of this
section which contained some material used in the poem about McElwee,
'From the very first coming down', which he wrote about six months later.
He also sent Isherwood a postcard with a version of the final six lines in
their present form, which was adopted, with one small verbal change, as the
ending of section 1 of '1929'.

This is a wry poem of separation during a Long Vacation. The loved-one
has his homologues, i.e. his own versions, of the signs of the local landscape
as the train takes him away, signs which are familiar to Auden as heralding
the approach to his home. This imagined sharing of images is replaced by
the memories of the visit that they share, the memories that are 'acceptable'
in family terms (i.e. harmless recreation with a holiday visitor, implicitly
contrasted with the more intimate memories that would be possible if the
mind were to 'build a house' for itself). Two of these memories, and the
sheering off 'like gull from granite' were reused in stanza 4 of 'Under
boughs between our tentative endearments'. This image of the gull and the
following double negative strikingly express the contrary impulses of the
conscious and unconscious mind. This duality is sharpened in the beautiful
final section. The poet is far from Oxford (bicycles, laughter, swept gown-
ends) and its systematising of human consciousness. The day is closed with a
sudden shower that does not have to choose to fall: for humanity the need

to make choices is, by contrast, an 'error' that alienates him from the natural world.

I shall sit here through the evening

?May 1927; 'Narcissus', *Oxford Poetry*, i, 3 (Spring 1984); *Juvenilia*, p. 185.

The epigraph from St Augustine (*Confessions*, ix.4) means: 'Seeing they that take joy in anything without themselves, do easily become vain, and spill themselves upon those things which are seen and are but temporal; yea, and with their hunger-starved thoughts lick their very shadows' (Loeb edn). It can thus be taken as an ironical excuse for a cautious cultivation of the self. Narcissus was also the earliest recorded Christian hermit.

After a glum and Eliotic first stanza (cf. 'I shall sit here . . .' in 'Portrait of a Lady'), Auden reviews his poetic past with allusions to 'Lead's the Best' (line 15) and 'The Sunken Lane' (line 17), the latter an apparently heterosexual poem. It is as if to blame his emotional isolation on various false starts, not least the unrecognised appeal of schoolboy heroes like Basley, Dickon and Thomas (lines 18–20, 26–7 occur in 'The spring will come'' and in *Paid*. Isherwood borrowed the name 'Basley' for the older boy who takes up with Victor Page in *All the Conspirators*, p. 117. 'The Ten' was a cross-country race at Sedbergh school). The third stanza confronts the true nature of the poet's left-handedness in love by playing on the mirror-effect of desiring your own sex (cf. 'The earth turns over . . .' and 'Fleeing the short-haired mad executives'). An asymptote is a line which approaches nearer and nearer to a finite curve, but which does not meet it within a finite distance (cf. the 'sigmoid curve, that dwindled suddenly' in 'Thomas Epilogises', line 19, and Auden's explanation of lines 41–2 of 'The crowing of the cock'). The Achilles-and-the-Tortoise paradox thus invoked lends further Eliotic timidity to the meeting of lovers (lines 35–6 are modelled on the last section of 'The Hollow Men') which in the final section becomes a kiss that seems barely to disturb the surface of Narcissus' pool.

It is possible that Auden continued to work on this poem. In a letter to William McElwee of Good Friday 1928, he writes: 'Narcissus gathers but so slowly, but I feel now that it will come to a head in the end.' There is a momentary farewell to the Narcissus figure in the person of the 'lolling bridegroom' of section IV of '1929'. Auden used the exhaling frogs of lines 4–5, and the whole final section of another poem for McElwee ('Out of sight assuredly, not out of mind', see above), in section I of '1929'.

Truly our fathers had the gout

August 1927; *Oxford Poetry*, i, 3 (Spring 1984); *Juvenilia*, p. 216.

Gnomic images of debasement and sterility reflect the influence of Eliot here. The final pair of lines (reused in 'The mind to body spoke the whole night through') suggest from that later context a climax of inevitable disintegration that awaits a failed and unheroic generation.

We, knowing the family history

August 1927; *Oxford Poetry*, i, 3 (Spring 1984); *Juvenilia*, p. 217.

This sonnet analyses a love affair as if it were a medical case-history. The 'lethal factors' and 'indolent ulcer' were reused in 'Because sap fell away' (a poem for Gabriel Carritt) and the final couplet in 'From the very first coming down' (a poem for William McElwee). Different loved ones, but an identical problem: they were both heterosexuals.

Deemed this an outpost, I

c. October 1927; *Oxford Poetry*, i, 3 (Spring 1984); *Juvenilia*, p. 225.

This poem was included in the original TS for *Poems* (1928) but was omitted by Spender with Auden's permission. Stanza 1 is about coming to terms with one's continued role within the family and its environment (cf. the beginning of Po's speech in *Paid on Both Sides*). In stanzas 2 and 3, the poet is wrestling with a traditional Antagonist ('roar' and 'scales' indicate an early appearance of Auden's dragon, and it is likely to be also in this sense that Auden referred Isherwood to 'The Laily Worm' as a possible subtitle for the poem; for the Laily Worm, see *Lions and Shadows*, p. 66). This has unmistakable sexual overtones, and what seems at first to be a struggle against erotic gratification becomes a celebration of a successful erotic encounter with the house-guest with whom after a concert the poet walks, the 'dead Spell' (i.e. magic suspended, because for the moment indulged) earning no rebuke from the neighbours who know him. The idea of dawn leaning in stanza 5 became the final image in 'Doom is dark and deeper than any sea-dingle'.

The weeks of blizzard over

c. December 1927; *Oxford Poetry*, i, 3 (Spring 1984) (line 9: for 'above' read 'alone'; line 14: for 'Teaser-Coop' read 'Tesser-Coop' [actually 'Jesser Coope', name of brothers at St Edmund's School); *Juvenilia*, p. 236.

This poem was in the original typescript for *Poems* (1928), but was omitted by Spender with Auden's permission. The image of the kestrel on the scar (i.e. crag), together with lines 12–13, 15 and 22–30, were used in the later poem 'Missing', conflated with material from 'I chose this lean country' in *Poems* (1928). The last lines help to explain the theme of lovers fated not to meet in 'Missing' (see p. 71). The candles and wine may be compared with the 'feast' provided for the poet's guest in 'Deemed this an outpost, I'. One note successfully absent from the later poem is Auden's pleasure at the names on the war-memorial, which he used in *The Enemies of a Bishop*. In 'Missing' these are simply, and with great legendary force, 'voices in the rock').

The colonel to be shot at dawn

Christmas Day 1927; *Oxford Poetry*, i, 3 (Spring 1984); *Juvenilia*, p. 234.

One suspects that this Christmas squib was prompted by thoughts of his father, and of his brother and himself, but it is not clear whether its symbolic significance is cultural or religious. The poem was written at the parental home at Harborne.

Across the Waste to Northward, go

?Winter 1926–7; 'Day-dreams of a Tourist', *Three Unpublished Poems* (1986); *Juvenilia*, p. 176.

This experiment in describing the process of memory in accurate sensory detail places its substantive images in an ascending order of significance: first the corrugated-iron shed (presumably a real one designed soon to become a symbol for a soon-to-be 'exhausted' infatuation), then the flooded football-fields (stanza 2) and the tolling bell (stanza 3) which take the memory back to a term-time setting, then in stanza 5 the 'you' who is, after all, the object of the mnemonic exercise. The poem is a serious examination of the psychological process of memory as well as a way of indicating, without unnecessary emotion, the progress of an affair.

Your shoulder stiffens to my kiss

?Winter 1926–7; 'The Evolution of the Dragon', *Three Unpublished Poems* (1986); *Juvenilia*, p. 177.

The title of this poem alludes to a book of the same name published in 1919 by G. Elliot Smith, the historical anthropologist and significant influence on the cultural theories of W. J. Perry which appear in Auden's 'O Love, the interest itself in thoughtless heaven' and other poems. The dragon in Smith's theory is related to the power of water, which links the turbine in the poem with such myths as Jason and the Argonauts which still have power to induce terror. The bathos of unheroic lives is remarkably Eliotic in this poem. The line from Verlaine's 'Sagesse' is a rebuke to youth, who is doing nothing with his life. The idea of the dragon being one of the 'specific projections of our human fears' is found in the later uncollected poem ' "Sweet is it", say the doomed, "to be alive though wretched" '.

The houses rolled into the sun

?1927; *Oxford Poetry*, i, 3 (Spring 1984); *Juvenilia*, p. 234.

This poem was included in the typescript of *Poems* (1928), but omitted by Spender with Auden's permission. Fagge in line 11 was a boy at St Edmund's School (*A Tribute*, p. 32). Lines 13–14 are borrowed from 'Consequences' (published 18 November 1926) and were later used in the chorus 'Can speak of trouble' in *Paid on Both Sides* (EA, p. 3). 'So it is with us' (line 7) may be an ironical allusion to the refrain in the Old English poem 'Wulf and Eadwacer'.

'Grow thin by walking and go inland'

April 1928; *Oxford Poetry*, i, 3 (Spring 1984); *Juvenilia*, p. 243.

This poem about the easier route taken has several resemblances to 'The Secret Agent', which also uses landscape for erotic allegory. Unlike the later poem's establishment of a controlling and betraying 'they', however, here the evasiveness is self-generated. Faced with the possibility of going further, he returns because 'Love is not there' (cf. 'Love by ambition', line 27). He lies, however, and is self-deceivingly proud of his evasiveness. Compare the 'hidden village' with the 'easy power' of 'The Secret Agent'. The line about lying about the cost of a night's lodging was reused in the chorus 'To throw away the key and walk away' in *Paid on Both Sides* (EA, p. 12), a version of which was written in Spa, Belgium, in the summer of 1928, that included the line about 'no case from Belgium to explain it by'. Auden stayed with a psychoanalyst on this visit (in a letter to David Ayerst he concludes: 'I find I am quite ambidextrous now': see Carpenter, p. 82; the psychoanalyst might have been Margaret Marshall). It would seem that an actual abortive possibility of a liaison with a friend on a walking expedition lies behind all these poems.

This morning any touch is possible

December 1928; 'Epithalamium for C. Day-Lewis', in Sean Day-Lewis, *C. Day-Lewis: an English literary life*, 1980, p. 307.

The poem was written for Cecil Day-Lewis on his marriage to Mary King at Sherborne on 27 December 1928. The stanza rhymes and half-rhymes with complexity: abacdcbd. The elevated tone of erotic celebration is maintained in the first two stanzas with images of hunting, and of pity for those unloved (there is an echo of the *Pervigilium veneris* in line 2). In stanza 3, using the opening phrase from 'Taller today, we remember similar evenings', Auden refers to the sexual scandals that haunted Day-Lewis's schooldays at Sherborne as hurt pride and lust (see Sean Day-Lewis's biography, p. 18). Most of stanza 4 reuses the opening lines of a poem of 1925, 'Punchard', and the third line of stanza 5 also comes from 'Taller today . . .' The last two lines of the poem were reused in the wedding scene of *Paid on Both Sides* (*Plays*, p. 32).

Time flies, Cecil; hardly a week ago

March 1929; 'Verse-letter to C. Day-Lewis', in Sean Day-Lewis, *C. Day-Lewis: an English literary life*, 1980, p. 309.

This verse epistle in couplets intended to be imitative of Dryden was written as a thankyou letter from Berlin after Auden had stayed with Cecil and Mary Day-Lewis at Helensburgh from 22 to 25 February 1929. It catches the homesick mood of 'It was Easter as I walked in the public gardens' with a fetching openness, and proceeds to an interesting critical survey of the modern poets ('Wolfe, the typists' poet' is Humbert Wolfe, extremely popular in the 1920s). Margaret Marshall and Christopher Isherwood are mentioned in terms similar to those in which they appear in 'I chose this lean country' (see p. 6). The three following friends mentioned are Rex Warner, Gabriel Carritt and William McElwee. The remainder of the poem analyses the career of the married poet (Auden was still engaged to Sheilah Richardson).

Father and mother, twin-lights of heaven

December 1929; *TLS*, 16 January 1976.

In many of Auden's early poems the insentient vegetable life is proposed as a kind of ironic ideal, but vegetation has no vision or memory. It is the incisiveness of the eye here which attempts to transcend the organic entropy (stanza 7) which threatens life. It does so by acting as a symbol of the submission of the powers of archaic darkness to the supremacy of light (stanza 6) and more particularly, in the opening stanzas, as a conditioned response to the sun and the moon seen in a Lawrentian way as male and female principles (compare the end of 'Statement' in *The Orators*). This is in effect presented as the primary duality which (like parentage) launches the human enterprise. In stanza 4, the 'face's primary division' probably refers to a received rule of proportion in drawing faces. The poem was written at Wescoe.

Having abdicated with comparative ease

January 1930; 'Interview', *Cambridge Left*, 1 (Summer 1933); *Westminster Magazine*, xxiv, 1 (Spring–Summer 1935); 'Half Way', CP, p. 69; EA, p. 45.

This surrealist briefing of a defecting enemy looks forward to *The Orators*. It is a high-spirited piece, though slight enough (its level is indicated, for example, in lines 11–12 by the comic conflation of Julius Caesar and freemasonry ritual). An omitted stanza helped, with its schoolboy nicknames, to identify both the humour and the imagery as essentially that of the school world. Auden had sight of the poem in 1964 when the MS notebook in which it appears was acquired by the British Library (Add. MS. 52430). In 1965 he allowed Laurence Scott to print seventy-five copies of it on his private press, in which it was described as 'Revised from an old notebook, *c*. 1931.' and slightly revised. This text was published in the 1966 *Collected Shorter Poems* with its present title, and it seems that Auden had forgotten its earlier appearances.

Pick a quarrel, go to war

?1930; the seventeen gnomic verses printed in EA, p. 50, were taken from the 1928–
?30 Notebook. A different but overlapping MS and TS collection was sent to
Isherwood. Nos 1, 2, 4, 10, 12, 13, 14 and 15 of the EA set had been published by
Auden himself in CSP66, p. 42, after he had sight of them in the notebook. Four
other similar poems had been published earlier: 'The Mother had wanted' and
'When I remarked at table' as 'Case Histories', *Adelphi*, ns ii, 3 (June 1931), p. 198;
'Why all the fuss' and 'New Life needs freedom first' as 'Cautionary Rhymes',
Adelphi, ns iii (3 December 1931) ('These ordered light' in the CSP66 set was also
one of the *Adelphi* 'Cautionary Rhymes' and was used in Ode IV of *The Orators*, EA, p.
103). Of the further set of eighteen gnomic verses printed in *As I Walked Out One
Evening* (1995), (d) 'Man would be happy, loving and sage', (f) 'Willy, finding half a
soul', (g) 'Desire for death in the morning', (o) 'Come kiss me now, you old brown
cow', and (p) 'Don't know my father's name', were previously unpublished, while
(e) 'Tommy did as mother told him' was first published in my *Reader's Guide to W. H.
Auden* (1970), p. 29.

No. 1 ('Pick a quarrel, go to war') is a simple exposition of the Auden–
Isherwood theory of the Truly Strong Man, who has no need for bravado,
but 'sits drinking quietly in the bar' (*Lions and Shadows*, p.207). Auden's
account of the same theory may be found in his review of Liddell Hart's
book on T. E. Lawrence (EA, p. 320). The quatrain also appears in Auden
and Isherwood's 'Preliminary Statement' (*Plays*, p. 46). Most of the
remaining shorts are rebukes to parental power or ineffectiveness, or rather
patly illustrate Homer Lane's theory of psychosomatic illness, though no. 13
('I'm beginning to lose patience') turns the despondency of the lavish and
unsuccessful wooer into a memorably wry witticism. Some of the others cast
a little light on parts of *The Orators*: No. 3 ('Schoolboy, making lonely maps')
makes explicit the homosexual scenario of the 'Prologue'; no. 16 ('There
are two kinds of friendship even in babes') was used in 'Argument' (for
comment, see p. 95); and the double-bind of 'Journal of an Airman' is
embodied in no. 7 (' "We take that hill" the colonel cried') (see also the
1929 journal, EA, p. 300). Compare (p) with 'The silly fool, the silly fool'.

'Renewal of traditional anger in peace'

January 1930; *Pearl* (Odense) 2, Autumn 1976.

This is perhaps Auden's first sestina, and interestingly shares one of its key-
words with the most interesting key-word of 'Hearing of harvests rotting in

the valley' (but see my argument about 'sorrow' on p. 154). The poem rehearses the idea of spiritual death as being akin to an 'entropic peace' (see 'It was Easter as I walked in the public gardens', part IV, completed about three months earlier).

Poems (1930)

Auden's first public collection was published by Faber and Faber in September 1930. He had submitted a collection to the then Faber and Gwyer in June 1927, but T. S. Eliot had declined the book. It is not known what it then contained. The dedicatory quatrain to Christopher Isherwood has sometimes been read as containing a sexual innuendo which, however, is utterly belied by the memorial tone of the verse: the contrast is between the living ('vertical') and the dead ('horizontal').

Will you turn a deaf ear

September 1929; P30, p. 37; 'The Questioner Who Sits So Sly', CP45, p. 177; CP, p. 41; EA, p. 35.

This poem was used as the Prologue to *The Enemies of a Bishop*, to be spoken by Bishop Law and addressed to a member of the audience. This context validates such lofty rebuke, for the character was intended in some sense to represent Homer Lane: the poem is addressed to those members of society who have perceived its malaise, but are too weak to do anything about it. The tone of the opening question should reflect a certain measure of derision ('How can you possibly . . .?'), and the title (first used in the 1945 *Collected Poetry*) reinforces this with its allusion to Blake's 'Auguries of Innocence' ('The Questioner who sits so sly | Shall never know how to reply'). Obviously, the 'questioner' is the enlightened but passive intellectual who is being addressed. He must do more than question, or he himself will not be able to stand interrogation (i.e. the poem).

The implication throughout is that if he can see why the rich are behaving as they are, he ought to act to cure them: i.e. he ought to wear a 'ruffian badge', etc. The rich are seen to be totally conditioned by their psychological state of mind, according to the theories of Lane and John Layard. Compare, for instance, the 'stork-legged heaven-reachers' with Auden's reported comment, as he expounded his newly discovered Lane doctrine, on Stephen Spender in 1928: 'Stephen's different. You know why he's so tall? He's trying to reach Heaven!' (*Lions and Shadows*, p. 303). 'Death' in stanzas 5–8 represents this overriding wish of a society to destroy itself (as in *The Dance of Death*) and is personified as hypochondriac, eccentric, a betrayer of youth. The invalid chair refers to Auden's employer, Colonel Solomon, war-wounded and confined like Lawrence's Clifford Chatterley (Carpenter, p. 108). Mendelson (p. 86) ingeniously suggests that Death's favourite colour might be blue because that is the colour of recent corpses, although blue is traditionally the male colour. Blue as the colour of distant bells may also have an association with Spender, whose eyes were the 'violent colour of bluebells' and who in a specially remembered incident gave 'a wild silly laugh' on hearing a carillon of bells destined for a war memorial in New Zealand tinkle out 'The Bluebells of Scotland' in Hyde Park (*Lions and Shadows*, pp. 281, 283). Blue overalls, uniform of working youth, turn up again in the opening chorus of *On the Frontier*.

Stanzas 8–10 give examples of the paradoxical position into which the sly questioner is forced (the infinitives are all dependent on 'Hard' in line 31), and the conclusion is that there is no reward for his attitude: the immediate result of such compromise is apparent failure, though to his descendants ('later other') the compromise might seem honourable. In stanza 12, Auden borrowed a phrase from Thomas Mann's *The Magic Mountain* ('history hermetically sealed') according to Charles Miller (Miller TS, p. 48). The poem succeeds by virtue of its curiously suggestive imagery rather than by its point or argument, and much of its persuasiveness lies in the half-rhymes.

Which of you waking early and watching daybreak

October 1929; P30, p. 39; EA, p. 41; omitted from P33.

Auden attempted to remove this poem from his first collection at proof stage, no doubt finding it too facile a celebration of 'peace' and 'truth's assurance of life'. Writing to Spender a year later, he was claiming that 'All poetry in our time is comic. There are two modes 1) The drunken prophetic 2) The legal disclaimer.' He went on to say that he ought to have written this poem in the first mode, but used the second instead: 'Result a pompous old gentleman' (*Auden Studies* 1, p. 60). The poem argues that such truth is there for the finding, natural as a grass-blade, for 'the mother of all life' ('Anima Mundi' in a draft sent to Isherwood) is omnipresent and sustaining. Mendelson has pointed out (p. 80) how the third section paraphrases Homer Lane's belief that any individual contains an organic accumulation of his predecessors' drive for perfection. It is only a short step from this belief to the assertion that the individual can recognise and share in that drive, rather than succumb to the collapse and alienation that is the outcome of the rake's progress of section four. The philosophical mood and insinuating arguments of the poem no doubt derive from Robert Bridges, whose *The Testament of Beauty* had recently been published (see Isherwood, 'Some notes on the early poetry', *A Tribute*, p. 77). Critics have been severe about this poem. Virginia Woolf remarked: 'I feel as if I had stubbed my toe on the corner of the wardrobe' (*Collected Essays*, 1966, ii, 187).

Since you are going to begin to-day

November 1929; P30, p. 41; 'Venus Will Now Say a Few Words', CP45, p. 109; CP, p. 43; EA, p. 44.

Here, in the compulsive and insidiously accusatory half-rhymed couplets of Owen's 'Strange Meeting', Nature explains to the happy games-playing lover how he represents only a momentary stage in her evolutionary plans, and how earlier forms of life, like his, were experimental and doomed to extinction. It is clear that the lover is being accused of selfishness. Compare 'Remembering everything you can confess' with 'Hushed for aggression | Of full confession' in 'Love by ambition'. And compare 'Relax in your darling's arms like a stone' with 'Stop behaving like a stone' in 'Get there if you can'. This phrase is explained by the 1928–?30 notebook, fols 11–12: 'That which desires life to itself, to arrest growth, is behaving like a stone and casts itself like Lucifer out of heaven.' The 'darling' was Robert Medley, according to Auden's annotation of a copy of the third printing of the US *Poems* in the Berg. In the final section, the phrase 'central anguish felt | For goodness wasted at peripheral fault' is a development of a remark in the 1929 journal: 'Man is relatively unspecialised at the periphery and highly organised at the centre, allowing a much greater freedom of environment than is possible to animals such as insects whose appendages are specialised' (*The English Auden*, p. 297). Such lack of specialisation leads to the starvation of the self, as in a besieged town. If the lover turns to religion, this merely means that the life force has moved on to another evolutionary stage, perhaps his son: and even he will be treated in the same way, 'tipped' (to win) and later 'topped' (hanged). The cycle seems inevitable. The poem shares a version of its ending with 'Consider if you will how lovers stand': the 'holders of one position' who now replace Solomon and Sheba are probably borrowed from Frost's 'Holding the curve of one position' ('Devotion' in *West Running Brook*, 1928).

Watch any day his nonchalant pauses, see

March 1929; P30, p. 43; 'We all Make Mistakes', CP45, p. 152; 'A Free One', CP, p. 40; EA, p. 31.

The careful lover of 'Upon this line between adventure' (also in five tercets) is paralleled here by a more dramatically caricatured member of the emotionally constipated middle-classes. Though 'the beggar's envy', this man is not free: an attitudinising chaperone is not a man of action and the country-house routine (like the undemonstrative camaraderie of 'Upon this line between adventure') is actually 'the longest way to an intrinsic peace'. The somewhat Yeatsian penultimate stanza proposes (vaguely) a solution: the 'buried' life and the 'warning' of war (compare 'iron wood' with Pope's 'iron harvests' in *Essay on Man*, iv.12) are twin symptoms of the middle-class death wish, and could possibly be healed by 'the song, the varied action of the blood'. Instead, however, we have the formalised gestures of that class, based at several removes upon the heroes they no longer resemble, now merely inflexible, evasive and precarious. The poem was written in Berlin.

From the very first coming down

Published in P28: see p. 12.

To have found a place for nowhere

November 1929; P30, p. 45; EA, p. 43; omitted from P33.

Mendelson (p. 88) has an ingenious explication of the first two sections of this difficult poem as 'a summary account of colonialism'. However, the lines in those sections that he does not accommodate within his reading, taken with the rest of the poem, suggests that 'the creation | Of nation from nation' might just as easily be the begetting of a new generation as the extension of empire. The tautologies and negatives of the opening define the etiology of a generation in spiritual limbo, just as the paradoxes of the ending define its teleology: it is a generation that was born in fear of fear and that lives by hoping in hope; indeed, forces hope to act as surrogate for true development.

Within this gnomic framework Auden has arranged his illustrative material in Skeltonic couplets, triplets and quatrains from which emerge two familiar Auden notions that amplify his understanding of the relationship between his own and earlier generations. The first is that the legendary has become the trivial and sporting ('girls and guns | And letters home') and that natural heroism has become a matter of anecdote or joke ('bending forks | And musical talks'). Here the ambience is, as so often in Auden, the country house and its convivial 'tables'. The 'vantage spots' (like the 'spots' in 'From scars where kestrels hover' from which the summer visitors come to view the 'prize competitors') are places where once 'mortal' fears were isolated. Now they are ripe for the bourgeoisification ('neighbour plots') which Forster feared in *Howards End* and which brings in its wake comparable quantities of mental instability and accumulating capital ('wards and banks'). The second notion is that, like it or not, we eventually turn into our fathers ('a mortal's heir | With loathing remembrance | And a growing resemblance'). In this sense, one may also become 'neighbour' to a previous generation and in one's turn become irrationally repressive, despite moments of erotic escape ('Pulling the cap down, tightening belt' seems to allude to Auden living cheaply in Berlin, where he wore a workman's cap). Auden uses words like 'mortal' and 'neighbour' impersonally to suggest, without directly invoking, the relationships and vulnerability of family life.

Upon this line between adventure

June 1929; P30, p. 46; 'Do be Careful', CP45, p. 151; 'Between Adventure', CP, p. 39; EA, p. 32.

It appears that this poem was written for Otto Kusel, one of the dedicatees of *The Enemies of a Bishop*, with whom Auden spent some time in an inn at Rottehütte in the summer of 1929 (Carpenter, p. 103). Kusel, who had escaped from a reformatory, probably helped to inspire the reformatory plot of that play and *The Chase*. Another poem to which Auden attached Kusel's initials, 'Sentries against inner and outer', also suggests the danger or fear of commitment, and again expresses it in imagery of combat. The injunction 'On narrowness stand, for sunlight is I Brightest only on surfaces' suggests the risk of exposure to snipers. Such military imagery is not new in Auden. The rhymes slow down the verse and cleverly mimic the cautiousness advocated for the lover: friendship is safe; it avoids a decision. On either side of that knife-edge lies commitment or rejection, each involving the world of emotion which is being avoided. Compare the ending with the last line of Robert Graves's 'O Love be fed with apples'.

Again in conversations

January 1929; P30, p. 47; 'Two's Company', CP45, p. 5; 'Never Stronger', CP, p. 35; EA, p. 27.

In this Berlin poem we are shown how the weak are again and again attracted to mere talk about love, instead of to the real thing. They may in conversation feel that they have grasped what it is all about, but this is imaginary. Gossip about other people's love affairs doesn't tell them how to embark on one themselves. They may leave the talkers and try to act, but out of timidity they usually return, because although they may seem to be defying their real natures by returning, they can escape judgement: at the heart of a hurricane there is always a womb-like calm ('the centre of anger I Is out of danger') in which they can hide. In 1933 Auden changed line 7 ('Than peace-time occupations') to 'Than boys' imaginations', probably feeling that the metaphor of love as war, widely used in the volume as a whole, was inappropriate here.

The crowing of the cock

Published in P28; see p. 11.

Love by ambition

March 1929; P30, p. 49; 'Too Dear, Too Vague', CP, p. 38; EA, p. 30.

Auden attached to this poem the initials of Kurt Groote, the young German friend mentioned in 'It was Easter as I walked in the public gardens'. It suggests that only our efforts to understand love taunt us with the possibility of its perfection and finality. We define it into yes and no – into, that is, reciprocated and unreciprocated love – as though these clear alternatives solved anything. Auden shows that love can destroy itself, whatever its circumstances: our insistent rationalisations are irrelevant to it. The second part of the poem carries echoes of Lawrence's arguments about 'sex in the head', and Auden may have in mind, in his lines about leaving 'the North in place | With a good grace', Lawrence's elaboration of his theory about the four poles of the dynamic psyche (*Fantasia of the Unconscious*, Phoenix edn, 1961, pp. 100ff). For 'Love has moved to another chair', cf. Emily Dickinson: 'I cannot live with You – | It would be Life – | And Life is over there.' 'Love is not there' are the words of the protagonist of Auden's ' "Grow thin by walking and go inland" ' (see p. 47).

The influence of Laura Riding is marked in the poem (see my commentary on 'Before this loved one', p. 65).

Who stands, the crux left of the watershed

Published in P28; see p. 8.

We made all possible preparations

December 1928; P30, p. 52; 'Let History Be My Judge', CP, p. 34; EA, p. 26.

The speaker proposes, with all the deadly reasoning of a self-righteous counter-revolutionary, a justification of repression and control by authority in the face of developing resistance to it. The 'situation' might be a generalised version of the General Strike; at least, there is some kind of emergency presented in the first two stanzas, which the speaker presumes is a challenge to a whole way of life, and must be met by force. Whose fault is this emergency? Stanzas 5 and 6 suggest that those in precarious control do have some inkling that the seeds of disruption are contained in the basic nature of society ('possibilities of error | At the very start'), so that finally the speaker is left clinging only to his self-respect and vested interests. After that, it appears, anything might happen. A psychological interpretation of this scenario is clearly intended.

Bones wrenched, weak whimper, lids wrinkled, first dazzle known

Published in P28; see p. 3.

Sentries against inner and outer

June 1929; P30, p. 53; 'Shut Your Eyes and Open Your Mouth', CP45, p. 104; EA, p. 33.

This is one of the more powerful of Auden's early love poems, depending for its effect on the reasonable Marvellian tone of the couplets up to the moment when the military metaphors yield gratefully to the erotic close. The psyche's defences are plotted like a graph ('stated interval') but the unarticled 'feature' is soon to be revealed as meaning the 'features' of the loved one's face (or possibly it is simply the teeth that are 'sentries' to the gate of the mouth: cf. Lawrence, *Fantasia of the Unconscious*, p. 57). It seems likely, though, that the 'sentries', whatever they are, militate against the perception of sensory wholes like love. Wolfgang Köhler used Goethe's words 'Denn was innen, das ist aussen' as a chapter heading in a work of 1920 and felt that it was misunderstood by some psychologists. Sensory wholes ('had it but known') originate in the nervous system of the individual, so the 'knowledge', being 'innen', is in consequence also 'aussen' (see Köhler, *Gestalt Psychology*, 1930, p. 133). You may 'parley' with the mouth, because only the mouth as an erotic centre can subvert the implacable opposition to love of the other features; but also because the mouth is the organ of speech, and the poem is really (despite its coolness and indirection) a wooing poem, written in Rottehütte, and like 'Upon this line between adventure', for Otto Kusel (see p. 56).

Control of the passes was, he saw, the key

Published in P28; see p. 14.

It was Easter as I walked in the public gardens

April–October 1929; P30, p. 55; '1929', CP, p. 45; EA, p. 37.

This key poem in its length, variety of detail and autobiographical allusions, breaks new ground (elsewhere in *Poems*, 1930, only 'From the very first coming down' and 'The strings' excitement, the applauding drum' use a reliably personal 'I'). It elaborates in an organised meditative framework, with its four parts corresponding roughly with the four seasons, Auden's central theory of social and psychological death and rebirth. Its later title emphasises the crucial role played in Auden's personal development by the year 1929, during which he (a) found personal liberation among the male prostitutes of Berlin; (b) established his critique of Freud's reliance on conventional morality; and (c) broke off his engagement with Sheilah Richardson. For Auden, the establishment of sexual identity was intimately bound up with his relationship with his family. The power of the family ('homesick') is replaced by the power of sexual exploit ('a fresh hand'), but at the same time actual homecoming is a motif in the poem with a contrary pull. Auden used to joke about his appetites ('Insufficient weaning . . . I must have something to *suck*', *Lions and Shadows*, p. 193), but weaning also becomes a serious poetic metaphor. If Freud was right in claiming that the ego can only give up a love object by identifying itself with it (as Auden noted in his 1929 Berlin journal), there is the danger that the insufficiently weaned son will 'become' his mother and seek new love objects that are like himself (one source for the idea in Freud is *Group Psychology and the Analysis of the Ego*, 1922, p. 66). Auden noted in his 1929 journal: 'One falls in love with people of that age at which one was most unhappy.' He also noted in the journal that 'The point of psychology is to prove the Gospel' and the particular psychology that Auden was anxious to prove is that which explains the necessity of escape from the family ('liberation from the superego, obeyed like the parents whom Christ enjoined us to abandon'). The poem is indeed full of such psychology, but its occasion is Christian.

Part 1 (April 1929). As the first line indicates, it is an Easter poem, and when he remembers 'all of those whose death | Is necessary condition of the season's setting forth | Who sorry in this time look only back | to Christmas intimacy', it is inescapable that he has the Christian story in mind. Indeed, he had something of a habit of writing Easter Day poems (see p. 37). Since he needs here to suggest a mysterious interrelationship of various cycles of change – personal, bodily, social and psychological – it is small wonder that the Resurrection finds a place. The poem's opening and closing paragraphs focus simultaneously on two myths that provide a sexual and spiritual framework for the poem: the death of Jesus and the death of Narcissus.

For Auden, the latter had become a convenient shorthand for the impasse referred to above, whereby in the process of inescapable identification with the mother the homosexual falls in love with images of himself. At Oxford he had attempted to exorcise his love for the heterosexual William McElwee with the poem 'Narcissus' (July 1927), which identified the love object with the poet's image in the pool ('my sterilised left-handed lover'), the pool itself representing the barrier between them, primarily a barrier of the will. Incidentally, this idea of the mirror-effect of desiring your own sex survives in 'The earth turns over' and 'Fleeing the short-haired mad executives' (both written in 1933). Auden did not abandon 'Narcissus'. He wrote to McElwee on Good Friday 1928 ('Jesus died today'): 'Narcissus gathers but so slowly, but I feel now that it will come to a head in the end.' Continuing to feel that 'homosexuality is an unnecessary form of narcissism, an attempt to complete oneself' (1929 journal), Auden gave his new poem a similar setting to 'Narcissus', with its abject grief and solitariness and its frogs exhaling from a pond. But he also borrowed images from stanza 1 of Hopkins's 'The Alchemist in the City', lending the setting the alchemist's detachment. It suited him, in his prediction of change, to put the solitary Narcissus figure at a distance: he encounters 'solitary man . . . weeping on a bench', and the generalising power of his omitted article elevates this image into a symbol of human despair. One is reminded of the 'solitary Man' of Wordsworth's Old Cumberland Beggar, for example, even, visually, via Grünewald, of the crucified Christ. The phrase 'like an embryo chicken' was used in the 1929 journal about John Layard after he had shot himself in the face, and it is Layard's analysis of his own failure that is referred to (Carpenter, chapter 5). Auden's relationship with the depressive Layard, and with 'new names', compliant German boys like Kurt Groote and Gerhart Meyer, allowed him the doubtful confidence of equating 'success' with 'happiness' and 'absence of fear', qualities which Homer Lane's teachings transmitted through Layard, but which were sadly not embodied in Layard's own life. Auden actually first met Gerhart Meyer on Easter Sunday, 1929. The contained and unassuming strength of the 'truly strong man' is intended to contrast with the impulse to rash exploit characteristic of the 'truly weak man', a significant theme in early Auden, deriving from the psychologist Bleuler (*Lions and Shadows*, p. 207). The once-hated master had rebuked Auden for writing poems during prep (*A Tribute*, p. 42). According to Auden's notes in the 1929 journal, cancer is the result of hatred of spiritual and creative love.

Part 1 ends with a strikingly metaphorical evocation of the peaceful scene before him: it is so natural that 'choice' (i.e. the efforts of the analysers and of the 'unforgiving' in Part 2 to rationalise their divided selves) seems inevitably mistaken, a 'necessary error'. However, 'O felix culpa! O necessarium peccatum Adae!' is part of the liturgy of Easter Saturday and is quoted in *Piers Plowman*, v. 610. Lines 27–33 are borrowed, almost unchanged, from the ending of another poem of the Long Vacation of 1927 written for McElwee, 'Out of sight assuredly, not out of mind'. The poet is far from Oxford (bicycles, laughter, swept gown-ends) and its systematising of human consciousness. The day is closed with a sudden shower that does not have to choose to fall: for humanity the need to make choices is, by contrast, an 'error' that alienates him from the natural world. For Narcissus, it was the difficult act of choosing ('Between the perception and the noun, | The desire, and the assurance, I and AM') that was symbolised as the surface of his pool, 'this film between us'. (Auden also used lines 27–33, and most of the material in the first section, as part of a verse letter to Isherwood intended to serve as a dedication of his play *The Reformatory*: this version gave an entirely different weight to the 'choice', which was the choice between poetry and life.) 'Sessile' here means belonging in one place (Auden used the word again of plants in the late poem 'Possible?').

Part 2 (May 1929). In Part 2 the instinctive natural life is embodied in the ducks which the poet observes in the harbour (their perfection perhaps indicated by the Yeatsian word 'paddle': cf. 'that mysterious, always brimming lake | Where those that have obeyed the holy law | Paddle and are perfect', 'Broken Dreams', lines 32–4). The ducks find the 'luxury' of the summer sun enough, and do not know the 'restlessness of intercepted growth' (cf. Trigant Burrow, *The Social Basis of Consciousness*, 1927, pp. 115ff). In the fourth stanza Auden elaborates this idea of arrested growth by giving a rather laconic Lawrentian account of the birth and growth of the individual (the central chapters of *Psychoanalysis and the Unconscious* seem relevant here). The failure is ultimately a sexual failure: 'Body reminds in him to loving, | Reminds but takes no further part.' In other words, reason and instinct are divided. As Auden himself comments: 'Body and mind are distinct but neither can exist alone, nor is there rightly a rivalry between them. Attempts to turn body into mind (Manicheeism) or mind into body (Arianism) lead to disease, madness, and death' (1928–?30 notebook, fol. 13). This is, of course, Lane's doctrine, too, and is associated with the Freudian death-wish. To have become 'other' and to fear 'other' is a state of primal anxiety, significantly different from, if etymologically identical to, the 'altering' things of Part 1 ('alter' means 'other'), for which an 'altering' speech must be found. Auden (with the help of Gertrude Stein) finds an altered abbreviated speech here for the organism's growing sense of identity and of being at peace with itself.

This concluding urgency 'To love my life' is given an added significance by the setting of this part of the poem in a time of political disturbance. The poet is naturally distressed to hear of police brutality in the May Day demonstrations by the communists, but pretends that he is pleased because this will accelerate the revolution (just as the Crucifixion is at once painful and joyful to a Christian, so the girl of nineteen shot through the knees takes on a significance that transcends the particular circumstances, a 'necessary error' of another kind). The last line of this section is borrowed from an unpublished poem 'Punchard' and originally referred to the impossibility of finding 'the word | Fit to speak of beauty and the dead'.

Part 3 (August 1929). Here the divided individual is seen desperately doing what he can to alleviate his loneliness. 'Order to stewards and the study of time | . . . in books' dignifies a railway lunch and the consulting of Bradshaw in an unexpectedly mock-heroic manner, but perhaps he is merely trying to reinforce the general feeling we have of the only half-consciously perceived passing of events. In late July Auden returned to England (to the family cottage, Far Wescoe, in Cumberland) and broke off his engagement. The development of the child from its mother in Part 2 is now specifically described in terms of weaning (cf. *Paid on Both Sides*) and colonising, both ways of achieving independent identity, both fraught with the insecurity of needing to face what one is leaving behind. Two lines cancelled from the P30 version at line 12 ('By opposite strivings for entropic peace, | Retreat to lost home or advance to new') emphasise two contrasts here (a) between the self-regulating conflicts that may lead to the unchangeable state of entropy and the real peace of 'absolute unity' in Part 2; and (b) between the home that has been left and which one may be homesick for and the home that has yet to be found (for psychological entropy, see Jung, *Contributions to Analytical Psychology*, 1928, pp. 27ff).

In fact, time irrevocably propels us along, and leaves us no idea whether what we cling to belongs to the past or the future. The ideas about love at lines 16ff are from Chekhov: 'Love. Either it is a remnant of something degenerating, something which has once been immense, or it is a particle of what will in the future develop into something immense; but in the present it is unsatisfying, it gives much less than one expects' (*The Note-Books of Anton Tchekhov*, tr. S. S. Koteliansky and Leonard Woolf, 1921, p. 36; Auden used this in a different translation in the *Faber Book of Aphorisms*, p. 180). It seems probable, however, that life will change, and by the end of the section Auden is clear that seasonal experience does prepare us for change, and for 'new conditions'. A couple of borrowings from the remarkably Eliotic 1 (c) in *Poems* (1928) gives a clue as to the kind of 'death' that Auden means here, although the last line of the section comes from J. W. Dunne's *An Experiment with Time* (1927), p. 181, where it refers to the foreknowledge of dreams in relation to actual death, a subject that Auden dealt with in the drafts to the section a few lines before the end (Mendelson, p. 75).

Part 4 (October 1929). Impending winter underlines the final decadence of society and the final madness of the psychologically ill, and at this moment of crisis the country-house guest and the closeted maniac can hardly be distinguished. Children playing in a depressing industrial environment are sensitive to the critical change: it is more than the year that is dying. In addition to natural forces there are supernatural ones, the dragon (Revelations xii.9) and the devourer (Malachi iii.11) whom the dead Christ has yet to defeat. In the original *Poems* text, ten lines at line 8 and six lines at line 20 supported the idea that real love needs death, too. Not the love of the 'frightened soul' of Part 3, who does not know if love 'be seed in time to display | Luxuriantly in a wonderful fructification', but a love completely reborn. 'You whom I gladly walk with' was Robert Medley, according to Auden's annotation of a copy of the US *Poems* (3rd printing, 1937) in the Berg.

Auden takes up this Chekhovian idea of love as a seed in the phrase 'death of the grain', referring to John xii.24: 'Except a corn of wheat fall into the ground and die, it abideth alone: but if it die, it bringeth forth much fruit.' Probably he was reminded of the biblical text by its use in Gerald Heard's *The Ascent of Humanity* (1929), p. 94. He was still ready to quote it ten years later in *The Prolific and the Devourer*, Part II, as a key example of the principle of spiritual growth that recognises change: 'We are not asked to destroy or deny any part of our nature but to allow it to grow and be converted' (p. 33). The allusion in Auden's phrase also perhaps invokes Gide's autobiography, '*Si le Grain ne Meurt*'. The Christian sense of life-in-death is provided in the same line by an echo of Eliot's 'Journey of the Magi' published a couple of years before: compare 'death, death of the grain, our death' with Eliot's 'This Birth was | Hard and bitter agony for us, like Death, our death', and therefore, proleptically, with the Resurrection. Though 'death of the old gang' seems merely to be thrown in for good measure, the poem ends by prophesying the burial of these beautifully selected representatives of their social class, 'The hard bitch and the riding-master', also pathic examples of confident sexuality. The unconfident example ('lolling', i.e. untumescent, where they are 'stiff') is also, as the syntax makes clear, to be forgotten in the spring: the 'lolling bridegroom' is the 'beautiful' Narcissus of the McElwee poem, now immersed in his own image 'deep in clear lake' along with other adolescent excitements and self-confidence (cf. 'No drowned hair crease the pond again' in an unpublished poem 'Before' of about 1925. There are other references to Narcissus in the juvenilia). Auden continued to acknowledge the seductive clarity of the reflective medium in which the narcissist lover perceives his dangerous love object (see *The Age of Anxiety*, CP, p. 365, and 'Dame Kind', stanza 5). Katherine Bucknell (*Auden Studies* 3, p. 202) argues for a fatalistic allusion here to Andersen's 'The Ice Maiden'. Rudy's reclamation by the Ice Maiden when he rows Babette to Chillon on the eve of his wedding and drowns in the 'clear' blue water of Lake Geneva is indeed strangely in keeping with the forward movement of this final section of Auden's poem: 'The prologue ended that the true drama of life might begin' ('The Ice Maiden', tr. Dulcken, repr. 1983, p. 689).

This lunar beauty

April 1930; P30, p. 61; 'Pur', CP45, p. 134; 'Like A Dream', CSP50, p. 145; 'This Lunar Beauty', CP, p. 55; EA, p. 52.

Auden took up his first job as a schoolmaster at Larchfield School, Helensburgh, in the summer term 1930, and wrote this poem during his first month there. The impact of the prepubertal beauty of twelve-year-olds (on a homosexual who did not, however, like 'chicken') has produced an elegiac distillation of its otherworldliness. The poem was written for 'J C', according to Auden's annotation of a copy of the US *Poems* (1934, repr. 1937). The difficulties of the poem are lessened if it is remembered that 'this' always refers to the innocent beauty and 'ghost' is the haunting of sexual desire. Only love can find 'features' in beauty to be loved, and only desire is disturbed by the passing of its featureless perfection: it is this eternal paradox that creates the 'sorrow' of the last two lines, which Isherwood quoted in 'Some notes on the early poetry', *A Tribute*, p. 77, as evidence of the influence of Emily Dickinson. 'Pur' (an earlier title) is an unusual word for a young boy which also, of course, carries a French meaning. The poem was set by Geoffrey Burgon in 1993.

Before this loved one

March 1929; P30, p. 62; 'This One', CP45, p. 19; 'This Loved One', CP, p. 36; EA, p. 31.

Auden's early reviewers noted that his syntax and absence of visual imagery in many poems recalled the work of Laura Riding (see, for instance,

Michael Roberts in *Adelphi*, December 1930). The evident debt was
nowhere more tendentiously expressed than by Robert Graves in *The
Crowning Privilege* (1955), p. 130: 'During 1928–9,' he wrote, 'I was printing
books by hand, and he subscribed to them. I had to suggest that the half-
guinea he paid for Laura Riding's *Love as Love, Death as Death* gave him no
right to borrow half-lines and whole lines from them for insertion in his own
verse.' Graves does not quote any whole lines borrowed (Riding's lines are
not anyway long), but certainly the influence is marked. This poem is a
notable example. Compare:

> And smiling of
> This gracious greeting
> 'Good day, good luck'
> Is no real meeting
> But instinctive look
> A backward love.

with the following from Riding's book (*Love as Love, Death as Death*, 1928,
pp. 19 and 57):

> The standing-stillness
> The from foot-to-foot,
> Is no real illness,
> Is no real fever.
>
> We shall say, love is no more
> Than waking, smiling,
> Forcing out 'good morning'.

Riding's style here owed something to E. E. Cummings, as Edgell
Rickword's parody in 'Twittingpan' (*Collected Poems*, 1947, p. 59) shows.
The parody comes near to early Auden, too, but on the whole Auden
jettisons the quaintness while preserving the edgy dignity and dark wisdom
of the Riding manner (see also my commentary on 'To ask the hard
question', p. 82). In 'This loved one', the lover is aware of everything that
has been done to escape family and history, the birthright as it were given
up ('the old loss', 'mortgaged lands'). Such sacrifice is pointless, a kind of
arrogant slumming (Auden said to his French translator of the line 'This
gracious greeting': 'I want something suggesting the seigneur here' – letter
to Edouard Roditi, Berg). By 'backward love' Auden probably has in mind
the idea that he should have had his homosexual friendships at a much

earlier age and was committing the error he noted when reading Trigant Burrow of thinking today in terms of what ought to have been yesterday (1929 journal). The poem is about Isherwood's boyfriend, 'Bubi' (see *Christopher and his Kind*, p. 12, and Auden's annotation 'B. von S[szczesny]' in a copy of the US *Poems* in the Berg Collection).

The silly fool, the silly fool

August 1929; P30, p. 63; 'Happy Ending', CP, p. 54; EA, p. 34.

Auden himself was a youngest son, and even once said that he tended to look upon himself as the youngest person in any room (*The Review*, no. 11–12, p. 8). It is the youngest son who is successful in fairy tales, where it is also a good thing to have obscure origins. In stanza 3 the drafts originally show 'good' for 'posh', and in answer to an enquiry about its meaning by the sister of Duncan Wood, Auden casually answered: 'Oh! The Virgin Birth' (Feild Memoir). At a later date, on the Virgin Birth, he said: 'What does it say but that no-one can acknowledge that his parents had sex!' (conversation with John Bridgen, *Auden Newsletter* 3). There is a serious point to the joke, however, for all mortals do in fact have fathers. As Freud had pointed out (*Group Psychology and the Analysis of the Ego*, 1922, p. 114), primitive stories such as fairy tales represent the rebellion against the father of the primal horde of his sons who have been forced into sexual abstinence and consequently into an emotional group identity. The youngest brother is stupid precisely because he is supposedly 'harmless' to the father, yet it is he who is the father's successor, symbolically aided by the brothers in the form of small animals and so on. Although such success is possible in life, this does not seem to include success in love: the sons of the primitive totemistic clan have in fact been compelled into homosexual object love. The odd syntax of the last stanza yields alternative explanations, of which the likeliest would seem to be: 'It is simple to prove that deeds can succeed in life, but it is only love which can succeed in love, and only 'tales' (i.e. art) which can be said to be achieving anything in tales of a world in which no one fails.' The repetition 'rather . . . rather' may be an echo of 'The Wreck of the Deutschland', stanza 10.

The strings' excitement, the applauding drum

April 1929; P30, p. 64; 'Family Ghosts', CP, p. 40; EA, p. 32.

This poem appears to be acknowledging the poet's predictable role as a
converter of emotion into art. The animal excitement of love (strings=
bowels, drum=heart) invokes an ancestral power to approve the love-choice:
the complex image is of the transmission of such psychic energy as a water
channel which the obsessive scribbling of poets chokes up with fancies even
when the imaginative source has dried up (a 'watercourse' is in fact a
ventilating device in lead-mining). Auden may have been reading Jung's
essay 'On Psychical Energy' in his *Contributions to Analytical Psychology*
(1928): Jung persistently uses the image of a water channel (or a stream
feeding a turbine) to explain the function of symbols in primitive
ceremonies as absorbing psychic energy from natural instincts (as in the
Watschandies' spring ceremonial, pp. 47ff). In modern life, Jung con-
cludes, such a process is transmitted through the generations: 'Although
our inheritance consists in physiological paths, still it was mental processes
in our ancestors that created the paths. If these traces come to conscious-
ness again in the individual, they can do so only in the form of mental
processes; and if these processes can become conscious only through
individual experience and thus appear as individual acquisitions, they are
none the less pre-existing traces, which are merely "filled-out" by the
individual experience. Every "impressive" experience is such an impres-
sion, in an ancient but previously unconscious stream-bed . . . The mind, as
the effective principle in the inheritance, is made up from the sum of the
ancestral minds, the unseen fathers, whose authority is born with the child'
(*Contributions to Analytical Psychology*, p. 61). In the third stanza, then, the
poet 'in love' is a victim of the unseen fathers, whose approval floods the
watercourse again. If the 'her' of stanza four is 'really' his fiancée, Sheilah
Richardson, Auden's substitution of 'that' in Maurice Feild's copy in 1933
(Bodleian) merely universalises for the homosexual what may indeed be a
non-exclusive psychic dilemma. In stanza 5 the sense of being beleaguered
by this dilemma, and still compulsively writing ('speeches', 'news'), is
expressed in lines drawn from the opening chorus of the first version of
Paid on Both Sides. At this point the terza rima breaks down in a rather
interesting way, reverting to the rhyme of the opening line. This seems to
suggest that when the 'ceremony' has worked, potentially sterile or
parnassian writing acquires an authentic sublimity. The characteristic

images of great poets of the past have, after all, been conditioned by real emotions like his own: Pope's insecurity in the image of the satirist swooping on his prey; Donne's grief in the image of tears as tides drawn by the moon ('lunatic'); and the blind Milton's lost Paradise in the image of the Golden Age which has become an Age of Ice.

On Sunday walks

August 1929; P30, p. 65; 'Such Nice People', CP45, p. 92; 'On Sunday Walks', CP, p. 51; EA, p. 33.

This casually assured portrait of the ebullient but vacuous heirs of the established gentry is very characteristic of Auden's ability to combine generalised insight and acute detail with a strengthening lightness of tone. The way in which a word like 'conquerors' goes beyond irony into myth is typical, too, of his infallible verve with his material. A poem which Auden sent to Isherwood with virtually the same opening suggests that the works are closed not through a strike or lock-out but because there has been an explosion: whatever the reason, the heirs seem blithely unconcerned: they 'know what to know' because they know what their fathers said and did, but they are visited by nightmares about tigers and bishops (the dreamlike atmosphere assisted by the half-rhymes). Traditions are handed on (perhaps an echo here of Hardy's 'Heredity'), and hereditary rights observed, but, like lingering superstitions, original virtues have dwindled to mere forms, 'all glory and all story, | Solemn and not so good'. Typically, the mother is given a large share of responsibility (lines 35–7): insufficient weaning is a cause of the fantasy world in which these substitutes for heroes find themselves (cf. *Paid on Both Sides*).

Get there if you can and see the land you once were proud to own

Easter Day, April 1930; *Twentieth Century*, March 1931; P30, p. 66; EA, p. 48.

This high-spirited harangue of the bourgeois 'dead' was written on Easter Day, 1930, and like Auden's Easter poem of the previous year ('It was Easter as I walked in the public gardens') is a poem of resolve: it involves a challenge to try to start living. The model is Tennyson's 'Locksley Hall Sixty Years After' (when sending an early thirty-four-stanza draft to Isherwood Auden referred to it as 'the Locksley Hall poem'). The forms of 'death' that

provide a comfortable alternative to this challenge are various in the poem
(and were to be Auden's major subject for the following few years), but
perhaps the most striking is the list of private and public enemies of the
achieved life introduced in stanzas 9–11. The list collocates the multiple
spheres of operation of these false mentors (private and public, sexual and
educational, philosophical and literary). These are the romantics, the
pessimists, the authoritarians. 'Newman' is the Rev. G. G. Newman, on the
staff at St Edmunds (see *A Tribute*, p. 36) and first in a list of sexual partners
on p. 2 of a 1943 notebook (Buffalo) – Auden told Ansen that his first
sexual experience was with an older man; 'Ciddy' is Cyril Morgan-Brown,
the headmaster of St Edmunds; 'Fronny' is Francis Turville-Petre,
eponymous hero of Auden's lost second play and model for Francis in *The
Dog Beneath the Skin*; 'Doctor Frommer' was a homosexual psychoanalyst
working in Berlin in 1929; 'Mrs Allom' was the mother of V. M. 'Peter'
Allom, a school friend, who wrote in an unpublished memoir: 'The real
trouble between Wystan and my mother was that the latter was a recent
convert to the Roman Church and was tactless in her references to religion'
(Carpenter, p. 128); 'The Baron' is Charlus in Proust's *A La Recherche du
temps perdu*. Brothel-crawling in Berlin, Auden brandished a cigar and
pictured himself as the Baron Charlus ('Actually I was a middle-class rabbit'
– 1929 journal). His journal found the first part of Sodom and Gomorrah to
be 'very inadequate' as 'a full analysis of the bugger'. Auden's reaction from
asceticism in Berlin would have induced a reaction to Flaubert, a writer he
had once enlisted as a spokesman for such asceticism (see my article 'Auden
and Flaubert', *Auden Studies* 1, pp. 135–46). Auden's later views of
Baudelaire may be found in 'Letter to Lord Byron', Part III ('How we all
roared when Baudelaire went fey') and 'New Year Letter', lines 1267–72;
his 1939 poem on Pascal similarly indicates a reversal of opinion: to the
Christian Auden, both geniuses, far from betraying progress or science,
showed that they could very well become saints. Freud had been discovered
to uphold conventional morality, and that to a disciple of Homer Lane
would never do. Lane, with Blake and Lawrence are presented as
contrasting cloak-and-dagger heroes, destroyed by the puritan middle-class
society that Auden is attacking from the inside. Lane actually died of heart-
failure after typhoid and pneumonia in Paris in 1925, but significantly his
mother was a strict Baptist ('In revolt against her authority, Lane became
the leader of a "tough" gang of boys in the town', A. A. David's
Introduction to Homer Lane, *Talks to Parents and Teachers*, 1928, p. 5). The
poem threatens revolution, and holds out the alternative of psychological

regeneration for the bourgeoisie in some of the plainest terms to be found in the early poems, while retaining a hectic invigorating diction that makes the poem excitingly bold, prophetic and assured. For 'stop behaving like a stone' see the 1928–?30 notebook, fols 11–12: 'That which desires life to itself, to arrest growth, is behaving like a stone and casts itself like Lucifer out of heaven.'

Nor was that final, for about that time

Published in P28; see p. 11.

From scars where kestrels hover

January 1929; P30, p. 71; 'Missing', CP, p. 30; EA, p. 28.

This poem written in Berlin introduces a theme of some importance in Auden's early poetry. What is heroism, he asks? The conclusion is simple: heroism does not lie in acts of bravery but in endurance, in 'resisting the temptations | To skyline operations'. These operations, visualised in the first section of the poem, evoke the feuding world of *Paid on Both Sides*. The landscape of these saga-heroes may be disciplined and austere; the leader may be 'unwounded'; but the little band are 'doomed' (an earlier version of the lines shows that the perpetual 'voices in the rock' is a metaphor for a war-memorial: see p. 46): today the tourists come with guidebooks to reconstruct the sagas in what is merely a holiday environment providing a spuriously exciting contrast to the bland elegance of the capital.

Some critics believe that this argument is contradicted by the line 'Leave for Cape Wrath to-night', and feel that this is a romantic celebration of saga-heroism (e.g. Spears, p. 43). This can hardly be so: the host is seen waiting for his guest, who does not arrive. He passes 'alive' into the house, in evident contrast to the guest who may be presumed dead as a result of his journey to Cape Wrath. (We remember that 'bravery is now | Not in the dying breath' but in a deliberate refusal to fight merely 'for no one's sake'.) It is a simple enough interpretation, but does depend upon an admitted obscurity in the Cape Wrath line. Its source lies in an account by Isherwood in *Lions and Shadows* (pp. 265–70) of a drunken journey north in Bill Scott's car. They have no idea where they are going, only that they have to keep on the move. 'These suddenly undertaken excursions exactly suited my escapist temperament,' Isherwood wrote. He had already (pp. 207–8) elaborated the conception of the Truly Strong Man and the Truly Weak Man, which he shared with Auden. The Truly Strong Man has no need to prove himself. Only the Truly Weak Man finds himself undertaking absurd heroics in an effort to master his real nature. The drunken journey in *Lions and Shadows* is just such an effort, and its climax is suitably melodramatic: 'We drove on, across the misty bog-plains, striped black where peat had been cut, in the direction of Cape Wrath. The coast was gashed into jagged fjords: under the cliffs, the water lay like ebony, with vivid jade shallows. The mountains were piled up in the west against an angry sunset' (p. 269). Isherwood realises how mad it all is ('One always has to go back, I thought, at the end of these little escapades') and soon afterwards makes his decision to study medicine. Auden's reference is inescapably ironic: Cape Wrath is an illusion, an unresisted temptation of the wrong sort. (In an attempt to show that this sort of urge is wilful rather than compulsory, Auden changed line 37 in Maurice Feild's copy to 'The leaders still migrate', but he never printed the emendation.)

And in any case, the line (as earlier versions make clear) is not an imperative, but an indicative statement, an intention from a telegram (' "Leave for Cape Wrath to-night, | Shall not arrive this week | Nor any week. Writing." ': draft sent to Isherwood). The telegram thus functions like the letter in 'From the very first coming down', while the source of lines 1, 17–18, 20, and 32–8 in another poem likely to have been written with McElwee in mind ('The weeks of blizzard over') and the source of lines 6–14 and the final line and a half in 'I chose this lean country' (see also 'the long slow curvings of the fells' in 'Alston Moor', Dodds notebook, p. 29) emphatically suggests that the heroism discussed in 'From scars where kestrels hover' is in one sense a metaphor for love. The endings of all three poems show that the 'host' is the poet himself, and that the migrating 'leaders' ('prophets' in 'The weeks of blizzard over') take on the characteristics of the unresponsive lover. The waiting 'host' then (like the poet 'Turning a stoic shoulder' in 'I chose this lean country' or, more particularly, moving 'decent with the seasons' in 'From the very first coming down') is a figure of rueful realism making the best of his loved one's message about non-arrival. Thus the subject of the poem, the hero, the loved one, is 'missing' both in the military sense, and in the sense of 'being missed': a masterful ambiguity conveyed in the later title of the poem.

Suppose they met, the inevitable procedure

Published in P28; see p. 7.

Taller to-day, we remember similar evenings

Published in P28; see p. 15.

No trenchant parting this

Published in P28; see p. 7.

Under boughs between our tentative endearments, how should we hear

March 1929; P30, p. 75; 'When the Devil Drives', CP45, p. 147; EA, p. 29.

The awkward beautiful rhythms of the seven-foot lines in these stanzas establish wistful hopes which are brutally abbreviated by the three-foot half-rhymed couplets. The sensitive lover might indeed hear drum-beats calling him to a decisive battle or ceremony, but they are imaginary and he presumably does not stir from his 'boughs' (compare 'Under the abject willow' in 'I chose this lean country'). Similarly, in stanza 2, happiness might be found by taking a branch line at a railway junction into mountainous country (which Auden later stated to be the ideal way of entering his dream Eden), but he does not leave the carriage of the express which has unexpectedly stopped at the junction. Stanzas 3 and 4 generalise the reasons for this timidity: we have no way of understanding our contemporaries because we are content with our own self-absorbed mental life. The images of bird's-nesting and the dog straining on the lead, and the phrase 'sheer off . . . like gull from granite', are taken from lines 10–12 and 15 of 'Out of sight assuredly, not out of mind', a poem of June 1927 written for McElwee. There, the images were the 'acceptable' memories of recreation with a holiday visitor in the family home, implicitly contrasted with the more intimate memories that would be possible if the mind were to 'build a house' for itself. In the present poem the constraining presence of the 'old' is more forcefully underlined and is developed in stanzas 5 and 6 into the familiar Jungian 'ancestral curse': we inherit all the weaknesses of our forebears just as we inherit their desires (this is the necessity alluded to in the 1945 title, cf. the proverbial 'He must needs go that the devil drives'). These inherited characteristics may not show themselves for years, like a carried disease: Auden's brilliant metaphor is of finding that you can do a jigsaw puzzle that has been put away because no one could finish it. In stanza 7 the 'cursed' heir to the dulled blood and sniffling mind of his ancestors is to be imagined having retired to a moorland market town (such as Alston) 'for work or love', but in fact unable to do either, escaping in his frustration to his favourite abandoned lead-mines ('sumps' are the short shafts that connect the horizontal mining 'levels': he is apparently to be imagined clearing them of debris in his emotional fury). In the final stanza he appeals again to those whom in stanza 3 he had professed not to understand, and attempts to give 'sharing' a new force in the context of an inscrutable pity and sorrow. In the following month he was to return again to old McElwee material in an attempt to argue beyond the passive endurance of this poem (see my commentary on 'It was Easter as I walked in the public gardens', p. 59).

Consider this and in our time

March 1930; P30, p. 76; 'Consider', CP45, p. 27; CP, p. 61; EA, p. 46.

Here we are shown the sick society 'as the hawk sees it or the helmeted airman'. Auden presents the cigarette-end smouldering on the border, the international set in the winter sports hotel, the farmers in the stormy fens and so on, cinematically, 'as the hawk sees the one concentrated spot where beats the life-heart of our prey' (Lawrence, *Fantasia of the Unconscious*, p. 62). The cinema was doubtless an influence in this kind of panoramic view, but there are literary parallels, too. For instance, Auden had first read Hardy in the summer of 1923, and later admitted: 'What I valued most in Hardy, then, as I still do, was his hawk's vision, his way of looking at life from a very great height, as in the stage directions of *The Dynasts*, or the opening chapter of *The Return of the Native*' (*Southern Review*, Summer 1940). The images are also linked in other ways: the guests at the garden party 'pass on' too, going south in the winter, and the playboys listen to the same band as the lonely farmers. The political implications in this nexus and its language ('smouldering', 'dangerous', 'stormy') are tense and unignorable.

The 'supreme Antagonist', like 'the Adversary' of 'Taller today, we remember similar evenings' or 'the Devourer' of 'It was Easter as I walked in the public gardens', has biblical force. Both the Old English *Bestiary* and *Paradise Lost* (1.200) also compare the whale with Satan. In Auden's glossary of Christian and psychological terms (1928–?30 notebook, fol. 44) Satan is seen as the Censor, responsible for repressing man's natural instincts and bringing about that self-consciousness which separates him from the rest of the animal kingdom. It is this division in men and society, keeping them from their real desires, that Auden is anatomising in the poem. The Antagonist's admirers, the ill, are in ascendancy and are themselves responsible for the malaise, the 'immeasurable neurotic dread', which has conditioned them and which spreads like a disease, 'scattering the people' in the triumphant diction of the Psalms (lxviii.1).

Auden omitted from collected editions lines 42–9, which attack financiers, dons, clergy and sportsmen, thus playing down the sense of impending social revolution implicit in the fates of the selfish which accumulate in the last lines. These fates take the form of psychological illnesses, and can all be found expounded in William McDougall's *An Outline of Abnormal Psychology* (1926). 'Fugues' (McDougall, p. 257) are a form of amnesia involving compulsive travel; 'irregular breathing' is a symbolic symptom in abnormal psychology (McDougall, p. 278); 'alternate ascendancies' (McDougall, pp. 483ff) are cases of alternating personalities with reciprocal amnesia like fugues; while for the 'explosion of mania' the reader may refer to McDougall's explanation (p. 360) of anger as a secondary feature of mania. This material had also figured in Auden and Isherwood's 'Preliminary Statement', a dramatic and psychological manifesto of 1929 (see *Plays*, p. 459). For the prizes being given to the ruined boys, see Dean Farrar, *Eric; or Little by Little*, chapter xv, where Eric comes second and is given more than one prize. Eric already has a foretaste of his doom: 'May every schoolboy who reads this page be warned by the waving of their wasted hands from that burning marle of passion where they found nothing but shame and ruin, polluted affections, and an early grave' (ch. ix). This was one of the young Auden's favourite books. He alluded to it in both *The Dog Beneath the Skin* and *The Age of Anxiety* (see pp. 142 and 381).

Sir, no man's enemy, forgiving all

October 1929; P30, p. 79; 'Petition', CP45, p. 110; EA, p. 36.

This is one of the more clinically diagnostic of Auden's early poems. A thirty-five-line draft version in a notebook given to Wendell Johnson (Berg) reminds us that physical death comes to 'all surfaces', including 'A gymnast's rhythm at Athens, or then | A celibate and certain faith at Tintern'. It shows us men leaving their clubs, 'washed to an assignation', and brides 'screaming'. The omission of this Eliotic material gives strength to the poem as we have it, and allows more controlling unity to the initial invocation. 'Sir', like 'Adversary', 'Antagonist', 'Devourer', reminds us that a respectful reappraisal of quasi-Christian terms is possible for a poet who has lost his faith. The urge to prayer and celebration was always as strong in Auden as the urge to ratiocination. 'Sir' is the God you can argue with of Herbert or Hopkins. 'God' forgives everything but man's will, which through sin has come to negate the divine will (in the draft it is 'negative principle of darkness') and yet is asked (like Adonis by Venus in Shakespeare's poem, line 755) to 'be prodigal', i.e. to forgive the denial of will and send 'power and light', as Adonis was urged to 'lend the world his light' (line 756). Auden wrote in a friend's copy: 'I bitterly regret the day I was snobbish enough to use an archaic genitive (= will's). I've been asked what this line means ever since' (Mendelson, p. 46). He changed 'will his' to 'the will's' in Caroline Newton's copy of *Poems* some time after 1937. Many of the images ('liar's quinsy' and so on) may be glossed by Isherwood's account of the effect of Layard's teachings on Auden (*Lions and Shadows*, pp. 299–304) so that the invoked power also takes on the role of psychiatrist (and at one point becomes perhaps a sentry on the perimeter: 'beams/spotted' refers to discovery by searchlight and enforced return rather than physical flaws). If will is the true negative of God (cf. the final sonnet of 'The Quest') as the Ego is the negative of the Id, then true change is to realise the authenticity of one's deepest desires, a Lawrentian message enforced by the allusion to the end of *The Rainbow* and its 'new architecture', an essentially mystical or apocalyptic conclusion belonging as much to Lawrence's being unable to conclude Ursula's story at that point as to a clear vision of a practical solution. It isn't a practical solution for Auden, either, since he was by no means an admirer of the Bauhaus ('I once expressed a desire for "New styles of architecture"; but I have never liked modern architecture. I prefer *old* styles and one must be honest even about one's prejudices': Foreword to the 1966 *Collected Shorter Poems*, p. 15). The point is somewhat disingenuous, however, since the 'architecture' in the poem is the architecture of the psyche (the change of heart has that Moral Rearmament ring typical of much early Auden). He had expressed serious doubts about the rest of that line as early as *The Dog Beneath the Skin* (*Plays*, p. 279), where the chorus say: 'Do not speak of a change of heart, meaning five hundred a year and a room of one's own, | As if that were all that is necessary.'

Poems (1933)

For the second edition of *Poems*, Auden omitted seven poems and added new ones in their place.

Doom is dark and deeper than any sea-dingle

August 1930; 'Chorus from a Play', *New Signatures*, 1932; P33, p. 43 (substituted for 'Which of you waking early and watching daybreak'); 'Something is Bound to Happen', CP45, p. 34; 'The Wanderer', CP, p. 62; EA, p. 55.

This poem, as its *New Signatures* title indicates, was used in the lost play *The Fronny*. Its present title stresses its Anglo-Saxon character: the poem's central part may be compared with lines 37–48 of the Old English poem *The Wanderer*. The first line is actually taken from a sentence in a Middle English homily, *Sawles Warde* (or from W. P. Ker's *Mediaeval English Literature*, 1912, p. 157, which happens to quote most of the sentence): 'Ha beoð se wise þat ha witen all godes reades. his runes ant his domes þe derne beoð ant deopre þen ani sea dingle' ('They are so wise that they know all God's counsels, his mysteries and his judgements, which are secret and deeper than any sea dingle'). 'Doom' is thus really the judgement of God. The Wanderer's compulsive exile also suggests Bunyan's Christian ('No cloud-soft hand can hold him, restraint by women'), though this rejection is present in *Sawles Warde* as well. Auden maintains the Old English mood with a minimum of the appropriate technical devices. These are kennings like 'houses for fishes', along the lines of 'hwaeles eþel' in *The Seafarer*, line 60; 'unquiet' is reminiscent of the Old English 'unstille' (in the *Maxims*); and there are one or two alliterating lines. However, the mood of the poem is largely created by the movement and cadence of the irregular verse, and by the ambiguity of its subject. Is this a lordless warrior or the emergent adolescent of the Prologue to *The Orators*? Is the exile an evasion of responsibility or a Quest? Is the doom a punishment or a providential directive? The suggestive vagueness of the poem's message is a large part of its strength. The bird in line 13 is a ring-ousel, incidentally, as the chorus in *The Dog Beneath the Skin* (*Plays*, p. 235) makes clear.

Between attention and attention

May 1930; P33, p. 48 (substituted for 'To have found a place for nowhere'); 'Make up your Mind', CP45, p. 27; 'Easy Knowledge', CP, p. 37; EA, p. 52.

A longer version of this poem exists as a chorus from the lost play *The Fronny*. It is a poem in the Riding manner, though beginning with an apparent echo of Eliot's 'The Hollow Men'. Love is assailed by indecisiveness (the earlier title, as so often, makes the point of the poem clear), and the lover's behaviour seems merely absurd and embarrassing. The examples of the hesitant lover's oafishness are borrowed from poems in the 1928 volume (lines 16–17 from 'The four sat on in the bare room' and lines 18–21 from 'Because sap fell away'). The 'snub-nosed winner' is 'snub-nosed Gabriel Carritt' of *Letters from Iceland*, p. 254, as the 1928–?30 notebook, fol. 65, makes clear. (Most references to Carritt in *The Orators*, together with the Ode dedicated to him, were dropped in the 1966 edition.) The second part of the poem typically uses the image of the loved one as a town to be visited: the lover loses his way, has to ask for directions. Again, love is talked about and rationalised ('registering | Acreage, mileage') but not felt ('the divided face | Has no grace'). The poem was written in Helensburgh.

Its no use raising a shout

November 1929; P33, p. 52 (substituted for 'The crowing of the cock'); EA, p. 42.

Auden had evidently first become interested in popular songs during 1929 (he twice wrote out the lyric 'He's Funny That Way', later immortalised by Billie Holliday; once in his 1929 journal, and once on the verso of a copy of 'Men pass through doors and travel to the sea' which he sent to Isherwood). The first line of the refrain in this poem resembles the elated 'You are here, so am I' in the song 'I only have eyes for you'. Here it is converted into the blank emotional impasse reached by a man oppressed by his mother's possessive love (stanza 2). The second line of the refrain may be compared with the opening of 'Address for a Prize-Day' in *The Orators*. The role of the lumbar ganglion (stanza 4) also relates to D. H. Lawrence, while the 'wish' of stanza 5 is Homer Lane's version of the Jungian ancestral inheritance:

'All organic life may be represented as a wish. Man, the highest form of life, is in himself the product of the cumulative wishes of all organic life in past ages' (*Talks to Parents and Teachers*, 1928, p.177).

What's in your mind, my dove, my coney

November 1930; P33, p. 58 (substituted for 'Bones wrenched, weak whimper . . .'); CP, p. 57; EA, p. 56.

This bold sexual invitation exposes the emotional limitations of the person addressed. It was a Helensburgh poem written for 'D. W.', according to Auden's annotation in a US *Poems* in the Berg Collection. In the first stanza love is sarcastically linked with materialism and acquisitiveness: this is sterile sex in the head. 'Do thoughts grow like feathers, the dead end of life' implies that rationalised love may, like plumage, be beautiful or protective, but is actually dead not living (cf. Lawrence's 'The mind is the dead end of life', *Psychoanalysis and the Unconscious*, p. 239). The loved one is then urged to become really aware through sight and touch of what love is about, until the phallic serpent rises, and sexual urgency takes over. The phrase 'great big serpent' is taken from Baudelaire (*Intimate Journals*, tr. Isherwood, 1930, p. 44), who comments: 'Such caprices of language, too often repeated, with an excessive use of animal nicknames, testify to a Satanic aspect in love.' This song was used in the lost play *The Fronny*. There is a later musical setting by Britten that remains unpublished, and it was set by Lennox Berkeley in 1960.

Look there! The sunk road winding

January 1931; P33, p. 77 (substituted for 'Nor was that final, for about that time'); 'The Bonfires', CP45, p. 77; CP, p. 50; EA, p. 56.

This poem seems closer to the metaphorical obscurities of *The Orators* than the essentially syntactical obscurities of *Poems* (1930), and indeed was written three and a half years later than the earliest poem in that volume. Auden now has the assurance to set his scene dramatically and fantastically with an ironically self-questioning use of heroic and surrealistic props. The point would seem to be that the lovers ('we') are not simple like heroes, and cannot cope with the usual trials and terrors. The pincer movement of 'the dark squadron' underlines the sense of being caught in a dilemma implicit in the frying-pan-into-the-fire sense of 'between the gin [trap] | And bloody falcon'. Phrases such as 'glaciers calving' and the Popean 'hedgehog's gradual foot | Or fish's fathom' maintain a balance between the sinister and the mocking. To descend into the strange valley would mean engagement. The lovers do not descend: the smoke rises to where they sit, smouldering with desire like the bonfires (irony is preserved in the cliché) and somehow satisfied with the 'bitter' smoke of the 'thorough' burning (suggesting the burning of Buddha's Fire Sermon and its hope for freedom from desire). The synchronised 'double beat' of hearts in achieved union is not for them.

Who will endure

?August 1931 (for problems of dating, see EA, p. 419 and Stan Smith in *RES*, 1990, pp. 357–62); P33, p. 80 (substituted for 'Suppose they met, the inevitable procedure'); 'Better Not', CP45, p. 176; 'No Change of Place', CP, p. 33; EA, p. 53.

It is a paradox that the improved communications of modern industrial society have in fact brought about a state of affairs where no one can any longer communicate except at a distance. Emotional energy is expended on the anticipation of love letters not on human contact, spring flowers arrive smashed, and the impersonality of the telephone reduces human sympathy to a merely functional response (pity is 'flashed', not, I think, like a morse signal, but like a pass or badge: it has become a shibboleth).

Auden intends the images in lines 4–9 to suggest, not *ennui* or anxiety, but a kind of vegetative calm. The scenario is not unlike that in Coleridge's 'Eolian Harp' and 'Reflections upon Entering into Active Life', but here the greater perception and understanding of life that will result from 'journey from one place to another' is simply not being risked: nothing better is known. As death in the dirge from *Cymbeline* (IV.ii) is the only respite from 'the heat o' the sun' and 'winter's rages', so here the calm is a form of anaesthesia, prior to all volition. The mood of Eliot's Prufrock is strongly present in this section.

In the third section (from line 20: a MS draft sent to Isherwood supports the white line in later texts) the 'professional traveller' is contrasted with those suffering from accidie: by making the journey, he has discovered some truth about life which they have not. He has nothing to say to them which they would understand, and their maps seem to bear no relationship to any reality they know. Thus perhaps the professional traveller represents the writer, and the maps in the 'ships long high and dry' of the *Poems* text represent modern literary culture (but cf. 'Schoolboy, making lonely maps: | Better do it with some chaps', EA, p. 50).

The final section develops this theme by indicating that the knowledge which the 'professional traveller' may have acquired has something to do with a possible change of social forms. The capital is waiting for conversion (perhaps this is a financial pun, too, but see Smith's argument in *RES* about the fiscal crisis of the summer). However, since nobody travels, nobody finds out: 'no one goes | Further than railhead' (cf. 'had they pushed the rail | Some stations nearer' in 'Control of the passes . . .'). The hint of decadence in the capital ('brilliant') is matched by corruption in the shires. The village band celebrates the 'ugly feast' of an aristocracy whose hirelings protect their privileges by force ('gaitered gamekeeper with dog and gun'). These terms may, of course, have a psychological meaning. The 'brilliant capital' may be the conscious mind and the unknown 'ugly feast' the primitive ceremony that is analogous to the transmission of ancestral desires which Jung writes about in his essay 'On Psychical Energy' (see my commentary on 'The strings' excitement . . .', p. 68). But the point of the poem is decisively and dramatically put: the retreat from life lived at first hand conspires to perpetuate the stagnation of the personal and social life. The words of the gamekeeper ('Turn back') echo the admonitions latent in the landscape of 'Who stands, the crux left of the watershed' written three years earlier ('Stranger, turn back again') but with a new externalised force (cf. 'The stocky keepers of a wild estate': one of the forms of the Lords of Limit in 'A Happy New Year', Part II). Smith persuasively relates many of these images to features of Helensburgh topograpy.

To ask the hard question is simple

?August 1930; P33, p. 83 (substituted for 'No trenchant parting this'); 'What Do You Think?', CP45, p. 141; 'The Hard Question', CSP50, p. 151; 'The Question', CP, p. 56; EA, p. 54.

Here Auden returns to the manner of Laura Riding (see my commentary on 'Before this loved one', p. 65). The poem captures the feeling that one also has in Riding's work of the poet taking from her experience only the absolutely necessary physical detail; it has the same reliance on infinitives and participles, the same kind of arresting opening, the same kind of exploration of existence as a precarious and elusive state which the individual happens to share with the whole race and must be careful not to make extravagant claims about. Riding's poems are about human consciousness of being bedevilled by space and time and needing to be cautious about making claims upon destiny. As in Riding, Auden's meaning unfolds beneath the sort of attention we give to aphorisms.

Trivial and conventional salutations like 'Where are you going?' or 'How do you do?' are here seen by Auden to contain real and difficult questions which the individual cannot answer, because he does not know anything about himself or his future, so he describes these salutations riddlingly as though they were the most penetrating kind of question about motive or state of being. Social forms stifle the individual's true nature and needs: the forms are represented by these 'hard questions', which tellingly reveal our anxiety about this stifling. The idea comes from Trigant Burrow's *The Social Basis of Consciousness* (1927) (from which Auden also borrowed material about the child's arrested development from the mother in 'It was Easter as I walked in the public gardens', Part 3): 'Upon our meeting, it is the accustomed reaction to make mutual inquiry into the condition of health of one another. "How are you?" or "How-do-you-do?" we ask . . . In the obvious apprehensiveness underlying this unconscious attitude of the social mind there is . . . the implicit conviction that we are . . . sick!' (p. 64).

Since the individual is 'Afraid | To remember what the fish ignored' (i.e. how to evolve from his environment, which he once did to escape from being a fish – the fish ignoring the impulse and therefore remaining a fish), he puts himself in the same category as a fish, and forfeits the memory of evolution which, as a human being, he might have had, seeing that the growing organism repeats the history of the evolution of the species (ontogeny recapitulating phylogeny). This idea is recounted in Homer Lane, *Talks to Parents and Teachers*, p. 85: 'Every child, between conception and maturity, is recapitulating in its own physical and spiritual growth, the history of the development of the race, from the life in water of the single cell to the self-conscious life of man. The recapitulation of those processes in our evolution which led to the human limbs and body – through the stages of fish, of bird, and the rest – is complete in the main at birth; but the main part of the spiritual evolution is the task of childhood.' Auden would probably have taken the idea about the organism's evolution relying on memory from William McDougall, *Modern Materialism* (1929), chapter v, 'Emergent Evolution', where 'memory' implies 'stability of organization in spite of change, a stability which enables it to survive change and to incorporate effects of change within itself' (p.136). Auden postulates an obstruction to man's development through 'forgetting'. Thus his progress is slow and painful. Instead of learning, remembering and developing, he longs, like the cowardly bird, for 'windy skies'; like the cold fish, for water;

like the obedient sheep, for a master (he had noted the sheep's embodiment of obedience in his 1929 journal, in which there is also a complex evolutionary chart setting out some of the other qualities characteristic of the ontogenic or phylogenic stages of existence, such as the jellyfish's indifference to life or the bird's flight from danger). In the last section of the poem, Auden hopes that love will have the power to restore to man his awareness of his inner nature, for it is love ('dark and rich and warm all over') which restores to him the condition of the womb in which he began his personal evolution (see Lane, p. 103).

The Orators

The Orators was written between March and November 1931 while Auden was teaching at Larchfield School, in Helensburgh, Scotland (see EA, p. 420, and Mendelson, pp. 95ff; some dates of composition of individual items are given below). The text was revised for the second and third editions (1934 and 1966). For details see *Bibliography*, pp. 8–10. My page references are to the text in EA.

It was the work which set the seal on Auden's early reputation. Subtitled 'An English Study', it appeared to early readers to present a surrealist anatomy of a country in crisis, while at its core lurked an elusive narrative of the failure of a neurotic hero. In some sense it is perhaps seriously a further experiment in drama (after *Paid on Both Sides* of 1928, *The Enemies of a Bishop* of 1929 and *The Fronny* of 1930): Auden told Naomi Mitchison on 12 August 1931 (Berg) while at work on Book II that formally he was trying to write 'abstract drama – all the action implied'. The conception is large-scale, the tone exuberantly varied and experimental. Though there is much in the work which is direct and satirical, the predominant allegiance evoked is to the European avant-garde of the 1920s, to the prose of Stein, Joyce and Wyndham Lewis, to the lingering influence of Baudelaire and Rimbaud, and to more recent poets like St-J. Perse. For Auden, working at close quarters with much difficult philosophical and sexual material, the temptation to shift gears sharply between the different levels of presentation seemed almost immediately to have been fatally irresistible. 'The Orators has been a success. I'm ashamed of its obscurity which is swank', he wrote to his brother four months after publication. Many reviewers emphasised this obscurity, but most came out in the work's favour. Bonamy Dobrée was enthusiastic in *The Spectator* (20 August 1932) and even included passages from it in his *Modern Prose Style* (1934). The ultimate accolade came in October 1932 when John Hayward wrote in *The Criterion*: 'I have no doubt that it is the most valuable contribution to English poetry since *The Waste Land*.' Dismembering and abandoning most of it for his 1945 *Collected Poetry*, Auden called it 'a fair notion fatally injured'; reprinting it in 1966 he looked on it with amused toleration. Some critics still throw up their hands in dismay, but most readers recognise its inspired originality, the poet poised on the half-lit threshold of public statement, exorcising his private ghosts.

By May, Auden had completed (and dedicated to Spender) what he called 'the Prose Poem *The Orators*'. This must have been what is now Book I, described in the letter to Mitchison as 'my memorial to Lawrence; i.e. the theme is the failure of the romantic conception of personality.' Auden went on to describe the four parts of Book I as 'stages in the development of the influence of the Hero (who never appears at all)'. Book II, 'Journal of an Airman' (which Auden called 'the second half', 'the situation seen from within the Hero'), was proving 'very difficult'. At some stage in the autumn he decided to add a third Book, consisting of six odes.

The work's title and subtitle indicate an area of concern larger than the immediate fate of its protagonist. Auden once wrote: 'One of the main differences between the Victorians and ourselves is that we have one more science, the science of anthropology' (*Town Crier*, 4 November 1938). He might with justice have added psychology, since the psychology of the time was often content to abandon medical groundwork for the excitement of anthropological speculations, and in many cases the psychologists were also anthropologists, like Auden's friend John Layard. This meant that the mental aberrations of individuals could often be explained with reference (however metaphorical) to social customs: this is precisely what *The Orators* is doing much of the time. Its originality lies in paying attention not to the customs of, say, New Guinea, but to English customs. The keynote is struck by the second of the orators: 'What do you think about England, this country of ours where nobody is well?' (p. 62). In general, the illness is characterised by the very oratory which describes it: Auden's personae orate but do not act; they live in a fantasy world, perceiving the need for a new life but secretly in love with the old.

It is 'an English study', then, in a number of senses: it is a portrait of a culture sketched both by social and political allusion, it is a self-referential display of literary and verbal forms, and it is a quasi-anthropological analysis of a variety of socially embedded rites of initiation, conflict and sympathetic magic. The orators are compulsive verbalisers, all with some apprehension of the malaise, some with a felt need for spiritual leadership; but all bound by their own social and psychological conditioning, and all doomed to failure. The Ciceronian political ideal, mirrored in the British educational and diplomatic system, may have provided an ironical justification for the work's final structure, with parallels to be found between *De Oratore*, on the orator's training (*inventio, dispositio* and *elocutio*), and Book I (Address, Argument, Statement); between *Brutus* and Book II; and between *Orator*, partly autobiographical and concerned with the ideal orator, and Book III. For Cicero the orator was a statesman, but Auden is looking to see how a writer/schoolmaster might be politically effective in a world where the existing orators are corrupt. By his virtuoso range of parody and stylistic allusion, Auden shows that he is as much concerned with rhetoric as with individual or social psychology; and of course the whole work shows a sustained interest in education. Indeed, the training of the ruling class provides an ambience of homoerotic *Kameradschaft* which on a number of occasions usefully underwrites the thematic core of the work which is involved with the ambivalence of joy and shame in homosexual attraction.

However bizarrely mythologised, this country of the unwell is at the same time a real environment that has produced for certain at least one bourgeois homosexual: the poet himself. Auden's notion of 'abstract drama' allows a strange kind of speculative and fictive attention to material that otherwise might have collapsed into a formless subjective panorama of local obsessions and observations (indeed, Auden's own notebook habits are in places given free rein in the text: Miller, p. 174, oddly suggests that 'Journal of an Airman' and 'Letter to a Wound' were originally part of one of Auden's own journals). The homosexual theme is, then, as might be expected, subsumed in a general analysis of the transmission of neurosis; but at the same time it is impossible for the reader not to feel that the author himself is his own major example of the felt paradoxes of such transmission. To that extent, *The Orators* has the same sort of psychological interest that a work like Byron's *Manfred* has, and one of the several kinds of critical interpretation possible would be a psychosexual one. The extraordinarily diversified play with public and private social organisations, for example, allows the anthropological eye to uncover unsuspected significance in the sometimes banal relationships between them. The thematic importance of codes and secrecy relates quite naturally to these latent conflicts between public and private worlds, and for Auden, of course, the greatest secret (and potential conflict) was homosexual identity, at that time carrying criminal status. In his 1929 journal he wrote of Proust: 'He rightly lays stress on two things. The Buggers as the great secret society and "the invert's terrible nerves".' Secrecy and neurosis are the twin driving forces of *The Orators*, and most of its implicit criticism of English society is conditioned by their occasionally manic, but ultimately fatalistic eruptions.

It is for this reason that the strange political attitudes of the work should be seen as tangential to the psychological ones. In the early 1940s, prior to the temporary dispersal of the work mentioned above, Auden wrote in Albert and Angelyn Stevens's copy: 'A catharsis of the author's personal fascism'. In his preface to the 1966 edition he could publicly confront this question with more equipoise: 'My name on the title-page', he wrote, 'seems a pseudonym for someone else, someone talented but near the border of sanity, who might well, in a year or two, become a Nazi.' In fact, the cohesion that he had desperately hoped for between the opposed private and public worlds was not to be secured by political means, and there is in any case a radical confusion between the health of the individual and the health of society. Some of Auden's best poems had fruitfully exploited this confusion, of course, but as his poetry became more open and vigorous it could not carry the prescriptive implications of some of his social 'cures'. In fact I do not believe that Auden was ever seriously misled by the appeal of fascism in 1931. Three years later he said that he opposed fascism because he knew from his experience of school what a fascist state was like (*The Old School*, ed. Graham Greene, p. 17). As a schoolmaster at the time of writing *The Orators*, such opposition was naturally put to an odd sort of symbolic test, and assumed the status of espionage, a prominent theme of the work itself. But the spy is shown to be an introvert and a failure ('Which Side Am I Supposed To Be On?'), incapable of serious political action. Much of the work is certainly about the need for revolution, but is concerned with revolution according to Blake, Lawrence or Homer Lane, not according to Marx, whose insistence on its proletarian character is effectively denied both by Auden's messianic mythologising and (in the fourth Ode) by the voice that addresses direct Skeltonic sneers at the working class.

The dedicatory verse to Stephen Spender may be found in the 1928–?30 notebook and is a near variation on the old proverb 'Fools' names and fools' faces | Are often seen in public places.' Auden's point is that society's health depends on the sum of the health of its members, not upon the rigidity and efficiency of its forms. It suggests, with memorable concreteness, that the community will benefit more from contributions from individuals than it will from an organised bureaucracy. It may also contain a sly apologia for the private references in the work. (Spender had dedicated his novel *The Temple*, finished in 1931, to Auden; it appears that *The Orators* was dedicated to Spender in recompense.)

The 'Prologue' (March 1931; entitled 'Adolescence' in collections after 1945) presents in miniature the half-hidden message of the whole work: that the introverted adolescent is obsessed and motivated by mother love, unable to free himself from it, deriving his neurosis from her and yet accused by her of it. The adolescent (like the Airman of Book II, and like John Nower in *Paid on Both Sides* and Michael Ransom in *The Ascent of F6*) is driven to exploits by his mother, and yet is ultimately destroyed by her. In Auden's mythology she becomes the Enemy, the Dragon, and in this 'Prologue', though she is first seen as a mammary landscape to which the adolescent is devoted, by the end of the poem she has become a shuffling giantess, crying 'Deceiver'. Her son is a deceiver because, like Nower perpetuating the feud or Ransom climbing F6, he believed that he undertook his quest out of choice, whereas it was really to please his mother.

Moreover, it is only the Truly Weak Man (see p. 194) who has to satisfy his weakness in this way. His Quest lends him a quasi-divinity as the biblical allusions in the second stanza imply (Psalms xxiii.2 and Matthew xxv.1–13 ironically conflate shepherd and bridegroom into an unrecognised role as redeemer) and this role-playing turns him into an impotent narcissistic Jove, 'worshipping not lying', whispering in girls' ears rather than going to bed with them (secondary sexual meanings of 'beak' and 'concha' suggest that we might instead have had the rape of Leda). He does understand that life should be natural and instinctive, unselfconscious as the roots of trees that the summer bands tell him about, but he does not put his knowledge into action. He tells others about it. He is, in fact, the first of the orators. The metaphor of the tree-roots in the third stanza probably derives from Lawrence: 'A huge, plunging, tremendous soul. I would like to be a tree for a while. The great lust of roots. Root-lust. And no mind at all' (*Fantasia of the Unconscious*, p. 39). The adolescent has too much of a mind, represented perhaps by the 'finest of mapping pens' with which he compulsively annotates a landscape as familiar to him as life itself. It is for this reason that though his Quest has taken him quite a long way, 'this prophet . . . receives odd welcome from the country he so defended.' This further biblical allusion shows why: 'A prophet is not without honour, save in his own country, and in his own house' (Matthew xiii.57). It is precisely 'in his own house' that his weakness lies, a weakness which is to be explored in Book II of *The Orators*.

Book I ('The Initiates') is largely about how the 'orators', with their varying degrees of perception and evasiveness, are trained in the specious rhetoric of self-justification. But as Auden suggested in his letter to Mitchison, there is an implied 'action'. His letter continued:

The four parts, corresponding if you like to the four seasons and the four ages of man (Boyhood, Sturm und Drang, Middleage, Oldage), are stages in the development of the influence of the Hero (who never appears at all).

Thus Part 1. Introduction to influence.

Part 2. Personally involved with hero. Crisis.

Part 3. Intellectual reconstruction of Hero's teaching. The cerebral life.

Part 4. The effect of Hero's failure on the emotional life.

The litany is the chorus to the play.

In Part I ('Address for a Prize-Day'; 'Speech for a Prize Day', *Criterion*, October 1931) we see psychological Phariseeism in a school; in Part II ('Argument') we see an adolescent day-dream about the elusive Leader, and the sanctimonious prayers which he inspires; in Part III ('Statement') we see a display of prophetic fatalism, the 'heroic' qualities so generalised that the doom seems unavoidable; and in Part IV ('Letter to a Wound') we see a secret devotion to the very illness which is sapping the individual's strength. Auden's schema suggests a greater coherence of 'action' than in fact exists. What he refers to as 'the Hero' is as much a set of attitudes as an individual like the Airman of Book II, attitudes, moreover, which the small band of followers (the 'initiates') can only discover in the course of learning the rhetorical forms with which to express them. The rich inclusivity of imagery ensures that these attitudes remain elusive: the 'crisis' is a crisis of understanding and the 'Hero's failure' relates to the fact that his 'teaching' can indeed only be 'reconstructed' by the 'intellect'. If life were whole, the 'cerebral' would not be opposed to the 'emotional'. The 'Hero' is attempting to solve this opposition, just as the Airman engages the Enemy in Book II: the effort is pointless, for the divided life itself has brought the symbolic protagonist into being, just as the work is finally 'only' a poem. The twin triumph of Book I is its stylistic virtuosity and its generous irony: like Swift's *Tale of a Tub* it presents us with an ever-shifting viewpoint in which, though the writer *in propria persona* is not present, many of his attitudes are. To a certain extent Auden is melodramatising aspects of his own intellectual beliefs: the analysis in the prize-day speech of the kinds of defective love, for example, or the fantastic catalogues of 'Statement' – these are in a basic sense obviously 'Auden's'. Auden as the author is an orator; Auden as a schoolmaster is an orator. But as both of these he is also a dissident force within the culture he is analysing. His 'Hero' is an embodiment of that dissident force.

The speaker in 'Address for a Prize-Day' is an old boy of a school. He has some of the right ideas (Homer Lane's), but ends in mere incoherence (he has a train to catch), urging the boys to bullying and persecution. Robert Medley claims that Auden catches the tone here of J. R. Eccles, the headmaster of Gresham's (*A Tribute*, p. 37) but Auden begins with a clear imitation of Cyril Morgan-Brown ('Ciddy'), the headmaster of St Edmund's (see *Lions and Shadows*, p. 184 for Ciddy's St Edmund's Day sermon: 'Nert – whur did it mean *to them, then, theah*? Bert – whur ders it mean to *ers, heah, nerw*?'). Auden was to develop the monologue as a form with some deftness (in the Vicar's Sermon in *The Chase*, for example, or in the cabaret sketch *Alfred*), so that in spite of its persona and occasion, it became primarily a vehicle for the ideas contained in it rather than an expression of character. In this case, the speaker's main purpose is to elaborate Dante's division of the sinners in *Purgatorio* xvii into 'those who have been guilty in their life of excessive love towards themselves or their neighbours, those guilty of defective love towards God and those guilty of perverted love'. His elaboration ascribes, on Lane's principles, various physical symptoms to each category, a procedure which Auden undertook in greater clinical detail in a diagram in the 1928–?30 notebook, fol. 48. A comparison of this preliminary zplan with the 'Address' will reveal the strength of Auden's suggestive inventiveness and imagery in the course of composition:

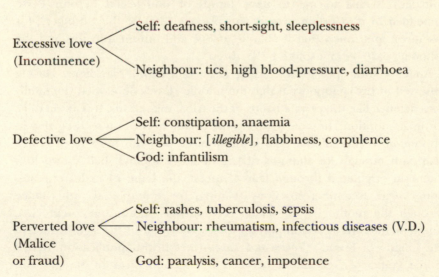

Excessive love
(Incontinence)
    Self: deafness, short-sight, sleeplessness
    Neighbour: tics, high blood-pressure, diarrhoea

Defective love
    Self: constipation, anaemia
    Neighbour: [*illegible*], flabbiness, corpulence
    God: infantilism

Perverted love
(Malice
or fraud)
    Self: rashes, tuberculosis, sepsis
    Neighbour: rheumatism, infectious diseases (V.D.)
    God: paralysis, cancer, impotence

There are similarities in the 'Address' to images in the early poems. Compare, for instance, 'Have you never noticed in them the gradual abdication of central in favour of peripheral control?' (p. 63) with 'central anguish felt | For goodness wasted at peripheral fault' in 'Since you are going to begin today'. Both are explained by Auden's 1929 journal, which remarks that man's peripheral specialisation required the development of intellectual memory ('Intellect alone can co-ordinate desires. It alone can set them at each other's throats': EA, p. 297). Thus the excessive lovers of their neighbours are particularly out of control. Such terms are part of a system that Auden is in the process of creating, and it has to be read as a poetically elaborated system. It is important to note that the theme, so early in the work, is love, and that the initiation is so radical. Lane (who once therapeutically offered one of his delinquents his own gold watch to be smashed) would certainly not have approved of the Black Hole: there are no prizes given to these ruined boys.

The second part of Book 1, 'Argument', begins with an arresting epic 'Lo!' (cf. Old English 'Hwaet!'), and images of birth introduce the theme of the establishment of a new order by a mysterious Leader. The speaker is affected, apparently in a dream, by the idea of the cycle of seasonal change, of death and life (the skull forced out of the dyke by growing bulbs is borrowed from 'We saw in spring', an image familiar from Eliot's 'Whispers of Immortality'). The theme of the Leader evidently derived from Perse's *Anabase*, recently translated by Eliot, who told Auden that Book 1, 'The Initiates', 'seems to me to have lumps of undigested St-John Perse imbedded in it'. Certain images and phrases (that of the 'stranger', for instance), and much that is oblique, exotic and liturgical in this and the following part, seem inspired by *Anabase*.

Auden's anthropological reading also comes into play here. Having observed in his 1929 journal that the middle classes developed the family 'as a defence like the private bands in the tribal migrations. It is afraid of its fortunate position', he now reinvents the primal horde as a secret group in opposition to this middle class institution. Freud, with hints from Frazer (curiously enough an alumnus of Larchfield Academy), had shown how totemism originated through fear of incest: the band of males operates under strict totemic restrictions relating, for example, to inheritance through the mother or to sexual relationships within the totem clan. These themes are clearly important to *The Orators*, as is the significance of the subtitle of Freud's *Totem and Taboo* (first British publication 1919): 'Some Points of Agreement between the Mental Lives of Savages and

Neurotics'. The secrecy of the Leader's name and meeting-place, the gender-differentiated dance and song, the cleansing ritual, the suggestion of exogamy: all these are totemic. The neurosis is soon to be made further explicit in the litany on p. 66.

The ambivalent relationship of the band of males to their womenfolk belongs, however, more clearly to the modern world. The alienation of the young men as they hand round tea is associated with being a stranger to their parents. The real bond is between friends (the 'third party' may be someone who often cannot even understand their conversation: cf. Auden's essay 'Writing', EA, p. 304; but see the fourth short poem appended to 'The Cave of Nakedness' for the idea that the 'third party' may in fact be silence). By virtue of their secret understanding with their Leader (capitalised pronouns suggest divinity) they 'smile inwardly': it is all very like Buchman's Group Movement (Moral Rearmament) which had been Oxford-based when Auden was an undergraduate and was rapidly expanding at the time *The Orators* was written (see *Oxford and the Groups*, ed. R. H. S. Crossman, 1934). In this secret confidence, the band feel themselves akin to the crofter 'working in sweat and weathers' (compare the fourth Ode, p. 105: 'All of the women and most of the men | Shall work with their hands and not think again'). A 'tin-streamer' is someone who gets tin by washing ore in a stream; a 'heckler' is a dresser of flax or hemp; and a 'blow-room major' is someone in charge of a tin-smelting house.

The passage beginning at the bottom of p. 64 suggests that all this might be still a dream of the speaker, who in his suburban home ('the laurelled drive') imagines, with the resources of a boy's adventure story, how the group will move into action to serve its Leader (interrogations take place at a folding card-table and a pair of goggles is 'a present from aunts'). Auden uses a complex of images here, some of which turn up elsewhere. The sawmill is a familiar property from earlier work; taken with the writing of 'reports' and waiting 'His word', it inevitably suggests the letter-hungry isolation of Auden's McElwee poems (e.g. 'Out of sight assuredly . . .', 'I shall sit here through the evening' or 'From the very first coming down'). Also compare, 'At the frontier getting down, at railhead drinking hot tea waiting for pack-mules, at the box with the three levers watching the swallows' with 'On the frontier at dawn getting down' (*Poems*, 1928) and compare these swallows and the next sentence but one ('The young mother in the red kerchief suckling her child in the doorway, and the dog fleaing itself in the hot dust') with 'Westland swallows swooped in and out of the eaves overhead. In a doorway opposite, a young mother looked down at her

suckling babe with ineffable Westland tenderness' (*The Dog Beneath the Skin,
Plays*, p. 229). Moreover, a little further on in this last passage is a reference
to new-mown hay which also turns up in *The Orators* (p. 64). Getting down
(from a train) at the frontier obviously provides a moment in the journey to
the new life for appraisal of what is to come. The swallows and the suckling
child symbolise the fruitfulness of the new life, the 'idea of building' which
governs the whole section. Nonetheless the images are personal, deriving
perhaps from a diary kept on the poet's 1927 holiday in Yugoslavia with his
father. Much of the density of *The Orators* appears to be maintained by
similar use of cannibalised material.

The whole long paragraph on p. 65 elaborates the imaginary world of the
small group (no more than seven?) waiting for action, a world familiar in its
outline from *Paid on Both Sides*. But the paragraph following shows that it is
all conditional. The absurd hero-worship and self-sacrifice are all in the
mind of the speaker. The tripod on the dunes is not the symbol of
inspiration which Faust carries back from the cave of the Mothers (its three
legs and its ring at the top uniting the male and female worlds) but the
shadow of the family camera. It is the 'world of the Spider, not Him', and
those who desire the new life are reduced to superstitious ritual. The
'vegetable offering' is probably only a loofah (Auden certainly used one: see
'In the year of my youth . . .', 11.45) but he may have had in mind Freud's
distinction in *Totem and Taboo* that unlike animal sacrifices which were
shared with his worshippers, the vegetable offerings were for the god alone.
The joke thus forces the schoolmaster to be fatally sacrilegious. 'Resurgam'
is another hopeful cry, but it is expressed by urinating in a patch of snow: a
more confident form of immortality can be obtained by a different sort of
'writing' with the penis.

The passage beginning at the bottom of p. 65 describes a journey, but it is
not clear that the journey is likely to accomplish anything ('Is it wise, the
short adventure on the narrow ship?'). The images of the dew-wet hare and
the emmet are borrowed from 'Upon the ridge the mill-sails glow' (*Poems*,
1928). The horns in the spring are reminiscent of *The Waste Land*, line 197.
Women are tender in the spring, but the group must leave them (cf. 'Doom
is dark and deeper than any sea-dingle') because 'it is your art just now
against the inner life'. In other words, it is the women who are preventing
the new life from coming about and must be abandoned. The group are
obedient to His will, but it is not clear that they really know what they are up
to.

The second section of 'Argument' (p. 66) consists of the group's prayers, a parody of the Anglican responses (and according to Auden 'the chorus to the play'). Prayer for delivery from various forms of neurotic illness is made to detectives of fiction, and prayer on behalf of defective lovers is made to a series of pubs: *private* detectives and *public* houses is, I think, the thematic joke. Most of the material here is plain enough. 'The drought that withers the lower centres' (p. 66) is the mother's inhibiting love (see Lawrence's *Fantasia of the Unconscious*, p. 119). The 'two against one' (p. 67) is illuminated by a couplet from the 1928–?30 notebook, fol. 43, and printed in EA, p. 51: 'There are two kinds of friendship even in babes | Two against one and seven against Thebes' (cf. p. 64: 'Our bond, friend, is a third party'). The source of the phrase may be an Icelandic proverb: 'Two are an army against one' (see *Racial Proverbs*, ed. S. G. Chapman, 1938) and it may allude to the exclusiveness of romantic love as opposed to the psychology of groups: i.e. the self-conscious mind's first task is to separate and destroy, to create the developed dualism that defeats psychology, health and group action. The 'seven against Thebes' is a symbol of the group outfacing the whole world (1929 Journal). In 1966 Auden omitted the invocation to Ferrers Locke for delivery from, among other things, 'the death-will of the Jews', which surely seemed tasteless after the Second World War. 'George' is a pleasant literalism for 'The King's Head'.

The third section of 'Argument' (p. 68) contains more than the usual share of writing that seems impenetrably stream-of-consciousness. Compare 'Shutting the door on machines, etc.' with 'The Engine House' (*Lions and Shadows*, p. 186). 'Love, that notable forked one, etc.' is adapted from 'Because sap fell away' (*Poems*, 1928). The section describes a time of crisis in the absence of the Leader, and it strongly evokes the meetings with Christ before the Resurrection ('Catching sight of Him on the lawn with the gardener . . . Hysterical attempts of two women to reach Him'). 'We who on the snow-line were in love with death, despised vegetation, we forgot His will' may allude to Eliot's 'Journey of the Magi', lines 21–2: 'Then at dawn we came down to a temperate valley, | Wet, below the snow line, smelling of vegetation.' The magi were similarly confused about the meaning of Christ, similarly involved with death, and are also alluded to at the end of Auden's 'It was Easter as I walked in the public gardens'). The Leader appears to have vanished as mysteriously as he came (or did he ever come?), leaving only legend behind him, and a stone whose inscription the children at play ignore (compare the war-memorial in 'From scars where kestrels hover', another poem about a doomed leader and a band of followers). The Christian implications of 'Argument' are no doubt fully intended by Auden to derive from its speaker. The final sentence appears to deliver a judgment upon his motivation and imagination: 'The priest's mouth opens in the green graveyard, but the wind is against it.' The 'crisis' of Auden's schema, then, involves the way in which the Leader's role, even his followers' understanding of who or what He might be, has become romanticised.

The third part of Book I, 'Statement' (p. 69), consists largely of laconic catalogues and gnomic observations which underline the idea of fate. The use of Perse continues (compare 'Summon. And there passed such cursing his father, and the curse was given him' with 'Stranger. Who passed, etc.' in Eliot's translation of *Anabase*, p. 15), but the basic debt is to Old English poetry. The three sections of 'Statement' are each built around a fairly direct pastiche of an Old English poem: the first uses 'The Gifts of Men', the second 'The Fortunes of Men', and the third 'Maxims'. These three poems appear in different parts of the Exeter Book, but are printed together in R. K. Gordon's *Anglo-Saxon Poetry* (1926), which Auden had probably used. 'The Gifts of Men' introduces the 'sum' formula. Compare (in Gordon's translation):

> He who has power of judgment scatters variously to dwellers throughout this world the bodily powers of men. To one on earth here He grants goods, worldly treasures. One is poor, an unfortunate man; yet he is wise in arts of the mind. One receives more bodily strength. One is beautiful, fair in form. One is a poet skilled in songs. One is eloquent in words. One is a pursuer in hunting of glorious beasts, etc.

Auden has converted the Old English ascription of men's gifts to God's providence into a purely materialistic and utilitarian generalisation: 'To each an award, suitable to his sex, his class and the power'. The resemblance of this to the famous dictum of Karl Marx is probably not accidental. 'Power' for Auden had a sexual implication (it was a word for the male genitals, see *A Certain World*, p. 269). In elaborating the catalogue, Auden may have been inspired by Perse (cf. p. 65, the passage about 'all conditions of men') or by Whitman's *Song of Myself*, but the 'sum' formula crops up in many places, in the *Iliad*, xiii.726–34, for instance, and in Corinthians.

Auden also continues to cannibalise earlier poems. Compare, for instance, 'one is skilful at improvising a fugue; the bowel tremors at the pedal-entry' with 'That pedal-entry in the fugue | Roared in, swept soul and knees away' ('In Spring we waited . . .', published in December 1926). One rich source was a poem 'Men pass through doors and travel to the sea' which Auden sent to Isherwood in July 1929 and which became Robert's speech in *The Enemies of a Bishop*, IV.iii). Its first four lines open the first section of 'Statement' and lines 6–8 may be found in the opening of section two. Line 18 also provides the 'influenza and guilty rashes' of the penultimate paragraph of 'Argument', together with an image of decline ('– speeding descent | Of noble mind, the brakes burnt out') the last four words of which followed the rashes in the first edition. Lines 21–8 were turned into most of the penultimate paragraph of 'Address for a Prize-Day'.

The contrasting implication of these first two sections, reliant as they are on the Old English 'Gifts' and 'Fortunes', is of the waste of a whole generation. A marvellously concrete evocation of the potential and variety of the human condition is quickly dispelled by the itemising of the disaster and illness which befall individuals, and of the often absurd and trivial compensatory luck of the survivors. It is, in effect, a memorialising enumeration. Its relevance is underlined by the reader's memory of the ignored war memorial at the end of 'Argument', and by the clinching image at the end of the second section of 'Statement': 'Have seen the red bicycle [of the telegraph messenger bringing the fatal news] leaning on porches and the cancelling out was complete.'

The final section of 'Statement' (p. 70) accentuates the inevitability of the process it has described so far, and its didactic tone supports Auden's claim that 'Statement' is an 'Intellectual reconstruction of Hero's teaching'. It describes the plenitude and continuity of life: 'Nothing is being done but something being done again by someone.' This sounds like a naïve description of the Mendelian chart later discussed by the Airman (p. 76). The first paragraph is a pastiche of Gertrude Stein (compare her *Useful Knowledge*, 1929, p. 1), whom Auden admired for a time while at Oxford (see *Lions and Shadows*, p. 214, and for a qualification, Stephen Spender, *World Review*, n.s. 6, 1949, p. 49). Compare also 'Two old things . . . with a new one' (Isherwood, *All the Conspirators*, p. 26).

In the following paragraph, Auden's model is the Old English 'Maxims'. Compare 'Fate is strongest. Winter is coldest; spring most frosty . . . The bird shall sport in the air. The salmon shall go darting in the pool, etc.' (Gordon, pp. 313–14). Auden used his image of the salmon again in *The Dog Beneath the Skin* (*Plays*, p. 206): 'Salmon leaping the ladder'. 'The belly receives; the back rejects' is reminiscent of Blake's 'Proverbs of Hell' ('The Cistern contains; the fountain overflows'). The absolute difference of the insect received Auden's definitive elaboration in his 1970 poem 'The Aliens'.

The third paragraph, while continuing to follow the Old English at random though sometimes closely (compare 'Two are consorts. A woman and a man shall bring a child into the world by birth', Gordon, p. 309), introduces some of Lawrence's educational ideas. When Auden wrote (p. 71) 'The boy and the girl shall not play together; they shall wait for power', he was probably thinking of something like 'Then keep the girls apart from any familiarity or being "pals" with the boys. The nice clean intimacy which we now so admire between the sexes is sterilizing. It makes neuters. Later on, no deep, magical sex-life is possible' (*Fantasia of the Unconscious*, p. 84; Auden often uses 'power' with a sexual meaning). 'The leader shall be a fear' was revised to 'The leader shall be a father' in the US edition of 1967. Substantive use of 'a fear' can be found, e.g. in Psalms xxxi.11. Such injunctions (and the 'sceal' formula which binds them, found not only in Old English but also in Leviticus) seem to suggest that fate has better things in store.

The final paragraph, reminiscent of 'Now from my windowsill . . .' written in February 1932, corroborates this by implying that out of the endless battle of contraries comes eventual good, 'Good against evil, youth against age, life against death, light against darkness', as the Old English puts it (Gordon, p. 314). Its terms are those of Lawrence's theory of the cosmological duality of life (*Fantasia of the Unconscious*, pp. 150ff) and it is an implication that Blake would have understood. Auden had elaborated the address to the sun and moon on the right and left in the poem 'Father and mother, twin-lights of heaven' of December 1929.

The fourth part of Book I, 'Letter to a Wound' (p. 71), is an imaginative leap of a high order. Auden's schema describes it as 'The effect of the Hero's failure on the emotional life'. The writer's wound represents his psychological illness, and he writes a love letter to it, full of relished intimacy and self-indulgent confidences, because he does not want to be cured. Indeed, the surgeon has no hope. The name 'Gangle' is a clue to the nature of the illness: it is Lawrence's lumbar ganglion that provides our sense of identity ('And it is from the great voluntary centre of the lumbar ganglion that the child asserts its distinction from the mother', *Fantasia of the Unconscious*, p. 31). The wound enables the writer to understand various other forms of perverted love (top of p. 73) such as that between the disgustingly named Offal and Snig. Although Auden uses 'Snig' elsewhere as an exemplary name ('Writing', EA, p. 304), there is probably an allusion here to anal intercourse ('offal' is waste, 'snig' an eel, 'the hardware shop at the front' the erecting genitals). According to Ansen, Auden said to him on 10 December 1947: 'I don't like being fucked, it's only happened to me once and I had to go to hospital'. Auden had an operation for an anal fissure in 1930 (this is the operation referred to in Ode 1, coincident with the death of Lawrence) and though Mendelson (p. 111) claims that Auden's real wound was not caused by sexual relations, the metaphorical drift is clear, and the whole work's rationale as a 'memorial to Lawrence' bizarrely underlined. Mendelson's ingenious suggestion (p. 102) that the wound is in some sense the 'open wound' of melancholia as described by Freud in 'Mourning and Melancholia' makes some sense if we follow the narrative line that the writer is unable satisfactorily to mourn for the dead leader (melancholia substitutes the lost love-object for the ego). However, we are not, I think, to identify the Leader with Lawrence. Auden had written of 'the difficult work of mourning' in 'It was Easter as I walked in the public gardens' (EA, p. 39) in a context that makes it clear that it is love for the mother which has died. If, in 'Letter to a Wound', the writer's emotional life is in ruins, then it might be precisely because (in Lawrence's terms) he had not asserted his distinction from his mother. He has, in fact, taken his mother as his ego-ideal, sought new love objects that are like himself and become homosexual (see Freud, *Group Psychology and the Analysis of the Ego*, 1922, p. 66). The adulation of the failed Leader is, throughout Book 1, coloured with homoerotic hero-worship. As if to counter the tonal distance of the letter's style, Auden has had no hesitation in introducing his own friends into it: Gabriel Carritt from Oxford (to appear more significantly in Book 11, and in Book 111); Olive Mangeot, Isherwood's employer; and Margaret Marshall (his brother's first wife, 'Margaret the brazen leech' of the poem 'I chose this lean country'). ('Molim' might be J. B. Malim, the headmaster of Wellington School.)

Book 11, 'Journal of an Airman', contains the central action of the whole work. As he explained to Mitchison in August 1931: 'I am now writing the second half, which is the situation seen from within the Hero . . . The flying symbolism is I imagine fairly obvious. The chief strands are his Uncle (Heredity–Matrilineal descent and initiations), belief in a universal conspiracy (the secret society mind), kleptomania (the worm in the root).' We have already seen how hard it is for the individual to break with his illness and embrace the new life, and we have seen how the mystique of a charismatic leader affects those who are thus divided. Now we have an account by such a leader of his understanding of the forces which prevent spiritual regeneration ('the enemy') and his programme of combat against them. But it transpires that this Truly Strong Man is a Truly Weak Man, his programme misconceived and doomed to failure. Auden later made a suggestive comment: 'The closest modern equivalent to the Homeric hero is the ace fighter pilot' (*The Portable Greek Reader*, 1948, p. 18), and of course the helmeted airman had turned up earlier in his poetry as a clinical observer ('Consider this and in our time'). But the drift of this book is anti-heroic as well as anti-romantic. The paranoia and kleptomania mentioned by Auden are the Airman's, and his flying is not the entirely straightforward military exploit that one might expect. Indeed, the flying symbolism is not obvious. Auden explained to Mrs Kuratt shortly after publication that 'The genesis of the book was a paper written by an anthropologist friend of mine about ritual epilepsy . . . linking it up with the flying powers of witches, sexual abnormalities etc.' (Buffalo). A series of papers about rites in Malekula in the New Hebrides had been published by Auden's friend John Layard (*Journal of the Royal Anthropological Institute* 58, January–June 1928, pp. 139–233, and 60, July–December 1930, pp. 501–24). These papers established that Malekulan priests, or 'flying tricksters', exploited the sensation of flight experienced by real epileptics in ritual self-induced pseudo-epilepsy. Their matrilineally transmitted rites concerned the reanimation of the dead; other characteristics of the flying tricksters included homosexuality, practical jokes and an individualism incapable of social organisation (see Mendelson, pp. 104ff). These ritual and neurotic elements are to provide a crucial fictive momentum to the Airman's circumstances.

Meanwhile, he begins his observations about 'the enemy' (p. 73) using the terms of a Gestalt psychologist. The first two pages depend very much on Wolfgang Köhler's *Gestalt Psychology* (1930), especially his chapter IV, 'Dynamics as opposed to Machine Theory', in which he attacks the main assumptions of introspective psychology and behaviourism. Köhler had already shown that introspection excludes experiences that are explained by the effects of meaning (e.g. optical illusions that we accept as real) and rely only on what physiologists accept as valid. Behaviourists are similarly concerned with measurable appearances (e.g. reflexes). The Gestalt psychologist, on the other hand, is concerned with the dynamic interaction of systems, not the artificially isolatable and measurable systems of machine theory. One of Köhler's examples in this chapter is of the difference between a drop of water in a pipe (which moves, 'aside from inertia', due to the higher pressure on one side) and a drop of water in the sea, where 'not only movement, or process as such, but also the direction and distribution of process is determined dynamically by interaction' (p. 102). Köhler's argument continues:

At each point the forces will produce changes of movement or process which, when considered in their totality, bring the system nearer to the balance of the forces themselves. The factor of inertia may cause the real course of events to deviate from the ideal exemplification of this principle. But where, as in most organic systems, inert velocities not corresponding to actual forces are destroyed by friction, the real distribution of processes will exhibit the principle perfectly, and will finally reach a state of stability, of rest or of stationary process . . . Therefore, by undisturbed interaction a system approaches order.

(p. 106)

This is the Airman's point of departure, and his first words ('A system organises itself, if interaction is undisturbed') are a rephrasing of Köhler's conclusion. Auden uses Köhler's 'inert velocities' and 'friction' in the following paragraph to establish 'the enemy' as an embodiment of everything that interferes with the natural tendency of the forces within a system to lead to stability. Auden's 'system' in this case is, of course, given the twin social and psychological orientation of *The Orators* already established, both the mind of the Airman and English society. The double role of the enemy is important. The Airman's observations establish the basic fact that the enemy's activities hinder the natural development of society and of the individual: there is a nervous evasive tone about these analogies drawn from physics and psychology (and, a page or two later, biology) as though the Airman, by seeking to establish an objective view of the enemy, is avoiding a subjective understanding. This is important for the Airman's drama of self-discovery.

The enemy, then, works by imposing artificial 'laws or habits' instead of allowing the system to mind its own business and reach the equilibrium posited by the second law of thermodynamics. The airman notes that an organically developing society must be based on the healthy self-sufficiency of the individual (self-care) and is weakened by the selfish demands of the neurotically introverted (self-regard). Self-regard is a sex-linked disease like haemophilia, he says, thus invoking the Mendelian theory of inheritance, where incidence of the characteristic is largely restricted to one sex. In these cases man is the sufferer, woman the carrier: ' "What a wonderful woman she is!" Not so fast: wait till you see her son.' The thematic outline of the 'Prologue' is already being filled in, just as the hints about the enemy in 'Argument' ('Their annual games . . . their day . . . their women') prepared for the significant female role.

Other sex-linked diseases include night-blindness, colour-blindness and

various ocular defects: this explains the diagrams that follow ('A Sure Test').
If you suspect someone of self-regard, you can give him an ocular test of the
kind used for colour-blindness. If he picks out an unlikely shape, it is, as the
Airman observes (p. 74), 'wiser to shoot at once', for his selection
represents his division of 'the unity of passion' (p. 78). The diagrams on
p. 74 are taken straight from Köhler (pp. 152–4) who uses the two crosses as
examples of 'real' forms (i.e. significant forms) immediately accessible to
the naïve observer. The unlikely shape is a 'learned' form. This simple
example is only a part of a complex argument in which Köhler is
investigating the problem of how we recognise 'real' wholes and how they
are invested with perceptual meaning. Auden's conclusion ('THE ENEMY IS
A LEARNED NOT A NAIVE OBSERVER') marks the enemy as a metaphorical
behaviourist, a kind of blinkered spy with no access to the insight of the
Gestalt.

On pages 74–6, Auden elaborates the Airman's idea of his role as an
agent of love ('central awareness'). The first analogy ('*The Circle*') proposes
the desirable interdependence of centre and circumference. The enemy's
ignorance of the Gestalt ('partial priority') disturbs this sympathy. The
second analogy ('*The Two Circles*') extends the example to human relation-
ships: the kinship of philia and the 'difference' of eros. It may be worth
pointing out that in the 1928–?30 notebook, fol. 8, what is there called
'Conjugative (Attraction) of cells of dissimilars' is associated with hetero-
sexual love. The metaphor of the circles, and the relationships between
circumferences and centres, also refers to Lawrence's upper and lower
centres of awareness, which Auden elsewhere called 'the duality of Higher
and Lower will' (EA, p. 300). The enemy's disturbance of these relation-
ships (in the individual, and between individuals) represents, as will be
made clearer, not only the ignorance of the true Gestalt, the divided psyche
of the spiritually ill, but also the mother's own 'partial priority', her love for
the son which strangles the deeper sensual centres (cf. *Fantasia of the
Unconscious*, p. 119).

At this point, Auden obviously felt that the insistent psychological
metaphors needed some relief, although the poem 'After the death of
their proud master . . .' (September 1931) was omitted by him in 1966. It
acts as an 'historical' illustration of the roles of the 'Higher and Lower will'
('Master' and 'Boots') in the shape of the thrashed and cowering children
of a proud paterfamilias who create bogeys to frighten the servants into
believing that it is not a social injustice which keeps them all in fear. The
legends deny 'weakness', but their demolition by a later pampered

generation does not redeem that weakness, since in denying legends in order to deny weakness you simply reintroduce the pride and envy which created the duality of 'Master' and 'Boots' in the first place. This crude but perhaps over-complex poem is Auden's first potted history of the Fall, of sexual repression and of the etiology of religious belief (the ogre has some of the characteristics of Dante's Lucifer: see *Inferno*, xxxiv): it would not have satisfied the Christian Auden.

The Airman then explores the relationship of the circles in time according to the Mendelism which he has already introduced, discovering that 'the true ancestral line is not necessarily a straight or continuous one'. His diagram, with the circle representing the zygote, the half-circles the gametes, and F1, F2 and F3 the various filial generations, demonstrates the basic Mendelian conclusion that where the inheritance of an alternative pair of characters is concerned, the effect of the cross in successive generations is to produce only three sorts of individuals, namely: dominants which breed true, dominants which give both dominant and recessive offspring in the ratio of 3:1, and recessives which always breed true. Thus the Airman is forced to conclude that his true ancestor is his uncle or great-grandfather.

Now the Airman has two uncles: Uncle Sam, who arranges sing-songs 'with all the assurance of a non-airman' (p. 78), and Uncle Henry, who committed suicide and appears to have been a homosexual (see pp. 84 and 85, and the poem 'Uncle Henry'). The Airman, fresh from his Mendelian charts, has a moment of doubt (p. 79: 'Uncle Sam, is he one too? He has the same backward-bending thumb that I have' refers to the tell-tale sucked thumb indicating deprivation of the breast at weaning), but he does assume that it is Uncle Henry who is his true ancestor. For this reason, the aeroplane becomes associated with homosexuality, and flying seems an unnatural activity: 'My mother's dislike of my uncle, the people's satisfaction at crashes. "If the Lord had intended people to fly He'd have given them wings" ' (p. 76). But the Airman is still primarily an agent of love, the central awareness: homosexuality is an enemy-created bogey (like the dragon in the marsh) irrelevant to the main problem of healing the individual and society. The Airman notes (p. 76) that the aeroplane is really only 'a guarantee of good faith to the people, frightened by ghost stories, the enemy's distorted vision of the airman's activities'. These ghost stories are clearly related to the Airman's note on p. 75 about ancestor worship: it is his recognition of his true heredity that is crucial to his programme of healing, not his flying.

The Airman begins now to look for bases from which to conduct his heroic campaign against the enemy (the names come from the Shetlands, where Auden took a summer holiday in 1931). Watching skuas (a kind of gull) he has an inkling that his role may involve self-deception: 'You are a man, or haven't you heard I That you keep on trying to be a bird?' We are reminded of Auden's adoption of Lane's theories as reported by Isherwood in *Lions and Shadows*, p. 303: 'epilepsy . . . was an attempt to become an angel, and fly.' There is no doubt that the Airman is in fact ill. He is probably a kleptomaniac (p. 79: 'Only once here, quite at the beginning, and I put it back'; p. 84: 'Yesterday positively the last time. Hands to remember please, always'; p. 86: 'Again. Always the same weakness. No progress against this terrible thing, etc.'; p. 91: 'Very little progress this year. Never quite as bad as that dreadful spring of 1927, but still generally at week-ends'; p. 93: 'The true significance of my hands . . . They stole to force a hearing'; p. 94: 'Hands in perfect order'), but we have to remember the connection between kleptomania and masturbation pointed out by Jung: 'When onanism confronts the physician it does so frequently under the symbol of frequent pilfering, or crafty imposition, which always signifies the concealed fulfilment of a forbidden wish' (*Psychology of the Unconscious*, 1917, p. 186). 'Pilfering' had already put in a significant appearance in 'After the death of their proud master . . .' on p. 75. In 1929 Auden had known a thief who falsely claimed to be a pilot (Margaret Gardiner, *New Review*, July 1976; see also Isherwood, *Christopher and his Kind*, p. 62). Katherine Bucknell has pointed out that Stekel connected kleptomania directly with homosexuality (unpublished Ph.D. thesis, Columbia University). Whatever the direct implication of kleptomania for Auden, it is a sign of a central weakness which (as with Nower and Ransom) forces the Airman to his exploits.

The airman then goes on (p. 76) to talk of the enemy as a philosopher who treats 'intellect–will–sensation' as separate entities, in defiance of the Gestalt. In a fine interpretation of the sestina which follows, 'We have brought you, they said, a map of the country' (September 1931, called 'Have a Good Time' in CP), John Blair shows how these three faculties correspond allegorically to the bay, the clock and the wood which appear in the poem. Blair interprets the vats as 'dyer's vats, which serve as an allegorical representation of art' (*The Poetic Art of W. H. Auden*, 1965, p. 80) and shows how the whole poem serves to describe the poet's (and by extension the Airman's) education and setting-out in life, and his attempts to integrate intellect, will and sensation. The mysterious vats are, however, less challengingly allegorical if they are seen as part of a whisky distillery (the landscape of *The Orators* is naturally mostly Scottish). The flying trickster in the wood is the most direct allusion to Layard's Malekula articles (see p. 100) and appropriately presides over the 'consummation' in the wood (i.e. initiation into the cult of reviving the dead and into the perception of 'real' wholes, both centre and circumference).

The 'terrible rat-courage' of the enemy (p. 78) was to be given a more explicit context in the poem 'Now from my window-sill . . .' (EA, p. 116), where it is a characteristic of the sick trying to evade the power of the Lords of Limit. The section '*The Enemy as Observer*' shows that the enemy are dangerous when cornered, and above all doggedly rational ('Their extraordinary idea that man's only glory is to think'), so that when their thinking goes wrong it takes on a belligerent prescriptive air. The remedy for the sick dog (p. 78) was compared by one contemporary of Auden's to the National Government's treatment of the unemployed with the Means Test and occupational centres (Fisher collection, Christ Church, Oxford). The enemy's perception of the passions is a 'learned' response to the more complex 'unity of passion' which (in Lane's terms) is the 'effort of a thing to realise its own nature'. The perversity of the 'learned' response (see the ideas of Köhler above) is like the private associations of rhyming slang (compare the form of back-slang employed by the Luder brothers in *The Enemies of a Bishop, Plays*, p. 48). These private and fixed associations need to be upset by practical jokes, which are 'contradictory and public' (one of the activities of Malekula's flying tricksters). At this point the first edition has an obscure poem 'Well, Milder, if that's the way you're feeling' (February 1931; dropped in 1934: EA, p. 442). Milder (from the folk poem 'The Cutty Wren', model for Auden's 'Epilogue') is a traditional questioner, perhaps, as in 'Epilogue', another role for the reader. The poem, then, appears to buttonhole the reader and suggest that it is not so easy to vow to abandon enemy characteristics. A 'windmill gesture' for Auden was probably a kind of shrug (as in the unpublished 'Landscape' of June 1925: 'once a ruined mill | Raised heavy hands'). Rather than smugly giving up stealing, the Airman now embarks on it (p. 79) in the hotel where he is gathering his forces.

'*The Airman's Alphabet*' (pp. 79–81; June 1931) is modelled directly on the Icelandic Runic Poem (*Runic and Heroic Poems*, ed. Bruce Dickins, 1915, pp. 78–81). Compare:

Wealth = source of discord among kinsmen
     and fire of the sea
     and path of the serpent.
Shower = lamentation of the clouds
     and ruin of the hay-harvest
     and abomination of the shepherd, etc.

Flying is a 'ghostly journey' because of its associations with the Malekulan rituals. Since a kiss is both 'Touch taking off' and 'Mark upon map', the Airman's flights seem to be defined by an erotic purpose, and the alphabet is scattered with *doubles entendres.*

The following definitions, '*Of the Enemy*' (pp. 81–2) are largely social and psychological. As Kathleen Hoagland has pointed out (*1000 Years of Irish Poetry*, 1947, p. 23), Auden wittily adapts the ninth-century Irish triad. The result is a comically elaborated list of personal *bêtes noires* reminiscent of Apollinaire's *merde | rose* or Wyndham Lewis's Blasting and Blessing. The phrase 'the fucked hen' was bowdlerised by Eliot to 'the June bride' in the first edition. Isherwood made Miss Belmare use it of Mr Charles's poor bowls playing in the Mortmere story 'The World War' (Christopher Isherwood and Edward Upward, *The Mortmere Stories*, 1994, p. 111). The Rev. Welken's Catullan gloss ('Gallina defututa') suggests a complex source (see 'The Megalopsych', no. II). The three results of an enemy victory are elsewhere explained as the consequence of a perverted love towards God (see chart on p. 91), though the sense of 'God' in this context is the true nature of the integrated organism. Although there are some definitions like this one which underline the psychological schema, the general picture that comically emerges is of the comfortable, cautious and stuffy bourgeoisie. For the enemy catchwords, see Forster, *A Room with a View*, chapter 17, where 'the armies of the benighted, who . . . march to their destiny by catchwords . . . have yielded to the only enemy that matters – the enemy within.'

The Airman's continued preparations and agitation are revealed by the week's timetable which follows, mentioning 'The Hollies', the house which becomes the centre of his operations. It appears that the 'E' who lives there is loved by the Airman, but is in danger because of this, and must be given up (pp. 83, 85, 91, 94: E's sex was changed for the second edition). Other allies of the Airman appear in the following pages: A, a scout; B, an indecisive and sceptical ally; Derek, a particular friend, killed through sabotage (in reality the 'D. W.' for whom Auden wrote 'What's in your mind, my dove, my coney'); and so on. The feuding atmosphere of *Paid on Both Sides* is again evoked ('A tells me they have been in Kettlewell and most of the outlying farms', p. 82; Kettlewell is in Wharfedale, scene of earlier Auden poems such as 'I chose this lean country'), and there are a number of philosophical jottings, lists of armaments, reported dreams and so on. The poem 'Last day but ten' (?1930) appears in the 1928–?30 notebook, fol. 15, a comment on a companion of the Airman whose escape is frustrated. Auden probably intended houses like The Hollies as allegorical representations of individuals in which a rallying integration is being attempted ('Cases of immunity, etc.'). In this case the efforts of the Airman on behalf of the blithely doomed E represent the circumference and centre of the human circle (p. 75) comparable to Nower and the Spy in *Paid on Both Sides*. (Auden's psychological allegorising was persistent: see for example 'The month was April . . .', *The Ascent of F6*, and *The Age of Anxiety*.) In the following section, '*Continuity and Discontinuity*', the enemy's opposition to such efforts at integration are represented as two forms of military opposition ('shock troops' and 'martial law') appropriate to combat the dissident activities of the Airman. This metaphor is once again from the psychological methods of introspectionists (flux-mongers) and behaviourists (order-doctrinaires) in relation to the nature of continuous wholes. The metaphor of 'drawing the line' is derived from Dedekind's Section, the method of defining irrational or transcendental numbers devised by the mathematician Dedekind.

The following section about Uncle Henry explains his influence over the Airman. The uncle's role, already given a 'public' scientific Mendelian significance (p. 76), has a 'private' anthropological one, as Auden acknowledged when telling Mitchison about the Malekulan rituals. But Auden had probably already been struck by this role in other matrilineal societies like that of the Trobriand Islanders as described by Bronislaw Malinowski in his *The Father in Primitive Psychology* (1927). In his letter to Mrs Kuratt he confuses Malekula with the Trobriand Islands. He would also have known about the influence of uncles from explanations of 'swustersunu' (sister's son) at line 115 of 'The Battle of Maldon', and he quotes this Old English poem later in *The Orators* (EA, p. 108). Uncle Henry is modelled on Isherwood's homosexual uncle, Henry Isherwood, who gave him an allowance to live in Berlin and was delighted to hear stories of his sexual adventures (*Christopher and his Kind*, pp. 34ff). Some details concerning his death are drawn from information given to Auden by Edward Upward concerning the suicide of the writer Allen Upward, cousin of Upward's father (Carpenter, p. 126).

Uncle Henry is clever and dissolute, feared and denigrated by the mother whose comfortable bourgeois standards he appears to threaten. He is the wicked bachelor who invites the sixteen-year-old nephew to his flat and gives him champagne for dinner. In the Airman's anxiety dream (p. 85), he appears as someone who has made a journey that the Airman is unable to make, even to save his loved one from a terrible danger (compare E as saboteur with the Spy in *Paid on Both Sides*). The journey turns out to be suicide, but the Airman does not realise the significance of this until later. 'I have crossed it' are the hero's words in Claudel's *The Book of Christopher Columbus* (New Haven, 1930), in the opening scene where the Chorus encourages Columbus to 'come to a higher region where a throne awaits thee . . . There is but one step to take and thou wilt be with us. Simply that narrow line to cross, that very narrow line which is called Death!' This ecstatic apotheosis supplies an important tonal colouring, for the Airman will later gladly follow the example of his uncle as the only means of achieving integration (for Claudel's importance to Auden in the following year, see p. 145).

The Airman appears at The Hollies (p. 85). The real 'The Hollies' (61 John Street, Helensburgh) belonged to Archie Stewart, a stockbroker and Larchfield parent. The Airman is drawn to the games-playing life of leisure that goes on there, but more and more uncertain as to his real position. Are the people that he meets on his side or not? He visits in order to 'acquire their ruses', and imagines that 'the spies have gone to phone for their police.' His kleptomania returns, and he has more bad dreams. The worrying mower is borrowed from 'Chloe to Daphnis in Hyde Park' published in 1926. 'Gonsil' and 'first-of-May' are both examples of tramps' cant, with homosexual implications (cf. 'The Duet' of 1947). 'Left-handed' suggests a narcissistic love (cf. 'I shall sit here through the evening' of 1927). 'Hygiene' and 'Newspapers' in '*Of the Enemy Gambits*' (p. 86) is explained by some remarks in the 1929 journal: 'We have tried to make the body more and more individualistic (hygiene) and the mind more and more communistic (newspapers). The result being that on the one hand we lose the capacity to love and on the other we lose the capacity to think' (EA, pp. 297–8).

'Hygiene' is here borrowed from Baudelaire's *Intimate Journals*, recently translated by Isherwood. The newspapers suggest a sexual joke: 'Hearts' and 'Queens' are football teams. And they also suggest a poem: 'Beethameer, Beethameer, bully of Britain' (p. 86; October 1931) is the first example of Auden's extensive use of rhyme royal (see also the Envoi to Ode IV, similarly written in October 1931, 'A Happy New Year' of the following

February, and 'Letter to Lord Byron'). The character of this satire on a Beaverbrook/Rothermere hybrid shows that Auden borrowed the form in the first place from Skelton's 'Speke Parrott' (which is also, of course, intermittently alliterative and at one point uses a refrain). Auden was reviewing Skelton's poems at the time: the review appeared in *The Criterion* (January 1932, pp. 316–19). His allusion is no doubt to the Beaverbrook/ Rothermere alliance of 1929 and the foundation of the United Empire Party. Stan Smith points out (*Critical Survey*, vi, 3, 1994, p. 320) that the Airman had to settle the bill (p. 94) for his 10,000 cyclostyle copies of 'Beethameer . . .' with a Helensburgh stationers owned by Samuel Bryden, local version of a newspaper monopolist.

At this point an outside voice breaks into the Airman's notes and meditations, interrogating him and encouraging free association in the manner of a psychotherapist. Much of the material looks as though it derives directly from Auden's own experience. 'Uncle Wiz' is one of Auden's Larchfield nicknames ('Audibus' was another); 'Uncle Dick' is Richard Crossman; 'Gabriel' is Gabriel Carritt, with whom Auden was unsuccessfully in love at Oxford; 'Do-a' is Carritt's father, and 'Do-ee' is Carritt's younger brother; 'Bill' is William McElwee, also loved by Auden, and like Carritt from Sedbergh; Roy Harrod was a Fellow in Economics at Christ Church; and so on. The point of this very personal passage (dropped in 1966) is to establish 'the interest' of the material that the creative process has abstracted from it. The Airman's story is as distant from Auden's as the Queen and her Laureate were from common realities (their beliefs about trains and cigars). Thus the interpolation re-insists upon the 'interest' in the sense of Auden's proprietory rights over this material and its relation to the actual world (the 'week the Labour Cabinet resigned', i.e. 24 August 1931, is reflected in the dating of the Airman's campaign on p. 91). The dream he can hardly remember is in fact very like the Airman's dream, suggesting that the whole allegorical phantasmogoria of the Airman may in a sense be a conscious piece of auto-therapy on Auden's part. Auden returned to this idea of 'the interest' in an important poem written in the following May, 'O Love, the interest itself in thoughtless heaven' (see p. 147 for the derivation from Henry James).

There is a further death among the Airman's companions, even as a new batch of initiates arrives (p. 88). The phrase 'Poor little buggers' is borrowed from a poem written for Gabriel Carritt ('Gabriel, fully occupied in either', 1928–?30 notebook) in which it specifically refers to his Larchfield pupils. Here, as elsewhere in *The Orators*, are passages of such mercurial transitions that one is reminded that automatic writing had been fashionable for a time. There are resemblances to examples of Isherwood and Upward's given in *Lions and Shadows*, p. 276. Compare:

> In the greenhouse they loiter, imagine coiled shapes, malignant, phosphorescent, in the zinc darkness of a tank. Come on, you chaps! After their change of heart, a desert silence, shadows of wool-white clouds. A caterpillar, lacking compass or guides, crosses the vast uplands of his shoe, whom bees ignore. They have all gone in to tea.
>
> (p. 89)

with Upward's reported exercise in *Lions and Shadows*:

> Rubber statuary in gardens of ice-cream roses bearing every imprint of foot and belly. Kissing beneath the jangling clock before the cinema doors are opened. Plush seats unbarred between, mumbling hands convolved in calico. Steady, chaps, go slow. Where were we?

This kind of writing does have a kind of internal coherence, but it is difficult to say exactly what it means. Much in *The Orators* might be ascribed to this method; Isherwood's piece of automatic writing contains a reference to a character in *Paid on Both Sides*; the first edition of *The Orators* made use of Mortmere characters (see p. 118). When, in the preface to his *Collected Poetry* of 1945, Auden spoke of *The Orators* as 'a case of the fair notion fatally injured', he may well have thought the fatal injury arose from the obscurity of such surrealist passages. As early as June/July 1936 in *New Verse* he was expressing pseudonymous 'Honest Doubts' about surrealism. 'Allen and Page' may allude to Allen Chalmers and Victor Page, major characters in Isherwood's *All the Conspirators*, although D. J. Allan and Denys Page, later Professors of Greek at Glasgow and Cambridge respectively, both matriculated at Christ Church in 1926 and were reputedly on bad terms with each other.

The Airman feels that he is likely to be exposed: the poem 'There are some birds in these valleys' (p. 89; May 1931) shows the 'spies' of The Hollies beginning to act as *agents provocateurs* (the poem was called 'The Decoys' in CP). Nonetheless he has day-dreams of victory, even though (p. 91) he realises that the crucial problem is 'group organisation (the real parts)' and (later) that through his weaknesses he is betraying his uncle. The relationship of 'real parts' to the 'real whole', instanced here by the unreliability of his comrades, is a paradigm of the relationship between the psychological centre and circumference (remembering the earlier definitions on p. 75: the Airman is the agent of the central awareness that the enemy attempts to disturb).

The poem 'The draw was at five. Did you see the result?' (November 1931; omitted in 1934: EA, p. 443) anticipates the twenty-eight-day mobilisation by linking the Airman's climactic preparations to the occasion of a full moon, when 'The power shall fill you, the touch be restored.' The drawing of lots during these crucial days is reduced to pavilion gossip by referring to a rejected recruit as 'that whipper-snapper Fleming'. This polarity of primitive ritual and public-school ethos is pervasive in the work as a whole. It is here linked to bourgeois caution, suggesting (as will be proved) that the enemy talent for camouflage is seriously capable of decoying the Airman. The 'rosebowl from Ardencaple', which the Airman has stolen, was a sporting trophy (the Larchfield Games, of which Auden on 11 June 1931 was one of three 'clerks of the Course', were held at Upper Ardencaple Park, the Old Larchfieldian Rugby Football Club ground).

Now he learns that the enemy are going to attack, forcing him to set in motion his plan for a twenty-eight-day mobilisation. This alludes to the mobilisation of the German army in preparation for the First World War, as recounted in General Ludendorff's *The Coming War* (1931), pp. 701ff: '[The Army] was able . . . at the beginning of the fourth week after the commencement of mobilisation, as a result of several great victorious actions, to force its way into France' (p. 71). Ludendorff's book also provided Eliot with sources for 'Coriolan', a contemporary poem which it is instructive to compare with the 'Journal'. Auden, however, conflates this historical mobilisation with Ludendorff's eccentric, doom-laden account of what he saw as the probable mobilisation against Germany of a Franco-Italian alliance. The tone of this latter account is recognisably a model for this part of the 'Journal': 'All payments from public funds, including of course unemployment benefits, pensions and salaries are suspended. Wages very soon cease to be paid and distress begins to stalk through the land' (Ludendorff, p. 105). Hair-raising enough in Ludendorff, with its allusions to a Jewish–Jesuit–Freemason conspiracy, this mobilisation is given a Bosch-like, apocalyptic turn by Auden that is directly reminiscent of Isherwood's and Upward's Mortmere stories, in particular Isherwood's 'The World War'. Its authors themselves recognised Mortmere as a 'special brand of mediaeval surrealism' and an indulgent escape from reality. In the 'Journal' the anarchy described is by turns jaunty, baleful, macabre, richly comic, momentarily disturbing: and of course it represents the Airman's own escape from reality.

It is at this point (p. 93) that he realises the significance of his earlier dream (p. 85). His uncle had not failed after all, because he had perceived a truth about the enemy which enabled him to pass beyond the vain struggle that the Airman is undertaking. At the centre of the enemy's world stands the mother, the bearer of the disease from which the hero suffers. As we have seen, D. H. Lawrence had said that the love-sympathy between parent and child aroused the deeper sensual centres but provided no outlet for them. This spiritual mothering is responsible for introversion and masturbation, 'enemy' traits which have been sublimated in the airman as spying and kleptomania, the latter being a subconscious cry for help ('They stole to force a hearing', p. 93) which seems to be his eventual undoing. The comfortable conventionalised world of the mother stifles, not only because it is bourgeois ('our homes and duty'), but because it transmits a 'learned' observation of parts that prevents the perception of real wholes. The Airman's real ancestor, his black-sheep uncle, has overcome this stifling by accepting it and by embracing his real nature ('self care'), rather than by trying to fight it as the Airman has been doing. Thus the sacrificed uncle becomes quasi-divine ('Uncle, save them all, make me worthy', p. 94), for his way out was to see that there is no way out. The Airman has learned that:

1. The power of the enemy is a function of our resistance, therefore
2. The only efficient way to destroy it – self-destruction . . .

This really only makes sense if we see it as the Airman's resistance to his mother-induced neurosis: the enemy is not an external enemy at all, but is to be found within himself, a part of his own nature. To maroon the enemy in a frictionless environment is indeed to give the enemy no opportunity to introduce 'inert velocities' into the system (see p. 73), but the only way to do that, and therefore to neutralise repression, is to destroy oneself. The enemy is simply the name given to one's conception of 'self', a fatally dualistic experience of the human organism. As Auden put it in his 1929 journal: 'A colonel captures a position, after receiving severe wounds himself and the loss of three-quarters of his regiment, to find that the enemy are his own side. Repression is equally heroic and equally foolish' (EA, p. 300).

At the end of the 'Journal' (p. 94) we leave the Airman about to make his final decision on the day fixed for the attack. In a letter of December 1932 Auden said: 'The airman's fate can be suicide or Rimbaud's declination' (to H. B. Parkes, Colby College Library), suggesting that the poet's vision is closely linked to the struggle for psychological integrity, both symbolised by heroic exploit (Ransom is a 'redeemer' in *The Ascent of F6* similarly tempted to declination, or vocational abdication; see p. 198). Auden said in his review of Liddell Hart's biography of T. E. Lawrence, upon whom Ransom is partly based: 'Lawrence's enlistment in the Air Force and Rimbaud's adoption of a trading career are essentially similar' (EA, p. 321). I think that we are meant to feel, in the ambiguous ending, that he accepts his abdication (even if it leads to death) as a necessary condition for future understanding and new life. After a list of readings from his instruments as he guides his machine at 10,000 ft, comes the phrase 'Hands in perfect order'. This implies that his weakness has disappeared, but it is also an interesting allusion to a phrase of Wilfred Owen's in a letter to Sassoon (which Owen repeated in a letter to his mother): 'The Battalion had a sheer time last week. I can find no better epithet; because I cannot say I suffered anything, having let my brain grow dull. That is to say, my nerves are in perfect order' (*The Poems of Wilfred Owen*, ed. Blunden, 1931 edn, p. 36. The allusion reappears in the last stanzas of 'Here on the cropped grass of the narrow ridge I stand'). It is likely that Isherwood's 'Test' complex, which conflated the missed 1914 war with challenges of sexual identity (*Lions and Shadows*, pp. 77–80), had its lasting effect upon others of his generation. Ending the 'journal' with this allusion to Owen, himself a victim of the airman-type, serves to throw the whole fantasy of guilt and exploit into a sharper relief.

Book III consists of 'Six Odes'. Despite the occasional nature of some of them, all are relevant to the theme of the whole work: the quest for social and spiritual health. The first (January 1931; 'January 1, 1931' in CP45; first printed in *Dope*, New Year 1932) recounts a dream in which the events of the previous year are weighed and found wanting. It is a very personal poem, establishing a mysterious connection between the poet's operation (see p. 99) and the death of D. H. Lawrence (on 2 March 1930), dramatising ideas of resurrection, and referring to the exploits in Germany of his friends, Isherwood and Spender. Embarrassment of personal reference haunted the poem. In Caroline Newton's copy of the third printing of the US *Poems* (1937) 'Seeker, Lightweight, Lolloper' are substituted for 'Wystan, Stephen, Christopher' and later 'Pokenose' for 'Stephen' and 'Oddfellow' for Christopher'. In the 1966 *Orators* 'Savers, payers, payees', 'Pretzel', and 'Maverick' are substituted. The night-nurse's words in stanza 2, 'We shall not all sleep, dearie', are those of St Paul (1 Corinthians xv.51), while Spender's words in stanza 4, 'Destroy this temple', were those spoken by Jesus in John ii.19 when the Jews asked for a sign ('Destroy this temple, and in three days I will raise it up'). Jesus was confusing his interlocutors by speaking of 'the temple of his body' and referring to the Resurrection. Spender's 1929–31 novel *The Temple*, (revised version published 1988) is about the poet's search for psychological integration as a writer and his corresponding mistrust of initially liberating physical pleasures ('I am beginning to tire of the selfconscious insistence of so many of these people in the body: of their worship of it, as though it were a temple': Texas). The novel was dedicated to Auden. Similarly Isherwood is shown insisting in stanza 5 that 'Man is a spirit' (perhaps alluding to 1 Corinthians xv.45). These biblical messages are not delivered with any more calm, authority or assurance than the Sophoclean mutterings of Perkins, headmaster of Larchfield Academy in stanza 3, or the drunken saluting of the moon of Auden's friend Arnold Snodgrass in stanza 5.

The alliteration and strange seasonal metaphors of the poem maintain a familiar tone of fatalism and compulsion: what the poet sees in his dream is a world of self-regard waiting for a spiritual leader. His reticence about proposing himself as one is justified by the bizarre troop of healers who do in fact rush forward (including not only John Layard, but 'the Mop', Arnold Snodgrass's mother), creating a chaos which breaks his dream. In the early morning he reflects upon the relative value of a psychological revolution and a political one, implying (rarely for Auden) that it is time for a firm decision about the latter. The dispossessed beggar wants to be told why the solution to the problem is not Communism, whose success is described metaphorically in the progress of constitutional democracy in Ancient Greece, reference being made to the overthrow of the Corinthian tyranny in the sixth century BC and the later ascendancy of the 'brilliant' democracy of Athens (the phrase is borrowed from Pindar's second Isthmian ode, line 20: λιπαραις ἐν Ἀθαναις).

Pindar is a more consistent model for the second Ode (April 1931; omitted in 1966), dedicated to Gabriel Carritt and celebrating a victory of the Sedbergh Rugby XV under his captaincy in 1927, although there is some doubt that Carritt was actually Captain and the other names appear to be fictitious. The 'propped-up cases' in stanza 5 could see the game because the school hospital stood on a rise overlooking the pitch. Auden's stanza is the stanza of the first and fifth Isthmian odes lengthened by one line, and his metre, at least in its initial intention, is their dactylo-epitritic metre. Some Pindaric features are preserved, such as the resort to myth in stanza 9 and the dejection of the failed competitors (compare stanzas 7–8 with the eighth Pythian, lines 84–7, and the eighth Olympian, line 68). But Auden is not content merely to use Pindar: he must locate a more bizarre model for his athletes' heroism, the exiled and drowned nuns of the *Deutschland*. Auden begins in outrageous parody. In stanza 18, Hopkins had button-holed his heart as follows, in cadences perhaps more than a little Welsh:

> Ah, touched in your bower of bone
> Are you! turned for an exquisite smart,
> Have you! make words break from me here all alone,
> Do you!

Auden begins his ode with an identical rhetorical question, screwed home, however, by a characteristically colloquial answer: 'Walk on air, do we? And how!' Oddly enough, the idiom is exhilarating rather than deflationary, and may have distracted Auden from remembering that currents of joy *would* indeed be incalculable in ohms, since electric current is calculated in amps not in ohms. 'Success my dears – Ah!' may remind us that 'The Windhover' at line 13 is arguing for a similar emotional response to a much more equivocal victory, but not only is a football score made mysteriously worthy of celebration (Auden's themes of hero-worship and the self-destruction of resisted sexual orientation seem to demand such a fruitful extension of subject) but the suggestion is that this subject is not, after all, unworthy of Hopkins himself. There is one moment, though, when the parody turns Hopkins into a victim. His habit of verbal insistence, as in the opening of 'Henry Purcell' ('Have fair fallen, O fair, fair have fallen, so dear | To me') is wickedly exposed in Auden's description of the beaten Sandroyd side ('Defeats on them like lavas | Have fallen, fell, kept falling, fell | On them, poor lovies'), but even here the respect is maintained, not least through affection for the fallen which closely parallels Hopkins's own. See also Joyce, *Portrait of the Artist as a Young Man*: 'The snares of the world were the wages of sin. He would fall . . . Not to fall was too hard . . . falling, falling but not yet fallen, still unfallen but about to fall.' Parody engineers a tonal stage on which Hopkinsian effects may be enacted afresh.

Phrases like 'poor lovies' or 'maundering chara', though imported for the first time into poetry, convey an entirely appropriate aura of dismissive but percipient empathy ('chara' perhaps licensed by Isherwood, see *The Memorial*, p. 120). Some of the diction should remind us that Auden was teaching in a Scottish school at the time of writing ('Regents' = teachers, 'gillie' = servant, 'elver' = new boy). Divinity is introduced in stanza 9 in Marxian terms that make it particularly a consolation in defeat ('Religion is the sigh of the oppressed creature, the heart of a heartless world and the soul of soulless conditions. It is the opium of the people': Karl Marx, *A Critique of the Hegelian Philosophy of Right*, 1844), but has created the world in seven days ('one little week of action'), is addressed like Hopkins's God ('sir') and made to act like Lawrence's lumbar ganglion ('Deep in their wheel-pits may they know you foaming'). Auden had already used this analogy in an unpublished 1926 poem 'Dethroned' ('The wheel-pit of the soul'). The ecstasy of fulfilment into which the Ode begins to modulate is made possible through the Hopkinsian orchestration which it employs. These half-mystical Lawrentian sentiments are found elsewhere in the work; here they are brought directly into line with public-school hero-worship. Later on, of course, Auden was highly critical of both Fascist and Lawrence-influenced educational practice (see *Education To-day – and To-morrow*, 1939, in EA, pp. 384ff).

The third Ode (October 1930; called 'The Exiles' in CP, and dedicated to Upward, drawing attention to the fact that he was then, like Auden, a schoolmaster) describes life in terms of arrival at a seaside hotel, barracks, school or sanatorium. By cunning ambiguity the extended metaphor acquires characteristics of all four of these establishments, the main point being that since this is life, 'These grounds are for good, we shall grow no more.' Upward claimed that Auden had been influenced by his 1929 story 'The Colleagues' (first published in *New Country*, 1932. See Upward, 'Remembering the early Auden', *Adam International Review*, 1973–4, p. 22) in which the new schoolmaster, Mitchell, reflects: 'I shall be here or in places similar to this for the rest of my life.' Mitchell's 'gladness' at his ironic epiphany in the final paragraph following this observation seems matched by the poem's cheery acceptance even of final atrophy, an effect due to the neat alliteration and half-rhymes of the shorter lines of Auden's stanza. For the image in stanza 10, compare a contemporary letter: 'In my life by this wonderful partic sea one gets egocentric mania. We live ghoulishly in the past, the flag at the golf-house flutters and nothing matters. I love it' (17 October 1931 to Spender, Berg).

The fourth Ode (October 1931; 'Birthday Ode', *Modern Scot*, January 1932, reprinted in *Whips and Scorpions*, ed. Sherard Vines, 1932) is one of the most interesting performances in the book and provides an important added dimension of topical social comment and sheer high spirits. Auden had written to John Pudney while working on *The Orators*: 'On the whole I believe that in our time it is only possible to write comic poetry; not the Punch variety, but real slapstick' ([April 1931], Berg). This ode is an example of what he means. It is addressed to John Warner, infant son of Frances Warner and the novelist Rex Warner, an Oxford friend, and treats him with friendly hyperbole as the expected spiritual leader. But though the ode is thus a kind of parody of the central concern of the work, it is also full of a serious and valid energy of its own, doggerel for the most part (with strong echoes of Skelton, the Lawrence of *Nettles*, and Vachel Lindsay's 'Brian, Brian, Brian, Brian') but compelling and persuasive. Auden condemns both the proletariat ('ugly and dirty', from a particularly Skeltonic passage) and the upper class ('Let's be frank a moment, fellows – they won't pass', p. 102). It is the cautious puritanism of the latter that is stressed ('Hush! not a word of the beast with two backs | Or Mead and Muskett will be on our tracks!' may be compared with Lawrence's 'Innocent England': 'A wreath of mist is the usual thing | in the north, to hide where the turtles sing. | Though they never sing, they never sing, | don't you dare to suggest such a thing | or Mr Mead will be after you.' Frederick Mead was the eighty-year-old magistrate who, on 8 August 1929, handled the case of Lawrence's paintings seized by the police for obscenity).

Edgell Rickword (in *New Verse*, November 1937) went further in seeing implications of Nazi 'degradation of women and regimentation of the Strength through Joy variety' in the following lines: 'Living in one place with a satisfied face | All of the women and most of the men | Shall work with their hands and not think again' (p. 105). This kind of prophecy, however, derives not from Nazism but from Lawrence (cf. '*The great mass of humanity should never learn to read and write – never*' and 'All schools will shortly be converted either into public workshops or into gymnasia', *Fantasia of the Unconscious*, pp. 83 and 77), and we have to remember the date at which it was written. Mussolini was an established 'ninny', Pilsudski a 'mawmet' (i.e. a puppet, an archaic contraction of 'mahomet', a word borrowed from Skelton) but Hitler was still only a 'false-alarm' (he did not come to power until January 1933) and Mosley had until only recently been thought of as a future Socialist Prime Minister. Some of Auden's poems (e.g. 'Get there if you can . . .') are apprehensive about a proletarian revolution: it is the invalids who are to blame, and they had better do something about it. Mosley's answer (the Corporate State) did not seem immediately fascist. In June 1931 Harold Nicolson had dreams of gaining the Foreign Office through the New Party, and in December Isherwood was singing the praises of the New German Youth Movement in Mosley's *Action* ('They are sombre, a trifle ascetic and absolutely sincere. They will live to become brave and worthy citizens of their country'). By the time Auden came to write 'A

Happy New Year' in February 1932, Mosley is consorting with thugs (stanza 27).

To his credit, Auden is sceptical about the cult of youth (p. 103: 'They're most of them dummies who want their mummies') and refers slightingly to Toc H, and to Beaverbrook's Empire Crusaders (who had made a determined effort to capture the Hiking Movement). He has nothing to say for any of the political leaders of the time. They are all presented as outdated (see 'These had stopped seeking', three stanzas first printed in *Adelphi*, December 1931, as 'Cautionary Rhymes'; compare 'Master Wet will show his pet' etc., with 'Mr Leach made a speech' etc., in the anonymous 'Forensic Jocularities' printed in Auden's *Oxford Book of Light Verse*, p. 272). England must be saved by the infant Warner. All false prophets, jealous of Warner's powers, must be discredited and the real Lawrentian revolution ushered in, 'The official re-marriage of the whole and part'.

In the printed texts prior to *The English Auden*, some of the false prophets were not clearly identifiable. 'The bugger magician with his Polish lad' ('nigger', 'bigger', or asterisks, in printed texts) probably refers to two stories of pederastic significance by Thomas Mann, 'Mario and the Magician' and 'Death in Venice'. The line about Middleton Murry was omitted. Robert [Graves] and Laura [Riding] became 'Bob and Miss Belmairs' (see *Lions and Shadows*, p. 104). [Wyndham] Lewis became 'the trained eye', and Eliot became 'Moxon' (see *Lions and Shadows*, p. 111). Bishop Barnes was a *bête noire* of Auden's mother. The possibility of being 'ducked' in a *Gletscher* suggests that all these people are extinct like animals found in glaciers. Auden indiscriminately lumps together 'the Simonites [dissident Liberals], the Mosleyites and the ILP [Independent Labour Party]' (p. 105). For this he was criticized. Edgar Foxall wrote in *The Bookman*, March 1934, p. 475: 'When Auden indulges in his indiscriminate sneers at all classes he misses the point. The Labour Party may be weak and the ILP insipid, but they represent the nearest point of contact with the masses. Those who worked in the Socialist movement before the first Labour Government know well that it was no mean achievement.' 'Pooty' is mid-Victorian slang for 'pretty', and 'piss-proud' means having a false erection due to the desire to urinate (it was an eighteenth-century term, used especially of an old man who marries a young wife). Auden almost certainly found it in Eric Partridge's 1931 edition of Francis Grose's *A Classical Dictionary of the Vulgar Tongue*, a work which accounts for a good deal of obsolete slang in the ode. From it come, for instance, 'rufflers' ('notorious rogues pretending to be maimed soldiers or sailors'), 'member-mugs' (chamber-pots) and 'quarrons' (bodies). Grose has succeeding entries 'Piss Prophet' and 'Piss-proud'. See also 'Lord Lobcock' and 'like a tantony pig' in the poem 'O for doors to be open . . .'. 'Smugging' is smartening oneself up (and was used by Joyce in *Portrait of the Artist as a Young Man*).

When Auden writes that John Warner will introduce the gauche and lonely to 'the smaller group, the right field of force', the phrasing comes from Gerald Heard, *The Social Substance of Religion* (1931), p. 212, where it refers in particular to the first Christian Agape: 'This is, on the psychic plane, analogous to, and as rare and as transmuting a happening, as the breaking down on the physical plane of the atom. An energy otherwise inconceivable is released. But we have seen it is essential for this that the "field", the group, be kept the right size.' While writing this ode, Auden also wrote to Isherwood: 'I've had a most important vision about groups which is going to destroy the church.' It seems likely that this 'vision' (unlike the later one at the Downs School, see p. 149) resulted from his first reading of Heard. The Airman was made to write towards the end of his Journal: 'Much more research needed into the crucial problem – group organisation (the real parts).'

Auden's images of the new life at the close of this ode are typical of his stylistic sureness of touch, a perfect modulation from the comic: 'Falcon is poised over fell in the cool, | Salmon draws | Its lovely quarrons through the pool.' The abbreviations intensify nature: without the article, these creatures cease to be mere species and impress their tangible qualities (we use the same process to talk of them as food). The Hopkinsian 'lovely' looks like a risk, but attached to 'quarrons' it comes off beautifully: the cliché and the obsolete thieves' slang justify each other, and the lines typify a perhaps not often remarked characteristic of *The Orators* in both its verse and its prose, that of its continual leaning towards the observed lyrical moment. The 'ENVOI' (p. 106) returns us to the poet's physical setting (cf. Part II after Part I of 'A Happy New Year') and continues the use of Skeltonic rhyme royal (see p. 108). 'Derek my chum' (line 7) is the 'D. W.' for whom Auden wrote 'What's in your mind, my dove, my coney'. The 'lamps of Greenock' (line 16) are the lights from Port Glasgow to Gourock, the longest such stretch in Europe. 'The Tower' (line 25) was a Helensburgh cinema. 'Darkmans' is thieves' slang for 'night'. Both 'darkmans' and 'quarrons' also appear in the second stanza of the anonymous 'The Maunder's Praise of his strowling Mort' which Auden included in the *Oxford Book of Light Verse*, p. 213.

The fifth Ode (November 1931; first printed in *New Signatures*, 1932, and called 'Which Side am I Supposed to be On' in CP) is dedicated to his pupils and extends the ambiguity of school and barracks to be found in the third Ode. His pupils are recruits on the side of repression, the schoolmasters merely veteran pupils perpetuating legends. The description in the second stanza (as if of the metalless Polynesian society described by W. H. R. Rivers in *Instinct and the Unconscious*, 1920) enforces a mysterious anthropological perspective upon this version of Auden's lost Eden. The wishing-well in the garden is described by Jung: 'The image of the temenos [region of taboo] with the well-spring developed in Islamic architecture, under early Christian influence, into the court of the mosque and the ritualistic washing place located in the centre. We have the same thing in the Occidental cloister with the well in the garden' (*The Integration of the Personality*, 1933). Auden reuses the idea to greater purpose in 'New Year Letter', lines 860 ff, and in *The Age of Anxiety*. In the ode, these secret legends maintain morale in the conflict with the 'They' who operate beyond the frontier. 'We' are the imperialists, the self-righteous ('When the bishop has blessed us'), but the imagery of class war is partly a metaphor, of course: what Auden is alluding to here is the divided psyche, the circumference and the centre, the repressive Censor and the rebellious Id. It appears from stanzas 10 ff that it is the Censor's fault that the Id is inspired by the Seven Deadly Sins to its heroic rebellion. The blinkered, defensive, 'frontier-conscious' routine of the Censor is contrasted with the suicidal determination of the Id to make itself felt, and Auden characteristically quotes some famous lines from the Old English *The Battle of Maldon* to make the point (lines 312–13, 317–19):

> Hige sceal þe heardra, heorte þe cenre,
> mod sceal þe mare, þe ure maegen lytlað
> . . . fram ic ne wille,
> ac ic me be healfe minum hlaforde
> be swa leofan men, licgan þence.

('Thought shall be the harder, heart the keener, courage the greater, as our strength grows less' . . . 'I will not leave, but by the side of my lord, so dearly loved, I intend to lie.')

But there is defection from one side to the other, efforts to unify the intellect and the senses by the few able to diagnose the illness and these 'speak of things done on the frontier we were never told'. Though the war continues, this knowledge forces the speaker to predict defeat for his side: 'We shall lie out there.'

The final ode (June 1931) similarly reflects the dawning self-awareness of the repressors, struggling against fate. In a parody of the contorted syntax of the Scottish metrical Psalms used at Larchfield School, it provides a vulnerable confession of weakness, a prayer for illumination rather than death. Auden quoted no. 121 of the Scottish Psalms to Theodore Spencer in 1943: 'Henceforth thy goings out and in | God keep for ever shall', adding: 'Like Mallarmé' (Harvard).

It is left to the 'Epilogue' (October 1931; called 'The Three Companions' in P58) to take up for the last time the possible optimism of the Quest theme, an optimism denied in the 'Prologue' and the 'Journal', but to an extent implicit in the deepest insights of the book, particularly in the thematic development of the odes: in the way in which the internally felt loss and defeatism of nos I and III passes alternately through the boisterous optimism of nos II and IV to become the externally seen defeat of nos V and VI. Now, in a form similar to the folk ballad 'The Cutty Wren', Auden shows the Quest hero disclaiming the qualities that have hitherto hindered him – intellectualism, fear and neurosis ('reader', 'fearer' and 'horror') – and setting out with a fresh determination. The symbolism in stanza 2 is strongly suggestive of a sexual choice ('midden' = anus, 'gap' = vagina, a grave where the tall return because the 'death' of orgasm creates a child who will exit from the womb), and the choice itself is symbolised in stanza 3 by the descent from mountain to valley, familiar enough in Auden's poetry. It will be remembered that the Airman's sexual identity was a matter of secrecy, shame and self-discovery, intimately bound up with his struggle for integration through a group.

Auden, it would appear, had not yet succeeded in working out the significance of his own sexual choices (see my discussion of 'It was Easter as I walked in the public gardens', pp. 59–65). In July 1932 he wrote a long letter to John Pudney on this subject. There are two complementary desires, he argued: the largely asexual desire to be part of a group and the desire to 'come into a particular woman and have a child by her. If you can't get one you intensify the other . . . Buggery is an attempt at a magical short cut: we choose those with whom we should naturally have an unconscious group relationship and try to get that by the personal conscious contact' (Berg). This makes plain what could not be so directly put in the 'Epilogue'. Faced with such a choice, Auden's instinct (as in 'It was Easter as I walked in the public gardens', the poem written in the year in which he broke off his

engagement) is simply to move on. And he moves on in a Kafkaesque spirit
that is to inform his Quest of ten years later (cf. Kafka's 'The Departure':
' "Where are you riding to?" . . . "Just away from here, away from here" ';
for 'Out of this house', see Isherwood's *All the Conspirators*, p. 14), seeking to
define authenticity by negation.

The Dance of Death

The Dance of Death was completed in the spring of 1933 and separately published in the same year. My page references are to the text in *Plays*, which incorporates material from the 1934 and 1935 Group Theatre productions (see *Plays*, p. 534).

As early as December 1926, Auden was deciding that 'the only remaining traces of theatrical art were to be found on the music-hall stage: the whole of modern realistic drama since Tchekhov had got to go; later, perhaps, something might be done with puppets' (*Lions and Shadows*, p. 215). His charade *Paid on Both Sides*, written in 1928, explored various kinds of dramatic symbolism and expressionism, but is still very much a closet drama. *The Enemies of a Bishop* (1929) and what remains of *The Fronny* (1930) similarly show him still tied to a cautious or inappropriate use of his poems within the dramatic text. It was not until 1932, when he founded the Group Theatre with Rupert Doone and Robert Medley, that the opportunity for writing plays for production actually arose, and his dramatic theories could be elaborated. It is clear from Auden's programme note for *The Dance of Death* that native dramatic forms (as in *Paid*) provided the most powerful stimulus for him: 'Drama is essentially an art of the body. The basis of acting is acrobatics, dancing, and all forms of physical skill. The music hall, the Christmas pantomime, and the country house charade are the most living drama of today' (*Plays*, p. 497).

The Dance of Death was written for Rupert Doone, who danced the main role, and the above programme note justifies the balletic nature of the piece. Doone had asked Auden in July 1932 for a ballet scenario on the story of Orpheus, but they had also discussed a play on the theme of the *danse macabre* (see Robert Medley, *Drawn from the Life*, 1983, p. 133). Auden abandoned the Orpheus idea in October, but finished what he called his 'Masque' in the spring of 1933. It was produced twice by the Group Theatre, in 1934 and 1935, with music by Herbert Murrill and costumes by Robert Medley, and dancer's mask by Henry Moore.

Actually, Auden disliked the ballet as a form (*Lions and Shadows*, p. 215) and never wrote anything quite so experimentally terpsichorean again, though as a device for symbolising the bourgeois death-wish and the protean role it assumes, the part of the Dancer is comparatively successful. The subject of the play, as is clearly announced, is the decline of the capitalist class: the ramifications of this subject could really only be tackled in the space of twenty-five pages with the use of a great deal of music-hall anecdote, potted history and mime. On the whole, the play was not well received. Leavis was polite but evasive (Auden was still writing for *Scrutiny*) and concluded that the drama remained not much more than schematic (June 1934). Kenneth Allott said in *New Verse* (November 1937): 'I think it is the worst thing Auden has done.' It remained out of print after 1953.

In fact it reads as an impressive attempt at popularising the Marxism in which Auden was currently interested. If it oversimplifies, this is no greater fault than the obscurity of *The Orators*. The comic Cockney characters planted in the audience have been attacked for the obvious social reasons, but they are no more embarrassingly out of Auden's range of experience and sympathy than, say, Eliot's Cockneys in *The Rock*. The choruses have been criticised as doggerel, but, again, this is what they are intended to be: parodies of musical comedy (p. 83), tin-pan alley (p. 86), the popular ballad (pp. 92, 104), the school song (p. 105, borrowed from *The Fronny*), and so on.

The allegorical action is simple. The Chorus (the bourgeoisie) are fun-loving until the Dancer (death-wish) steals their clothes (p. 86). These are replaced with military uniforms (p. 88) by the Manager (capitalism). Angry, and encouraged by the Audience (the proletariat), they threaten revolution, until the Announcer (nationalism) persuades them instead to turn against 'the dictatorship of international capital' (p. 90). They agree, and beat up the Jewish Manager. At this point they form themselves into a 'ship of England' (p. 92) and mime a journey (reminiscent of a similar device in Brecht's *Mahagonny*, II.xvi) whose progress is threatened by the Audience, representing storm and rocks. The Dancer falls in an epileptic fit (cf. *The Orators*) and is advised to take it easy (p. 95). The Chorus then pursue various forms of the inner life (Lawrence's 'will of the blood' and his view of the role of women are here satirised), but, as members of the bourgeoisie, are incapable of mysticism: the climax of this part of the play is the Dancer's attempted flight as a Pilot into 'the very heart of Reality' (p. 100). The mystical proposal to 'fly alone to the Alone' refers to the final phrase of Plotinus' *Enneads* (VI.9), φυλὴ μόνου πρὸσ μόνον, 'a fairly commonplace Greek phrase', according to A. H. Armstrong in his Loeb edition (1988, vii.344) and 'the only words of Plotinus at all generally known'. This, according to Armstrong, is 'the common translation'. Auden may possibly have remembered Lionel Johnson's recipe for avoiding the temptation of lust in 'Dark Angel' ('Lonely, unto the Lone I go') when looking for a way of expressing the idea of leaving a life of earthly pleasure. Eight lines of early notes on Plotinus survive in Auden's hand. Auden used the phrase again in 'Brothers, who when the sirens roar', stanza 9.

The Dancer fails, as the Airman of *The Orators* failed, and becomes paralysed from the feet up, sign of a fraudulent love of God. The Manager feels it politic at this point (p. 102) to provide a panacea in the form of a night-club called the Alma Mater (a final nostalgic appeal to patriotism and social solidarity), and the Audience come up on to the stage. Their speech (to portray both the rooted compulsions of the sexual instinct and their bewilderment at this situation of being wooed by the bosses) is reflected in fragments of stream-of-consciousness prose, and literal translations, as from a phrase-book, of idiomatic German phrases (e.g. 'self-understandingly' is *selbstverständlich*, 'of course'; 'Thou seest dreadful out' is *Du siehst schrecklich aus*, 'you look terrible'; and 'swindle not' is *schwindle nicht*, 'no kidding'). In a state of spiritedly expounded decadence and criminality (pp. 104–7) capitalism expires, and Karl Marx pronounces upon the Dancer's corpse: 'The instruments of production have been too much for him. He is liquidated.' Auden later annotated Albert and Angelyn Stevens's copy: 'The Communists never spotted that this was a nihilistic leg-pull.' In fact the nihilism is limited to the relative crudity of the political analysis as compared, for example, with the anthropological and psychological analysis of *The Orators*. But it was, for the purposes of Auden's 'masque' celebrating a shared and complicit guilt, equally functional and equally serious.

The Dog Beneath the Skin

The Dog Beneath the Skin was the first published collaboration with Christopher Isherwood, more or less completed by January 1935 and published in the spring of that year. My page references are to the text in *Plays*, which for the first time printed the new ending written for the first Group Theatre production in January 1936.

The genesis of the play is lengthy and complicated. Auden distilled several substantial earlier works over a period of half a dozen years to arrive at the rich brew of *Dog*. These abandoned works have by now been published (*Plays* prints *The Enemies of a Bishop* (1929), fragments of *The Fronny* (1930), and *The Chase* (1934); 'In the year of my youth . . .' (1932–3) appeared in the *Review of English Studies*, August 1978), thus providing the reader with a confusing history of borrowed plots, developed characters, transformed symbolism and cannibalised passages. The textual and historical substance of the dramatic rewriting is set out in detail in *Plays*, to which the reader is therefore referred. For myself, I prefer not to think of these earlier plays as surviving works at all (in the sense in which they are presented in *Plays*) but simply as material which feeds the canonical *Dog*. Much the same is true, I feel, of 'In the year of my youth . . .'. Within a dozen years, Auden himself had become confused (in 1947 he told Alan Ansen that the original title of *Dog* was 'The Fronny'). I shall therefore now say something about these works but for the most part only insofar as they throw light on the meaning of *Dog*, or on later canonical works of Auden's.

The Enemies of a Bishop

Auden and Isherwood had admired a play they saw together in Berlin, Peter Martin Lampel's *Revolte im Erziehungshaus* ('Revolt in the Reformatory'). Auden seems to have planned a reformatory play on his own, but the reformatory plot appears in *The Enemies of a Bishop*, written with Isherwood in 1929. This Mortmerean farce, described as a 'morality', is concerned to unravel various forms of sexual blindness. Robert Bicknell becomes manager of a lead-mine (suddenly profitable in a way borrowed from one of the anecdotal voices in the poem 'Lead's the Best'). Among the actions to which he is urged by his 'Spectre' is an affair with his under-manager's wife, which nonetheless takes the form of the wooing of a shop-window mannequin (cf. *Dog*, p. 271). The Spectre is a realised psychic force which has an ironical insight into Bicknell's desires (cf. Shadow in *The Rake's Progress*. It may be that Auden had the Blakean sense of 'Spectre' in mind, as in *Jerusalem*: 'Man is born a Spectre or Satan and is altogether an Evil, and requires a New Selfhood continually, and must continually be changed into his direct contrary', quoted in *The Enchafèd Flood*, p. 53). Bicknell's Spectre recites poems as a serious commentary on the essentially ludicrous action (among them, eight from Auden's 1930 *Poems*) and is eventually murdered by Bicknell.

Robert's brother Augustus Bicknell (the name is made up of Auden's father's second name and his mother's maiden name) is the Governor of Templin Reformatory, from which George and Jimmy escape. In their disguise (Jimmy as a woman) they arrive at the Nineveh Hotel (cf. *Dog*, p. 258) and are taken up respectively by the homosexual Colonel Tearer and by Augustus himself. Homer Lane, whose ideas permeate the play, was himself the superintendent of a self-governing reformatory, closed in scandalous circumstances in 1918. The charge was of assault of runaway girls (E. T. Bazeley, *Homer Lane and the Little Commonwealth*, 1928).

The third eponymous and weakest plot concerns a young woman detective who, ignoring the obvious villains, falsely accuses Bishop Law of being a white slave trafficker. Her officious psychoanalytic insinuations are very like those reported of Auden at this time, and, insofar as the latter were stimulated by the ideas of Homer Lane, the authority of Bishop Law as a Lane type is somewhat blurred. Moreover, the crimes and penalties of the Bishop's 'enemies' do not engage with the psychological implications of the poems at any level deeper than that of the immediately effective joke, whether self-directed or not. The interplay between Robert and his Spectre is in itself a promising notion, but the remaining material is more superficial.

The Fronny

Auden's play *The Fronny* was finished in October 1930, but the text has been lost. What clearly emerges from the surviving fragments printed in *Plays*, however, is that it first introduced the missing heir plot that survives in *Dog*. It also contains a Villonesque Testament, a form which Auden later used in *Letters from Iceland*. 'The Fronny' is in Berlin bar-parlance ('Der Franni') Sir Francis Crewe, a character based on the archaeologist Francis Turville-Petre. 'Alan' 's involvement with 'Lou' also survives in *Dog* (pp. 266ff) as does an abbreviated version of the epithalamium (which was originally written for Alan and Iris Sinkinson). For further details, see *Plays*, Appendix II.

'In the year of my youth . . .'

For a full discussion of this important uncompleted poem, see Lucy McDiarmid's Introduction and Notes in the *Review of English Studies*, August 1978. The poem, begun in September 1932, is a Dantesque journey through the modern city, with the character Sampson (based on Gerald Heard) as Auden's Virgil. Some of its characters, or versions of them, survive in *Dog*: 'Admiral' Hotham and his wife, and the German-hating Mildred Luce. A major episode of the poem was also clearly going to be a 'Chase', although not the search for the missing heir in the play of that name, but a kind of establishment man-hunt for disaffected workers. To a certain extent, therefore, this theme (barely touched on in what survives of the poem) does have important links with the two 'armies' of the published version of *Dog* and the defections at its conclusion. The most important way in which the poem feeds the play (via *The Chase*) is, however, in providing material for the choruses. Auden had some difficulty in finding the right tone of public distance for his dramatic choruses, a difficulty exacerbated by his weakness for the ready-made lyric. The most striking material is largely sociological and descriptive, but there is also the song sung by Titt and Tool, separately reprinted as 'The Witnesses'. The Witnesses themselves survive in *The Chase*, but although their effect is vestigial in the text of *Dog*, I shall discuss them and their song in my commentary below on the opening chorus.

In order most effectively to summarise the cannibalising of material from the poem, I shall list all the examples I have traced, including works other than choruses of *Dog* (the numbers are page references of *Dog* and *The Chase*, and canto and line numbers of poems; 'Commentary' is that to 'In Time of War'):

1, 5	sixteen skies of Europe: 'Easily my dear . . .' 5.
46	talkative city: 'Oxford' 41.
62–70	Goods . . . wiped away: *Dog* 257.
73–4	those . . . alone: *Dog* 257.
76	west of the cathedral: *Dog* 218.
92–101	Spacious and gilded . . . tore away: *Dog* 258.
132	Hotham . . . Honeypot Hall: *Dog* 190.

493–508 But O you are young . . . more like men: *Dog* 204–5.

813–29 You are the town . . . lighted inn: *Dog* 193–4.

836–65 But do not imagine . . . Remember the Two: *Dog* 194.

904–10 last ferrule . . . touching sides: 'The latest ferrule now . . .' 1–6 [EA, p. 147].

905–6 The tiny noises . . . ear: 'Commentary' 257–8.

911–15 Dear Sleep . . . struck off: *Dog* 254.

922 vigorous shadows: *Dog* 191.

925 Rushed towards Lyra . . . charge: 'Certainly our city . . .' 33.

II, 37 Fathoms of earth . . . air: 'Here on the cropped grass' 2.

144–5 shadow . . . world: *The Chase* 149; 'Commentary' 124–5.

152–5 That which . . . friends: *The Chase* 149.

154 mad executives: 'Fleeing the short-haired mad executives' 1.

159–60 unprogressive . . . veto: *The Chase* 149; 'Commentary' 79–80.

161 Hills . . . like a Shelley: *The Chase* 149; 'Commentary' 126.

164–6 The timely . . . stolid perish: *The Chase* 149.

202–4 lad of seventeen . . . gladly: *Dog* 273.

206–8 men . . . recesses of the sea: *Dog* 273.

213 luckless poor: *Dog* 273.

218–19 invalid poets . . . classroom: *Dog* 273.

274–5 shooting sticks . . . in a circle: *Dog* 218.

279–81 From Puffin Conyers . . . wife: *The Chase* 128–9.

285, 287 Then driving . . . Daimler, From Honeypot . . . doves: *The Chase* 128.

285 blue Daimler: *Dog* 195.

287 haunt of doves: *Dog* 195.

290–93 From deep-walled Larchwood . . . sister: *The Chase* 129.

294–6 Young Dr Slag . . . shirt: *The Chase* 129.

299 A dried boy . . . bicycle: *The Chase* 129.

301–10 Mrs Aster-Lynch . . . heaps more: *The Chase* 129.

The Chase

The Chase brings together the reformatory plot from *The Enemies of a Bishop* and the missing heir plot from *The Fronny*. It also preserves in some scenes the setting of a lead-mine from *The Enemies of a Bishop*, but substitutes for plot a strike and lock-out resulting from Fordham's automation of the mine in place of Robert Bicknell's infatuation with Mrs Stagg. Colonel Tearer disappears, so that George (now disguised as a dog) can be attached to Alan Norman. The interlocking of these plots is more maturely handled than is the case in *The Enemies of a Bishop*, and their politicising is a significant stage towards the European scale of *Dog*.

With the addition of choruses spoken by the Witnesses from 'In the year of my youth . . .', and a number of elements that survive into the published *Dog* (such as the General's 'special record' intended to 'call the audience round' in III.v, which had been published in *Life and Letters*, May 1934, as 'Sermon by an Armament Manufacturer' and became the Vicar's Sermon), the text of Auden's *The Chase* was clearly a significant staging post in the creation of the later collaboration with Isherwood. The texture is much closer to it in many places (e.g. the opening scene, with its pantomime doggerel, parody of Kipling and a song-and-dance), while the crucial dialectic between the exemplary knockabout scenes and the lyrical and analytical choruses is already in place. Indeed, in many ways *The Chase* is a politically more ambitious play than *Dog*, but it has a far less interesting dramatic texture and range, even though it may be said to fairly bulge with theatrical devices. This is probably due to a sharp division of interest between the reformatory revolt and the search for the missing heir. Moreover, the relation of both these themes to the industrial unrest in the background is sketchy in the extreme, though it is intended to provide the point behind the violent and pessimistic climax to the play. The answer lay in telescoping the plots: thus, in *Dog*, George, Jimmy and Augustus Bicknell disappear, and Francis Crewe himself becomes the dog who accompanies Alan Norman on his quest. Although this telescoping means that the action of *Dog* is compelled to become much more episodic than that of *The Chase*, it does allow for the Ostnia/Westland enlargement introduced by Isherwood, and it does also provoke the central message of the play in its new form: that only by an act of imaginative sympathy and self-abnegation (becoming the dog) can the hero come to understand his predicament and escape from it. Francis becomes the veritable, though occluded, Leader of *Dog*, and the new title (which Robert Medley claimed that he provided) emphasises the centrality of this developed idea.

The Dog Beneath the Skin

As far as the collaboration goes, Isherwood once said: 'I have always thought of myself as a librettist to some extent with a composer, his verse being the music; and I would say "Now we have to have a big speech here", you know, and he would write it' (*London Magazine*, June 1961, p. 51). The crucial extent of Isherwood's prescriptions in November 1934 may be judged from his long letter to Auden (*Plays*, p. 557). Isherwood's share of the actual composition was as follows, as reported by Auden to Spender in June 1935:

Scene 1.	W.H.A.
Steamer scene.	C.I. (except song)
Ostnia scenes	W.H.A.
Red Lamp scene.	W.H.A.
Asylum scene.	All except the Leaders speech. C.I.
Financier scene.	C.I. (except song)
Paradise Park.	
Operation scene.	mostly, W.H.A.
Foot scene.	Poetry. W.H.A. Foot Dialogue. C.I.
Nineveh Hotel scenes.	Destructive Desmond, quarrel with dog, and dialogue after Francis discovery. C.I. The rest. W.H.A.
Last scene	[i.e. of the published version] Vicars sermon. W.H.A. The rest. C.I.

(*Auden Studies* 1, 1990, pp. 64–5)

The last scene of the text in *Plays* (i.e. as prepared for Group Theatre performance) was written by Auden.

The dedicatory quatrain may be found in the 1928–?30 notebook on a page (fol. 85) much influenced by Blake. It invokes the revolutionary as a healer or a poet, who, in his anatomy of a corrupt society, comes to understand the powerful role played by the bourgeoisie ('the genteel dragon'), just as Francis Crewe comes to see through the villagers of Pressan Ambo.

The name *Crewe* was probably taken from an inn at Blanchland ('It is a number of years now since I stayed at the Lord Crewe Arms, but no other spot brings sweeter memories', *Vogue*, 15 May 1954, p. 63; Alan Myers, in *Auden Newsletter* 12, argues that Blanchland is a model for Pressan Ambo). *Francis* is from Francis Turville Petre, *Iris* and *Alan* from Iris and Alan Sinkinson, friends from Helensburgh. *Luce* is the maiden name of Isherwood's father's mother (see also Captain Edward Gervase Luce who is remembered by the Fronny in his will, *Plays*, p. 479). *General Hotham* is a real General from the Thirty Years' War (Norman Williams, *Auden Newsletter* 10–11, p. 15). *Madame Bubbi*: although 'bubby' is a breast, 'Bubi' was the nickname of Berthold von Szczesny, a boyfriend of Isherwood's. *Honeypot Hall* is the vagina. *Vipond* is the modern form of the name of the eleventh-century Barons of Veteripont: the Viponds held the manor of Alston,

Auden's sacred lead-mining area (Sopwith, p. 20; Caesar Caine, *Capella de Gerardegile*, 1908). For the significance of *Pressan Ambo*, see p. 142.

The opening chorus is in Auden's characteristic panoramic–descriptive mode, with imagery developed to a musical simplicity and accuracy that was to become more and more common in his middle period. To the opening chorus of *The Chase* Auden has added significant elements (St Paul's hypothetically showing its gold cross through the shallow Dutch sea, the deep water dividing us from Norway, the journey from Scots Gap to Bellingham with the black-faced rams defying the panting engine, the lilting speech and magician face of the Welsh border, the shorthorn and the map-like Friesian, and the Soar gliding out of green Leicestershire to swell the ampler current) borrowed directly from Anthony Collett, *The Changing Face of England* (1926; page references to 1932 edition), pp. 3, 4, 125, 244, 245 and 166. Whatever may seem of largely biblical cadence in Auden's new choric manner is also afforced by the grander periods he had learned from Claudel and first put into practice in 'O Love, the interest itself in thoughtless heaven'. This initial idyllic appeal to a genuine love for England provides a perfect dramatic contrast to the agricultural desolation and chaotic proliferation of exurbia which follows. He continues from line 23 in an occasionally Jeremiad tone perhaps influenced by Eliot's attacks on the complacent suburban life in *The Rock*, which had been published in May 1934. This is the landscape of decadent capitalism grinding slowly to a halt, the outward manifestation of an inner anxiety which is presented in the semi-choruses as the insomnia of the young men from among whom is about to be chosen a hero to undertake the quest for Sir Francis Crewe, the missing heir of Honeypot Hall. Correspondingly the chorus creates the archetypal English village as a kind of predicated correlative of Eros: 'you are loving towards it.' The actual village of Pressan Ambo is very different.

The Witnesses who play such a large role in *The Chase* as representatives of Necessity are reduced here (p. 192) to one embodiment only: they appear as the chorus leaders who conclude the chorus by singing eight of the ten stanzas of the third section of Titt and Tool's song in 'In the year of my youth . . .'. This song (a version of which, called 'The Witnesses', had been published in *The Listener* in July 1933) elaborates and explains the function of the Witnesses 'to curse and bless'. It describes the despair of the hero, Prince Alpha, who discovers that he is not 'the truly strong man'. 'Alpha' is the principal star of a constellation (compare 'It's farewell to the drawing-room's civilised cry', stanza 13: 'my name shall be Star'). As Auden was later to write in his essay on Grimm and Andersen (*Forewords and*

Afterwords, p. 203), 'the fairy tale is a dramatic projection in symbolic images of the life of the psyche.' Crucial to the emptiness of Prince Alpha's life is his strident defiance of necessity (i.e. his 'offending' the Witnesses, the forces of time and space which set a limit on all human actions). The true hero, as later writings of Auden's such as 'The Quest' make plain, accepts these limitations ('one must not be anxious about ultimate success or failure but think only about what it is necessary to do at the present moment': *Forewords and Afterwords*, p. 204). This is one of the first of Auden's many uses of the desert as a place of anxiety. For a probable source, see Gerald Heard, *The Social Substance of Religion*, 1931, p. 147:

> The primal conflict which gives rise to the individual finally drives one stock, the more active, as an Ishmael to the desert under patriarchal rule. His hand against every man, he wanders in dry places seeking rest and finding none. Meanwhile the more stable stock has, also under the stress of conflict, but a state subacute, built up under an elaboration of the matriolatry the first stages of civilization. On this the patriarchies fall. So we have at this level, on the one hand the patriarchate, nomadic, authoritative, ultra-repressed, excessively active and warlike. On the other side we have the erotic, inventive, self conscious, creative.

Like 'Comrades, who when the sirens roar', it uses a stanza distantly related to the Burns stanza, and diction ('swish', 'foozle', 'a looker') deliberately demotic. Prince Alpha's exploits, then, though heroic, have been in vain, for the Witnesses are displeased. Auden seems to have taken these figures from D. H. Lawrence's *Apocalypse* (1931). The two Witnesses come from the Book of Revelation, and orthodox commentators identify them with Moses and Elijah. Lawrence associates them with the more ancient myth of twins: the Tyndarids, Dioskouroi or Kabiri (cf. Auden's 'Atlantis'). They have power over rain, power to turn water into blood, and to smite the earth with plagues. In Auden's unfinished epic they are also the female and male principle ('Titt and Tool') who are 'simply the servants of a system' (line 663). In the *Dog* chorus, as Necessity and Time ('the clock'), they create for the guilty quest hero (the restless neurotic or radical bourgeois) an atmosphere of indefinable menace which Auden evokes with allusions to Egyptian plagues, fire falling on the sodomites in the *Inferno* (Canto xv), Birnam Wood coming to Dunsinane in *Macbeth*, and the Scissor Man from Hoffmann's *Struwwelpeter*. But this nursery ghoulishness enforces a serious point. As Lawrence wrote, possibly with some debt to Frank McEachran's *The Civilized Man* (1930), pp. 82ff:

A creature of dual and jealous consciousness is man, and the twins witness jealously to the duality . . . they are 'witnesses' to life, for it is between their opposition that the Tree of Life itself grows, from the earthly root . . . all the time, they put a limit on man. They say to him, in every earthly or physical activity: Thus far and no farther – They limit every action . . . to its own scope, and counterbalance it with an opposite action. They are gods of gates, but they are also gods of limits . . . They make life possible; but they make life limited. [cf. Gerald Heard's idea of the 'limen' used 'In the year of my youth . . .' and the Lords of Limit in 'Now from my window-sill I watch the night'].

The action begins in 'a musical comedy or pantomime village garden' (stage direction from *The Chase*), with the stereotyped characters introducing themselves in verses reminiscent both of Gilbert and Sullivan and of the doggerel of Lyceum pantomimes in the 1930s (see A. E. Wilson, *Christmas Pantomime*, 1934, pp. 247ff). Auden said that pantomime was 'the most important single influence' on *Dog* (Breon Mitchell, *Oxford German Studies*, 1967, p. 169). Dick Whittington was a popular pantomime subject at the time (Wilson, p. 165). The fragments of villagers' overheard talk are modelled formally on Firbank.

When Alan Norman is chosen to find Sir Francis Crewe, the chorus invoke Love (p. 201: 'Enter with him', called 'I shall be Enchanted' in CP45 and 'Legend' in later collections) to accompany him on his quest. Love is seen as the archetypal bewitched fairy-tale figure who accompanies the hero, helping him with his tasks, and then demands to be sacrificed in order that he may return to his real shape (cf. *The Frog Prince*). In this sense, therefore, the 'love' of the chorus is (a) the quality a successful hero needs in order to pacify the Witnesses; and (b) the dog, Francis, the real hero who assists Alan, and who is seen sniffing about, being kicked and patted, throughout the chorus. (On p. 202 it is still being called George, relic of George's disguise in *The Chase*.) Mildred Luce's speech embodies the kind of vengeance that Auden was writing about in *Paid on Both Sides*. Her vain appeal to her watch shows that the Witnesses ('we are the clock') are not responsive to such vindictiveness. The 'Grimaldi infants' were among the then earliest specimens of *homo sapiens*, found in the Grottes des Enfants near Menton (G. Elliot Smith, *Human History*, 1930, pp. 132, 143).

Alan's journey has all the inconsequential logic of a dream. Indeed, some of the scenes suggest the direct influence of Lewis Carroll: compare the King of Ostnia with the King of Hearts (p. 213) or the Poet with Humpty

Dumpty or the White King (p. 242). Alan's naivety and obstinacy are exactly suited to the kind of revue-sketch world he moves through. The didactic point of these scenes is clear enough, so that Auden is able to concentrate his more complex elaboration of their relation to his theme into the choruses which punctuate them. The scene is the Europe of the inter-war period, typified by Ostnia, a corrupt East European monarchy, and Westland, a fascist dictatorship, countries which were to reappear in the later Auden and Isherwood plays.

The scene on the boat where Alan meets the two Journalists was written by Isherwood (except for the Cowardesque song 'They're in the racket, too'). With its neat and very conventional characterisation, its well-observed dialogue which isn't afraid to take ironic short-cuts across the pages of middle-brow fiction, and its continual undercurrent of light farce, this scene sets the general tone of the play. The description of Ostnia, for instance (p. 209), creates an expectancy of something not far removed from the Fredonia of the Marx Brothers' film *Duck Soup*. Indeed, the whole scene in the Palace at Ostnia (p. 213), with its parody of the Mass, and the King's fussy, apologetic execution of the workers, has a violence and offhand illogicality reminiscent of the Marx Brothers. And yet in the introductory chorus (p. 212) Auden holds up Ostnia and Westland as serious types of contemporary communities, whose follies are similar to England's, and whose poverty, expanding 'like an air-bubble under a microscope slide', will soon affect England's 'treasure and . . . gentlemanly behaviour'. The old man 'of the sobriquet of Tiger senilely vain' is Clemenceau, whom, in a review in *Scrutiny* (March 1933, p. 413), Auden had called a senile homicidal maniac, and the 'naughty life-forcer in the Norfolk jacket' is Bernard Shaw.

The King has directed Alan to Ostnia's Red Light district, and the chorus on page 218 describes his journey through the city ('where loyalties are not those of the family') to find it. The descriptions of cruel poverty and deprivation here are borrowed from Auden's version of the *Inferno*, 'In the year of my youth . . .', and have a force and a pity which sets the scene at the brothels (p. 219) at an ironical distance, although when making emendations to the latter, Isherwood attempted to preserve the Dantesque atmosphere that Auden required (*Plays*, p. 564). Cosy Corner was a gay bar in the Zossenstrasse, Berlin. Mother Hubbard's was a nightclub run by Kate Meyrick (see James Laver, *Between the Wars*, 1961, p. 100). For Yama the Pit, see the book by Alexander Kuprin (1930). The Second Tout's offer of 'Jig-a-Jig' is Indian Army slang (a supposed exclamation of pleasure by

Indian women during intercourse). Those who visit the brothels are 'rebels who have freed nothing in the whole universe from the tyranny of the mothers, except a tiny sensitive area': the Chorus's accusation is suggestive and characteristically phrased, and bears enough weight to allow the predicament of Sorbo Lamb, former heir-finder turned dope-addict, and therefore abandoned by 'Love', to be presented on the same ironical cartoon level as the brothel proprietors' songs.

The following scene in the Westland lunatic asylum (about half of which was written by Isherwood) is an evident satire on German nationalism. Spender criticised the scene (*New Writing*, Autumn 1938), saying that it was not frightening because the Nazis were not really lunatics: perhaps the point is rather that the lunatics of *Dog* are not frightening because they are not as mad as we now know the Nazis to have been. The scene is high-spirited, not bitter, and its prophecy of doom seems too genially dismissive. The First Mad Lady's Song was adapted from an uncollected sonnet in *New Verse*, October 1933, now reprinted in the notes to EA, p. 423. Isherwood said that the mock-aeroplane scene was 'cribbed from [J. R.] Ackerley's "Prisoners of War", but who cares?' A similar device is found in Brecht's *Mahagonny*.

In the intervening chorus, the place-names at the end locate the road from Penrith to Alston (see Norman Williams, *Auden Newsletter* 10–11, p. 14) and the line about the ring-ousel may also have been suggested by Collett (p. 105), although when Auden added the line to the *Fronny* chorus 'Doom is dark and deeper than any sea-dingle' before putting the poem into the second edition of *Poems* he made it apply to a chat. On their way out of Westland, Alan and the Journalists encounter the financier Grabstein, a figure probably based roughly on Sir Alfred Mond, industrialist, politician and one of the architects of ICI (compare 'President of the XYZ'). Auden had reviewed Hector Bolitho's biography of Mond in *Scrutiny*, December 1933. Compare Grabstein's 'I've founded hospitals and rest homes' (p. 239) with Bolitho, p. 219, where a similar point is made about Mond; and compare Grabstein's 'I've studied all the Italian Masters' with Auden's point in his review that Mond was no artist and that his taste for Italian painting was not relevant. The reminiscence of Eliot's Bleistein among the Canalettos is regrettable. Eliot also wrote about Mond (in 'A Cooking Egg').

The chorus on page 240 (called 'The Cultural Presupposition' in CP45) is one of Auden's most famous poems, famous rightly for the way it moves triumphantly from its point about man's self-consciousness and knowledge of death to its point about the dependence of a flourishing highbrow culture upon a slaving and oppressed proletariat. It does this not by any facile neatness or didacticism, but by a simple rhetorical appeal to biblical authority. Again, Auden may have been influenced by Eliot's *The Rock*. More particularly, the echoes of the Beatitudes here may have come via Owen's 'Insensibility', which Auden included in *The Poet's Tongue*, published in the same year as *Dog*. The idea for the chorus may have been suggested by the work that was such an influence on 'In the year of my youth . . .', Gerald Heard's *The Social Substance of Religion* (1931), p. 203: 'Hear Abu Bekir, uncle and faithful follower of the Prophet, who on this point was spiritual brother of Augustine: "Happier were a man as a beast or a bird, than all his days to live, as live he must, with this consuming fear [of eternal torment]"'.

In his search for Sir Francis Crewe, Alan had been told by Grabstein to try Paradise Park (Hegel said that Paradise was a park, where only brutes, not men, could remain, in his *Philosophy of History*, tr. J. Sibree, 1900, p. 414). The brutes that Alan meets here are all solipsists and self-deceivers. The Poet, Grabstein's son, is a Poundian egotist: he is 'the only real person in the whole world' and insists on speaking in several languages, quoting Aeschylus and Catullus and Villon (a line already used by Pound in *Mauberley*). When Alan doesn't understand, the Poet is forced to speak English and quotes Dryden's 'Secular Masque'. '*Cinders*' (p. 242) is the title of an early Auden poem (in *Oxford Poetry 1926*). The two lovers are similarly self-absorbed: their song is a loose variation on Lear's *The Owl and the Pussycat*, and manages to include an allusion to *Sweeney Agonistes* ('Two as one and one as two', p. 244). Neither they nor the invalids know anything about Sir Francis Crewe. The self-consciousness defined by the previous chorus, and demonstrated in Paradise Park, assumes the extreme form of absorption in disease, the Lane theory finally coming into the open in the chorus on p. 247.

If disease has a psychosomatic cause, as Lane's theory holds, it follows that conventional surgery is a waste of time. The belief 'in the physical causation of all phenomena', exposed by the parody of the Creed in the next scene, underlines the futility of the Surgeon's quasi-religious procedure (Isherwood had compared an operation to a religious ceremony in *Lions and Shadows*, p. 294.). It is hard to see how the bullet in Chimp Eagle's bowel could have a psychosomatic origin, especially as he got it during strike action at the docks (p. 246). However, in his Wagnerian duet with Alan (pp. 251–2) he knows that Francis is in England, and that he (Chimp) has forgotten his 'choice and lot' (it is Francis disguised as the dog disguised as the nurse, curiously enough, who hastens his death by giving him an injection of hydrochloric acid). Chimp thought that he could succeed by simple political action.

The night interlude which follows (pp. 253ff), though it contains two of the most striking choric passages in the play, is merely marking time on Alan's journey back to England. The dialogue between his two feet is taken from *The Chase*, now given a quasi-political point by Isherwood's addition of Cockney dialect. Isherwood wrote to Auden, 11 December 1934: 'What was Homer Lane's theory about the two sides of the Body? The Left instinct and the Right reason? This is just a hint. But couldn't the attitudes of the two feet somehow express this?' See also Layard on Isherwood's hairy shoulder (*Christopher and his Kind*, p. 13). The view was more or less traditional. Compare Gregory the Great's commentary on Jacob wrestling with the angel: one foot is love of God, the other love of the world (*Homiliarum in Ezechielem*, 11.2.113). The dialogue also attempts to maintain interest in the mystery of Francis's whereabouts, but the melodramatic confidence about the roller-skates has a limitingly Mortmere air. The choric 'Now through night's caressing grip' may owe a debt to Oberon's final speech in *A Midsummer Night's Dream*, and its opening lines to Collett, p. 9 ('Capes push seaward . . . like the shadow on a dial'). It was set by Britten as part of *On this Island* (1938).

In the following Act III chorus (p. 256) the hawk's eye moves in from 'Villas on vegetation like saxifrage on stone' down through the suburban 'sorrow' clinically catalogued, into the heart of the city as Alan and the dog make their way to the Nineveh Hotel, symbol of capitalist excess. In the vestibule he meets the two Journalists, and the Second Journalist is given the opportunity to sing his rhyming-slang song 'Alice is gone' (to the tune of 'Jesu, the very thought of thee' according to *The Chase*). For two songs in the restaurant scene Auden made use of material he had written for the Downs School Revue (there are twenty-two sides of notes in a Texas notebook, including 'Quick boys, slick boys' etc., and 'By the Rhondda': see *Plays*, p. 508, and Gurney Thomas, 'Recollections of Auden at the Downs School', *Auden Newsletter* 3). The scene burlesques the sexual tyranny and (Isherwood's notion, this) the militant philistinism of the rich: Destructive Desmond's appeal to the cabaret audience as he is about to slash the Rembrandt is borrowed from the presentation of Christ to the Jews, and the cry of 'Barabbas! Barabbas!' Alan's involvement with this world is represented by his affair with the film star, Lou Vipond. To the accompaniment of an ironic epithalamium sung by the hotel staff, he makes love to her as a shop-window dummy ('*When the dummy is to speak,* ALAN *runs behind it and speaks in falsetto*'), a device borrowed from *The Enemies of a Bishop*, II.i, which represents the isolated self-regard of conventional romance. Sex is thus (as the speech by the dog's skin, p. 272, makes clear) merely an 'idea in the head'.

The skin represents the instinctive life, and it draws the contrast between itself and the clock in the hall, which represents fate. Francis's assumption of the skin (which is revealed to the audience in this scene) is therefore essentially an attempt to break out of duality. However, he later (p. 285) hints at social reasons for the disguise (reasons more elaborately expressed in the published version) and when he helps Alan to escape from the Nineveh Hotel in the skin, and Alan is kicked by the Manager, says 'Ha ha! Now you know how it feels!' The underlying metaphysical meaning, however, with its implications for human culture and even the form of the drama itself, remained of importance for Auden. He obviously proposed the duality in just these terms as a set subject for his Downs School pupils (see R. Goldsborough, 'Dog and Clock', *The Badger*, iii.5, Spring 1935).

The chorus on p. 279 re-emphasises the inevitable conditioning and fate of the divided individual. Auden drew on Georg Groddeck's *Exploring the Unconscious* (1933) for some of the significant detail. Compare 'his first voluptuous rectal sins' with 'The earliest sins . . . are connected with the rectal tract' (Groddeck, p. 89), and 'the greater part of the will devoted | To warding off pain from the water-logged areas' with 'certain lower parts of the adult body always contain an excess of fluid . . . A great part, a very great part of our unconscious mental energy is used up merely in warding off pain from these water-logged places' (Groddeck, pp. 51–2). The last notion is a particularly dotty one, since Groddeck proposed that the water-logging was due to the effect of gravity. At first the chorus seems to have Bloomsbury in its sights, as though writers like Eliot ('his favourite pool between the yew-hedge and the roses') or Virginia Woolf ('five hundred a year and a room of one's own') had some false idealised notion of the challenge, which would receive an uncomfortable shock when death inevitably landed on the beaches of their love 'like Coghlan's coffin' (see J. Forbes-Robertson, *A Player Under Three Reigns*, 1905, pp. 165–6: the actor's coffin was washed out to sea and carried two thousand miles to his birthplace, from Galveston, Texas, to Prince Edward Island). But Auden does not exclude himself from the escapism and optimism of those who imagine that five hundred a year and a room of one's own are a sufficient 'change of heart' (Auden's own Downs School salary at the time was £220, according to his Guggenheim application of 8 October 1941). The allusion to the final poem of *Poems* (1930), 'Sir, no man's enemy', shows a fresh awareness in Auden of the difficulties in which the individual is involved: he may easily be able to beware of others, whose illnesses he can correctly ascribe to their various spiritual failings, but will he be able to beware of himself, whose own heart whispers: 'I am the nicest person in this room'? Two years later, in a broadcast, Auden was still tackling solipsism in much the same terms (*The Listener*, 22 December 1937, p. 137). The solution in this chorus looks rather perfunctory: in a pastiche of the 'Give. Sympathize. Control' passage from *The Waste Land*, Auden resorts to an abbreviated didacticism.

At this point the problem about the alternative endings must be confronted. In *Plays* (pp. 281ff) III.v is the previously unpublished version prepared by Auden for the Group Theatre production of 1936. It is very different from III.v as printed in the Faber edition of 1935 (and the paperback reprint of 1968) and therefore as known to readers for well over sixty years. In the published version, the village establishment is first unwittingly betrayed by the Vicar's mad Sermon and then directly denounced by Francis himself, who with Alan and a handful of recruits leaves through the auditorium to join what he calls the 'army of the other side'. All the villagers turn into animals. In the later ending as it appears in *Plays* the Sermon disappears, Francis is killed by Mildred Luce, and the whole thing is covered up by the Journalists. Mendelson argues, with perfect cogency, that the scene he prints more accurately represents final authorial intentions. Auden, for example, made similar changes to the published text for a New York production in 1947, and it is undeniable that the elegiac admonitory choric passages on p. 289 (which form the Epilogue in the published version) 'really' refer to the situation in *The Quest* from which they were borrowed, where Francis dies on the operating table and Alan is machine-gunned to death in the aisle of the theatre. However, at Oxford in the early 1970s Auden authorised and enjoyed an undergraduate production which used the published ending, and is known to have sponsored a contest in 1953 for a new comic ending.

It is characteristic of much of his work in the 1930s (*The Orators* is a notorious example) not to have really made up his mind between spiritual tragedy and an invigorating call to order (this of course represents a conflict in his thinking which could only be resolved later by the adoption of Christian belief). The *Plays* text (which was further adapted for the actual Group Theatre production) is patently attempting to reconcile this equivocation and to tidy things up, but the result is flat and unexciting.

The loss of the Sermon, for example (which was the best thing in the play, according to Isherwood, who never expected it to be dropped from the revised ending), in favour of lengthy explanations of what might happen to Mildred Luce, is simply disastrous. And of course the coded political outcome, which in its way is no small part of the received meaning of the work, quite evaporates. I would urge producers at the very least to look seriously beyond the *Plays* text (Mendelson does print the published version in his notes) and I will take the liberty of continuing my commentary with reference to the 1935 published version alone.

Alan and Francis have returned to find Pressan Ambo in a fit of jingoism. The Vicar, who with General Hotham has founded a rather Mosleyite Boys' Brigade, delivers a sermon on the origins of sin, or more particularly on the revolt of Satan against God, which he compares to the growth of international Communism (p. 575). His conviction that God is on his side in this new battle develops into self-righteousness, and the self-righteousness into hysteria. It seems fitting that one of Auden's greatest prose set-pieces should thus act as a climax to the play, evoking as it does the ironical fifth Ode in *The Orators*, where the psycho-political struggle is suddenly seen from the side of reaction. The ambiguities of the subject and the form of address may even have influenced the name of the village Pressan Ambo, for 'ambo' means (a) on both sides; and (b) a kind of pulpit. Auden reprinted the sermon in the 1945 *Collected Poetry*, and the view once circulated (probably due to Beach) that Auden had come to approve of the witch-hunting Vicar. Quite on the contrary: a prefatory note in the *Collected Poetry* makes it plain that the subject of Auden's satirical attack is still the same as it was when the piece appeared as 'Sermon by an Armament Manufacturer' in *Life and Letters*, or as the General's gramophone record in *The Chase*: that is, the type of the Super-Ego convinced that it is the Voice of God.

Not surprisingly, Auden borrows the high Victorian tone of Frederic W. Farrar for much of this sermon about fatal choices. Farrar's *Eric, or, Little by Little* was one of Auden's favourite childhood books. With its motto from *Measure for Measure* (' 'Tis one thing to be tempted, Escalus, | Another thing to fall.'), its melodramatic hints about homosexuality, and its concern with the narrow line dividing virtue from vice, it seems an ideal source for a prose of grandiloquent rectitude and regret. In particular compare the end of the Vicar's long paragraph on p. 576 about Azazael and Abdiel ('This is your only chance', etc.) with chapter 9 of *Eric* ('Now, Eric, now or never!' etc.). For his final paragraph, Auden moves from Farrar to Gogol's *Diary of a*

Madman (tr. Mirsky, 1929) in order to heighten the manic pitch of the sermon, and to hint at the maternal conditioning of repression which had figured in *The Orators* and was to recur at the end of *The Ascent of F6*. Compare the Vicar ('Oh Father, I am praising thee! . . . running to Thy arms! . . . Admit him to the fairs of that blessed country . . . the blue sky! . . . Mother is waving from the tiny door! . . . my beautiful blue and gold room!') with Gogol's government clerk in his asylum ('Oh Lord! the things they are doing to me! . . . Save me, take me away! . . . Carry me from this world! . . . There is the sky whistling before me . . . blue mist . . . Is that my home in the blue distance? Is it my mother sitting before the window?'). Among other possible models, see Father Arnall's hellfire sermons in chapter III of Joyce's *Portrait of the Artist as a Young Man*.

Francis reveals himself and denounces the village. He has observed them 'from underneath', recording his observations in a diary, and did not like what he saw. He is like Stearn in the Mortmere stories (see Brian Finney, 'Laily, Mortmere and All That', *Twentieth Century Literature*, 22, 1976, pp. 287–302) or like the Tutor in Upward's *Journey to the Border*. The idea of the diary may have come from 'Joanna Field' [Marion Milner], *A Life of One's Own* (1934), chapter II, which Auden had reviewed and praised in *The Listener*, 28 November 1934, p. viii. For 'You are all units in an immense army', see Lenin's 'What is to be Done?' in *Selections from Lenin*, ed. P. Pascal (1929), p. 107. With a handful of recruits from the village he leaves to join 'the army of the other side', passing out through the auditorium while the Journalists photograph the villagers, who have all turned into animals.

Spender criticised *Dog* (*New Writing*, Autumn 1938) on the grounds that it presented 'a picture of a society defeated by an enemy whom the writers have not put into the picture because they do not know what he looks like although they thoroughly support him'. It is plain, however, just as it is plain in another parabolic work of fantasy like Upward's *Journey to the Border*, that the hero joins the Communist Party. The vagueness (as in Upward) is part of the mysterious inevitability of it all, an inevitability supported by the final line of the 'Epilogue', a version of the words Bakunin spoke at his trial in 1870, a formula picked up by Marx five years later: 'To each his need: from each his power', and by the whole drift of this deliberately grand and rhetorical chorus in which love is urged to wake from its dream and prove its vigours ('Love, loath to enter' was originally part of a longer poem published in *New Oxford Outlook*, May 1934, pp. 82–4). It is amusing to note that one line of this chorus is based on a phrase of Winston Churchill's in *The World Crisis* (1923), his history of the First World War, describing

Germany's March offensive: 'It was an hour of intolerable majesty and crisis' (see Auden's review in *Scrutiny*, March 1933, p. 413). The play's extraordinarily lively and eclectic means to this serious end has deceived many into thinking less of it than they might. Curiously, it was not entirely well-received at the time (the range of critical attention is well exemplified by Kenneth Allott in *New Verse*, February/March 1936, and Ian Parsons in the *Spectator*, 28 June 1935), but it is the sort of long-gestated work that improves with keeping: what may originally have seemed raw and youthful has now attained a fine period flavour, and it deserves frequent revival.

Look, Stranger!

The title of the volume was foisted on Auden by Faber and Faber, who published it on 22 October 1936. He said that it 'sounded like a vegetarian lady novelist' (letter to Frederic Prokosch, 16 March 1937). The US title was *On this Island* (published 2 February 1937).

The dedicatory poem to Erika Mann celebrates 'a narrow strictness' as a call to order in the face of a pan-European chaos that Auden characterises (perhaps because Mann was an actress in satirical cabaret) in terms of display ('extravagant', 'baroque', 'surrealist'). Auden married Mann on 15 June 1935 in order to provide her with a British passport.

O Love, the interest itself in thoughtless heaven

May, 1932; 'Poem', *New Statesman*, 16 July 1932; 'Prologue', *New Country*, 1933; LS, p. 11; 'Perhaps', CP45, p. 89; EA, p. 118.

The title given to this poem in *New Country* as well as in *Look, Stranger!* has confused some readers (e.g. Carpenter, p. 154) into believing that it was originally intended for a play. In fact, the volume contains both 'Prologue' and 'Epilogue', and it seems most likely that in 1933 Auden already recognised in the case of the 'Prologue' that it had a thematic and structural importance for the work as a whole. There is not obviously any play that it might have belonged to.

It is perhaps the most significant of the new kind of fully argued and rhetorical poem that he had been writing for about a year. Structure freed Auden's observation and invention; it provided new and liberating ways of putting poems together. The old understated poetic models were now superseded by writers unafraid of magnificence; here, in particular, Pindar and Paul Claudel. Auden had already discovered Pindar while writing the Odes in *The Orators*. Claudel was the great master of psychic geography, invocations and sea-voyages. If time has pardoned him (see 'In Memory of W. B. Yeats', Part 3) it has pardoned him for giving this crucial lift to Auden's choric manner in 1932.

So much of his that is eloquent, ecstatic and admonitory comes from Claudel. In particular, see Claudel's play *The Satin Slipper: or, the worst is not the surest*, translated by the Rev. Fr. John O'Connor (1931). This play appears on a list of 'Required Reading' that Auden wrote out as part of the reading list for the Fall 1941 course 'Fate and the Individual in European Literature' when he was teaching at the University of Michigan. In the play the two lovers Roderigo and Prouheze are separated by the Atlantic like the continents Africa and America. The Jesuit's Chorus on p. 3 may be compared with line 4 of Auden's poem ('Fill these lovers with such longing as shall involve, in the deprivation of each other's presence through the daily play of circumstance, | Their primal integrity'). Phrases from St James's Chorus on p. 97 may be compared with lines 8–9 of the poem ('this donjon-keep'; 'On this Atlantic rose which . . . closes up Europe's basin'; 'on that half-sunken mole') and on pp. 97–8 with lines 44–5 ('beating heart'; 'one ship drives straight towards America'; 'All the walls that keep your hearts asunder cannot prevent your existing at the one time'). Indeed, there is much beating of hearts and many prows of ships in the play. Claudel's 'unwavering keel' is directed, as it were, at Roderigo's heart, giving Auden's poem an erotic subtext which it perhaps otherwise would not quite have, while the theme at the close of the poem of a cultural pilgrimage out of the Mediterranean is given force by the fact that Claudel's St James is a personification of the constellation Orion, and is a figurehead on the Jesuit's ship which is setting out through the Pillars of Hercules.

Another specific source for this richly allusive poem was Anthony Collett's *The Changing Face of England* (1926; page references to the 1932 edn). Stanza 5, see Collett, p. 197: 'Modern Lancashire grew out of a wild moor fringed by bare mosses and sand-flats.' Stanza 6, see Collett, p. 198: 'The extreme instance of topographical overcrowding is, perhaps, in the narrow parallel valleys of the Glamorganshire coalfield.' Stanza 12, see Collett, p. 91: 'Chester knows Moel Fammau, the mother mountain of the little hills of the border, and divines the coming weather by the clearness or withdrawal of her bare crown.' Stanza 13, see Collett, pp. 121, 115: 'A likely dream'; 'Magical are those secret and winding valleys, where in the miry oakwoods every pit is full of coiled ammonites in eternal snakelike slumber.'

The poem appears to take off from an abandoned line in the penultimate stanza in a draft of 'Me, March, you do with your movements master and rock', written the previous month: 'O Love, sustainer of the unbreakable atomic ring'. This ring is primarily the psychic field formed by the early Christians at their agape or love-feast (see my commentary on 'Out on the lawn I lie in bed', p. 149), although the phrase 'atomic ring' is later specifically scientific in a draft of 'New Year Letter' (see p. 336). The ring survives in the present poem as the 'ring where name and image meet'. Obviously Auden's analogy with such ecstasy entirely defeats the position of the intellectual, who habitually thinks and talks. In the argument of this and of other poems of the time he is forced to abandon 'talk and kindness' as a liberal illusion. Love is 'thoughtless' ('careless' in a never-printed MS revision of 1965). In the poem, even England's greatest scientist didn't have to 'think' his theory of gravity: Newton in his orchard simply becomes aware of the eternal tie between himself and England, as Auden himself seems to have done at this time, albeit with the help of Collett.

This psychic ecstasy, this thoughtlessness, is given a respectable literary shape in Auden's strange first line. It was Henry James who complained about Arnold Bennett (in 'The New Novel'): 'Yes, the circumstances of the interest are there, but where is the interest itself?' Auden quoted this more than once as a validation of literary or political authenticity (cf. 'But where is the interest' in 'I have a handsome profile', stanza 10). The interest, he claimed to Ansen, was the central kind of excitement that induced you to write, as opposed to 'amusing wayside stimuli'. It is the very power that enables you to come to terms as an artist with your environment. See his address on James, *Gazette of the Grolier Club* II, 7 (January 1947): 'The interest itself is the freedom of the individual will, not to deny the field of fated facts within which it operates, but to create, with them and in spite of them, a human character.' Compare also the Freudian meaning of 'interest', i.e. the ego's conception of itself. By analogy with the novelist, then, who must, as it were, 'love' his subject, all men and women need this appeal to a numinous power to convert 'thought' into the wholly natural. Auden's image for this natural pattern of thought is borrowed from Caxton's 'murmeracion of stares' (see OED). The metaphor suggests that it is the starlings' joy which thus becomes an image of 'Heaven'. 'Name' and 'image' have become lovers, like Claudel's Roderigo and Prouheze, and it is their longing that will bring man's thought alive. Love is therefore at the service of the highest human power.

One significance of this poem is that having begun by talking about love it manages to talk about history as well. The poem contrasts two dreams. The first is a real dream that has gone wrong: Whig history, perhaps, in an age of industrial depression. The second is a 'possible' dream, history as individual choice can make it, invoking the necessity of change and suffering, perhaps, just at this moment for Auden, Marxist history. Just as the first dream shows the stultified heritage of the entrepreneurial classes who have crippled the mines of Lancashire and Glamorgan, so the second dream shows that a new beginning can be made out of that very urge to mine the earth ('And out of the Future into actual History' replaced 'And called out of tideless peace by a living sun' in the *New Country* text: compare 'tideless heaven' in Gerald Heard, *The Social Substance of Religion*, 1931, p. 147).

Auden had been intrigued by the theory of W. J. Perry in *Children of the Sun* (1923), *The Origin of Magic and Religion* (1923) and *The Growth of Civilization* (1924) that the origin of all archaic civilisation was in Egypt, and that megaliths such as Stonehenge evolved via the dolmen from the Egyptian mastaba tomb. Perry acknowledged the influence of G. Elliott Smith's book *The Evolution of the Dragon* (1918), which argued that English long barrows were modelled on the mastaba tomb. (Auden appears to have known Smith's work, incidentally, for he wrote a poem at Oxford called 'Evolution of the Dragon'). The reason Perry suggests for this great wave of Egyptian culture is connected with ideas of ritual rebirth of the dead, a central theme in Auden's poem. Such rebirth depends upon the search for life-giving magical substances such as precious metals, and would therefore account for the presence of dolmen builders in Tintagel, centre both of the Cornish mining region, and the castle of King Arthur, central figure in the myth of the search for the Holy Grail. The final stanzas of Auden's poem can thus be explained as a metaphor of a daring risk to redeem the living dead. Pindar had written in his Fourth Isthmian, lines 12–14: 'And by far-reaching deeds of native valour, did they touch the pillars of Hercules; and let none pursue prowess that passeth beyond that bound! Aye, and they became breeders of horses . . .' (Loeb edn, 1915, p. 461). Auden's 'Merlin, tamer of horses' is thus a kind of coded symbol of Perry's ideas. 'Tamer of horses' is a Homeric epithet, actually the very last words of the *Iliad*, thus conflating Merlin with Hector and suggesting a dispersal of the megalith-building culture beyond the Pillars of Hercules (like Dante's Ulysses or Layamon's Brutus) to create British culture, through magic, and through mining. For further speculations about the Egyptian origins of Stonehenge, see Robert Graves, *The White Goddess*, chapter 16. Auden's characterisation of this second dream in terms of 'military silence' and a 'surgeon's idea of pain' is in accord with the 'narrow strictness' of the dedicatory poem of the whole volume. It is challenging in erotic terms, but is still in line with the discipline of initiation that runs through *The Orators* (according to Perry, initiation into totemic clans and secret societies was a means of handing on the esoteric wisdom of the archaic civilisation).

Out on the lawn I lie in bed

June, 1933; 'Summer Night', *Listener*, 7 March 1934; LS, p. 13; 'A Summer Night 1933', CP45, p. 96; 'A Summer Night', CP, p. 117; EA, p. 136.

This poem, written in the stanza of Smart's 'Song to David' and with a nod towards the equally moonlit landscape of Arnold's 'A Summer Night', is, in its consideration of the continued opposition of the private and public worlds, a key poem. In his introduction to Anne Fremantle's book *The Protestant Mystics* (1964), p. 26, Auden refers, as an example of the Vision of Agape, to 'an unpublished account for the authenticity of which I can vouch'. The quoted account begins: 'One fine summer night in June 1933 I was sitting on a lawn after dinner with three colleagues, two women and a man . . .', and tells of a mystical sense of communal awareness shared by them on the occasion. It then goes on to say: 'and among the various factors which several years later brought me back to the Christian faith in which I had been brought up, the memory of this experience and asking myself what it could mean was one of the most crucial' (see *Forewords and Afterwords*, pp. 69–70). The account fits Auden's own circumstances and is taken as his own. He was prepared for this experience by his reading of Gerald Heard (*The Social Substance of Religion*, 1931, chapter ix) who drew his account of the agape or love-feast of the early Christians from Percy Dearmer's *The Church at Prayer* (1923). The agape consisted of dinner, followed by singing, the forming of a ring which acted as a psychic field, a kiss of peace, and spiritual exercises. The 'ring' is specifically mentioned in stanza 3. The dove-like light in that stanza seems tellingly divine. The post-prandial context is important. Auden wrote about eating as a symbol of universal love in *The Prolific and the Devourer*, pp. 32ff ('even a Rotary Club dinner is nearer my intention than the Mass', p. 39).

The poem therefore relishes such a magical moment with a full consciousness that it is the privilege of those 'whom hunger does not move' and are as vague as any newspaper reader about details of the European situation (the reference to Poland may ultimately involve the dispute over the Polish Corridor, but it *says* no more, according to the metaphor of the drawn bow, than that the situation is 'taut' – a journalistic cliché revived by poetic figuration). The privileged are protected from hunger by their limited decencies (compare 'Our kindness to ten persons' with Ricky in Forster's *The Longest Journey*: 'He believes in humanity because he knows a dozen decent people', or possibly Auden had Proust's Baron

Charlus in mind), but it is not quite clear whether the 'intentions not our own' are those of the hungry, 'The gathering multitudes', or of the future. This distinction is crucial in Auden's poems of the mid-1930s , and involves the paradox to be explored in 'Spain, 1937' about whether we are responsible for history or not. I believe that this poem is still mindful of the multitudes, and of the cultural gulf between the classes. It would account for the substitution in collected editions of 'butcher' for 'orphan' in stanza 7, originally perhaps a memory of Rimbaud's 'Les Effarés' (see Auden's copy of *On This Island* at Texas), and for the dropping of the centrally important stanzas 10–12. The poem weighs present harmony against future change, that 'crumpling flood' soon to 'force a rent . . . through dykes of our content'. Auden is still thinking of the social revolution: the poem proposes that the (largely erotic) delights it describes will always be the objective of men, as natural as heredity (stanza 15) and powerful to assuage the violence which will necessarily come to an unjust world. The final stanza is partly modelled on one from a poem of about 1928 ('The trees are alive in the forest'): 'They shall outlast the tiger | His swift motions | Their slowness tune the heart-beat | Of nervous nations'. The 'they' in this instance, of course, are not the 'delights' of 'A Summer Night' but trees. Auden may have changed the tiger to a tigress under the influence of Owen's 'Strange Meeting', line 28 ('They will be swift with swiftness of the tigress').

The opening of stanza 6 is modelled on the white paternoster ('Matthew, Mark, Luke and John | Bless the bed that I lie on,' etc.). That Auden was in the habit of entrusting his sleeping soul to 'the Gospel Makers' is suggested by 'The Cave of Nakedness' in *About the House*. Auden borrowed the birds of Wicken Fen in stanza 12 from Anthony Collett, *The Changing Face of England* (1926; repr. 1932), p. 67. The poem is dedicated to Geoffrey Hoyland, headmaster of the Downs School, Colwall. Although Auden was happy and fulfilled there as a teacher (he actually took his bed out into the garden during the summer), he was at first conscious of the particular atmosphere of a Quaker school. On 4 October 1932 he wrote to Alan Sinkinson: 'The atmosphere I find a little intense. I suppose its what the communist state will be like: one feels it isn't done not to be enthusiastic about everything.'

Part of the poem was set by Britten in his 'Spring Symphony' (1949).

Our hunting fathers told the story

?May, 1934; 'Poem', *Listener*, 30 May 1934; published as a pamphlet by Frederic Prokosch, November 1935; LS, p. 17; 'In Father's Footsteps', CP45, p. 95; 'Our Hunting Fathers', CP, p. 122; EA, p. 151.

This poem consists of two stanzas, each of which is made up of a single sentence: the total effect is of an immensely involved couplet. It is an intellectual statement of some complexity, and the effect is somewhat deceptively formalised by the elaborate prosody and orotund Yeatsian diction (the poem acted as the epilogue to Britten's eponymous symphonic cycle of 1936, though its obscurity makes it an odd choice as a text for music). The poem contrasts two views of love. The first stanza shows how in the eighteenth and nineteenth centuries it was felt to be the driving power which, tempered by reason, provided the individual with his basic motivation. It is like Pope's Ruling Passion, or Shaw's Life Force. The animals are to be pitied because in them the quality is innocent and undirected: only man can consciously put it to a purpose. The second stanza develops the modern view that love is, on the contrary, not a noble force at all, but one to be denied because it inevitably leads to the guilt of individualism and self-regard. 'His southern gestures modify' means to sublimate love's genital impulses into not a selfish love, but a universal, social love. The last two lines, according to Auden in his review of Basil Liddell Hart's book on T. E. Lawrence (EA, p. 320), are a quotation from Lenin (similar to the one already made by Brecht in *Die Massnahme*, 1930). Lenin certainly stressed the importance of secret trade unions and illegal literature (see *Selections from Lenin*, ed. P. Pascal, 1929, 1.132, 147) but Nicholas Jenkins has shown that the words are actually those of Nadezhda Krupskaya, Lenin's widow (*Auden Newsletter*, 10–11). The stanzas contrast reason's collaboration with reason's modification, individualism with collectivism, Victorian *laissez-faire* with the Communist revolution.

Let the florid music praise

February, 1936; 'Song', LS, p. 18; CP45, p. 213; CP, p. 137; EA, p. 158.

This poem was written for the same boy for whom 'The earth turns over . . . ', 'Dear, though the night is gone' and 'Lay your sleeping head my love' were written. It demonstrates Auden's power, at its height in the mid-1930s, to expose, within the space of a brief lyric, the dreadful dichotomy between the outward and the inward impulses of love, between the positive aesthetic sense of the lover and his negative needs. It depends upon the poised diction ('florid', for instance, suggests not only the decoration of baroque music, but the healthy radiance of his loved one's face) and upon the sense of grand public statement which the contrasted stanzas imply; but it also depends upon an uninsisted yet consistent use of metaphor which, in the Augustan manner, barely conveys its vehicle at all. Thus, Beauty's conquest of the citadel of the loved one in the first stanza creates the terms whereby in the second stanza Death may be seen as able to reassert his power easily through the allegiance of the unloved, who have no encouragement to pay homage to beauty: 'Their secretive children walk | Through your vigilance of breath | To unpardonable Death'. The submerged metaphor is of a secret betrayal to a greater power which, in the last line of the poem, is even acknowledged by the poet. This is not merely Death in the temporal sense, but Death as a psychological state of the selfish will ('The weeping and striking') which the absence of love encourages.

Britten set the poem as part of his song cycle *On this Island* (1938).

Look, stranger, at this island now

November, 1935; 'Seaside', *Listener*, 18 December 1935; *Living Age*, June 1936; LS, p. 19; 'Seascape', CP45, p. 214; 'On This Island', CP, p. 130; EA, p. 157.

This poem, which provided the titles for both the English and American editions of Auden's second collection, and for Britten's song cycle of 1938 in which a setting of it was included, is rightly celebrated, not only for the superb imitative and descriptive language that reads like for once properly digested Hopkins, but for the delicately prophetic suggestions in the final stanza. The ships are engaged in 'voluntary' errands, as though coercion were soon to come (though compare the 'involuntary errands' of all the hot stars in 'The latest ferrule now has tapped the curb'). The ships are like 'floating seeds' in another sense: they may themselves germinate into quite different instruments. The vague echoes of Shakespeare in the first stanza reinforce the poem's sense of rediscovered Englishness (a feeling very much present in the contemporary *Dog Beneath the Skin*). The 'stranger' of the opening line may be ultimately the same as the 'stranger' of 'Who stands, the crux left of the watershed', but he is a stranger who has a simpler, more instinctive feeling that he could belong somewhere, and may therefore respond more responsibly to the veiled warning of the last stanza.

In fact, the vocative formula seems to bear some sort of relationship to memorial epitaphs (cf. 'Stranger, this still | Museum exhibits | The results of life' etc., in *The Age of Anxiety*, CP, p. 501) where the passer-by is enjoined to empathise fully with what is memorialised. To that extent the symptomatic English landscape is already distanced and historical, the 'delight' turning to instant nostalgia. Auden was a great admirer of E. M. Forster, and it may be that there is here a substantive influence of the rhapsodic opening and closing paragraphs of chapter xix of *Howards End* ('If one wanted to show a foreigner England . . . It is as if a fragment of England floated forward to greet the foreigner . . . Does she belong to those who have . . . seen the whole island at once', etc.). The 'pluck' of the tide is borrowed from Anthony Collett, *The Changing Face of England* (1932 edn), p. 9. The poem was written for a documentary film by Marion Grierson, *Beside the Seaside*, but the film used no more than a few phrases from it.

O what is that sound which so thrills the ear

October, 1932; 'Ballad', *New Verse*, December 1934; LS, p. 20; CP45, p. 222; 'The Quarry', SP58, p. 27; 'O What Is That Sound', CP, p. 120; EA, p. 125.

This is a much anthologised and compelling ballad whose point appears to lie in one's initial presumption that the eighteenth-century soldiery were as likely as not to be the instruments of repression, and that therefore the second speaker of the poem is an honest rebel for whom the cause of continued resistance is more important even than the girl he loves (the situation might be imagined as taking place at any time between the first Jacobite uprising and the American War of Independence). 'Drumming, drumming' sets up an iterated effect which greatly assists the drama and suspense of the poem. Paul Haeffner has pointed out a similarity to Ella Wheeler Wilcox's 'The Arrival' in *Notes and Queries*, no. 207, March 1962.

However, the rebel's scale of values is not approved by Auden: the poem is an important political comment appropriate to his developing emphasis on love and individual values, and it has a crypto-Christian element. Hermann Peschmann wrote to Auden in 1938 asking about the Freudian element in the poem. Auden replied: 'Freud if you like. The idea came from a picture I saw of the Agony in the Garden, with the soldiers in the distance.' Auden's Freud Lecture of 12 March 1971 delivered at the Philadelphia Association for Psychoanalysis ('Phantasy and Reality in Poetry') refers to 'O What is that Sound' in these terms:

For dramatic purposes, I wanted a second person in the poem beside the dreamer, so, for the disciples who ran away, I substituted a single figure, whom the dreamer loves and trusts – i.e. the reader can choose whatever image suits him or her – but who in the end deserts the dreamer leaving him to face the terror alone.

The lecture (now published in *Auden Studies* 3, p. 177) also refers to a painting of soldiers coming to arrest Jesus. The painting that Auden had in mind is likely to be either the one by El Greco (in which, as the lecture describes, the soldiers are actually crossing a little bridge) or by Bellini. Both are in the National Gallery, London.

Thus the poem successfully works at many levels: the archetypal dream of desertion, the icon of Christian betrayal, the pastiche Jacobite ballad, the contemporary application of Nazi gun-butts on the door with its attendant political dilemma, and so on. Britten attempted a setting of the poem, but it is incomplete and unpublished.

Hearing of harvests rotting in the valleys

May, 1933; *Criterion*, July 1933; published as a pamphlet by Frederic Prokosch, November 1933; LS, p. 22; 'Paysage Moralisé', CP45, p. 104; CP, p. 119; EA, p. 135.

This was Auden's second published sestina. William Empson had complained that the capacity to conceive such a large form as the sestina had been lost since the age of Sidney, whose double sestina in the *Arcadia* he had been discussing (*Seven Types of Ambiguity*, 1930, chapter 1). Auden's sestina shares two of its six key words with Sidney's (*Sidney*: mountaines, vallies, forrests, musique, morning, evening; *Auden*: valleys, mountains, water, islands, cities, sorrow) and therefore looks like a conscious effort to rebut Empson. However, as with the earlier sestina in *The Orators* (see p. 104) the complex exploration of the concepts embodied in the key words is allegorical rather than emotional: the poem is an ingenious exercise in the suggestiveness of multiply defined symbols.

One significant aspect of this departure is found in Auden's choice of his most interesting key word. Empson had reflected on the cumulative power of the sestina's structure in Sidney, and concluded: 'So that when the static conception of the complaint has been finally brought into light . . . a whole succession of feelings about the local scenery, the whole way in which it is taken for granted, has been enlisted into sorrow and beats as a single passion in the mind.' Although Auden had already used 'sorrow' as the key word in the unpublished sestina of 1930, 'Renewal of traditional anger in peace', I believe that it is Empson's suggestive 'enlisting into sorrow' which prompts him to use it again here in the way that he does and which gives him the idea of 'local scenery' becoming 'a single passion in the mind' that is implicit in the concept of 'paysage moralisé'. What is most notable about the nature of this sorrow is that it is enlarged from the simple love-sickness of Arcadian shepherds into a sorrow, like anxiety, which represents for Auden the general spiritual condition of man. In moving to this sublimated meaning it is remotely possible that Auden was influenced by Heidegger's use of *Sorge* in *Sein und Zeit* (first published in *Jahrbuch für Phänomenologie und phänomenologische Forschung*, ed. Husserl, Spring 1927), particularly in the striking annunciatory use of it in the coda, although he would already have been familiar with Pound's translation of the Old English 'sorge', in 'The Seafarer', line 42, = fear, anxiety) as 'sorrow'.

Auden has also borrowed from Sidney the natural pairing and mutual definition of the key words. In Sidney there is a polarity of place (mountaines/vallies) and a polarity of time (morning/evening) which frames in the first stanza a conceptual polarity of vocation (forrests/ musique) appropriate to the pastoral life, since a forest lies outside the boundary of the world that is fenced and farmed and tamed by the pipes of the Orphic shepherd-poet. The stanzas of a sestina, like the excursions of a pair of compasses creating patterns from overlapping circles, naturally contain three distichs, in each of which the fresh order of key words develops this sense of mutual definition. After six stanzas the scheme would, of course, return to the initial pairings in their initial order.

The structure of the poem is doubtless to a degree historical, a dry-run in a sense for the more explicit 'Memorial for the City', Part II, but it is this exhaustive sense of definition and redefinition which forbids a detailed understanding of the key concepts of the earlier poem, even though the related failure of both founding heroes and artist-prophets is clear enough. *Valleys* are places of origins and of comfort, one might suggest, representing the protection, maternal or erotic, of the womb. *Mountains* could symbolise the phallic motif of the Quest. Indeed, taken together, the valleys and mountains could be the female and male principles (like Lawrence's moon and sun) which govern human behaviour. However, the poem insists on qualifications: the valleys are wretched places (stanza 5) that the wretched refuse to leave (stanza 6), where the harvests rot (stanza 1) and where villagers mope (stanza 4). They may be places of projected civilisation (stanza 2) and of nostalgic dreams (stanza 3), though both these kinds of dream are almost certainly illusory. Mountains also feature in these false dreams (stanza 3), but more commonly are barren (stanza 1), unmined (stanza 4) or places of failure (stanza 6), haunting as regrets (stanza 4), where originating impulses have been forgotten (stanza 2).

In the civilising journey of human history we might expect such negatives, for they characterise the restlessness of man and his uncertain aims, just as the contrary urges of solitariness (*islands*) and gregariousness (*cities*) convey the social paradox of human existence. Islands are places of mysterious origin (stanzas 5 and 6) and of equally unknown destination (stanzas 1, 3 and 4), but they are also places to wish to be rescued from (stanza 2). This is presumably because they represent the dangers of solipsism or an impossible dream of escape from society. You cannot escape from cities (stanza 4). They are unredeemed (stanza 5). Their founders expected them to be places of culture (stanza 2) but they are now places of guilt (stanza 3), starvation (stanza 1) and unhappiness (stanza 6).

What, then, is to give this poem its sense of hope? *Water* is the medium that defines islands, and therefore is a principle of the growth and development of the individual human spirit. However, on its very first sudden appearance in stanza 1 its role seems to be ambiguously deployed, both to heal the sterility of the preceding line and to drown the voyagers of the following line. We have, in fact, the scenario of Eliot's *The Waste Land* in miniature. In all the other stanzas, though, it is in one way or another a medium of enchantment, and in particular in stanza 3 its one appearance as a river turns the sorrow of that stanza unmistakably back into Sidney's erotic melancholy. From 'Control of the passes was, he saw, the key' to 'In Praise of Limestone', running water is a symbol of trust in love for Auden. The relative consistency of this key word in the poem prepares us for the coda, where it is enjoined (like the flood in 'Out on the lawn I lie in bed', written the following month) to irrigate and destroy, so that the city may be rebuilt, sexual harmony restored and individual isolation ended. If the shades of Eliot, and perhaps also of Tennyson and Baudelaire, have haunted earlier parts of the poem, it is now the turn of Hopkins, and it is Hopkins's presence that is possibly the most significant at this moment of exclamation and accelerated pace. Reaching for a pitch of language to express the revolution that water could bring about, Auden wittingly or half-wittingly but unmistakably echoes the bittersweet meaning and over-powering conviction of the crucifixion of Christ in Hopkins's analogy of the sloe in stanza 8 of 'The Wreck of the Deutschland':

How a lush-kept plush-capped sloe
    Will, mouthed to flesh-burst,
Gush! – flush the man, the being with it, sour or sweet,
Brim, in a flash, full! – Hither then, last or first,
    To hero of Calvary, Christ,'s feet –
Never ask if meaning it, wanting it, warned of it – men go.

It cannot be that we are intended by this to think of water as specifically sacramental, but it does seem clear that the Vision of Agape that lies behind 'Out on the lawn I lie in bed' prompted more than one poem in which Auden guardedly alluded to the origins of the Christian sacraments. To support the idea that this occluded Christian meaning may be discovered in the text, it may be noted that the title was added in 1945, after Auden had written the Rilkean and specifically Christian sestina sequence 'Kairos and Logos', charting different historical aspects of the revelation of truth and man's incompetent handling of it. Critics (e.g. Spears, p. 142, and Blair, p. 88) ascribe the creation of the genre of allegorised landscape to Rilke himself, following Auden's remarks in *The New Republic* in September 1939 ('One of Rilke's more characteristic devices is the expression of human life in terms of landscape', etc.). However, despite Auden's extensive debt to Rilke, it seems likely that his title, 'Paysage Moralisé', actually alludes to a famous poem by an anonymous fourteenth-century friar in which the classical poet Ovid is made fit for Christian readers (see *Ovide Moralisé*, ed. Cornelis de Boer, Amsterdam, 1915, 1920).

Now the leaves are falling fast

March, 1936; *New Statesman*, 14 March 1936; LS, p. 24; 'Autumn Song', SP58, p. 32; CP, p. 139; EA, p. 159.

This lyric is one of the best examples in Auden's work of the combination of musicality and pictorialism with an essentially angular and symbolical imagination. The result, as critics have remarked, reminds us of Blake. And the theme is a Blakean one, too, of the daunting and reproving bonds of environment, and of the ideal world of the imagination, 'From whose cold cascading streams | None may drink except in dreams.' In Kallman's copy of *Look, Stranger!* Auden noted: 'cribbed from a pupil 10 yrs old'. See the untitled poem by R. H. Corson in *The Badger* I, 1 (Spring 1933): lines 5–6 run 'Now the snow is falling fast, | Nurse's flowers will not last.' In general, the quality of contributions to *The Badger* suggests that Auden was as likely to

contribute to his pupils' work as to steal from them. The poem was set by
Britten in his song cycle *On This Island* (1938).

The earth turns over, our side feels the cold

December 1933; *New Verse*, February 1934; LS, p. 25; 'Through the Looking-Glass',
CP45, p. 113; CP, p. 122; EA, p. 144.

The situation behind this poem (Auden's love for the fourteen-and-a-half-
year-old boy whose portrait, painted by the Downs School art master, is
described in the second stanza) has to be understood before the poem itself
can be fully understood. The first stanza, with its atmosphere of Donne's
'Nocturnal upon St Lucy's Day', sets the tone of cold and stasis within which
operate the 'shifts of love' to which the poet has been put. The setting is an
end-of-term Christmas party, a moment of necessary decision about what
the poet's love is going to mean. It can be 'wooded' or 'stony' (stanza 2),
depending not so much on conventional good fortune in love but on the
poet's decisive attitude to what he sees in the 'looking-glass' of the boy's
portrait. Essentially the twenty-six-year-old poet is in danger of seeing a
younger version of himself ('the mirror world where logic is reversed')
because as his reading of Freud had clearly taught him, in the process of
inescapable identification with the mother, the homosexual falls narcissis-
tically in love with images of himself as he was when his ego originally failed
satisfactorily to give up his first love object, the mother (see Freud, *Group
Psychology and the Analysis of the Ego*, 1922, p. 66). The forceful presence of
the poet's family in this dream scenario (stanza 3) acknowledges that the
problem is a psychological one belonging to the poet, and that the
quotidian reality of the boy (stanza 4: 'Love's daytime kingdom which I say
you rule'), though it is as morally censored as the school environment itself,
is as equally real as the world of the poet's family in which the poet is the
one who is loved. Thus loving and being loved are distinct and alike only in
being 'dreams' (stanza 6), within which the poet might pretend that he is
still a child, and outside which time moves inexorably onwards, the boy in
danger of losing his beauty while nothing in the relationship is accom-
plished. The final stanzas, with their beautiful images of life as a journey by
sea in which all landmarks have been lost, break away from this dream-
haunted dilemma. If you try to steer in a storm, you will break your rudder.
Better to let the storm blow itself out, and you may still reach your
destination. In practical terms, this means waiting until the poet and the boy

can meet as equals (in the final stanza 'Free to our favours' was 'Meeting as equals' in a draft) since the age difference between, say thirty-four and twenty-two is not so threatening as that between twenty-six and fourteen (Auden was thirty-two when he later met the eighteen-year-old Kallman). Among others, the poems 'Let the florid music praise', 'Dear, though the night is gone' and 'Lay your sleeping head, my love' were written for the same boy.

Now from my window-sill I watch the night

February 1932; 'A Happy New Year' (Part II), *New Country*, 1933; LS, p. 28; 'Not All the Candidates Pass', CP45, p. 83; 'The Watchers', CP, p. 63; EA, p. 115.

This second part of 'A Happy New Year' provides a meditation and prayer appropriate to the return to the real world of Larchfield School, Helensburgh, after the surreal visionary satire of Part I, but Auden never reprinted the latter after the complete poem's appearance in *New Country* and reduced the former's fifteen stanzas to thirteen and finally to eight in the collected editions, losing the school setting entirely. Writing to his brother John on 20 November 1931, he remarked: 'To-night is Friday night when the chaps come to play Badminton and to talk about big-ends.' The line in the poem about the badminton players (line 65) was borrowed from the dedicatory verses to *The Fronny*, addressed to John Auden, as also were lines 11–12, 14 and 48–9 (see *Plays*, p. 486). The names in stanza 13 may all be fictional: Alexis is a traditional pastoral name, and Favel is the figure of Flattery found in many medieval poems, notably in Skelton's *The Bowge of Court*, a poem which also influenced 'A Happy New Year', part I.

If 'the Great Bear | Hangs as a portent' it may be intended to allude to Soviet Russia. 'China's drum' is also a prophecy ignored by the 'blood [moving] strangely in its moving home'. China was virtually in a state of civil war in 1931. Auden borrows a phrase here from M. Hutton's translation of *Agricola* (Loeb edn, 1914), 35: 'he was more sanguine than they and deaf to all prophecies of ill [*firmus adversis*].' Agricola, of course, was notably successful in crushing the last Scottish resistance at Mons Gropius. The prospects of political revolution are considered with greater scepticism than in the other poems of Auden's in *New Country*. Auden makes his appeal elsewhere, to the 'Lords of Limit', begetters of Titt and Tool in 'In the year of my youth . . .' and of the Witnesses in *The Chase* and *The Dog Beneath the Skin*.

The particular appellation 'Lords of Limit' may derive from Blake, in whose system the Limits of Opacity and Contraction (Satan and Adam) were 'fixed as an act of mercy by the divine Savour, to put bounds to error'. But as the Witnesses (cf. the latest title, 'The Watchers') these 'influential quiet twins' are more particularly the ancient Kabiri, mysterious watchers at the procreation of children, the gods of gateposts, guardians of things held apart to make a space. They are the originators of 'property' in the sense of propriety, that which makes something itself and not something else ('From whom integrity begins' in the draft). Auden got these ideas from D. H. Lawrence's *Apocalypse* (1931), chapter xiv, and something of the sexual implications must have appealed to him in his own stated role as a 'watcher', a beneficent guardian in an institution of male adolescents. 'Witnesses' or 'twins' are Latin euphemisms for testes (see J. N. Adams, *The Latin Sexual Vocabulary*), so that the acquired integrity of his pupils ('Who to their serious season must shortly come', line 55) is only superficially the vocational future that the following stanza describes. In reality it is their sexual integrity that Auden is talking about (Lawrence described the twin gods as '[holding] the phallic balance forever', *Apocalypse*, p. 69).

In a stanza cancelled from the *New Country* text, Auden asks the Watchers to especially remember 'The Lindens, Ferntower, Westoe'. These were local houses: 'The Lindens' (3 Victoria Road) belonged to Arthur Wedgwood, Chairman of the Directors of Larchfield School, whose son Derek was a friend of Auden's and had been a pupil at Larchfield between 1919 and 1926: 'Ferntower' (6 Woodend Street) belonged to the Snodgrass family (Mrs Snodgrass is 'the Mop' in the first ode of *The Orators*, and Auden was very friendly with her son, Arnold); 'Westoe' (55 John Street) belonged to John Heys Strang.

In the final stanzas Auden alludes to Lawrence's description of death in terms of its ultimate violation of the twin gods in a 'pagan Saturnalia' (for the idea behind lines 68–9 see *Apocalypse*, p. 69: 'The bodies of the slain two lie unburied for three and a half days . . . when all decency and restraint has departed from among men'). It is because they are the enemies of licence that the twins make life possible: they are enabling but also limiting forces. Auden sees them as entirely necessary (compare his 'Ode to Terminus') and appeals to them to continue to use their power so that none 'break uncontrollably away'. Lawrence was more ambivalent:

The Apocalypse shows us what we are resisting, unnaturally. We are unnaturally resisting our connection with the cosmos, with the world,

with mankind, with the nation, with the family . . . we must break away
. . . we call that being free, being individual. Beyond a certain point,
which we have reached, it is suicide. Perhaps we have chosen suicide.

(*Apocalypse*, p. 103)

But Auden had already moved away from Lawrence on this issue. The
Airman in *The Orators* was a particular example of the fatal result of
breaking uncontrollably away.

Just as his dream foretold, he met them all

May, 1934; *Bryanston Saga*, Summer 1934; LS, p. 31; 'Nobody Understands Me',
CP45, p. 72; 'A Misunderstanding', CSP66, p. 77; CP, p. 125; EA, p. 148.

This sonnet had a passing existence in a longer sequence (see EA, p. 423)
confirming its ultimate role as a poem of frustrated love (the loved one is
the loved one of 'The earth turns over . . .', 'Lay your sleeping head, my
love' and other poems of this period). It begins with the elusive sense of *déjà
vu* of dreams: the garage-boy, the botanist and the deaf girl symbolise that
power of the external world to conspire with the individual's intuition of the
ordained, which itself is a metaphor for the inevitability of love. This
meaning is made evident in the sestet, where the lovers' roles are not clearly
understood: which is the strong partner, most fitted to give the 'stroking
and advice'? It should be the dreamer (i.e. the poet) because he is wiser and
older, but the dream is telling him that he should not be so sure.

The final line suggests a psycho-political context for the dream's
metaphor: compare 'physician, bridegroom and incendiary' with the
'lancet, speech or gun' of the dedicatory poem to *The Dog Beneath the Skin*,
a roughly contemporary piece which is quite clearly about the resources
needed to redeem a dangerous and corrupt society. This triad is capitalised
in a copy of the poem sent to *Life and Letters*, underlining the unignorable
riddling subtext of Father, Son and Holy Ghost. The dreamer may then
have the typical inflated super-ego of the Auden ante-type who believes
himself to be God, or at least a welcomed redeemer (for a discussion of this
tempting role, see Mendelson, chapter xi). The professor may in reality
have 'been' a characteristic Auden father-figure (T. F. Coade, headmaster
of Bryanston School, where Auden had recently failed to secure a job: see
Carpenter, p. 174). The fairy-tale green château out of *Beauty and the Beast*
may in the terms of the dream be 'really' a nursing home and the girl
apparently deaf because she is a nurse trained to ignore the ravings of the

patients. Interpretations of such contributory elements are very much left to the individual reader in this poem. What is important is that the mood of mystery and anxiety in the vehicle is seen to contribute to the elusive sense of reversal in the tenor of the poem: any confidence of spiritual enrichment in the relationship is thwarted by the undermining of the lover's confidence. Auden considered the title 'At Each Meeting' for the 1966 *Collected Shorter Poems.*

As it is, plenty

Summer, 1936; LS, p. 32; 'His Excellency', CP45, p. 17; CP, p. 145; EA, p. 163.

In his 'Letter to William Coldstream, Esq' Auden wrote: 'And we read the short stories of Somerset Maugham aloud to each other I And the best one was called *His Excellency*' (*Letters from Iceland*, p. 225). In the story, a suave ambassador, Sir Herbert Witherspoon, admits to an affair with Alix, a music-hall acrobat. This affair had for him a challenging erotic vibrancy that leads him to conclude that the rest of his professionally successful life, with its calculated marriage to a beautiful woman from a good family, has been so much waste and boredom ('sometimes it seemed intolerable to live for ever and ever behind a mask, sometimes he felt he couldn't bear it. But he bore it.') Auden returns to the short line and half-rhyme for this oblique portrait, in which the generalised detail ('the work and the banks', 'the betraying smile' and so on) suggests a recasting of the attitude in *Poems* (1930), or at least a desire to escape too specific a reliance on the Maugham story. However, its elements are recognisable, particularly in the second stanza, where elegant and uncompromising ruthlessness is held in balance with a sense of lightly accomplished betrayal – a perfect match for the tone of bitter comedy in Maugham. The homosexual application needs no comment: Auden said to Ansen on 17 December 1946 that the ambassador's girl was really a boy. 'Venal' was corrected to 'venial' in later collections. The lyrical repetitions were finely underlined by the sinisterly jaunty syncopations of Britten's setting in his song cycle *On this Island* (1938).

A shilling life will give you all the facts

?1934; *Rep*, April 1934; LS, p. 33; 'Who's Who', CP45, p. 17; CP, p. 126; EA, p. 150.

This sonnet seems to have been prompted by Basil Liddell Hart's biography of T. E. Lawrence, which Auden reviewed in *Now and Then*, no. 47, Spring

1934 (EA, p. 320) and by a passage in Proust's *Sodome et Gomorrhe* (see Davenport-Hines, pp. 123–5). It examines the real nature and desires of the popular hero, desires which, like Lawrence's, are seen finally to be for the ordinary and the mundane. The contrast between the athletic and the suburban conforms absolutely to Auden's theory about the Truly Weak and the Truly Strong Man, while the poem's temporary appearance in a sequence of ultimately personal love poems (see EA, p. 423) suggests that the 'astonished critics' represent the poet's own ironic sense of the disproportion between the strength of his feelings and the loved one's ultimate obliviousness to them. Auden developed this idea of the really heroic appearing unexceptional in a number of different ways. Compare 'The Quest' in *The Double Man*, especially Sonnet XVI. Davenport-Hines, p. 123, has pointed out that the relationship is based on an episode in Proust.

Brothers, who when the sirens roar

August, 1932; 'A Communist to Others', *Twentieth Century*, September 1932; *New Country*, 1933; LS, p. 34; EA, p. 120.

Auden cut six stanzas from this poem and made other significant changes before putting it into *Look, Stranger!* He entirely deleted it from the copy of the collection which he gave to Kallman in September 1939, and never reprinted it (when allowing it to appear in Robin Skelton's Penguin *Poetry of the Thirties*, 1964, it was on condition that it was made clear that it was one of five poems which were 'trash' that he was ashamed to have written: the other four were 'Sir, no man's enemy, forgiving all', 'August for the people and their favourite islands', 'Spain 1937' and 'September 1, 1939'). The *Twentieth Century* text is reprinted in a twenty-page symposium in *Auden Studies* 1, pp. 174–95, to which the reader is referred for its extremely detailed commentary.

The poem is an exercise in ventriloquised vitriolics. Auden was not a communist in any actual sense ('No. I am a bourgeois. I shall not join the CP': letter to Rupert Doone of October 1932). Whatever now seems inconsistent or self-deceiving about the political attitudes revealed in the poem, there is no doubt of its contemporary shock-value and the uncompromising terms in which the 'enemy' is identified ('the great malignant | Cambridge ulcer', etc.). Critics of its mixed diction might remember, too, that poetic language before Auden was rarely so rich. 'Cops' and 'talkie-houses' in stanza 1 may suggest Americanisms, but the

latter was the way the Helensburgh cinemas were described on posters at
the time. 'Done . . . brown' (stanza 4, misprinted in LS) means cheated.
'Columbines and pathics' (stanza 14) mixes centuries and jargons to refer
to female and male prostitutes. 'Stuma' (stanza 12) is stumer, a dud. The
language doesn't really pretend to be other than public school, as if to make
its gut-appeal to the objects of its hatred through an infection of their
idiolect ('sacked', 'buffers', 'it isn't cricket', 'bounder', 'little squirt', 'aren't-
I-charming', 'smarmy', 'jolly decent', etc.). The style itself ranges from
Shakespeare ('Their daughters sterile be in rut', stanza 15) through Skelton
('That army intellectual/ Of every kind of liberal', stanza 9) to Ira Gershwin
('which we enumer', stanza 12). The form of the poem is not the Burns
stanza, but it was certainly one that had been used in Scotland in the
eighteenth century (e.g. by Mary A. Barr). The attitudes themselves were to
be dramatised in *The Dance of Death*, and some details are similar (including
the echo of Plotinus in the attack on mysticism in stanza 9; see p. 124).
Mysticism is a failure. What the capitalist classes really require are the
ordinary pleasures of self-regard: 'Love and music and bed and board |
While the world flounders' (stanza 10). This view is instructive to compare
with that of 'Out on the lawn I lie in bed', whose own 'vision' is self-
confessedly the privilege of those 'whom hunger does not move'.

The chimneys are smoking, the crocus is out in the border

April, 1932; 'Poem', *New Country*, 1933; LS, p. 38; 'Two Worlds', CSP50; EA, p. 116.

The opening lines of the *New Country* text ('Me, March, you do with your
movements master and rock | With wing-whirl, whale-wallow, silent budding
of cell') were obviously abandoned as too ecstatically Hopkinsian. Curiously
enough, however, as if to maintain the tribute, Auden substituted a more
direct allusion to Hopkins (the 'blue March day' comes from 'The Loss of
the Eurydice', line 21, where it is named a 'a liar'; similarly for Auden, the
early spring brings only loss). He then changed the 'communist' into the
'political' orator and 'our Reds' to 'the Reds', perhaps because the earlier
epithets gave too loaded a distinction between the 'two worlds' of the later
title. These worlds are the public and private world each concerned in its
different way with the mysterious 'carried thing' of stanza 3, i.e. one's share
of the Life Force which (by analogy with Plato's theory of the split soul) 'fits'
with that of the loved one. Solving the sublime jigsaw brings an illusory unity
with nature (stanza 4), the widest form of the public world, illusory because

it is governed by 'the white death', who is seen in stanza 6 to have the cruel interest of a Thomas Hardy in the ironies of the human condition. Auden's proposal, in the rest of the poem, is to defeat death's hideous little scenario by affecting an unconcern at separation. He trusts that if millions like himself have the desire to transcend fate through love, that trust itself (including his equivocal love of nature which, being stronger than they are, takes no interest in the lovers' separation) will in some strange and devious way ('crooked'), perhaps like the communism which lurks as a sub-text in the poem, achieve a co-operative end. It perhaps should be noted that although the political orator lands 'like a sea god' (stanza 1), the sea is actually 'ungovernable' (stanza 7). The poem therefore ends with a dance, not of death but of life, celebrating the joy that cannot be suppressed by estrangement. It is a joy in plotted routes and boundaries, games, channeled forces, and chance (stanza 10), all ways of acknowledging the real power of what is ungovernable in nature but at the same time of taking human pleasure in pretending to circumvent it.

May with its light behaving

1934; *Listener*, 15 May 1935; LS, p. 41; CP45, p. 214; 'May', CSP66, p. 79; CP, p. 127; EA, p. 152.

Auden's genius for parading dense meaning in the pictorial lyric reached a high point in the mid-1930s. Spring is conventionally regenerating, and here seems to symbolise a dawning of maturity ('The real world lies before us'), both personal and historical. On the personal level, the awakening is sexual. The ambiguous grammar of 'light' in line 1, and the double meaning of 'vessel' (implying both yachts in the sun, and tumescence), give to the 'careless picnics' a particularly erotic flavour. Stanza 2 shows that idyll is predicated by the historical landscape, by the escape from medieval forests and by the *felix culpa* of the enlightenment ('The dangerous apple taken' is itself taken from 'Adam lay ibowndyn', which Auden printed in *The Oxford Book of Light Verse*, p. 50: 'ne hadde the appil take ben, | the appil taken ben'). The idyll is therefore an illusory one; this is because the 'real world' is now one in which the subconscious motive is understood, and love no longer compellingly self-sufficient. The neuroses laid bare in stanza 3 lurk behind the natural impulses in stanza 4 to bring home the insufficiency of those natural urges; these cannot account for the lost world of traditional morality represented earlier by the fairy-tale 'angel vampires'. The freedom gained is seen as debilitating: the psychologically ill are only 'willing' to recover, the picnics are 'careless', because sex has become a recurrent panacea, an indulgence.

Here on the cropped grass of the narrow ridge I stand

1933; 'The Malverns', *New Oxford Outlook*, November 1933; *Dynamo*, Summer 1934; LS, p. 42; EA, p. 141.

In this poem Auden has begun to move confidently from his analysis of the psyche to his analysis of the country at large, with his customary panoptic view, the tone very much that of the healer precariously healed, momentarily confident to offer a general diagnosis. One can see this tone in the opening here, where the scenarios of earlier poems like 'Who stands, the crux left of the watershed' or 'Taller today, we remember similar evenings' have been reinterpreted in the light of a confident, inquiring simplicity. The irony of 'happy each thought the other, thinking of a crime' (stanza 2) is much more than the mere coming to terms with a sexual proclivity that was indeed a criminal offence at the time. It is part of a continued suggestion in his poetry that man is conscious of his fallen situation, conscious of belonging and not belonging to the nature he has ruined.

It is this inescapable tie that produces some of the most poignant moments in Auden. For a time in the 1930s, England itself became a kind of macro-symbol of fallen nature, and to express it, Auden had to learn a new kind of geographical language. The range of reference he found possible in 'In the year of my youth . . .' helped him, and passages from that poem found their way into this one (line 2 from 11.37; lines 30–34 from 1.251–3; lines 53–4 from 1.474–5). Abergavenny's Sugarloaf mountain is borrowed from Anthony Collett, *The Changing Face of England* (1932 edn), p. 94. For lines 55–6, 'The high thin rare continuous worship | Of the self-absorbed' see Gerald Heard, *The Social Substance of Religion* (1931), pp. 274ff: Christian worship once it had become the Mass and ceased to be Agape became a solitary and continuous activity, instead of a group celebration. It is linked with cinemas as part of Heard's attack on 'city culture'.

The geographical range natural to the poet's position on the Malvern Hills is now matched by a similar range in time: images of the hope and deceit of history are a natural consequence of musing upon archaeology and upon the civilisation of the Greeks (stanzas 6–7) and Auden returns to the theme of *The Dance of Death*, his class's love-affair with their own spiritual defeat. The stanzas in tercets are borrowed from an unpublished poem, 'Friend, of the civil space by human love' (see Mendelson, pp. 241ff), and they provide an analysis of the 'fall' in terms that were to become familiar in Auden's work: it is an alienation aggravated by the Enlightenment, when 'luxury', science and progress induced men to believe themselves heroes of reason but led only to a mechanised hatred and (in particular) to the First World War (in the LS text, 'war' at line 101 should be 'the war'). To remind us that the writer himself must be heroic, Auden reintroduces the Owen allusion with which he had concluded the 'Journal of an Airman' in *The Orators*: 'my nerves in order'. Owen himself ('Wilfred') and Katherine Mansfield ('Kathy') are adopted as intimate colleagues in this literary endeavour of forever 'returning' to the real world in order to redeem it in art (see *Lions and Shadows*, p. 72, for Isherwood's and Upward's adoption of these writers at Cambridge).

The sun shines down on the ships at sea

July 1932; 'To a Young Man on his 21st Birthday', *New Oxford Outlook*, May 1933; LS, p. 47; EA, p. 120.

The seven-stanza version of this poem in *Look, Stranger!* was cut down from the fifteen-stanza version in the *New Oxford Outlook*, and apparently omitted in error this final stanza which Auden added to the copy he gave to Kallman in 1939 (before deleting the whole poem, which he never reprinted):

> If we can't love, though miles apart,
> If we can't trust with all our heart,
> If we can't do that, then we're in the cart.

Presumably Auden felt that the poem with its popular idiom (and uncertain tone) looked a little facile in its reduced form. The Lady Diana/banana rhyme was borrowed from a song of the period. He more effectively used 'Let wishes be horses' for Tom Rakewell coming dangerously into his inheritance in *The Rake's Progress*, 1.i. There is an unpublished setting of the poem by Britten.

To lie flat on the back with the knees flexed

?1933; LS, p. 48; 'What's the Matter?', CP45, p. 143; EA, p. 149.

This was another sonnet which Auden put into the sequence he sent to Isherwood in 1934. It was set by Britten, but the setting remains unpublished. The speaker and a friend are sunbathing on a roof, cocooned from the 'casual life outside the heart' but aware of a mounting sexual tension that returns them in a new sense to the social roles ('to cower or to bully') which they had been able to abandon in their relaxation. 'Sidewalks' is an unusual Americanism.

Fleeing the short-haired mad executives

?Summer 1933; 'Poem', *New Oxford Outlook*, November 1933; LS, p. 49; 'The Climbers', CP45, p. 41; 'Two Climbs', CSP50, p. 56; CP, p. 124; EA, p. 149.

This sonnet was included in the 1934 sequence sent to Isherwood, and was written for the same person as 'The earth turns over . . .' with which it shares the idea of a mirror image of love revealing confused psychological motivation in the lover. The 'mad executives' come from 'In the year of my youth . . .' II.154 (the convincing 'made executives' in the 1950 *Collected Shorter Poems* is a misprint). In the source poem, as Lucy McDiarmid has shown, the 'lonely unstable mad executives' derive from Gerald Heard's *The Social Substance of Religion*, p. 66 ('the growth of an outer, executive, unstable side of man's nature'). Here, the 'short-haired . . . executives' may owe something to P. C. Wren's preference for the 'short-haired executive type' of novelist (Q. D. Leavis, *Fiction and the Reading Public*,, 1932, p. 52). The allegorical mountain is the inherent difficulty of the relationship (see my commentary on 'The earth turns over . . .'). In the octave the poet fails on his own to achieve a transcendent sublimation of his love and his consolation is a relapse into the pride of possessiveness. In the sestet sublimation seems hardly the point, but the mirror of their eyes (in which they see themselves 'left-handed') creates a barrier beyond which sexually ('the rich interior') they dare not go. Auden had written about this barrier in an early poem 'Narcissus', where the 'left-handed lover' is despaired of not only because heterosexual (as is the case in this sonnet) but because he is an image of the poet himself cast in a narcissistic role (see also 'left-handed and ironic' in *The Orators*, EA, p. 86). See also my commentary on 'It was Easter as I walked in the public gardens' (p. 59).

Easily, my dear, you move, easily your head

November 1934; 'A Bride in the 30's', *Listener*, 20 February 1935; LS, p. 50; CP, p. 128; EA, p. 152.

This poem was also included in the 1934 sequence that Auden sent to Isherwood, and the same young man is in question, not a 'bride' in the usual sense (see Mendelson, pp. 222ff) but someone who is similarly entering upon his maturity and sexual heritage. The dedication to Isherwood's friend and employer Olive Mangeot is something of a red herring. The European scale of this poem was afforced (as was *The Dog Beneath the Skin*) by Auden's visit with the young man (and one other) to eastern Europe in the summer of 1934. See 'In Search of Dracula', *The Badger* II, 4, Autumn 1934, pp. 21–4 and III, 5, Spring 1935, pp. 16–18, reprinted in *Auden Studies* 2 which suggests that there would actually have resulted a shared album of photographs ('Mutual photography'), and the poem 'Since' (commentary on p. 513). The 'sixteen skies of Europe' were borrowed from 'In the year of my youth . . .' 1.5, and probably represent Portugal, Spain, France, Switzerland, Italy, Belgium, Luxemburg, Netherlands, Germany, Austria, Czechoslovakia, Poland, Hungary, Yugoslavia, Albania and Greece (omitting Britain, of course, and also Bulgaria and Romania, the countries of 'the Danube flood').

The poem elaborates in a wider personal and public context the conclusion of 'May with its light behaving': 'Before the evil and the good | How insufficient is | Touch, endearment, look.' It explores this insufficiency by showing that love both retreats from the world of public morality and is yet, half-aware, the creator of it. It is easy to feel that love has no responsibility to its environment (stanzas 2 and 3) and exists for itself alone. It is able to ignore the architecture of Nazi Germany, even to make fun of it, as Auden tended to do, albeit for a schoolboy audience, in 'In Search of Dracula' (despite its homosexual sense, the 'pansy' railway in line 9 is merely affectedly dolled up; compare the Germans who go off to have their hair done 'All pansied up in helmets, goggles and fur coats', *Auden Studies* 2, p. 23). For the 'terrifying mottoes' of line 13, see *ibid*, p. 21: 'One Folk: One Leader: One Yes', etc.

And yet the music of love's dance summons unignorable images of reality. The enlarged sensibility (stanza 4) cannot avoid contemplating the real world (stanzas 5 and 6) from which images like newspaper photographs press in upon the rapt lover (in the draft at Texas it is 'Stalin at the microphone' and in the following pages of the notebook Auden proceeds significantly to draft the Westland dictator's speech from *The Dog Beneath the Skin*). Stanza 7 asserts that society is conditioned by the will of the individual, that Hitler and Mussolini and the rest are somehow the product of inadequate and stunted private love, and that the child's conditioning narrows his choice and puts limits to his natural desires (stanzas 8 and 9). If our love-choices are even to this extent determined (and stanza 10 is very like Donne's theory in 'Air and Angels'), it is imperative that the individual should be aware of the deep division between his private desires and the public good that should result from them. Erotic love is insufficient because it does not care (and Auden wishes it did) if its object is van der Lubbe or Hitler, scapegoat or tyrant (stanza 11). These symbolic examples come from a political world that did affect Auden deeply (Maurice Feild remembered: 'When the Reichstag was burnt down most people thought it was the work of the communists, Wystan was furious and deathly white: he knew better'). Eros is like the civil servant who can do nothing but put into effect a particular political programme (stanza 7). If 'the engaging face is the face of the betrayer' (stanza 13), as it was to an extent to be for Auden in the case of Kallman, there is nothing to be done about it (for 'the beautiful interest', see 'O Love, the interest itself in thoughtless heaven'). Eros cannot itself recognise (stanza 14) that man is a superior animal with a moral sense and 'the language of learning' and, above all, with a power to choose, through love, the kind of society he wishes to have. The poem ends by stressing what seems to be a quasi-religious choice in quasi-religious terms, and it should be stressed that 'crooked' and 'straight' here should have no sexual connotations (as in 'crook' for homosexual in a quatrain about Robert Bridges printed in *A Tribute*, p. 79). The choice is a straightforwardly ethical antinomy making humanity the toy of the gods, on trial for its life.

Night covers up the rigid land

March 1936; 'Two Songs' 1, LS, p. 53; EA, p. 162.

The first of 'Two Songs' dedicated to Benjamin Britten and set by him (although the setting of this one was not known in Britten's lifetime) laments an unreciprocated love in terms of the solipsistic isolation of dreams. Auden has returned to his Housman manner of ten years earlier, and had obviously been rereading the early poems he wrote in German:

lines 13–15 and 19–20 derive from lines 5, 6, 8 and 12 of 'Lacrimae Rerum' ('Denn jede Liebe hat ihr eigene Lage | Und jeder Art von Liebe denkt an sich . . . Du liebst dein Leben und ich liebe Dich . . . Mein Traum von Dir mit Dir hat nicht zu tun.' See *Auden Studies* 1, p. 4. It would appear, in addition, that Auden translated parts of the sonnet back into English. See the 1928–?30 notebook, the draft of the last poem, 'My love has its own habitation'). In a Berg notebook the drafts of 'Night covers up the rigid land' follow the poem 'Dear, though the night is gone', itself specifically modelled on a real dream about the young man of 'The earth turns over . . .' and other poems. It is not at all certain therefore (*pace* Carpenter, p. 188) that it is addressed to Britten himself.

Underneath the abject willow

March 1936; 'Two Songs' 2, LS, p. 54; CP, p. 140; EA, p. 160.

Britten's setting of this second of 'Two Songs' was published in 1937. He scores it for two voices, thus giving a societal emphasis to what in the poem might read as a simple *carpe diem* injunction. The poem reflects the predominantly tranquil passionate mood of Auden's love lyrics in this period. The first line is taken from the early poem 'I chose this lean country' in *Poems* (1928), where in a rather less convincing mood of prophetic gloom Auden had reflected 'how everyman | Shall strain and be undone, | Sit, querulous and sallow | Under the abject willow.' Though it ignores arguments about the gulf between the human and the instinctive life which so frequently figures in Auden's poetry, this later lyric is an invigorating attack on the lover's 'unique and moping station', and has been taken by critics to be addressed to Britten, at that time notoriously timid in affairs of the heart. Auden remembered the image of the brooks meeting together in the ocean of the general human life in his words for the lonely Inkslinger in *Paul Bunyan* (*Libretti*, p. 28).

To settle in this village of the heart

May 1934; 'Poem', *New Verse*, June 1934; LS, p. 55; 'It's So Dull Here', CP45, p. 144; EA, p. 151.

This poem was included in the sequence of love poems which Auden sent to Isherwood in 1934, and therefore is about the young man of 'The earth turns over . . .' and other poems. The *New Verse* text is much more explicitly a *paysage moralisé* with its 'trunk-roads of fear', 'greed's thin cafés', 'sham ornamentation of the feelings', 'strident swimming-pool of the senses', and 'thoughts | Dressed up identically in townee smartness'. No doubt Auden felt that the autobiographical allegory was in danger of being over-explicit: the manor house turned into a commercial pub already clearly represents the substitution of casual affairs for the unique parental love of pre-adolescence in the 'heart' of the speaker. The ultimate appeal is close in intention to the final stanzas of 'Easily, my dear, you move, easily your head', with its assertion that love should be the desire for true neighbour-hood not 'the irresponsible beauty of the stranger'.

O for doors to be open and an invite with gilded edges

?Spring 1935; 'In the Square', *Spectator*, 31 May 1935; LS, p. 56; CP, p. 135; EA, p. 154.

This poem is about art as wish-fulfilment. We are all in a sense beggared cripples, and their fantasies are our fantasies. But ultimately art cannot make these fantasies real: the statue is silent. The title suggests that the public, even political standing of the statue might give credence to the beggars' appeal. However, the personal nature of the wishes and the colourfulness of their attendant myths more or less prevent the poem from having a political force. Even the surprising fifth stanza, with its anti-Semitic nuance, cannot carry that suggestion powerfully enough outside the fairy-tale terms of its dream-metamorphosis: these are 'beggared cripples' not 'crippled beggars', i.e. it is psychology not economics which first defeats us. Though it is largely an exercise in an inventively sensuous exuberance, the Yeatsian refrain and its symbolism reinforce the serious meaning of the poem. Some of the phrases come from Grose's *Classical Dictionary of the Vulgar Tongue* which Auden had read when writing *The Orators*: 'lobcock' (a large relaxed penis) occurs there, as does 'To follow like a tantony [St Antony] pig', i.e. to follow close at one's heels.

Only the hands are living; to the wheel attracted

April 1936; 'Casino', LS, p. 58; CP, p. 146; EA, p. 164.

Auden here uses the metaphor of gamblers to represent a lost generation; fortune to them is an oasis in a waste land, to which they are attracted as to a religion (stanza 3). The poem proposes that they have resigned their will, and retained only their appetite (which remains unsatisfied, stanza 2). The casino is sterile: no Minotaur, no clue; not even the consolation of art (the fountain, the laurel). The gods have departed, 'and what was godlike in this generation | Was never to be born' (compare the refrain of ' "O who can ever gaze his fill" ', written later in the same year).

That night when joy began

November 1931; *Twentieth Century*, November 1933; LS, p. 59; CP, p. 58; EA, p. 113.

These twelve brief lines yield a most ingenious metaphor. Night is associated with sexual tumescence ('narrowest veins'), morning with the end of the one-night stand. The lovers expect to be challenged by the morning as by a sentry, but, unbelievably, peace has been made: now they can see no end to their love. The poem was written for his Helensburgh 'chum' (see Carpenter, p. 131).

Fish in the unruffled lakes

March 1936; *Listener*, 15 April 1936; LS, p. 60; CP, p. 138; EA, p. 162.

This fine lyric (set by Britten, who published the setting in 1937) celebrates an act of love in terms of a union of human attributes with animal ones: the beautiful animal merely acts and is gone, despite its beauty; man is self-conscious, aware of time and of the obligations of morality, envious of the animal. But the third stanza shows that man does have animal beauty, and that his conscious surrender to its powers ('voluntary love') can have a beauty of its own. It may be argued that this surrender must be contrasted with the unwilled appetites of the creatures, but Auden makes it an addition to his lover's animal gifts.

Dear, though the night is gone

March 1936; 'The Dream', *New Verse*, April–May 1936; LS, p. 61; 'A Dream', SP58, p. 30; CP, p. 137; EA, p. 161.

The dream presented here shows itself capable of the Freudian interpretation that the loved one confessing another love must mean the unconscious desire of the lover to break off the affair himself. The pressures inherent in the situation are symbolised in the poem by the presence of the other couples, inert and hostile: though the room is timeless ('Our whisper woke no clocks'), it is crowded with beds and 'lofty as | A railway terminus', cunningly suggesting that it is here that partners are changed like trains. The dream was a real one, and is described, with interpretations, in a notebook (Berg). The loved one is the young man of 'The earth turns over . . .' and other poems of the early 1930s. The drafts of the poem follow after one intervening leaf in the notebook, beginning with the final stanza.

Love had him fast, but though he fought for breath

?Summer 1933; 'Five Poems' v, *New Verse*, October 1933; LS, p. 62; 'Meiosis', CP45, p. 79; CP, p. 125; EA, p. 150.

Auden included this sonnet as the final poem in a sequence of love poems which he collected together in 1934 (see EA, pp. 423–4). The subject of the sequence was the young man addressed in 'The earth turns over . . .'. It elaborates, with a full biological symbolism, the theory lurking in so many poems of the period that love can be an essentially selfish and predatory force, working to obstruct the free and natural development of society. The lover is ensnared by his struggle 'to possess Another' because he imagines that his goal is possession, whereas the final purpose ('the snare') is forgotten in the pleasure of orgasm ('the little death').

The purpose is the evolutionary development of the species, advanced by the cycles of reproduction which 'love' controls. Auden addresses the spermatozoon which has been set free by the love that it has never heard of, and which can now 'set up building', i.e. impregnate the ovum. There the sense of useless heroic endeavour signalled by the allusion to the North-west Passage (cf. Isherwood's unfinished novel and the theory behind it in *Lions and Shadows*, pp. 206ff and Auden's essay 'Writing', EA, p. 309) is more appropriate to the doomed *Fronny*. The strange line about 'the all-night journey under sea' is an allusion to Frobenius, *Das Zeitalter des Sonnengottes* (1904) where the hero is born anew by virtue of eviscerating a monster who has swallowed him and swum east with him all night, symbolising the unconscious robbed of its energy. Auden could have read this account of 'the "night-journey under the sea" of Frobenius' in Jung's *Two Essays on Analytical Psychology*, trans. H. G. and C. F. Baynes (1928), p. 105. Lines 7–8 and a version of line 4 of the sonnet had been used in a long poem of February 1930 drafted in a Berlin notebook given to Wendell Johnson, p. 89, and also in stanza 3 of 'With northern winter snowballing season' from *The Fronny* (*Plays*, p. 477).

Behind this heroic act of the spermatozoon lies the whole of human history, which has, in a biological sense, only been a preparation for it ('Cities and years constricted to your scope'). At this moment the condition of man ('sorrow', cf. 'Hearing of harvests rotting in the valleys') is reduced to a single impulse of fertilisation: it is in this act that the future of the human race resides. And yet, when the fertilised egg is born and grows up, human history and human desire will once again seem as complex as before ('Shall be as subtle when you are as tall'), since the son will share all the delusions about love that the father was seen to have had at the beginning of the poem. But not quite all, the poem concludes, since evolution works continually to improve the race: the life force ('The flood on which all move and wish to move', a line that Auden seems to have borrowed from somewhere in Nietzsche) cannot be impeded by individual selfish demands of love ('Hopeful falsehood').

'Meiosis' is the process of chromosome reduction in gametes which are undergoing maturation. The son may be superior to the father since the spermatozoon only carries half the male chromosomes, and may therefore very well carry the better half. Auden had a few years earlier contrasted meiosis with mitosis in their psychological implications in a notebook diagram, concluding: 'The course of every natural desire is that of the orgasm. Being satisfied they desire their own death' (1928–?30 notebook). This comment provides a useful gloss on the sonnet, which in its temporary role in the sequence provided a culminating complex analysis of the relationship between the erotic urge and biological destiny. No doubt Auden had somewhere in mind Shakespeare's injunction to his heterosexual young man to have children.

August for the people and their favourite islands

August 1935; 'To a Writer on his Birthday', *New Verse*, October–November 1935; LS, p. 63; EA, p. 155.

Dedicated to Christopher Isherwood, this is one of the key autobiographical poems, consciously, even programmatically, dividing early Auden from the Auden of the later 1930s. Its rhetorical balance and open sense of structure and argument are based on a multitude of brilliantly observed details (a few of which are again borrowed from Anthony Collett. See *The Changing Face of England*, 1932 edn, pp. 245–6 for the origin of lines 5 and 65).

Nine years before, he and Isherwood became absorbed (wrongly, he concludes) in the fantasy worlds of *Paid on Both Sides* and of Mortmere, both merely reflections of their privileged environment. Isherwood has described Auden's visit in 1926 to the Isle of Wight, the poem's 'southern island, | Where the wild Tennyson became a fossil':

> I see him striding towards me, along Yarmouth Pier, a tall figure with loose violent impatient movements, dressed in dirty grey flannels and a black evening bow-tie . . . The black hat caused a considerable sensation in the village where I was staying. The village boys and girls, grouped along the inn wall by the bus stop, sniggered loudly as we got out of the bus. Weston was pleased: 'Laughter,' he announced, 'is the first sign of sexual attraction.'
>
> (*Lions and Shadows*, pp. 188–9)

It is plain that such Freudianism is one key to Auden's early use of fantasy. The felt hat appears in the poem, too (stanza 5), but it is turned into part of the apparatus of the spy, a direct conflation of disguise and erotic challenge. In the same stanza we hear that 'one laughed, and it was snow in bedrooms'. The allusion is to drugs, for 'coke', another slang word for cocaine, is mentioned in the preceding line. No doubt Auden's abundant sense of the sinister and unconsciously meaningful demanded that the sniggers at his hat should have this sexual, even unlawfully sexual, significance.

But this is dismissed, and so is the maturer role that 'love' played in his Homer Lane period: 'five summers pass', and love becomes an easy panacea, taming even the dragon of fascism (stanza 6). And yet the following stanza shows how even love is diverted by 'nerves' into jokes and lies (for 'thrushes' compare 'In the year of my youth . . .', 1.310, 'she sang like a bloody thrush'). The poem makes it clear that such 'flabby' fancies can no longer serve a poet who has responded to the urgency of social and political reality. It is almost suggested that poetry itself must yield to the documentary novel, to the 'strict and adult' pen of Isherwood, the task of making 'action urgent and its nature clear' (he also used this phrase in his introduction to *The Poet's Tongue*, 1935, where he was concerned to show how art must avoid being propaganda). However, the poem itself sweeps on to a strikingly personified anatomy of the current crisis modelled on Shakespeare's sonnet no. 66. Auden later singled out this effect as something impossible in the Petrarchan form: 'Shakespeare is able to give twelve single-line exempla of the wretchedness of this world and the horrors of lust, with an accumulative effect of great power' (*Forewords and Afterwords*, p. 96). Some of the details of stanzas 9 and 10 perhaps need comment: to stand at Weeping Cross is to fail badly, 'the green thumb to the ledger knuckled down' trades natural growth for financial drudgery (cf. Eliot's *The Confidential Clerk*), 'till St Geoffrey's Day' means never. Auden himself wrote to Nob Snodgrass on 21 February 1933 (his birthday): 'I am living miserably like a hen scratching miserably for food.' The feeling of justice and satirical understanding that Auden's exempla provide, combined with the sensuously evocative and frequently antithetical lines of the poem generally, gives the poem an Augustan flavour and therefore an unusual authority and directness in demanding, as a substitute for immature daydreams, a wholly committed literature.

Certainly our city – with the byres of poverty down to

Spring 1936; 'Europe 1936', *Time and Tide*, 23 May 1936; 'Epilogue', LS, p. 67; 'As We Like It', CP45, p. 25; 'Our City', CSP50, p. 41; EA, p. 165.

If *Look, Stranger!* began with the strangest of possible dreams, the transmission of love like an ancient culture (see the Prologue: 'O Love, the interest itself in thoughtless heaven') then it ends pessimistically in the real world with the healers dead and hatred in the ascendancy. The generalised portrait of the city in the opening stanza is reminiscent of that in 'In the year of my youth . . .', with its slums, cathedral and plate glass, and at the climax (line 33) Auden actually reuses the line from the end of the first canto of the earlier poem which sets human life in the context of a giant impersonal astronomical destiny: 'Rushed towards Lyra in a lion's charge' (1.925). The deeply ironical concluding phrase ('It's a world. It's a way'), implying that it's the only world we have and that our way with it had better change, was, so Auden noted in Kallman's copy of *On this Island*, 'A misheard crib from Stephen's translation of a poem of Hölderlin's'. This is likely to be 'The Short Poems' (*New Writing* 1, Spring 1936, p. 116) which contains, amid many rhetorical questions, the phrase: 'it's away, and the earth is cold'. The bulk of the Epilogue laments the passing of modern cultural heroes, now either dead or unheard, with material taken from an unpublished poem, 'Sweet is it,' say the doomed, 'to be alive though wretched' (posthumously printed in the *TLS*, 16 January 1976). The 'neat man' in stanza 4 is Lenin, who in 1932 had renamed the modernised Nizhny Novgorod as Gor'ky. Auden also said in a contemporary review (*Listener*, 22 April 1936) that the schoolmaster must be one of those who 'towards the really better world have turned their faces'.

Uncollected Poems 1930–36

Listen, Norman Wright

8 November 1930; *Auden Newsletter* 1, 1988, p. 3; *Auden Studies* 2, p. 17.

These sixteen lines using only one rhyme were written for Auden's Helensburgh pupil Norman Wright, an attempt to win over a boy who frankly found his English master unsympathetic (see Wright's account in the *Auden Newsletter*).

These also told their secrets to the hazels

?May 1931; *TLS*, 16 January 1976.

Much of this half-sympathetic, half-clinical observation of the 'warm lives coming into touch' of the young found its way into *The Orators* (for lines 2–3 and 7–8, see 'Journal of an Airman', EA, p. 85, and for lines 13 and 20, see Ode IV, antepenultimate and final lines, EA, p. 106). The suggestion is that their lives are being lived by forces that they do not acknowledge. For 'weasels' compare 'the confabulations of weasels' (*Plays*, p. 299).

For what as easy

October 1931; 'Poem', *New Signatures*, 1932; 'To You Simply', CSP50, p. 57; CP, p. 58; EA, p. 113.

This oblique lyric with its deliberately stumbling mode of expressing the difficulties of expression ('To you . . .', 'From me . . .') recreates a sense of instinctive gratitude for a happy love affair. It was written for his Helensburgh 'chum' (see Carpenter, p. 131) and might have found a place with 'That night when joy began' in *Look, Stranger!* were it not for its reliance on the Laura Riding manner, which he had at that time largely given up. Sex is seen as a necessary exchange, the inevitability cunningly suggested by the tautologous 'data given': data have to be given, therefore the senses have to be 'even', with the double sense of reciprocated and pacified. This idea is enforced by lines 14 and 16, omitted from the text in *Collected Shorter Poems*: the spirit ('ghost') has found a home and the tongue (mediating both between 'speech' and 'word', and 'ghost' and 'heart') its twin desire ('list'). In this way the early tentativeness is redeemed by the incisiveness of the final lines which are still about saying but in which the act of speech is wholly unified. The triangle of speaker, subject and listener is identical ('heart').

Bourgeois why are you looking so gay?

?1931; *TLS*, 16 January 1976.

Introducing the poem's first appearance, Edward Mendelson described it as 'perhaps a fragment from . . . *The Fronny*', but did not include it among the surviving fragments twelve years later in *Plays*. The poem is as simple and direct as it is possible to be in its attack on middle-class values, particularly on the bourgeois assumption of having a private pact with God. For 'Smoking, smugging, and self-regard' (stanza 2) compare 'smugging, smartness, and self-regard' in Ode IV, of *The Orators* (EA, p. 105). 'Safety-first' (stanza 4) was one of the enemy catchwords in *The Orators* (EA, p. 82).

When the Flyin' Scot

?1931; 'Uncle Henry', CSP66, p. 48; CP, p. 60; omitted from EA.

This exercise in English Sapphics (actually written in the same metre as Campion's 'Rose-cheek'd Laura, come') seems to be spoken in the character of the Duke in 'The month was April . . .' ('cweature') or of Colonel Tearer in *The Enemies of a Bishop* ('amusin', 'delicious', etc.), although when in the mid-1960s Auden had sight of the 1928–?30 notebook in which it appears (before it was acquired by the British Library) he gave as its title the name of the Airman's homosexual uncle (his 'true ancestor') in *The Orators*. This is odd, since the uncle's presentation there is without concession to stereotype, far from this lisping upper-class pederast, scouring North Africa in the manner of Wilde or Gide. In 1966 Auden substituted 'Kosta' (a boyfriend of Kallman's) for the MS's 'Otto' (a boy-friend of Isherwood's), 'Manfwed' (one of his own Berlin call-boys) for 'Gerard' and 'Nino' for 'Jimmie' (a boyfriend of Stephen Spender's). He also changed the MS 'All they have they give' (with its echo of Ulysses on Troilus, 'what he has he gives', *Troilus and Cressida*, IV.v.101) into 'All they have they bwing' (closer to Christina Rossetti's 'All that I have I bring' in 'Twice', line 45).

The third week in December frost came at last

February 1932; 'A Happy New Year' (Part I), *New Country*, 1933; EA, p. 444.

Apart from four introductory stanzas, the eighth stanza, and one final eight-line stanza rhyming or half-rhyming aabbcddc, Auden uses thirty-eight stanzas of rhyme royal for this long satirical dream-vision. In the previous month, Auden's review of John Skelton's *Complete Poems* appeared in the *Criterion*; it seems quite clear that he was much taken with the descriptive energies of 'The Bowge of Courte', 'Speke, Parrot' and in particular 'The Garlande of Laurell', and that the first part of 'A Happy New Year' is written in the same form and spirit. He had used the stanza a couple of times before in *The Orators* ('Beethameer, Beethameer, bully of Britain' and the 'Envoi' to Ode IV, see EA, pp. 86 and 106). These earlier examples date from October 1931, and it is possible that Auden was reading Skelton for his review at that time. He reused rhyme royal for 'Letter to Lord Byron'.

Contrasting his meditative mood with the suspended but still 'dangerous' (i.e. dominant) power of the erotic, and leaving the boys to their examinations, Auden climbs above Helensburgh. Larchfield School was already some way above the level of Gare Loch, and not far from the Luss Road (B832) which leads north-east out of Helensburgh and down into Glen Fruin. After about a mile and a half, Auden would have had sight of Loch Lomond. Magically he hears a voice in the telephone wire which urges him to look down at his 'promised land'; it is as though from such a height, even though in Scotland, he can see the whole of England. The beautiful kinetic observation at work in stanzas 9–11 about the motor-cyclist softens the reader up and allows a gear-change into colourful buffoonery. Soon the plain below him is populated by a Langlandesque field of folk (he was more specifically to imitate the opening of *Piers Plowman* in 'In the year of my youth . . .' begun later in the same year). The jazz band in stanza 14 may be compared with the minstrels in stanza 39 of 'The Garlande of Laurell'. Then comes a grotesque array of the physically awkward and psychologically repressed. Stanzas 16–17 in particular use Skelton's 'So many . . . So myche . . . was nevyr sene' formula ('Speke, Parrot', lines 442ff). T. E. Lawrence had by this time joined the RAF in the doubtful obscurity of the ranks; to make him a fighter pilot (stanza 18) is a peculiar irony (but compare 'The Journal of an Airman' in *The Orators*).

Soon the individual politicians, generals, financiers and writers and so on arrive, and Auden enters the exalted mood of semi-surrealist anarchy that he had begun to practise in the fourth Ode of *The Orators*. He borrows Skelton's manner of recounting his meeting with the poets in 'The Garlande of Laurell'. The officers are attended by distinguished physicians, the ranks by music-hall artistes (stanza 20). In stanza 21 Thomas, Baldwin, Snowden and Churchill appear. J. H. Thomas had supported Ramsay MacDonald's National Government in 1931 and had been hounded by the railwaymen's union for doing so. Stanley Baldwin was Lord President of the Council in the National Government, but could easily have claimed the premiership for himself. Philip Snowden as Chancellor of the Exchequer had proposed a future tax on land values in the April 1931 Budget and it was this as much as anything else which had led to the formation of the National Government, which he supported. Churchill had resigned from the Shadow Cabinet in January 1931, and was forever issuing warnings of the threat posed by a rearming Germany. Lord Kitchener died (stanza 22) when the HMS *Hampshire* struck a mine in June 1916. Sir Oswald Mosley (stanza 27) was soon to create the British Fascist Movement, the 1931 election results having been disastrous for his New Party. Rothermere and Beaverbrook eating bananas probably reflects on their Empire Free Trade Campaign. Sir Owen Seaman was the Editor of *Punch*. Sir Alfred Mond (stanza 28) was one of the architects of ICI, a model for the Financier in *The Dog Beneath the Skin*. 'Sir Austen' is Austen Chamberlain. One 'cocktail' on offer from the sanctimonious Sir Benjamin Drage half a dozen years later was the panacea of a universal language (see *Looking Forward: A Great Opportunity for the League of Nations*). The Dolmetsch family (stanza 29), especially Arnold Dolmetsch (1858–1940), were pioneers in the re-creation and use of early musical instruments. Lord Baden-Powell started the Boy Scout movement. Major Clifford Douglas (stanza 30) was the originator of the theory of Social Credit, which proposed to subsidise production to enable prices to be set lower than costs and so remedy the supposed chronic deficiency of purchasing power. His ideas had been formally rejected by the Labour Party in 1922, but were revived during the Depression. Sir Montagu Norman was Governor of the Bank of England.

Auden's writers, who appear next (stanza 31), unlike Skelton's are not in this context particularly admired and not addressed. In the case of Eliot, for example, fastidiousness is linked with an unhappiness which must be intended to be personal (the recent *Ash Wednesday* is probably in Auden's mind; compare the 'unhappy' poet in the cancelled stanzas of 'Brothers, who when the sirens roar'). Pound and the Sitwells are guilty of escapism and privacy (compare the solipsistic poet in *The Dog Beneath the Skin*, 11.3). Auden seems more sympathetic to the violence and dissidence of Wyndham Lewis, who had many admirers in the 1930s (e.g. Geoffrey Grigson and Julian Symons). Fr. Martin D'Arcy was not quite yet Master of Campion Hall, but had received many contemporaries (including Evelyn Waugh) into the Roman Catholic Church. Horace Joseph (stanza 32) was Tutor in Philosophy at New College and the principal Oxford lecturer on Plato. He was also a devoted Wykehamist and was made a Fellow of Winchester shortly before his death in 1943. Maynard Keynes's latest book was his *Treatise on Money* (1930) which among other new ideas canvassed the likelihood that there was no automatic tendency to full employment inherent in the economic system.

There is something of Firbank's manner with dialogue in stanzas 34–5 and 37, while the vague drawing up of battle-lines of the Eagles and the Tigers, together with the admonitory voice of the little man with field-glasses at his elbow (introduced in stanza 22), and his sudden disappearance (in stanza 43), and in particular the throbbing of the drums (stanza 43) is very close in mood to *Through the Looking Glass*, chapter vii. 'Gup' in stanza 37 means 'Gee-up' and is a skeltonic word (see 'Gup, Scot!' in Auden's *Oxford Book of Light Verse*, p. 72). Ernest Jones was a psychoanalyst, and biographer of Freud. In stanza 43, the Eagles depart northwards for Arrocher at the head of Loch Long, while the Tigers head southwards towards Dumbarton, while the snow falls like a final curtain. There is little left to say, and the reader like the poet himself is left to 'moralise | Upon these blurring images | Of the dingy difficult life of our generation'.

I have a handsome profile

September 1932; 'Song', *New Verse*, January 1933; *New Republic*, 12 July 1933; EA, p. 123.

When Auden sent this poem to Arnold Snodgrass in October 1932 he said that it was intended to go to the tune of 'Frankie and Johnny'. The music to which Auden sang the song to Maurice Feild as they walked down to the cricket field at the Downs School is (as transcribed with apparent care by

Alexandra Feild) partly recognisable as a version of that traditional tune, but suggests that Auden did not know it or sing it well. Like 'Brothers, who when the sirens roar', the poem's routes of bourgeois escape have a chilling answer. At the heart of all the responses is the familiar shrug: 'But where is the interest' (cf. Henry James on Arnold Bennett in 'The New Novel': 'Yes, the circumstances of the interest are there, but where is the interest itself?').

In the year of my youth when yo-yos came in

For this poem, and the ballad 'The Witnesses' contained within it, see pp. 128 and 133.

The month was April, the year

April 1933; *New Statesman*, 25 February 1977; EA, p. 130 ('Printed from a notebook, extensively emended by the editor').

Auden never published this dream allegory in which the captain of the ship *Wystan Auden Esquire* is a commandeering woman with a musket somewhat like the undisciplined 'wyf' of the Middle English homily *Sawles Warde* (i.e. the Will). If Auden had such a model in mind, then the mate, timid and bow-legged, would be the equivalent of Wit, who in the homily is the true master of the household (Auden seems to have had *Sawles Warde* in mind when writing 'In the year of my youth . . .', 1.174–81). The respective characters of the captain and the mate correspond closely to those of Auden's parents. The captain's map (stanza 9) is borrowed from the Ocean-Chart in *The Hunting of the Snark* 'representing the sea | Without the least vestige of land'. She is determined to take a straight course to the land of Cockayne regardless of storm threats, and ignoring the suggestions of the wireless operator (stanza 20) that the journey will be safer 'If we steer our course to the east' (i.e. Communism?). The allegory of the crew is by contrast physiological. In their various ways the engineer (cardio-vascular system), the stoker (libido) and the cook (digestive system) play no part in the problem of route and destination, while the Duke (sexual orientation), who is only a passenger, makes a play for the cabin-boy. The other passenger is the Professor (art) who spends his time playing cat's cradle (in stanza 16, 'Navaho' is a verb imperative meaning to lift one loop over another over the top of the finger: see Kathleen Haddon, *Artists in String,*

1930, p. 156). He is also unconcerned when the storm arrives. (Auden left a
string figure to Professor Richard Dawkins in 'Auden and MacNeice: Their
Last Will and Testament' and was still playing cat's cradle in October 1947
in a restaurant with Alan Ansen.) The poem is a comic plea for the psychic
wholeness that alone can redeem a sick world. The self-analysis appears to
issue not only in another version of the Terrible Mother, but also in an
attack on the class exploitation of certain kinds of homosexuals and the
political irrelevance of poetry itself (compare the unhappy poet in the
cancelled stanzas of 'Brothers, who when the sirens roar' who also 'fled . . .
To islands in your private seas | Where thoughts like castaways find ease | In
endless petting').

Sleep on beside me though I wake for you

?Summer 1933; 'Five Poems' I, *New Verse*, October 1933; EA, p. 146)'Turn not
towards me lest I turn to you').

The *English Auden* text is that of the sequence of love poems which Auden
sent to Isherwood in 1934, addressed to the boy of 'The earth turns over
. . .'. Auden returned to something of the situation and argument of the
poem in 'Lay your sleeping head, my love', though here the form (and
attitudes) of the Shakespearean sonnet encourage a greater openness
about the guilt of the lover and the pressure of outside circumstances.

On the provincial lawn I watch you play

?Summer 1934; 'Sonnet', *Rep*, October 1934; published as a pamphlet by Frederic
Prokosch, 1935; EA, p. 146.

Auden included the sonnet in the sequence addressed to the boy of 'The
earth turns over . . .' which he put together in 1934. The speculation about
his loved one's future (and, in the sestet, the corruptions of Eros) involves
Shakespearean abstractions which the sonnet form allows Auden to borrow
freely: 'world', 'time', 'power', and so on. Lines 6–8 again refer to the
disparity of age between them (see my commentary on 'The earth turns
over . . .', p. 158).

I see it often since you've been away

?Summer 1933; 'Five Poems' II, *New Verse*, October 1933; EA, p. 423.

The essence of the sestet of this sonnet was distilled into the First Mad Lady's song in *The Dog Beneath the Skin*, II.i. In both printed texts the semicolon at the end of line 3 should clearly be omitted.

At the far end of the enormous room

?Summer 1933; 'Five Poems' III, *New Verse*, October 1933; EA, p. 147.

Both the situation in the octave and the argument in the sestet are here achieved with notable force and simplicity, with the sestet's diction in particular staying close to its Elizabethan model. The wish of love not to be (line 10) is not, I think, the natural oblivion of orgasm (compare 'Love had him fast . . .'), but the wish not to betray, a theme running through many of the sonnets of this sequence written for the boy of 'The earth turns over . . .'.

The latest ferrule now has tapped the curb

?Summer 1933; 'Five Poems' IV, *New Verse*, October 1933; EA, p. 147.

The first six lines of this sonnet, also part of the 1934 sequence, were developed from 'In the year of my youth . . .' 1.904–10, and lines 2–3 reused in the Commentary to 'In Time of War'. Compare line 12 with the 'voluntary errands' of the ships in 'Look stranger, at this island now'. The isolation of this night-piece is sensitively conveyed both by the scrupulous atmospheric detail in the octave and the terrors of the galaxy in the sestet. The contrast between them is dramatic, the link ('shivering') establishing the connection between the two kinds of isolation, the solitariness of the lover and the relative unimportance of human life.

One absence closes other lives to him

May 1934; EA, p. 147.

This sonnet was part of the sequence of love poems which Auden put together in 1934 (see EA, p. 423). He returned in 1948 to a more elaborate psychological allegory of a 'household' in the poem of that name. The loved one is merely the occasion here ('one absence') for an analysis of the poet's predicament as a would-be 'redeemer' who cannot heal others until he can wake from his own self-absorbed dream of love.

The fruit in which your parents hid you, boy

?Spring 1933; 'Poem' II, *New Verse*, July 1933; EA, p. 148.

This sonnet became part of the sequence of love poems addressed to the boy of 'The earth turns over . . .'. It was intended for *Look, Stranger!* (as no. iv) but omitted at proof stage. The holograph copy which Auden had sent to Grigson in 1933 was reproduced in the Auden double number of *New Verse* in November 1937. Line 4 was transported into the penultimate stanza of 'Journey to Iceland' and the last three lines were rearranged and became the ending of the same poem: the 'deadly journey' may derive from the 'Todfahrt' of 'Ich weiss dass Du bist weg . . .' written three years earlier (see *Auden Studies*, 1, 1990, p. 12). In the *New Verse* text it is a 'mad' driver, suggesting a closer analogy with the infantile desperation of 'howling': the 'rich' of the *English Auden* text is more reminiscent of the Cambridge escapade to Cape Wrath (see my commentary on 'From scars where kestrels hover', p. 71). In the *New Verse* holograph the driver was originally an airman. It is, in any case, an example of the uselessly heroic journey of the Truly Weak Man, one of the perturbations of Eros. The inheritance of the opening is explored with greater biological detail in 'Love had him fast . . .', once part of the sequence but separately published in *Look, Stranger!*

Dear to me now and longer than a summer

?1933; EA, p. 149.

This sonnet was included in the sequence of love poems addressed to the boy of 'The earth turns over . . .' and put together in 1934. Auden reused the third line in *The Ascent of F6* (*Plays*, p. 316). The admission of betrayal surfaces more directly in this sonnet, and is more specifically shown to relate to promiscuity; on the other hand, the appeal to the loved one's power to redeem that infidelity is more nakedly expressed in the final line than anywhere else in the sequence.

The dawn of day had scarce broke through

1933; 'Lament', *The Badger*, Autumn 1933; *Auden Studies* 2, 1994, p. 18.

Though signed 'Anon', this poem about a matron at the Downs School is probably by Auden.

'Sweet is it,' say the doomed, 'to be alive though wretched'

March 1934; *TLS*, 16 January 1976.

This long poem in tercets was not accepted by the *Criterion* when submitted there for publication, and Auden made use of some of its lines and ideas in other poems. Lines 1–4 became lines 16–19 of the Commentary to 'In Time of War', lines 5–9 and lines 13–18 were used in Ransom's first prose speech in *The Ascent of F6*. Lines 28–30 were used in Sonnet XII of 'In Time of War'. Lines 47–8 and 51 became lines 11–12 of 'Certainly our city . . .'. Some of the healers who 'without reproaches show us what our vanity has chosen' were borrowed for the same poem ('Sweet . . .': Freud, Homer Lane, Groddeck, Matthias Alexander, Marx, Lenin, both T. E. and D. H. Lawrence, Gerald Heard, Nansen, Schweitzer, Einstein, Planck, Rutherford; 'Certainly . . .': Nansen, Schweitzer, Lenin, Freud, Groddeck, Lawrence, Kafka, Proust). Lines 90–96 and 100–103 became lines 10–19 of Ransom's speech after his interview with the Abbot in the first edition of *The Ascent of F6* (*Plays*, p. 612). Lines 102–3 then became the last two lines of the Commentary to 'In Time of War'. The poem is basically a history of the enlightenment and of human uprootedness, a subject that was more and more to concern Auden in the late 1930s, though rarely dictated in so preachy a tone. The crucial point in the poem is perhaps lines 88ff: 'O luckiest of all the ages for a pioneer, | When the choice is simple and important, and all must choose.'

This is the night mail crossing the border

July 1935; 'Night Mail', GPO *Film Library Notes and Synopses*, 1936, p. 11; TPO: *the Centenary of the Travelling Post Office*, 1938, pp. 15, 18; CSP66, p. 83; CP, p. 131; EA, p. 290; *Plays*, pp. 422, 667.

The revised text which Auden printed in 1966 is nineteen lines shorter than the eclectic text printed by Mendelson in *The English Auden* (the material in the notes to *Plays* is more complicated still). It represents quite closely the words actually used in the film, except that the line 'Notes from overseas to the Hebrides' has been omitted. This is restored in the main text in *Plays*. Auden sent '3 Fragments for films' (no. III is 'Night Mail') to John Lehmann for *New Writing*, but withdrew them in April 1936, perhaps because some of the material had been used in *The Ascent of F6* (although he claimed that it was because he thought they were not good enough). In 1935 Auden had worked for six months with the General Post Office Film Unit. He produced a song for the film *Coal Face* (1935) ('O lurcher-loving collier, black as night', printed in *Another Time*), this verse commentary for *Night Mail* (1936), and a commentary for *God's Chillun* (1939). This last film was developed out of an earlier project for a film to be called *Negroes*. He played the part of Father Christmas in *Calendar of the Year* (1936). He also wrote commentaries for *Beside the Seaside* and *The Way to the Sea* (1937), films made by the Strand Film Company, and for *The Londoners* (1939), a film made by John Grierson for the British Commercial Gas Association. In *Coal Face*, *Night Mail*, *The Way to the Sea* and *God's Chillun* he collaborated with Benjamin Britten, whom he had first met on 4 July 1935.

Night Mail was originally to be entitled *Scottish Mail-bag*, and was a dramatic account of the nightly journey of the LMS postal special from Euston to Glasgow. The verse commentary in the last third of the film is a striking performance, full of perceptive detail and evocative rhythms, some of them perhaps borrowed from R. L. Stevenson (cf. 'From a Railway Carriage': 'Faster than fairies, faster than witches, | Bridges and houses, hedges and ditches', etc.). It has probably not been realised, however, what a feat it represents, for Auden's images did not, as in a scenario, prescribe the images on the screen: he fitted the verse to an edited version as a composer does. In 'Poetry and Film' (*Janus*, no. 2, May 1936) he was reported as saying that he 'even found it necessary to time his spoken verse with a stop-watch in order to fit it exactly to the shot on which it commented' (*Plays*, p. 513). Although the film was largely directed by Harry Watt, much credit for its success must be given to Alberto Cavalcanti, who was responsible for the Sound Direction. Auden had written another poem on this subject in 1924 ('The Mail-train, Crewe', *Juvenilia*, p. 76). In the earlier poem the train is headed south rather than north, and the poet's speculations about the various messages delivered by postmen are highly generalised.

Now is the time when all our spirits mount

July 1935; 'Epilogue', *The Badger*, Autumn 1935; *Auden Studies* 2, p. 29.

This is an end-of-the-year tribute to boys and schoolteachers at the Downs School, written in heroic couplets. Richard Davenport-Hines and Nicholas Jenkins have supplied detailed notes to accompany the *Auden Studies* text. The various persons addressed who are not directly named are the Headmaster, Geoffrey Hoyland (line 11), Mrs Hoyland (line 23), the second master E. C. Coxwell (line 29) and the Latin master, Mr Day (line 39). The final line of the poem alludes to the school motto, 'Aedificandum Est'. The *Auden Studies* emendation of line 26 is not necessary, since Auden would have intended 'mamma' to have the English pronunciation, with the accent on the second syllable.

Still at their accustomed hour . . .

1935; 'Negroes', *Plays*, p 424.

This commentary for a film to be called 'Negroes' (eventually used in *God's Chillun*, 1939) was included in '3 Fragments for films' but never printed (see my commentary on *Night Mail*). Auden is perhaps returning to the long periods of Claudel for his expansive transatlantic subject in the paragraphs beginning with the Bass Recitative on p. 426 (see my commentary to 'O Love, the interest itself in thoughtless heaven', p. 145). The text otherwise treats the economic facts of West Indian agriculture and manufacture with elaborate factuality, counterpointed for irony. There is little generalised or summarising comment until the last dozen verse lines, themselves so gnomic that they could be adopted virtually unchanged for the final scene of *The Ascent of F6*.

This coast is continuous . . .

1935; 'Beside the Seaside', *Plays*, p 429.

Auden probably wrote this commentary for Marion Grierson's film for the Strand Film Company, although he is not credited on the film itself. Certainly he admitted to contributing to the film (see *Plays*, p. 512) and the first section contains a deployed paraphrase and elaboration of significant parts of his poem 'Look, stranger, at this island now', with certain memorable phrases intact. Note the telling phrase about 'daily decisions'. And compare the formula in the last sentence ('Under these roofs one cannot tell how many people . . .') with Ransom's remark about the stupid peasants in the first scene of *The Ascent of F6*.

When I was only so high, I was amiable and gay

March 1936; *Auden Studies* 2, p. 69.

This song was printed from the notebook largely used for *The Ascent of F6*. It marks a transition in Auden's work from the generalised songs of the early 1930s portraying the deficient bourgeoisie to the specific case-histories of the ballads of 1937.

I'm a jam-tart, I'm a bargain-basement

March 1936; *Auden Studies* 2, p.76; *As I Walked Out One Evening*, p. 34.

Although this is one of the liveliest of Auden's unpublished songs, its debt to Cole Porter (particularly to 'You're the Top' from Act 1 of *Anything Goes*, 1934; Auden may have seen the film version of 1936) probably kept it from publication. The magic casement (line 2) is from Keats's 'Ode to a Nightingale'; the umbrella and sewing machine (line 3) from Lautréamont's *Les Chants de Maldoror* (the classic 'chance encounter on a dissecting table of a sewing machine and an umbrella'); a dog's nose (line 8) is a cocktail (gin and beer). Britten's music has been lost.

From the moment that I saw you

?April 1936; *Auden Studies* 2, p. 78.

These two stanzas are almost certainly part of the following song.

It's not easy to begin to describe the state I'm in

?April 1936; *Auden Studies* 2, p. 79.

 This song, first printed from *The Ascent of F6* notebook, shares its refrain ('[But] What do I care I I'm having an affair') with an unpublished poem of March 1930 in the notebook which Auden gave to Wendell Johnson (Harvard), 'There's mutiny in the Palace Guard'. This later version is much more developed, but the point is the same: love pays no attention to politics. The frequent interpolation of the phrase 'I don't care' is probably derived from such dismissive duet-lyrics by Ira Gershwin as 'So What?' in *Pardon My English* (1933) and 'First Lady and First Gent' in *Let 'Em Eat Cake* (1933).

When you're feeling like expressing your affection

?1936; *Plays*, p. 673.

This brief encouragement to use the telephone was set by Britten: the presumption is that it was Auden who provided the words and the GPO Film Unit who provided the occasion. *Pace* Donald Mitchell in his comments accompanying the first recording (Unicorn–Kanchana DKP(CD)9138), Button A was nothing to do with international calls: it was the button you pressed finally to make your connection (Button B gave you your money back).

The line waits

1936; 'The Way to the Sea', Donald Mitchell, *Britten and Auden in the Thirties: The Year 1936*, p. 90; *Plays*, p. 430.

This film was directed by Paul Rotha for the Strand Film Company, on a commission from Southern Railways to celebrate the electrification of the line from London to Southampton. Rotha has acknowledged the ironic intent of the makers of the film (see Mitchell, pp. 88–9, 101). Britten's score is one of his most parodically elaborate. Auden's 'End Commentary' is a penny plain version of the style of his dramatic choruses of the period and therefore as it stands not self-evidently deflationary. It is true that the tone which Eliot introduced into his choruses of *The Rock* for admonishing the suburban mentality is not very far away, and when the phrase 'People like you and me' is twice repeated we can hardly believe it, but at the same time Auden's analysis of escapism is utterly straightforward and characteristic. Much of it reads like a generalising version of the observations in 'August for the people . . .'. Also compare 'Here are all the varieties . . .' with 'Here are all the captivities . . .' in 'Schoolchildren'. The text in *Plays* is six lines longer than Mitchell's text, and other variants are given in the notes.

Time will make its utter changes

1936; 'Raynes Park School Song', *The Spur*, October 1936; 'A School Song', *The Badger*, Autumn 1937; *Auden Studies* 2, 1994, p. 32.

This school song was commissioned by John Garrett, headmaster of Raynes Park County Grammar School, and dedicated to him. Dr Thomas Wood wrote the music. Garrett had been co-editor with Auden of *The Poet's Tongue*, published in 1935. The lines 'Man must live among his neighbours | For he cannot live alone' are an early instance of the sentiment that reaches its boldest expression in stanza 8 of 'September 1, 1939'. 'The diver's brilliant bow' is borrowed from 'No trenchant parting this'.

The Ascent of F6

The Ascent of F6 was written with Isherwood in Portugal between March and April 1936, and published by Faber and Faber in September of that year. Soon afterwards it was considerably revised. In particular, as was the case with *The Dog Beneath the Skin*, there were significant changes to the final scene. These changes were incorporated into the Random House and second Faber editions of March 1937, and further changes were made before the first performance by the Group Theatre in February (with music by Benjamin Britten). Auden and Isherwood continued to work on the ending of the play for American productions in 1939 and for the Group Theatre revival in the same year, and Auden wrote yet another ending for a production at Swarthmore in 1945. I shall refer to the text in *Plays*, which is essentially that of the second edition. The relatively complicated textual history is fully set out by Mendelson (*Plays*, pp. 598–652).

Isherwood has described their collaboration in *Christopher and His Kind* (p. 180):

> Wystan did act one, scene one; the dialogue between Ransom and his Mother in act one, scene three; the dialogue between Ransom and the Abbot in act two, scene one; Ransom's monologue in act two, scene two; the whole of act two, scene four; all songs and choruses, the speeches by the A's and all other speeches between the scenes. We interfered very little with each other's work. The only scene on which we really collaborated was the last. It was understood, throughout, that Wystan's speciality was to be the 'woozy' and mine the 'straight' bits.

Isherwood glosses 'woozy' as 'grandiloquent, lacking in substance, obscure for obscurity's sake'.

The hero of *The Dog Beneath the Skin* was an innocent who led a charmed life. There was little dramatic conflict; the stage was free for incidental social satire. *The Ascent of F6* is another matter: the plot (for which Isherwood was responsible) is more involved, the dramatic conflict is uppermost, and social satire is confined to the margins of the play – that is, to the boxes on either side of the stage where the main action takes place.

The hero is a man of action, and his problem is one of motivation: what lies behind Michael Ransom's lifelong ambition to climb F6? Is he the Truly Strong Man or not? For Isherwood the provenance of their hero was plain. The truly strong man is 'calm, balanced, aware of his strength, sits drinking quietly in the bar; it is not necessary for him to try to prove to himself that he is not afraid, by . . . leaving his comfortable home in a snowstorm to climb the impossible glacier', whereas the truly weak man 'prefers to attempt . . . the laborious terrible northwest passage . . . The Truly Weak Man was represented by Lawrence of Arabia, and hence by their character Michael Ransom in *F.6.*' (*Christopher and His Kind*, p. 192). His character may, then, be based on T. E. Lawrence, but his predicament owes something to Mallory's or Captain Scott's and his moods to Hamlet's. At bottom, Ransom is a character we have met before in Auden: in his attempt to deny and rationalise the powerful influence of his mother, he is merely John Nower or the Airman in another guise. The influence of the mother takes a different form in F6: Mrs Ransom had deliberately withheld her love from Michael and lavished it on his twin brother, James. Instead of this making Ransom strong and independent as she had hoped, it left in him an unconscious desire to replace James in his mother's affections, a desire which expressed itself in the aggressive mammary symbolism of climbing the mountain. The play was appropriately dedicated, without apparent irony, to Auden's brother John, himself a geologist and mountaineer, a founder member of the Himalayan Club, who had mentioned the mountain K2 to Auden in 1929 (*A Tribute*, p. 27). The allusion in the dedication to the 'stricken grove' is from Dante's *Inferno* xiii.

Ransom's first soliloquy establishes and explains his devotion to mountaineering ('the impassive embraces of this sullen rock', p. 296) as his rejection of the real world, which he finds irredeemably sordid and corrupt. Reflecting upon a passage from Dante (*Inferno* xxvi) where Ulysses is exhorting his men to undertake their last journey 'to follow virtue and knowledge', Ransom concludes that the world is not motivated by virtue and knowledge at all, but by power. Even Dante himself used his poetic gift for this purpose, 'power to exact for every snub, every headache, every unfallen beauty, an absolute revenge'. This is the Freudian view of the role of art, and it has a crucial thematic importance at this point in the play; we cannot help reflecting throughout the action that Ransom's attempt on F6 and all it implies is in fact an international symbol of the creative act of the poet. A. E. Housman quotes the Dante passage in his *Introductory Lecture* of 1892 (*Collected Poems and Selected Prose*, Penguin, 1989, p. 271). So does Eliot in his 'Dante' (1929). So for that matter does Frank McEachran in his *The Civilized Man* (1930), p. 60. McEachran was an influential teacher at Auden's school, Gresham's, and Ransom's Freudian interpretation looks like a designed refutation of McEachran's cultural argument. However, Auden refers approvingly to McEachran's views on Dante and tragedy in the 1929 Journal. The passage is also quoted in Italian as epigraph to Leishman's translation of Rilke's *Sonnets to Orpheus* (1936), p. 8.

Ransom's observation about the 'stupid peasants' is borrowed from a line in one of Auden's early German sonnets ('Im Dorf die dofen Bauern machen Kinder': see *Auden Studies* 1, 1990, p. 12). It is a view that would, I think, be intended to place Ransom politically for the audience. Compare Auden in *New Era in Home and School*, January 1939, p. 6: 'People who believe that the poor are poor because they are stupid, and that they will have stupid children, will not adopt a democratic form of government.' Ransom's disillusionment in fact prevents him from seeking the political leadership that he seems fitted for and secretly to desire. His speech ends on the most nihilistic note struck by a 1934 poem of Auden's ' "Sweet is it," say the doomed, "to be alive though wretched" ', borrowing its lines 5–9 and 13–18. These contain dramatic irony as well: it is because Ransom still can, as it were, cry 'Mama' as the frozen idiot cannot that he is fatally to respond, like Coriolanus, to his mother's appeal on p. 314.

The next few scenes sketch in the political situation that underlies the Government's desire to conquer F6 before the Ostnians. The reason is no more complex than it need be: according to native legend, the first white man to reach the summit will rule both British and Ostnian Sudoland, on whose common border the mountain lies. Power is therefore the ultimate motive: power which will satisfy a nation deprived of virtue and knowledge, symbolised by the petit-bourgeois Mr and Mrs A who act as chorus, bored and unhappy; power which will satisfy the vested interests of the politicians and generals, represented by Ransom's brother James, Lord Stagmantle, General Dellaby-Couch and Lady Isabel.

The jingoistic colonialism behind all this is perhaps too obvious, and the dialogue of the expository scene (pp. 299ff) is based largely on the clichés of the middlebrow novel ('Aha, so that's their little game', 'Look here, Ransom', and so on); but this is quite deliberate ('Very chinny', Auden wrote to Dermott Grubb on 25 May 1936, 'like *Journey's End*'). The method makes these exemplars of naked power appear clearly as stereotyped bogeys. They are only marginally more realistic than the villagers of Pressan Ambo, and only marginally less mad and threatening. Behind the cartoon manner is a serious authorial attitude. As Auden was to write a few years later in *The Prolific and the Devourer*, p. 14:

> The Enemy was and still is the politician, i.e. the person who wants to organise the lives of others and make them toe the line. I can recognise him instantly in any disguise, whether as a civil servant, a bishop, a schoolmaster, or a member of a political party, and I cannot meet him however casually without a feeling of fear and hatred and a longing to see him (or her, for the worst ones are women) publicly humiliated.

The Enemy fails to persuade Ransom to undertake the expedition, even though F6 is his 'fate'. It is only when Mrs Ransom reveals how she has concealed her love for him in order to make him 'truly strong' that Ransom consents (p. 314). The rest of the first act shows how the expedition provides vicarious excitement for Mr and Mrs A (they continue to react throughout the play), and it also shows how Mrs Ransom is mysteriously influencing her son. Her song (p. 318), taken from Augustus Bicknell's song to 'Miss James' in *The Chase*, II.iv, perfectly expresses her deadly possessiveness. Before she can reassert her power over Ransom, he must conquer the Demon reputed to live at the top of the mountain. Since, as we have seen, his ascent of the mountain is, as Auden later put it, 'a symbol of the geste . . . a symbol of the act of aggression' (*Hudson Review*, Winter 1951, p. 575), the demon must represent the ultimate source of responsibility for his aggressiveness, i.e. the mother who conditioned the rivalry of the brothers for her love (Freud had something to say in *Totem and Taboo* about the association of fear of demons with veneration of ancestors). Ransom is therefore climbing F6 to face the past, or to obtain, like Dante, not virtue or knowledge, but revenge. The artist cannot be organised by politicians, but is, on the other hand, driven by his personal psychological demon.

It has been presumed that the ascent was based on the Everest expedition of 1924. This is probably correct, but the action also reflects aspects of Scott's expedition to the South Pole: the rivalry with the Ostnian Blavek, for instance, and the choice of companion for the final assault on the summit (compare the disappointment of Wright at not going on to the Plateau with Shawcross's jealousy of Gunn). Gunn and Shawcross are both weak characters, who conceal their weaknesses in boyish bravado and head-prefect priggishness respectively. Gunn was based on a friend of Isherwood's called Orpen, and the authors evidently had some fun with him and with his songs and jokes (there is a fuller version of his song 'The chimney sweepers' (p. 306) in *Auden Studies* 2, p. 70, and of 'Some have tennis-elbow' (p. 341) in *New Verse*, April–May, 1936, 'Foxtrot from a Play', also printed in *Auden Studies* 2, p. 72). He is a compulsive stealer, too (cf. *The Orators*), while Shawcross idolises Ransom to compensate for his own inadequacies. Lamp and the Doctor are less interesting characters, but their presence is necessary.

These four companions of Ransom's symbolise his four faculties: Intuition, Feeling, Sensation and Thought. Auden seems to have attempted such symbolism before (see 'The four sat on in the bare room' and 'The month was April, the year') and was to do so again with some elaboration (see *The Age of Anxiety*, where the faculties are represented by the characters Quant, Rosetta, Emble and Malin. See also 'For the Time Being', CP, p. 355). This symbolism was probably suggested by Jung's *Modern Man in Search of a Soul* (1933), p. 107 (in his review of Liddell Hart's book on T. E. Lawrence, EA, p. 320, Auden claimed that Lawrence, with Lenin, came nearest to exemplifying 'most completely what is best and significant in our time, our nearest approach to a synthesis of feeling and reason, act and thought'). In *F6*, Intuition is represented by the Doctor, vegetative and worried about his fatness; Feeling is represented by Shawcross, who is entirely motivated by his hero-worship of Ransom and his jealous hatred of Gunn; Sensation is represented by Gunn, who lives for thrills, sex and fast cars; and Thought is represented by the botanist Lamp, in single-minded pursuit of his Polus Naufrangia (a significantly-named plant in the circumstances, 'pole of shipwreck'). By treating these faculties in isolation in this way, Auden emphasises the expedition's representation of the imprisoned will seeking liberation upon the mountain of its choice (as the four faculties are made to say in *For the Time Being*: 'We who are four were | Once but one, | Before his act of | Rebellion; | We were himself when | His will was free, | His error became our | Chance to be', CP, p. 355). Naturally, this symbolism is hardly one of which an audience would be aware, but it is evidently one of those classifying principles upon which Auden liked to build the development of his themes.

The allegorical pattern is reflected in II.i, where in the monastery half-way up the mountain the climbing party each look into the monk's prophetic crystal; the faculties desire their limited satisfactions, but Ransom himself feels called to the spiritual leadership of the multitudes of the weak and deprived (p. 324) as if to fulfil his ironical name, as a redeemer. In his following interview with the Abbot, this wish is elaborated and exposed for the self-deception that it is. If Ransom is to conquer the Demon and save

mankind, he can only do so by the exercise of power ('government requires
the exercise of the human will: and the human will is from the Demon',
p. 327). This dilemma, according to the Abbott, admits of only one
solution, and that is to renounce the world and become a monk. Ransom,
however, has gone too far already merely to 'return to England and become
a farm labourer or a factory hand' (alluding to Lawrence's escape into the
ranks of the RAF). Ransom provokes the Abbot to admit that he himself, as
ruler of the monastery, has not succeeded in making a complete abnegation
of the will, and is in fact subject to visitations of the Demon described in
terms that are close to a parody of Housman's definition of poetry in *The
Name and Nature of Poetry*, p. 47. (Jung's *Commentary on the Tibetan Book of the
Dead*, 1935, is the probable source of the funeral rite and its meanings.)
Ransom's speech after the Abbot's exit contains (p. 329) some more
prosified material from the eminently 'woozy' 1934 poem ' "Sweet is it," say
the doomed, "to be alive though wretched" '. In the first edition this was a
fuller verse borrowing (lines 9–19 in F6 were taken from lines 90–6 and
100–103 in the earlier poem. The earlier version is in *Plays*, p. 612). The
whole scene was one of the most heavily revised. The revisions effectively
elaborate the Abbot's offer and clarify Ransom's predicament.

Ransom is in a quandary: he wants to climb F6, but recognises that in
doing so he will be playing a corrupt and spurious role. On the other hand,
how can he be certain that renunciation of the will is not itself an act of the
will, a subservience to the Demon? Ransom's 'woozy' appeal to 'the history
and the creator of all these forms in which we are condemned to suffer'
reveals at this point what is an essentially religious despair. Soon, in 'Spain
1937', Auden was to imagine such a force being invoked 'as a dove or | A
furious papa or a mild engineer' as if to reinvent the structure of the
Trinity. In *The Prolific and the Devourer*, Part IV, p. 53, he wrote: 'If anyone
chooses to call our knowledge of existence knowledge of God, to call
Essence the Father, Form the Son, and Motion the Holy Spirit, I don't
mind.' Ransom has not yet begun this process of reinvention. Auden later
wrote in Albert and Angelyn Stevens's copy of the play: 'The end . . . is all
wrong because, as I now see it, it required, and I refused it, a Christian
solution.'

In the end, his 'faculties' decide for him. News comes through that
Blavek and his party have reached F6 and are 'hammering the whole south
face full of pitons and hauling each other up like sacks!' (p. 330), an
unethical procedure which was adopted by the Germans in the 1930s out of
their intensely nationalistic competitiveness. Gunn, Lamp, Shawcross and

the Doctor (the faculties) are outraged and excited. They now want to beat Blavek. Ransom (the will) wearily concludes: 'Very well then, since you wish it. I obey you. The summit will be reached, the Ostnians defeated, the Empire saved. And I have failed.' He fails because it has become an inauthentic choice. It is significant that when Auden came to write his sonnet about the Pelagian heresy ('The Quest', no. 2, 'The Preparations') his metaphor was of an expedition like Ransom's. Ransom's motivation is psychologically conditioned, but it is also without grace.

The action is now comparatively straightforward until the denouement. Ransom plays Hamlet to a discovered skull (p. 334) which provides opportunities for dramatic irony ('those to whom a mountain is a mother') and a potted history of mountaineering, drawing heavily (as did the potted biography of Ransom towards the end of Act 1) on R. L. G. Irving's *The Romance of Mountaineering* (1935), especially pp. 8, 12, 18–29, 46, 82, 142–3 and 175. Antoine de Ville climbed Mont Aiguille in Dauphiné with 'subtilz engins' in 1492; Horace de Saussure (1740–99) was the creator of scientific mountaineering; Balmat was the Swiss guide who accompanied Dr Michael Paccard on his conquest of Mont Blanc (Marc Bourrit jealously exaggerated Balmat's part in the climb); W. F. Donkin and Henry Fox were lost in 1888 attempting Mount Dychtau in the Caucasus; Marie-Couttet, nicknamed 'Moutelet', discovered the route up Mont Blanc by the Bosses du Dromadaire; Edward Whymper conquered the Matterhorn in 1865 after many attempts (Hadow slipped on the way down, and four of the climbers were killed); Franz and Toni Schmid climbed the North Face of the Matterhorn; and the 'pair . . . whom Odell saw' were George Leigh-Mallory and Andrew Irvine, last seen on 6 June 1924 attempting Everest (N. E. Odell was a day behind them, collecting geological specimens).

After this, an avalanche kills Lamp (Thought) moving Mrs A to couplets (p. 336) with a note of Housman (*Shropshire Lad*, xix); Shawcross (Feeling) commits suicide; the Doctor (Intuition) is left behind; and Gunn (Sensation) finally gives up, collapsing through exposure. Though it is not a very close allegory, this seems to be the right order for the loss of the faculties, and it leaves Ransom alone for another Shakespearean soliloquy (p. 344, cf. *King Lear*, III.ii.1–9). (There is a fuller version of the Announcer's song, p. 343, in *Auden Studies*, 2, p. 74). Such a sober and dramatic moment is uneasily served by pastiche of this kind, and the uncertainty of tone is maintained in the following passage of voices from the stage boxes (compare 'Snow on the pass. Alas' with Gertrude Stein's 'Pigeons in the grass – alas' in *Four Saints in Three Acts*). Ransom himself collapses at this point (p. 346), and the remainder of the play is an expressionistic enactment of his psychological predicament, with which one might compare the central scenes of *Paid on Both Sides*. Rupert Doone once complained that all Auden's plays were resolved 'in dream'.

The chorus refers to the Dragon of Revelation (cf. the poem in 'Journal of an Airman', EA, p. 75) as an opportunity for a quest hero. These roles are taken in the fantasy by James and Ransom. Ransom is imagining how his expedition is being exploited by his brother as a panacea for the unhappy lives of the oppressed. They play chess, and though James wins, Ransom, by an appeal to the mysteriously veiled figure on the summit, challenges the victory. James collapses, saying: 'It was not Virtue – it was not Knowledge – it was Power!' (p. 349). Ransom in his delirium is evidently wishing that his brother might die instead of him, but he blames this guilty fantasy on the veiled figure: 'It wasn't my fault! The Demon gave the sign.' That is to say, he is not responsible for the conditioning in infancy which made him jealous of his brother. There was to be a revised version of 'Stop all the clocks, cut off the telephone' (p. 350) in *Another Time* ('Funeral Blues').

The Abbot then proceeds to judge the case, calling as witnesses the victims of the Demon: Shawcross, Gunn, Lamp and the Doctor. These do not wish to accuse (it was only the subconscious that recognised his guilty desires) and Ransom is now sorry that he has blamed the Demon. He rushes to the Demon's defence. This recognition that the Demon is of his own making (and represents his reasons for climbing the mountain) dismisses the other figures in his fantasy, and leaves him alone at last in peace with the Demon. The final scene, with its reminiscences of Ibsen and the grand gestures of the chorus (albeit borrowed from a text written for a film to be called *Negroes*) gives him an illusory triumph at the moment of his death.

The real difficulty about this ending is that of wanting to turn the tragedy that it claims to be into a kind of comedy, like *Peer Gynt* (a new translation of which by Randall Swingler had been read at the Group Theatre in the 1935–6 season). The diversion from Demon to Dragon allows a maternal reunion and release that clearly had great force for Auden: when the veil is removed, Mrs Ransom is revealed 'as a young mother', an Aase turned Solveig who presides over his death with an enchanting lullaby. Auden must have been influenced by Groddeck here, in his identification of death with the eternal mother. Groddeck wrote about Ibsen's play:

Here then once again we have the mother and child situation. Peer ranges the whole world about, and at home there waits one who is at the same time mother, wife and woman. That is the essence of life, except that man is not always fortunate in finding a Solveig to be both wife and mother to him. As a rule he finds the second mother, the eternal mother, only in that dark kingdom whither we all descend, our common home.

(*Exploring the Unconscious*, 1933, p. 159)

Letters from Iceland

Auden visited Iceland between June and September 1936 with a commission from Faber and Faber to write a travel book. He asked Louis MacNeice to collaborate with him on the book, and was also joined for part of the trip by a party of boys from Bryanston School. *Letters from Iceland* was published in August 1937, with MacNeice responsible for one-third of the authorial text (see Auden's letter to *Time and Tide*, 21 August 1937). In the preface to the 1967 paperback edition, Auden wrote: 'Though writing in a "holiday" spirit, its authors were all the time conscious of a threatening horizon to their picnic – world-wide unemployment, Hitler growing everyday more powerful and a world-war more inevitable. Indeed, the prologue to that war, the Spanish Civil War, broke out while we were there.'

Excuse, my lord, the liberty I take

Part I: July; Part II: August; Part III: August; Part IV: September; Part V: October 1936; 'Letter to Lord Byron', LI, at pp. 17, 49, 99, 200 and 232; CP, p. 79; EA, p. 167; *Prose*, at pp. 179, 208, 249, 326, 354.

The texts in collected editions restore a line at 1.15.4 that had been altered to avoid libel. The *Collected Poems* text was first revised for the Penguin *Longer Contemporary Poems* (1966) and incorporated into the Faber paperback of *Letters from Iceland* (1967); it is twenty-seven stanzas shorter, having lost 1.6, IV.7–16 and 54, and V.1–15. The omitted stanzas in Part IV contained some of the more personal and physical aspects of his autobiographical sketch. Auden seems to have lost patience with the concluding part, which turns from autobiography to the state of England and the fate and conditioning of poets in its final address to Byron; he simply omitted it all, adding its final stanza to the end of Part IV.

Auden explains himself (1.22) why he chose rhyme royal rather than Byron's *ottava rima*, although he doesn't remind the reader that he had already used rhyme royal extensively in 'A Happy New Year' and other earlier poems, albeit in a largely Skeltonic manner. When preparing his

1945 *Collected Poetry* he wondered if it wasn't 'too yppity-tippity' to be
included (letter to Kallman) and in the end did not do so. However, its
lightness of tone and openness of subject was a major factor in the success
of *Letters from Iceland*. Auden's civilised, ironic distance of style was a daring
but appropriate accompaniment to his geographical distance, and the
poem made its effect as a masterly innovation. This was the right moment
for Auden to be informative about his life and ideas in a mode that allowed
him to be funny as well (the parallel is with Isherwood's *Lions and Shadows*,
which had been brewing for a number of years: see IV.16). However, the
poem takes in more than the merely personal or literary, showing a sharp
nose for cultural pretentiousness and socio-political lies, a dislike of the
direction that poetry has taken since the eighteenth century and above all a
suspicion of technology and the antiseptic habitat of Economic Man.

1.1.7 Father Charles Coughlin was a popular radio preacher in the
USA.

1.1.7 Canon H. R. L. ('Dick') Sheppard had initiated the Peace
Pledge Union in 1934.

1.3.1 cf. Pope, 'Epistle to Dr Arbuthnot'.

1.6.2 Sir George MacKenzie, *Travels in Iceland* (1812).

1.6.3 'I have a gramophone at home'.

1.6.4 'English kids are keen on machines'.

1.6.5 Το καλov is the Greek concept of beauty and order, often
quoted by Pound (e.g. in *Hugh Selwyn Mauberley*, III.15).
'Glubit' is from Catullus, Carm. lviii.5: '[Lesbia] . . . Nunc in
quadriviis et angiportis | glubit magnanimos Remi nepotes'
('Now at street-corners and in alleyways she peels back the skin
of the great-hearted descendants of Remus'). Auden had
quoted the line with relish in a letter to Isherwood of 1927.
Compare all this with the Poundian polyglot poet in *The Dog
Beneath the Skin* (*Plays*, p. 242).

1.7.7 A sleeping lexicon (compare 'sleeping dictionary') is a bed-
companion from whom one picks up a language.

1.9.1 See Housman's lecture 'The Name and Nature of Poetry'
(1933): 'I have seldom written poetry unless I was rather out of
health', etc. (*Collected Poems and Selected Prose*, Penguin, 1989,
p. 370).

1.11.1 Richard Jeffries, the Wiltshire writer and naturalist. Auden
wrote a sonnet about him in May 1925 (*Juvenilia*, p. 92).

1.11.4 Marie Stopes (1880–1958), pioneer of family planning and sex education.

1.13.7 The moral failings of Henry Crawford and John Yates were exposed in *Mansfield Park*, those of Charles Musgrove in *Persuasion*.

1.16.2 The four great Russians are presumably Turgenev, Gogol, Dostoyevsky and Tolstoy.

1.16.4 The original line 'The Book Society had not been bought' was replaced, for fear of libel, by 'The help of Boots had not been sought'. The presence of Day-Lewis on the selection committee of the Book Society (for which he had been much vilified, e.g. by Grigson in *New Verse*, May 1937) ensured that *Letters from Iceland* was itself recommended to the Society's members.

1.16.7 Henry James had said that the novel was 'the most independent, most elastic, most prodigious of literary forms' in his Preface to *The Ambassadors*.

1.19.5 T. E. Lawrence adopted the names first of J. H. Ross and then of T. E. Shaw when he enlisted in the ranks of the RAF in 1922.

1.23 Auden elaborated his view of light verse in the introduction to his *Oxford Book of Light Verse*. He thought that Belloc was one of the two best writers of light verse of the time.

1.24.1 See the poem of that title by W. B. Yeats in his collection *The Green Helmet* (1910).

1.24.3 'Quicunque vult' is a key phrase of the Athanasian creed meaning 'Whoever wishes [may be saved]' See also 'New Year Letter', line 1033, where it is also used in a secular sense.

1.24.5 See Goethe, *Faust*, I.xxv.208–9. When Mephistopheles says of Gretchen in prison: 'Sie ist gerichtet!' ('She is condemned!'), a voice is heard from above saying: 'Ist gerettet' ('She is redeemed').

1.24.6 'Et cetera, et cetera' cf. *Don Juan*, III.i, XIII, 284, etc.

1.25 John Bradford (1750–1805), dissenting minister and hymn-writer; Thomas Cottam (1549–82), Jesuit martyr; John Dyer (1699–1758), poet; Matthew Prior (1664–1721), poet.

1.26.7 Faber and Faber's address in 1936 was 24 Russell Square.

1.29 Auden used the translations of the sagas by G. W. Dasent, and in his Bibliography (p. 89) refers to William Morris's *Journal* (1871–3), Lord Dufferin's *Letters from High Latitudes* (1858), and Hooker's *Journal of a Tour in Iceland* (1812). Peter Fleming (1907–71) was author of *Brazilian Adventure* (1933) and correspondent of *The Times* in China from the same year. Auden and Isherwood were to encounter Fleming in China (see *Journey to a War*, p. 207).

1.30.4 Auden's father believed that the Auden family was descended from Auðun Skökull, who was one of the first Norse settlers in Iceland in the ninth century.

11.4.2 See *Don Juan*, 1.lxiv: 'Happy the nations of the moral North!' etc.

11.6.1 'Eotechnic' is a term coined by Patrick Geddes. Auden probably intended 'neotechnic', which was Lewis Mumford's term for the new economy based on electricity and lighter metals (see *Technics and Civilization*, 1934).

11.10.2 This was his father's mother, who lived at Horninglow, near Repton.

11.18.3 Andrew Carnegie (1835–1919), wealthy manufacturer and philanthropist, who had started work as a bobbin-boy in a cotton factory.

11.19.7 The Leicestershire hunt.

11.22.7 Ely Culbertson was an authority on Contract Bridge.

11.23.2 i.e. a chorus girl. C. B. Cochran (1872–1951) was a theatrical impresario, particularly of musicals and revues.

11.24.6 Vilfredo Pareto (1848–1923), Italian economist and sociologist.

11.33–5 Despite the characterisation in terms of Mickey Mouse or Strube's cartoons, Auden's little man here is a version of Organisation Man (eventually, perhaps, of someone like Adolf Eichmann) and the 'ogre' is a version of the state bureaucracy which manipulates him. Auden was to return to another aspect of the ogre in his poem 'Autumn 1968'.

11.36.1 Compare Wordsworth on Milton.

11.37.6 Sir Oswald Mosley, leader of the British Fascist Movement.

11.37.7 Gleichgeschaltet: made to toe the line.

11.38.3 The upper-class religious revival represented by the Oxford Group Movement had achieved greater notice after its Albert Hall meeting of July 1936.

11.38.4 W. R. Morris (Lord Nuffield), car manufacturer.

11.38.5 Stanley Baldwin, the Prime Minister.

II.38.7 Richard Tauber, tenor.

II.40.7 Gide supported the Communist-inspired United Front against fascism, but in 1936 after his visit to the USsr became disillusioned.

II.41.4 cf. Milton, 'On the Morning of Christ's Nativity', line 172: 'Swinges the scaly Horror of his folded tail.'

II.44.3 cf. Tacitus, Agricola, 30: 'ubi solitudinem faciunt, pacem appellant', from the speech of the British chief Calgacus.

II.45.4 Set and Horus, brother and son of Osiris, were the Egyptian deities representative of the cult of death and immortality.

III.1.6 See the headnote above.

III.3.6 This is probably the Oxford philosopher, H. A. Prichard.

III.10.7 Storm's was a café near the railway station in Keswick.

III.11.1 See *Areopagitica* (1644), but Milton was ironically referring to the licensing authority's interference with a teacher's credibility. The reference probably derives from Charles Whibley's Introduction to W. P. Ker's *Essays*, p. xii, referring to Ker's use of the phrase in his lecture on Joseph Ritson.

III.11.7 As Arnold did.

III.20.4–5 Diderot had claimed that he would exchange ten Watteaus for one Teniers (quoted in Anita Brookner, *Jacques-Louis David*, 1980, p. 15). Auden had borrowed two volumes of caricatures at Akureyri 'and spent a very happy evening with Goya and Daumier' (p. 123).

III.20.7 A version of this line in quotation marks appears in Auden's essay on Pope in *From Anne to Victoria*, ed. Bonamy Dobrée (1937). His intention was to contrast the human poetry of Pope or Byron with the nature poetry of someone like John Clare, who is the only poet I have found who uses all these words. Pudge: puddle; pilewort: the Lesser Celandine, Ranunculus Ficaria; petty-chap: the Garden Warbler or Chiff-chaff, Sylvia Hortensis; pooty: the girdled snail shell, Helix Nemoralis.

III.30.1 Thomas Savery, Thomas Newcomen and James Watt were pioneers of the steam-engine.

III.33.5 Auden returned to this joke about Baudelaire in 1938 in the Introduction to the *Oxford Book of Light Verse* (EA, p. 366).

IV.7.5 Rassenschänder: defiler of the race.

IV.9.6 Georg Groddeck believed that the 'It' controlled not only an individual's illnesses but also his or her physique or bodily characteristics.

IV.10.2 St John Ervine (1883–1971), playwright and critic. He was drama critic of the BBC from 1932.

IV.10.3 See John Sparrow, *Sense and Poetry* (1934).

IV.11.3 i.e. Dante, Goethe and Shakespeare (Joyce's words in *Finnegans Wake*, p. 539, line 5).

IV.13.2 referring to the confessional house-parties of the Oxford Groups.

IV.15.1–3 See Shakespeare, Sonnet 121, lines 9–11.

IV.16.5 i.e. *Lions and Shadows*, eventually published in 1938.

IV.19.3 The customary saying is 'All Lombard Street to a China orange', the former being the centre of banking and trade in London.

IV.21.3 The terrier was called Vigi.

IV.25.5 The word is *bellum.*

IV.27–9 Captain Reginald Oscar Gartside-Bagnall (see *Forewords and Afterwords*, p. 505).

IV.39 The friend was Robert Medley.

IV.41.4 The poem referred to is probably 'The Darkling Thrush'.

IV.41.7 Alluding to the penultimate line of Rupert Brooke's 'The Old Vicarage, Grantchester'.

IV.42.4 i.e. because he was a follower of Eliot.

IV.43.5 i.e. the generation of Waugh and Brian Howard.

IV.44.3 When Augustine came to Carthage, he found it a 'cauldron of unholy loves' (cf. *The Waste Land*, line 307).

IV.44.6 John Layard, the anthropologist.

IV.45.1 Homer Lane, American psychologist and educationalist. For the impact of Layard and Lane on Auden, see Carpenter, pp. 85ff.

IV.47.7 i.e. Gabbitas and Thring, educational agency.

IV.51.2 See Mendelson, *Early Auden*, pp. 281–3.

IV.52.7 greens: sexual intercourse.

V.4.3 Dura Virum Nutrix: stern nurse of men.

V.8.4 Sir Frederic Truby King (1858–1938), author of *Feeding and Care of Baby* (1913) and *The Expectant Mother and Baby's First Month* (1924).

V.10.2 The words of Henry James addressing the guardian angel of his inspiration in French in his journal entry about *The Ivory Tower* on 4 January 1910.

v.11.1 'The wise are susceptible to the beautiful' (Hölderlin, 'Sokrates und Alcibiades', lines 7–8, with omissions). Auden quoted the whole of the second stanza of the poem in his review of Laurence Housman's *A.E.H.: A Memoir* in *New Verse*, January 1938, and also referred to its concept of 'Das Lebendigste' ('what is most alive') in 'Last Will and Testament', where it was bequeathed to Nevill Coghill.

v.13.4 'Ganymed' is the penultimate of Hugo Wolf's Goethe songs, one of three on aspects of the relationship of man to God. The cry is that of Ganymede, yearning to embrace the beauty of nature in his arms.

v.15.3 cf. 'stolen waters are sweet', Proverbs ix.17.

v.15.7 Henry Pye (1745–1813), Poet Laureate.

And the traveller hopes: 'Let me be far from any

July 1936; 'Journey to Iceland', *Listener*, 7 October 1936; *Poetry*, January 1937; 'Journey to Iceland: A letter to Christopher Isherwood, Esq.'', LI, p. 25; CP45, p. 7; CSP, p. 23; CSP66, p. 100; CP, p. 149; EA, p. 203; *Prose*, p. 185.

The poem is an investigation of this statement, taken from the prose letter to Isherwood which follows it: 'We are all too deeply involved with Europe to be able, or even to wish to escape.' The celebrated misprint 'ports' for 'poets' is also explained in this letter. Iceland represents the traveller's 'limited hope' that there is somewhere 'where the affections of its dead can be bought | By those whose dreams accuse them of being | Spitefully alive' (probably a joke about spiritualism. Auden wrote to E. R. Dodds on 10 July: 'Spiritualism is the commonest religion, but I haven't been to a séance yet'). It is the North which means 'Reject', providing an ascetic refuge for 'the pale' who 'from too much passion of kissing feel pure in its deserts' (cf. 'Letter to Lord Byron', II.4.2: for further elaboration of North/South symbolism, see 'England: Six Unexpected Days', *Vogue*, 15 May 1954). It is also Auden's ethnic homeland (since his father claimed their family's Icelandic descent), his favourite saga world and a place of 'natural marvels'.

In stanzas 4–6 are the following allusions. The 'horse-shoe ravine' is Asbyrgi, a rock island shaped like a hoofmark of Sleipnir, Odin's horse. The bishop who 'was put in a bag' was Jon Gerreksson, who was drowned in a sack in the river Bruara near Skalholt in 1433. The 'great historian' is Snorri Sturluson (d. 1241), whose bath may be seen at Snorralaug. The outlaw who dreaded the dark is Grettir and the rock ('fort' in later texts) is perhaps Grettishof (see *The Saga of Grettir the Strong*, tr. G. A. Hight, 1914, chapters lv and lix). The doomed man thrown by his horse is Gunnar (see *The Story of Burnt Njal*, tr. G. W. Dasent, Edinburgh, 1861, 1.236: 'Fair is the Lithe; so fair that it has never seemed to me so fair . . . and now I will ride back home, and not fare abroad at all'). The 'old woman confessing "He that I loved the I Best, to him I was worst"' is Gudrun in the *Laxdaela Saga*, speaking to young Bolli about Kjartan (tr. Muriel Press, 1899, p. 271). Auden writes at length about this saga in *Secondary Worlds*, Lecture II. But behind the tourist front and the heritage of the sagas is eternal human nature (stanzas 8–10). The poem concludes with some borrowed lines from 'The fruit in which your parents hid you, boy' (for details, see p. 186) and offers no actual location for the romantic wish for a 'fabulous country'; this is the illusion of the escapists, the mad driver (the type of the traditional hero, a Truly Weak Man, a Gunnar rather than a Njal perhaps) and the writer who 'runs howling to his art'. The poem 'Hammerfest' provides an interesting comparison with the conclusions of this poem.

A glacier brilliant in the heights of summer

July 1936; 'Letter to R. H. S. Crossman, Esq.', LI, p. 91; *Prose*, p. 241.

This poem was written to former Oxford friend and later politician, Richard Crossman, while Auden was in 'the Njal country', and makes references to that saga. The thrust of the poem's familiar argument in favour of the 'uniqueness' (stanza 7) of the individual instance as opposed to the larger generalisations that create our sense of 'fate' (stanza 17) is here dependent on the example of photographs, the very photographs that Auden took to illustrate *Letters from Iceland*, in particular of a village festival at Mulakot, as described in stanzas 1–3 and exemplified in the photographs following p. 96 (the photographs were unfortunately omitted from reprints of the volume). The pure excitement of accurately capturing any image, however unimportant, 'through the glass' is dramatically described in stanza 9 (the cellophane from a cigarette packet 'like glittering butterflies'), even though the series of images from Njal's Saga in the previous stanza is deliberately and contrastingly matter-of-fact. These refer to Gunnar's death at Hliðarendi (see *The Story of Burnt Njal*, tr. G. W. Dasent, Edinburgh, 1861, 1.246). The ripe barley fields of Hliðarendi (which is only about two miles from where Auden is writing the poem) are 'white to harvest' in Dasent,

1.236. Flosi rides to Threecorner Ridge before the burning of Njal's house (Dasent, II.165). Auden has confused 'Little Daimon [sic]' with 'Big Dimon' (Storn Dimon), called Rauðaskriður in the sagas ('Redslip' in Dasent). He is referring to Njal's and Gunnar's wives fighting by proxy when their serving men Kol and Swart meet on Rauðaskriður (Dasent, I.107ff).

Auden was later to reverse this argument about photography entirely (e.g. in the Christian evaluation of the 'meaningless moment' of the camera's eye in 'Memorial for the City' or in Rosenstock-Huessy's view, elaborated in 'I am not a Camera', that photographable life is always either trivial or already sterilised, lacking our crucial moral evaluation), but in 1936 it suited the general feeling of the time that individuals could be too easily defeated by their received understanding of impersonal forces like 'the law' (stanza 12), 'Time' or 'history' (stanza 15). In the poem these come to constitute a flood (cf. the last stanza of 'August for the people and their favourite islands') which anaesthetises the human will, dismisses the value of making choices and encourages a compensatory fantasy and false heroics (stanzas 16–17). The reference to Oxford in stanza 16 alludes to Crossman having become a don there, and the final stanza brings the last-ditch heroics of *The Battle of Maldon* into play (he had already quoted lines 312–13 in Ode v of *The Orators*).

For who is ever quite without his landscape

July 1936; 'Detective Story', LI, p. 122; CSP66, p. 42; CP, p. 151; EA, p. 204; *Prose*, p. 267.

The poem is introduced in the letter to 'E. M. A.' (Erika Mann) in which it appears as being about 'why people read detective stories'. Really, of course, it is about guilt, for in Auden's parable the murderer and his victim are ultimately the same: 'Someone must pay for | Our loss of happiness, our happiness itself.' As usual in this period, Auden's casual relish in making the allegory work prevents the poem from becoming too soberly moralising. It is interesting to compare it with his later essay 'The Guilty Vicarage': 'I suspect that the typical reader of detective stories is, like myself, a person who suffers from a sense of sin' (*The Dyer's Hand*, p. 157). See also 'To T. S. Eliot on his Sixtieth Birthday (1948)'.

O who can ever praise enough

July 1936; *Poetry*, January 1937; LI, p. 143; CP45, p. 226; CSP, p. 255; 'The Price', CSP66, p. 105; CP, p. 154; EA, p. 205; *Prose*, p. 281.

This is another poem from the letter to Erika Mann, and in *Letters from Iceland* is introduced by some remarks to her as follows:

> Went for a short walk in the afternoon to the bridge over the half-lake, half-river which fills this valley. I was thinking about a picture of the seven ages of man I saw in some book or other. A girl playing a flute to a young man, two infants wrestling in a meadow, and an old man staggering to a grave, you know the kind of thing. After tea the thoughts developed into a poem.

Davenport-Hines (p. 159) has suggested that the painting is Titian's *The Three Ages of Man*. The poem evidently contrasts in its two Blakean stanzas the cherished order of life created by the imagination, and the price paid by the individual organism which houses that imagination. Some critics (Beach, p. 141; Robert Bloom, *Shenandoah*, pp. 40–1) take the second stanza to indicate the penalty of 'experience', as though the first stanza represented only a childhood world. It seems to me, however, that the second stanza is about gestation and birth (nine nights representing nine months, in a slight parody of the Creation), and that to be 'Bride and victim to a ghost' is not so much a Gothic symbol as a riddle for the body being invested by the soul. The pit and the ghost were no doubt suggested by the Icelandic lullaby that Auden refers to in the letter ('Far i fulan pytt | Fullan af draugum'). This, then, is the somatic reality behind the 'fantasy' of the seven ages view of life. It opposes to the comforting landscape the essential solitariness of the human condition.

'But Landscape,' cries the Literary Supplement

September 1936; LI, p. 220; *Prose*, p. 344.

The general letter to the painter William Coldstream begins with a short prose introduction in the style of the sagas and concludes with a poem each from Auden and MacNeice. This 'little donnish experiment in objective narrative' comes between. Doubtless in using the phrase 'objective narrative' Auden had somewhere in mind the camera-eye technique of John Dos Passos's trilogy *USA*, whose third part, *The Big Money*, appeared in

1936. But the procedure of the poem constantly evokes the making of a documentary film. Auden had known Coldstream well when they both worked for the GPO Film Unit, and as the poem suggests, both 'were suspected, quite rightly, of being disloyal' (line 35). Auden's objections to the documentary film movement to which he made such a notable contribution were both aesthetic and sociological (they are clearly enough set out in his review in the *Listener*, 19 February 1936, of Paul Rotha's *Documentary Film*, EA, p. 354) and the poem good-humouredly makes much of film's necessary traffic with externals. There is much characteristic complaint about absence of human interest (at line 57, the sailors he sympathises with are those in the 1936 film *Follow the Fleet*, and a quotation from its Irving Berlin song 'We Saw the Sea' follows. Auden always hated the sea).

If, as Coldstream claimed, the artist 'is both perceiver and teller, the spy and the gossip' (line 64), the poem makes it clear that 'telling' barely gets closer to the human truth than 'perceiving'. Auden produces first (lines 72–108) an array of discrete images of Icelandic life like the rushes of a film that could only be 'saved' by editing (or perhaps by commentary; Stuart Legg had spoken Auden's verse commentary to *Night Mail*). Then he produces, in heroic parataxis, a jumble of personal gossip (lines 116–60), much of it funny, but none of it designed to explain anything at all about Iceland. Auden plays Sarastro's aria from *The Magic Flute*, II.i, on the farmer's harmonium, they read a story by Somerset Maugham (which Auden used for his poem 'As it is, plenty') and MacNeice mutters Greek on the quay (some very relevant lines from the *Odyssey*, v.219–20, Odysseus to Calypso, saying that she may be more beautiful than Penelope: 'But even so, I wish and long day by day to reach my home, and to see the day of my return'). The slightly hysterical mood which all this induces is compounded by what Auden calls the equivalent of 'orchestral background' in the form of political and economic comment from Europe, really the theme of the whole book: 'Your case is hopeless. I give you six months.' Purely subjective feelings are the responsibility of music (cf. Auden's poem 'The Composer') and therefore, by implication, it is left to poetry to provide, in symbol and generalisation, its larger human interpretation, vindicating at last the earlier preference for 'Subject' over Roger Fry's 'Significant Form' (line 40) as a means of 'stating experience' (line 174). Auden's poem follows.

'O who can ever gaze his fill'

September 1936; 'Song', *New Statesman*, 16 January 1937; LI, p. 227; CP45, p. 224; CSP, p. 253; 'The Dead Echo', SP58, p. 52; 'Death's Echo', CSP66, p. 103; CP, p. 152; EA, p. 205; *Prose*, p. 350.

This is the poem which immediately follows the 'Letter to William Coldstream, Esq', fruit of a fortnight in which nothing very remarkable happened. Its immediate context is the mention of grave news from Europe (among other things, of course, the announcement of the outbreak of civil war in Spain) which the Coldstream letter treats with comic despair (see p. 212). Thus Death's mysterious and insistent injunction in the refrain to 'dance while you can' acquires a sinister overtone of evasion as well as being in a Yeatsian sense a call to order. The farmer and the fisherman, the travellers, the lover, the dreamer and the drunkard have all embraced life with enthusiasm, but Death's answer underlines the ultimate emptiness of their various objectives: 'Not to be born is the best for man.' This, we feel, is *not* Auden's conclusion, but he is showing how the pastoral, social, erotic or spiritual utopias are all irrevocably bonded to their negative motivations or conditions: the despair of lean years, loneliness, post-coital sadness or the morning-after hastens man's awareness of his mortality. For a somewhat later view of the Death Wish as part of the concealed puritanism of Freud's opposition of the Pleasure Principle to the Reality Principle, see *The Prolific and the Devourer*, p. 7.

We, Wystan Hugh Auden and Louis MacNeice

?December 1936; 'Auden and MacNeice: Their Last Will and Testament', LI, p. 236; *Prose*, p. 357.

Letters from Iceland was virtually complete by the beginning of December 1936, but seemed to require a larger and more generalised statement (Auden wrote to E. R. Dodds on 8 December: 'The whole thing is finished except the testament we are going to do together'). Auden had used Villon's *Petit Testament* and *Grand Testament* as models before, in the climax of the early play *The Fronny* (see *Plays*, p. 478). Here, however, instead of an eight-line tetrameter stanza like Villon's, Auden and MacNeice use *terza rima*. This technical change allows a slightly more expansive modulation from the itemised comedy of ironical bequest into more significantly quasi-Dantesque passages of 'testament' (i.e. of affirmation). At the end, for example, the tone is not far from the 'wooziness' (Auden's terms for high-minded generalising) of the tercets of the Commentary to 'In Time of War'. It is perhaps partly for this reason that the poem, otherwise a *tour de force*, was never reprinted. Another reason may have been proprietorial difficulties due to joint authorship. But undoubtedly Auden came to feel that the poem was obscure. In the Foreword to the 1967 paperback edition of *Letters from Iceland* he wrote: 'One chapter jointly written, *Last Will and Testament*, seems to me excessively private in its jokes, and I wondered whether I oughtn't to cut it. But American friends to whom all the Proper Names are unknown have told me that they enjoyed it, so I have left it as it was' (pp. 8–9). It is something of a special case in terms of commentary, going beyond 'A Happy New Year' and parts of *The Orators* in relying on elusively local material. Even those allusions which are still possible to recognise or reclaim are, many of them, either ruined by explanation or simply too tortuous to explain, like most good jokes. And the reader has to remember that 1936 was the year of the International Surrealist Exhibition. The following notes on Auden's contributions may, however, be of assistance. Page references are to the first edition.

p. 239. Auden's first bequests are to his parents. The fifteen-foot Cross at Bewcastle, near the site of a Roman outpost of Hadrian's Wall, is carved with seventh-century runic inscriptions. Auden's father was Professor of Public Health and School Medical Officer at Birmingham, also much interested in Norse antiquities and the supposed Icelandic origins of the family. The high-church St Aidan's, Small Heath, suited Auden's mother's religious practices. Auden's brother John was working with the Geological Survey of India at the time (see p. 194 for his relationship with *The Ascent of F6*) and his brother Bernard farming in Canada.

Stanley Baldwin, the Conservative leader, was returned as Prime Minister in October 1935. Kipling was a cousin, and he supported Dominion status for India. The National Government had been formed in August 1931 to save the pound. Churchill had been a member of the delegation who signed the Irish Peace Agreement on 6 December 1921, insisting that naval facilities be granted to the British at four strategic points around the Irish coast. Ballinrobe, however, is a town on the River Robe near Lough Mask, County Mayo, inaccessible by navigation, so that its 'dry harbour' (a place where ships may be repaired) would have little military significance. The allusion may be to Churchill's drinking. Randolph Churchill had publicly ridiculed Auden's friend E. R. Dodds's appointment as Regius Professor of Greek at Oxford on the grounds of his pacifism ('un bel pezzo' is a well-endowed man). Sir Maurice Hankey created the Cabinet secretariat in 1916 and had served governments of all parties since. George Lloyd, former Governor of Bombay, led the opposition in the House of Lords to the 1935 India Bill which gave India the right to self-government.

p. 240. The Gran Chaco is the central South American plain over which Bolivia (supplied by Vickers armaments) had fought against Paraguay. 'The Balkan Conscience' alludes to the Balkan Conference of 1935 which was designed to promote trade, not excluding arms. The stones of Kaldidalur ('Cold Dale', see *Letters from Iceland*, p. 187) are in a valley between the mountains of Langjökull and Ok, and Hambros Bank was Iceland's largest creditor. Ramsay MacDonald was the Labour leader who seemed to many in his party to have betrayed it by setting up the National Government in 1931 (in 1935 he became Lord President of the Council *vice* Baldwin on the grounds of ill-health); the allusion is to his 'soft-soaping' his supporters. Of the surrealist assortment of bequests to the Church of England, Austin Lee was Vicar of Pampisford, near Cambridge, a friend of Isherwood's who in 1932 had compromised his career as a naval chaplain by singing 'The Red Flag' in a pub in Malta. The Chief Scout was Robert Baden-Powell: at the bottom of p. 240 the scouting movement's notorious obsession with knots is alluded to. The puritanical Old Marlburian Arthur Winnington-Ingram was Bishop of London from 1901 to 1939: at the age of seventy-eight he had only recently given up playing hockey. 'The Grouper's Pope' is Frank Buchman, founder of the Oxford Group (known after 1938 as Moral Rearmament). The movement had gone public with a meeting in the Albert Hall in July 1936. W. R. Inge, Dean of St Paul's, was known for his gloom and exposure of popular illusions in weekly articles for the *Evening Standard* since 1921.

p. 241. Cosmo Gordon Lang was Archbishop of Canterbury from 1928 to 1942; his broadcast on the Abdication on 13 December 1936 was widely criticised for its attack on Mrs Simpson's social circle. Pat McCormick, Vicar of St Martin's-in-the-Fields, was a regular religious broadcaster. James Craig, first Viscount Craigavon, had been for fifteen years the first Prime Minister of Northern Ireland; he stubbornly refused a commission into the 1935 sectarian riots. Eamon De Valera was the Premier of the Irish Free State whose long-standing trade disputes with Britain led to the signing of agreements with Belgium, Germany and Spain in 1935, though the latter was no particular reason for embarrassment about his inherited Spanish surname (he was generally supported by the Labour Party, but its leaders were at times critical of his policies). The proctors at Oxford are, among other duties, responsible for undergraduate discipline, and the bulldogs are their bowler-hatted police (the New Zealand runner J. E. Lovelock set up a new world record of 3 minutes 47.5 seconds in the 1500 metres in the 1936 Olympic Games). A copy of *Excerpta de Statutis* (i.e. those rules relevant to Junior Members) were given to each matriculating member of the University.

p. 242. The OTC is the Officers' Training Corps. Of the useless places to send Oxford graduates, 'Calaguttis' may be a misunderstanding of 'Calagurris', a Roman town in the valley of the Ebro, Spain. Sir Farquhar Buzzard, Regius Professor of Medicine at Oxford since 1928, had played a leading part in the foundation of the Nuffield Institute for Medical Research in 1935 but no doubt gets his raspberry for standing as a Conservative candidate in the forthcoming Oxford University by-election. Wittgenstein had rooms above MacNeice's friend Anthony Blunt at Trinity College, Cambridge, and was one of Blunt's *bêtes noires*. Blunt's view seems to have prevailed here. Julian Huxley had become Secretary to the Zoological Society in April 1935, the year that he published *Ants*; he was well-known for inducing the axolotl to develop into a salamander by giving it thyroid extract (work that his brother Aldous clearly drew on when Lord Edward Tantamount in *Point Counter Point*, chapter iv, is shown cutting up 'salamanders and all that'). Lady Astor campaigned for teetotalism. The journalist Basil de Sélincourt receives the mock-Parthenon in Edinburgh for his pretentiousness; some of his *TLS* essays on Tolstoy, St Francis, Beethoven and others were collected in *Towards Peace* (1932). Cyril Norwood had been Master of Marlborough in MacNeice's time and was now President of St Johns College, Oxford. His *English Tradition of Education* had appeared in 1929, and its ideals of Service in education were attacked by Auden (see *The English Auden*, p. 384). The Rev. Philip Clayton was the founder of the teetotal organisation, Toc H. General Eoin O'Duffy was elected leader of the Irish Army Comrades Association in July 1933 and changed its name to 'the National Guard', a near-fascist organisation that used blue for its flags and shirts; 'the Harp That Once' alludes to the song by Tom Moore ('The harp that once in Tara's halls | The soul of music shed').

p. 243. The public-school writer par excellence Ian Hay (Major John Hay Beith) had the dubious distinction of having two West End plays running at the same time in 1936 (*The Housemaster* at the Apollo, and *The Frog* at the Princes). The three broken promises which Auden leaves to his own public school were '(1) Not to swear. (2) Not to smoke. (3) Not to say or do anything indecent' (see 'Honour', *The English Auden*, p. 325). J. A. Smith had in 1936 just retired as Waynflete Professor of Moral and Metaphysical Philosophy at Oxford. The 7 and 5 Abstract Group was an innovative group of artists directed by Ben Nicholson. The new Geological Museum at South Kensington had taken over the Jermyn Street Museum of Practical Geology's collection of fossils in 1935. Frederick Lindemann, Dr Lee's Professor of Experimental Philosophy since 1919, and Student of Christ Church since 1921, had become a member of the Tizard Committee on air defence in 1935. The *Observer*'s review pages had given Auden a fairly consistent bad press on the whole (if philosophers are fossils, then critics are dinosaurs). J. B. Morton, a disciple of Hilaire Belloc, took over the 'Beachcomber' column in the *Daily Express* from D. B. Wyndham Lewis in 1924. Shell-Mex House on the Embankment was built in 1931, the sort of modern architecture that Auden disliked. Wells had written the futuristic screenplay for the 1936 film *Things to Come*, based on his book *The Shape of Things To Come*. The Central School of Speech-Training and Dramatic Art was founded by Elsie Fogerty, who also worked for the Group Theatre; she would have disliked the heroic couplets of the minor Augustan poet Thomas Tickell, author of *Kensington Garden* (1722), the earliest known poem about Kensington Gardens (where Sir George Frampton's statue of Barrie's *Peter Pan* was erected in 1912; this is one of the obscurer jokes). The child Christopher Robin in A. A. Milne's stories is asexual; on the other hand, the sex-life of *Sunday Chronicle* diarist and prodigy Beverley Nichols already caused consternation at the time of his attachment to the War Office at the age of eighteen.

p. 244. Margot Tennant (married H. H. Asquith in 1894 and became Countess of Oxford in 1925) always minded about her figure, and was well-known to be a model for Dorothea Vane, the beautiful wilful heroine of E. F. Benson's first novel *Dodo* (1893). J. L. Garvin, a strong supporter of the National Government, was the Editor of the *Observer*. Rupert Doone was Director of the Group Theatre (see Jon Stallworthy, *Louis MacNeice*, 1995, p. 191, for his statement to MacNeice during preparations for *Agamemnon* in MacNeice's translation: 'Aeschylus is static, and I'm dynamic, so fuck all!'). Daan Hubrecht was at Trinity College, Cambridge, in Blunt's time there; Stephen Dedalus lived in a Martello Tower in Joyce's *Ulysses*. Hugh McDiarmid, the Scottish poet, is appropriately given a cheap drink made of red wine and methylated spirits because of his politics, his drinking and Auden's opinion of his poetry. Sir Archibald Flower was Chairman of the Trustees of Shakespeare's Birthplace and of the Council of the Shakespeare

Memorial Theatre at Stratford. Lieut.-Col. Ross McGillicuddy was a member of the Irish Senate. The homosexual novelist Norman Douglas was also a keen cook. John Fothergill owned the Spread Eagle at Thame and had written anecdotal name-dropping volumes of his memoirs (see MacNeice, *The Strings are False*, p. 258); Lyons Corner Houses were popular cafeterias. Maurice Bowra is left 'Life' as opposed to 'Eternity' (the allusion is to Shelley's 'Adonais'). Ronald Knox not only translated the Bible, but published detective stories and a *Book of Acrostics* (1924). The novelist Compton Mackenzie had helped to found the Scottish Nationalist Party in 1928 and had been Rector of Glasgow University between 1931 and 1934. James Douglas was a literary journalist. Roy Campbell continued to attack the work of Auden and his friends in his *Mithraic Emblems*, published in October 1936, and was notorious as a self-advertising macho poet (see *The Prolific and the Devourer*, p. 21). The Sunday theatre critics James Agate and Ivor Brown had both been dismissive about the Group Theatre. The implication in Edith Sitwell's bequest is that her obituary would at last tell the truth about her literary standing. Naomi Mitchison's 'faith period' was perhaps realised sooner than Auden suspected: in 1939 she published *The Kingdom of Heaven* and *The Blood of the Martyrs*.

p. 245. Sir Oswald Mosley, founder of the British Union of Fascists, had remarried in October 1936 with Hitler as a witness; in December Parliament had empowered the police to forbid political processions as a result of his East End marches. Anthony Ludovici was an eccentric and prescriptive eugenicist. He believed that classical ideas of female beauty were basically homosexual, and stressed the different trunk-leg ratios in men and women (see his *The Choice of a Mate*, 1935, pp. 482ff, where the desirable features of breast, hips and legs are comparable to those found in the Venus of Willendorf). The King's Proctor was left a skeleton key because his office was concerned to prevent false evidence of adultery (as a result of complicit access to hotel rooms) from being used in divorce cases (in which he traditionally intervenes on behalf of the Crown). *Die Untergang des Abendlandes* ('The Decline of the West') was a book by Oswald Spengler. The music-hall singer Douglas Byng was famous for sexual innuendo. Geoffrey Mure was MacNeice's philosophy tutor, 'one of Oxford's few remaining neo-Hegelians' (*The Strings are False*, p. 125). MacNeice distrusted the fashionable semantic philosophy and found Mure, translator of Aristotle, sympathetic. Barrie's sentimental view of babies in *Peter Pan* was diametrically opposite to the scientific one of Sir Frederic Truby King, according to whose regime the infant MacNeice was raised (see *The Strings are False*, p. 147). Sir Bindon Blood (born 1842) had only recently been appointed chief royal engineer; Bernard Shaw (born 1856) was as vigorous as ever. Marie Stopes had founded the Mother's Clinic for birth control, and cocoa-butter was a recommended method. The 'most mischievous woman now alive' was Marie Beazley, MacNeice's mother-in-law (for her numerous interferences in her daughter's affairs, including a specially commissioned Jewish curse, see Jon Stallworthy, *Louis MacNeice*, 1995, pp. 176–7). Evelyn Underhill was a prolific writer on mystical subjects. Osbert Lancaster, artist and writer (his first books had appeared in 1936), appreciated Victoriana. He was to design *The Rake's Progress* for Glyndebourne in 1953. Nervo and Knox (along with Flanagan and Allen, Naughton and Gold, and 'Monsewer' Eddie Grey) were members of the Crazy Gang, formed in 1931 under Val Parnell, and appearing frequently at the London Palladium; the Eisteddfod is the annual Welsh celebration of the national achievements in poetry and music. 'Ladislas Peri' is László Peri, the sculptor. Bryan Guinness the poet is left bitter because his family made the best-known brand of stout.

p. 246. For 'the Interest itself', see p. 147. William Coldstream was a member of the London Group of painters from 1933 and was the recipient of one of the letters in the volume (see p. 211). He did become Slade Professor of Fine Art at University College, University of London, in 1949. The proceeds of the Entertainment Tax are left to the Group Theatre because the tax was abolished or reduced in theatres in April 1935. John Grierson was the director of the GPO Film Unit for which Auden had worked in 1935–6 (see pp. 188 and 212). 'Long Meg and her nine daughters' is a megalithic circle near Little Salkeld, just north of Penrith, appropriately left to the sculptor Barbara Hepworth. Clive Bell was the apostle of Pure Form. Ben Nicholson's carved reliefs bear a resemblance to the design of certain contemporary wireless-sets, such as those produced by Murphy Radio Ltd. Ian Parsons had given *The Dog Beneath the Skin* an extremely unsympathetic review in *The Spectator* (28 June 1935). Herbert Read had in 1935 published his *Poems 1914–1934*, much of which seemed at odds with his most recent ideas about art. Peter Fleming's travel books greatly understated the difficulties he encountered; Auden and Isherwood were to encounter him in China (see p. 235). The Martyr's Stake at Abergwili was near Carmarthen, where Bishop Ferrar was burned in 1555; Wyndham Lewis was at cultural odds with the world and had a notorious admiration for Hitler. Alexander Korda (Sandor László Kellner) formed London Film Productions in 1932. His recent films included *Rembrandt* and

Things to Come (both 1936). The 'Balcon Boys' were recruited to work at Gaumont-British Studios by Michael Balcon, its director of productions. *Sabotage* (produced by Balcon) was Hitchcock's vastly simplified version of Conrad's *The Secret Agent*. Hitchcock is appropriately left 'the Stavisky Scandal' as a subject (Stavisky had been involved in a 200 milliard-franc financial fraud in 1933; police tracked him to his Chamonix villa where he met with a violent death; the magistrate in charge of the papers connected with the affair was later found dead in mysterious circumstances, and the scandal had wide political repercussions). Berthold Viertel was the film director whom Isherwood worked with and wrote about in *Prater Violet*. The 'cottage' is the public lavatory at Piccadilly Circus Tube Station, used for homosexual pick-ups; the 'certain novelist' is Charles Morgan, whose recent 'spiritual cry' was made in his novel *Sparkenbroke* (1936). Lord Berners (Sir Gerald Tyrwhitt-Wilson) was a composer, novelist and landscape painter who had built a folly near his house in 1935; the 'King and Queen' would presumably be the recent and respectable Duke and Duchess of York (Edward VIII had renounced the throne on 10 December).

p. 249. John Waterhouse was a Lecturer in English at Birmingham (see *The Strings are False*, pp. 148–9) and Gordon Herrickx a sculptor ('Wimbush' in MacNeice's *Autumn Sequel*, canto I: see *The Strings are False*, pp. 155–6). The 'Hammerklavier' is Beethoven's Sonata in B flat major, Opus 106. 'The Isle of Capri' was a popular song of 1934. The painter Robert Medley (school friend of Auden's who had prompted him to write poetry in 1922) was the designer of the Group Theatre production in November 1936 of MacNeice's translation of the *Agamemnon*, in which the chorus wore goggles and Agamemnon a jester's cap. Geoffrey Tandy was a curator at the Natural History Museum. Humphrey Thackrah was the solicitor who arranged MacNeice's divorce; 'Numero Cinq' is the perfume Chanel no. 5. Isaiah Berlin was left a saucer of milk perhaps because he had acted like a witch's cat for MacNeice's mother-in-law (see Stallworthy, p. 176).

p. 251. There is a sexual innuendo in the remarks about John Betjeman (the story about Auden and Betjeman and the bribed scout was suppressed with a cancel in Charles Osborne's biography); Pugin (1812–52) was a church architect and Gothic revivalist.

p. 252. Harold Acton, the Oxford Aesthete, had lived in China since 1932; a 'goose' is a pinched buttock. Heinz Neddermeyer was Isherwood's boyfriend in the early 1930s and had many problems in travelling to evade military service. John Andrews was a ballet-dancer who had an affair with Isherwood early in 1937; 'L. M. S.' is the London, Midland and Scottish

Railway. St John Ervine was the *Observer*'s drama critic, and had mounted several attacks on Auden and MacNeice in 1935–6. Auden had made use of J. W. Dunne's *An Experiment with Time* (1927) in his poem 'It was Easter as I walked in the public gardens'. The geologist Andrew Corry had been a Rhodes Scholar at Merton; a belemnite is an extinct cephalopod (like a cuttlefish), or more particularly its fossilised internal bone shaped like a bullet (there is an inevitable sexual innuendo here). Noël Coward would have recognised that the sun must set on the British Empire after all. The bequest to the cadging Dylan Thomas supposes that his Welshness is to a degree *voulu*. Charles Madge's first Mass Observation publications were not to appear until 1937. The *New Statesman* is attacked for appearing to be self-righteous, and John Sparrow for being unsympathetic to Auden's generation (in his *Sense and Poetry*, 1934). The birthrate was down to just over sixteen per thousand in the 1920s, and under fifteen per thousand for most of the 1930s. The causes were felt to be economic, although there is again an absurd sexual innuendo in the thought of the economists Roy Harrod and Maynard Keynes 'pulling together' to reverse the trend. Brian Howard was a greatly indisciplined writer, but enjoyed travel; the 'painted buoy' is a less subtle innuendo than the previous one.

p. 253. Father Martin D'Arcy had been Master of Campion Hall since 1933, and in 1935 had been preaching in the US. He made so many converts into the Roman Catholic Church that it was sometimes known as 'doing a D'Arcy'. Nevill Coghill had been Auden's English tutor at Oxford; 'Das Lebendigste' means 'what is most alive', a quotation from Hölderlin's 'Sokrates und Alcibiades' (see also my note to 'Letter to Lord Byron', v.11, p. 208). In his 1965 'Eulogy', Auden supplies an interesting gloss on his bequest here by claiming that Coghill was 'not a disciple-hunting | Socratic bully, | not a celibate glutton'. Richard Dawkins had been Bywater and Sotheby Professor of Byzantine and Modern Greek at Oxford since 1920. He may have introduced Auden to string figures (see 'The month was April'), having published an article on them in *Annals of Archaeology and Anthropology* xviii (1931), p. 39 (for 'The Fighting Lions' figure, from Portuguese East Africa, see Kathleen Haddon, *Cat's Cradles from Many Lands*, 1911, p. 41). Richard Best, son of Lord Justice Best of Belfast, had come up to Christ Church in 1927. Geoffrey Grigson, poet and editor of *New Verse* was a particularly acerbic critic. William Empson's *Seven Types of Ambiguity* appeared in 1930. Gerald Heard (the Sampson of 'In the year of my youth . . .') was a significant influence on Auden from 1931. He had recently taken up yoga. Maurice Feild was the art master, and Geoffrey Hoyland the headmaster, of the Downs School, Colwall, where Auden had taught between 1932 and 1935. John Davenport was a freelance writer and bohemian. Tom Garland was an old school friend of Auden's ('Wreath' in the essay 'Honour', see *The English Auden*, p. 324). His wife Peggy recalled that he provided Auden with a warm coat and a supply of painkillers for the wounded before the poet went to Spain on 13 January 1937. Nancy was the wife of William Coldstream; she was to collaborate with MacNeice on *I Crossed the Minch* and had an affair with him. John Layard, the anthropologist and disciple of Homer Lane, had once been immobilised with a psychosomatic paralysis. Olive Mangeot was the wife of André Mangeot, leader of the string quartet for whom Isherwood had acted secretary. There is a reference to her in 'Letter to a Wound', and Auden made her the public dedicatee of 'Easily, my dear, you move, easily your head'.

p. 254. Peter Roger was a former Downs pupil who lived there with Auden in a cottage in the grounds of the school. He was one of the two who accompanied Auden on the trip to eastern Europe commemorated in 'In Search of Dracula' (see *Auden Studies* 2, pp. 19ff). Robert Moody was a medical student. He was the dedicatee of *The Dog Beneath the Skin*, and his brother John acted the part of Alan Norman in the first production on 12 January 1936. Graves and Riding had lived on the Spanish island of Mallorca until August 1936. The Channel Islands are a notorious tax-haven. The Laxey Wheel is an overshot waterwheel built as a power source for local lead mines. It puts in an appearance in 'Homage to Clio', stanza 19. Sean was the five-year-old son of Cecil Day-Lewis. Auden had spent a holiday with Michael Yates and his family on the Isle of Man in 1935; they lived in Brooklands, a suburb of Manchester. The novelist 'Sapper' (Cyril McNeile) wrote the Bulldog Drummond thrillers. Hilaire Belloc, author of such poems as 'Tarantella' ('Do you remember an inn, | Miranda?'), his sole contribution to Yeats's *Oxford Book of Modern Verse* (published in November 1936), would have loathed the modern ex-urban roadhouse. Quintin Hogg was then a barrister and a Fellow of All Souls. His book *The Law of Arbitration* had appeared in 1935. The Wardenship of the Cinque Ports has no serious executive function. St Clether's Well is in Cornwall, Betjeman country. Sebastian Sprott (Walter John Herbert Sprott) taught psychology at Nottingham University. At the time he was reputed to live in a working-class slum. Mortimer's Hole in Nottingham Castle is so called from the imprisonment of Roger Mortimer after the murder of Edward II. Gabriel Carritt (see pp. 12, 109 and 114) stayed with Auden at the Beetle and Wedge in Moulsford-on-Thames near Oxford, having (chastely) to share a bed. 'T. F. C.' is T. F. Coade, Headmaster of Bryanston. For Auden's letter about putting an onion in the chalice, see p. 161 and Carpenter, p. 174. Richard Crossman was one of the recipients of letters in the volume, and at the time was a member of Oxford City Council. John Cowper's Powys's *A Glastonbury Romance* appeared in 1932. The 'White Horses' are the chalk figures found in the Vale of the White Horse. The Vale of Evenlode contains the village of Adlestrop famously celebrated by Edward Thomas's poem of that name during the First World War (and MacNeice stayed in nearby Oddington in August 1934).

p. 255. Offa's Dyke was constructed by Offa, King of Mercia, to keep out the Welsh. The Castleton Caverns are in the Peak District, the Blue John area of Derbyshire, extending 2,000 feet below ground and first used by eighteenth-century lead miners. P. Sargant Florence was Professor of Commerce at Birmingham, a friend of E. R. Dodds and author of *The Logic of Industrial Organization* (1933), a book utterly opposed to the ideals of the Elmhirsts of Dartington Hall, a cultural, educational and craft community based on that of Tagore's Santiniketan. However, Auden failed to get a job at Dartington School because Leonard Elmhirst didn't like his pink shirt. Frederick (not Herbert) Pethick-Lawrence was imprisoned in 1912 for suffragist activity. The poet Rex Warner was also a keen ornithologist. Wicken Fen was an insect sanctuary in Cambridgeshire (see 'Out on the lawn I lie in bed', stanza 12) and Hillborough Dovecote belongs to Hillborough Manor, Temple Grafton, near Stratford. Sidney Newman was an organ scholar of Christ Church, and an Oxford friend of Auden's. Edward VIII abdicated before the new Coronation Organ in Westminster Abbey could be used. The Crystal Palace at Sydenham had burned down on 30 November 1936, leaving only the water towers at each end. Boston Stump is the 272 foot lantern tower of St Botolph's, Boston, Lincs. The psychoanalyst Ernest Jones's most recent work was *On the Nightmare* (1931). Michael Roberts, poet and editor of *The Faber Book of Modern Verse* (1936) was also a keen mountaineer. The composer Constant Lambert was neither traditional, provincial or German-influenced enough to have been performed at the Three Choirs Festival; his most recent choral work was *Summer's Last Will and Testament* (1932–5). The Vale of Eden in Cumbria was one of Auden's sacred landscapes. John Masefield, Poet Laureate, lived at Boar's Hill, near Oxford, as had Robert Bridges. The Birmingham Hippodrome was a music-hall (MacNeice describes a visit there in 1938 to see George Formby and Florrie Forde, see *The Strings are False*, p. 174).

p. 256. 'At the butts', i.e. shooting game. Their 'islands of Langahans' (i.e. 'islets of Langerhans') are parts of the pancreas that secrete either insulin or glucagon. 'Major Yogi-Brown' is Francis Yeats-Brown, author of *Yoga Explained.* The Thames Conservancy Board was opposed to nude river bathing of the kind practised at Parson's Pleasure in Oxford. F. R. Leavis, the critic and editor of *Scrutiny,* made a public point of finding Auden's work immature. On 1 December 1936, the Bishop of Bradford (A. W. F. Blunt) made some remarks on Edward VIII's need of God's grace for his office which precipitated open discussion in the *Yorkshire Post* and elsewhere of his affair with Wallis Simpson and led to the abdication. Gilbert Murray was the Regius Professor of Greek at Oxford before E. R. Dodds; he was a vegetarian. 'In Chancery', i.e. until their lust came of age.

It might be added, in case the spirit of *vive la bagatelle* of this poem (or its aforementioned 'wooziness') should be thought to amount to a serious self-contradiction, that Auden wrote his share of it with the full (and announced) intention of offering his services in Spain. When, therefore, in lines 10–13 he sets down his 'will and testament: | Believing man responsible for what he does, | Sole author of his terror and his content. | The duty is to learn, to make his choice', he knew precisely what he meant. This comic portrait of the year 1936 provides a moral context for a choice of this kind.

Alfred

The cabaret sketch 'Alfred' was written for the actress Therese Giehse, who acted with Erika Mann in her cabaret company, Die Pfeffermuehle. Auden had married Mann on 15 June 1935 to provide her with a British passport, and it was later arranged that Giehse should similarly marry John Simpson, a friend of E. M. Forster, on 20 May 1936. 'Alfred', perhaps intended as a kind of wedding present, was completed by 15 July, when it was accepted by John Lehmann for *New Writing*. It appeared in the issue of Autumn 1936, and was never reprinted by Auden. The text may be found in *Plays*, p. 437.

Isherwood describes Giehse in Amsterdam in *Christopher and his Kind* (p. 156) as an 'unforgettable actress'. Die Pfeffermuehle was touring in countries bordering on Germany where German was understood, and having a great success with its anti-Nazi satire: 'My most vivid memory of her', he recalled, 'is in a scene in which she nursed the globe of the world on her lap like a sick child and crooned weirdly over it.'

Auden's sketch has some similarity to this in tone. The old woman alternately cajoles, threatens and confides in the goose, whispers sexual secrets to it and ends up with it on her lap, a knife in readiness, saying: 'Auntie loves her Alfred. He knows she wouldn't hurt him, not for anything in the world . . .' A goose is a less obvious symbol than a globe, but the intention is comparable. According to the initial stage direction, the old woman 'has something about her that reminds us of certain prominent European figures'. She is the fairy-tale woman who kills the goose that lays the golden eggs. If she is Hitler, then the goose may be the German people who have been stupid enough to give him power. Perhaps more particularly he represents the Jews (the eggs being cultural or financial prosperity). The old woman is shown to be in the grip of a manic-sexual jealousy, a motif which the brevity of the piece doesn't allow credible development. Other possible allegorical details are thin in number and effect (does her secretly allowing the fox in, for example, allude to the Reichstag fire?).

The sketch does, however, have a memorable grotesqueness and sense of menace. Auden always had a gift for monologue (compare the Prize-Day speaker in *The Orators*, the Vicar of Pressan Ambo in *The Dog Beneath the Skin* or Herod in 'For the Time Being'), and here the combination of fairy-tale, crude political allusion and cartoon choreography (e.g. '*Looks round the stage on tip-toe*') suggests that he is attempting something in the classic popular vein of Disney or Chaplin. He revised the piece as a radio play, *The Dark Valley*, in 1940.

Hadrian's Wall

Hadrian's Wall was a radio documentary commissioned by the BBC and broadcast on their north-eastern Regional Programme on 25 November 1937. The incidental music was by Benjamin Britten.

Auden's script is largely a compilation, including space left for recorded talks by an archaeological excavator and a local farmer. He relied heavily on historical sources such as R. G. Collingwood, *Roman Britain* (1932). Much of the narration at *Plays*, pp. 443 and 447, is from Collingwood, pp. 18, 21 and 34–5, for example, and Joyce's guidebook on p. 445 is indebted to Collingwood, pp. 30–31. The verse 'Enos lases juvate' ('Help us, O household gods') on p. 441 is the sixth-century BC song of the Arval Brothers (see *Remains of Old Latin*, ed. E. H. Warmington, IV.250–52). The poem 'Now is the time to twine the spruce and shining head with myrtle' on pp. 442–3 is a translation of Horace I.iv.9–20 by Louis MacNeice (*Collected Poems*, p. 549). Auden was pleased enough with the sentence 'Plump little Horace composed his civilized song' to echo it in the last line of 'Voltaire at Ferney'. There are quotations from Tacitus: on p. 444, for example, all three of the rebellious speeches by a Male Voice are taken directly from M. Hutton's Loeb translation of the *Agricola*, 30 and 32 (Calgacus's speech before the battle of Mons Graupius). Auden also appears to have borrowed from Hutton in 'Now from my window-sill I watch the night' (see p. 158). The stanzas on pp. 443 and 448 are the first and last of Venus' aria from Dryden's *King Arthur*. The verse 'Jam lucis orto sidere' is an anonymous sixth-century hymn for Prime (see *The Oxford Book of Mediaeval Latin Verse*, ed. F. J. E. Raby, 1959, p. 53). The ballad on p. 450 is the anonymous 'The Fray of Support' (see *The Poet's Tongue*, p. 136).

Auden was no doubt attracted to this commission because the Wall was part of his sacred landscape (see 'New Year Letter', lines 1100 ff) but in the final two paragraphs of his dramatised guidebook he draws a serious Forsterian lesson that is central to his thinking at the time: political virtue is a matter of private, even anonymous, endeavour; political idealism is a frequent cover for barbarianism.

Caesar leaned out of his litter, shouted,
'How're we doing, boys?'

October 1937; 'Song of the Legions', 1972 TS; *Plays*, pp. 443, 444 and 446.

In the radio programme the three stanzas of the song are separated:
between the first and second stanzas is a statement about the geographical
dispersal of the legions, and between the second and third is a dramatised
account of the activities of the ninth legion from the battle of Mons
Graupius under Agricola to the construction of Hadrian's Wall under the
legate Aulus Nepos. Auden typed the poem up in 1972 after discovering a
copy of the script of *Hadrian's Wall* among his papers, giving it the title
'Song of the Legions'.

The manner of this poem is that of Kipling, the supreme celebrator of the
humour and endurance of the infantrymen of empire. Although most of
Kipling's examples concern the British in India, he did also produce the
'British-Roman Song' in *Puck of Pook's Hill* and 'Rimini' ('It's twenty-five
marches to Narbo. | It's forty-five more up the Rhone, | And the end may be
death in the heather | Or life on an Emperor's throne'). Auden was to
return to the Kipling manner for several poems in 'For the Time Being', his
other major work with a Roman Imperialist setting. 'Song of the Legions' is
written in trochaic octameter couplets (the form of 'Get there if you can
and see the land you once were proud to own') although the Kipling
flavour encourages the metre to collapse (as it tends to do in any case) into
galliambics. The second stanza refers to Agricola's completion of the
conquest of Britain, first in Wales (the Silures) and then in the North of
England (the Brigantes). Eboracum is York, headquarters of the ninth
legion.

Over the heather the wet wind blows

October 1937; 'Roman Wall Blues', AT, p. 94; CP, p. 121; EA, p. 289; *Plays*, p. 447.

This poem was all that Auden published from *Hadrian's Wall*. The opening
line echoes a line from *The Ascent of F6*, II.5: 'Over our empty playgrounds
the wet winds sough' (*Plays*, p. 346). If the legionary's girl was in Tungria
(in Germania), then he was doubtless quartered in the Tungrian garrison
of Housesteads, which the family in the radio programme are so eager to
see when they are introduced to us (p. 445) and which is the scene of the
eighteenth-century saga of the Armstrongs (pp. 450ff). From inscriptions at

Housesteads, it would appear that the legionary would have worshipped a Germanic god called Hueter. He is scornful of his puritanical Christian comrade Piso who 'worships a fish' because the Greek 'ichthus' was an acronym for '*Je*sous *CH*ristos, *TH*eou *U*ios, *S*oter' (Jesus Christ, Son of God, Saviour).

Journey to a War

In 1937 Auden and Isherwood were commissioned by Auden's publishers to write a travel book about the East. The outbreak of the Sino-Japanese War in August determined them to go to China, which they visited between January and July 1938. *Journey to a War* was first published in March 1939. The prose 'Travel-Diary' (from Hong Kong to Macao) which forms its bulk was written up by Isherwood from their separate journals, as was a piece called 'Escales', a travel-diary from Marseilles to Hong Kong (*Harper's Bazaar*, October 1938, reprinted in *Exhumations*). 'Escales' was not reprinted in the book, since some of its material is duplicated in Auden's poems in the section 'London to Hongkong'. Auden's verse contributions, which include this sequence, the volume's dedicatory poem to Forster and the concluding sonnet sequence, 'In Time of War', were much rearranged and revised in collections from the mid-1960s (including the paperback of *Journey to a War* in 1973). The verse 'Commentary' to 'In Time of War' was dropped from the sequence's separate reprintings as 'Sonnets from China'. General details of these changes are given below.

Here, though the bombs are real and dangerous

Summer 1938; 'To E. M. Forster', JW, p. 11; revised as Sonnet XXI of 'Sonnets from China', CSP66, p. 138; CP, p. 195; EA, p. 249; *Prose*, p. 494.

The dedicatory poem brings into play right at the outset a significant theme of the book: the conflict between the dangerous, apparently unavertable reality of the external political world and the continuing moral challenge of the 'inner life'. Auden locates evil in the genteel prejudices of the English middle-class that Forster exposed in his novels: the prejudices of Lucy Honeychurch (*A Room with a View*), Turton (*A Passage to India*) and Philip Herriton (*Where Angels Fear to Tread*). There is possibly some textual doubt about the real nature of this evil. For a travel book (and indeed, for a writer as significantly travelled as Forster) it is no doubt useful to claim that 'we | Wish international evil'. But what Caroline Abbott actually says in chapter 9 of *Where Angels Fear to Tread* is 'I will have no more intentional evil'. Clearly, what one intends is more crucial to Auden's scenario of moral choices than the international implications of those choices. Since the line would still scan if 'intentional' were substituted for 'international', it is possible that this is an unnoticed compositor's error. If so, it would not stand alone in Auden's work. The sonnet has other references to Forster's novels: Margaret and Helen Schlegel discover that the 'inner life had paid' in chapter xxxvii of *Howards End*; Lucy Honeychurch joins 'the vast armies of the benighted' when she sins against 'Eros and Pallas Athene' ('Reason . . . and Love' in the sonnet) in chapter 17 of *A Room with a View*, and the sword is the one with which Charles Wilcox has felled and accidentally killed Leonard Bast in *Howards End*. Miss Avery's silent accusation is turned into a general symbol here (we cannot escape our actions) which the role of this sonnet as the final one of 'Sonnets from China' made more specifically Christian, as though the housekeeper were an angel guarding Eden (cf. Sonnet II, line 13) against any human return.

Where does the journey look which the watcher upon the quay,

January 1938; 'The Voyage', JW, p. 17; 'Whither', CSP66, p. 119; CP, p. 173; EA, p. 231; *Prose*, p. 496.

This poem of embarkation and departure on 'the false island' of the ship bound for Hong Kong reiterates the point made in 'Journey to Iceland', and to a certain extent in 'Dover', that truth and falsehood go everywhere and that travelling discovers nothing. Auden's notion of 'the Good Place' in stanza 2 may be influenced by Henry James's story, 'The Great Good Place' (cf. 'At the Grave of Henry James', stanza 15). For the medical metaphor, compare 'Escales' (*Exhumations*, p. 144):

This voyage is our illness: as the long days pass, we grow peevish, apathetic, sullen; we no longer expect, or even wish, to recover. Only at moments, when a dolphin leaps or the big real birds from sunken Africa veer round our squat white funnels, we sigh and wince, our bodies gripped by the exquisitely painful pangs of hope. Maybe, after all, we are going to get well.

Did it once issue from the carver's hand

January 1938; 'The Sphinx', JW, p. 19; CP, p. 175; EA, p. 232; *Prose*, p. 496.

The macabre directness of 'The Sphinx' is to some extent due to the large amount of descriptive drafting which was ultimately condensed into sonnet form: the perceptions are strikingly distilled. There is an eighty-one-line quasi-Lawrentian poem in MS which contains the essence of the later sonnet's conception of Egypt as the uncomprehending cradle of Western civilisation. Some of the phrases of this poem get into the prose account in 'Escales' (*Exhumations*, p. 145):

> There it lies, in the utter stillness of its mortal injuries: the flat cruel face of a scarred and blinded baboon, face of a circus monstrosity, no longer a statue but a living, changing creature of stone. A camera, if cameras had been invented, could have shown how that face has changed through the centuries, growing old and blind and terrible in the blaze of the sun, under the lash of the wind and the desert sand. Once, no doubt, it was beautiful. Long ago, it could see. Now it lies there mutilated and sightless, its paws clumsily bandaged upon bricks, its mane like an old actor's wig, asking no riddle, turning its back upon America – injured baboon with a lion's cruel mouth, in the middle of invaded Egypt.

There is a comic account in Isherwood's *Christopher and his Kind*, p. 221, about whether the Sphinx actually faced west or east. The Sphinx represents an older fatalistic way of life, with no conception of progress and no possible understanding of the brash optimism of the latest civilisation ('shrill America'). It therefore becomes a numinous reminder of the eternal possibility of suffering, and offers no consolation to the ephemerality of power (the 'success' of line 10 is in the draft poem that of the successive conquerors of Egypt; in the sonnet there is a further suggestion of the admonition of the writer's pride). A sonnet requires a sonnet structure, however much it may be disguised as it is here by abruptness and enjambements; the questions in the sestet therefore turn the sphinx into a kind of generalised oracle, dramatising its function in a way which the lengthy early versions, for all their fullness and explicitness of writing, cannot begin to do.

The streets are brightly lit; our city is kept clean:

January 1938; 'The Ship', *Listener*, 18 August 1938; JW, p. 20; CP, p. 174; EA, p. 232; *Prose*, p. 497.

Like 'The Voyage', this sonnet exploits a somewhat obvious though ultimately powerful metaphor (here of the ship as European society; one of many possible sources for the idea is actually mentioned in *Journey to a War*, p. 187, the dictum of Anatole France that 'A British boat is a floating democracy. A French boat is a drifting demagogy'). The unnerving outcome is due to a discrepancy between the vagueness of the 'test' that Europe will be put to, and the laconic, matter-of-fact tone. We are certainly prepared for an Augustan neatness (e.g. 'One doubts the virtue, one the beauty of his wife') and yet the sentiments at the end strike deeper than this: 'no one guesses | Who will be most ashamed, who richer, and who dead'. The added room allowed by the six-foot line that Auden has chosen here contributes to the slightly menacing and obtrusive rhythm of the poem.

Holding the distance up before his face

January 1938; 'The Traveller', *New Statesman*, 27 August 1938; JW, p. 21; EA, p. 234; *Prose*, p. 497.

This sonnet (dropped after 1966) is about the effort of the traveller to maintain his identity. The readiness of the earth to accept man as a denizen is an illusion particularly attractive to the traveller, deriving from his perception that cultures are similar. However, in the sestet the traveller is significantly absorbed as an anonymous unit ('cities', 'crowds') not as the individual of the second quatrain, desperate to retain his unique identity.

A weed from Catholic Europe, it took root

December 1938; 'Macao', JW, p. 22; CP, p. 176; EA, p. 235; *Prose*, p. 498.

The imperialist origins of the great Eastern ports is given a half-comic turn in Auden's sonnets. In the case of Macao, the pioneering settlement of the Portuguese, this means that the Roman Catholic influence will ensure that evil is reduced and localised to manageable and pardonable proportions: 'nothing serious can happen here.' In fact, Macao saw the setting up of the first lighthouse, the first printing-press and the first foreign hospital in China.

The leading characters are wise and witty

December 1938; 'Hongkong', JW, p. 23; CP, p. 173; EA, p. 235; *Prose*, p. 498.

The comic view of Hong Kong is here conveyed through the theatrical metaphor, by which the financiers have created a sophisticated world where the 'servants' (i.e. the Chinese) are suggestively silent and where violence is forced to take place off-stage. It was the Japanese gun firing at the second line up from Ma Yuan that was 'like the slamming of a great door' (see *Journey to a War*, p. 110). The rebuke in the close of the sonnet to Rousseau's *volonté generale* is echoed in the 'Commentary' to 'In Time of War', line 158, in a more explicit context: the message of fascism is that man can have unity if he will give up freedom (at Swarthmore Auden taught a course entitled 'Romanticism from Rousseau to Hitler').

So from the years the gifts were showered; each

November 1938 (no. XII: 1936, no. XVIII: April 1938); no. XI: 'Ganymede', *Common Sense*, April 1939); no. XII: 'The Economic Man', *New Verse*, June–July 1936; no. XVIII, *New Statesman*, 2 July 1938, *Living Age*, September 1938, *China Weekly Review*, 29 October 1938, *New Republic*, 7 December 1938; no. XXI: 'Exiles', *New Writing*, Autumn 1938, *New Republic*, 7 December 1938; no. XXVII: 'Sonnet', *Listener*, 3 November 1938; 'Press Conference' and 'Air Raid' in *New Republic*, 7 December 1938 contain material that became nos XIII and XIV (see EA, pp. 426–7); 'In Time of War: A Sonnet Sequence with a verse commentary', JW, p. 259; no. VII: 'The Bard', no. XI: 'Ganymede', no. XII: 'A New Age', no. XVIII: 'Surgical Ward', no. XIX: 'Embassy', SP58, pp. 60, 54, 55, 56, 57; 'Sonnets from China', CSP66, p. 128 (omits nos IX, X, XIV, XV, XX, XXV and XXVI, reverses the order of nos XVII and XVIII, adds the dedicatory sonnet to E. M. Forster as the new no. XXI, and extensively revises the remainder. The 1973 paperback of *Journey to a War* uses this text without the Forster sonnet); CP, p. 183 ('Sonnets from China'); EA, p. 251 ('In Time of War'); *Prose*, p. 667.

'In Time of War' represents a new scope of historical understanding and new powers of generalisation and condensation in Auden's work. The 'Commentary' makes it clear that the sonnet sequence is an attempt to evaluate man's predicament in 'the epoch of the Third Great Disappointment' (the first two being the collapse of the Roman Empire and of medieval Christendom). The Sino-Japanese war thus becomes the main exemplum of a far more ambitious account of the vagaries of human destiny in the machine age than any kind of verse journalism would have allowed. Indeed, the Rilkean obliquities of the sequence and the occasionally grandiose and didactic paragraphs of the 'Commentary' have a particular function in the context of *Journey to a War* that are lost when they are abstracted from it. They are calculated to counterbalance the self-deprecatory comedy of the central 'Travel-Diary', where the authors' pretended ignorance of Chinese politics, awareness of war as a personal 'test', friendly rivalry with professionals like Peter Fleming, obsession with clothes, food and illness, and so on, sometimes goes to an extreme of the journalistically ingenuous (though without any loss of brilliance, charm or insight).

Auden's poems are thus structurally licensed in their longer perspectives and sometimes oracular or sermonising tone. It is this contrast, in fact, which gives *Journey to a War* its real distinction as a travel book. In its discussion of evil, of human nature and society, 'In Time of War' is Auden's *Essay on Man*, a seriously secular theodicy. It never loses sight of the ultimate problem of how human happiness and justice are to be achieved, even when it is dazzling the reader with its mercurial insights into dramatised history and its boldly symbolised cultural phenomena. The title itself may have been suggested by the English translation of the oratorio by Haydn. Auden's stylistic revisions for 'Sonnets from China' are mainly concerned to correct false rhymes (done with some ingenuity and slight loss of clarity) and to reduce the occurrence of the definite article (with largely disastrous effects). The revisions obscure the extreme and deliberate simplicity of much of the sequence, some of which has a quasi-biblical authority due to parataxis and basic vocabulary. Indeed, the core stylistic effects of the sequence are quite often achieved without straying much beyond the currently fashionable Basic English (some of the implications of Basic English for poetry were discussed by A. P. Rossiter, *Statement and Suggestion*, 1935).

No. 1 ('So from the years the gifts were showered; each') begins with the Creation, where the material world is seen to achieve its nature effortlessly, merely by existing in time ('the years'). In contrast with the vegetable and animal worlds, man is an unformed creature, capable of creating vastly different civilisations ('On whom the years could model any feature') and not easily classifiable as gregarious or predatory. Despite his error and mistrust, however, man is still (and this forms the leitmotif of the sequence) capable of shaping his own future: he 'chose his love'.

In no. 11 ('They wondered why the fruit had been forbidden') the lost Eden is interpreted as the impossible arcadia/utopia of 'the poet and the legislator': it is impossible because it is the way back and not the way ahead (compare Auden's much later distinction in 'Vespers' between 'my' Eden and 'his' New Jerusalem). The true way ahead is described as a kind of anti-Wordsworthian 'maturity' which 'as he ascended, | Retired like a horizon from the child' (surely a sort of answer to *The Prelude*, i. 322ff and 381ff where the hills follow the young Wordsworth with moral intent). Man is thus in a state, not of Being, but of Becoming, and his world is fraught with danger.

One of the dangers is language. In no. III ('Only a smell had feelings to make known') language gives man power, but exercises its own tyranny ('They' of line 9 are words) by obsessing man with ideas far removed from observable reality. Man is defeated by abstract thinking. The point about smell itself may have been suggested by Gerald Heard, *The Ascent of Humanity* (1931), p. 266: 'Smell is essentially a racial matter: through it passion must dominate.' For 'the interest' in line 6, see p. 147.

Auden then contrasts the unprogressive life of the Noble Savage in no. IV ('He stayed: and was imprisoned in possession') with the epic life of the *comitatus* in no. V ('His generous bearing was a new invention'), when the migrating tribes settled in Europe; the hero's decline into a stagnant authoritarianism represents the period of political growth and consolidation of the early Middle Ages. Some of Auden's abbreviated lines may have been achieved by accident: 'offices' in line 12 was originally 'hideous offices'. The epithet was deleted in draft and the missing foot never replaced.

No. VI presents the monastic tradition's pursuit of truth in solitude, from astrological prophecy to the first glimmerings of humanism. Auden avoids specific Christian references here, to allow the possibility of the generalisations being applicable to China as well as to the West. This is, of course, one of the obvious reasons for the general use of symbols and formulae in this first part of the sequence. No. VII is a history of poetry in any culture, whereby the intuitive and prophetic becomes the rational and satirical; Hesiod to Juvenal, say. No. VIII ('He turned his field into a meeting-place') is a brief description of the City in terms of capitalism, democracy, science and paper credit. Here is Auden's account of the 'Third Great Disappointment' in the sestet of the sonnet, where industrial urbanisation is the price paid for the advances of the Enlightenment described in the octave ('He gathered into crowds and was alone'), a theme which was to become an important element in Auden's work of the 1940s. No. IX ('They died and entered the closed life like nuns') is about the development of a consciousness of history, within which any dead individual becomes only the sum of an achieved life. The heroes of history (the 'kingly' and the 'saintly') are those whom we live up to in making our choices, those whom we correspondingly could 'free' by embodying their principles in our own lives and whom we in fact 'betray' by never doing so. 'Airs, waters, places' (line 8) is the title of a Hippocratic treatise, ΠΕΡΙ ΑΕΡΩΝ ΥΔΑΤΩΝ ΤΟΠΩΝ, on the distinctive contributions to the health of different environments, indicating a kind of 'climate' of the dead as we might talk of a 'climate' of opinion.

In no. x ('As a young child the wisest could adore him') Auden writes about the Logos and the secularisation of the church. 'The beautiful stone courts' (line 7) are built to contain this spirit of the Word or the Law, thus confining it and turning it into the exclusive property of the powerful. By a neat structural device the sacrificial 'poor' and 'martyrs' of the first quatrain become the oppressed 'poor' and 'martyrs' of the second tercet, suggesting that a systematised religion has changed nothing. No. xi ('He looked in all His wisdom from the throne') uses the myth of Zeus and Ganymede to account for man's misuse of his powers, again perhaps in the context of church history: conversion by compulsion (and therefore by violence) can only breed further violence. No. xii ('And the age ended, and the last deliverer died') looks in a different way at the similar theme of how we account for evil in an age of disbelief: the external powers of myth are interiorised into the compulsions of our own psyche, the results no less devastating. In line 13 'the sons who strayed into their course' was in the *New Verse* text 'the son, indifferent to the mother's curse'. Three lines were borrowed from ' "Sweet is it," say the doomed, "to be alive though wretched" ' (*TLS*, 16 January 1976).

At this point the historical preamble is really over. Man is now at a stage of civilisation at which consciousness of his failure to create a just society is equally mixed with his hope that he may eventually do so (no. xiii: 'Certainly praise: let the song mount again and again'). The opening of this sonnet is borrowed from the opening of the seventh of Rilke's *Sonnets to Orpheus*, Part i ('Rühmen, das ists!') although Auden's 'certainly' contains a strong sense of 'nonetheless', as in the 'dennoch preisen' of *Sonnets to Orpheus*, ii.xxiii. The structure is 'Certainly . . . But . . .' Despite the fragility of men's achievements 'all princes must | Employ the Fairly-Noble unifying Lie.' This is a reference to Plato's justification in *The Republic*, iii.414–15 of the Noble Lie which will convince the whole community that the Guardians rule by some natural right and not by virtue of being educated to rule. This 'lie' is the myth of a common birth of all citizens in mother earth, with a natural hierarchical differentiation according to the presence in them of gold, silver, iron or bronze. Its purpose is to increase loyalty to the state and to each other. Clearly myths of this sort are a function of admonitory 'history' which is opposed to the 'buoyant song' of praising (i.e. art). This opposition becomes the underlying theme of the remaining sonnets, which now turn to the actual situation in China.

Auden begins in the air. No. XIV ('Yes, we are going to suffer, now; the sky') was slower to take its final shape than most of the sonnets (see EA, pp. 426–7). The sonnet is answering a hidden question which effectively links the historical preamble with the present war: if suffering is indeed a consequence of the human errors which have been committed in the past, then 'Yes', we are going to suffer now. Auden may be remembering Bernard's empathy with Percival in *The Waves* (Penguin 1992, p. 202): ' "Now in this drawing-room he is going to suffer. There is no escape." ' There is a double meaning in 'the little natures' of line 4: in one sense they are like the now invisible powers of Sonnet XII, but they are also, of course, Japanese pilots. It is our manipulation of the earth we dwell on that is now in question, since this earth has few effective defences (the searchlights are 'groping' in the dark) against attack from the air. The sestet is curiously circular, since the aeroplane itself is an example of highly developed 'earth' (in the mineral sense) obedient to the 'intelligent and the evil'. We cannot escape responsibility ourselves, since the implicit connection between intelligence and evil condemns all human civilisation, and the octave has already established the air raids as something we recognise like our own illnesses or dreams. In the second sonnet about the air raids (no. XV: 'Engines bear them through the sky: they're free') Auden uses an extraordinary image of biological necessity to enforce another version of this circular argument. Thus, the pilots chose their fate (line 8), but if they are like 'the very rich' (line 1) they must also be like the 'heiress in her mother's womb' (line 13) and therefore bound and helpless after all. This link between rich and poor is pure metaphor for a psychological necessity, but it allows Auden's last line a sociological point in its own right. The Japanese airmen not being compelled to fly is perhaps suggested by Yeats's 'An Irish Airman foresees his Death', line 9 ('Nor law, nor duty bade me fight') since the Japanese 'skill' is as aesthetically detached as the Irish 'delight' in the task of military flying.

In no. XVI ('Here war is simple like a monument') the verse itself is simple like a monument. Though war is terrible, Auden retains a sense of the justice of a cause: 'Yet ideas can be true, although men die' (cf. 'Spain 1937'). Those ideas which are not true (i.e. Japanese imperialism) are therefore those which create the evil, and Auden links East with West at this juncture: 'And maps can really point to places | Where life is evil now. | Nanking. Dachau.' This abbreviated close is admirably pungent, and was probably borrowed from Rilke. No. XVII ('They are and suffer; that is all they do;') is set in the military hospital in Shang-kui (see *Journey to a War*, p. 93) where the isolation of suffering cannot be imagined by the uninjured. For line 9, 'For who when healthy can become a foot?', compare *The Prolific and the Devourer*, pp. 7–8: 'if we have a toothache, we seem to be two people, the suffering "I" and the hostile outer world of the tooth.' No. XVIII ('Far from the heart of culture he was used:') pays rather obvious respects to the fate of the common man in war: 'And added meaning like a comma, when | He turned to dust in China that our daughters | Be fit to love the earth, and not again | Disgraced before the dogs' smacks a little of questions about rape at a tribunal for conscientious objectors. It took Auden some time working on lines 9–10 to introduce this idea. He called it 'a Sassoon sonnet' in a letter of 20 April 1938 to Mrs Dodds (but in fact the whole sequence is a remarkable departure for war poetry).

In no. XIX ('But in the evening the oppression lifted;') the conferring leaders are perhaps rather melodramatically seen as out of touch with the armies waiting for their orders. (In lines 10–11, incidentally, are two examples of revision leading the poem astray: 'The armies' becomes 'two armies' in 1966, and 'all the instruments' becomes 'well-made implements': the later readings are obvious and/or overspecific). No. XX ('They carry terror with them like a purse') is about civilian refugees for whom the means of escape have come to signify the dispersal of their settled communities. Auden's *faux naif* similes do their familiar work here (for example, if terror is like a purse it has become something that you have come to need to underwrite your journey, cannot lose even if you would like to be without it, and therefore must be kept hidden; the metaphor riddlingly rewrites and occludes all sense of *value*. If we 'lie in the Present's unopened | Sorrow' then the Present is like an unopened present and we shall never know what it really is, i.e. the Future, which actually is unlimited, and need not be sorrowful at all). In no. XXI ('The life of man is never quite completed;') Auden takes a look at another example of the uprooted: the European exiles who 'walk the earth and know themselves defeated'. A 'shadow-wife' is probably to be taken in a Jungian sense of 'shadow'. i.e. all that one most does not wish to be.

No. XXII ('Simple like all dream wishes, they employ') is about popular tunes and the way in which they appear to ignore political events. The metaphor for this 'elementary language of the heart' or 'joy' is the primitive enthusiasm of 'the dancers' (cf. the escapist death-wish of the Dancer in *The Dance of Death*) which has fascist implications. While in China Auden heard that Franco had retaken Teruel from the Republicans on 22 February and that the Germans had marched into Austria on 11 March. The final tercet contrasts the essentially national self-regard of appeasement or isolationism in terms of the personal emotions of particular songs. The French one was popularised by Charles Trenet; the American one is from 'In the Still of the Night' by Cole Porter (written for *Rosalie*, premiered in 1937). No. XXIII ('When all the apparatus of report') is Auden's tribute to Rilke who is perhaps the principal stylistic influence on the sequence. Muzot (line 10) is the country house in the Swiss Valais where in February 1922 Rilke completed the *Duino Elegies*: 'I have gone out and stroked my little Muzot for having guarded all this for me and at last granted it to me, stroked it like a great shaggy beast' (*Selected Letters of Rainer Maria Rilke 1902–1926*, tr. R. F. C. Hull, 1946, p. 354). Rilke thus becomes a symbol of possible fulfilment even at a time of apparently total evil and violence.

No. XXIV ('No, not their names. It was the others who built') contrasts two kinds of forebears, the 'unloved' who 'had to leave material traces' in the form of imposing public monuments, and those whose only memorial is their posterity, content to remain unknown, and therefore still likely to be a living force in life through their transmission in the blood (compare *Sonnets to Orpheus*, I.v). No. XXV ('Nothing is given: we must find our law') describes Shanghai, which was at that time effectively in Japanese hands (in the 1966 *Collected Shorter Poems* the sonnet was attached to the initial sequence and entitled 'A Major Port'). In this city Auden and Isherwood found 'the gulf between society's two halves . . . too grossly wide for any bridge' (*Journey to a War*, p. 252) and the 'Travel-Diary' itself ends with the liberal and humanitarian intellectual wringing his hands and exclaiming: 'Oh dear, things are so awful here – so complicated. One doesn't know where to start.' There is a straight answer to this, and Isherwood alludes to the introduction of Chinese members on to the Council of the International Settlement in 1927. This hopeful beginning has been broken off by the actions of the Japanese. In Auden's sonnet the 'answer' is more generalised. In a beautifully condensed Rilkean last line he economically sets out the three necessary stages of making an informed political choice; understanding, feeling and action: 'We learn to pity and rebel'. No. XXVI ('Always far from the centre of our names') expands upon the second and most crucial of these, in an extended metaphor of manufacture. The 'minor item', the 'unsaleable product' is not named and is taken little account of, but in a period of economic disaster it shows 'a steady profit'. It is, therefore, in effect the ability to endure disaster, the recourse to something as private and enduring as a sacred landscape (lines 3–4), the emotion that will feed a beggar rather than find him picturesque (line 8), i.e. love.

The final sonnet (no. XXVII: 'Wandering lost upon the mountains of our choice') pictures the redeemed instinctive life in which love would be a free spirit. The 'warm nude ages of instinctive pose' are borrowed from the 'époque nues' of Baudelaire (see Auden's Introduction to his *Oxford Book of Light Verse*, p. xv), an image of the unattainable Golden Age (cf. Sonnet 11). We cannot return to this life, since we are 'articled' (like a trainee lawyer) to error. Turning our sinfulness into a vocation, therefore, Auden ends the sequence with a powerful expression of the duality which he conceives to be at the heart of the human experience, the double-bind of the Double Man which gives him through his superior faculties a tragic understanding of his divorce from nature, but still in the terms of Engels in *AntiDühring*: 'We live in freedom by necessity.'

Season inherits legally from dying season

Autumn 1938; 'Commentary', JW, p. 289; EA, p. 262; *Prose*, p. 680.

The 283-line 'Commentary' to 'In Time of War' picks up this notion of human duality so powerfully expressed in its final sonnet: we are our galaxy's rarest product, both judge and victim of the universe we contemplate. Lines 1–15 elaborate our evolutionary distinction, rehearsing the point made in Auden's early poetry that ontogeny repeats and advances upon phylogeny. At lines 16–19 he borrows the opening of his poem of March 1934, '"Sweet is it," say the doomed, "to be alive though wretched"' (see *TLS*, 16 January 1976), to remind us of Rilke's injunction to praise the world in spite of its imperfections.

At line 25, the poem turns to the Chinese themselves, first to their origins (Tarim is the river to the extreme west of China; most of the earliest settlements have been found in the valley of the Yellow River, i.e. the Huang Ho; Auden may well have found this in Perry, *The Growth of Civilization*, Pelican 1937, p. 127); and then to their enemies (especially the Chin Tartars and Mongols, who threatened from the north from the twelfth

century, and now, of course, the Japanese). The 'travel-diary' (p. 237) also
mentions the Japanese 'blood-spot flag' flying brazenly everywhere on the
Whangpoo River outside Shanghai. Line 45 ('The innocent and short
whose dreams contain no children') was described by Auden (to Aurora
Ciliberti) as 'A sort of Dante periphrasis for describing children.' Lines 37–
9 refer to the alliance between the Communists and the Nationalists in the
face of their common foe. In lines 52–3, Hongkew and Chapei are districts
of Shanghai, whose International Settlement and French Concession were,
of course, unoccupied by the Japanese. Auden now builds up a long
sentence (lines 52–71) which asserts that the Sino-Japanese struggle is
merely one example of a 'general war' between past and future, between
ideals and practicalities (lines 67–8) that is the permanent condition of a
creature who can make choices and act upon them, and has been since the
Laufen Ice Retreat (i.e. the temporary melting of the fourth glaciation
during the Upper Palaeolithic era, when the earliest man-made dwellings
and examples of art were found). Nothing, therefore, has essentially
changed, in either time or space, as Auden makes clear by saying in line 84
that Jen is still unachieved. Jen is the fundamental virtue of Confucian
philosophy, originally a quality of humaneness, particularly of rulers to their
subjects (contrast lines 160–74), and eventually of love for all mankind,
something more familiar to Auden as Agape.

As Auden moves into a rehearsal of his view of human history he now
begins to use material from an earlier sketch of the subject in 'In the year of
my youth . . .' (see *Review of English Studies*, xxix, 115, August 1978). The
'Commentary' lines 79–80, 103–4, 112–17 and 124–6 derive from 'In the
year of my youth . . .' II.159–60, I.164–5, I.211–16 and II. 144–5 and 161.
Lines 85ff describe the Three Great Disappointments (the collapse of the
Roman Empire, the end of medieval Christendom, the failure of the
Enlightenment). Lines 94–6 show that Christendom was inadvertently
defeated by the growth of science and individualism, which has only
succeeded in stunting 'brotherhood and feeling' (line 111), was respon-
sible for the Industrial Revolution (lines 112–15) and therefore has sown
the seeds of revolution (lines 116–18). ('The Hundred Families' is a
traditional Chinese term for the Chinese nation.) This is our angst, which
the base and the violent (line 133) take the opportunity to exploit. Their
message comes from the three fascist countries of Italy, Germany and Japan
(lines 137–44) and offers all the mindless comforts of totalitarianism (line
158: 'You shall be consummated in the General Will' is a further rebuke to
Rousseau: cf. 'Hongkong', line 13).

Lines 160–74 offer thumb-nail sketches of celebrated proto-fascists from history. Ch'in Shih Huang Ti, the first sovereign emperor of the Ch'in dynasty, unified the writing system, built the Great Wall and in 213 BC ordered all books (excepting some on useful subjects like medicine) to be burnt (the Nazi burning of the books had taken place on 13 May 1933). Chaka (*c.* 1787–1828) was the psychotic founder of the Zulu Empire. Genghis Khan (1155–1227) unified Mongolia, consolidating his power with large-scale massacres. Diocletian (AD 243–316) reorganised the Roman Empire with extensive domestic and military reforms. Napoleon and Frederick the Great also of course used military power to put France and Prussia more securely on the European map (Frederick, like Chaka, was probably a homosexual, and is actually more famous for saying: 'My people and I have come to an agreement which satisfies us both. They are to say what they please, and I am to do what I please'). Their despotism is seen to be licensed by political philosophers from Plato to Bosanquet (another approver of the communal will, author of *A Philosophical Theory of the State*, 1899). By 'Shang-tzu' Auden might mean Shang-Yang (d. 338 BC), the authoritarian Chinese philosopher who endorsed military power, strict enforcement of the law, mutual spying and directed labour. The Fertile Crescent (line 176) is the irrigable land of the valleys of the Tigris, the Euphrates and the Nile, cradle of the earliest human cultures of Babylonia, Assyria, Egypt and Phoenicia. It was a term popularised by J. H. Breasted (1865–1935). The stanza about Pascal's wager and the will of God at line 187 was omitted from the 1945 *Collected Poetry*. The stanza at line 193 about 'Fahrenheit in an odd corner of great Celsius' kingdom' is borrowed from the poem 'Kronprätenden' by Morgenstern (used or referred to by Auden on three other occasions: see p. 3).

From line 196, Auden turns to 'our faithful sworn supporters' who have worked for the good in conditions tending towards the anonymous. It is here that the tone becomes most preachy, but unlike some earlier exercises in the genre it does not include lists of prophets and gurus. Only one is named, and that is the Northern Sung artist Kuo Hsi (fl. *c.* 1060–80). For his waiting for inspiration like the coming of an honoured guest, see *Lin-ch'uan kao-chih*, his collected notes on landscape painting. Auden reused the phrase in 'In Memory of W. B. Yeats', III.1. Thus the 'Invisible College of the Humble' is rather like the Just exchanging their messages in 'September 1, 1939' and Auden's description of it accords with positions like that of Forster in the thirteenth paragraph of his essay 'What I Believe' (1938): the college is invisible because 'their temple . . . is the holiness of the Heart's affections, and their kingdom . . . is the wide-open world' (*Two Cheers for Democracy*, Penguin edn, 1965, p. 88). The wish of the humble is to rebuild the unity that the Great Disappointments lament (for example like that of the Christendom of Dante, 'the flint-faced exile' of line 240). Auden's position requires unity to be compatible with freedom 'among the just' (line 248) but only stirring rhetoric can relate freedom to truth, truth to justice and justice to freedom (lines 229–31) and does not attempt to say how you can bypass the General Will and convert individuals into a unity without becoming a fascist. After the exhortations of the Humble, the 'Commentary' winds down, but the poetic pressure is increased.

The final eleven stanzas from line 250 were separately published in Auden's *Some Poems* (1940), p. 79 ('Night falls on China; the great arc of travelling shadow'), where their peroratory character seems more buoyant in their lyric isolation, a more high-minded version, perhaps, of 'Now through night's caressing grip' from *The Dog Beneath the Skin*. There is a nice descriptive touch at lines 257–8 from 'In the year of my youth . . .', II.905–6, also used in the 1933 sonnet 'The latest ferrule now has tapped the curb', and generally the pace and variety of the busy world is finely conveyed as a backdrop for the third speech of the poem, the voice of Man at line 270 (with its possible nod to Browning's 'Apparent Failure', stanza 7, at lines 271–3). Man's appeal for the construction of a 'human justice' is, in the context, unexceptionable if 'woozy'. Auden's conversion of the phrase to 'Justice' in the 1945 *Collected Poetry* was, given the sermon-like character of the speech in the first place, understandable (but see the first chapter of J. W. Beach's persistently unsympathetic *The Making of the Auden Canon*, 1957, where it is pounced on as ideological sleight-of-hand). Auden was doubtful about the tone of the poem from the beginning. When sending it to the Dodds he wrote: 'I am very uncertain whether this kind of thing is possible without becoming a prosy pompous old bore.'

On the Frontier

The Ascent of F6 was subtitled a tragedy, but *On the Frontier* is with greater humility described on its title-page as 'a melodrama in three acts'. Isherwood claimed that 'there's more of Auden's work in *On the Frontier* than any of the plays, because he not only wrote all the poetry but also a big share of the prose' (*London Magazine*, June 1961, p. 51). The play was planned in the Lake District in the spring of 1937, and a first version was finished in Dover in the autumn. However, the play was substantially revised in 1938, largely in June while travelling from China to Vancouver on the *Empress of Asia* after visiting the Sino-Japanese war. It was published in October by Faber and performed by the Group Theatre in Cambridge in November 1938, and in London in February 1939 (for textual details, see *Plays*, pp. 653ff).

Thus since writing *The Ascent of F6* Auden had seen both the civil war in Spain and the front line in China, and no doubt felt authorised to tackle the subject of two countries entering upon a war. As a bold and simple, even simplistic, dramatisation of the European situation of the time, it is undeniably their most topical play, and some critics (e.g. Francis Scarfe in *W. H. Auden*, 1949, p. 24) dare to think it their best. But Eliot, their publisher, was disappointed (Virginia Woolf, *Diaries*, v, pp. 192–3), feeling that they didn't take politics seriously enough. It is, in fact, its very political awareness (its direct exposure of leader-worship, senseless preparation for war and the impotence of the man in the street) that makes it less suggestive than their previous work. It is dramaturgically neat and evidently sincere, but it lacks a myth. It is a play that leaves no clear images in the mind. Auden was to write in Cyril Connolly's copy 'I do not like this.' Ishwerwood appended: 'But we had a lot of fun doing it.' With it, one of the most promising collaborations in theatrical history came to an end.

The dedicatory verse (p. 357) is to Britten, who wrote the music, and uses that art in a metaphorically uncomplimentary way. The drums are the 'horrible drums' of the fascist army that the Thorvalds hear in II.i. The violins are similarly seductive: in trying to drown 'the song behind the guarded hill' they are concealing a truth that looks riddlingly like Agape (guarded hill = Eden?). The 'dancers' should be compared with the dancers in Sonnet XXII of 'In Time of War', who in a context of unignorable political violence are 'pleased' only by the erotic.

On the Frontier focuses sharply on two families in the two imaginary countries that appear in all the published Auden and Isherwood plays: Ostnia, the decadent monarchy, and Westland, the fascist dictatorship. The action takes place in the 'Ostnia–Westland Room', a symbolically divided setting where the Vrodnys and Thorvalds live, the members of each family (except Anna Vrodny and Eric Thorvald) remaining unaware of those of the other; and in the house of Valerian, a cultured Westland industrialist, *éminence grise* behind the mad Leader.

The first scene establishes this Krupp-like figure as superbly authoritative and perceptive. He is a talkative Shavian character, who casually exposes his secretary as an Ostnian spy (p. 363) and goes on in a long monologue to justify the present regime and his position in it. This speech (pp. 364ff) is a good example of Auden's aphoristic expository prose. The remark about wanting to have been a bishop in the thirteenth century is a wish of Auden himself (cf. *A Certain World*, p. 38) but in other respects the tone of the speech is as though the Devourer had written *The Prolific and the Devourer* with some help from Wilde and from Shaw's Andrew Undershaft. Such a set piece may be an impediment to the dramatic development of the story, but it does mean that Valerian is someone in whom one is interested, and this can be said of hardly any other character in the play, not even Eric and Anna (who are much more conventional than their protoypes John and Anne in *Paid on Both Sides*, and seem merely functional).

Indeed, the roles of Eric and Anna, by approaching the symbolic, stand out uneasily in the context of the scrupulously naturalistic and antiphonal Vrodny–Thorvald scenes. When they first step into the light-circle that marks their mystical consciousness of each other (p. 388), Eric identifies it as the 'good place', a concept already capitalised and docketed by Auden as an illusion (in Sonnet XIII of 'In Time of War'). Their idea of the inimical 'They' (p. 389) seems consciously more élitist than Auden's commoner use of the term for hostile philistines. Eric's pacifism provides no useful occasion for a dramatic predicament (Auden is more interesting on the subject in *The Prolific and the Devourer*, pp. 56ff) so that his love for Anna emerges as a grateful objective correlative for a solution which has no real political meaning: 'We found our peace | Only in dreams' (p. 417). To an extent their separation by a frontier expressed Isherwood's feelings about his friend Heinz (see *Christopher and his Kind*, p. 214).

Similarly, the psychological motivation behind the puppet Leader (a manic-depressive peasant, tamed by recordings of Rameau), or behind the storm-trooper Grimm, who is finally goaded to the point of killing Valerian, has a facile dramatic convenience that gives little real insight into the fascist mentality, or into the causes of war. Only Valerian, magnificently calm and cynical in a disintegrating world, is conceived with a genuine imaginative control of both his political function and his personal values, his public and his private face. And even so, the character remains largely on the level of inspired caricature, perhaps so very witty and ironical only because the play would otherwise have no real intellectual or choric centre.

The actual choruses are more brief and more detached from the main action than in the earlier plays, though they provide a skilfully varied commentary from an important social class not otherwise represented in the play, the dissident proletariat. The first chorus, of workers (p. 361), uses the same rhythmical formula for its refrain as 'Refugee Blues', but, in accordance with its function as a text for music, it is much less expressive, and its very flatness mirrors the weary desperation of industrial regimentation. The next chorus, of prisoners (p. 373), echoes the repressed defiance of the first in terms which are prophetic rather than inspiring. The rather perfunctory allusion to Shelley's *Mask of Anarchy*, line 155 ('You are many, they are few'), in the third chorus, of dancers (p. 390), similarly suggests that working-class resistance is based on slogans rather than on intelligence or energy. It seems to take the outbreak of war to stir them to action. The fourth chorus, of soldiers (p. 402), is much the most sympathetic, and much the most satisfying poetically. The first song has an ingenious deadpan metric based on a traditional folk-song, 'The Horse Named Bill' (*The American Songbag*, ed. Carl Sandburg, 1927, p. 340: 'Oh, I had a horse and his name was Bill. | And when he ran he couldn't stand still. | He ran away – one day – | And also I ran with him', etc.). The second, with some resemblances in mood to 'Roman Wall Blues', follows the poem 'Passenger Shanty' in being modelled on 'Mademoiselle from Armentières' and may have been written at the same time. The fifth chorus, of journalists (p. 413), replaces a chorus of newspaper readers in the first edition. The prescribed lighting is 'as for the witches in *Macbeth*' and therefore the feeling of the piece is very close to that of Coleridge's 'Fire, Famine and Slaughter'. The range of reference here is a useful contextualisation of the Ostnia–Westland conflict, although the chorus is less specific about an outbreak of world war than the chorus of newspaper readers that it replaced.

The final impression of the play is that the millions who suffer are not in

control of their destiny, and that despite the broadly Marxist terms of the
political analysis, the 'full flower and dignity of man' will not be attained
without the 'will of love' (p. 417). As agents of that will, Eric and Anna dwell
uneasily within the brisk realism of their dramatic context, and the tone of
their final *Liebestod* points forward – in its stylistic gestures towards emotion,
as distinct from a stylistic embodiment of emotion – to the medium of
opera.

Another Time

The volume was first published by Random House in February 1940, the first of Auden's books to be first published in the US. Its ironical title is drawn from the last line of the poem 'For us like any other fugitive' (see p. 274) and means that we cannot forever put off living our lives in the here-and-now ('another time' was a contemporary idiom like taking a raincheck, i.e. declining an invitation but wanting to be asked again). The volume has a fair claim to contain the best of Auden's work in the 1930s and possibly to be the best of all his collections of shorter poems.

The dedicatory poem (EA, p. 456) is to Chester Kallman, whom Auden first met in April 1939 and to whom he came to regard himself as inalienably married, through many trials, for the rest of his life. The poem weaves variations on the states of the ego. Auden's 'I Will' and 'I Know' and his 'I Am' and 'I Love' seem to relate to Buber's basic words I-It and I-You (Martin Buber, *I and Thou*, tr. Ronald Gregor Smith, 1937). Buber's idea was that in every You we address the eternal You and indeed for Auden, Kallman became a kind of Messiah (see, for example, the poems 'Perhaps I always knew what they were saying' and 'Not as that dream Napoleon, rumour's dread and centre'). Auden was to stress in works like 'The Quest' the fatal temptations of the Will, but this quest is of course never-ending: thus it is that the dedicatory poem's operative verbal mood is 'can', and its form is palindromical, returning at the end to the solipsistic premise of its opening.

Wrapped in a yielding air, beside

June 1937; 'Poem', *New Writing*, Autumn 1937; AT, p. 15; 'As He Is', CP45, p. 179; 'Able At Times To Cry', SP58, p. 39; CP, p. 172; EA, p. 217.

The opening of this quest poem in the *New Writing* version was 'Under the fronds of life', a phrase borrowed from the poem 'The Seven Virgins' (see *Come Hither*, ed. de la Mare, p. 489). The poem makes great play with the anomalies of man's position in the animal universe, a subject which was as fascinating to Auden in this period as it once had been to Pope. In stanza 2, the distinction of 'gun and lens and Bible' (perhaps only an imperialist version of the earlier dissident 'lancet, speech and gun' in the dedicatory verse to *The Dog Beneath the Skin*) gives man his particularly paradoxical status: he is a 'militant enquirer' and also 'Able at times to cry'. Unlike the larger phenomena of nature, he has a highly developed social organisation in which time is ordered by money (stanza 3) and allows both a sense of the past and of ideals (stanzas 4 and 5). Parental forces ('dull', 'legal', 'pious') condition the ambiguous bequest of his true nature (the locked tower) so that he is divided between madness or desolation on the one hand, and a grandiose vision of love on the other. The fairy-tale images are suggestively sexual, but in stanza 6 they shift gear into the heraldic. The dualities here are Blakean and suggestively cyclic: the symbols are 'determined' like geometrical facts on Time's shield, lamb v. tigress (the innocent and the devouring mother?), lion v. adder (God and Satan?) and adder v. child (evil finally outwitted by innocence restored?). For man, reconciliation of these contraries is merely a dream. All he can do is, as it were, to take up this shield that he inherits, be faithful to the dualities it represents and do battle with it. In ordinary life his condition is that of grief: he simply suffers a succession of personal defeats in this war (the betraying love is a 'deserter') until death finally defeats grief itself.

Law, say the gardeners, is the sun

September 1939; AT, p. 17; 'Law Like Love', CP45, p. 74; CP, p. 262.

'Law Like Love' is based on Auden's distinction between human and natural law, which is also treated in *The Double Man* (p. 112). See also his distinction in the essay on Kierkegaard: 'God's love is not a law at all, that is to say, Laws *of* are aesthetic, Laws *for* ethical' (*Forewords and Afterwords*, p. 177). Awareness of this distinction prompts the lovers to avoid the bland assertions used by other members of society ('Law is . . .') and to state only 'a timid similarity' ('*Like* love . . .'). Auden would quote Rosenstock-Huessy on the problem: 'Monism was the bent of the whole nineteenth century, always willing to pervert . . . love into law' (Eugen Rosenstock-Huessy, *Out of Revolution*, 1939, p. 190). Actually he would probably have followed D. H. Lawrence in seeing the poem itself as a possible accommodation of the two principles: 'Artistic form is a revelation of the two principles of Love and Law in a state of conflict and yet reconciled' (*Study of Thomas Hardy*). For

Lawrence it was only in the Spirit that such reconciliation was possible (i.e. the resolution of the Joachite triad of Father [Law], Son [Love] and Holy Spirit). Human love is only a pale and fallible reflection of the latter. To say that the Law is 'like love' is to say that human love is as fallible as human law, and the whole procedure of the poem therefore partakes of the admonitions of nursery didacticism (stanza 4, for example, is pure A. A. Milne). Finally, perhaps, it reduces all kinds of men to the common human condition of puzzlement and death (stanza 8's 'unconcerned condition': compare 'the Country of Unconcern' in 'The Cave of Making').

They are our past and our future . . .

?February 1936; 'The Creatures', AT, p. 20; EA, p. 158.

This poem was written for Britten's song cycle *Our Hunting Fathers*, to which it acted as Prologue. Its form is that of the psalms (Auden had modulated into psalmody before, in another poem about the insentience of animals: the chorus 'Happy the hare at morning' from *The Dog Beneath the Skin*). Although the song cycle was about man's relationship with the animals, this Prologue naturally ranges somewhat more widely. Its starting-point is an electromagnetic metaphor for desire. The positive and negative poles which create the magnetic field and therefore constitute the very principle of attraction (desire) are both defined as 'they', i.e. the creatures. The implications are threefold. The basis of every human impulse, from lust to metaphysical yearning, is dependant on our animal nature; that animal nature cannot differentiate morally between love and hate; and we perceive our animal perfection to have existed in the past or to be recoverable in the future. The grand rhetoric with which Auden accomplishes this complexity of idea is remarkable. Animal 'Pride' is amoral, but it is a pride in just that unity of being which human beings want to recover, and can only recover through the 'Charity' of a moral vision which is very close to Christian. At the centre of the poem's six lines are two key functions of the animal in history. The first (line 3) reminds us that because of their amoral pride they are of no real assistance as models to any kind of political theorist or activist: thus they cannot provide a viable Utopia. The second (line 4) exposes the romantic absurdity of yearning for primitive or classical simplicities in the Machine Age: thus they cannot provide a viable Arcadia. The allusion in the latter to 'nude and fabulous epochs' is to Baudelaire's 'J'aime le souvenir de ces époques nues'. This is a perfectly serious appeal to the Golden Age of naturism as Baudelaire saw it, where men and women could freely and openly exercise 'la santé de leur noble machine', but Auden always took his Baudelaire with a pinch of salt. He quoted the lines in his Introduction to the *Oxford Book of Light Verse* (1938) in a paragraph designed to expose the different ways in which the Romantic poets turned their backs on the real world. For Auden, the real world always contained men's minds, not only their bodies. It is interesting that when inscribing a collection of his poems in 1933 to the artist who had produced the portrait of the boy described in 'The earth turns over . . .', he should call painting (weirdly relapsing into the tongue of Baudelaire) 'cet art plus primitif, auquel le corps sain est plus éxcitant que les malaises de l'esprit' (Maurice Feild's copy, Bodleian). The point about the creatures for Auden is not so much that they have healthy bodies, but that they are without anxiety.

Here are all the captivities; the cells are as real:

June 1937; 'Hegel and the Schoolchildren', *Listener*, 21 July 1937; 'Schoolchildren', *Junior League Magazine*, December 1939; AT, p. 21; CP, p. 126; EA, p. 126.

After Auden's visit to Spain early in 1937, he returned for the summer term to the Downs School, Colwall, where he had previously taught. This perhaps explains the idea of the two kinds of captivity developed in the first stanza: the world of the fifth Ode in *The Orators* is being reassessed; the schoolmaster has seen a real war. The poem's urgency and simplicity of style underlines the direct emotional nature of its statement.

The original title explains many of the ideas in the poem about the merely potential freedom of the child: 'the bars of love are so strong' and 'the tyranny is so easy' because, according to Hegel's *Philosophy of Right*, it is through love and obedience that the groundwork of the ethical character is laid in childhood. The aim of education is to enable the child to stand by itself, and to become a free personality. The purpose of authority is to cancel itself. The pathos of this process is very delicately delineated by Auden. Relevant, too, is the Freudian notion of infantile sexuality: 'the professor's dream is not true' (originally 'the dream of the don . . .') perhaps refers to Lewis Carroll's obsession with the child's innocence (compare 'Eros Paidagogos' in 'Oxford'). The dream is not true, because 'the sex is there.' Auden is questioning the validity of Hegelian education in the light of a real 'rebellion': how can the child become a free personality, as Hegel professed, when the educators are themselves 'condemned' and unable to become free? How can the child's touching trust and fidelity ever of itself germinate 'the new life', when adults themselves are unable to break loose from the easy tyranny?

Nature is so near: the rooks in the college garden

December 1937; 'Oxford', *Listener*, 9 February 1938; AT, p. 22; CP, p. 147; EA, p. 229.

Auden probably revisited Oxford in connection with his editorship of the *Oxford Book of Light Verse*. He seems to have remembered the significant periphrasis for his old university town in his abandoned epic 'In the year of my youth . . .', lines 45–6: ' "Where have you been and what doing | Tell me, since you left the talkative city?" ' His poem investigates the relationship between the home of the intellect (and of talk) and the natural world outside. When finally reducing the poem to four stanzas in 1966 and attempting to expunge definite articles, Auden forgot that 'the tower' (i.e. Magdalen's unique Great Tower) is not the same as 'towers', which could not therefore be so 'utterly' satisfied with their weight. In the first two stanzas the setting is purely natural. To the 'minerals and creatures' of the Oxfordshire landscape are comically ascribed that most monkish of sins, accidie (sloth). Then in stanzas 2, 3 and 4 a larger environment is sketched. The colleges came into being through their founders' wealth, obtained in the real world of Success and Violence, and thus Wisdom and Knowledge have an unignorable relationship with that outer reality of 'glittering prizes'. The metaphors of benediction (stanza 3) or of the spoilt child (stanzas 5–6) link learning and power with the sly implication of duty to some grave authority rather than to the 'sharp sword' of the public world. Through metaphor knowledge has turned into a child, and remains a lover of children in stanza 7 ('Eros Paidagogos', love as the teacher of boys). For Auden this was a force like charity which could lead to the cure of evil through the removal of fear ('The Good Life', 1935, EA, p. 346) and he admitted it into his own vocation as pedagogue (as late as 1963 he signed a postcard to Orlan Fox 'εροσ παιδαγογοσ'). To present it as 'virginal' is as much a calumny upon dons as it is to suggest that Oxonians in general do little but 'poke' (stanza 7), but Auden's argument requires this barrier between Eros and Nature (stanza 8). The division is as radical in 'the talkative city' as in any other (stanza 9), and even here, as Mendelson has shown (p. 295), Freud's 'soft and low' voice of the intellect 'continues until it has secured a hearing' (*The Future of an Illusion*, 1928, chapter 10).

No one, not even Cambridge, was to blame

December 1938; 'A. E. Housman', *New Writing*, Spring 1939; AT, p. 24; CP, p. 182; EA, p. 238.

The starting-point of this sonnet is perhaps Auden's remark in a letter to E. R. Dodds in December 1936, that if Housman had had self-knowledge we shouldn't have had the poems. Laurence Housman's *A. E. H.* (1937) made clear, with diplomatic indirectness, some of the reasons for the split between the scholar and the poet, what Auden in his review (*New Verse*, January 1938) called 'Jehovah Housman and Satan Housman'. The review elaborates a duality of the writer and the integrated personality which parallels both the mutual enmity of the Prolific and the Devourer, and such later variations on the love of the homosexual for the heterosexual man as the treatment of Falstaff and Hal in *The Dyer's Hand*, e.g.: 'Socrates will always fall in love with Alcibiades: Alcibiades will only be a little flattered and rather puzzled.' Housman's love for Moses Jackson does not appear to have been declared, and his life exhibits various kinds of compensation for his much-thwarted homosexuality. 'Food was his public love' may have been suggested by Laurence Housman's remarks on his brother's atheism, remarks which elaborate A. E.'s observation that there was no word for 'God' in a certain South African tribe: 'I have myself heard a similar story of the trouble missionaries have had to find the word for love, "appetite for food" being the nearest equivalent' (*A. E. H.*, p. 115). Housman considered himself something of a gastronome (see Grant Richards, *Housman 1897–1936*, 1941, especially chapters 5, 11 and 26).

Auden himself provided a comment on lines 9 and 10 of his sonnet:

The inner life of the neurotic is always projecting itself into external symptoms which are symbolic but decipherable confessions. The savagery of Housman's scholarly polemics, which included the composition of annihilating rebukes before he had found the occasion and victim to deserve them, his obsession with punctuation beyond the call of duty, are as revealing as if he had written pornographic verse.

(*New Statesman*, 18 May 1957, p. 643)

The sonnet concludes with an explanation of Housman's obsession with death, with which one might compare Auden's *New Verse* review, where he linked Jehovah Housman and Satan Housman: 'But they had one common ground upon which they could meet; the grave. Dead texts; dead soldiers; Death the Reconciler, beyond sex and beyond thought. There, and there only, could the two worlds meet.'

Left by his friend to breakfast alone on the white

January 1939; 'Edward Lear', *TLS*, 25 March 1939; AT, p. 25; CP, p. 182; EA, p. 239.

Auden owes much to Angus Davidson's *Edward Lear* (1938) for details of Lear's life. Indeed, to read Davidson's biography and then to read Auden's interpretation of it is to see something of the poet's skill in posing and lighting his significant detail like a photographer. Sometimes this skill leads to distortion. Fear of dogs and dislike of Germans, for instance (Davidson, pp. 79 and 224), suggest greater vulnerability and contemporaneity than the facts warrant. The anecdote (Davidson, p. 47) of two young Englishmen overheard in Calabria ('Why, he's nothing but a d—d dirty landscape painter': a title gleefully adopted by Lear himself) is combined with Lear's sensitivity about his ugliness (Davidson, p. 15) to produce the celebrated thumbnail line: 'A dirty landscape painter who hated his nose.' Here something of Lear's intelligence and humour is lost for those who do not know the source: he becomes instead a lachrymose melancholic afflicted by epilepsy (this is his 'Terrible Demon', Davidson, p. 93), an almost theatrical presence, a pantomime Romantic. Auden builds his caricature upon Davidson's commonplace observation that 'whimsical humour is closely allied with tears' (p. 197), and that Lear's comic verse was, like Housman's scholarship, a compensation. The 'cruel inquisitive They' of the limericks are seen as the adults that Lear himself cannot bear to face. Davidson had made the point thus (p. 196): 'What a world of implication there is in Lear's "they"! "They" are the force of public opinion, the dreary voice of human mediocrity: "they" are perpetually interfering with the liberty of the individual: "they" gossip, "they" condemn, "they" are inquisitive and conventional and almost always uncharitable.' (The idea also got into *On the Frontier*, II.i, which Auden was working on during 1938.) Like Housman and like Rimbaud, Lear was a victim of society: but as Auden was to write in 'New Year Letter', lines 111–12, 'the live quarry all the same | Were changed to huntsmen in the game.' Compare this with Ransom's view of Dante's art as a form of revenge (*The Ascent of F6*, I.i).

It's farewell to the drawing-room's civilised cry

January 1937; 'Song for the New Year', *Listener*, 17 February 1937; AT, p. 26; 'Danse Macabre', CP45, p. 59; CP, p. 154; EA, p. 208.

This ironical oration is the poet's farewell on the eve of his departure for Spain, where 'matters are settled with gas and with bomb.' Indeed, the copy he sent to E. R. Dodds is entitled 'Recruiting Song for 1937', as if its analysis and proposals were not deeply pessimistic about the confusion of ends and means in war. Auden himself was to insist that unlike ideas men can die too soon ('In Time of War', Sonnet XVI). The fanatical speaker on the other hand (deliberately an *alter ego* of the poet, himself a 'spoilt Third Son') represents that puritanical intolerance of human nature which finds totalitarianism so attractive. The parole-breaking Devil is a red-herring; like the Vicar of Pressan Ambo, the speaker uses the myth of the Fall of the Angels to account for human sin, and to excuse his need to conquer and to punish that sin by destroying individuals. He is, like the Vicar, a type of the Super-Ego convinced that he is the voice of God. Entitled 'Dance of Death', the poem was used in the Scherzo of Britten's 1939 *Ballad of Heroes*.

Perhaps I always knew what they were saying:

May 1939; 'The Prophets', *Spectator*, 25 August 1939 (reprinted in *Southern Review*, Autumn 1939); AT, p. 29; CP, p. 255.

This is one of the earliest poems written for Chester Kallman. It tries to show that the poet's love for Kallman was foretold, not by earlier human loves, but by his worship of abandoned lead mines and the machines which used to work them. Auden used to joke about this. In November 1946, for example, with a great air of revelation he showed Ansen photographs of his former loves. Ansen, expecting beefcake, saw pumping engines (cf. 'Heavy Date', stanza 15). 'The Prophets' is quite deliberate about the disproportionate character of these harbingers, which patiently convey a sense of the numinous to the only partially enlightened worshipper. In *The Dyer's Hand* (p. 34) Auden comments that his early reading consisted of books like *Machinery for Metalliferous Mines* or *Lead and Zinc Ores of Northumberland and Alston Moor*. 'Worship' in the poem was really a matter of reading 'the technological prose of my favourite books in a peculiar way. A word like *pyrites*, for example, was for me, not simply an indicative sign; it was the Proper Name of a Sacred Being, so that, when I heard an aunt pronounce it pirrits, I was shocked. Her pronunciation was more than wrong, it was ugly. Ignorance was impiety.' The deserted mines had a meaning for Auden, but they let it be, as it were, the meaning which he at the time was prepared for; they taught him 'gradually without coercion'. They are like Rilke's *Dinge*. The *Ding*,

> is ready to simplify everything, made you intimate with thousands through playing a thousand parts, being animal and tree and king and child, – and when it withdrew, they were all there. This Something, worthless as it was, prepared your relationships with the world, it guided you into happening, and among people, and, further; you experienced through it, through its existence, its anyhow appearance, through its final smashing or its enigmatic departure, all that is human, right into the depths of death.
>
> (Rilke, *Puppen*, quoted in *The Double Man*, pp. 88–9)

The concluding section shows how the 'answer' is revealed in terms of the human love which could not be given by the 'book' or the 'Place'; only this can lead to the love which is not selfish ('vain') or unrewarded ('vain'). The title of the poem strongly and daringly suggests the Messianic nature of this love ('asks for all my life') and so does the argument, for as *Ding* to Kallman, so Kallman to the divine. (See also 'In Praise of Limestone' and 'Amor Loci' and in particular Auden's Christmas poem to Kallman in Farnan, p. 65.)

Wandering the cold streets tangled like old string

December 1938; 'Brussels in Winter', *New Writing*, Spring 1939; AT, p. 30; CP, p. 178; EA, p. 236.

This is a characteristic portrait of the modern city, where the sociological implications implicitly enforce themselves on the reader despite the riddling surface. There are riddles in both octave and sestet: what would the city be able to say if you could untangle it? What is the significance of the 'phrase' and the 'look'? If you solve the second, you can begin to answer the first. The phrase and the look are sexual. It is within the lit units of rich apartments that the only warm relationships possible in the city are conducted, through prostitution. Therefore (to turn to the first riddle) the city must have lost its heart. Its cold, isolating presence is seen paradoxically as a gigantic illusion, so that the old, the hungry and the humbled are absorbed in the hardships of life as they might be at the opera (paradoxically the traditional entertainment of the rich). It is the familiar Audenesque figure of the 'stranger' whose negotiation earns him, as it were, the freedom of the city, though even as he warms it, it remains heartless. The 'fountains' and the 'ridges of rich apartments' evoke the area in which Auden was staying in December (Marie-Louise Square and Rue Palmerston, rather grander than 83 Rue des Confédérés, where he stayed in August).

The nights, the railway-arches, the bad sky

December 1938; 'Rimbaud', *New Writing*, Spring 1939; AT, p. 31; CP, p. 181; EA, p. 237.

Auden's sonnet about Rimbaud contains imagery that inevitably suggests Blake's 'The cistern contains; the fountain overflows' – a thought that Auden takes up again in 'New Year Letter' (line 199), where he describes Rimbaud as having 'strangled an old rhetoric'. Not only did Rimbaud help to break the tyranny of the alexandrine; he helped to free truth from its confinement in art, to bring the experience of poetry into real life as a 'dérèglement de tous les sens' (cf. line 6). The 'weak and lyric friend' is, of course, Verlaine. But finally 'integrity was not enough'. The new life as merchant and explorer is seen as the failed visionary's second attempt at wholeness (Enid Starkie's work on Rimbaud began with her monograph on the African period, and it was Starkie's biography of Rimbaud that Auden reviewed for the *New Republic* in 1939). The poem was later set by Hans Werner Henze.

Hell is neither here nor there

September 1939; 'Hell', *Harper's Bazaar*, January 1940; AT, p. 32; CP, p. 278.

Beginning with the Renaissance commonplace about a personal hell (cf. Marlowe and Milton), the poem continues with a wry complaint about the sheer effort involved in most forms of human weakness. Relying on the reader's inability to remember whether six monkeys and six typewriters could or could not in time produce the works of Shakespeare, Auden uses the example to undermine the real relevance of language altogether: it contrives, the ensuing stanzas say, to assist pride in supporting our pretensions to heroic grandeur (that Hell exists to contain us). Thus we theatrically revel in our supposed wretchedness, whereas if we were really wretched 'there'd be no living left to die.' The form of the poem takes on for significantly long enough in stanzas 2–4 the naïve insistence of Tennyson's rhymed tercets in 'The Two Voices', a poem which similarly contrives to be at once both inside and outside its misery.

Towards the end he sailed into an extraordinary mildness,

March 1939; *Southern Review*, Autumn 1939; AT, p. 33; CP, p. 251.

The poem refers to the fact that, after his adventurous youth, Melville settled down as a New York customs inspector. Auden sees this 'extraordinary mildness' as a kind of love, a state of achieved goodness which could be reached only by exorcising the terror which produced his early books (a terror also seen as Moby-Dick, 'the rare ambiguous monster that had maimed his sex'). Auden writes brilliantly about the psychosexual implications of *Moby-Dick* in the third lecture of *The Enchafèd Flood* (1950). This storm had to blow itself out, a metaphor which also effectively describes Melville's literary career (six books in six years). *Billy Budd* was written in his last years, and presents the discovery that 'evil is unspectacular', i.e. that we are all Claggarts, that we all help to crucify Christ (Billy) and cannot escape from our destiny. (In *The Enchafèd Flood*, Auden is more specific about Claggart's unconscious homosexuality). In the final stanza God is seen as a projection of parental images; Melville's friendship with the older Nathaniel Hawthorne prompted his discovery that 'his [i.e. Melville's] love was selfish', that the real love is Agape, the Christian charity, and that man must surrender to this love so that the City of God can be re-formed ('"The Godhead is broken like bread. We are the pieces"').

Quarter of pleasures where the rich are always waiting

December 1938; 'The Capital', *New Writing*, Spring 1939; AT, p. 35; CP, p. 177; EA, p. 235.

This is one of Auden's most obsessive subjects, the alienation of the big city (once again it is Brussels, cf. 'Brussels in Winter'). Here it is turned into a fairy-tale. The wicked uncle hints at forbidden pleasures, and the farmer's children are lured to the flattering city, where each selfish illusion is shattered and the pieces are swept out of sight. Auden's consummately simple and easy similes and metaphors can distil some complex meanings, e.g. in stanza 3, where a disjunction of time-scale (the slow wearing-down of the sea, the speed of the factory conveyor belt) enhance his vision of the perplexity of the deprived urban life. The 'quarter of pleasures' is probably the area around the Rue des Bouchers.

The hour-glass whispers to the lion's paw,

September 1939; AT, p. 36; 'Our Bias', CP, p. 118; CP, p. 277.

The octave of the sonnet is some sort of riposte to Shakespeare's Sonnet 19 ('Devouring Time, blunt thou the lion's paws'), though whether it intends to undermine Shakespeare's main point (that poetry can outlast the destruction of love by time) is uncertain. The sestet certainly turns to language, as Shakespeare's does, but does so principally in order to contrast its ludic role in human affairs with the economical directness of nature in the lion's leap or 'the assurance of the rose'. The final two lines look forward to an important theme in 'The Quest', and may have been written with Melville in mind: 'Round the world! There is much in that sound to inspire proud feelings; but whereto does all that circumnavigation lead? Only through the numberless perils to the very point whence we started, where those that we left behind secure were all the time before us' (quoted in *The Enchafèd Flood*, penultimate page).

O had his mother, near her time, been praying

August 1939; 'Pascal', *Southern Review*, Autumn 1939; AT, p. 37; EA, p. 451.

On 8 June 1939, Auden wrote to Mrs Dodds: 'I am studying Pascal for a future poem' and then on 29 August: 'Done a lot of pensees and a poem on Pascal.' Nine years earlier Pascal had for Auden been an example of the false prophet in 'Get there if you can . . .', along with a dozen others who were 'boon companions who devised the legends for our tombs' and 'betrayed us nicely while we took them to our rooms'. (Auden mentions the *Pensées* as early as 1927, in a letter to his brother.) Now, in a subtle contrast, Pascal provided Auden not only with the literary model for *The Prolific and the Devourer* ('my pensees') but with the more personal model of the 'genius attempting sainthood', the view of Pascal put forward in Morris Bishop's study of 1937, which Auden had surely been reading. Auden abstracts from the facts of Pascal's career in order to discover the essential lineaments of a life involved in religious discovery.

The essence of Pascal's story is that the mathematical prodigy had a two-hour vision on the night of 23 November 1654, at the age of thirty-one, which prompted him to the abandonment of science and the writing of Christian apologetics. The appeal of such a story to Auden at this date is obvious (Auden was thirty-two). Of all his biographical poems of these years, with their examination of how a creative genius can be true to his gift, only this poem finds the abandonment of the gift for religious revelation wholly satisfactory: 'round his neck | Now hung a louder cry than the familiar tune | Libido Excellendi whistled as he wrote | The lucid and unfair.' Pascal had transcribed his vision (Auden's stanza 10) on to a parchment which he wore sewn into his doublet for the last eight years of his life (e.g. 'From about half past ten in the evening until about half past twelve, | . . . . . . FIRE . . . . . .| God of Abraham, God of Isaac, God of Jacob, not of the philosophers and scholars. | Certitude, certitude, feeling, joy, peace. | *God of Jesus Christ*' etc.).

Auden takes up Pascal's quotation from Mark xii.26 here to describe the vision as like that of the burning bush. 'Libido Excellendi' is the form of 'Libido dominandi' (intellectual pride) which Bishop chooses to use in his discussion of Pensée 696 (p. 197; see also pp. 307, 338, 353). Pensée 696 (the numbering of *Oeuvres Complètes*, ed. Chevalier, Paris, 1954) refers to the *libido sentiendi, libido sciendi* and *libido dominandi* ('the lust of the flesh, and the lust of the eyes, and the vainglory of life') of 1 John ii.16 (although Auden uses the form 'Libido Dominandi' in *The Prolific and the Devourer*). It is implied that Pascal's scientific achievements (such as his invention of the calculator, proof of the vacuum, or the early work on conic sections, which Descartes said was derivative – none of them alluded to by Auden, curiously enough) were entirely a product of his worldly egotism.

Auden's total silence on the colourful details of Pascal's secular career is replaced by an odd concentration (throughout the first four stanzas) on Pascal's mother, about whom almost nothing is known except that she was very pious, and that she visited and loved the poor. She died when Pascal was three. The point of this, and of the marvellous description of pregnancy with which the poem opens, is, I think, to establish her as a typological representative of the Virgin ('Love' lifting up 'Knowledge') and the infant Pascal a Christ announced to a superstitious and barbaric age, a Christ leaving her maternal comfort to 'build a life upon original disorder'. There is a hint for this in Bishop (p. 339): 'After all, he was a little like Jesus.' The husband's role (Etienne Pascal was Second President of the Cour des Aides at Clermont, a post perhaps equivalent to Commissioner of Taxes) is similarly of a Joseph-like adoration. In stanza 5 this daring parallel is abandoned, and the young Pascal is shown realising how his particular mission, his scientific talent, is to set him apart from ordinary people.

In the following stanza the idea of the 'ferry' of the happy and ignorant is drawn from Pensée 696, and the distracting flies from Pensée 96. In stanza 7 there is an allusion to the celebrated Pensée 91: 'The eternal silence of those infinite spaces strikes me with terror.' In stanza 8, the idea of his Gift being able 'To use the echo of his weakness as a proof | That joy was probable' refers, in appropriately mathematical language, to those arguments for Christianity in the *Pensées* which were drawn from gaming and chance. The Gift is inalienably a gift of the Enlightenment, I think, letting Pascal believe that it was his own 'finesse', i.e. intuition, which prepared for his restoration of faith (the reference is to the distinction between *esprit de géomètrie* and *esprit de finesse* in Pensée 33). There are other Pascalian ideas here (such as that in the penultimate stanza that the only excuse for sex is that it has made the saints) but the structure of the poem concentrates on the sometimes obscure 'crooked custom' of the truth. As an exponent of Jansenist rectitude and mystical certitude, Pascal is really only interesting for his continued intellectual strategy as a child of science. Auden's long sentences and avoidance of the specific militate against the sort of encapsulation successful in the shorter biographical poems of this period, and this may be one of the reasons why, after *Another Time*, he never included it in any of his larger collections.

Auden's considered criticism of Pascal's position is perhaps worth quoting here. It comes from *The Prolific and the Devourer*, II, p. 34:

> I feel about Pascal as Pascal felt about Montaigne. Of all the dualists he is incomparably the noblest and most seductive. Like most of us he exalted the faculty he lacked over the faculty he possessed, the heart over the reason, and fashioned an image out of his opposite. The neurotic who as a child was thrown into fits by the sight of his two parents together was truly a split being with a corrupt heart and an uncorrupt intelligence. By all appearances he should have been damned, but he was saved, and saved not as he thought by his heart but by his reason, for it was his reason that told him that his heart was corrupt and that therefore the love of human beings was not for him.

In Auden's poem, such elements as the role of the mother, of the Gift, and of the *libido dominandi* suggest that elements personal to Auden's life could be used to dramatise the religious predicament of the dualist. He was to exploit this method in the sonnets of 'The Quest'.

Perfectly happy now, he looked at his estate.

February 1939; 'Voltaire at Ferney', *Listener*, 9 March 1939 (reprinted in *Poetry*, June 1939); AT, p. 41; CP, p. 250; EA, p. 240.

'Voltaire at Ferney', with its picture of the collaborators in *L'Encyclopédie* as rebellious schoolchildren, assumes a subtly damaging attitude to its subject-matter. Voltaire is presented as the 'cleverest of them all'. His model estate at Ferney, with its agricultural experiment, social progress and benevolent concern for the local inhabitants, is only one aspect of his desire to defeat 'the infamous grown-ups', the superstitious and fanatical Establishment of his day. Auden had been reading N. L. Torrey's *The Spirit of Voltaire* (his review of it appeared in *The Nation*, 25 March 1939). The 'blind old woman' is Mme la Marquise du Deffand. Of the writers with whom Voltaire is compared in stanza 4, D'Alembert 'was in essential agreement with Voltaire's point of view, but . . . was "under the monster's claw", was drawing a pension from the Court, and did not dare to compromise himself' (Torrey, p. 173). Pascal, according to Voltaire, was someone who, like Plato, had mistaken his vision for the Truth: 'Voltaire admired the mysticism and the style of his great predecessor, and at the same time he saw in him the doctrinaire whose influence it was most important for him to combat' (Torrey, p. 185). Diderot's materialistic atheism seemed too narrowly systematic to Voltaire, while Rousseau had given in by becoming a sentimentalist, a rather puritanical defender of the goodness of God. Pascal was wrong about sex, too (stanza 5). The women mentioned are his lover Emilie du Châtelet, and Olympe Du Noyer with whom he attempted to elope.

In his stand against 'superstition', Voltaire becomes a near relation of Herod in *For the Time Being*, except that Auden still at this date seems to see such humanism as a possible stance. Its relevance to the period just before the outbreak of the Second World War is obvious: 'still all over Europe stood the horrible nurses | Itching to boil their children' (a sly piece of Struwwelpeter, this: they are doubly horrible, because boils itch). Voltaire is right to try to prevent them, but is he not guilty (according to Auden's later beliefs) of denying 'the Multiplicity, asserting that God is One who has no need of friends and is indifferent to a World of Time and Quantity and Horror which He did not create . . .'? (*For the Time Being*, CP, p. 389). The poem ends with a bland and limiting comment on such purely secular efforts to achieve the Just Society: 'Overhead | The uncomplaining stars composed their lucid song', which is a reminiscence of 'plump little

Horace composed his civilized song' in *Hadrian's Wall* (*Plays*, p. 442).
'Civilize' (stanza 2) is Voltaire's watchword, too. Civilised song was in a
certain sense just the kind of poetry that Auden was beginning to mistrust
in himself.

Lay your sleeping head, my love,

January 1937; 'Poem', *New Writing*, Spring 1937; AT, p. 43; 'Lullaby', SP58, p. 35; CP,
p. 157; EA, p. 207.

This poem, written for the young man who was the subject of 'The earth
turns over . . .', is one of the best-known of Auden's lyrics. It achieves the
beauty of its effect by the way in which the moment of happiness is weighed
gravely and consciously against an awareness of all that can threaten it. The
delicately hinted rhymes, the harmony between the musical line and the
extended statement, and the careful epithets: all these reinforce the poem's
gravity. The first stanza establishes the essential fragility of beauty within the
temporal and moral universe and celebrates it with a Yeatsian emphasis (in
'A Prayer for my Daughter', Yeats walks and prays over the sleeping Anne,
wishing 'natural kindness' for her rather than beauty, since 'Hearts are not
had as a gift, but hearts are earned | By those that are not entirely beautiful';
by contrast, Auden's sleeping love is 'Mortal, guilty, but to me | The entirely
beautiful'). Faithfulness haunts this poem, but its aura of beneficent charm
('till break of day') enforces the tonal resemblances to Oberon's blessing of
the couples at the end of *A Midsummer Night's Dream*.

The second stanza proposes that on the one hand Eros can lead to
Agape, and on the other that 'abstract insight' can induce Eros: the lover
and the desert saint are closer than they might appear. The parallelism
reappears in the final stanza, where the two extreme states are guarded by
the types of love they can induce ('involuntary powers' are powers not of
the human will, i.e. providence). One may object that the loved one is not
convincingly present in the poem, and certainly the 'dreaming head' of the
final stanza moves nearer to being a stage property than its appearance in
the first stanza, but the poem is rightly considered one of Auden's greatest
achievements in the genre. It was later set by Hans Werner Henze.

What does the song hope for? And the moved hands

April 1937; 'Orpheus', *London Mercury*, June 1937; AT, p. 45; CP, p. 158; EA, p. 212.

Auden wrote this poem shortly after his return from Spain, as if to ask oracular questions of an invisible oracle about the function of poetry. It is a marriage of two of his most admired German poets: the subject-matter of Rilke, the stanza and rhetoric of Hölderlin. In fact, the position of Rilke in the *Sonnets to Orpheus* is under scrutiny. Is art a celebration of life, or a desire to control it? Why celebrate life at all, when those who live it have no need of art ('content with the sharp notes of the air')? The final question opposes the power of natural circumstances ('the weak snowflake') to the greater power of human desire for knowledge ('the wish') and human creativity ('the dance') but leaves them, as it were, in the air. After all, the snowflake is a classic, and minuscule, form of unique natural beauty; no wonder if it content the 'beautiful' who appear to be content without 'knowledge of life'. In its ambiguities this poem is perhaps something of a critique of the words of Keats's urn if they are applied to poet or audience rather than merely to the poem.

Encased in talent like a uniform,

December 1938; 'The Novelist', *New Writing*, Spring 1939; AT, p. 46; CP, p. 180; EA, p. 238.

'The Novelist' shows how at this time Auden professed a belief in the superior powers of the novelist, who by a process of sympathy and self-abnegation can understand, interpret and create human character in all its variety, whereas a poet merely generalises. The idea is found, for example, in 'Letter to Lord Byron' 1.14. This view of the novelist is clearly influenced by his admiration for Isherwood, to whom, in the previous year, he had written a comic verse tribute that similarly stressed the novelist's ambassadorial role, 'pretending to be nobody' (see p. 299). It may also be a comment on Matthew Arnold's point in 'The Strayed Reveller' that the price poets pay for their art is to 'become what we sing' or his remark in his sonnet about Shakespeare, that 'All pains the immortal spirit must endure'. It seems likely, too, that Auden would have recognised Henry James's claim that Flaubert 'is for many of our tribe at large *the* novelist, intent and typical' (see my comments on Auden and Flaubert, p. 342). In the sestet the ideas approach a redemptive position where the novelist is almost a type of Christ.

About suffering they were never wrong,

December 1938; 'Palais des Beaux Arts', *New Writing*, Spring 1939; 'Musée des Beaux Arts', AT, p. 47; CP, p. 179; EA, p. 237.

Auden wrote to Mrs Dodds from Brussels on 31 August 1938: 'I have been doing the art gallery and trying to appreciate Rubens. The daring and vitality take one's breath away, but what is it all ABOUT?' When Auden turned from Rubens to the Bruegels in the Musées Royaux des Beaux-Arts he soon found a style of painting that was *about* something. It was, he concluded, 'about' suffering, and in this poem he deliberately inverted the word order of the opening statement so as to begin with this important word. It is likely that in his initial effort of appreciation he came across the little 12-inch Rubens sketch of Daedalus encouraging Icarus as his wings begin to melt. The heroic subject is an excuse for a pair of spreadeagled male nudes seen from below with groin-concealing drapery: not really about anything very much.

There is a rich double meaning in this opening word, for it is Bruegel's very circuitousness of approach ('about' in a different sense) that Auden is interested in. (Interpreting the poem in relation to the paintings by Bruegel Senior and Brueghel Junior is tricky, and Auden himself may have confused them). In Bruegel's *Landscape with the Fall of Icarus*, the painter presents a momentous event in a world of diurnal unconcern. Trade and agriculture can take no account of individual fate, not the corpse in the thicket (typically illustrating a proverb: no plough ever stops just because a man dies), not even a boy falling from the sky. An 'important failure' would be something like the failure of a harvest.

Besides the explicit mention of *Icarus*, the poem contains imagery that appears to refer to three other Brueg(h)els: *The Numbering at Bethlehem* and *Winter Landscape with Skaters and a Bird Trap* (lines 5–8), and *The Massacre of the Innocents* (line 12). In a TS interview of 1951 with S. Raichura and A. Singh, p. 10, Auden said: 'Musée was inspired by two pictures, *Winter* and *The Mask of Innocence* [misheard], I saw in Brussels.' It is strange that *The Numbering at Bethlehem* is left out of this account, since most of the details can be found in that painting, and only one (doubtfully) in *The Massacre of the Innocents* (and none at all in *Winter Landscape*, or at least, none that are not in the others). Auden is therefore being circuitous himself here, since the events surrounding the Nativity should be of much greater cultural concern than the fall of Icarus. And indeed, the reader naturally comes to feel that the allusions to the Nativity create the poem's concealed subject, what it is really *about*. *The Numbering* of course evokes the position of Jews in the Third Reich, as Auden was with tact to bear in mind when writing his Christmas oratorio *For the Time Being*. To what extent, the reader wonders with biographical hindsight, was the poet himself 'reverently, passionately waiting | For the miraculous birth'? Like Icarus' disappearing legs, the Nativity is marginalised in the poem itself. Auden himself has 'somewhere to get to', like the ship which in the painting is by no means (as one might imagine from the poem) setting out on a quest, but returning to harbour (the sun is setting: it has taken time for Icarus to fall after the melting of his wings). The process of returning to Christian belief would at one level for Auden have involved an appraisal of the relationship between the miracle of the Incarnation and the suffering of mankind. Such relationships attain great significance in his Christian poetry (as between the individual's daily life and the events of the Crucifixion in the sequence 'Horae Canonicae').

Auden's argument is elaborated to the point at which the poem's centre of interest has become art criticism. John Press (*The Fire and the Fountain*, 1955, p. 210) pointed out that the observation may have come from Lewis Namier (though it is not one to have escaped admirers of Bruegel's painting). Namier used it as an example of ironic humour, what he called 'historical comedy': 'at close quarters, the actions of men are in no way correlated in weight and value to the results they produce' (*England in the Age of the American Revolution*, 1930, p. 148).

This is one of Auden's most celebrated short poems. Its long irregular lines create an illusory casualness of argument, which the rhymes subtly enforce (the one in line 4 narrowly escaping the alarming sweet reason of Ogden Nash). It also pays tribute to the form of the sonnet, 13:8 instead of 8:6, although a 'sonnet' of half as many lines again as a regular sonnet might be expected to divide 12:9 (as does Sonnet III of 'The Quest'). However, Auden deploys the rhymes to enforce a subdivision into something like quatrains and tercets (abca | dedb | fgfge || hhij | kkij) with the widely-separated 'e' rhyme acting as a unifying link.

All the others translate: the painter sketches

December 1938; 'The Composer', *New Writing*, Spring 1939; AT, p. 48; CP, p. 181;
EA, p. 239.

'The Composer' celebrates the purest of the arts, music. However, Auden
reinforces this notion, curiously, by imagery which, in contrast to the
practical clumsiness of the poet ('rummaging', 'painstaking'), presents the
composer's skills as being like the skills of the seducer (the 'gift', the sensual
liquid caresses, the pouring out of wine). Indeed, the composer seems to be
credited with very little: the cliché overtones of 'absolute gift' suggest that
he would be a fool not to take his chances; his techniques come naturally to
him. It is clear that music is here intended to be seen as instinctive,
generous, even sanctifying, but one cannot help feeling that there is
something unconsciously lowering in that last line, despite its evidently
intended sacramental allusion. The point in the penultimate line ('unable
to say an existence is wrong') was more subtly elaborated in *Secondary
Worlds*, p. 91, where Auden remarks that it makes no sense to ask of a piece
of music if the composer means what he says, since music is always
intransitive and in the first person, having only the present indicative tense
and no negative.

Not as that dream Napoleon, rumour's dread and centre

May 1939; 'The Territory of the Heart', *Southern Review*, Autumn 1939; AT, p. 49;
'Please Make Yourself at Home', CP45, p. 82; 'Like a Vocation', CSP50, p. 98; CP,
p. 256.

The abandoned titles of this poem make it much clearer that it is a love
poem (one of the first written for Chester Kallman). It takes up the central
metaphor of 'To settle in this village of the heart', written five years earlier,
but makes its invitation with a much greater sense of confidence and
inevitability, despite its replacement of the fear of infidelity and the self-
deprecatory 'gaucheness' of the earlier poem with a terrified existential
weeping (stanza 5) that might seem more challenging to the object of love.
The metaphor is treated with a greater complexity: the lover is invited to
enter the country of the spirit not as a temporary conqueror or tourist
(stanza 1) but with a full right of inheritance, of permanent possession
(stanza 5), 'like a vocation' (i.e. to be called to the relationship in an
absolute, even divine sense).

The poem makes much of its distinction between the uniqueness of this calling and the dull relationships of the thousands who have 'their moderate success' (stanza 3). This is not to say that Auden is not aware of the paradox inherent in this attitude, for every member of a crowd is unique, and though he is not the crowd itself, he knows that 'the meek inherit the earth' (stanza 5). There is a kind of argument with Jung going on here. When writing about vocation Jung had asked: 'What, in the last analysis, induces a man to choose his own way and so to climb out of unconscious identity with the mass as out of a fog bank? . . . What is it . . . that inexorably tilts the beam in favour of the *extraordinary*?' (*The Integration of the Personality*, 1939, tr. S. Dell, p. 291). Auden was, of course, inclined to doubt the virtues of the exceptional (cf. 'The Quest') and in a letter to Theodore Spencer of 20 February 1943 said: 'a sense of vocation should be the normal not the exceptional thing. A vocation is like falling in love with the princess's picture.' Auden intends to suggest the mysterious way in which the predestined seems perfectly natural (cf. 'The Prophets'), but ends up trying to have it both ways: what if you are the wrong woodcutter's third son?

Where do They come from? Those whom we so much dread

April 1939; 'Crisis', *Atlantic*, September 1939; AT, p. 51; 'They', CP, p. 253; EA, p. 243.

Auden wrote on 7 August 1939 to Mrs Dodds (who was clearly puzzled by the poem): 'The Crisis is just the spiritual crisis of our time, i.e. the division between the reason and the heart, the individual and the collective, the liberal ineffective highbrow and the brutal practical demagogue like Hitler or Huey Long.' In fact, 'they' are what we have become through our inattention to the division which Auden describes (e.g. stanza 4) and through our own misplaced ideals (e.g. 'money' and 'culture' in stanza 6). They are what we have always been, though we did not know it, the fatal flaw or curse of myth (stanza 2), our family conditioning (stanza 9), our instinctive desire to change (stanzas 11 and 12). Above all, perhaps, they are what we will become, i.e. our children, telling us what we are really like after all. All this breeds a violence that we like to think we have outgrown, but have not, because we have not freely chosen the good life. The words that Auden puts into Jesus's mouth in *The Prolific and the Devourer*, II, provide an interesting gloss on the final stanzas:

You can love your neighbour, not because you ought to, but because you really want to, because that is the nature of the particular biological species to which you belong. You are neither an ape nor a tiger by nature [referring to *In Memoriam*, cxviii.27–8, just quoted], and if you want proof of this, if you want to know what your biological nature is like, look at your children, whom you must admit do love and trust their neighbour naturally unless their trust is betrayed, and quite irrespective of their sex or class or colour or morality, to your great embarrassment.

To that extent, our 'embarrassment' is perfectly conveyed on the eve of the Second World War by Auden's astonishing notion that 'even our armies | Have to express our need for forgiveness.' On its first magazine appearance the poem was prefaced by a quotation from Dante's *Purgatorio*, xiv.85–7: 'Of my sowing such straw I reap. O human folk, who set the heart there where exclusion of partnership is necessary?' (the words of Guido of Duca, who was consumed with envy where he might so easily have loved). The present title derives from a TS found among Auden's papers after his death. He also made some emendations to the text in 1965, but did not include it in the *Collected Shorter Poems* of the following year.

A nondescript express in from the south

December 1938; 'Gare du Midi', *New Writing*, Spring 1939; AT, p. 54; CP, p. 180; EA, p. 236.

'Gare du Midi' was one of a number of poems written during his most productive month in Brussels. The suggestion in this economical little drama is that the 'infection' of the city from the south (i.e. arriving at this *particular* Brussels terminal) is somehow connected with time-saving Nazi diplomacy in western Europe in the post-Munich period; that the man is not a spy but a bureaucrat. His anonymity has a kind of sinisterly shabby respectability of a Graham Greene kind (Auden had in fact just finished reading *Brighton Rock* in 1938). Perhaps the point is simply that, as with many of the best Auden poems of this scale, one can imagine a variety of backgrounds which would give life to the symbol. He might even be literally employed in germ warfare (cf. the sinister, tall-hatted botanist in 'Certainly our city . . .').

As I walked out one evening

November 1937; *New Statesman*, 15 January 1938; AT, p. 55; 'One Evening', SP58, p. 33; CP, p. 133; EA, p. 227.

'As I walked out one evening' was described by Auden himself as a 'pastiche of folksong' (Spears, p. 110). This is evidently what it is, though the later sophistications of the ballad stanza (as found in, say, Burns or Housman) are clearly acknowledged, and the illusions of love are as subtly qualified as they are in other poems of Auden's in this period. The imagery in the first two stanzas, for instance, while indicating fullness and fruition (crowds as harvest wheat, the river brimming), suggests at the same time the levelling in store (the harvest to be cut down, 'brimming' not only like a cup, but as in 'brimming with tears'). The lover's vow is magnificent, but the railway arch may be intended to signify a comparatively sordid rendezvous, and anyway Time's winged chariot is hurrying near, as it must in a poem of this kind. Clocks began to 'whirr' in Auden's poetry in the unpublished 'Elegy' of September 1924. The city's clocks, so whirring and chiming, produce reserved admonitions rather different from Marvell's thundering chariot, and introduce a note of social realism foreign to folk-song but characteristic of the 1930s. Auden's Nightmare is perhaps an extension of Matthew Arnold's Darkling Plain (Arnold is the subject of the following poem in *Another Time*) and what Auden insisted upon at this time was that the private good which erotic love represented had nothing to do with Justice.

The imagery in this central section is typically striking, and complex without being obscure. A phrase like 'appalling snow', for instance, is literal (the snow makes the valleys pale) and yet reinvigorates a common cliché about bad weather; the careful doubleness of the epithet manages to recapture its most useful sense of 'dismaying'. The following lines, too, create a complex movement of thought: Time destroys youthful joy in two ways; it destroys actual manifestations of it in physical exuberance and prowess (in the 'dances' and in the action of the diver), and it also destroys it in the metaphor of a girl's party dress, breaking her necklace and her 'brilliant bow'. The fusion of these different images is very casually done, and in fact the phrase 'the diver's brilliant bow' is taken from a poem of 1927, 'No trenchant parting this'. Stanza 10 may have been influenced by Hardy's 'Under the Waterfall' ('Whenever I plunge my arm, like this, | In a basin of water . . .' etc.).

The clocks continue with their message of doom and impotence in stanza

12, introducing a world where nursery-rhyme morality has been thrown to the wind. The Lily-white Boy, like the seven stars of stanza 4, is from the song 'Green grow the rushes, O'. The nursery-rhyme formula is continued in stanza 14: 'You shall love your crooked neighbour | With your crooked heart', a prescription which echoes the 'Be Lubbe, be Hitler, but be my good, | Daily, nightly' of 'A Bride in the '30s'. The possibility that you could fall in love with Hitler seems to render the Arnoldian gesture of 'Ah, love, let us be true | To one another' faintly ridiculous. The conflict between the lover's ironical idealism and life's unhappy perversion from its possible ends is not resolved in the poem; the poet, hidden listener of the dialogue, is left alone, aware only of the continued Arnoldian flow of the river, the eternal progress of human life towards its future. There is a 1942 setting of the poem by Elisabeth Lutyens.

His gift knew what he was – a dark disordered city;

February 1939; 'Matthew Arnold', *Listener*, 14 September 1939 (reprinted in *Nation*, 30 September 1939); AT, p. 58; EA, p. 241.

Arnold is described as 'a dark disordered city' here in two senses. First, the phrase describes the psychological 'homelessness' of Arnold as an individual, against which he asserted his father's moral authority in order to condemn facile Victorian optimism, denying the poetic gift which could have been used for self-analysis. This metaphor may be compared with Sonnet v of 'The Quest', where a theological 'Necessity' corresponds to the poetic 'gift', but where the City is still essentially misunderstood by the grown boy. Secondly, the phrase alludes to that idealistic conception of the state as an organic entity to which Arnold's denial of his gift led him. As Auden put it in 'Whitman and Arnold' (*Common Sense*, April 1939): 'Arnold attempted the impossible task of writing as if Victorian London were Fifth Century Athens, and in consequence his inspiration ran dry.'

Steep roads, a tunnel through the downs are the approaches;

August 1937; 'Dover', *New Verse*, November 1937; AT, p. 59; CP, p. 148; EA, p. 222.

Auden once wrote: 'I cannot believe . . . that any artist can be good who is not more than a bit of a reporting journalist' (*New Verse*, April–May 1936, p. 24), a view which is faithful to some of his ambitions at this time, and which underpins his approach in 'Dover', a poem which depends upon its accumulated sociological analysis of the ethos of a frontier town (where, incidentally, Auden wrote much of *On the Frontier*). Its function as a frontier enables Auden to turn it into a symbol of how man exists in time, as a traveller, facing the future and the past, a victim of forces outside his control. Auden brilliantly expands the significance of man's predicament from the local to the cosmic ('tides warn bronzing bathers of a cooling star, | With half its history done') without straining the vivid descriptive links in the chain of argument, the adroitly varied word-play: the eagerness and frustration of travel is expressed by train smoke that 'fumes' in two senses (stanza 2); an oracle may seem to promise exotic sexual success ('Arabia found in a bed', stanza 4) but allows for the contrary interpretation of sterility (cf. 'The desert sighs in the bed' in 'As I walked out one evening', stanza 11); the symbols of authority that are sometimes woven into military insignia are also the names of pubs (stanza 7); and so on. Like so much of Auden, its appeal lies very much in the understated air of laconic understanding, somewhere between tenderness and impartiality ('Nothing is made in this town', 'Some of these people are happy'). In 1965 he changed the last phrase to 'Not all of us are unhappy', perhaps in an attempt to seem less aloof, though it could be argued that the change has the opposite effect.

Warm are the still and lucky miles,

September 1939; 'Song', AT, p. 61; CP, p. 267.

In this ecstatic lyric the regenerative power of love is celebrated. The image of light predominates: the sun in the first stanza lends its power metaphorically to the embracing lovers, macrocosm to microcosm; the bonfire in the final stanza illuminates a new trust by destroying a sterile past. Is there something heartless in burning all that is 'dumb'? The present, curiously enough, is voiceless, too: in the Marvellian green shade of the second stanza the only human language is a smile. This is the difference: the first is the silence of sterility, the second the silence of sexual fulfilment. The play in the last stanza of turning a common phrase 'live-long day' into 'life-day long', makes of the new noun not merely a rich moment but a kind of festival that can be celebrated forever, like a birthday. It is easily missed (e.g. misquoted in Carpenter, p. 263). The phrase 'live day long' occurs in Blake's 'A Mother's Lament for the loss of her only Son', line 12.

The poem is interesting for its complex pattern of cross-assonance on the stressed syllables (e.g. in each stanza, the first of line 1 with the last of line 5; the last of line 2 with the second of line 4; the first of line 2 with the last of line 4; the second of line 1 with the last of line 3; the first of line 3 with the last of line 4).

For us like any other fugitive

October 1939; AT, p. 62; 'Another Time', CP45, p. 41; CP, p. 276.

'Another Time' is in a sense the title poem of the 1940 collection, although it was not so titled until the 1945 *Collected Poetry*. It supports the volume's acute sense of the present moment and its demands upon the individual to justify his way of life. Auden had been vastly impressed by the recently published *Out of Revolution* by Eugen Rosenstock-Huessy (1939) and some of the ideas about time in this poem and others of the same period seem influenced by it (e.g. for stanza 2, cf. Rosenstock-Huessy, p. 114, on 'timeliness', and p. 513: 'In war there is no time. In war people have lost control over time. Then it is that the wheel of nature grinds us in its turning. Peace restores to us the room for free action. But unless we carry into this action an idea of the future, of final values, or direction, our liberty will not be of any use'). The poem proposes that those who live in the past, respecting the established forms which are in fact breaking up around them, are living a lie. The poem might perhaps be compared with a much earlier one, 'Will you turn a deaf ear'.

Underneath the leaves of life

June 1939; 'The Leaves of Life', *New Republic*, 26 July 1939 (reprinted in *New Writing*, Christmas 1939); AT, p. 63; 'The Riddle', CSP50, p. 157; CP, p. 257.

'The Riddle' concerns man's double nature in relation to God. This idea is best explained in Auden's own words in his essay in *Modern Canterbury Pilgrims* (ed. James A. Pike, 1956):

As a spirit, a conscious person endowed with free will, every man has, through faith and grace, a unique 'existential' relation to God, and few since St Augustine have described this relation more profoundly than Kierkegaard. But every man has a second relation to God which is neither unique nor existential: as a creature composed of matter, as a biological organism, every man, in common with everything else in the universe, is related by necessity to the God who created that universe and saw that it was good, for the laws of nature to which, whether he likes it or not, he must conform are of divine origin.

Thus the 'Duality' of the first stanza is the duality of freedom and necessity, whose origin is located with the fall of man in the Garden of Eden. Auden's ideas on this subject are more fully expounded, and clarified, in Simeon's speech in *For the Time Being*, and lie at the back of many of the poems of the 1950s. Eden in this poem is portrayed in visual terms reminiscent of Dürer's engraving of Adam and Eve. In imagination, the angelic sword guarding Eden against Adam and Eve's return becomes 'bayonets glittering in the sun'; the judgement of God turns into the human judgement of 'soldiers who will judge' because the world of Necessity, a world linked to the laws of nature, does not involve the individual in a personal reward of Grace (i.e. 'the Smile'). In his free existential relationship with God, the individual must act out of love and conviction of the truth, but in the world of necessity this is not so: 'Even orators may speak | Truths of value to the weak, | Necessary acts are done | By the ill and the unjust'. This duality ('the Judgement and the Smile') is unavoidable. The Kingdoms of the Short and the Tall in the third stanza remind us of the Truly Weak and the Truly Strong Man, a concept which Auden revived in metaphysical terms in the sonnet sequence 'The Quest' in *The Double Man*.

As with many of Auden's half-lyrical, half-philosophical poems of this sort, it turns in the last stanzas into a love poem. The inevitability of the duality prompts the argued reflection that Eros is thus the essence of human life. This is both because it is our greatest contentment, and because it shows us this limitation ('That we love ourselves alone') as a preparation for a spiritual development which the poem is not concerned with exploring, but which lies suggestively behind it: that reconciliation which is the subject of the related poem 'As He Is'. 'The Riddle' borrows its initial phrase via an earlier version of 'As He Is' (*New Writing*, Autumn 1937, pp. 170–71) from the ballad 'The Seven Virgins': 'All under the leaves and the leaves of life'. Auden would probably have known this ballad from de la Mare's *Come Hither*, p. 489.

Sharp and silent in the

October 1939; AT, p. 67; 'Heavy Date', CP45, p. 105; CP, p. 259.

With its insistent trochaic rhythm and brief lines, the poem achieves an effect which is appropriately careless, a kind of halting ruminative pattern evading the demands of the metre. Indeed, the fact that the syllabic pattern is absolutely regular suggests that the poem is not really intended to be read with a full eye on the traditional prosody that it is still theoretically invoking. Though the poem pretends to be the 'purely random thinking' of the poet as he awaits a prearranged sexual encounter, it does emerge as a perfectly coherent discussion of the nature of love.

Auden begins as he looks out at the skyline of Manhattan's business district from his apartment in Brooklyn Heights. Discussing his dreams is a distraction from concentrating on his lover (the poem is about Kallman) since, as Goethe had said, no one can watch a beautiful sunset for more than quarter of an hour (stanza 3). If the dreams leave the poet guessing, then there is not much that anyone else can do with them, although the bull-dog and trombone (stanza 5) suggests the old HMV gramophone label, and in his Freud Lecture of 1971 he discussed the dream about the steamroller and said that it represented a malignant power (*Auden Studies* 3, p. 193). The argument of the poem really begins at stanza 8 with Malinowski's anthropological observation that the typical Oedipus dream of killing the father and committing incest with the mother occurs only in patriarchal communities (cf. Auden's essay 'The Good Life', EA, p. 352). Auden concludes that the erotic object is purely relative and subjective, and may develop in unpredictable ways. Spinoza's idea of the 'intellectual love of God' (stanza 13) demands that the individual recreate in his own mind some part of the self-creative activity of nature, and thus transcend his mortality. This objective may have suggested the argument of the remainder of the poem, that 'Love requires an Object' (cf. Spinoza, *Ethics*, III, 'Definition of the Emotions', no. vi, Everyman edn, tr. Boyle, 1910, p. 130). Auden, however, playfully reminds us in stanza 15 that 'anything will do', even a pumping-engine (which turned up in early poems such as 'Lead's the Best' and 'Who stands, the crux left of the watershed'). Love, he goes on, does not merely require an object; it requires mutual need, and the poem bows gracefully out by observing that the actuality of sex has nothing whatever to do with intellectual justification of it.

Let me tell you a little story

April 1937; 'Miss Gee', *New Writing*, Autumn 1937; 'Three Ballads: 1 Miss Gee', AT, p. 73; CP, p. 158; EA, p. 214.

In a television interview with Richard Crossman in January 1973, Auden said that the character of Miss Gee was 'based on a governess we had'. The idea that if you refuse to make use of your creative powers you produce a cancer instead was one of those implicit in the psychosomatic theories of Homer Lane (see *Lions and Shadows*, p. 303). Auden would have found it also in Groddeck, who makes much of the idea that even male cancer can be a compensation for the inability to become pregnant (see *Exploring the Unconscious*, p. 80). Auden had something of this sort in mind when he wrote to William McElwee in December 1928: 'The sort of Homosexuality which should remain when I have done [i.e. indulged himself in Berlin] has the same cause as cancer, the displaced wish to have a child.' Miss Gee represses her sexuality into guilty dreams about the Vicar, and thus develops an incurable tumour (on the liver, as an extra stanza 17 in the Texas draft makes clear). Auden believed that our natural desires may defeat us if we deny them. John Lehmann, politely urging Auden to change the ending in his letter of 28 June 1937, claims licence to do so because, as he says: 'One or two people (who admired the new ballads enormously) have suggested to me that the end of Miss Gee doesn't seem quite right. I know that it originally had a different end.' No alternative ending survives. The point about the Oxford Groupers dissecting her knee is that such a pious and sanctimonious movement as Moral Rearmament has a totally irrelevant notion of where the cause of moral distress and psychological unhappiness really lies.

This was one of four similar ballads (see 'James Honeyman', 'Victor' and 'Sue'), most of which raised critical opposition, some of it fierce. It was not intended to be a psychologically subtle or sympathetic character study but a direct piece of polemic, rather Brechtian in tone. Another possible influence was William Plomer, whose ballad 'The Murder on the Downs' Auden had praised in a review of Plomer in *Poetry*, January 1937. The tune to which 'Miss Gee' should be sung is 'St James's Infirmary', as Auden's earliest text makes clear.

James Honeyman was a silent child

August 1937; 'James Honeyman', *Ploughshare*, November–December 1937; 'Three Ballads: 2 James Honeyman', AT, p. 76; EA, p. 223.

The tune for this ballad, according to the magazine text, is 'Stagolee'. In this text, too, the quatrains are written out as couplets (as is 'Stagolee' itself: see the *Oxford Book of Light Verse*, no. 245). Honeyman is an introverted scientist, so without emotion that he only looks at his mother 'with curiosity' (stanza 1) and in order to finish an experiment neither goes to bed for sex (stanza 17) nor illness (stanza 18). Having been thinking about phosphorus ever since his mother found him striking matches on the nursery floor, he invents a new kind of poison gas, a phosphorus compound, because Lewisite was 'not nearly strong enough' (stanza 9). Lewisite was an arsenic compound invented in the early 1920s. It is true that some opinion thought it treatable with soap and scrubbing brush if tackled soon enough, but Honeyman's ambitions are clearly signalled by such a comparison, and his neglected invention is snapped up by a foreign agent (stanzas 27–9). The outcome is simple: when war is declared, Honeyman and his very ordinary suburban family are killed by his own gas. It is odd that Auden never reprinted the ballad, when in the following decade debate about science's whole involvement in war after Hiroshima became critical. Perhaps the very fact that the new armaments were to make Honeyman's N.P.C. seem as archaic as gunpowder was a reason for feeling that the poem was too simplistic, even though the moral retains a crude force. The idea may have been suggested by some lines in Day-Lewis, *The Magnetic Mountain* (1933), 20, stanza 3: 'That young inventor – you all know his name – | They used the plans and he died of their fame.'

Victor was a little baby

June 1937; 'Victor', *New Writing*, Autumn 1937; 'Three Ballads: 3 Victor', AT, p. 82; CP, p. 167; EA, p. 218.

This ballad's tune is 'Frankie and Johnny' according to the text in *New Writing* (Auden has already used this tune for his poem 'I have a handsome profile'). Like 'Miss Gee', it shows what happens when a repressed personality is faced with a sexual situation it is unable to control. In Victor's case it is religious mania. His impulse to murder his faithless wife arises both from a hinted sexual inadequacy (he is presented as a typically anal-erotic personality) and from what Auden later called 'the constant tendency of the spiritual life to degenerate into an aesthetic performance' (note in the 1945 *Collected Poetry* prefixed to the Sermon from *The Dog Beneath the Skin*). His spiritual dialogues with nature (stanzas 22-6) confirm only the projection of his own neuroses into the real world, the Super-Ego acting as a supposed agent of the divine (the general psychological procedure of these stanzas was to be reused by Auden in the scene of the mocking of Hel Helson in *Paul Bunyan, Libretti*, p. 34). Anna is promiscuous and must die (the card she turns over in stanza 28 is appropriately a reversed Ace of Spades, a name for the female genitals, see *A Certain World*, p. 269). The violence of this story is possibly more suited to the genre of popular ballad than are the more commonplace, and therefore more distressing, circumstances of Miss Gee; but it should be remembered that the tone of these poems is deliberately exaggerated and distancing. 'Victor' was originally conceived with a refrain ('Have mercy, Lord, save [his] soul from Hell') and according to Ansen, Auden said that 'Victor was really somebody by that name.'

O the valley in the summer where I and my John

April 1937; 'Four Cabaret Songs for Miss Hedli Anderson: 1 Johnny', AT, p. 88; CP, p. 142; EA, 213.

All of the four cabaret songs were set by Britten, this one on 5 May 1937 (*Britten Letters*, p. 545). The settings were published in 1980. Hedli Anderson was born in the same year as Auden, had worked in the Group Theatre since *The Dance of Death*, played the Singer in *The Ascent of F6*, performed in revue and was leader of the chorus line in the late-night cabaret at the Trocadero Grillroom, Piccadilly Circus. This ballad gets close to the feeling of popular song in many of its images and epithets, but the deflationary refrain puts it in a different class (cf. the effect of the refrain in ' "O for doors to be open and an invite with gilded edges" '). The title and the mood of frustration seem reminiscent of Brecht (cf. 'Das Lied vom Surabaya-Johnny' in *Happy End*).

Some say that Love's a little boy

January 1938; 'Four Cabaret Songs for Miss Hedli Anderson: 2 O Tell Me the Truth About Love', AT, p. 89; CP, p. 143; EA, p. 230.

Eros of classical myth or Dove of the Holy Spirit? This cabaret song begins with its most serious question, as if to get it out of the way, before accumulating the pure comedy. And then again at the end, when the reader is softened up by the absurdities, Auden introduces a personal note, another kind of seriousness, in stanza 7. As he said to Ansen, 'For me personally it was a very important poem.' The manner is, I think, Noel Coward rather than Cole Porter. Auden always liked to vary his effects, and his Porter song is the unpublished 'I'm a jam tart' (now in *Auden Studies* 2, 1994, p. 76).

Stop all the clocks, cut off the telephone,

April 1936; version in *The Ascent of F6*, II.5; 'Four Cabaret Songs for Miss Hedli Anderson: 3 Funeral Blues', AT, p. 91; CP, p. 141; EA, p. 163.

The poem is a fair pastiche of the stoical lament and flamboyant imagery of the traditional blues lyric, but like many of Auden's blues it is not modelled on the classic form. In *The Ascent of F6* it is sung by Stagmantle and Isabel following the phantasmogoric 'death' of James Ransom, and the first two stanzas are followed by three quite different ones referring to members of the climbing party. The ironic effect of the hyperbole is much changed when the song is sung by a single singer lamenting the death of her lover. In stanza 3 compare 'Out on the lawn I lie in bed', stanza 6: 'Now North and South and East and West | Those I love lie down to rest.'

Driver, drive faster and make a good run

May 1939; 'Four Cabaret Songs for Miss Hedli Anderson: 4 Calypso', AT, p. 91; CP, p. 266.

The last of the group of four cabaret songs is appropriately one of celebration and anticipation, written after Auden had met Kallman. Its exuberance and rhythmical oddity give it great charm. Some of the themes of poems like 'Heavy Date' and 'Law, say the gardeners, is the sun' are to be found here in simpler form, which, given the emotional directness and angularity of the calypso style, makes it a moving poem. Auden was teaching at St Mark's School, Southborough, Massachusetts, and would have made trips to New York as described here in order to meet Kallman.

O lurching-loving collier, black as night

June 1935; 'From the film "Coal-Face" ', *New Verse*, Summer 1938; 'Madrigal', AT, p. 93; CP, p. 136; EA, p. 290; *Plays*, p. 421.

This charming poem in the Elizabethan manner exploits the theme of *carpe diem* rather unusually in relation to a miner's working week. A lurcher is a poacher's dog, used for catching rabbits and hares; the metaphor in line 4 is from hare-coursing. A version of line 6 may be found in *The Ascent of F6*, 1.3 (*Plays*, p. 318). The poem was written for the GPO film *Coal Face* (directed by Alberto Cavalcanti; first shown in October 1935) and was set by Britten for a female chorus. This was Auden's first collaboration with Britten. It was also set by Lennox Berkeley in 1960.

Over the heather the wet wind blows

October 1937; 'Roman Wall Blues', AT, p. 94; CP, p. 121; EA, p. 289; in *Hadrian's Wall* (*Plays*, p. 447).

For commentary on this poem, see p. 228.

Perfection, of a kind, was what he was after,

January 1939; 'Epitaph on a Tyrant', *New Statesman*, 31 January 1939; AT, p. 95; CP, p. 183; EA, p. 239.

'Epitaph on a Tyrant' portrays a simple dictator, flattered, manipulated and ultimately innocent, very reminiscent indeed of the Leader in *On the Frontier* (published three months previously), although 'senators' may be intended to place the poem metaphorically in the context of the Roman Empire. Real understanding or real exposure of motivation is perhaps sacrificed to the rhetorical device of the last line (a form of hypallage) in which the expected verbs are exchanged. This reversal of expectation is very striking, and was no doubt the donnée of the poem. The allusion is to J. L. Motley, *The Rise of the Dutch Republic*, III.481: 'As long as he lived, he [William the Silent] was the guiding star of a brave nation, and when he died the little children cried in the streets' (from the official report of 11 July 1584: 'Dont par toute la ville l'on est en si gran deuil tellement que les petits enfans en pleurent par les rues'). Auden and Isherwood were reading Motley in China (see *Journey to a War*, p. 184: 'Motley depressed us both intensely with his catalogue of tortures, massacres, and battles. 'And it's exactly the same nowadays,' Auden exclaimed. 'Really, civilization hasn't advanced an inch!').

He was found by the Bureau of Statistics to be

March 1939; 'The Unknown Citizen', *Listener*, 3 August 1939; AT, p. 96; CP, p. 252.

'The Unknown Citizen' sketches in, with the lightest of ironies, some details of 'the average man . . . put through the statistician's hoop' ('New Year Letter', lines 1366–70). Bureaucracy cannot be concerned with the happiness of the individual, cannot indeed be concerned with any of the things that make him individual. Thus the title of the poem (parodying the grave of the Unknown Soldier) suggests an administrative chimera, whose predictability Auden wittily laments. He may have remembered Brecht's 'Anleitung für die Oberen', which provides an analogous argument for a ceremony to honour the Unknown Worker, 'Irgendein Mann . . . Dessen Gesicht nicht wahrgenommen' ('Some man . . . Whose face no one noticed'). 'Fudge Motors' is a portmanteau of Ford and Dodge.

Say this city has ten million souls,

March 1939; 'Song', *New Yorker*, 15 April 1939; 'Refugee Blues', *New Writing*, Autumn 1939; AT, p. 98; CP, p. 265.

Auden sent this poem to Britten ('Dear Bengy, | Here is a blues for Hedli, or whatever you think best') but there is no evidence that Britten set it. It was, however, set for Hedli Anderson by Elisabeth Lutyens in 1942. The hypothesis of the opening line is genuinely hypothetical; it is a prognostication by Lewis Mumford. The necessity of a passport for a refugee (stanza 4) was well-known to Auden: he had married Erika Mann in 1936 in order to provide her with one. The refrain skilfully accommodates a varying tone of resignation, disturbance and menace. Its form is similar to that in the Blues sung by the Quartet of the Defeated in *Paul Bunyan* (*Libretti*, p. 15).

Yesterday all the past. The language of size

March 1937; *Spain*, Faber pamphlet published May 1937 (reprinted in *Deux Poèmes* by Nancy Cunard's Hours Press, in the *Saturday Review*, 22 May 1937, and in *Poems for Spain*, 1939); 'Spain 1937', AT, p. 103; EA, p. 210.

Auden visited Spain between January and March 1937, having decided that 'the poet must have direct knowledge of the major political events' (letter to E. R. Dodds, 8 December 1936). He went out with a medical unit organised by the Spanish Medical Aid Committee, and told friends that he was going to drive an ambulance (he had driven for the TUC during the General Strike) but never did. For his period in Spain and his reaction to the anti-clericalism of the Communists, see Carpenter, pp. 206–16. For further details of his movements, see Nicholas Jenkins, 'Auden and Spain' (*Auden Studies* 1, pp. 88–93).

Auden was a poor driver, but a great poet; whatever precise attitudes to the political struggle in Spain that may lie behind it, and however disappointing it may have seemed to some people as propaganda, the poem is a large-scale rhetorical structure containing a powerful argument on behalf of individual responsibility. This structure, contrasting past and future, necessity and the political will, fully supports the poet's call to action. It underlines the need for choosing personal involvement and risk in the fight against fascism, while recognising that for every individual the motivation and circumstances of the choice will be different. Without this, the Just City, the whole premise of the needs of humanity, is an impossible dream.

The starting-point of Auden's structural procedure is a concentration upon this ever-present moment of choice in human life. Indeed, such a consciousness of the overriding demands of the present lay behind his whole conception of history and its making. He would have learned this from Jung, for whom it was a key to the spiritual problems of modern man. Jung's very terms provide the rhetorical basis of the poem:

It is sheer juggling to look upon a denial of the past as the same thing as consciousness of the present. 'Today' stands between 'yesterday' and 'tomorrow', and forms a link between past and future; it has no other meaning. The present represents a process of transition, and that man may account himself modern who is conscious of it in this sense.

(Jung, *Modern Man in Search of a Soul*, tr. Dell and Baynes, 1933, p. 229)

The first pamphlet text, containing twenty-six stanzas, is so symmetrically structured as to allow the central response of history ('I am whatever you do') to be positionally at the very centre of the poem itself, namely:

1. Yesterday . . . but to-day   6 stanzas
2. Invocations of 'the life'   6 stanzas
3. Its reply   2 stanzas

4. The call to arms   5 stanzas
5. To-morrow . . . but today   6 stanzas
6. Conclusion   1 stanza

My commentary is therefore based on this original text, and will use my numbering of the hypothetical sections.

(*1*) In the first stanza we can immediately see that Auden's view of the past is influenced by W. J. Perry's theory of the transmission of culture ('Spreading . . .'; 'diffusion . . .'). Civilisations do not arise independently and in isolation. Auden had already used Perry's theory of the Egyptian origins of Western civilisation in 'O Love, the interest in thoughtless heaven' as a means of suggesting that we can inherit a tradition by which the dead may be reborn. That theory informs Auden's account here of the origins of mathematics ('the language of size') and of the solar calendar (see W. J. Perry, *The Growth of Civilization*, 1924, Pelican, 1937, p. 53). The counting-frame and the cromlech link science with religion (the cromlech owing its form, according to Perry, to the Egyptian mastaba tomb), and Perry is not above speculating on the Egyptian origins of Chinese civilisation (p. 125). These early signs of civilisation are succeeded by more recognisable evidence of the development of Mediterranean civilisation, particularly in stanzas 3–4 of the peculiar ecclesiastical history of Spain. The 'struggle' in this context at first seems like a resistance to superstition, a struggle for rationalism, and it continues to retain some kind of dual meaning: the struggle against authority and the struggle for existence, the struggle against Franco and the struggle to make the right choice, and so on. In the context of Auden's adroit potted history in this section it continually, above all, suggests progress.

(*2*) In this section, Auden's representatives of the limited human view of destiny, the poet (stanza 7), the scientist (stanza 8) and the poor (stanza 9), invoke their individual view of the force that they believe can reveal it to them. The poet is contrasted with the inhuman world he celebrates (the pines, too, may whisper, but they cannot be startled; where the waterfall is loose, his body is compact; he is upright where the tower leans) and though the comparison is to his advantage, he needs something more, a vision, something like an intuition by which he can direct his life, like a sailor. The scientist is contrasted with the inhuman world that he investigates. The germ or the planet are 'finished' in the sense of being wholly complete in themselves (compare the 'finished' features of the animals in 'Our hunting fathers told the story'), whereas humanity ('the lives of my friends') is restlessly incomplete. The poor, without a vocation that links them to the world, are merely victims of it, and appeal to History as a manager of their lives and to Time as a refreshing power (though you cannot step into the same river twice). In stanzas 10–11 these representative appeals are combined into a single human appeal for intervention, particularly for the gift of successful social organisation comparable to that effortlessly achieved by the sponge, shark, tiger and robin (cf. the 'Just City' of stanza 14). The appeal is to an undifferentiated 'life', which may be the Life Force or even Groddeck's It (i.e. 'the life | That shapes the individual belly'), but which is asked to 'descend as a dove or | A furious papa or a mild engineer'. These terms are quite clearly a parody of the Trinity (holy spirit, angry Jehovah and merciful creating Logos) and are presumably intended in the spirit of hypothesis. Compare his remarks about 'existence' in *The Prolific and the Devourer*, p. 53 ('If anyone chooses to call our knowledge of existence knowledge of God, to call Essence the Father, Form the Son, and Motion the Holy Ghost, I don't mind: Nomenclature is purely a matter of convenience'). This 'life', or 'existence', has really nothing to say on its own behalf at all, as stanza 12 makes clear, but its crucial reply follows.

(3) The reply begins with an important demurral, since 'the Mover' is unequivocally a term for God. If 'the life' is not God, it is at least History, i.e. in Tillich's sense 'the reality of decisions rooted in the Unconditioned' (Paul Tillich, *The Interpretation of History*, 1936, Part Two, chapter ii). To this extent, History as a 'yes-man' is careless of human destiny: 'I am whatever you do' (cf. *Paul Bunyan, Libretti*, p. 46). Does this absolve us from agonising for too long over our decisions? Stanza 14 implies not; it offers two explanations for any individual choosing to fight in Spain, and one of them is wrong on two possible counts: (a) it is romantic self-aggrandising, and (b) it might easily lead to fighting for Franco, as a poet like Roy Campbell did (see *The Prolific and the Devourer*, p. 21). One must make the right decision, the decision to build the Just City.

(4) The call to Spain is expressed in terms of natural movements like migration, germination and blossoming. The civil war (on both sides) is an embodiment of ordinary emotions, e.g. in stanza 19 the people's army is seen as the flower of 'hours of friendship'. This and the previous stanza were cancelled in the text in *Another Time*, and Auden's proviso found embodiment in 1938 in Valerian's words in *On the Frontier*, III.2 ('You will imagine that, in a People's Army, it is against your principles to obey orders – and then wonder why it is that, in spite of your superior numbers, you are always beaten').

(5) Auden's vision of the future ('To-morrow . . .') has come in for criticism. Not so much the applied science of stanza 20, but the ravens, the pageants, the trades-union meetings of stanzas 21 and 22. Some of these details are eccentric and evocative in the manner of *The Orators*. Some, certainly, were foreign to Auden's personal tastes. The opening of stanza 22, for example, seems close to the improper catharsis discussed in 'Writing' (*The Dyer's Hand*, p. 27). In 1940 he scrapped that stanza. In stanza 23 the idyllic images carry the slightest of ironic quotation marks as they evoke poems by Spender and Day-Lewis.

Two lines in stanza 24 brought a particularly hostile reaction from George Orwell which has been thoughtlessly echoed by later critics. In 'Political Reflections on the Crisis' (*The Adelphi*, December 1938, p. 110) Orwell quoted 'To-day the deliberate increase in the chances of death, | The conscious acceptance of guilt in the necessary murder' as an example of the 'utterly irresponsible intelligentsia', the alliance of 'the gangster and the pansy'. Orwell was stressing the gulf between murder as a word and murder as a fact (which as a combatant in Spain he had witnessed); though when he later elaborated the criticism in 'Inside the Whale' (1940) he largely interpreted 'murder' as Stalinist liquidation (*Collected Essays*, 1.516). When preparing *Another Time*, Auden changed these lines, probably in response to the *Adelphi* article (but not to 'Inside the Whale', which was published in March 1940, a month later than *Another Time*): 'deliberate' became 'inevitable' and 'necessary murder' became 'the fact of murder'. Auden thought that Orwell had been 'densely unjust'. In a letter to Spears of 11 May 1963 he explained the obvious, that he was not excusing totalitarian crimes but 'only trying to say what, surely, every decent person thinks if he finds himself unable to adopt the absolute pacifist position'. Even in a just war, he goes on to say, both sides effectively 'murder' each other. 'Murder' to mean 'killing in war' is not being disingenuous; it is making a moral point. Auden's arguments about pacifism may be found in *The Prolific and the Devourer*, pp. 56ff.

(6) Auden maintains the sense of drama to the end. 'The stars are dead; the animals will not look' really means that only mankind is forced to make moral choices, but it also manages to imply the arrival of a moment of stasis and horror. The final stanza is insisting that if the struggle fails (through the implied failure of the political will) then 'History to the defeated | May say Alas but cannot help or pardon.' In his Foreword to the 1966 *Collected Shorter Poems*, Auden quoted these concluding lines and wrote (p. 15): 'To say this is to equate goodness with success. It would have been bad enough if

I had ever held this wicked doctrine, but that I should have stated it simply because it sounded to me rhetorically effective is quite inexcusable.' In Cyril Connolly's copy, Auden has annotated more simply: 'This is a lie.' In 1937, of course, the lines could refer to Franco or the Loyalists, or to anyone else, for that matter, i.e. those who never made up their mind which side they were on in the first place. If it means 'defeated by war', and since Franco won, then Auden's 1966 remark has some point. But if it means 'defeated by choice, or by not choosing' (compare the 'Quartet of the Defeated' in *Paul Bunyan, Libretti*, p. 15, who have failed to 'make' America), then History has become what it often is, a merely directionless accumulation of random events. No wonder that it could not then 'help or pardon', since that would be a role for some mysterious power that could indeed decide what the right choices had been, i.e. the divine Mover. Compare 'that unseen target where all | Our equivocal judgements are judged and resolved in | One whole Alas or Hurrah' in stanza 10 of 'At the Grave of Henry James'.

He disappeared in the dead of winter:

February 1939; 'In Memory of W. B. Yeats', *New Republic*, 8 March 1939 (reprinted in *London Mercury*, April 1939); AT, p. 107; CP, p. 247; EA, p. 241.

'In Memory of W. B. Yeats' was the first poem that Auden wrote in the US. It contains two basic, related points: that a poet's work ultimately becomes independent of him, because he has no control over the interpretation which posterity will give it; and that therefore it is conditioned by society, and its role in society can be no more than a passive one. The rather sinister dramatisation of Yeats's death in the first section is thus an essential part of the mystery of a poet's destiny, and the numb elegiac tone reinforces the sense that the external world, in the grip of winter, is quite irrelevant to the internal world of poetry. The external 'instruments' measure the fact of the weather and the fact of Yeats's death, but the internal 'guts' receive and modify his life's work (this 'scattering' and 'modification' in lines 18 and 23 may be intended as a kind of sacramental metaphor of sowing, reaping and digesting bread).

Similarly, the metaphor of revolution represents the purely material fate of the poet's body: the city is in revolt, but the countryside (the poetry) goes on as usual (in the fourth stanza, about the scattering, the line about finding his happiness 'in another kind of wood' may be a riddle for paper;

'unfamiliar affections' are admiration for his work; 'a foreign code of conscience' is criticism of it). The poems, by being still read, continue to live ('By mourning tongues | The death of the poet was kept from his poems') and the poet, in ceasing to be a physical being, takes on the affective value of his oeuvre ('he became his admirers'). Howard Griffin's notes on a class of Auden's in the early 1940s elaborate this idea: 'Symbol of immortality – symphony orchestra. The idea that a person survives in his work. You have the music, the score, the instruments, the aesthetic whole, i.e. the intention of the artist. Up there on the stage is Beethoven; idea of resurrection as understood by Western Christians similar.' An interesting parallel to the poem is provided by Mittenhofer in Auden's and Kallman's libretto *Elegy for Young Lovers*: as a character, he was derived in many ways from Yeats.

Part 2 begins with a statement ('You were silly like us') which asserts that the writer in his person has no moral distinctiveness (Maud Gonne called Yeats 'silly'; compare Auden's Lawrentian poem for Isherwood, 'Who is that funny-looking young man . . .', line 10: 'Anonymous, just like us'). In an article entitled 'The Public v. the late Mr William Butler Yeats', which was written at about the same time as the poem, Auden elaborated some of the arguments about Yeats's talent and beliefs which are alluded to in the second and third parts. 'You were silly like us' is echoed by the words of the 'Public Prosecutor': 'But, you may say, he was young; youth is always romantic; its silliness is part of its charm' (EA, p. 391). It is more seriously explained by the 'Council for the Defence', who tries to show that Yeats's interest in fairies and the Anima Mundi was in a sense a search for a binding force for society in the face of social atomism. The poem's answer in Part 2 ('poetry makes nothing happen'; cf. 'Tolstoy knew that art makes nothing happen', *The Prolific and the Devourer*, p. 22) is further enlarged upon by the Defence Counsel: 'art is a product of history, not a cause. Unlike some other products, technical inventions for example, it does not re-enter history as an effective agent, so that the question whether art should or should not be propaganda is unreal. The case for the prosecution rests on the fallacious belief that art ever makes anything happen' (EA, p. 393). The whole idea is a rebuke of Yeats's speculation in 'The Man and the Echo' about the effect of his play *Cathleen ni Houlihan* on the Irish rebellion. The section also takes up the image in Part 1 of the 'peasant river' (Yeats's ambitions for a folk poetry) and shows it surviving without value for the 'executives' of history, flowing away from the raw realities of life, simply 'a mouth' (i.e. both Yeats's 'voice' and the mouth of the metaphorical river).

Auden moves into measured trochaic tetrameter couplets for Part 3. In stanza 1 Yeats's body becomes an 'honoured guest' like the inspiration that the painter Kuo Hsi waited for ('Commentary' to 'In Time of War', line 200) or more appropriately like Wellington in his cortège (Tennyson, 'Ode on the Death of the Duke of Wellington', line 80). The river is transformed into the sacred life-blood of Yeats's poetry, emptied from the vessel that is his body, and to become in the final stanza a healing fountain (the unfrozen pity of stanza 6, and a melting inversion of the snow-covered proleptic public statues of the opening winter scene of Part 1). Stanzas 2–4 were omitted in the 1966 *Collected Shorter Poems*. The case for the prosecution in the article claimed that 'a working knowledge of and sympathetic attitude towards the most progressive thought of his time' is one of the three requirements of a great poet. Those stanzas had shown how such a requirement might be circumvented. Time worships language, has therefore pardoned Kipling and will pardon, indeed does pardon Claudel 'for writing well'. Both right-wing writers influenced Auden (see pp. 228 and 146). In *The Prolific and the Devourer*, p. 20, writing of the difference between artists and ecclesiastical or political dogmatists, Auden said: 'There is more in common between my view of life and that of Claudel than there is between Claudel's and that of the Bishop of Boston.' There are allusions to Yeats's work in the following stanzas. 'A Prayer for my Daughter' connects hatred and the intellect; 'The Gyres' and 'The Man and the Echo' contain the injunction to rejoice. The allusion in stanza 8 is to Genesis iii.17. The real point about the value of art that Auden is making is that it teaches 'the free man how to praise' (stanza 9), i.e. how in this eve-of-war malaise to begin to value order above disorder, even though that order is only the order of art.

The shining neutral summer has no voice

May 1939; 'In Memory of Ernst Toller', *New Yorker*, 17 June 1939 (reprinted in *New Writing*, Christmas 1939); AT, p. 111; CP, p. 249.

Ernst Toller, the Expressionist playwright, hanged himself in New York on 22 May 1939. He had fled from Nazi Germany, was perhaps uncertain of his future and certainly short of money, but on the other hand had talked of suicide long before. He once wrote: 'If an intellectual man yields to death, the compelling motive will be the need of knowledge' (quoted in W. Willibrand, *Ernst Toller and his Ideology*, 1946, p. 30). Auden had met Toller and his wife in Portugal in 1936, and had translated the lyrics of Toller's play *Nie Wieder Friede!* (published in translation by Edward Crankshaw as *No More Peace!* in 1937). Auden uses as an image of Toller's thoughts of suicide the pair of swallows that had nested in his cell in the summer of 1922 in the Stedlheim prison in Munich, where he had been imprisoned in 1919 for his part in attempting to set up a soviet republic in Bavaria. It was here that he wrote most of his plays, and also *Das Schwalbenbuch*, a book about the nesting swallows. In the second and third stanzas Auden introduces the idea of the 'shadow', borrowed from Jung. The shadow is everything that the individual does not want to be, the negative side of the personality ('Everyone carries a shadow, and the less it is embodied in the individual's conscious life, the blacker and denser it is', Jung, *Collected Works*, 11, para 131). The third to fifth stanzas ask what possible psychological or political reason could account for Toller's death. The questions are purely rhetorical. Auden's real answer is contained in the fatalistic seventh stanza: 'We are lived by powers we pretend to understand', a turn of phrase pretty damning to psychology, it seems, but clearly referring to Groddeck's It (see also Auden's review of de la Mare in the *New Republic*, 27 December 1939, p. 292: 'we . . . are content masochistically *to be lived*'). Just before the quasi-religious peroration to 'New Year Letter', written a year later, Auden could put this with a significant difference: 'the powers | That we create with are not ours' (lines 1649–50).

I sit in one of the dives

September 1939; 'September 1, 1939', *New Republic*, 18 October 1939; AT, p. 112; EA, p. 245.

Auden had thoughts of dedicating this poem to Thomas Mann, but changed his mind. Its title is the date of Hitler's invasion of Poland, and therefore the 'clever hopes' in stanza 1 have much to do with the appeasement of Munich (this was in fact clearer in an earlier MS draft which read 'last mad hopes'). Auden's 52nd Street 'dive' may have been the gay bar, the Dizzy Club, on West 52nd Street, known at the time as 'Swing Street' for its many small jazz clubs and bars (see Harold Norse, *Memoirs of a Bastard Angel*, 1989, pp. 78–9). Perhaps the crush of bodies there prompted the advertising metaphor in line 10 (though see the reference in 'In this epoch of high pressure selling', lines 5–6, to such a contemporary advertising campaign). This bar-stool, bar-mirror setting for obsession with the war (there is a reminder in stanzas 4 and 5) was to be the starting-point of *The Age of Anxiety*. Auden may have remembered the opening of Dashiell Hammett's *The Thin Man* (1934): 'I was leaning against the bar in a speakeasy on Fifty Second Street' (see Alan Parker, *Auden Newsletter* 9).

In face of this expiry of hope, it seemed more than ever necessary to make some affirmation. The direct inspiration for this central theme in the poem seems to have been the dancer Nijinsky. On 27 June 1940 Auden explained to E. R. Dodds: 'The day war was declared I opened Nijinsky's diary at random (the one he wrote as he was going mad) and read "I want to cry but God orders me to go on writing. He does not want me to be idle".' This is the vocational message for Auden, but the poem itself, enacting the injunction to 'go on writing' is compelled to survey the reasons for 'the whole offence' of Nazism. The central error is found in stanza 6. The basis of the Just Society is universal love, the Christian Agape, which is denied by the Eros of the individual corrupted by sin: 'For the error bred in the bone | Of each woman and each man | Craves what it cannot have, | Not universal love | But to be loved alone.' Auden borrowed these last two lines from Nijinsky: 'Some politicians are hypocrites like Diaghilev, who does not want universal love, but to be loved alone. I want universal love' (*The Diary of Vaslav Nijinsky*, 1937, p. 44).

Stanza 2 suggests that the immediate evidence of this 'error' could be traced in theory by psychoanalytic investigations of Hitler's formative experiences in Linz and of his 'huge imago' (i.e. those of Hitler's subjective experiences, probably of parental authority, which caused him to be a psychopath: 'imago' is a Jungian term). It could also be uncovered by a historical study of German nationalism ('the whole offence | From Luther until now | That has driven a culture mad') and it is possible that Auden had a recent specific example in mind, Eugen Rosenstock-Huessy's *Out of Revolution*, chapter 7. The stanza concludes with a simple answer, with a strongly Christian flavour: 'Those to whom evil is done | Do evil in return').

Actually, the mention of Luther was probably intended to indict far more than Nazism, for Auden at this time blamed the anxiety of modern life largely on those thinkers of the Renaissance and the Enlightenment who were responsible for Economic Man. A passage from Auden's preface to his *Poets of the English Language* (1950) bears a very direct relationship to the meaning of 'September 1, 1939': 'The dualism inaugurated by Luther, Machiavelli and Descartes has brought us to the end of our tether and we know that either we must discover a unity which can repair the fissures that separate the individual from society, feeling from intellect, and conscience

from both, or we shall surely die by spiritual despair and physical
annihilation' (p. xxx). In the words of the poem: 'We must love one
another or die' (stanza 8). It is worth making clear at the outset that Auden
means both these kinds of death. The idea is by no means unique in
Auden's work. A dry-run for the line put in an appearance a few months
earlier, for example, in his revisions for a Group Theatre production of *The
Ascent of F6* at the Old Vic on 27 June 1939: 'ABBOT. What did you see in
the crystal? What did you see? | RANSOM. I saw written: Man is an animal
that has to love or perish' (*Plays*, p. 648).

The stanza in which this celebrated line occurs is introduced by the final
line of stanza 7, alluding to Proverbs xxi.8: 'Who can speak for the dumb?'
Auden's answer is 'All I have is a voice | To undo the folded lie' etc. Selden
Rodman wrote in his diary:

> Last July he told me he would be impelled by collective responsibility to
> enlist in the ambulance corps: he wouldn't fight under any conditions.
> Today he seems to have rationalised his pacifism. 'People have different
> functions,' he says, 'mine is not to fight; so far as I know what mine is, I
> think it is to see clearly, to warn of excesses and crimes against humanity
> whoever commits them.'

The 'folded lie' of the 'man-in-the-street' suggests the image of a man who is
carrying a message which he does not really understand, instructions for
living which are impenetrable, like a map that needs to be spread out to be
interpreted. Probably in fact the 'folded lie' is a kind of kenning for a
newspaper, tucked under the arm of the commuter of stanza 7. In contrast
to the headline lies of Authority, Auden's prescriptions in this stanza are
simple but also paradoxical. The first two (at lines 7–8 and lines 9–10) are
equivalent to the 'We live in freedom by necessity' of Sonnet XXVII of 'In
Time of War'. Of the third, Auden came to write (in his Foreword to the
first edition of Bloomfield's *Bibiography*, p. viii):

> Rereading a poem of mine, *1st September, 1939*, after it had been
> published, I came to the line 'We must love one another or die' and said
> to myself: 'That's a damned lie! We must die anyway.' So, in the next
> edition, I altered it to 'We must love one another and die'. This didn't
> seem to do either, so I cut the stanza. Still no good. The whole poem, I
> realized, was infected with an incurable dishonesty – and must be
> scrapped.

Since this is Auden's most notorious revision, it is worth pointing out that his statement here does not seem supported by the bibliographical facts. The stanza was omitted in the 1945 *Collected Poetry*, whereas the variant 'and die' (which Beach thought must be a misprint) seems not to occur until 1955 in Oscar Williams's *New Pocket Anthology of American Verse*. The variant itself may, according to Kallman, have been suggested by Cyril Connolly as a joke (see *Libretti*, p. 739). The tone of Auden's explanation and in the first case, his 1955 emendation, is curiously predated in two novels: (a) Randall Jarrell, *Pictures from an Institution* (1954), 1974 edition, pp. 173–4: 'Flo Whittaker had once gently reproved Dr. Rosenbaum for his attitude towards politics. She had done so by quoting to him, in tones that rather made for righteousness, a line of poetry that she had often seen quoted in this connection: "We must love one another or die." Dr. Rosenbaum replied: "We must love one another *and* die." '; and (b) John Bowen, *The Birdcage* (1962), p. 207: ' "I think that what you're really saying in your plays, if I'm any judge," he said, "is that we must all love each other or die. Isn't that it? – Really?" | "We've got to die anyway". Triumphantly. "But we've got to love *too*?" ' The concept is subtly adjusted in the *Audi, ne moriamur* of the late poem 'Aubade', also influenced by Rosenstock-Huessy.

At any rate it is a stanza that concentrates all the Yeatsian postures of a poem which Auden called the most dishonest he had ever written (to Naomi Mitchison, 1 April 1967). It is, of course, a parade of rhetoric designed to question the function of rhetoric, something that the 'old Cagliostro' himself, as Auden called him (letter to Louise Bogan, 17 November 1941), could be accused of. The deliberate choice of the elevated assertive trimeters of 'Easter 1916' (the century's most attractive model for the reserved dispassionate indirect political poem) makes no secret of Auden's strategy, after all, and the character of the poet's 'voice' once it has been introduced as a subject into the poem itself is unchallengably modest; it is presented at its most urgent and laconic in stanza 9 as being, like the underground morse code of the dispersed community of the Just (cf. Forster, 'What I Believe'), a single ironic (originally 'little') point of light. In essence, the position is very far from the grandeur of the tone in which it is expressed. Part of the continued appeal of the poem lies in this contrast.

When there are so many we shall have to mourn

November 1939; 'In Memory of Sigmund Freud', *Kenyon Review*, Winter 1940; AT, p. 116; CP, p. 273.

'In Memory of Sigmund Freud' is more discursive than the previous elegies in *Another Time*, and for that reason seems less occasional, although possibly it is thereby a greater tribute. Auden wished to 'place' the role of psychology more exactly within the ideas he was developing about the importance of moral choice. In stanzas 9 to 11 the poem develops, like 'Spain', a normative scenario based on Past, Present and Future. Freud 'showed us what evil is: not as we thought | Deeds that must be punished, but our lack of faith' (stanza 15. Cf. *The Prolific and the Devourer*, p. 26: 'To do evil is to act contrary to self-interest', etc.). That is to say, psychotherapy can reveal the distinction between causal necessity and logical necessity more clearly, so that the responsible moral choice can be disentangled from circumstances which confused it. There is an interesting elaboration of this argument in *The Double Man*, p. 130, using Kierkegaard's distinction between tribulations and temptations as a starting point. Freud, in just this way, was 'doing us some good' by helping to turn tribulations into temptations as any good scientist should.

The secondary theme of the poem, developed in the last half-dozen stanzas, is that Freud also helped to 'unite | The unequal moieties' of intellect and feeling (the use of the originally legal term 'moiety' creates an oxymoron that must be mutually resolved by these, as though by reconciling the unequal mental virtues of parents and children). It is for this reason that he is mourned by 'the household of Impulse', the sexual motive that both binds men together socially and creates discord between them personally. As early as 1929, Auden had been naturally critical of Freud's attitude to unconventional sexual behaviour (e.g. in his 1929 Journal: 'The trouble with Freud is that he accepts conventional morality as if it were the only one') and had been more impressed by psychologists who allowed men to accept their natural urges rather than to expect them to be curable.

This poem appears, incidentally, to be the first that Auden wrote in syllabic metre, under the influence of Marianne Moore. It uses the same syllabic stanza pattern (11/11/9/10) as the Prologue and Epilogue of *The Double Man*. In *The Dyer's Hand*, p. 296, Auden wrote that when he first began to read Moore's poems in 1935 he 'simply could not make head or tail of them', although he had previously been well acquainted with the experiments of Robert Bridges.

Some poems of 1936 and 1937 ('Casino', April 1936; 'Journey to Iceland', July 1936; and 'Schoolchildren', May 1937) he printed from 1966 without capitals at the beginning of the lines, a practice normally indicating syllabics. If he had reprinted 'Certainly our city . . .' (Spring 1936) I suspect that it would have received the same treatment. The looseness and odd enjambements of these poems are, however, related to the freedom of poems like 'Spain', a freedom which is traceable back to the Odes of *The Orators*. Auden may well have been attempting something like the Marianne Moore touch in these poems without the necessary strict counting of syllables, or he may have been using a classical model, perhaps via Hölderlin, whom he probably first read in March 1936. The Freud elegy, already begun in late October, may possibly have been syllabified after he dined with Marianne Moore and her mother on 13 November 1939. His letter to her of the following day expresses his admiration for her work, admits to his earlier bafflement and asks some technical questions.

While explosives blow to dust

September 1939; *Epithalamion commemorating the marriage of Giuseppe Antonio Borgese and Elisabeth Mann at Princeton, New Jersey November 23, 1939*, pamphlet, 1939; 'Epithalamion', AT, p. 121; EA, p. 453.

Auden went to a little printer in New York, and had the printed poem distributed to the wedding guests. He retained the dedication to the Borgeses in *Another Time* (Elisabeth Mann was in effect his sister-in-law) but its position as the culminating poem of the volume and its inclusion in lists of poems that constitute 'l'affaire C' show that he also had himself and Kallman in mind (one of the lists is among the Ansen letters, the other in the 1947–64 notebook, p. 300). In particular, the dismissal of the angels of erotic attitudinising in stanza 6 seems inappropriate in a public poem, and the 'heaven of the Great' in stanza 8 is one personal to Auden. The most extraordinary phrase in the poem is the 'lamb | With haemorrhages' of stanza 3, which represents together with the 'ascetic engineer' the dual view of God arranged by the Enlightenment. The stanza that Auden employs has a complex rhyme-scheme that appears to be his own invention. The metre, however, provides in this instance an interesting link between the celebratory tetrameters of poems like 'Lay your sleeping head, my love', modelled on Oberon's marriage-blessing, and the expository tetrameters of 'New Year Letter', which he was to begin in a few months.

Uncollected Poems 1937–39

Ladies and Gentlemen, sitting here,

?early 1937; 'Blues', *New Verse*, May 1937; EA, p. 209; *Auden Studies* 2, p. 81.

Despite the dedication to Hedli Anderson, there appears to have been no setting of this song, and she herself had no recollection of it (*Britten Letters*, p. 545). It is a weaker text than those that were set, even than some (e.g. 'Jam Tart') whose texts Auden never published. The US slang (e.g. 'subway', 'sugar daddy', 'G-man' [i.e. federal agent], 'hot-seat', 'real-estate') sorts uncomfortably with idiom that is plainly British ('my lad', 'simply grand') and the ending is understated even for a blues. In its personification of a bourgeois spiritual death, it looks like a poem that Auden might have written four years earlier.

You would go raving mad if I told you all I know

?April 1937; *Auden Studies* 2, p. 82.

Auden here satirises paranoid fear of Communism in the nonsense style that he developed for a good deal of his light verse ('If you sneeze you are thrashed with a bakelite truncheon | Babies are pickled and eaten for luncheon'). The scare word 'Reds' is also used by the First Old Tree of the Young Trees in *Paul Bunyan* (*Libretti*, p. 6).

Cleopatra, Anthony

?April 1937; *Auden Studies* 2, p. 84; *As I Walked Out One Evening*, p. 42.

This is another of the cabaret songs written for Hedli Anderson. The setting by Britten has not survived.

Education's in its infancy as yet

?April 1937; *Auden Studies* 2, p. 86.

According to the educational ideas of Hegel, with which Auden was debating at the time (see 'Schoolchildren'), the groundwork of the ethical character is laid in childhood through love and obedience to authority. The absurdity of applying these terms to non-human nature (in a comic poem of extended and fetching invention) is partly intended as ironical regret that they must ever be applied to us, who cannot so effortlessly discover our own true natures.

The Ostnian Admirals

?Summer 1937; *Auden Studies* 2, p. 89.

A song doubtless destined for *On the Frontier*, but never used.

Once upon a time there was a girl called Sue

1937; *Sue*, Sycamore Press broadsheet, January 1977; *Auden Studies* 2, p. 91.

Of all Auden's cautionary case-histories notable for their rough metre, black humour and deliberate malice, 'Sue' has a special place in the poet's affections ('the best one I ever did' as he told Alan Ansen). When a woman friend tore up his only fair copy, Auden never bothered to reconstruct it. The version published forty years later is a conjectural approximation from barely legible drafts and fragments in a notebook that belonged to Christopher Isherwood. 'Sue' is about the empty, fashion-conscious life of a society girl and her subsequent suicide. The outraged friend might be forgiven for thinking it misogynistic: 'I don't despise women. They terrify me, are far too expensive and love rows' he told Mrs Dodds in a letter of 15 December 1938. Auden's case-histories (cf. 'Miss Gee', 'James Honeyman' and 'Victor') are a fair cross-section of the repressed or errant bourgeoisie. One of the features of the poem is its extensive use of phrases culled from fashion magazines, which Auden jotted down in the notebook with evident delight, preparatory to tracing Sue's decline. At the conclusion of the poem, her possessions (including a box of fatal sleeping-pills) are brought to life to complain about her – a device which Auden probably borrowed from James ('B. V.') Thomson's poem 'In the Room'. The form of the ballad, in lines of four stresses arranged in couplets, sounds similar to the form he used in the narration of *Paul Bunyan* and in 'The Ballad of Barnaby' (both using guitar accompaniment). The resemblance, in subject, phrasing and metre, to William Plomer's 'Mews Flat Mona: A Memory of the 'Twenties' is remarkable, although 'Mews Flat Mona' was not published until February 1940. The text of 'Sue' cannot be regarded as authentic: the guesses stand out like plaster limbs on a statue.

My love is like a red red rose

?Summer 1937; 'Nonsense Song', TS; *Auden Studies* 2, p. 95; *As I Walked Out One Evening*, p. 44.

This poem was sent to a Miss Boyd (along with 'James Honeyman', 'Stop all the clocks . . .' and 'Johnny') for a children's anthology. The nonsense is Carrollian in spirit, though the tradition of such poems goes back a long way (see, for example, John Gay's 'A New Song of New Similies').

There are millions of things that we want to make

?Summer 1937; *Auden Studies* 2, p. 96.

After the multiple zeugma in the first line, this popular lyric slightly runs out of steam until the enjambement and caesura in the third stanza leading up to 'O enter', which was a word of charged significance for Auden (see, for example, 'Enter with him' and 'Love, loath to enter' at the beginning and end of *Dog, Plays*, pp. 201, 289, or 'this full view | Indeed may enter' in 'Look, stranger, at this island now').

As I look in the fire I remember

?Summer 1937; *Auden Studies* 2, p. 97.

Auden fully embraces all the clichés of a socially-dazzled romance in this sentimental ballad of a summer affair. It seems likely that it was in fact the 'Berk[e]ly' they dined at.

His name was John, a charming child,

1937; 'Johnny (A Cautionary Tale by Request)', *Badger*, Autumn 1937; *Auden Studies* 2, p. 34.

The only text known appears in the Downs School magazine: the poem is signed 'Rather Anon', and followed by 'A School Song', signed 'Very Anon'. The latter is certainly by Auden (see p. 192). The poem is in three parts, and is written in couplets in the Belloc manner. Johnny's significant failing is lack of punctuality. His parents in despair send him to the Downs School to be put in hand, but he dies after becoming stuck in a tree: no one rescues him because no one ever expects him to turn up anyway. Richard Davenport-Hines and Nicholas Jenkins have supplied detailed notes on school characters and customs in the *Auden Studies* printing, many of which derive from E. J. Brown, *The First Five: The Story of a School* (1987). In Part III Booge is E. C. Coxwell, the Second Master; Pup is F. M. Day the Latin Master; Brown is E. J. Brown, the Science Master; Grassy is Maurice Feild, the Art Master; and Hoyland is Geoffrey Hoyland, the Headmaster. Wizz is Auden himself.

Who is that funny-looking young man so squat with a top-heavy head

August–September 1937; printed in Brian Finney, *Christopher Isherwood: A Critical Biography* (1979), and in Charles Osborne, *W. H. Auden: The Life of a Poet* (1980).

This poem for Isherwood was written, in an effortless pastiche of D. H. Lawrence, in the preliminary pages of a copy of Lawrence's *Birds, Beasts and Flowers* which Auden gave to Isherwood on 3 September 1937. The view of the novelist's art is rather different from the birthday poem written two years previously ('August for the people and their favourite islands'): instead of pointing to the obligation of warning and insight, Auden now stresses the writer's necessity to act as 'our great ambassador to the mad'. This function of social camouflage is taken even further in the sonnet 'The Novelist' of the following year, where Auden claims that the novelist must actually and mysteriously *become* the experience that is the material of his art. This, perhaps, is a greater effort of imagination on the writer's part than Isherwood's 'anonymity', which in the Lawrence poem seems simply to be an aspect of his general pose of disguise and temperamental detachment. The phrase 'Anonymous, just like us' seems to be the seed of the famous phrase in the Yeats elegy, 'silly like us': the writer in his person alone has no moral distinctiveness.

When a little older, Robert,

December 1937; *Three Unpublished Poems*, 1986; *Auden Studies* 2, p. 41.

Written for Robert Russell, a Downs pupil (see *Auden Studies* 3, p. 327), in a copy of John Betjeman's *Continual Dew*. The Betjeman pastiche is nicely maintained.

I sit in my flat in my newest frock

1937 or 1938; 'My Love Stolen Away', TS; *Auden Studies* 2, p. 98.

This is one of the better of the unpublished Auden songs, written in the persona of the jealous older woman. It was given to Britten, but apparently never set (see *Britten Letters*, p. 548).

A city is the creation of the human will

?1938; 'The Londoners', *Plays*, p. 433.

Auden is credited with sections of the commentary to this film produced by Basil Wright and John Grierson for the Gas Light and Coke Company on the occasion of the jubilee of the LCC. The director was John Taylor. Auden's most blandly grandiose rhetoric conveys some unexceptionable truths about town planning.

The poets have taken their quick myopic walks

January 1938; 'Paris', *Oxford Poetry*, Winter 1985.

Auden spent the night of 19 January in Paris, *en route* with Isherwood for Marseilles, where two days later they set sail for Port Said on the first leg of their trip to China. In the notebook which contains poems written during the voyage, the text of 'Paris' comes before the early long draft of 'The Sphinx'. It is a sonnet appropriately written in syllabic alexandrines in acknowledgement of the common French verse measure. The opening lines appear to be a tribute to Rilke's poems written from the Jardin des Plantes and the Jardin du Luxembourg in Paris (Rilke is the presiding model for Auden's sonnets in *Journey to a War*) and in the last line there is a probable nod to Rilke's 'Du musst dein Leben ändern' from his sonnet on the archaic torso of Apollo, with the public statue of Napoleon in the Invalides having to stand duty for Rilke's god of poetry and healing. The tribute to the humble dead in lines 8–10 may have been the seed of the long passage in lines 196–249 of the 'Commentary' to 'In Time of War'. The 'blank wall' in line 13 is the 'Mur des Fédérés' in the Père Lachaise Cemetery, where 147 Communards were executed in 1871.

The ship weighed twenty thousand ton

January 1938; 'Passenger Shanty', EA, p. 233.

This poem is also taken from the notebook which contains the work written on the voyage to China. It is modelled on the First World War song 'Mademoiselle from Armentières'. Some of the passengers described also appear in Isherwood's account of the voyage in *Christopher and his Kind*, pp. 220–23. The rubber merchant Mr Jackson is there called 'Potter', and the sex-starved planter is called 'White'. Auden and Isherwood introduced them to each other, and they left the ship together at Singapore. Capa is the celebrated Hungarian press-photographer. Teruel was taken and retaken in the Spanish Civil War. Auden met Capa again in China (see *Journey to a War*, pp. 53 and 165; Auden also took his photograph for the book). In the penultimate stanza Christopher is still longing for Heinz, and Wystan repeats the phrase 'Love is exceedingly rare' more or less verbatim from one of his early poems (see 'The four sat on in the bare room'). 'Annam' is central Vietnam under French colonial rule.

When the postman knocks

?Autumn 1938; *Auden Studies* 2, p. 99.

This confession to falling out of love has a prose setting (probably intended to be spoken above the musical introductions to the verses) and aural effects. It was given to Britten, but apparently never set. The Munich Agreement was signed on 29 September 1938, and Capt. G. E. T. Eyston dramatically increased the land speed record on 27 August (previously held by Sir Malcolm Campbell since 1935).

O What's the loveliest thing the eye (the eye)

?May 1939; 'Song (after Sappho)', MS; *Auden studies* 2, p. 101.

Auden sent this brief lyric to Britten with 'Calypso', but unlike the latter its setting has not survived, even though the words were written for an existing tune (see *Britten Letters*, pp. 657–8). Auden regarded it as a brief encore piece. The poem on which it is modelled is the sixteenth fragment of Sappho, which begins 'some say a host of horsemen, others of infantry, and others of ships, is the most beautiful thing on the dark earth: but I say, it is what you love' (Denys Page's translation in his *Sappho and Alcaeus*, 1955, p. 52).

The movies and the magazines are all of them liars

May 1939; 'Love Letter', *Hika* (Kenyon College), June 1939; reprinted in *Illuminations*, Spring 1984, in *The Chatto Book of Love Poetry*, 1990 and in *Auden Studies* 2, p. 42.

The circumstances of this early poem to Kallman are those of 'Calypso', to which it is a kind of palinode. Kallman was enrolled as a student at Brooklyn College while Auden was teaching for a month at St Mark's School, Southborough, Massachusetts. The exuberant anticipation of meeting in 'Calypso', where Kallman's love for Auden is said to be 'an admirable peculiarity', becomes here a wretched agony of estrangement, concern and jealousy, where Auden asks 'after all, what reason have you to love me . . .?' The nadir of erotic self-abasement and physical disturbance comes in the powerful third stanza, with its echo of Hopkins's 'No worst, there is none'. The simple passion of this poem, and the degree to which it makes plain that the poet needs love as a kind of cure, gives it an importance in Auden's work in the light of which its having been discarded is all the more puzzling. Phrases from it reappear in later poems by Auden (line 3 in 'Christmas 1940'; lines 18–19 in the 'Prologue' to *The Double Man*; line 23 in Sonnet XII of 'The Quest'; line 27 in Sonnet VI of 'The Quest').

The vacation at last is approaching

May–June 1939; 'Ode', *Vindex* (St Mark's School), June 1939; *Auden Studies* 2, p. 44.

Auden's contribution to the Massachusetts school where he had been teaching for a month was signed 'The Feather Merchant' (term from a contemporary comic strip for someone who has an easy job). This is vintage light verse, modelled on Praed. Despite the private nature of most of its references and allusions, it is a delicate and resourceful poem, worth reading. Full references are supplied to the *Auden Studies* text by Richard Davenport-Hines and Nicholas Jenkins. The backhanded implication that the pupils of St Mark's might have learned more at Eton (stanza 4) accords perfectly with his known view of the low standard achieved by American private schools ('The boys nice but quite helpless', as he wrote to Mrs Dodds). In the penultimate line, τον ευτοπον = the Good Place. The last line ('*Et le vert paradis des amours*') is adapted from Baudelaire's 'Moesta et Errabunda' (*Les Fleurs du mal*). The lines in Baudelaire mean 'But the green paradise of childish loves, the innocent paradise, full of furtive pleasures'.

My thoughts lie topsy-turvy and pell-mell;

October 1939; 'Ballade of a Disappointed Man', *Adam*, 1973 (printed in Edward Mendelson, 'Auden in New York: 1939–1941').

The refrain of this ballade is 'The truth is not the proper thing to tell' appropriate to its circumstances: 'Walter Louch[h]eim' was the Federal official with whom Auden stayed in order to be coached for an interview with the immigration authorities about the violation of the terms of his entry visa concerning gainful employment. 'Mr Houghteling' was James Houghteling, the Commissioner of Immigrants at Washington who interviewed Auden. Auden found that he had to dissemble in some way about his payment for teaching at St Mark's School in May. Though the poem is in the nature of a thank-you note (Louchheim's wife Katie wrote a piece about it in the *Washington Post* magazine, 5 November 1978) there is a small but genuine core of moral upset in it.

In this epoch of high-pressure selling

?October 1939; 'Ode', *New York Times Book Review*, 8 March 1981 (reprinted in Farnan, p. 93; *As I Walked Out One Evening*, p. 67).

Auden again uses the twelve-line anapaestic stanza modelled on Praed that he had used for the St Mark's 'Ode' and that he was soon to use for Inkslinger's song in *Paul Bunyan*. The poem was written for the manager, Donald Neville-Willing, and for the staff, of the George Washington Hotel, on Lexington Avenue at 23rd Street, where Auden and Isherwood had stayed between January and March. The poem, a little shakier metrically than his other contemporary *vers de société*, is little more than a very elaborate visitors book contribution. S. A. = sex appeal.

The Dark Valley

This monologue for radio was commissioned by CBS (to whom Auden, eager for work when he first settled in New York, had already submitted a script entitled *Song*, never produced). Auden worked on the play during the spring of 1940, and it was broadcast by the Columbia Workshop on 2 June 1940, performed by Dame May Whitty, and with music by Britten. It was published in *Best Broadcasts of 1939–40*, edited by Max Wylie (1940), and a slightly revised text appears in *Libretti*, p. 371.

Auden was clearly interested in the medium of radio and had a gift for it. In the historical documentary *Hadrian's Wall* of 1937 he had exploited a montage technique learned from film; and in 1941 he was (with James Stern) to adapt D. H. Lawrence's story 'The Rocking-Horse Winner' with distinct expertise in translating the abstract psychological motivation of prose fiction into the purely aural effect of disembodied voice. But in general he found it an unprofitable medium for serious work. In an interview with Horst Bienek for Deutschlandfunk on 9 September 1965 he said: 'Ich habe ein Radio-Stück geschrieben. Aber das ist so, in Amerika ist das nicht sehr gut bezahlt. Das ganze Radio ist kommerciell. Das ist schwer.' However, as he confessed in a letter of 5 May 1963 to Monroe Spears, Auden cherished a secret affection for 'The Dark Valley', and even considered including it, between the Notes to 'New Year Letter' and 'The Quest', in *The Double Man*.

In such a position it might have usefully mediated between the largely sociological and psychological substance of the Notes and the fairy-tale character of the sonnets. But Auden must have decided that its subject, despite some significant parallels with material in *The Double Man*, would have been too distracting. Originally entitled (according to Max Wylie) something like 'The Psychological Experiences and Sensations of the Woman who Killed the Goose That Laid the Golden Eggs', it is a complete revision and expansion of Auden's 1936 cabaret sketch 'Alfred'. The new title may well be borrowed from Dante's *Inferno*, xii, stanza 29.

Although the cartoon political symbolism of the cabaret sketch (essentially conveyed by make-up, i.e. Therese Giehse looking like Hitler) has been necessarily abandoned in 'The Dark Valley', Auden maintained some sort of socio-political intent at least during the drafting of the play. Writing to Wolfgang Koehler at the time, he said: 'I have been struggling to finish a radio play. It's supposed to be an old woman talking to a goose, but I believe she's really Knut Hamsun.' Hamsun, the Nobel Prize-winning chronicler of Norwegian rural life, had become a notorious admirer of the Nazis who occupied his country.

To compare the old woman of the play to Hamsun is to lend some serious contemporary interest to a situation which is always in danger of lapsing into the archetypal. To kill the goose that lays the golden eggs is a vast mistake. In 'Alfred' (specifically anti-Nazi) it is easy to imagine that the gander represents the great genius of the Jewish race. In 'The Dark Valley' the goose's sex has been changed, and the quite elaborate family history of the old woman makes it clear that it is her own mother's puritanical repression that has conditioned her to a multiple hatred of (in the words of Auden's own preliminary MS notes) 'the women, the young, Liberalism, Government, Culture, Life'. This is not the first life-denying mother in Auden's work by any means, but in this case the ultimate victim is no putative male hero like Nower, the Airman or Ransom but a female goose, a symbol of the innocent and unfallen world itself. What the fairy-tale suggests is, therefore, that but for our stupidity the world is redeemable, and bears infinite riches that we are bent on destroying. Isherwood remembered Therese Giehse in cabaret in Amsterdam 'in a scene in which she nursed the globe of the world on her lap like a sick child and crooned weirdly over it' (*Christopher and his Kind*, p. 156). 'Alfred' was conceived with such an image in mind, but it is in the last lines of 'The Dark Valley' that the scene is most vividly realised: 'What have I done? Father, why are you looking so fierce? Father, don't you remember, I'm the world you made. Father, I'm so young and white, I don't want to die. Father . . .' (p. 381).

A few months after the broadcast, Auden published a hard-hitting 'Open Letter to Knut Hamsun' in *Common Sense* (August 1940) in which his tone of rage and regret is sufficiently elevated to project Hamsun's example on to a larger stage of human failing. He makes the point that Hamsun's fiction had established that 'physical toil and poverty do not necessarily debar man from leading a noble and beautiful, a *civilized life*.' This is, of course, precisely the milieu in the play of the old woman's mining father, who is presented in high poetic style as a Blakean force of energy and love. Auden's preliminary notes are quite specific about this ('Mine (Father)

Love') just as they associate the 'pious strait-laced' mother with 'Government'. Auden's setting, though beautifully exploiting the derelict valley of his own sacred mining landscape, may be intentionally a nod at the fictional world of Hamsun. In the 'Open Letter' he goes on to accuse Hamsun of ambitions beyond his gift, indeed of succumbing to temptations ('a lust for prophetic fame . . . impatience with social evils that baffle even the experts') which had tempted Auden himself.

Auden, like Hamsun, was waiting for some kind of answer, but he had avoided falling for fascism eight years earlier: 'Some worm there must have been, lying dormant in the heart which even while the life affirmed life, denied it, and only waited for the hour to strike, to rear its ugly little head and declare its blind animus against the human spirit.' It is such a blind animus that the old woman of 'The Dark Valley' reveals. And she reveals, too, an admiration for Hamsun's New Man (e.g. on p. 377, the punctual aeroplane, ferrying its millionaires, linked in her mind with respect for the authority of government and statistics). Auden worked into the text of the play a great list of civic employments representing 'the boys and girls of the city' as if to underline his claim that Hamsun was now appealing not to the fishermen and farmers of his novels but to 'the oversophisticated, the mentally lazy, the hopeless; above all to the brutalized masses of great industrial cities, the lumpenproletariat of a machine age'. And in a final ironic twist (considering that Auden was on the eve of conversion) the old woman kills the goose to the sound of church bells which represent, as Auden's draft notes make clear, the 'paternal authority behind Christianity', a substitute for the true natural authority of her real father ('He was a stag among sheep, a star among tapers').

In several passages of the draft Auden moves into alliterative verse of the kind that he was to employ more formally in *The Age of Anxiety*, although these passages are published as prose. The old woman sings two songs to the music 'of folk song character' which Auden had required from Britten. These songs were reprinted in collected editions of Auden's poems. 'Eyes look into the well' (CP, p. 269) has suggestively Christian and Dantesque imagery. It was also set by Lennox Berkeley in 1960. 'Lady, weeping at the crossroads' (CP, p. 279) is a more substantial ballad. The theme of suicide with the penknife clearly underlines the larger allegorical theme of political destiny in the play. The movement of the ballad also relates closely to the illusory dream-quest of the goose (p. 372) in which there is similarly no waiting fairy prince. An assignation at twilight is suspicious (cf. the horror of the heroine in stanza 12 of Coleridge's 'The Ballad of the Dark Ladie') and the journey, like Prince Alpha's in 'The Witnesses', becomes one of fatal self-discovery.

May Whitty, best-remembered now as the engaging spy in Hitchcock's *The Lady Vanishes*, was at the time of the broadcast playing the Nurse in *Romeo and Juliet*. This was quite fortuitous, but it must have lent a frisson to her voicing of the confused sexuality of Auden's sinister old woman.

Paul Bunyan

Paul Bunyan has the troubled distinction of being the first and last operatic collaboration between a librettist and a composer who were later to produce some of the greatest twentieth-century examples of the genre. Auden and Britten had only been in the USA for a matter of months, and though it now seems natural that they should have chosen the mythical subject of this American lumberjack folk-hero ('It is certainly up Wystan's tree and also up mine' was Britten's appropriate way of putting it to Ralph Hawkes on 19 October 1939), it is clear that their elusively parabolic and eclectic treatment of it was puzzling to audiences. Auden was at work by mid-October, and a typescript of the substantially finished libretto was ready by the middle of January 1940. The operetta was first produced by the Columbia Theater Associates of Columbia University on 5 May 1941, but reviews were not on the whole favourable. The work remained unpublished (and was not further performed) for thirty-five years. Towards the end of his life, Britten made some revisions and reissued the operetta as his opus 17. The revised version of this libretto was published by Faber in 1976, and in an edited version (with omitted material in an appendix) by Donald Mitchell in 1988. Edward Mendelson's text in *Libretti* establishes the libretto that Auden intended Britten to set, and differs in many respects from the words of the musical work as we now know it. Nevertheless, this is the text that I shall refer to.

When the Nazis invaded Poland, Auden wrote in 'September 1, 1939' of New York's many languages rising into 'this neutral air | Where blind skyscrapers use | Their full height to proclaim | The strength of Collective Man.' Whatever had seemed exciting and positive to the *émigré* about the freedom of a rootless and polyglot community was momentarily, on the eve of war, a frightening illusion. He rapidly came to realise, as the stanza goes on to show, that 'international wrong' is everyone's burden (the phrase was reused in 'Music is International', line 71). The haunted wood has roots after all, and the novelty of the new country lay principally in its providing a fresh context for the analysis of a universal problem. As Auden was to put it in 'New Year Letter' (lines 1519ff): 'More even than in Europe, here | The choice of patterns is made clear I Which the machine imposes, what I Is possible and what is not, I To what conditions we must bow I In building the Just city now.'

It is with precisely this notion of the 'Collective Man' and human destiny in the machine age that *Paul Bunyan* is concerned. It starts with virgin forest (a beautiful chorus in slowly advancing Lydian scales) and ends with the giant Bunyan bidding farewell to the community which has already cleared a continent and begun farming, and which has therefore no longer any need of his initiative and benign authority. Auden's 'Prologue' is typically a version of the Fall, and in one abandoned version introduces an actual 'lapse' of the botanical into the biological (*Libretti*, p. 540). It presents the arrival of man as a piece of frightening news brought to the self-sufficient forest by three Wagnerian-sounding wild geese: 'A man is a form of life I That dreams in order to act I And acts in order to dream I And has a name of his own.' The name is, of course, 'Paul Bunyan', representing the collective dream of the human endeavour, and he is due to be born at the next Blue Moon (clearly there is no place in the scenario for any Native Americans). When the moon obligingly does turn blue, to an early example of Britten's heterophonic gamelin-inspired music, the forest chorus grudgingly accepts the development with a big show-stopping number: 'But once in a while the odd thing happens, I Once in a while the dream comes true, I And the whole pattern of life is altered, I Once in a while the Moon turns Blue' (p. 7).

In the score there is a big reprise of the opening chorus in the final 'Litany'. This follows 'Bunyan's Farewell' (p. 44), a thematically important speech spoken in Shakespearean tetrameters that are subtly different from the tetrameters of 'New Year Letter' (see my first paragraph above) that so closely borrowed from them: 'Now the task that made us friends I In a common labour, ends I . . . All I had to do is done, I You remain but I go on, I . . . Here, though is your life, and here I The pattern is already clear I That machinery imposes I On you as the frontier closes, I Gone the natural disciplines I And the life of choice begins.'

In other words, nature has been tamed and its collective dream ended: now it is the individual human relationship that is of importance (a precise inversion of the anthropological emphasis of *The Orators* eight years earlier, when Auden was seeking a satisfactory group life) while the emphasis on 'pattern' already implies a pre-existent future to be discovered or traced by each individual. The life of choice begins, but it has to be the right choice.

There is no doubt a paradox here, perhaps akin to that of free will and divine foreknowledge (though Auden is yet to be converted). At the core of the 'Litany' is a significant echo of an earlier poem. When Bunyan is asked what is to become of America, he replies: 'Every day America's destroyed and re-created | America is what you do | America is I and you, | America is what you choose to make it.' This is 'Spain 1937' 's 'I am whatever you do' with something of a difference, just as 'whatever' is different from 'What'. The 'life' in the earlier poem is History as a yes-man, careless of human destiny. Bunyan has become a far more concerned and numinous symbol, still removing himself, it is true, from the arena of human choice, but embodying the means to create the future as a father looks benevolently on his children. In a production of the operetta he *sounds* like a father or a schoolmaster ('Goodnight, Mr Bunyan', the lumberjacks call out at one point, like boy scouts planning a midnight feast) but he is, of course, as one knew all along, an Abstraction. When, in the final scene, he is asked who he is, he replies: 'Where the night becomes the day | Where the dream becomes the fact | I am the Eternal Guest | I am Way | I am Act' (p. 46). Bunyan is not only the sum of human endeavour (i.e. all lumbermen), but a principle of human endeavour (i.e. freedom to choose). But a 'guest' arrives from elsewhere, and is surely close to the principle of Grace.

Despite its eclectic and parodic nature, the operetta proceeds in a confidently and subtly unified manner. An example is in the first stanza of the Prologue (p. 5) where the Arnoldian notion of time as a river reaching the sea is to be echoed later in 'Johnny's Regret' (p. 28). In the second stanza the waves are 'glad-handed' presumably because they extend an eager welcome to the beach (cf. Caliban's 'facile glad-handed highway' in 'The Sea and the Mirror', CP, p. 442). The global processes of nature enforce necessity upon organic life, but organic life rebels. Urged by the gossip of the progressive geese, the younger trees actually want to turn into wooden artefacts (p. 7).

Bunyan's early life is recounted in the first of the three ballad interludes (p. 8). These narrations are sometimes overlong, but they are necessary to convey the story of a superhuman being who never appears on stage. Auden's style here is the loose ballad couplet he had used for 'Sue' and was to use for 'The Ballad of Barnaby' (also accompanied by guitar). The blue ox, Babe, who advises Paul (stanza 14) was taken by Auden (arbitrarily as he admitted, though he was certainly in a Jungian frame of mind in these years) to be a symbol of his anima. The anima is Jung's 'soul-image', usually appearing to males in dreams or poems in female form.

Act 1 opens with Bunyan's first meditation, describing the innocent landscape ('It is America but not yet'). Bunyan's invisibility and prescience allows Auden the full exercise of his grand choric manner. Bunyan's call to the pioneers is strikingly modelled on Ransom's reflections on Ulysses' address to his crew in *The Ascent of F6* (*Plays*, p. 296). The Lumberjacks' Song (p. 10) establishes the various reasons for emigration to America with a refrain that alludes to *Acis and Galatea* (compare 'We are handsome and free and gay' with 'Harmless, Merry, Free, and Gay', perhaps a nod to Gay himself). The musically memorable Western Union Boy (p. 12) brings a telegram announcing the first of the three most important human characters, the logger Hel Helson. This is followed by the duet for the two bad cooks, with its pastiche of Donizetti and satire on media advertising and salesmanship (a running theme in Auden's original conception).

The arrival of the second important human character, Johnny Inkslinger (p. 13), suggests that Auden conceived the work with an earlier opera about lumberjacks in America in mind: Brecht and Weill's *The Rise and Fall of the City of Mahagonny*. In fact, *Paul Bunyan* reads very much like an answer to the profound pessimism of *Mahagonny*. Johnny Inkslinger is introduced hungry, but unable to pay for the beans and soup that Bunyan can provide and unwilling to work for him because 'This is a free country.' Bunyan's emphasis on 'no work, no pay' is a dramatised illustration from *The Prolific and the Devourer* (p. 9: ' "Work" is action forced on us by the will of another. "Unless you do this, I won't give you anything to eat" '). In *Mahagonny* the lumberjack Jimmy Mahoney is condemned to death for being unable to pay for three bottles of whiskey (and a curtain rod) consumed in the Here-You-May-Do-Anything Inn. Brecht's America is a commercial and moral trap. Jimmy is seeking a destiny entirely confined by the sordid pleasures of the city. 'Choice' for Brecht (in the central chorus of the work) is a matter of exploitation:

> Denn wie mann sich bettet, so liegt mann,
> es deckt einen da keiner zu,
> und wenn einer tritt, dann bin ich es,
> und wird einer getreten, dann bist du's.

> (For as you make your bed, so you lie in it,
> No one gets covered up there,
> And if anyone's going to do the kicking, it'll be me,
> And should anyone get kicked, it'll be you.)

For Auden, choice is a matter of collective co-operation. Brecht's is the

City of Nets; Auden's is already the City of Possibility, the Just City postulated by 'New Year Letter'. All the material about discriminatory feeding in *Paul Bunyan* that seems so incidental to the work's theme (see also pp. 18–21) may in fact be an answer to the scene in *Mahagonny* where one of the lumberjacks eats himself to death. The Christmas Eve celebration is, in this context, almost a sacrament.

It is also interesting, if not surprising, that Auden's camp is free of prostitutes (Brecht is full of them) and that therefore the high-voiced roles have largely to be provided by animals (this suits Auden, of course, as the relationship between animals and men is an old theme that gets a significant showing in the operetta). Fido, Moppet and Poppet are introduced in the next scene (p. 14), a Trio of sopranos singing 'The single creature lives a partial life' (reprinted in *Harper's Bazaar*, April 1945; CP45, p. 230; CSP, p. 259; CP, p. 268). The two cats perhaps owe something to Baudelaire's 'Les Chats', lines 3–4 ('Orgueil de la maison', etc.) and their dialogue is reminiscent of the Kitchen Cat and the Parlour Cat in Andersen's 'The Ice Maiden'.

The following Blues sung by the Quartet of the Defeated (p. 15) was also reprinted in some of Auden's collected editions (CP45, p. 202; CSP, p. 232). It is written very much in the mould of 'Refugee Blues'. For the first line, compare 'Gold cometh from the North' (Job xxxvii.22). The varied refrain ('You don't know all, sir, you don't know all') suggests both that these immigrants were lured by the material promises of know-alls and that they were themselves recklessly deaf to advice. The great climax in the final stanza ('Like butterflies they're pulled apart, | America can break your heart') turns the young continent into a cruel god, like the famous simile in King Lear, though Auden in a letter to E. R. Dodds of 16 January 1940 wrote: 'America may break one completely, but the best of which one is capable is more likely to be drawn out of one here than anywhere else.' It is quite possible that the Quartet is yet another example of the schema of the Jungian division of the psyche into its four faculties (which Auden later used in 'For the Time Being' and *The Age of Anxiety*). If so, then the Alaskan gold speculator would represent Intuition, the Western gunman Sensation, the Alabaman suicide Feeling (like Rosetta, the only woman of the quartet), and the Wall Street speculator Thought.

The second ballad interlude (p. 16) covers at some length Bunyan's marriage, the death of his wife, Carrie, and the birth of his daughter, Tiny. Back in the camp in the second scene of Act I, the loggers dispense with the services of the bad cooks (Britten's setting of the Cole Porterish Food

Chorus is a little too unrelaxed), paving the way for the arrival of the cowboy Slim, who can cook well, and is the last of the trio of important human characters (p. 21). Slim's song has several themes currently of personal interest to Auden. In his offstage introduction there is a significant zeugma introducing his quest: he must hunt down his shadow and hunt out his missing self. The shadow is Jung's term for 'the thing a person has no wish to be' (*Collected Works*, 16, para. 470). Auden very often referred to it at this time as the 'lame shadow', i.e. that part of oneself that represents one's inferior qualities manifested in uncontrolled emotions. Finding Kallman was for him an act of liberation from the attentions of his own lame shadow (e.g. writing to Margaret Gardiner on 19 November 1939: 'The Lame Shadow, dear thing, has gone back to the Unconscious where it is at home'). In the song itself, Slim is free but vulnerable. In stanza 1 he dances between the horse-hooves like one of the butterflies that America can break apart (according to the Alabama woman in the Quartet of the Defeated, p. 15). In stanza 3 he is (in the words that Auden famously applied to himself in line 3 of 'September 1, 1939') 'uncertain and afraid'. Slim compares himself to a lost child needing to lay ghosts, an image that Auden had also used in stanza 5 of the earlier poem.

Johnny Inkslinger's Song (p. 23) is written in a brisk Praed-like form that Britten nonetheless set at a somewhat graver pace. It asserts the classic dilemma of the artistic soul who is convinced that success in any cultural medium would be his if only he weren't distracted by the necessity of earning a living. His Love Song to Tiny which follows (p. 25) is a lexical patter-song once again with Cole Porter mannerisms, curiously prophetic of the double dactyl invented by Hecht and Hollander (see p. 524). 'Occi-parietal', which is not in the OED, may be a portmanteau of 'occiput' (back of the head) and 'parietal' (as used of bones of the skull). The song was omitted by Britten from the 1976 production. The wooing of the individual lumberjacks (p. 27) resembles the refrains of Ira Gershwin's 'How About A Man?' in *Strike up the Band* (1927). Tiny's Song (p. 27) was written overnight when it was discovered that the actress playing the part in 1941 could actually sing. Its coda interestingly identifies the bone of the dead mother with limestone (cf. 'In Praise of Limestone').

'Johnny's Regret' (p. 28) picks up an idea from the opening stanza of the Prologue, but it also remembers the third stanza of 'Underneath the abject willow' of 1936, written for Britten, where the brooks flowing to the ocean are also metaphors for love coming into its satisfaction. After warning Bunyan about Helson, Johnny has his dream of Hollywood, a Lullaby and

Chorus of Lame Shadows and Animas (see p. 311 for comment). Britten called them 'Dream Shadows, Film Stars and Models', but seems to have cut the whole scene before the first night in 1941. The introductory Lullaby (p. 29) is full of conscious echoes of seventeenth century poems (e.g. 'fear no more' from the Act IV, sc. 2 song in *Cymbeline*, Sabrina's 'translucent wave' from *Comus* and 'the drumming of an ear' from Marvell's 'A Dialogue between the Soul and the Body'). The following Chorus (p. 30) was published in the *New Yorker*, 24 August 1940, under the title 'The Glamour Boys and Girls have Grievances too.' The point for Auden about these 'grievances' of lame shadows and animas is that they embody the false ideals in real life of beauty and self-image (stanzas 1–4), maternally conditioned perversions (stanza 4), or fantasised heroism (stanza 5). These illusions must be replaced by what the following words of Bunyan describe as the 'exchange' of 'the Actual and the Possible' (p. 31). This exchange is mysterious because it requires a night of religious testing for the individual, even a 'return to the humble womb'. If the possible is to become actual, therefore, something more than mere rational choice is needed. The will must be 'pacified and refreshed' by some external and supernatural initiation or rebirth. It is perhaps at this moment (originally spoken, but beautifully scored for the 1976 production) that Bunyan seems most like God.

Act II opens with Bunyan's words at dawn (p. 32) predicting a new stage in the civilised life of the continent. He is now able to allow agriculture, and so goes off with the potential farmers to clear the Topsy Turvey Mountain, leaving Helson in charge. Helson's cronies urge him to rebellion (p. 34). When, in the aftermath of the perceived failure of the first production, Auden drafted a new text (drastically cutting most of the best scenes, e.g. the dog and cats, the Western Union Boy, the cooks, etc.) he was intent on elaborating this element of the plot (see *Libretti*, p. 555). The cronies (in symbolic terms playing the part of the Devil) are given a much more calculating role in their plotting against Helson and Bunyan. They are represented in an oddly jacobinical way, talking speciously about Liberty, Equality and Fraternity. A suggestion here that Auden intended a subsidiary allegory of a subversion of the profitable relationship between the boss (Bunyan) and the worker (Helson) need not be anti-communist, though it is true that Auden was at this time disillusioned with the communist League of American Writers (Carpenter, p. 294).

The Mocking of Hel Helson (p. 34) owes something to Victor's spiritual dialogues in stanzas 22 to 26 of Auden's earlier ballad of that name: both Victor and Hel are essentially projecting their own neurotic fears on to various aspects of the natural world. Unlike Johnny Inkslinger, Helson will not confide in the dog, even though it appears to be possessed of a great deal of psychiatric insight. The response of the Cat's Creed (p. 36) is to see human beings as riddled with romantic aspirations and delusions which they share with dogs (this symbiotic relationship has already been established in 'The single creature lives a partial life', p. 14). Cats, on the other hand, are not Platonists but Aristotelians, i.e. they are firm believers in the material world. Cats are different from men just as Ibsen's Trolls are: the human creed is 'Man, to thyself be true!', the Troll creed 'Troll, to thyself be – enough.' (*Peer Gynt*, II.6).

While Helson fights Bunyan (p. 37), Slim and Tiny consolidate their love in a brief lyric. The idea of the trysting stone in the first stanza is that on midsummer eve (i.e. when the sun has departed) lovers would meet by a stone to pledge their affection to each other. Auden may, for example, have known the standing stones of Stenness in the Orkneys, through a hole in one of which the lovers joined hands when they made their binding oath (see also Scott, *The Pirate*, chapter xxxviii). Helson loses (a 'picayune' is a six-cent piece, i.e. something quite insignificant) and is struck with remorse. The reconciliation of Helson and Bunyan (p. 39) is treated like a Revivalist conversion ('O great day of discovery'), and after the final ballad interlude with its perfunctory account of further episodes in Bunyan's story, the stage is set for the final scene (p. 41), set at a festive Christmas dinner (not of course without deep significance to the religious level of the operetta's meaning: this is in a sense the *agape* which brings the celebrants together before the final departure of their strange *deus absconditus*, Paul Bunyan). The events of this scene are a straightforward exposition of the future of the human characters in the story.

If events in the camp so far have seemed to be something of a distraction from the point of the work as I initially described it, it is here that Auden's plan becomes clearer. The trio of Slim, Hel Helson and Johnny Inkslinger represented for Auden a folk-tale version of what he described in *The Prolific and the Devourer* (p. 8) as the three categories of roads to salvation:

There is only one salvation but there are as many
roads thither as there are kinds of people.
> Three kinds of people: three roads to salvation.
> Those who seek it
>> 1) through the manipulation of non-human things: the farmer,
>> the engineer, the scientist

    2) through the manipulation of other human beings: the
       politician, the teacher, the doctor

    3) through the manipulation of their own phantasies: the artist,
       the saint

At the party we finally see the particular destiny of the three characters who exemplify these types:

(1) Slim has already become a cook ('manipulation of non-human things') and fallen in love. He has also discovered himself in Tiny (their charming engagement chorus, 'Carry her over the water', was reprinted in collected editions, CP45, p. 199; CSP, p. 229; CSP66, p. 160; CP, p. 268; it has just the right amount of compressed metaphor for a lyric, as in the stanza in which leaping fish are compared to the shutters of cameras. It was also set by Lennox Berkeley in 1960). Together they are put in charge of a mid-Manhattan Hotel (possibly a tribute to Donald Neville-Willing, manager of the George Washington Hotel on 23rd and Lexington, in which Auden stayed early in 1939 and recommended to Britten as able to provide him with a decent piano).

(2) Hel Helson is the foreman of the loggers ('manipulation of other human beings') who broods about his lack of brains, who fights Bunyan and has to be reconciled with him (i.e. power requires the direction of the rational Will, or possibly, political choice is useless without Grace). He goes to Washington to help in the administration of the New Deal.

(3) Johnny Inkslinger is the camp book-keeper, but he is also a would-be artist ('manipulation of their own phantasies') and Auden oddly envisaged him as 'satisfying Henry James's plea for a fine lucid intelligence as a compositional centre' (*New York Times*, 4 May 1941). Not surprisingly, after his dream at the end of Act I, he is summoned to Hollywood as technical adviser on a lumber picture. Whether this is a satisfying opportunity for him (Isherwood, Huxley and others were, after all, working in the movies) or whether it represents the classic material compromise of the intellectual (one which Auden himself never made) is not quite clear.

Bunyan makes his farewell (p. 44) in the celebratory metre of Oberon, leaving the loggers on the threshold of the Machine Age. Some of the superficial aspects of this self-deceiving age are satirised in the otherwise elevated Litany, in which Bunyan goes out of his way to declare that he cannot bless Slim and Tiny ('May you find the happiness that you possess'; cf. 'Heavy Date', stanza 17, 'We can only love what- | -ever we possess', i.e. blessedness is found and not given). In the penultimate scene of

Mahagonny, incidentally, the 'Play about God in Mahagonny' seems to enact a bizarre reversal of Bunyan's role among men. 'God' (enacted in lurid *Sprechgesang* by Trinity Moses) is a suddenly-revealed presence chillingly ignored by the already-damned of the city; Bunyan is an ever-immanent absence who makes the recalcitrant lumberjacks love him, and who therefore creates the conditions for the very founding of cities. The human task is now, in the words of Auden's 1941 programme note, 'how to live well in a country that the pioneers have made it possible to live in'.

The Double Man

The Double Man is made up of a 'Prologue'; the 1707-line poem 'New Year Letter' followed by its 'Notes' (commentary and short poems by Auden, with extensive quotations from other writers); the sonnet sequence 'The Quest'; and an 'Epilogue'. It was published in the US in March 1941, and in England (under the title *New Year Letter*) in May. Auden dismembered the book for subsequent collected editions (details of the reprinted material will be given in my commentary) but did allow a new English impression to be issued in May 1965. The different English title arose because in December 1938 he had almost certainly in violation of his Faber contracts accepted an advance for a prose book from the Hogarth Press. In about March 1940 he described such a new book to John Lehmann: 'It will be in the form of Pascal's Pensées or Kierkegaard's journal, i.e. a series of Reflections on art, politics, life and death etc. As a title, I suggest, a phrase of Montaigne's "*The Double Man*"' (Wichita). Hogarth listed the proposed book, causing Faber to remind Auden of his contractual obligations to them and to avoid using the title that Hogarth had inadvertently advertised. Auden was in fact describing to Lehmann the book that became the unpublished *The Prolific and the Devourer*. T. S. Eliot as the Faber director responsible for poetry took the liberty of removing Auden's only textual use of the phrase 'the Double Man' from the antepenultimate line of the 'Prologue' and substituting the phrase 'the invisible twin'.

Auden's ascription of the phrase to Montaigne is misleading: it actually occurs in Charles Williams's discussion of the quotation from Montaigne (in *The Descent of the Dove*, 1939, p. 192) which Auden borrowed for the epigraph of the book. Auden admitted to being extensively influenced by Williams, but he might as easily have found a version of 'the double man' as haunted dualist anywhere (e.g. in Flaubert's 'homo duplex', *Bouvard et Pécuchet*, Garnier edn, Paris, 1954, p. 266). Callan (p. 170) points out that Williams also quotes Athanasius on becoming 'a double man' through Christian neighbourly empathy (i.e. suffering imaginatively in another's body as in one's own), though whether this sense was intended to be operative in the title is doubtful.

Auden wrote 'New Year Letter' between January and April 1940. He then wrote and assembled the 'Notes', and completed 'The Quest' during the summer, and the book was finished by October 1940. At times during the year he considered including in *The Double Man* other works of his which he had to hand, such as 'The Dark Valley', his St Cecilia's Day ode and the poem to Henry James. There would have been a certain appropriateness in some of these inclusions, e.g. in the quest material or mining symbolism (cf. 'New Year Letter', lines 1100 ff) of 'The Dark Valley' or the view of James as a pure apostle of art, but the work is compendious enough as it is, though successfully and suggestively so.

'New Year Letter', the core of the book, was addressed to the fifty-six-year-old Elizabeth Mayer, wife of an expatriate Jewish psychiatrist then living in Amityville. Auden had met her through Peter Pears (who had met her through Basil Douglas in 1936) and therefore knew her very much in the context of the kind of family music-making described at lines 47ff of the poem. Mrs Mayer was a mother-figure to him, a real exile and a patron of the purest of the arts which had this strange ability to create in the mind 'a *civitas* of sound'. For Auden she seemed a fit recipient of a poem which was to argue itself into a position of detachment and worship of 'the powers that we create with'. Why not a letter to his real mother, who would have needed it more? He had, after all, just spent Christmas with the Mayers; this was an unlooked-for kind of thank-you letter. The answer must be that he was sensitive of his new proto-Christian position, and it was his first truly Christian work, 'For the Time Being', that was to be Constance Auden's memorial.

The central appeal of *The Double Man* lies in the particular tone of the discourse of 'New Year Letter' and its odd relationship with the 'Notes' which follow. The octosyllabic couplet is perhaps just too narrow for discursive verse without descending into quaintness or whimsy (just as the heroic couplet is too broad: tailoring of resources gives these forms their distinctive features) and thus in order to be serious appears to be continually pushing further and further away the decisive statement. The examples of Swift and Gay, of Butler perhaps, and above all of Prior's *Alma* seem relevant to the tone here. Prior was a great favourite of Auden's (letter to Spears, 3 May 1963) and his great poem on the mind gives licence in its freedom with psychological arguments to Auden's similar freedom with sociological ones. Auden's natural critical categorising and qualifying accentuates this effect of postponing the decisive statement, and so do the 'Notes'. The reader turns to the back, as if to find the answer, but usually finds an extension to the problem. This applies even in cases where the meaning is transparent: are the 'Notes' authorities or examples, analogues or applications of the ideas which the poem is exhibiting with such fertility? It is not certain. The familiar accusation that the 'Notes' are merely undigested material which the precipitous prosody of the 'Letter' could find no room for is only a half-truth, for without the resources of the 'Notes' the 'Letter' would be over-burdened, not only with material, but with the necessity to furnish at every point its awareness of the dialectic; the reader's mental energy is better deployed (by doing more creative work) in interpreting the 'sources' for himself. The 'Notes' have been compared with Eliot's in *The Waste Land*, but these, we know, were a distinct afterthought. One may better compare them with Pope's notes to *The Dunciad*, which are similarly deployed contributive material. Auden is, I think, almost light-heartedly aware that he is having it both ways, that the work is something between Blake's *Marriage of Heaven and Hell* and a metaphysical treatise, with nutshell political theory and the pragmatic philosophical discoveries of a great talker thrown in for good measure. And all the time we must remain aware that the principal section of the work is an informal neo-Augustan epistle, because this safeguards the aphoristic tone of the whole.

Auden's permanent settlement in the United States at this time (he became a naturalised citizen in 1946) is clearly connected with *The Double Man*, if only because his choice of New York, the world's most notoriously alienating metropolis, the city of Lorca, Mayakovsky, Hart Crane, seemed a deliberate act of self-discovery, an environmental act of good faith in respect of his personal quest for truth, a decisive acknowledgement that 'Aloneness is man's real condition' (line 1542). Thus the 'Letter' ('addressed to a Whitehall' but 'under Flying Seal to all', lines 315–16) is a public explanation of what to many in wartime England seemed a kind of defection. Auden is here struggling for a system of belief more coherent than the 'pink liberalism' which had shown itself powerless to avert the war. He is concerned to elaborate with greater rationality the human situation as outlined in the potted history of 'In Time of War', particularly in the context of metaphysics. America seemed the most typical human environment in the epoch of the Third Great Disappointment, and the 'Letter' makes this quite clear (lines 1519–24). Auden no doubt felt he had seen enough of two wars against the fascists profitably to face a third; what seemed necessary was to explore a state of affairs in which there were no effective sanctions that civilisation could use against the Nazis. If this involved him in a study of metaphysics, particularly of existential philosophers like Kierkegaard and theologians like Niebuhr, well and good: the conditions for building the Just City had to involve a new, unified sense of man's purpose and man's needs, something of greater authority than the monistic systems of Marx and Freud.

The goal is Christianity, but one of the agreeable strengths of *The Double Man* is that its proto-religious conclusions are less diplomatically argued than honestly sought. Indeed, the seeking is an important thematic element in the whole work, not only in the sonnet sequence 'The Quest', where it is dramatically embodied, but incidentally even in the relaxed 'Letter' itself. When MacNeice reported: 'Auden, for example, working eight hours a day in New York, is getting somewhere' ('Traveller's Return', *Horizon*, February 1941), he was doing more than justifying a regretted absence; he was respecting the single-mindedness of spiritual purpose in Auden's retreat. Auden's poetry had been fully concerned with the European situation for a decade. The war itself barely modified his experience of this situation. 'To go in quest means to look for something of which one has, as yet, no experience', he later wrote, apropos of the Quest Hero (*University of Texas Quarterly*, Winter 1961, p. 81) and much of his later poetry is involved in this search for the Just City, a search which is not private, but shared.

The 'Prologue' is an early use of syllabics, but *pace* Blair, pp. 150–51, not the earliest. (For a discussion of Auden's early syllabics, see p. 294.) 'Prologue' was first printed in the Allied Relief Ball Souvenir Program, 10 May 1940, and was called 'Spring in Wartime'. It was reprinted in *Horizon*, July 1940. As a poem of war, it argues that although war is so antisocial that it betrays even the simplest forms of organisation, and brings the kind of chaos that even a beehive has progressed from (stanza 7), it is not man's greatest fear. It is a poem of spring (stanzas 1, 5) and also of morning (stanza 3) when the primitive energies assail us in dreams and sexual renewal. The glimmer of biological unwillingness in stanza 5 is fortified by the borrowing of the 'truculent sailors' and 'plump little girls' from the poem 'Love Letter' of May 1939; however, it is hardly possible to be sexually jealous of a dinosaur. A better sense of the renewal of spring makes the poem a summary of one aspect of the position reached in the 'Letter', where in the last lines a skilfully periphrased God is enjoined to make himself manifest. As the final stanzas of 'Prologue' put it, 'neither a Spring nor a war can ever | So condition his ears as to keep the song | That is not a sorrow from the Double Man.' This song (and the knowledge that invests the reassembled bones of the previous lines, in allusion to Ezekiel xxxvi.7) is man's involuntary awareness of a transcendental reality which makes him weep by reminding him that his imperfections are not essential qualities (double meaning of 'accident') but an aberration from his true nature, his 'substance'. It is this double nature of man (expressed in the Montaigne epigraph) that is his central alienation.

'New Year Letter' falls into three parts, which Callan (p. 183) aligns with Kierkegaard's three categories of the aesthetic, the ethical and the religious. Perhaps not too much should be made of this correspondence. Part I is little more than a poetic apologia, and Part II, though a concentrated exposure of the dualism which Kierkegaard opposed, is none the less only a very tentative espousal of the existentialist position; its focal point is the apology to Marx. Part III corresponds even less obviously to Kierkegaard's category of the religious. It is longer than Parts I and II together, and more varied, including a good deal of generalised history and political theory, some spiritual autobiography and a description of America. Its conclusion is, admittedly, an appeal to God, but it is to God seen first of all as a unicorn; the quest imagery reminds us that Auden's ideal here is still 'Our faith well balanced by our doubt' (line 962), a line pleasantly glossed in the 'Notes': 'With what conviction the young man spoke | When he thought his nonsense rather a joke: | Now, when he doesn't doubt any more, | No one believes the booming old bore.' Kierkegaard's categories should be taken, not as a hidden key to the work, but as a parallel expression of ideas that have already deeply influenced the argument.

Part I. Lines 1–29: Auden begins Part I by presuming a shared anxiety and a shared interest in finding life's true direction. The poem at line 13n (note material will be indicated by n after the line number) shows how this sought direction needs to be continually reviewed (it was called 'We're Late' in the 1945 *Collected Poetry*, and was set by Lukas Foss). 'The sleepless guests of Europe' cannot see what may be done, and 'the dead say only how'. That is to say, history will describe what has been chosen in the past, but is not concerned with current choices. This is exactly the main point of 'Spain 1937'. The term 'wishful-thinking' at line 13 seems to have originated in the 1930s, perhaps by analogy with German *das Wunschdenken*.

Lines 30–55: Personal order is possible, especially through the medium of art (the same sun shines on the Nazi invasion of Poland as on Auden playing Buxtehude in a cottage on Long Island).

Lines 56–98: Order is the aim of both Art and Life, but it is something which cannot be willed (man's condition, in other words, is of Becoming not Being) because the state of Being is a whole which must comprehend all contraries. The account of Choice at line 63n reinforces this view, because our 'free-will' is really only our subjective view of the complex influence of Causal and Logical necessity. Moreover, the order of art is concerned with 'autonomous completed states' (line 86), which Auden ingeniously glosses by reference to Hans Spemann's account of embryonic induction and to Henry James's account of the 'casual hint' which produced *The Spoils of Poynton*: in other words, the 'hint' for the poem corresponds to the frog ectoderm which is transplanted into its field of induction (the *Triton* head = feeling) and produces the words of the poem (i.e. 'the presumptive primordia', the first rudiments of the organ being induced, whose pattern of growth is the meaning of the poem). What I think Auden means to imply by this devious analogy is that poetry is as factitious as *Triton* with a tadpole's horny jaws instead of teeth. His gloss (line 78n) about the political inadequacy of artists is more straightforward but less convincing; and his sidetrack about the Spanish War (line 87n) merely amusing. Why should writers be expected to 'be | Of some use to the military'? Auden's own parable about the duck-shooters and tree-fellers (EA, p. 368) is the best refutation of that. Auden's general position is sound enough, and his expression of it much-quoted: 'Art is not life and cannot be | A midwife to society.' Not a midwife, but a nurse, perhaps?

Lines 99–126: Writing can be a compensation for life's oppressions or inadequacies, a Freudian theory familiar to Auden (e.g. in the biographical poems of *Another Time*). This digression is an opportunity for an important account (line 109n) of Kierkegaard's categories of the aesthetic and the ethical, and a brilliant set of definitions of the different kinds of artist.

Lines 127–232: This is a personal passage in which Auden acknowledges as judges sitting in perpetual session those poetic mentors whose achievement he most wishes to be measured by. Compare Shelley's *Defense*. 'The jury which sits in judgement upon a poet, belonging as he does to all time, must be composed of his peers; it must be impanneled by Time from the selectest wise of many generations' (*Critical Prose*, ed. McElderry, 1967, p. 11). The first judge is Dante (the account of Amor Rationalis may be found in *Purgatorio*, xvii; 'Malebolge's fissure' is rather misleadingly singular: the 'malebolge' in the eighth circle of hell in *Inferno* xviii are ten stone ravines) and the other two are Blake and Rimbaud (who had strangled eloquence in Verlaine's poem 'Art poétique'). It is clear that the further poets mentioned, Dryden, Catullus, Tennyson, Baudelaire, Hardy and Rilke, are merely present in the court and are not judges, of whom, according to mythology and the Quorum, there should be only three. The confession involved here is not undefiant, especially in the notes.

Lines 233–318: The time's malaise is here seen in terms of a detective mystery, a particular form of the quest. The mystery cannot be solved, because the democracies are inefficient, and the dictatorships ('one inspector dressed in brown' = Hitler) capricious. The malaise is essentially a personal guilt: these are 'vast spiritual disorders' (line 266). Auden manages to suggest this within the context of the decade's violence (lines 267–78) through his gloss on Nazi persecution of the Jews at line 275n. This is the sonnet entitled 'The Diaspora' in the 1945 *Collected Poetry*. The diaspora is the dispersion of the Jewish tribes (see John vii.35), and Auden's fusion here of Christ with the Jewish victim has a Rilkean obliqueness: what the oppressors are denying is their human nature, their common citizenship. Our recognition of the guilt which we, as human beings, hold in common with the oppressors tempts us to perform useless sacrifices (compare lines 280–84 with 'the minotaur of authority' in 'The Sea and the Mirror', CP, p. 438) or to indulge in dreams of revenge (lines 289–94). The poem about Nietzsche at line 280n (printed in *Common Sense*, August 1940, as 'Elegiacs for Nietzsche') is at once an unrhymed sonnet and seven classical elegiac couplets. It praises him for debunking 'our liberal fallacies', but doubts that Hitler ('This tenement gangster with a sub-machine gun in one hand') is the kind of Superman that he intended. In fact, as Part I concludes, 'No words men write can stop the war' (line 296), and yet the 'candid psychopompos' (Hermes, as conveyor of souls to the place of the dead, as god of dreams) can satisfy with oracular riddles, even where a direct solution is impossible – a defence of the poem itself, a private letter whose public interest is indicated by being despatched 'under Flying Seal' (line 316), i.e. with a seal attached but not closed, so that it may be read by any person handling it even though it has significant diplomatic import ('addressed to a Whitehall').

Part II. Lines 319–82: Auden begins Part II with a landscape of self-discovery which can ossify those obsessed with the past (lines 337–40: the image is of Lot's wife). We fear the future because we desire stability of one sort or another, and do not wish to change. Line 348: Willem de Sitter (1872–1934), whose cosmological model was based on Einstein's theory of relativity. Major Peter Labellière (line 368) and Sarah Whitehead (line 376) were borrowed from Edith Sitwell's *English Eccentrics* (1933), pp. 23 and 30–36 (see Nicholas Jenkins in *Auden Newsletter* 15, p. 23).

Lines 383–426: Embodying this fear of having to make choices is the

Devil, but the Devil is unwittingly the agent of God (in the words of the prophet Habbakuk at line 406, he is symbolised by the 'fiery bolts' that go forth at God's feet). But he has 'no positive existence' (line 414) presumably because, as Auden would have learned from Tillich, 'the Satanic . . . in order to have existence . . . would have to be able to take on form, i.e., to contain an element of creation' (*Interpretation of History*, 1936, p. 81). The Devil is actually a projection of our inauthentic self (line 411: for the Jungian 'lame shadow', see p. 314) and represents 'fear and faithlessness and hate' (line 416). The injunction 'retro me' at line 411 therefore links Jung and the Bible: it was spoken by Jesus to Peter, who tried to argue (Matthew xvi.23) that Jesus would not have to be killed. Thus the Devil is the voice that, by luring us from our real choice, shows us what our real choice is. Auden says 'credo ut intelligam', that he believes in order to understand: the phrase is Anselm's, quoted by Williams, p. 109: 'Credo ut intelligam, said Anselm, and defined the wiser method. Intelligo ut credam, Abelard almost said, and might have added dubito ut credam.' Auden was to be critical of Abelard, founder of the dialectical method, in 'Memorial for the City', Part ii.

Lines 427–66: This passage examines the subjective world of the individual, which, Auden says, lives 'in eternity' because it has no real contact with events beyond its own continuum, not even much control over its own physical habitat, as the poem at line 453n elaborates (the genteel 'sex' was replaced by 'prick' in the text in the 1966 *Collected Shorter Poems*, p. 189). This poem is a versification of the ideas in *The Prolific and the Devourer*, pp. 7–8. The passage about Berkeley at lines 459ff refers to Ronald Knox's Berkeleyan limerick 'There was once a man who said 'God'' '.

Lines 467–527: The Devil's cunning enables him to agree with us when 'we contradict a lie of his': thus he develops a flatteringly co-operative argument from the valid premise that the intellect 'parts the Cause from the Effect' (i.e. is guilty of the dualism of empirical science), and ends by urging men to throw away intelligence altogether and rely upon 'the *Beischlaf* [sexual intercourse] of the blood' (line 524). In other words, the Devil becomes D. H. Lawrence. 'Barbara' (line 505) is a mnemonic for certain kinds of logical syllogisms: it suggestively evokes the 'barbaric' world outside a hypothetical non-dualistic paradise.

Lines 528–56: The Devil also quotes one's favourite authors against one. He is ironical, prodding, reactionary, and to Auden in particular, in Rilke's lines about the gnat in the eighth Duino Elegy he offers the instinctive life as an escape from responsibility. See also Rilke's letter to Lou Andreas-

Salome of 20 February 1914. At line 553n is a versification of ideas in *The Prolific and the Devourer*, p. 7.

Lines 557–630: Auden now examines the paradox of dualism and monism. In our retreat from the necessity of having to make our choice, we try to create a world in which we can account for our sin. The Devil does this for us in two ways: by dualism, by denying any relationship between the universal and the particular; and by monism, by turning the particular into the universal. Auden's allegory here is playful and difficult: he presents the Devil as defeating his own ends, because he cannot be both God and dualist. 'Pure evil would be pure passivity, a denial by an existence of any relation with any other existence; this is impossible because it would also mean a denial of its own existence' (line 563n). The Devil has to keep us doubting in order to keep us sinning (and not merely doing evil, as deterministic monistic systems might allow). Compare *The Prolific and the Devourer*, p. 26. Pisgah (line 618) was the mountain from which Moses glimpsed the Promised Land (Deuteronomy, iii.27). For 'the bottom of the graves' (line 629) see Blake's *Jerusalem*, Plate 48: 'Beneath the bottoms of the Graves, which is Earth's central joint, | There is a place where Contrarieties are equally true.'

Lines 631–64: One of the Devil's methods is to associate the truth with a lie, make us recognise the lie and so 'treat babe and bath-water the same'. Auden gives two examples of disappointed milleniallists, the early Christians and Wordsworth ('Parousia', the Second Coming, is a term borrowed from Williams; the 'agape' is the celebratory love feast of the early Christians).

Lines 665–750: This provides a reason for being unnecessarily disillusioned with Karl Marx (line 680). Marx destroyed the Rousseauistic political philosophy (lines 709–11) which had come to justify totalitarian regimes, but the millennium which his theory predicated never arrived. In *The Prolific and the Devourer* III, paras 3ff, Marx's contribution to history is seen to be his emphasis on Man the Maker, the producer of wealth, as opposed to Man the Politician, the consumer (i.e. on the Prolific rather than the Devourer). The poem does not quite decide if the thrust of Marx's discoveries is due to his psychological 'despair' or his 'heroic charity', but does conclude that he establishes the primacy of a 'universal, mutual need' (line 732) that is not inconsistent with the positions of Wordsworth or the early Christians. To some extent, he is an example of Tillich's 'demonic' creativity (*Interpretation of History*, pp. 83, 85), destroying forms through an eruption of the creative basis of things and challenging through 'catabasis' (way of descending) into the abyss of exhaustibility and emptiness that,

Auden says, 'always lies just underneath | Our jolly picnic on the heath | Of the agreeable' (lines 701–3). Together with Galileo (line 739), Newton (line 742) and Darwin (line 745), therefore, Marx has rightly marked the end of an era. Auden was influenced in this latter idea by Rosenstock-Huessy: 'The leaders of a revolution re-name the era. That is all they do' (*Out of Revolution*, p. 560). In the UK edition, 'Pinuccini's monument' is a misprint for 'Rinuccini'. Archbishop Rinuccini's tomb is near the main entrance to the Cathedral at Pisa where Galileo observed the pendulum in 1581. Unfortunately Rinuccini did not die until 1582. Auden redeemed the error in the US edition.

Lines 751–86: The reason for this is that human law will always be imperfect, and the law of God elusive. This is one of the keynotes of Pascalian thinking. Cf. Pensées 335 and 591 which quote Isaiah xlv.15: 'Verily thou art a God that hidest thyself.' The rondeau at line 761n glosses this serene impersonality of the *lex abscondita* (cf. 'Law Like Love'). Here Auden returns to the failure of hopeful political systems. The 'centrosome' (line 786) is a small nucleus of material in a male cell necessary for biological development. It organises the web of protein filaments that form the cellular skeleton and is active in the process of mitosis, or cell division. Its existence is taken by Auden as evidence that a quest for authenticity (i.e. throwing out the 'dwarf mutations' of the inauthentic) is a sign of the workings of the Logos.

Lines 787–833: Disappointed political idealism is like a terrible hangover, where the Devil is able to secure our exaggerated retreat into the teetotalism of reaction or conformism. The gloss at line 803n points the contrast between the political realist and the political idealist (see *Hudson Review*, Winter 1951, p. 590, for Auden's reference to Fouché as the originator of the police state and to Napoleon as someone who merely 'wanted to astonish his mother'), and at line 818n he notes how a society's expectations can be turned inside out ('Hans-in-Kelder' is interpreted as 'penis' in Auden's notebook of 1965–73 (Berg), although in 1940 he may have found it in Grose, who defines it as 'Jack in the Cellar', i.e. the child in the womb). Perhaps this is the lesson to be learned from opposing industrial production with the apparently futile 'vorpal sword' of Agrarianism, but perhaps Auden had forgotten that the Jabberwocky was killed in Carroll's poem (from which the phrase was taken). Out of the Devil's juggling with ideas and possibilities (his 'hocus-pocus') comes, however, a possible dialectic for the 'either/ors' who can see only one side of the paradox. Since Kierkegaard's *Enter/Elle* had not yet been translated into

English, these were probably borrowed from Rosenstock-Huessy's phrase 'The Voltairian "either-or"' (see *Out of Revolution*, p. 189: 'Either (1) God once created it [the machinery of the world] and nature has obeyed ever since, or (2) God unceasingly gives existence and changes of existence to everything. A third point of view would be inexplicable.' Rosenstock-Huessy comments: 'Law and love, nature and creation, are in perpetual opposition and struggle with each other. The third viewpoint, which was inexplicable to Voltaire, is the viewpoint practised by everybody every day'). However, the capitalised phrase 'Either/Or' was used in 'In War Time', written in June 1942. The Devil is even, in a sense, the father of poetry (line 829n), for poetry can 'be defined as the clear expression of mixed feelings'. Thus the diabolic gift of hocus-pocus (which is, after all, the priest's half-understood 'hoc est corpus') might be identified with art, a magic lamp which if used properly might be 'a sesame to light'.

Part III. Lines 834–59: The introductory passage restates the subjective value of the experience in art and friendship of 'the privileged community'. It does so in guardedly religious terms (the Mayers' Christmas feast has become a bridal occasion, as perhaps did the Christmas Eve dinner for Tiny Bunyan who is the invisible God-like Paul's normal human offspring; 'shining garments' are the clothes of angels, as in Luke xxiv.4).

Lines 860–913: But, he continues, these moments of harmony and love may come to anyone, even though they do not mean that the state of Being is thereby permanently possible for man. The temenos (line 863) is a region of taboo, here a garden with a well which turns up elsewhere in Auden (e.g. in stanza 2 of Ode v of *The Orators* and the hermetic gardens in *The Age of Anxiety*, also entered through the John Bunyan-derived wicket gate). Auden read about the temenos in Jung's *The Integration of the Personality* (1933). If man imagines that Being is possible then he creates the hell of denying his own nature: man is imperfect. The sinister events that symbolise this hell are reminiscent of the apocalyptic climax of 'The Witnesses'. Line 898n, however, suggests that this hell is not really binding; the paradox is that man knows it is not, but is unwilling to admit that his existence might be different.

Lines 914–74: Being is beyond our will, therefore we are thrown back into the Purgatory of trying to come to terms with our lives (lines 924–5: 'We . . . need their stratagems to win | Truth out of Time'). Auden uses the metaphor of climbing a hill to suggest once more that life is a quest and a renunciation. A cancelled MS note to line 931 quotes *Wuthering Heights* here: '– "What are beyond those hills?" | – "More hills"'. 'Doubt' at line

962n is a Pascalian virtue: the 'booming old bore' of public life is a characteristic Devourer (see *The Prolific and the Devourer*, 1, para 43).

Lines 975–1000: Auden pauses to describe himself in the act of writing, 'A tiny object in the night', and states his determination to act for himself alone, wary of the claims of political causes. The 'Socratic Sign' (line 986) is the inner oracle or *daimon* which deterred Socrates from taking certain actions. Since it never actually encouraged him to do anything, Socrates said: 'This it is that opposes my engaging in politics, and a very good thing it is' (Plato, *The Apology of Socrates*, 31D, Woodhead's translation). An 'athlon' (line 988) is a prize for which one contends. Line 990n refers to Hitler, who is reported to have said in the ruins of Warsaw 'Why do they try to resist my destiny?' (cf. Auden's article 'Mimesis and Allegory' in the *English Institute Annual*, 1940, a parallel to many of the ideas in the 'Notes' to Part III). Hitler is thus, as a determinist, a 'particle who claims the field': Auden's responsibility can be only to his friends.

Lines 1001–33: This passage takes up the idea of Hitler as a denial of more than twenty centuries of Europe: this decadence is not comparable even with the fall of Rome, because at least the barbarians expressed 'the pure instinctive joy | Of animals', whereas the present destruction is 'the refined | Creation of machines and mind'. Our 'evil *Daimon*' (line 1022) is not like the divine *daimon* of Socrates (see above, line 986). The 'metaphysics of the Crowd' is the result of 'Industry's Quicunque Vult' (line 1025, literally, 'whosoever wishes'): that is to say, its power, a parody of the Athanasian Creed, gives a hope of materialist salvation to the individual.

Lines 1034–86: Auden contrasts the private and the public life: each demands allegiance from us, and neither is escapable. The two worlds are distinguished in a geometrical metaphor (line 1060) which only underlines the general principles which unite them.

Lines 1087–152: Auden elaborates his own loved English landscape into a *paysage moralisé* (Rookhope is the setting of *Paid on Both Sides* and 'Who stands, the crux left of the watershed'), whereby the geological history of the Pennines comes to represent man's impulse towards civilisation, an impulse which is nonetheless felt as a 'fault', cause of a primary division between mind and heart. In the drafts (Berg) the fault is equated with 'the break with self-communion'. At lines 1134ff the division is more particularly ascribed to the recognition of the mother as the Not-self in infancy, and therefore to primal dread, and the first intimations of mortality. This passage has the force of profound revelation. The child Auden at the edge of the lead-mining shafts feels *Urmutterfurcht*, that fear of the primeval mother characteristic of the Earth-goddess Erda in *Siegfried* (line 1114n).

In Wagner's opera Wotan predicts the death of the gods and the emergence of a hero Siegfried who will waken Erda's daughter Brunnhilde and redeem the world through love. Siegfried indeed kisses Brunnhilde awake (as does Ferdinand Miranda in 'The Sea and the Mirror', CP, p. 422), but Auden recasts their dialogue at lines 1,149ff in order to deconstruct the heroic heterosexual transfiguration of the opera's ending. Brunnhilde says: 'Your mother will never come back to you. Your own self am I.' For the sake of a necessary rhyme Auden interpolates 'your allegiance and love', and then adds a line from much later in the scene: 'though it shatter my image'. The effect of this conflation is to ironise Brunnhilde's pleas to Siegfried that precede their union. Don't touch me, she says. Have you never seen your pleasing image in a clear stream? It disappears, doesn't it, if you disturb the water's surface? And Siegfried replies that he is burning to plunge into her delicious wave, even though it will shatter his image. Auden's own context turns him into a boy dropping pebbles into the flooded shafts, conscious not of heroic joy like Siegfried's, but only of guilt. Auden appears to be claiming that his fear of the mother drives him into knowledge, that his civilising creativity, his very vocation, is powered by fear of the mysterious and unknown.

In lines 1137ff, the terms all suggest roles for the actual mother as representative of mysterious authority and an alien sex, but the actual terms have various origins. The 'Outlawed' ('Forbidden' in the drafts, like the fruit of Genesis) suggests the incest taboo. The 'Others' may among many other things be a concept derived from Heidegger's notion of the 'they-self' contrasted with the 'authentic self' ('As they-self, the particular Dasein [Being] has been *dispersed* into the "they", and must first find itself', Martin Heidegger, *Being and Time*, tr. J. Macquarrie and E. Robinson, Oxford 1962, p. 166). This Heideggerian idea of discovering the authentic self within a situation of dispersal into a 'they' seems certainly present in the schema of 'The Quest'. See also Isherwood's *Down There on a Visit* (1962), p. 141. 'The Terrible, the Merciful' represents the dualism of Christian divinity. Lastly 'the Mothers' locates more precisely the vocational urge. In Goethe's *Faust*, II.1.v, Mephistopheles gives the hero a key with which to descend to the realm of the Mothers so that he can bring back a tripod whose incense smoke can shape itself into the ideals of human beauty. Goethe told Eckermann that he found the Mothers mentioned in Plutarch as the name under which the ancient Greeks worshipped certain goddesses. For Goethe they represented a necessary concentration on the infinite and the eternal, and therefore on the world of truth and art. Auden probably had in mind the vast multiple anthropological significance of the word in Robert Briffault's *The Mothers: A study of the origin of sentiments and institutions*, 3 vols (1927), which refers in its final pages to Goethe, quoting this same passage of *Faust* which is also quoted by Auden in a cancelled MS note to the line 1149 of 'New Year Letter'. See also Groddeck, *Exploring the Unconscious* (1933), p. 196: 'It is almost staggering to find in this poem the Unconscious designated as "the Mothers". The teaching of Freud lies hidden in Faust.' Groddeck interpreted Mephistopheles's key as a phallic symbol.

The latent meaning of Auden's scenario in these lines is complex. If there is an unconscious sexual drive behind art, the homosexual artist's guilt is double. Not only will the mother never return, but neither will Brunnhilde be rescued from her circle of fire. There are connections between the boy dropping pebbles into the flooded shafts and the Narcissus figure of Auden's earlier poems (see my 'Pleasing Ma: The poetry of W. H. Auden', the 1991 Kenneth Allott Memorial Lecture, University of Liverpool, 1995). Auden refers again to 'the Mothers' in the 1972 poem 'A Lullaby'.

Lines 1153–77: Auden has already (lines 553n) said that a return to the womb is impossible. Having acknowledged the power of umbilical Nature, he concludes that it does not have to be obeyed. We must become 'patriots of the Now' (line 1169).

Lines 1178–230: This passage rather fatalistically describes the aimlessness and inevitability of violence. Auden is now concerned with the development of 'Economic Man' (phrase first used in 'In the year of my youth . . .', 1.198), who has arisen since the Renaissance, since the time of 'Luther's Faith and Montaigne's doubt'. The sonnets at line 1213n encapsulate in the manner of the biographical sonnets in *Another Time* the philosophies of these individuals. The first sonnet, 'Luther' (*Christian Century*, 2 October 1940), makes the point which is reinforced in the note at line 1220 – a quotation from Kierkegaard, ' "The Just shall live by Faith" ' (quoted by Williams, p. 165) – that there may arise a situation in which 'worldliness is honoured and highly valued as piety.' Montaigne gave 'The Flesh its weapons to defeat the Book' by a retreat from authority into intelligence. Many of the ideas for the second sonnet come from Williams, e.g. p. 194: 'though Letters are not and never can be Religion, yet style has had an immense influence on Religion', and p. 192: 'He found two sources of the world's distresses: "Most of the grounds of the world's troubles are matters of grammar" and "The conviction of wisdom is the plague of man"' (see Auden and Kronenberger, *The Faber Book of Aphorisms*, p. 155).

Lines 1231–52: Economic Man, therefore, reached the stage of being able to examine ideas for their utility: their justificatory purposes could no longer disguise their falsehood (line 1232n). Line 1244n explores the limited value of science from an ethical point of view by reference to Kierkegaard's distinction between tribulations and temptations (cf. line 63n with its distinction between Fortune and Virtue, between causal and logical necessity). Psychology, for instance, is dangerous because it tempts man to think that since the suffering of his tribulation can be removed, he will not have to suffer at all (see 'Mimesis and Allegory', pp. 13ff). Protestantism, as line 1245n goes on to expound, 'remains in nature as the sphere of decision', fighting the tendency of reason to turn 'useful concepts' into 'universals', 'the kitsch'. This idea is ironically brought out at line 1245n in the poem about the Council of Trent (called 'For the Last Time' in the 1945 *Collected Poetry*), at which, though invited to attend, the Protestants were not able to vote, and where – far from the relaxation of formalism that one might have expected – many of the dogmas under examination were defined more rigidly than they had ever been defined before. The poem describes how, just at the moment of this 'success', four heralds gallop up with their news. They represent the world of nature in which decisions have to be made, in which, in Tillich's words, 'the Kairos determines the Logos', Time governs the Word. The words that compose the last lines of the poem (*Postremum Sanctus Spiritus effudit*: 'Here the Holy Spirit spoke for the last time') are those that were written up on the wall of S. Maria Maggiore at Trent, when the Council's sittings had finished, and are quoted by Williams, p. 187.

Lines 1253–331: Auden charts the opposition of the intellectuals to Economic Man, now in the guise of the nineteenth-century bourgeois, and concludes that the Verbürgerlichung (say, suburbanising) of 'joy and suffering and love' cannot be counteracted by so simple a means as the impulse towards chaos of the Romantics: 'The bourgeois were not real devils but false angels' (line 1277n). Also at line 1277n the idea that only God can tell the saintly from the suburban is derived from Kierkegaard's *Fear and Trembling*, and for the quatrain about intellectuals, cf. *The Prolific and the Devourer*, I, para 17 (in Spring 1940, writing to Wolfgang Köhler, Auden said that 'the man-in-the-street is not altogether wrong in thinking that intellectuals are usually immoral for few of them seem able to take experimentation beyond the destructive stage', a less bathetic form of the accusation). In any event, the warnings of Blake, Rousseau, Kierkegaard and Baudelaire were ignored, and Economic Man has become ruled by his environment (lines 1285–301). There follows a briskly satirical passage exposing man's lack of freedom in all its variety. At line 1312, for *dialegesthai*, Greek for thinking, see Williams, p. 77, on Augustine being amazed that Ambrose read silently: 'thinking was still *dialegesthai*, talking.'

Lines 1332–75: This lack of freedom is blamed on society and on politicians, but these are only projections of the individual will (lines 1366–7: 'The average of the average man | Becomes the dread Leviathan'). Thus the current war is a result both of individual English hypocrisy and of individual German apathy.

Lines 1376–443: The idea of an intellectual élite and the idea of an indiscriminate identity of individuals both lead to tyranny. In the case of the first, Auden appears to allude in line 1378 to the 'lie' in *The Republic*, III.414–5, where Plato justifies the innate superiority of the Guardians. Auden had alluded to this passage in Sonnet XIII of 'In Time of War' (see p. 237 for further details); in the case of the second, to Rousseau's primitivism. The individual should be not 'dissociated', not 'integrated', but 'differentiated' (line 1388n). It is the Ego which is responsible for this double 'social lie'. If the Ego denies *amor naturale* (line 1402n), there comes a time when realisation of selfish isolation produces a reaction in favour of a belief in fate, as typified in Wagner (compare line 1432n with 'Mimesis and Allegory', p. 7), who carried the Romantic heresy of exalting causal necessity over logical necessity further than anyone else. Siegfried or Tristan, the huge doll roaring for Death or Mother at line 1440 is a 'mental hero' like Ransom in *The Ascent of F6*, existing only for his suffering. Auden's note claims that Wagner was only any good when dealing with suffering (which helps to explain his strange deconstruction of the ecstatic ending of Act III of *Siegfried* at lines 1149ff of the poem).

Lines 1444–524: Auden breaks off again here to remind the reader of the setting of the poem: New York in the small hours of New Year's Day. This gives him the opportunity to characterise America and its past. The Massachusetts immigrants between lines 1473 and 1477 are Anne Hutchinson (1591–1643), the Antinomian; John Cotton (1584–1652), the Puritan divine who tried her for sedition; John Winthrop (1588–1649), first Governor of the Massachusetts Bay Company and founder of Boston; and Roger Williams (1603–83), who, exiled like Hutchinson, founded a democratic commonwealth on Rhode Island. It was Hutchinson who contrasted 'the voice of my beloved' (Christ) with that of Moses, i.e. that of Love with that of Law. Lines 1481–3 refer to the political arguments

between Thomas Jefferson and Alexander Hamilton at the end of the
eighteenth century, federalism versus republicanism, a struggle equated in
the notes to that between the 'Haves' (Pelagians) and the 'Have-Nots'
(Jansenists). America therefore may not have Europe's history, but shares
the same heresies, and makes even clearer 'The choice of patterns . . .
Which the machine imposes' (lines 1520–21, borrowed from *Paul Bunyan*,
Libretti, p. 45). This Goethean view of the USA is echoed by Rosenstock-
Huessy (*Out of Revolution*, pp. 117–18).

Lines 1525–72: It is the machine which compels us to admit that
'Aloneness is man's real condition.' Auden justifies this in terms of both
American life and American literature, locating the spiritual destiny of the
common man within the quest myth or the parabolic situations of the novel.

Lines 1573–650: As dawn breaks, the Good Life seems, as ever, so
desirable as to be possible, but 'wishes are not horses' and the facts of war
and the humiliation of civilisation are undeniable. Zola's toad, incidentally,
appears to be really Chamfort's (see *The Faber Book of Aphorisms*, p. 18: 'A
man must swallow a toad every morning if he wishes to be sure of finding
nothing still more disgusting before the day is over'). Man cannot escape
from his predicament. The labyrinth of line 1629n ('The Maze' in the 1966
Collected Shorter Poems) is of his own making; if he were a bird he would know
what to do, but he is not ('apteros', wingless, a Daedalian predicament). All
he can say is that every individual is different, and that real unity begins
there (lines 1641–2, 'That all have needs to satisfy | And each a power to
supply' is a Marxian formula). The idea at line 1649 is originally
Groddeckian (cf. 'In Memory of Ernst Toller', line 19). In a contemporary
elaboration of this passage Auden wrote: 'In the last analysis we do not live
our lives, but are lived. What we call I, our little conscious ego, is an
instrument of power outside itself. But it is an unconscious instrument. To
reason and obey logical necessity are its functions.' And he adds a gloss to
the story of Mary's spitting at line 1649n: 'That is the attitude we need. To
listen always for the voice of the unknown, and then have our little ideas'
(*Smith Alumnae Quarterly*, August 1940, p. 358). The strange poem at line
1650n gives examples of bodily energy which symbolise both the death-wish
and a desire for spiritual renewal, enacting a rite of religious redemption.

Lines 1651–707: The final invocation avoids addressing God directly,
though the images of unicorn, dove, fish and so on are traditionally
Christian (one excised couplet, however, originally between lines 1666 and
7, was not: 'O order the electrons sing | Dancing in their atomic ring'). In
1967 Auden thought the cedars/lead us rhyme the 'worst crime he'd ever

committed' (Memoir by Richard Hoggart of Auden in Birmingham). Line 1668 (*Quando non fuerit, non est*: 'There is not when he was not') is quoted by Williams (p. 39) and explicitly refers to Origen's belief in the co-eternity of the Son with the Father. *O da quod jubes, Domine* at line 1684 ('Give what thou commandest', Augustine, *Confessions*, x.xxix) is also quoted by Williams (p. 66). Auden also quoted it in a contemporary view: ' "O Thou who commandest Chastity, give what Thou commandest" – not denying free-will, but only saying that in order to will you must first believe that you can' (*Common Sense*, November 1940). The success of the ending lies in the way in which Auden has been able to merge this affirmation (vague as it is) with the reiterated need for a quest for the New Life. The poem at line 1708n (November 1939; 'Nativity', *Harper's Bazaar*, December 1939; 'Blessed Event', CSP66) takes the Christian family out of the context of man's fallen nature, shows it as contriving 'to fumble | About in the Truth for the straight successful Way | Which will always appear to end in some dreadful defeat', and leads directly into 'The Quest', the Rilkean sonnet sequence which follows.

'The Quest' first appeared in the *New Republic*, 25 November 1940, with the following prefatory note: 'The theme of the Quest occurs in fairy tales, legends like the Golden Fleece and The Holy Grail, boys' adventure stories and detective novels. These poems are reflections upon certain features common to them all. The "He" and "They" referred to should be regarded as both objective and subjective.' What Auden means by this is indicated when, after listing the essential elements in the typical Quest story, he asks: 'Does not each of these elements correspond to an aspect of our subjective experience of life?' ('The Quest Hero', *Texas Quarterly*, Winter 1961, p. 83. See also 'K's Quest' in *The Kafka Problem*, ed. A. Flores, 1946). In other words, the sequence is intended as a heavily conceptualised account of a personal quest for 'true happiness or authenticity of being'. To a great extent, then, the 'He' and 'They' correspond to the self's discovery of its own true ground of being through the rejection of false paths. The 'Letter' has already established modern man as an existential hero (lines 1543–4: 'each must travel forth alone | In search of the Essential Stone'), and it remains for his predicament to be analysed with the particular kind of dynamic obliqueness and metaphysical symbolism which the Rilkean sonnet provides, to be embodied in a moral landscape which owes as much to fairy-tale and to Kafka as to theology. I do not wish to suggest that the sequence is circumstantial spiritual autobiography to be decoded; on the other hand, it is clear that 'He' and 'They', though needing reappraisal in each context, are distinguished through a process of refinement from life's temptations or of confrontation with unavoidable failure or merely through fairy-tale 'luck'. Above all, 'He' is not exceptional, and sometimes 'They' take on the banal public colouring of Edward Lear's 'they' (see p. 255), although in fact the stimulus behind the distinction is closer to that between Heidegger's *eigentlich-selbst* ('authentic self') and *Man-selbst* ('they-self'), in which the ground of Being has been dispersed (see my note to the 'Letter', line 1137 above).

The framing sonnets present the object of the quest (authenticity of being) in traditional terms of a garden. No. 1 'The Door' ('Out of it steps the future of the poor') shows what normally happens when we have only a partial insight into it: we attempt to arrange the future by codifying these insights into systems (lines 1–4: metaphysics, law, political philosophy) which allow us to live; and we fear those intuitions which undermine our confidence in the future (lines 5–8) by showing us the real past as something threatening which we attempt to suppress. Of course, the door itself (the riddling 'it' of the poem) is something like a real riddle whose answer is 'time'. If it were really open, time would be transcended. Since it isn't, we see time as an inscrutable authority, the closed door outside which we wait as in the Kafka parable. In the second quatrain it becomes a key to what we like to think we have achieved, subject to the destructive flood of memory (the strange line 7 is probably intended to typify a disgraceful episode in life that one would attempt to suppress); in the first quatrain it acts as a continuum in which we can comfortably appeal to authority as a guiding principle (the Queen of Hearts, based on Richard III) or subvert it if we wish (Lear's Fool). There is a suggestion in this Shakespearean contrast of a deliberate political metaphor: we can imitate the God either of the Old or of the New Testament, so that 'the future of the poor' is therefore within our power to make a matter of repression or of humane understanding. The sestet, with its shift to images of death and revelation, shows that we cannot outwit time simply by social engineering: we know that even in a utopia the door will remain shut.

The irrelevance of politics is to a certain extent further pursued in No. 11 'The Preparations' ('All had been ordered weeks before the start') which again deals with man's mistaken sense of self-sufficiency. Auden is here writing about the fifth-century Pelagian heresy, as the sonnet's evident source in Williams's *The Descent of the Dove* makes clear. Williams (p. 66) wrote of St Augustine's reaction to Pelagianism and the question of sin: 'Man precisely was not in a situation – not even in a difficult situation. He was, himself, the situation.' Augustine felt that only the grace of God could alter the situation, but Pelagius (i.e. the Welsh monk Morgan) thought that virtue was easily attainable through reason. There may be some relevance here of Heidegger's treatment of 'The Situation' (see *Being and Time*, tr. Macquarrie and Robinson, p. 346: 'The "they" knows only the "*general situation*", loses itself in those "*opportunities*" which are closest to it'). Auden's final three lines (not to give a poisoner medicine, etc.) intend to show that it isn't valid for fallen man to take up a means to salvation which is itself similarly related to his disease, this means being his own will. Auden had already rehearsed this argument in *The Ascent of F6*, ii.i, where the Abbot underlines Ransom's 'situation' of being unable to renounce the will through an act of the will (a similar double bind lies behind the crisis of the Airman in *The Orators*). As if remembering this scene, Auden clothes the sonnet in the metaphor of an expedition like Ransom's. Incidentally, in the drafts a version of the final line was, until a late stage, the more logical but unsubtle 'Put a cocked rifle in a tiger's paw.' However, it is not clear that the substituted pun ('rifle'/'bore') is preferable, since a melancholic bore is not self-evidently suicidal.

No. iii 'The Crossroads' ('The friends who met here and embraced are gone') uses the fairy-tale or Arthurian formula of the year and the day as the time allotted to complete a task. A year is thought to be sufficient for moral reform, but it never seems to be enough, even though it 'should take no time at all'. The axes of the crossroads (fame/torpor; joy/betrayal) are suggestive of distinctions between both public (i.e. literary) and private (i.e. erotic) careers, and of connections between them (i.e. that even joy like fame could be 'flashy' and need atonement, or that 'a village torpor' like Gray's 'village-Hampden' is at least safe from the ruin that attends a public figure). The deepest link is contained in the notion of 'friends'; these can be both rivals and lovers. All this suggests, perhaps, a touch of autobiographical meaning. The sonnet is an expanded one, using half as many lines again as the conventional sonnet, in the proportion 12:9 (rhyming aabcbcddecec/fghifgigh). Auden's rhyming cunningly offsets the potential bulkiness of the form, for the 'octave' is constructed of two sestets and is both musically effective and reminiscent of familiar sonnet rhyming, while the 'sestet' is of an original arrangement whereby weak h rhymes ('impossible'/'all') and enjambement at line 19 allow the strong g rhymes ('say'/'betray'/'day') and f rhymes ('fear'/'year' with a firmly end-stopped line 17) to do all the work.

No. iv 'The Pilgrim' ('The Traveler', *New Republic*) ('No window in his suburb lights that bedroom where') describes the landscape of sin which makes the hero homeless. Auden is visualising his own childhood, since a mill makes a significant appearance in some of his early poems. However, the metaphor here is complex: the meadows suggest territorial and therefore erotic conquest, as though in a desperate effort to inherit the mysterious grown-up world without recognising that that world had been maintained through love, i.e. by turning the wheat of the fields into bread. The point is that his 'Greater Hallows' (relics of saints, therefore any sacred object) have not been stolen by evil powers, but have been lost through sin (see 'K's Quest', p. 48) and are only waiting to be reclaimed by innocence. The final line establishes these relics as powerfully parental.

No. v 'The City' ('In villages from which their childhoods came') shows the effect of the fragmentation of the community of seekers: each believes himself insignificant within the anonymity of the metropolitan crowd and does not see that Necessity is, after all, precisely the need to confront the unique predicament. The sonnet prepares for the more personal sonnets on the three temptations that follow.

These temptations are related to the three temptations of Christ as recounted in Matthew iv (discussed by Auden in *The Prolific and the Devourer*, II as the temptations of childhood, adolescence and maturity). No. vi 'The First Temptation' ('Ashamed to be the darling of his grief') is about the artist, whose 'gift for magic' tempts him to turn 'his hungers into Roman food', i.e. to relish and re-relish aesthetically what should have been a spiritual discipline. Auden is glancing at his own career here, particularly in lines 3–4, where joining 'a gang of rowdy stories' allows him to avoid a serious confrontation with his 'grief'. This corresponds to the biblical temptation to perform miracles, to turn the stones into bread (cf. Shadow's machine in *The Rake's Progress*, and *The Prolific and the Devourer*: 'There is only one way in which stones can be turned into bread, and that is by phantasy stimulated by hunger').

No. vii 'The Second Temptation' ('The library annoyed him with its look') is about a nihilistic disgust with the material world and with the body (feminine, as so often in Auden: see line 13). It is the temptation of suicide ('And plunged into the college quad, and broke'). This corresponds to the biblical temptation of Christ to prove his godhead when placed on the pinnacle of the temple; the temptation involves spiritual pride in both cases. Like the 'Hero' of No. xvi he appears to equate God with 'Nothing', although for the former such negativism is a matter of wry Flaubertian detachment rather than the direct invocation that we have here in the interrupted syntax of the Metrical Psalms (compare *The Orators*, Ode vi).

This second quatrain was originally, in draft: 'Swaying upon a parapet he cried: I I was a fool to think I had to think I I feel much better since my logic died I And gravitation ended with a drink.' In the printed version, while retaining the ambience of the academic philosopher, Auden has put less emphasis on intellectual pride (this temptation is close to the *libido dominandi* examined in Auden's poem on Pascal) and has introduced in 'Thy perfect' the notion from Denis de Rougemont's *Love in the Western World* (1940) of the Catharist *perfecti*, the élite Christians who scorned the world.

No. VIII 'The Third Temptation' (*Poetry*, October 1940) ('He watched with all his organs of concern') is the temptation to selfish isolation, which appears to provide the discipline that gives power ('soon he was king of all the creatures') but which is merely an obsession with self. This corresponds to the biblical offer of the kingdoms of the earth, the temptation to worship Satan in return for power. Appropriately enough, Auden concludes with an allusion to Henry James's 'successful' Spencer Brydon confronting an image of himself in 'The Jolly Corner'.

No. IX 'The Tower' ('This is an architecture for the odd;') shows how the artist tries to have it both ways. Like Plato's watch-tower of the soul, or like Acrisius' tower where Danaë was imprisoned, the tower of the artist provides at once a challenge to the divine and a retreat from it. It is a retreat because it is a retreat from life ('For those who dread to drown of thirst may die'; for life as the sea, cf. 'The Sea and the Mirror' and *The Enchaféd Flood*) which is none the less as compulsive as a magic spell.

No. X 'The Presumptuous' ('They noticed that virginity was needed') are those who are induced to imagine themselves able to act as heroes because they have not accurately observed the qualities necessary for heroism (Auden's metaphor in the first quatrain suggests yet again the traps that spiritual wilfulness springs for us, i.e. to stay virgin if we are good-looking is not likely to trap the unicorn). The presumptuous also fail to note the once-bitten hero's caution and attempt to emulate him without his experience (second quatrain). Inevitably they fail.

No. XI 'The Average' ('His peasant parents killed themselves with toil') is another false hero conducting an abortive quest: the average man who is educated to believe himself exceptional. He is the opposite of the presumptuous of the previous sonnet, and structurally faces them across the exact centre of this twenty-sonnet sequence.

No. XII 'Vocation' ('Incredulous, he stared at the amused') exhibits another closed circuit, that of the cynic: the Kafkaesque official is 'amused', not because the request to suffer is presumptuous, but because the refusal of it is believed. One is, of course, going to suffer in any case. But to will suffering is to be a false martyr (this was the problem of Eliot's Becket in *Murder in the Cathedral*) and is probably another example of the Pelagian reliance upon reason instead of grace. Considering the ambiguities of the title, and Auden's consciousness of the need to be true to one's gift, the hyperconsciousness here of what may be spiritually required also constitutes the difference between impassioned art and the 'caustic tongue' of satirical, intellectual art. The amusement becomes, then, amusement at oneself, at the predicament of wanting something more than irony with which to 'keep the silences at bay', the sonnet itself ironic.

No. XIII 'The Useful' ('The over-logical fell for the witch') elaborates upon the Falstaff/Hal suggestion of the previous sonnet that failures still have something useful to teach those who are still trying.

No. XIV 'The Way' ('Fresh addenda are published every day') points out the dangers in the idea of the previous sonnet as a negative rather than a positive encouragement: 'how reliable can any truth be that is got | By observing oneself and then just inserting a Not?' The chapel in the rock is from the Grail legend, the Astral Clock is the fourth dimension of theosophists like Ouspensky, and for the Triple Rainbow see C. M. Doughty, *Arabia Deserta* (1888), ii.305: 'These were the celestial arches of the sun's building, the peace in heaven after the battle of the elements in a desert-land of Arabia.' Auden was reading Doughty in 1928, according to MacNeice (*The Strings are False*, 1965, p. 114).

In No. XV 'The Lucky' ('Suppose he'd listened to the erudite committee') the traditional luck of the third son in fairy-tales is equated with Grace: in other words, the Lucky are the Elect, and the failed are those who fail in No. 11, the Pelagians (their torment, it is implied, is not to be able to believe in Grace).

No. XVI 'The Hero' ('He parried every question that they hurled') is one of the more interestingly obscure sonnets of the sequence. This hero has a Kierkegaardian patience and humility, remaining laconic under a barrage of questions. Auden described line 4 to Aurora Ciliberti as an 'English proverbial way of refusing to answer an impertinent personal question', though he clearly was also attracted to it as a kind of absurdist Christian answer to the question that precedes it: to go home by Beggar's Bush means to be ruined, so that the reduced nakedness of unaccommodated man really is, as it was to Lear, 'the greatest wonder of the world'. Auden described Kierkegaard's ideal Christian as 'happily married, looks like a cheerful grocer, and is respected by his neighbours' (*Forewords and Afterwords*, p. 192). However, the questioners feel that the hero 'owes a duty to his fame'. They are like the 'astonished critics' of the popular hero described in the sonnet 'Who's Who', who cannot believe that having been the greatest figure of his day he can long for someone who does little more than potter around the garden (cf. 'Only God can tell the saintly from the suburban', 'New Year Letter', line 1277n).

Allusions to Flaubert run through this sonnet (for a full discussion of the implications of this, see my article in *Auden Studies* 1, 1990, p. 135), some of them from Francis Steegmuller, *Flaubert and Madame Bovary* (1939), pp. 301, 314–18 and 358 (Steegmuller is quoted in the 'Notes', lines 856n and 1271n): (a) Flaubert's letters to Louise Colet reveal an ambiguous attitude to the Emperor Napoleon III's *coup* and its resulting literary censorship. The lesson that Flaubert learns from the Emperor is, therefore, a carefully cultivated independence from commitment. 'Not to push' (i.e. to conclusions) is in effect Flaubert's 'ne pas conclure', that ability to express a variety of points of view, like Negative Capability, which he considered the only motto for a sensible man; (b) Flaubert was aggrieved at a misprint of his name at the time of the publication of *Madame Bovary*: 'Faubert' was the name of a grocer in the Rue de Richelieu; (c) Flaubert looked at the landscape through pieces of coloured glass to be able to describe the effect in an omitted episode of *Madame Bovary* where Emma on the day after the ball walks in the grounds of La Vaubyessard and contrasts the view through the stained glass of a small pavilion and then through a pane of clear glass in order to see things as they are, symbolising the point-of-view technique; (d) The immediate source of the mundane decanting of the penultimate line was in Chekhov (Letter to A. S. Souvorin, 1 December 1895: 'I have just poured castor oil from little bottles into a large one'), but in his researches for the novel Flaubert could just as easily have tried such pouring of liquids in an attempt to 'become' the pharmacist Homais as he clearly felt he could 'become' Emma. Homais is, perhaps, the fullest representative of the bourgeois in *Madame Bovary*. He wishes to label all experience and contain it in his bottles (III.2). Homais' objective decanting is, in a sense, the opposite of Emma's subjective vision through the glass, but Auden shows that the novelist must transcend both attitudes by absorbing them, just as he must maintain an aesthetic detachment from doctrinal or political positions. Auden is doing this, of course, in a verse form which traditionally requires argument, condensation, parallelism and effective conclusion. In these last two lines the whole of the bourgeois tragedy of the novel is implicated (it is with Homais' arsenic that Emma kills herself) so that Auden's Flaubertian 'hero' is enabled to reach his strange Christian conclusion beyond the self-destructive scenario of dualism. He wants to be not the Double Man, but the bare man Nothing.

No. XVII 'Adventure' ('Others had swerved off to the left before') shows further how, in the face of the unaccountably dislocated behaviour of outcast questors, the crowd plays for safety (the racing imagery underlines the notion of a Pascalian wager). Pascal himself had quoted in Pensées 335 and 591 the words of Isaiah xlv.15: 'Verily thou art a God that hidest thyself' which help to explain the last line of the sonnet about the Absconded God.

No. XVIII 'The Adventurers' ('Spinning upon their central thirst like tops') takes up the contrast in Williams (pp. 57–9) between the Affirmative Way and the Negative Way. The Negative Way is the way of the ascetic desert fathers, whose fruition is seen in the sestet only in art and superstition, and leads only to the Dry.

In No. XIX 'The Waters' ('Poet, oracle and wit') the metaphor of the uncaught fish inevitably recalls 'New Year Letter', lines 1659ff (the 'Icthus' of the early Christians). A 'vector' is basically an imaginary line connecting a planet with the centre of its orbit, and therefore becomes the fisherman's line as it stretches to its focus of interest in the 'ponds of apperception'. The fishermen tell lies because they cannot bear to think that the fish got away. The conditions of modern life ('With time in tempest everywhere') treat the saintly and the insincere alike, and even obliterate the traces of the suffering that they share. This is because the right question has not been put (cf. the Grail legend). In terms of the metaphor, the right question would produce Icthus. This sonnet ends, like Humpty Dumpty's recitation about the obstinately inaccessible little fishes of the sea, on a 'but'.

The final sonnet, No. XX 'The Garden' ('Within these gates all opening begins:') describes the world of innocence which must be recaptured if the quest is to be successful. The garden is a state of authenticity of being that is achieved largely through love. It is not unrelated to other poetical gardens such as the one in the *Roman de la Rose* or in Eliot's *Burnt Norton* (which as Eliot admitted also made use of the rose-garden in *Through the Looking Glass*, see Sonnet I) The synaesthesia of line 2 recreates the confused sense of the primal world (cf. the opening of the 'Prologue'). In line 3 the sins are not deadly, but merely the 'earnest' (i.e. not deadly earnest) subject of children's play; in line 4 the body ('dogs') is free of the interfering super-ego ('their tall conditions', i.e. their masters); and in the second quatrain love casts aside all duality. The concluding lines of the sequence confirm for the reader Auden's insistence that the state of authenticity can only come about by an abnegation of the will and a complementary recognition of a reality lying outside the world as we know it. Maintaining the submerged level of spiritual autobiography to the last, the conversationalists 'blush' in a moment of transcendence not unlike the Vision of Agape that Auden described in his introduction to Anne Fremantle's *The Protestant Mystics* (1964), p. 26. This shifting of one's 'centre of volition' is something which might be described as yielding to the will of God, but Auden avoids such clearly recognisable terms.

The 'Epilogue' (*Nation*, 7 December 1940; 'Autumn 1940', CP45; 'The Dark Years', CSP66) reiterates with melancholy riddling the need for humility and striving in the face of certain violence and probable death ('the narrow gate where | Events are traded with time' of stanza 13). The syllabics contrive to be dignified and elegiac, even when absorbing jokes; in stanza 2 when the ego 'does not like the noise or the people' this is because of the state of war (see the story in *A Certain World*, p, 383, about the Guards officer who was asked what war was like: "Awful!" he replied. "The noise! And the *people*!" '). The 'websters' of stanza 4 are nothing to do with lexicographers: they are weavers, i.e. the three Fates. In stanza 6 'this year the towns of our childhood | Are changing complexion along with the woods' is saga-stoicism for fearing that Birmingham is being bombed. There is much real feeling in this grim mélange, even though the final injunction can do little more than grandly invoke the attitude to time and spirit of Eliot's *Burnt Norton* (e.g. stanza 16).

For the Time Being

When applying for a Guggenheim Fellowship on 8 October 1941, Auden proposed in his project statement 'a long poem in several parts about Christmas, suitable for becoming the basis of a text for a large-scale musical oratorio'. In the week before Christmas he told Ursula Niebuhr that he was slowly pegging away at it and that it would be 'very theological'. Although there should have been no theoretical conflict between these two intended aspects of the work, it was clear when finished in July 1942 that it was far too long to be so set to music. It was first published on 6 September 1944 in a volume of the same title that also included 'The Sea and the Mirror'. Some parts (indicated in the commentary below) were first separately published. My page references are to the text in the 1991 edition of the *Collected Poems*.

'For the Time Being' carries the argument of *The Double Man* one important stage further, directly into the Christian faith. It might be said that argument is therefore left behind, and it is patently true that there is a world of difference implicit merely in the form of the Christmas oratorio, as distinct from that of the digressive verse epistle or the mythopoeic sonnet sequence. But even so, the sense of exploratory didacticism, of justified and expository faith, is continually lurking in the later work; and the fact that its metaphorical terms happen to be the Christian story of the Incarnation does not hinder Auden's compulsive urge to use these terms as parable, that is as a description of the continual demands of the Eternal upon an individual living in Time. There is nothing merely functional or celebratory about the oratorio: it uses the traditional formulae to present a spiritual predicament, and it is therefore the same *kind* of formal discovery as its companion piece, 'The Sea and the Mirror', even though as an objective correlative the Bible or the Corpus Christi play is more closely relevant than *The Tempest*.

It is precisely because the Christian story is itself already, after centuries of theological comment, so heavily endowed with symbolic significance that 'For the Time Being' sometimes falls comfortably (in a way that 'The Sea and the Mirror' does not) into its received terminology. Auden would probably have been the first to admit that subject-matter of this kind offers no particular head-start to poetry concerned with the problems of faith, and may even, in a sense, be too easy a way out. As Auden himself wrote (almost certainly borrowing the idea from David Jones's 1955 essay 'Art and Sacrament'): 'There can no more be a "Christian" art than there can be a Christian science or a Christian diet. There can only be a Christian spirit in which an artist, a scientist, works or does not work. A painting of the Crucifixion is not necessarily more Christian in spirit than a still life, and may very well be less' (*The Dyer's Hand*, p. 458).

Thus Auden is concerned throughout the oratorio to make it clear that he is writing about his contemporary civilisation. Simeon's meditation elaborates the basic belief that man must reach spiritual impasse before he can be saved. Auden was influenced here by Reinhold Niebuhr's view of Protestantism as the continuous process of voluntary assent. The predicaments of the characters in the oratorio therefore provide a dramatised analysis of the predicament of modern man, who is continually faced with the choice of accepting or rejecting the Word made Flesh. What this really means must remain a theological mystery to the non-Christian, but it is apparent from Auden's treatment of it in this and other works (even some early ones) that it represents *a point of view* from which the social and psychological malaise of the world is susceptible of being transcended. It is not a rational point of view, because reason has failed: 'The liberal humanism of the past had failed to produce the universal peace and prosperity it promised, failed even to prevent a World War' (Auden in *Modern Canterbury Pilgrims*, 1956). The presentation in the oratorio of Herod as such a liberal humanist may be flattering to Herod (and the joke is a good one), but it is unflattering to liberal humanism.

Auden wrote the oratorio while he was teaching at Ann Arbor in the aftermath of two events significant to its composition: the first infidelity of Kallman in July and the news of the death of his mother in August. Of the first he later wrote that it made him 'the prey of demonic powers . . . stripped of self-control and self-respect'; of the second that 'when mother dies, one is, for the first time, really alone in the world and that is hard.' Auden had already chosen intellectual solitude as the seed-bed of a working-life and he had already reasoned himself into the Christian belief, but these events provided a significant emotional need for religious consolation. The oratorio is dedicated to his mother and suffused with an eagerness to make the sort of difficult peace with the Flesh (and, interestingly enough, peace with the mother) that is found in Augustine's *Confessions*.

In November Auden and Britten discussed the oratorio as a musical collaboration, but it would not have been clear at that stage how impossibly long it would have had to have been. Only 'Chorale' (i.e. 'The Summons', v) exists in a musical setting by Britten. Britten also set 'Shepherd's Carol' ('O lift your little pinkie') which at one stage, e.g. in a transcript made by Angelyn Stevens, was part v, section 2. Both of these settings were broadcast in a BBC radio programme, 'A Poet's Christmas', in 1944. Auden was still optimistically sending sections of the work to Britten a few months before the composer left the USA in March 1942. The section 'At the Manger' contained vocal directions when it appeared in Commonweal in December 1942. An abridged version of the whole was set by Marvin Levy, and performed at the Carnegie Hall on 7 December 1959.

The oratorio falls into nine parts, most of which correspond to the traditional division of the Nativity story in the Church festivals and the medieval drama. The first part, 'Advent', is an essentially choric dialogue on man's condition (p. 349). The first chorus (Yeatsian trimeter in a rondeauesque stanza) describes the emptiness and apathy of a society in the grip of winter and of war. Auden's talent for evoking doom is evident in his description of the impotence of progressive political power, a Hercules who is 'utterly lost', aware like Childe Roland 'of | Being watched from the horrid mountains | By fanatical eyes' but of seeing no one, 'only hearing . . . the poisonous rustle | Of famishing Arachne'. The rare transitive sense of this participle lends force to the archetypal spider. 'The eyes huddle like cattle' suggests the despair of Hopkins in 'No worst, there is none', and Auden had used a similar phrase in 'Love Letter', a poem of 1939 expressing alarm at Kallman's absence. All belief has been undermined. 'The watchman's tower' and 'the cedar grove' suggest Greek philosophy and the Greek gods, the terms in which Auden expounded the first two Kierkegaardian categories of the aesthetic and the ethical in his introduction to *The Living Thoughts of Kierkegaard* (1952). 'The civil garden' is thus left vulnerable to 'a wild passion' which is both objective and subjective, i.e. is both Hitler and the individual's tendency to nihilism and self-destruction.

This power is glumly delineated by the Narrator (p. 351) in a familiar context of bourgeois life. He is a kind of flat Eliotic version of Auden's earlier dramatic anatomisers of doom, out of the Witnesses by the choruses from *The Rock*: the grisly embodied threat has been replaced by a problem of identity and by a sharp sense of the terror of 'the Void', which is Paul Tillich's notion of the 'sacred void', the Christian's time of waiting that has replaced the concept of *kairos*.

In the following chorus (p. 352), modelled on Baudelaire's 'Réversibi-lité', this state of despair is seen as self-induced: it arises from an unwillingness to believe ('Dreading to find its Father lest it find | The Goodness it has dreaded is not good') and the demand for the absolute conviction of a miracle. In stanza 3, 'The Pilgrim Way has led to the Abyss' is a notion which may owe something to Heidegger's pun on the ground ('Grund') of Being and the 'Abgrund' (abyss) of meaninglessness (*Being and Time*, p. 194).

The following recitative makes clear Auden's attitude to such a rational search for God (e.g. of Joseph in the third section) by stating that 'The Real is what will strike you as really absurd'. The garden, which is described in *The Enchafèd Flood*, p. 29, as the innocent earthly paradise where there is no conflict between natural desire and moral duty, can only be reached through the desert ('the place of purgation for those who reject the evil city because they desire to become good', *The Enchafèd Flood*, p. 24). Although these symbols seem very Eliotic (the waste land, the rose-garden from *Burnt Norton*, I, the interpenetration of desert and garden in *Ash Wednesday*, V, etc.), it is clear from the discussion of them in *The Enchafèd Flood*, that they are intellectual, even rather bookish, symbols, unlike the numinous locations of Eliot. The elegiacs of the chorus on p. 354 contrast man, in familiar Auden fashion, with other forms of life, and hope for the 'magic secret of how to extemporize life'.

The second section, 'The Annunciation' (p. 355), introduces a device from the morality plays in its personification of the four faculties. If man is to 'extemporize' life (and the word suggests not only the recapturing of an unselfconscious natural innocence of action, but also the existence of such an action 'out of time', i.e. extemporizing, redeeming the Time Being), he must attain that wholeness of personality which was fragmented by the Fall. Thus Intuition, Feeling, Sensation and Thought are the means by which he may get glimpses of that redeemed life which his fallen nature denies him ('We alone may look over | The wall of that hidden | Garden whose entrance | To him is forbidden'), though of course he can be misled by the information which these faculties separately give him. Auden probably found these ideas originally in C. G. Jung, *Modern Man in Search of a Soul* (1933), p. 107, because he seems to have used them in *The Ascent of F6* and perhaps in *Paul Bunyan*, but see also Jung's *The Integration of the Personality* (1940). The speeches of the faculties describe the exclusive limitations of their separate points of view, and in style and import (the fantastic and symbolic landscapes with Bosch-like incidents, the heresies of the divided personality) may be compared with the third part of Caliban's speech in 'The Sea and the Mirror'.

Gabriel then tells Mary that she has been chosen to do 'the will of Love', and therefore may repair the sin of Eve (p. 359). This moment of the supernatural cannot be said to be very convincingly done. Auden is plainly more interested in the idea of the encounter of the Eternal and the Temporal: as a mysterious marriage and a divine gestation, it predictably calls forth the familiar sensuality, paradox or homely detail of the seventeenth-century baroque, and this not even the musical gusto (and quasi-Revivalist refrain) of the final solo and chorus can do much to enliven (p. 360).

It is as if aware of this that Auden insistently modernises the third section, 'The Temptation of St Joseph' (p. 362). What was familiar to medieval drama as 'Joseph's trouble about Mary' is inevitably (at all events to an audience that would take such an attitude to cuckoldry) seen as comic (*'Mary may be pure, | But, Joseph, are you sure?'*). Auden, however, takes the opportunity of using Joseph as an example of someone who needs to have a demonstrable reason for believing (compare the second chorus, p. 352), someone who is unwilling to take the leap of faith. He is not to be satisfied, but must behave as if nothing unusual had happened. This is Auden's saintly response to what he later referred to as 'l'affaire C', i.e. Kallman's devastating unfaithfulness of the previous summer. Auden told Ansen: 'Joseph is me.' The parallel may seem bizarre, but Auden's other significant Nativity poem, the poem of Christmas Day 1941, written for Kallman (a bowdlerised version appears in *Auden in Love*, p. 65), provokes a creative confusion between the Incarnation and his relationship with Kallman of much greater daring. The Joseph of the oratorio must atone for all men's habitual domination and patronising of women: 'you must be | The Weaker Sex whose passion is passivity.' This speech of the Narrator at p. 364 is doubly amusing in that the examples of men's aggressive masculinity are on the whole so absurdly and vulnerably Thurberesque. The 'Irish charm | That hides a cold will to do harm' refers to an earlier boyfriend of Kallman's (Auden to Ansen, 17 May 1947). Joseph and Mary becomes types of the ideal couple prayed to by 'common ungifted | Natures': by the romantics, 'enchanted with | The green Bohemia of that myth | Where knowledge of the flesh can take | The guilt of being born away'; by the bourgeoisie, 'whose married loves | Acquire so readily | The indolent fidelity | Of unaired beds'; even by unborn children, for 'in | The germ-cell's primary division | Innocence is lost.'

In the fourth section, 'The Summons' (p. 368), the star of the Nativity, the sign of the Incarnation, serves also as a symbol of man's discarding of classical self-control ('orthodox sophrosyne') and his beginning in the way of faith, which must take him into a state of dread. The 'Glassy Mountain' is borrowed from Grimm's 'Die Sieben Raben' in the *Kinderhausmärchen* and a 'Brig o' Dread' leads to Purgatory in the anonymous ballad 'A Lyke-Wake Dirge'. This is like Kierkegaard's 'dizziness of freedom', the state of fear and trembling in which the choice is made.

The three wise men are types of the various intellectual heresies of denying the 'extemporized' life. The experimental scientist proves that objective reality can provide no clear answers about the truth; the philosopher discovers that the present does not exist; and the sociologist tries to make Eros ('the Venus of the Soma', the body) instead of Agape the basis of the just society by a simple smokescreen of utilitarian political theory. All three have reached a stultifying impasse in their knowledge and use of nature, time and love: the star provides them with a totally new possibility, the chance of discovering 'how to be human now'. Auden had underlined the bewilderment of Eliot's magus to the point at which the three wise men seem merely puerile ('At least we know for certain that we are three old sinners, | That this journey is much too long, that we want our dinners'), but this is evidently a deliberate ploy, for the following speech of the Star takes up the idea of the Quester as a bewildered child taking 'the cold hand of Terror for a guide'.

The Fugal-Chorus and its ironical praise of Caesar which follows (p. 371) is indebted to the caesuras, parallelisms and antitheses of Arthur Waley's translations of the Chinese poet Po-Chu-i (which Auden had first read at school). It thus enlarges with delicate civility upon that world of material progress which the wise men have created, and which can no longer satisfy. Caesar's seven kingdoms – Philosophy, Physics, Mathematics, Economics, Technology, Medicine and Psychology – have all developed in modern times to an advanced degree of impersonality and artificiality (e.g. 'Last night it was Tom, Dick and Harry; tonight it is S's with P's' alludes to the development of philosophical language: the everyday human examples which were used by the eighteenth-century philosophers have largely been superseded by the mathematical symbols used in symbolic logic: S = subject, P = predicate). Auden admitted that in stanza 5 the word 'Whee-Spree' (everything going on simultaneously) 'doesn't sound quite right' (to Theodore Spencer, Harvard). The Narrator observes in his exposure of the delusion inherent in such notional progress (p. 373) that we cannot trust material ideals. They lie behind any 'Perfect State', even the Third Reich. The already Eliotic tone of the Narrator becomes particularly appropriate with the mention of 'aliens and free-thinking Jews' (p. 373), an allusion to a notorious passage in *After Strange Gods*. Auden told Ansen in May 1947 that Eliot had not been annoyed by the reference, which after all is appropriate to Auden's ironical purpose of making the numbering at Bethlehem vivid for the modern reader. The Narrator introduces the Chorale, which prays 'that Thy Primal Love | May weave in us the freedom of | The actually deficient on | The justly actual' (i.e. 'actual' in the double sense of 'at the moment' and 'active'). This was the only part of the finished oratorio to be set by Britten (see p. 347).

The fifth section, 'The Vision of the Shepherds' (p. 375), completes the picture of a generalised humanity awaiting the Good News. Unlike the wise men, the shepherds know nothing except how to keep the 'mechanism' going, and yet they, too (perhaps they especially), 'know that something | Will happen'. The mechanism tempts to nihilism (the lever that nudges the aching wrist, p. 377, could be a trigger, or simply the lever that keeps the wheels turning, as for example in Lang's *Metropolis*). The modern shepherd is part of a mechanised work-force, but also to an extent symbolical; in a contemporary review Auden wrote of the civilised world at the moment of the Incarnation, 'Its philosophical dualism divided both society and the individual personality, the wise from the ignorant, the Logos from the Flesh' ('The Means of Grace', *New Republic*, 2 June 1941, p. 765). Thus the words of the angelic chorus on p. 377 have a particular relevance to the poor and oppressed of society (as shepherds in the Corpus Christi play traditionally were, e.g. in the two Wakefield Shepherds' Plays of the Towneley Cycle), in that 'the old | Authoritarian | Constraint is replaced | By His Covenant, | And a city based | On love and consent | Suggested to me.'

The sixth section, 'At the Manger' (p. 379), begins with Mary's lullaby (published in *Commonweal*, 25 December 1942: 'At the Manger') predicting that the human element in Christ's nativity which she has contributed will bring him anxiety and death. This anxiety is not shared by the Father, showing that Auden maintained the orthodoxy observed by Anne Fremantle when they discussed the Patripassian heresy in 1931 (*A Tribute*, p. 80). By 1971, however, he may have changed his mind (see John Bridgen in *Auden Newsletter* 3, p. 3). The lullaby is followed by a duet of wise men and shepherds (p. 380), contrasting the paths by which they have been brought to the threshold of the truth: the 'impatience' of the intellect and the 'laziness' of the flesh (Auden cheerfully uses the tomb/womb rhyme that he had exposed in 'New Year Letter', line 552). They conclude (p. 383) with an address to the Child in the person of that Love which 'is more serious than Philosophy'. It is, however, defined in relation to the philosophical ideas of Martin Buber. The 'Otherness that can say I' (p. 384) is a version of Buber's 'I-You' spoken by grace and with the fusion into the whole being that the speaking of it accomplishes: 'I require a You to become; becoming I, I say You' (Buber, *I and Thou*, 1970, p. 62). Auden came to use this idea as a definition of the authenticity of our individuality as persons (e.g. in his radio talk 'Nowness and Permanence', *Listener*, 17 March 1966, p. 377: 'each of us is a person, a being who is able to answer "I" to the "thou" of other persons').

'The Meditation of Simeon' which follows (p. 385) continues to demonstrate that the philosophical meaning of the Incarnation is considered very much of importance. Auden's Simeon is not a weary old man like Eliot's Simeon (whose peace was granted through his intuition of the Incarnation) but an earnest theologian whose conversion must be insistently and rationally explained, so that his meditation becomes much more like a sermon, punctuated by alliterative summary exclamations from the chorus ('The chief reason for the choral interjections in Simeon's prose', wrote Auden to Theodore Spencer in 1943, 'is to give the audience's attention a moment's rest'). Simeon traces different attitudes to the Fall, and shows that only when man's sense of sin is complete can the Word be made Flesh (the double sense of the Incarnation as a historical event and as a continual discovery of the individual is clearly intended). At this moment the unknown is no longer to be feared, and necessity is seen only as the freedom to be tempted, something which occurs to every man and woman, so showing the traditional truth about fairy-tales where heroism and success are not the prerogative of the exceptional. Dualism and monism are confounded, the universe is revealed as being real and various at the same time as being a divine totality, and art and science are justified. The 'Meditation' is a condensed and exhaustive statement of Auden's religious position at the time, a time when he was reviewing and thinking about Niebuhr (see Ursula Niebuhr's memoir in *A Tribute*, pp. 104–118). As such, it is probably more valuable for its ability to illuminate other writings of Auden's, for in itself it is an example of that weakening tendency to abstraction, only occasionally revitalised by *ad hoc* metaphor, which almost seems to make the Nativity drama an excuse and not an end in itself.

Much more imaginatively telling is the eighth section, 'The Massacre of the Innocents' (p. 390). It begins with a complaint from Herod (published in *Harper's Magazine*, December 1943: 'Herod considers the Massacre of the Innocents') that the rumour of the Incarnation is a threat to the orderly rational world which he has so patiently constructed and wishes to continue to govern. Christianity after all (as Auden pointed out to his father in a letter of 13 October 1942) regards the state as playing a negative role, and Marcus Aurelius, whom Auden had been reading, provided a model of the cultured, rational preserver of civic order who was instinctively suspicious of the dangerous irrationality of Christianity. Herod's credentials (in a bizarre parody of Marcus Aurelius' memorialising of his mentors in *Meditations*, Book I) are those of Nature and Necessity. Compare his opening paragraph with Marcus Aurelius: 'The gods . . . have not been wanting to help me to realise the life conformed to nature.' Auden called him 'that horrible old Marcus Aurelius' to Ansen. Herod has tried to stamp out superstition, but without much success, and now he predicts that belief in the Incarnation will mean that 'Reason will be replaced by Revelation . . . Idealism will be replaced by Materialism . . . Justice will be replaced by Pity' (p. 393). The elaboration of this state of affairs in a fantasia of specific examples gives the speech its particular flavour of wit and hidden irony that links it with earlier prose set-pieces of Auden's. Herod is not far from the truth, if one considers, for example, Auden's remark about the history of the Church being strewn with its scandals in *Oxford and the Groups*, ed. R. H. S. Crossman (1940), p. 90. His childlike dismay and petulance make him a momentarily sympathetic figure ('Why can't people be sensible? I don't want to be horrid').

However, in supposing that the rumour might be true, he is forced to face his terrible predicament: God has given him the opportunity to kill God. The alternative would be the (to him) impossible demands of belief: 'once having shown them how, God would expect every man, whatever his fortune, to lead a sinless life in the flesh and on earth. Then indeed would the human race be plunged into madness and despair' (p. 394). Herod is rational, liberal and humane: he cannot bring himself to believe without proof, and so unhappily is forced to order the Massacre of the Innocents that his reasoning demands. What one admires about this part of the oratorio is that Auden has resisted the temptation to make Herod into the traditional raging tyrant. Herod is more effective for Auden's purposes, not as Hitler, but as a representative of those attitudes which have no ultimate sanction against a Hitler. The Shavian final lines show Herod to be 're-enacting the myth of Don Juan' (see Auden's Introduction to *The Portable*

Greek Reader, 1948), and according to Ansen, Auden envisaged him as Sidney Greenstreet (who played the homosexual Fat Man in John Huston's *The Maltese Falcon*). The creative tensions of the characterisation at this point (perhaps a little too late for the success of the oratorio) guarantee the interest of the non-Christian.

The following somewhat Plomeresque soldiers' chorus (p. 395) maintains the humour and intensifies the colloquial. A comic soldier was traditional in this part of the Corpus Christi play (e.g. Watkyn in the York cycle) and George is the archetypal amoral adventurer who finds a cheerful refuge in the army. The camp tone and camp references seem designed somehow to exonerate individuals in the matter of military atrocities. Auden explained to Theodore Spencer in April 1943 that the chorus should, in his and Britten's view, be set for girls' voices, in high register: 'The lament [i.e. of Rachel] will then be in the richest Mahleresque style.' The massacre itself would have been represented by an orchestral interlude between the soldiers' chorus and the lament (letter to Britten of 11 September 1942). The massacre is described in Matthew ii as the fulfilment of the prophecy in Jeremiah xxxi ('Rachel weeping for her children, | And would not be comforted, because they are not'). Auden again uses dogs and sheep as symbols of the self-absorption of flesh and intellect (compare in 'Musée des Beaux Arts' the 'doggy life' which goes on while the dreadful martyrdom runs its course).

The final section, 'The Flight into Egypt' (p. 396), takes up Rachel's description of 'these unending wastes of delirium', and treats the desert through which the holy family must pass as a symbol of the lifeless and commercialised decadence of the modern world (the geysers and volcanoes turn up again in Caliban's speech in 'The Sea and the Mirror'). The voices of the desert tempt with an alliterative surrealist fantasia punctuated by quasi-limericks like jingles in a travel brochure. The last of these, p. 398, remembers Scott Fitzgerald's 'The Crack-up', where 'in a real dark night of the soul it is always three o'clock in the morning, day after day' (Bodley Head Scott Fitzgerald, 1958, 1.279).

Once the holy family is conducted to safety in a recitative, the Narrator breaks in with a speech (published in *Harper's Magazine*, January 1944: 'After Christmas') describing the end of a modern Christmas, when all the decorative paraphernalia is put away: 'Once again | As in previous years we have seen the actual Vision and failed | To do more than entertain it as an agreeable | Possibility' (p. 399). The Narrator has taken us back to 'the modern Aristotelian city', with 'bills to be paid, machines to keep in repair, |

Irregular verbs to learn, the Time Being to redeem | From insignificance'. Auden defended this effect to Theodore Spencer in a letter of April 1943:

> The Egypt–Christmas tree transition. The madness does not belong to Egypt but to the desert on the way there (a parallel to the temptation in the Wilderness). The Light may shine in darkness but to us its light is hid, because we have sent it away, i.e. the immediate post-Christmas temptation is that of the emotional let-down of an intense experience which is then suddenly over. I tried to introduce the sweeter note in the last section, i.e. if the light is to be seen again, it is by going forward (to the Passion perhaps) and not by nostalgic reminiscence. One cannot be a little child; one has to *become like* one, and to do that one has to leave home, to lose even what seems now most good.

The Atonement is still to come, then, for Auden, like Milton before him, evidently (despite that 'to the Passion perhaps') found the Incarnation a more intellectually entertaining proposition than the Atonement. The 'agreeable possibility' (glimpsed in Buber's terms of 'Everything became a You and nothing was an It') seems to be something that cannot be faced without the corresponding appeasement of guilt. The time-scale invoked here applies at once to the life of Christ, to the history of man and to the life of the individual; and Auden ends the speech with an aphorism from Kafka ('One must cheat no one, not even the world of its triumph') which reinforces the necessity for endurance, endurance of the mundane rather than the endurance of the suffering one might be tempted to pray for. (One of the differences between Auden and Niebuhr was that Auden would 'allow a little more place, perhaps, for the *Via Negativa*': *A Tribute*, p. 106).

The final chorus celebrates the transformation of the mundane by the Incarnation. Christ is traditionally 'the Way . . . the Truth . . . the Life'. To follow him in this world of ungodliness, of anxiety and of the body, is to convert it to the fulfilment of a fairy-tale dream. The phrase 'the Land of Unlikeness' was borrowed (via Kallman) from Augustine's *Confessions*, Book VII, section x (ed. Watts, 1.373): 'et inveni longe me esse a te in regione dissimilitudinis' ('I found myself to be a long way from thee in the region of unlikeness'). This is from the climactic passage where Augustine first finds God, and provides a suitable locus for Auden's 'sweeter note' in which the quester has a chance of discovering his authenticity through grace and forgiveness. Here, if anywhere, we may imagine Auden on his knees. Indeed, he wrote to Britten on 11 September 1942: 'it strikes me that you might want some *Amens*.'

The Sea and the Mirror

Auden started 'The Sea and the Mirror', his self-confessed *ars poetica*, in August 1942 after finishing 'For the Time Being'. By 9 January 1943 he told Elizabeth Mayer that it was 'going quite nicely so far', and he had finished the first two parts by early March. He found Part III difficult (see below) and could not see how to proceed until October. The work was finished by February 1944 and published together with the oratorio in *For the Time Being* in the same year. It was republished in the 1945 *Collected Poetry* (p. 349) and in the 1968 *Collected Longer Poems* (p. 199). Publication of individual sections is noted below. The text referred to is that in the *Collected Poems* (1991), p. 401.

As is the case with all the long poems of the 1940s, there is an autobiographical thrust to the work, endorsed here perhaps by the ending of a poem he admired by Rilke, 'Der Geist Ariel': 'Nun schreckt mich dieser Mann, | der wieder Herzog wird. Wie er sich sanft | den Draht ins Haupt zieht und sich zu den andern | Figuren hängt . . .' ('Now he terrifies me, | this man who's duke again. The ways he draws | the wire into his head, and hangs himself | beside the other puppets . . .', Leishman's translation). In Auden this self is clearly the poet's self, and the puppets are both the characters he borrows from Shakespeare and various reactions to the power of art. In a 1943 notebook in which he drafted much of the work (Buffalo) these characters are also listed as parts of the body, faculties and activities, while in a contemporary letter to Isherwood they are categorized in normative terms relative to anxiety or to modes of conduct. On occasion, as we shall see, they may also suggest relationships personal to Auden. However, since the work is a semi-dramatized discussion of the relationship between life and art in the context of spiritual possibility, one obvious starting point is Prospero's Epilogue:

> Now I want
> Spirits to enforce, Art to enchant;
> And my ending is despair,
> Unless I be reliev'd by prayer,

Which pierces so, that it assaults
Mercy itself, and frees all faults.

Prospero's words are, of course, a kind of pun, an actor's appeal for applause, but for Auden their suggestion that the artist as a maker of illusions is in need of supernatural grace when his belief in these illusions has been shattered, is a powerful one. It is one which is heavily reinforced by the allegorical interpretations of *The Tempest* which circulated in the nineteenth century, that Prospero is the artist, Ariel his imagination, and Caliban his animal nature. Although these interpretations seem to have lost their critical following in the twentieth century (certainly since the work of Wilson Knight) they are present in D. G. James's *Scepticism and Poetry* (1937), a book which, in its attempt to show Shakespeare tending towards a Christian symbolism, may have stimulated Auden at this date. Lecturing on *The Tempest* in the 1940s, Auden would mention treatments by Dryden, Renan, Browning and Wilson Knight. He pointed out to Alan Ansen that in fact Dryden was the first to see Prospero as the Artist ('But *Shakespeare's* Magick could not copy'd be, | Within that circle none durst walk but he'). If we accept a crude identification of Prospero with Shakespeare, then it is possible to see the familiar Kierkegaardian categories lurking in Auden's interpretation of Prospero's course of action: his enchantment belongs to the aesthetic, his forgiveness to the ethical, and his abdication to the religious sphere, and the whole action of the poem (taking place immediately after the end of Shakespeare's play) symbolises a similar process of self-awareness, in a vocational context, going on in Auden's own consciousness. To this extent, 'The Sea and the Mirror' is not only a commentary on Shakespeare's play but a completion of it. As Auden remarked to Ansen on 30 April 1947; 'Shakespeare really left it in a mess.'

The work falls into three main parts: (I) Prospero gives Ariel his freedom: i.e. Auden feels that his spiritual quest takes him beyond a reliance on art. (II) The other characters soliloquise in celebration of their regeneration, though they are negated by the unrepentant Antonio: i.e. man's pride is beyond the reach of either the aesthetic or ethical appeal. (III) Caliban addresses the audience about his own role, and that of Ariel: i.e. he discusses what is expected from art in its treatment of reality, and of the rival worlds of the flesh and the spirit.

The dedication is to James Stern, the short-story writer, and his wife Tania, née Kurella. Auden had met the Sterns in Paris in 1937, and in 1941 had collaborted with James in a radio adaptation of a story by D. H.

Lawrence, 'The Rocking-Horse Winner'. The quotation from Emily Brontë is the final stanza of her poem 'Plead for Me', in which she makes a powerful case for the authority of her imagination.

The 'Preface' of the Stage Manager to the Critics (p. 403) suggests that art, by presenting its audience with the surprising fulfilment of their secret wishes (stanza 1), reveals the human motive behind it. With reality it is a different matter (stanza 2). Rational explanations do not ultimately help, and art, because it is human, can only evoke emotions from its presentation of the human predicament; it cannot arouse the will or account for our sense of being victims of life (stanza 3). In the end, the religious sense has no need for art ('the smiling | Secret he cannot quote'), for it is the Unknown which has supreme importance. The last half-dozen lines blend Shakespearean quotations (*The Tempest*, IV.i.142; *Hamlet*, V.ii.372; *King Lear*, V.ii.11) with the garden quest of Eliot's 'Burnt Norton', I.

'Prospero to Ariel' (p. 404) begins by establishing the basic terms on which the Unknown must be approached: the creative imagination is responsible for the denial of a reality that has to be faced ('I am glad I have freed you . . . | For under your influence death is inconceivable'), and is ultimately a poor exchange for life itself (mere shadows compared with the city of common warmth). Art is basically a compensation for life, 'the power to enchant that comes from disillusion' (cf. 'New Year Letter', Part I), and it has great power to reveal and explain life's disorder.

Prospero's first song is based on this idea (p. 406). Art's function as truth is so powerful, he says, that we cannot bear too much of it. The sexual ambience within which this truth may be glimpsed is interesting here. Auden revealed himself to Ansen as a 'oncer', frightened of any deeper relationship than a one-night stand, hurt by Chester Kallman's defection. The holiness of his love for Kallman prompts complicated metaphors of Rome facing the barbarians and Andromeda chained for the dragon. The obliqueness of Prospero's songs may be due to their originating in part in 'l'affaire C', as 'Prospero to Ariel' in general certainly did. As Auden admitted to Isherwood: 'It's OK to say that Ariel is Chester, but Chester is also Caliban, "das lebendigste"' (the phrase is from Hölderlin, and means 'what is most alive'). This seems to imply that Auden conceives the duality of the imagined life and the lived life to be unbridgeable, even in art.

Prospero turns to the other characters of the play (p. 407), admitting his own responsibility for Antonio's treason. Here, I think, is a suggestion of the failure of liberal humanism to avert Hitler. This is not the particular responsibility of the artist though in the second part of the work Antonio, in

his arrogant self-sufficiency, stands outside Prospero's power, and, while he
denies it, will continue to call it forth. Prospero's 'impervious disgrace' is,
however, not the defiant tempted Ego of Antonio, but the recalcitrant Id of
Caliban, whose 'absolute devotion' Prospero has himself desired. All the
other characters have 'been soundly hunted | By their own devils into their
human selves' and are returned to the sea of existential living from which
they lately swaggered. Thinking of Miranda and Ferdinand leads him into
his second song (p. 408) about the erotic ideals of youth, middle age and
old age. Its imagery circles suggestively around the Falstaff / Hal situation,
where for Auden the erotic is as significant as the political. It casts the
shadow of Falstaff's rejection over the remainder of Prospero's speech: as
an old man, he will find it hard to embark on his spiritual quest without
being able to speak about it. The Kierkegaardian leap ('seventy thousand
fathoms') demands suffering 'without saying something ironic or funny |
On suffering' (cf. 'The Quest', no. XII). Prospero's final song (p. 410)
shows him, even as 'trembling he takes | The silent passage | Into
discomfort', still wishing for Ariel's song, as though at the moment of
rejection art had attained a fresh poignancy and power.

Part II, 'The Supporting Cast, Sotto Voce' (p. 410) is something of a
virtuoso performance as, 'dotted about the deck', the changed characters
deliver, each in an appropriate verse-form, an account of how the magic has
changed them and how they mean to pursue their destinies. Auden may
have been saving up his technical idea for some time. Reviewing Philip
Henderson's edition of Skelton in the *Criterion* (January, 1932), he wrote: 'I
am glad that Mr Henderson has called attention to the use of different
kinds of verse for different characters in *Magnificence*. As far as I know
Skelton is the only English poet who has done this' (Auden then makes a
point about the similarity of Shakespeare's blank-verse climaxes).

Antonio sets the scene, referring in his first stanza to the 'calm seas,
auspicious gales' promised by Prospero in *The Tempest*, v.i.316, ironically
equating Prospero's magic with Circe's (whereas it is Sycorax, Caliban's
mother, who is closer to Homer's sorceress) and later, in stanza 6, with the
saccharine property of popular song ('What a Little Moonlight Can Do',
from the obscure film *Roadhouse Nights*, but popularised by Billie Holiday).
His refrain ironically dominates the whole section in its expression of his
unregenerate will. Antonio represents man's freedom to create the disorder
which exists for art to put in order. *The Tempest* is about the purgation of
evil, but Antonio's virtual silence in Act v could indicate that he has not, as
the personal agent of the evil, repented. In his stanza about Hitler in

'September 1, 1939' Auden seemed uneasy with the facile assumption that evil is begotten only of evil. But here it is certainly the natural outcome of temptation. Prospero is responsible for his brother, because he put the temptation to usurp in his way: in other words, it is the irresponsibility of art in the real world which guarantees art's continuing importance as a means of healing the errors which its isolation has created. As long as Antonio exists, Prospero will not be able to give up his role. Auden sees Antonio as a man made demonic by art, a failure because he cannot forgive forgiveness. As Antonio says, 'while I stand outside | Your circle, the will to charm is still there' (cf. 'New Year Letter', lines 64–75). Prospero's 'all' is 'partial' because it is not a 'true gestalt', and Antonio feels justified in his sarcastic view of it as a Circean charm which can easily be resisted by the unaccommodating will. The last line of the *terza rima* was originally in the draft 'As a little child into the joy of heaven'; in the text it becomes an allusion to one of Auden's favourite Baudelaire lines, 'Le vert paradis des amours enfantines' (from 'Mœsta et Errabunda'). He also quoted the Baudelaire line in the Preface to his edition of Tennyson and in the poem 'Ode' ('The vacation at last is approaching').

Ferdinand's sonnet in alexandrines (p. 412) takes a hint from the involved syntax of his language in *The Tempest* (e.g. at III.i) to create a tone of innocent obscurity which pleasantly borders on pastiche (Auden told Isherwood that Ferdinand 'describes fucking in completely abstract words'). The sense in lines 3–6, however, of his discovery in Miranda's *Thou* of the fullness of his own *I* probably derives from his reading of Martin Buber. And in its final tercet the sonnet's awareness of 'another tenderness', a Light which enables the lovers to possess the 'Right Required Time' of the Kairos, shows it to be seriously Christian. The other phrase in the final line ('The Real Right Place') is similarly Jamesian. One James story, 'The Real Right Thing' (1899), is conflated with another, 'The Great Good Place' (1900). Auden praised the latter as a religious parable and contrasted it with James's unspeakable view of America in *The American Scene*: the 'Great Good Place' is 'nearer everything' (*Town and Country*, June 1946).

Stephano's ballade (p. 412) involves his search for identity. The belly ('bride' and 'daughter' in the opening lines, ambiguously 'Child' or 'Mother' in the envoi) is an early representation of the feminised body in Auden (cf. 'No, Plato, No' and the later 'Lullaby'). See also the remarks about Falstaff in *The Dyer's Hand*, pp. 195–6. Auden associated Stephano with Falstaff in his comments made to Isherwood: both take that flight from anxiety into the unconsciousness of which only the body can be the instrument. Stephano's belly, heavy with drink, exchanges cravings with his mind, not only in the sense that it wishes to get rid of the alcohol as fast as Stephano wishes to consume it ('Between the bottle and the "loo"', the quotation marks for this newish word appearing to be an editorial intrusion), but because it is the belly which has learnt to need the alcohol through the mind's desire to escape from its 'disappointments' and 'ghosts'. The search for identity is assisted by drink, because it dispels melancholy. ('The high play better than the blue') and imparts the illusion of a unity of mind and body, even though 'The will of one by being two I At every moment is denied').

Gonzalo (p. 413) is representative of the interpretative reason 'in whose booming eloquence I Honesty became untrue'. His 'prediction' (of the ideal Commonwealth) did come true in a sense, but he is guilty of making the song of the Absurd sound 'ridiculous and wrong' because of his compulsive and pedantic rationalisation (the reference is to his vision of the political threat in *The Tempest*, represented by Ariel's song at II.i.295). As Auden explained to Isherwood, he is the man who makes goodness easy by blinding himself to evil.

Adrian and Francisco's camp couplet (p. 415) expresses their realisation that their superficial life must come to an end; their appalled resignation is largely a theatrical gesture (as Antonio's comment acknowledges), a reaction of the corrupt court. According to Ansen, Auden heard the phrase 'madly ungay' at a lunch party in the South of France applied to conditions in Spain at the time of the civil war. Auden used it himself, for example in 1942 on discovering that his Swarthmore class consisted of twenty-six girls and one boy. However, the only earlier use in print that I have found is in Cyril Connolly's 'Where Engels Fears to Tread' (in *Press Gang*, ed. Leonard Russell, 1937), reprinted in *The Condemned Playground* (1945): 'Harold said Balliol was perfect for case-histories like mine, but I realized I should find it madly ungay.' An earlier longer version of this section appears in *As I Walked Out One Evening* (1995), and contains material (similar to parts of 'Under Which Lyre') critical of contemporary education.

Alonso's speech (p. 415) is written in lines of nine syllables with a seven-syllable line at the end of each stanza, and is a letter intended to be opened by Ferdinand after his death. It was first published in *Partisan Review* in October 1943. Its central image is of the 'Way of Justice' as 'a tightrope I Where no prince is safe for one instant'. On one side is the sea, on the other the desert, each lying in wait to tempt the prince from his path, or to purge him of his error if he does stray. In ideal terms, the sea represents the life of the senses, the realised; the desert represents the life of the spirit, the potential. One is reached by the *via activa*, the other by the *via contempliva*. Each should ideally balance the other. As temptations here, they offer 'vagueness' and 'triviality' (compare the 'primitive potential power' and 'actualized triviality' in Auden's elaboration in *The Enchafèd Flood*, 1951, p. 28). As always in Auden, the nightmare has elements of the surrealistic (with a flapping horror perhaps out of M. R. James's ' "Oh, Whistle, and I'll Come to You, My Lad" '). Ecbatana in stanza 5 was the capital city of the Medes, the earliest inhabitants of Persia. The statue in the final stanza is borrowed from *The Winter's Tale*.

The Master and Boatswain (p. 418) sing of the prostitutes of Stephano's song in *The Tempest*, II.ii.47. They take a hard, practical, even Freudian, view of the consolations of sex. They see it fatalistically as a kind of chain reaction stemming ultimately from a hopeless search for a lost maternal love ('nightingales' is slang for prostitutes; cf. Eliot's 'Sweeney among the Nightingales': 'The nightingales are singing near | The Convent of the Sacred Heart').

Sebastian's sestina (p. 419) shows him glad to have been found out before he was able actually to murder Alonso ('my proof | Of mercy that I wake without a crown'). His guilt has only been a dream, his error in a sense exposed by the sword which he took up against his brother; now he has woken from his dream, and ceased to be a negative personality even though his nature has been revealed in its full weakness. The sestina form here accidentally gives the appearance of being much looser than usual: the order of the key words, in relation to those of the preceding stanza, is either 364125 (stanzas 2, 4 and 5) or 246531 (stanzas 3 and 6) instead of the entirely conventional 615243. The reason for this is simply that the originally drafted order was changed during composition: stanzas 2 and 3 were reversed, and so were stanzas 5 and 6.

Trinculo (p. 420), as a jester, is a type of the artist, whose loneliness is symbolised by his tallness. As Stephano retreats from anxiety into unconsciousness, so Trinculo retreats from anxiety into wit, and his humour is seen as a nervous reaction to his alienation from life: 'A terror shakes my tree, | A flock of words fly out, | Whereat a laughter shakes | The busy and devout.'

Miranda's villanelle (p. 421) expresses her certainty of love in fairy-tale terms, as Ferdinand had done in terms of striving for a vision of the Logos. The 'Black Man' may be an allusion to the King of Tunis to whom

Ferdinand's sister Claribel has just been married, but the elder tree links him more firmly with Othello, who in his last speech in the Folio text compares himself with Judas: the somersault turns any threat of betrayal into a clownish game. The Witch melts away like the Wicked Witch of the West in *The Wizard of Oz* (filmed 1939). In the drafts, the 'Ancient' was successively 'the patriarch' and 'Grandfather'. Of course, the three characters may more simply be Miranda's dream conceptions of Caliban, Sycorax and Gonzalo. The 'high green hill' is suggestive of Calvary ('There is a green hill far away'). Ferdinand is Miranda's 'as mirrors are lonely' in the sense that since a mirror doesn't fulfil its function unless someone is looking into it, and yet cannot itself see its own reflection, it is inevitably lonely, whereas lovers who belong to each other are mutually reflected in each others' adoring eyes. The mutuality of 'mine' was a late thought in the draft: Auden originally wrote 'true'. The conceit is a familiar one in Elizabethan poetry, and its use as a refrain enforces what the other images also propose, that her love is largely an aesthetic pleasure ('O brave new world') and is expressive of a magical harmony ('children in a circle dancing'). For 'He kissed me awake', Auden borrowed 'Ich küsste Sie wach' from Siegfried's aria in *Götterdämmerung*, III.i.

Antonio's last words in Part II were altered from 'the Royal O, | Dances all day alone' to 'Creation's O | Dances for Death alone' in galley proof, a thematic deepening of some importance, linking the ring of Agape with a negative solipsism, and with the Dance of Death.

Part III, 'Caliban to the Audience' (p. 422), is much the longest section, and it was also one of Auden's favourite pieces of work. He chose to reprint it, for example, in his Penguin selection of 1958, where it takes up twenty-three pages of the selection (pp. 103–25). It is an insistent, amusing and exhausting prose disquisition on the role of art, written in the style of Henry James. Auden is concerned to examine art's particular place in society (as he must be concerned to defend the aesthetic character of the individual creative consciousness), but the admonitory and ventriloqual voice of Caliban, forever confiding, cajoling, comforting and castigating, forces a recognition of the unbridgeable gulf between what people wish to be like and what they really are. According to Auden's explanations at the time, Caliban is a representation of nature who has the power of individuation but no power of expression, while Ariel is a representation of the spirit, who has the power of expression, but no power of individuation. Caliban is therefore Ariel's 'oracle', possessed by him just as Socrates was possessed by Diotima (the analogy suggests that Auden considered his spiritual conclusions here to be of the same order of significance as those of Plato in the *Symposium*). His speech concludes that for the artist or for any human agent these opposed contraries of life are almost impossible to reconcile; only the Supreme Artist is able to create 'the perfected Work which is not ours', of which art itself is only a 'feebly figurative sign'.

The argument, as in earlier prose pieces such as the 'Address for a Prize-Day' in *The Orators* or the Sermon in *The Chase*, is imaginatively detached from the normal functions of the kind of rhetorical prose it resembles; the Caliban persona ensures that what is said derives from the point of view (however imaginatively varied) of man's fallen sensual nature, his 'impervious disgrace', which still imagines that its attempted transformation by the imaginative order of art is something whose failure is a suitable subject for a sermon. Behind Caliban's unearthly style are the intuitions of Ariel; behind both, of course, is Auden himself, attempting in this way to define the longing of Ariel for perfect embodiment. This is to be most movingly expressed in the 'Postscript', brief as it is; for the moment, and at great length, the unassimilable and natural is allowed a voice and a role in front of the theatre curtain (for this Caliban can be neither left on the island nor taken on board ship for the new life). The limbo in which Caliban exists is in Auden's mind specifically a sexual limbo. He was conceived as 'the Prick', as letters to Isherwood and to Theodore Spencer tell us. Phallic utterance demanded an original and ornate style as far removed from nature as possible. 'From May to October', Auden wrote to Spencer, 'I was completely stuck with Chap. III. I knew what I wanted to say, I had the images, but every treatment went wrong, until I suddenly got the James idea: it seemed blindingly "right".' The Buffalo drafts indeed show a good many false starts, among them (a) a speech by Ariel himself, 'Kiss me, Caliban, curse no more', much of which ends up in the final paragraph of 'Caliban to the Audience', including the significant final line which becomes the latter's last seven words; (b) a version in verse of a speech by Caliban, 'Ladies and gentlemen, please keep your seats'; and (c) an entirely different prose draft about Setebos, Caliban's God, a devil who has bewitched the real world ('the task is to break the spell of Setebos'). This draft introduces the imaginary landscapes, and experiments with versifying them. The Henry James idea took Auden usefully right away from his own style, and he came to feel that in a strange way it was therefore more authentic. Auden did not say so, but what better ironical prose voice might there be than that of a supreme stylist also rumoured to have been emasculated in an accident? Of course, Auden did also believe that James's

Prefaces were 'the best stuff I know about the nature of the creative act' (letter to Ursula Niebuhr, 19 June 1946). Even at the level of a literary joke, this is a very good one, and it sustains the theme admirably.

Caliban's speech falls into three main parts. First of all he assumes the audience's role in enquiring of Shakespeare why he should have introduced Caliban into *The Tempest* at all. 'Our native Muse' is presented as a hostess faced by an unwelcome guest. Although she doesn't, for instance, have any suburban worries about 'what the strait-laced Unities might possibly think', she does draw the line at Caliban, and so do the audience, because to them Art is a wholly other world of which they feel privileged to have glimpses, and in which opposites are reconciled and time is in control (p. 426: 'what delights us about her world is just that it neither is nor possibly could become one in which we could breathe or behave'). Caliban in such a world appears as a distorted parody of what he is in real life, 'a savage and deformed slave', i.e. the penis, instead of the 'nude august elated archer of our heaven', i.e. Eros (p. 429). In the mirror of art, Caliban appears 'incorrigibly right-handed' (i.e. untransformed by reflection. Left-handedness is a symbol of absorption in the lover's eyes in 'Fleeing the short-haired mad executives' and other earlier poems). The address to Shakespeare ends lightly with a parallel possibility (p. 430): 'Is it possible that, not content with inveigling Caliban into Ariel's kingdom, you have also let loose Ariel into Caliban's? We note with alarm that when the other members of the final tableau were dismissed, He was not returned to His arboreal confinement as He should have been.' This joke about the Crucifixion (if such it is) is crucial: it prepares us for the survival of the aesthetic in the religious sphere (and no doubt also for a Christian Auden continuing to write poetry). Prospero may drown his book, but Ariel is not returned to his pine-tree.

The second part of his speech is addressed, on Shakespeare's behalf, to young poets for whom Ariel, the creative imagination, is at first a faithful servant (p. 432: 'the eyes, the ears, the nose, the putting two and two together are, of course, all His, and yours only the primitive wish to know'). In time, the partnership goes sour, but Ariel refuses to be set free (p. 433):

> Striding up to Him in fury, you glare into his unblinking eyes and stop dead, transfixed with horror at seeing reflected there, not what you had always expected to see, a conqueror smiling at a conqueror, both promising mountains and marvels, but a gibbering fist-clenched creature with which you are all too unfamiliar.

The artist, in other words, may too easily ignore his Caliban nature. Auden is alluding perhaps to Wilde's paradoxical aphorism about Victorian literature: 'The nineteenth century dislike of Realism is the rage of Caliban seeing his own face in a glass. | The nineteenth century dislike of Romanticism is the rage of Caliban not seeing his own face in a glass' (Preface to *The Picture of Dorian Gray*). To have chastised the flesh, or to have given it complete freedom, might have been ways of reaching the truth, but these would have distracted the artist *qua* artist, who must steer his way between Realism and Romanticism. For 'the reverent rage of the highest-powered romance' (p. 434) compare 'The reverent fury of couples . . .' (New Year Letter', lines 1649n). When the poet's 'charms . . . have cracked' and his 'spirits have ceased to obey', then he is left alone with 'the dark thing' he 'could never abide to be with' (pp. 434–5).

The third part of Caliban's speech is *in propria persona* as he addresses the audience on the subject of himself and Ariel (p. 435). The first two parts of the speech have shown that he can upset both the work of art and the artist by his eventually unignorable presence: now it is the audience's turn to be brought face to face with the choices they must make in real life. In childhood there is no distinction between the miracles of life and play (the coal-scuttle Hector suggests another Shakespearean character, Don Armado as Hector in *Love's Labour's Lost*) but in adult life the duality of Caliban and Ariel is enforced.

Caliban then (p. 436) describes life as a journey in which the actual moments of travel are few; even when the right step is taken, this only brings the traveller so 'far outside this land of habit' that he immediately becomes vulnerable to the twin heresies of desiring either a retreat into the actual (via Caliban) or an escape into the possible (via Ariel).

The first of these courses was described by Auden to Isherwood as 'The flight from God into Nature as immediacy. It gives him an opportunity to indulge in a version of his own Eden (cf. *The Dyer's Hand*, p. 6) in a surrealistic dream landscape which represents the childhood nostalgia of those who 'have never felt really well in this climate of distinct ideas' (p. 438). The slightly deranged tone of ecstatic homecoming (like the end of the Sermon in *The Chase*) is out of Gogol's *Diary of a Madman*. Caliban responds to those making this nostalgic plea by conducting them instead to what is really 'the ultimately liberal condition', an arid solipsistic universe, 'where Liberty stands with her hands behind her back, not caring, not minding *anything*'. The result is the despair of having nothing to choose because you are the only subject in the world. Curiously enough, this landscape is distinctly Icelandic.

The second course (described by Auden as 'The flight from God into Spirit as possibility') is taken by those who wish to escape from the chaos of life to 'that Heaven of the Really General Case', a Platonic universe of transcendental reality, to which they imagine Ariel is able to lead them. Instead, they arrive in a world without causal necessity, without objectivity, in which events may have any interpretation because all sense of *haecceitas*, or Thisness, has been lost ('A sugarloaf sea' on p. 439 is a rough sea with pointed waves; on p. 441, a 'fish-tail burner' is a kind of gas lamp; for 'bisson eye' compare 'bisson rheum' (blinding tears) in *Hamlet*, II.ii.502; 'bevel course' means at an obtuse angle). This is the Quest's Negative Way, and, like the first course, leads to an annihilating despair, 'the love nothing, the fear all' (cf. Lady Macbeth's 'All is the fear, and nothing is the love').

Caliban presents these alternative routes ('the facile glad-handed highway or the virtuous averted track') as the horns of a dilemma which faces the artist, too, for he cannot successfully portray both the truth and man's condition of estrangement from it; and worse, where he is successful in doing this, 'the more he must strengthen your delusion that an awareness of the gap is in itself a bridge, your interest in your imprisonment a release' (p. 442). This is what Auden described as 'The flight from God into self-reflection'.

Thus art can in a sense be self-defeating, for an awareness of life's inadequacies can itself become an interesting game. And in life itself the irreconcilable categories, Ariel and Caliban, act out in *ad hoc* fashion (the metaphor, apparently borrowed according to Ansen from Trotsky writing about Kerensky, being of 'the greatest grandest opera rendered by a very provincial touring company indeed', p. 443) fallen man's version of the perfect life, Becoming not Being. At the moment of realisation that this is such a shoddy performance, we are aware (Auden asserts) of 'that Wholly Other Life': 'it is just here, among the ruins and the bones, that we may rejoice in the perfected Work which is not ours' (p. 444).

The reader has a slight sense of the *deus ex machina* at this point. Auden has subtly and brilliantly exposed the contradictions that govern both art and life, but he has not (despite Caliban's confident and persuasive rationality) been able to show how they may be resolved, except by this gesture towards deity. However, in the 'Postscript' (p. 445) the totality of the individual is lyrically and mysteriously expressed by Ariel's love for Caliban, and reinforced by the Prompter's echo '. . . I'. It is perhaps cast as an aria as a tribute to Kallman, who could well recognise the opera's urge to transcend the passions it exploits, just as Auden could ruefully acknowledge that poetry could still be made out of sexual unhappiness (the body's lameness casts its shadow, the ideal that it can never be). The aria puts man firmly at the centre again, his body and spirit precariously but tenderly united.

The Age of Anxiety

Although this, the fourth of Auden's long poems of the 1940s, did not appear in England until well into the post-war period, he had started work on it in July 1944, and at least half of it was written by 1945 (Spears, p. 230). It was finished in November 1946, published in 1947 in the US, and in 1948 in England. The war itself plays an important part in the poem, through the radio announcements which continually break in upon the characters' explored consciousnesses to remind them of the violence and frivolity of the material world. The setting, a New York bar on the night of All Souls, thus provides an atmospheric link with other wartime meditations of Auden's, 'September 1, 1939' and *The Double Man*. Here, though, he is not much concerned with rationalising the immediate predicament of the individual or the world, or of applying to it the terms of art, philosophy or Christian revelation. It is a sign of the highest invention and genius that Auden should have produced so soon after 'For the Time Being' and 'The Sea and the Mirror' another major work which embodied his convictions in such radically different terms, those of Jungian psychology and the allegorised interior consciousness. The page references in my commentary are to the text in the 1991 edition of the *Collected Poems*.

The principal idea of the work (that of representing the four faculties of the fragmented psyche by four different characters) was not a new one for Auden (see my discussion of *The Ascent of F6*, p. 197). What he seems to have done here is to elaborate a hint from 'For the Time Being' (The Annunciation', CP, p. 355), where a morality-play personification of these four faculties allowed him to demonstrate how the Fall destroyed the wholeness of man's personality, and how the separate faculties allow him only glimpses of the redeemed life which his fallen nature denies him. In *The Age of Anxiety*, this Christian application is not stressed. Auden is much more interested in the complex relationship between the four faculties indicated by Jung's *t'ai chi t'u*, a diagrammatic representation of the processes of the psyche (see Jolande Jacobi, *The Psychology of C. G. Jung*, 6th edn, pp. 10 ff) and in embodying this relationship in the thoughts of the four 'real' characters who represent the faculties. This interior nature of the work makes it in parts almost as difficult as *Finnegans Wake* (published in 1939 and evidently an influence on Auden here), and allows his talent for fantastic and symbolic landscape its full rein.

The work is subtitled 'A Baroque Eclogue', and the traditional pastoral concerns may be intermittently glimpsed throughout its six parts. The baroque element makes reference to the appeal to the senses characteristic of the religious art of the seventeenth century known as baroque, and seems an appropriate term for Auden's ingenious discovery of metaphor applicable to the elusive states of mind he is concerned with. In poetry, the baroque uses wit as an instrument of vision, and works upon the reader through extravagance and shock. A relevant discussion of the style may be found in Austin Warren, *Richard Crashaw: A Study in Baroque Sensibility* (1939), chapter 3 'Baroque Art and the Emblem'. The formality and the lexical oddity of style has deterred many readers, but it is clear that its self-consciousness is quite deliberate. Auden wrote to Theodore Spencer:

> Re the 'made-up' feeling of some of the verse, I've probably failed to do what I wanted which is a difficult thing, namely to devise a rhetoric which would reveal the great vice of our age which is that we are all not only 'actors' but know that we are (re-duplicated Hamlets) and that it is only at moments, in spite of ourselves, and when we least expect it that our real feelings break through.

To Alan Ansen, he said: 'I think we're due for a revival of Gothic, baroque prose. I do something with that. Of course, it'll go too far. But we've had enough of Hemingway.'

The dedication to John Betjeman is significant: in its noticeable attention to the distinctive features of name and place, part-nostalgic, part-quaint, *The Age of Anxiety* seems designed to provide some kind of version of the topographical poetry that Auden claimed he could not write and of which Betjeman was an acknowledged master (see Auden's Introduction to his selection of Betjeman's poetry, *Slick but not Streamlined*, published in the same month as *The Age of Anxiety*). In particular, there is much in Rosetta's memories that is Betjemanesque. Nevill Coghill thought that Auden was also 'excited by the topographical interest discovered by [A. H.] Bright in *New Light on Piers Plowman* (1928)'.

The epigraph is from Thomas of Celano's thirteenth-century Latin hymn on the Last Judgement ('That day will be full of tears when man shall rise again from his ashes to be judged in thy court'). The 'Dies Irae, Dies Illa' was the crowning hymn of All Souls, with its celebration of brotherhood in death and hope of release from Purgatory. There is a partial translation of it by Auden in the Buffalo notebook containing drafts of 'The Sea and the Mirror'. The institution of All Souls in 998 was, for Auden, of revolutionary significance (see my discussion of 'Horae Canonicae', p. 461) and the setting of the action *The Age of Anxiety* on All Souls' Night should be kept in mind: after 998, in the words of Eugen Rosenstock-Huessy (*Out of Revolution*, 1939, p. 509): 'every Christian anticipated, through the common purgation of death, what we would call the final judgement of world history . . . Odilo of Cluny discovered world history as a universal order and fact, when he ordered the whole religious fraternity to pray for the liberty of "*omnes omnimodo fideles*".' 'Last Judgement' conveyed more than terror, it revealed man's dignity, his claim not to be thrown into the fire like a weed, but to be judged, and (p. 513): 'In anticipating the lessons of death, Europe learned democracy, she learned Unity, she learned Universality. All Souls is the cornerstone of all our modern civilization.'

The four characters are Malin, a medical officer in the Canadian Air Force who represents Thinking; Rosetta, a Jewish department-store buyer who represents Feeling (these according to Jung are the rational, evaluative faculties); Quant, an elderly Irish shipping-clerk representing Intuition; and Emble, a teenaged naval recruit representing Sensation (these are the irrational, perceptive faculties). At the allegorical level, these four closely follow in attitude and sensibility the various mental processes they represent, in which a commoner distinction is between Thinking and Sensation as objective and Feeling and Intuition as subjective processes. They do, however, exist as characters in their own right, and the nature of their encounter is the classic pastoral one (the erotic triangle Malin–Emble–Rosetta evoking, say, Spenser's Hobbinol–Colin–Rosalind). It is also a mystical encounter like that described by Auden in his Introduction to Anne Fremantle's *The Protestant Mystics* (1964), p. 26, where four school-teachers feel a mystical communal awareness which he takes to be proto-Christian, a Vision of Agape. The description is taken to refer to a real experience of Auden himself, and to lie behind the 1933 poem 'A Summer Night'. Auden always regarded himself as a Thinking-Intuitive type, an assessment which governs the respective roles of the characters in the scenario of *The Age of Anxiety* (e.g. to Spender in 1940 he wrote: 'As you know my dominant faculties are intellect and intuition, my weak ones feeling and sensation. This means that I have to approach life via the former; I must have knowledge and a great deal of it before I can feel anything').

Two of the characters have partial originals in real life. Malin appears to be based on Dr John Thompson, a Canadian Air Force medical officer who used to teach at Harvard. Auden knew him slightly in 1943, used some of his experiences in the poem, and 'checked the associations [of the Seven Stages] against' him (Auden to Ansen, 8 October 1947). There was also a history instructor at Swarthmore called Malin (a man who thought that 'Letter to Lord Byron' was in *ottava rima*). Rosetta inevitably brings to mind Rhoda Jaffe, with whom Auden had an affair during the period of the poem's composition. Ansen heard from a friend 'Annette' that Rhoda was planning in about 1945 to be a department store buyer. There seems to be no model for Quant, but Emble might be any of Chester Kallman's conscripted pick-ups. Ansen's diaries reveal that Auden had a well-tried domestic procedure for young men who passed out on the sofa.

Of course, the allegorical intensity of the work requires Malin, Rosetta, Quant and Emble to function also as representatives of the poet himself. A parallel and probable source of such an arrangement is provided by Kierkegaard's *Stadier paa Livensveget* ('Stages on Life's Way'), which introduced invented characters to embody aspects of Kierkegaard himself (Johannes the Seducer, Victor Eremita, Constantine Constantius, 'the young man' and 'the Ladies' Tailor'). By way of introduction to the three main parts of Kierkegaard's book, these characters arrange a banquet at which Constantine proposes that they should all deliver speeches on the subject of love, and after which they all set off in carriages. The resemblance to the scheme of *The Age of Anxiety* is obvious, and the title of Part Three is also borrowed from the *Stadier*.

In *Auden: A carnival of intellect* (1983), Edward Callan suggests the following interpretations of the characters' names: *Malin* from the French 'malin', meaning clever, mischievous; *Rosetta* from the Rosetta Stone, suggesting, through the link with the mouth of the Nile and prehistory, the feminine principle, the past, the unconscious; *Quant* from quantum, referring to the intuitive perception of things as wholes; *Emble* from emblem, a device which makes concepts manifest to the senses (as in emblem books, characteristic of baroque literature).

Drafts of the poem show that these names were conceived at a relatively late stage of composition. In a notebook fair copy in ink (Texas) used as a basis for late revisions, Malin is 'J', Rosetta is 'A', Quant is 'M' and Emble is 'B'. Indeed, on p. 112 of this notebook, in a fragment of unused dialogue, the characters are labelled respectively 'C', 'G', 'D' and 'B'. Soon after this the initials of the final names begin to be written in blue biro, probably

Auden's earliest use of the newly invented ballpoint pens. The earlier initials might, if they could be explained, give us further insight into the sources or significance of the characters beyond that already sketched above. However, although 'J' might be John (Thompson), the other initials of each set are difficult to ascribe. There is in the Buffalo notebook an even earlier plan for a work of a similar kind using four characters (a Civilian, a Merchant Seaman, a Corporal and a Woman) with intervention from a radio, but it does not yet have the Jungian differentiation and its story was to contain a murder.

The need for an extra-human solution to the problems which the poem explores seems to be appreciated only by Malin. The 'anxiety' of the title (according to such Protestant theologians as Niebuhr, by whom Auden was much influenced at the time) is itself a characteristic of the human condition indicating an awareness of the need for God, a characteristic identifiable with the 'dread' of Kierkegaard or the 'angst' of Heidegger. Niebuhr saw man as living a two-dimensional existence of necessity and freedom; he is both a spirit, and a child of nature, compelled by its necessities: 'In short, being both free and bound, both limited and limitless, is anxious. Anxiety is the inevitable concomitant of the paradox of freedom and finiteness in which man is involved. Anxiety is the internal precondition of sin. It is the inevitable spiritual state of man' (*Nature and Destiny*, 1.194–6). It is interesting to compare with this Malin's long final speech (pp. 534–6): the Christian choice is his, and is therefore considered by Auden (as we have seen in *The Double Man*) as essentially an intellectual choice.

However, the spiritual is (as so frequently even in the Christian Auden) subservient to the psychological, and this emphasis links *The Age of Anxiety* firmly with earlier works concerned with the quest for integrity, like *The Orators* or *The Ascent of F6*. Seen from this point of view, the central figure is not Malin but Rosetta, the representative of Feeling, who leads the others in the central journey through the unconscious in the important third part of the work, 'The Seven Stages'. Her personal quest is for an emotional fidelity to experience (in this case her childhood in England, which she glamorises and misrepresents); but the larger quest (suggested perhaps by Dante's seven cycles of purgation and the vision of Paradise in Canto XXVIII of the *Purgatorio*, and by aspects of the Zohar: see below) leads to the hermetic gardens which each of the characters in their roles as mental faculties has power to glimpse (cf. 'New Year Letter', lines 86off). The Vision of Agape, uniting the faculties in mystical communion, brings them to the hermetic gardens, as to a lost Eden which the fragmented psyche has left behind.

Part One, the 'Prologue', describes the characters, and charts their gradual process of awareness. Their initial monologues reveal the habits of thought which are most typical of their natures. Quant's quizzical interrogation of his mirror-image as he sits drinking in the bar (p. 451) shows how he is sharply aware of possibility. Auden has some fun with this looking-glass world. As Martin Gardner has shown in *The Ambidextrous Universe* (1967), p. 133, the line 'What flavour has | That liquor you lift with your left hand?' makes a serious point, because alcohol contains carbon compounds called 'esters' which give it flavour, and most of which are asymmetrical. Thus Gardner concludes: 'No one knows what flavour Looking-glass liquor might have.' Malin rationalises man's predicament in scientific aphorisms which cut bluntly across the alliterative lines of the verse: this is familiar Auden subject-matter, here introduced to stress man's peculiarity as an inquisitive, self-conscious creature, and to prepare for Malin's application in his final monologue of the idea of the inexplicable enrichment of 'novelty', the fact that 'Nature rewards | Perilous leaps', to Christian thought. Even at this stage of the poem, the leaps seem insistently Kierkegaardian.

Rosetta describes her ideal landscape, a stylised and cute version of pre-war England: this is her obsession, as unreal, say, as the English sets of the Americanised Hitchcock, but representing symbolically an important fantasy about her deepest feelings and origins. Auden has dropped a clue about his intentions here by referring the reader to English detective stories (p. 450) and their 'lovely innocent countrysides' into which a 'horrid corpse' suddenly intrudes. As the earlier poem 'Detective Story' (CP, p. 511) makes clear, Auden looks upon these elements of the genre as representative of the archetypal awareness of sin and guilt, even as a type of the lost Eden. Rosetta's awareness in her final long speech of a need for a paternal deity resolves her self-delusions, and explains their symbolism. Compare the churches (p. 453) with *Finnegans Wake*, p. 569. Emble's speech, as is proper to the representative of Sensation, analyses the spiritual loneliness which he does not really share.

The radio breaks in upon their soliloquies at this point, making them aware of the world around them. Malin's reaction (p. 455) is an interesting application in a realistic context of the mythical inventions of *Paid on Both Sides* and other early poems, but his role as airman has little significance in the poem as a whole, except to corroborate his representation of the high-flying intellect (similarly Rosetta as buyer for a store is fulfilling her role as representative of taste and feeling, and Quant as a clerk that of the literary imagination). The verse takes on an epic colouring in the Old English manner (compare 'Many have perished; more will' with 'þaes ofereode, þisses swa maeg' in *Deor*, a rare instance of a refrain in Old English poetry). Bert's words 'Why have They killed me?' come from an anecdote supplied by Dr John Thompson about an aircraft gunner he had treated, mortally wounded over Cologne. Quant may imagine the war he has not experienced, and Emble has the disasters of a convoy to recount with all the brashness of his youth (victims of a torpedo are 'exposed to snap | Verdicts of sharks'), while Rosetta's thoughts naturally turn to a besieged England and an occupied Europe.

They begin their dialogue (p. 459) by applying the general principle of the failings of the human will to the specific situation of the war. Emble describes the passing of cultures in the face of the barbarian, while Malin points out that the Nazis are not in this sense barbarians, but a product of the city (p. 460). Thus the point of the argument, and Rosetta's consequent avowal of personal guilt and responsibility, is essential (a) to the conditions which the 'Prologue' is concerned to elaborate as urging and defining the investigations of the work which follows; and (b) to Auden's own principal reason for rejecting the liberal humanism which had failed to prevent Nazism, and could of itself provide no real validity for its values (see his essay in *Modern Canterbury Pilgrims*, ed. James A. Pike, 1956). More simply, perhaps, as Malin states, 'A crime has occurred', and judgement is required. On All Souls' Night the Christian soul needs to be judged. The original epigraph to Part One ('O opportunity, thy guilt is great' from Shakespeare's *The Rape of Lucrece*) was cancelled in draft, as perhaps not wholly unambiguously referring to the human condition itself.

Malin proposes a conversation: shall it be about past or future, atom or star? They decide instead to discuss 'the incessant Now of | The traveller through time', who is 'in quest of his own | Absconded self' – that is, his real self, which, like the elusive law of God (cf. 'New Year Letter', lines 751–86), remains hidden from him by reason of his sin. Quant's speech silencing the radio (p. 464) describes the quartet as united in their sense of being removed from their proper environment ('the Ganymede Club for home-sick young angels', etc.). They propose, then, to investigate man's nature, his sense of alienation and his guilt in time. They leave their bar-stools and move to a booth.

Part Two of the work, 'The Seven Ages' (p. 465), examines the condition of man at both the generic and the personal level, with the Shakespearean hint (*As You Like It*, ii.vii.139ff) providing a bold metaphorical brilliance.

(George Rylands' anthology, *The Ages of Man*, had recently been published.) Malin leads the investigation. He introduces each stage, which the other characters then describe in relation to their own experience. The effect is remarkably like the formally stated experiences of the characters in *The Waves*, and it is a tribute to Auden's powers to find that his descriptions of childhood in the first two Ages rival Virginia Woolf's. The theme is the loss of innocence. Malin's terms ('that ban tempts him; | He jumps and is judged') are quasi-theological, and the individual developments are all concerned with the vagaries of the will and of love, the paradoxes of 'anxiety' (p. 469: 'So, learning to love, at length he is taught | To know he does not'). The verse in this part is among the most striking in the work. It ranges from Quant's surrealist vision of an adolescent's sexual discovery (pp. 469–70) to the neat, symbolic songs from the Wallomatic, a device (like the radio in the 'Prologue') which enlarges the significance of the statements to include the social environment of what would otherwise be nakedly psychological organisms; in a sense, the baroque in the work evokes the specific world of urban America. In 1944, Auden's view of the only eatery in Swarthmore included the comment, 'The jukebox is really an invention straight out of hell.' Quant's speech mingles Baudelaire and Botticelli's *Primavera*, according to Auden reported by Ansen. There is also some Bosch and Hogarth. 'Scivvies' are undershorts worn by sailors, 'herms' figures of Hermes with an erection, used as boundary-markers. The 'indolent ulcer' dates back to the 1929 Journal: it was what Auden claimed he got from travelling with his family. He also used the phrase in the poem 'Because sap fell away.'

Rosetta's torch song in lines of seven syllables (p. 470) shares some of the syntactical pastiche of Ferdinand's sonnet in 'The Sea and the Mirror', and is in fact imitative of the kviðuháttr metre used in the Icelandic poem *Sonatorrek*. Line 12 is reminiscent of line 13 of 'Turn not towards me lest I turn to you' (EA, p. 146). Emble's song (p. 471) is an ingenious application of the terms of the game 'Consequences' (Auden had written a poem based on this game twenty years earlier; see p. 41). Both songs destroy the illusions of romantic love, the first by describing a brief affair of unequal love, the second a 'sensible' divorce. This process of disillusion in the first three Ages yields in the fourth to the 'mutable circus' and its 'real world of | Theology and horses' (p. 472). This represents a Roman circus and its chariot-racing, where sides must be taken. The sides are in effect the newly developed technique of dialectic at the service of theological debate (cf. 'the yes and no | Of a rival allegiance' in 'Memorial for the City', II.4) seen in terms of sporting partisanship. Green and blue were the colours of the different racing factions, although Auden seems also to have associated 'heretic green' with the monophysites, who believed that there was only one nature in Jesus. The laps of each race were measured by movable eggs and dolphins (emblems of the horse gods Castor and Pollux, and Neptune). Auden knew about this from reading about the Hippodrome at Constantinople (letter to Carlo Izzo, 9 April 1952). Thus Malin's real world of the fourth Age is one of a personal awareness of duality presented in a complex historico-cultural metaphor. This is a world where commitments must be made, but where a revelation is missing. 'We are mocked by unmeaning.' The speeches of the fourth Age show man's growing awareness and expectation of the Kairos of 'the Absolute Instant' (p. 473). For 'kairos', see below, page 389.

This itself is reflected in the strange communion which the characters experience, but in the fifth Age the adult is aware of the numinous merely in terms which reflect back on his own needs and ego: 'that Generalized Other | To whom he thinks and is understood by' (Malin, p. 474); the 'Personal Call | From Long Distance . . . the low voice that | Defines one's future' (Emble, p. 474); 'the wheel' (Quant, p. 476). Quant's long speech here tells how man has always been like this, how his failed aspirations are reflected in the stories of Narcissus, Polyphemus (the One-Eye of the final sentence) and Orpheus (mythology is one of Quant's specialities) and condemns him to the eternal revolutions of the wheel.

The sixth Age introduces the doubtful poise of middle age, where 'clandestine under | The guilt and grime of a great career, | The bruise of his boyhood is as blue still, | Horrid and hurting' (p. 477). This makes man pine 'for some | Nameless Eden', which the characters describe in terms of their personal quests. In Quant's case, failure is reminiscent of 'Journal of an Airman' from *The Orators* ('on the thirteenth day | Our diseased guide deserted with all | The milk chocolate'), with a gallery of eccentric allegorical characters, representing the selfish postures of the will, and a landscape of spiritual endeavour nearer to C. S. Lewis than to Bunyan. Quant has only one glimpse of the Good Place, and then he wanders back, 'whistling ruefully' (p. 479). For Rosetta, the Primal Age she is nostalgic for is symbolized by the Rilkean dolls, who are simply themselves 'so clearly expressing . . . the paternal world'. The child is like a mechanical doll wound up by the father (who is also God) and working through nature. To her, as Feeling, the lost condition of Being is symbolised by images of dancing animals from childhood and myth, and the failure to obtain it is symbolised by the decay of the great country house, and the unwinding of the clockwork doll ('Wafna. Wafna.' is borrowed from the *Carmina Burana*, and is an expression used in connection with a hangover). Emble (p. 480) takes up this idea when he says that he has lost 'the key to | The garden gate', an image by 'Burnt Norton' out of *Alice in Wonderland* that has already appeared in Auden (cf. *The Double Man*). The Eliotic note is maintained when Quant refers to reproaches 'Emanating from some hidden center . . . The Accuser crying in a cocktail glass' (p. 480). 'The Accuser' is taken from the Zohar (IV.63), and is the Devil, particularly in his role as tempter.

Such a glance at the bourgeois limbo is a cue for another song from the Wallomatic (p. 480), a dense and witty encapsulation of the Fall of Man ('jilted his heirs') and of the Seven Ages, reviewing man's desire, will and intellect (stanzas 2–4) and concluding that his mortality is the most significant thing about him (stanzas 5 and 6). Malin's brief description of the seventh Age ('he | Joins the majority, the jaw-dropped | Mildewed mob and is modest at last') underlines this. The discussion ends, and while fresh drinks are fetched, the characters review their obsessions: Rosetta's parody world of the pre-war English upper classes, Emble's fear of fading into the crowd like his contemporaries, Quant's fear of age. Quant then asks Rosetta to show them the path to 'hope and health'. He does this in somewhat whimsical terms of pastoral chivalry, but Rosetta comments that she has no special gifts to lend them in their next journey: 'the sole essential a sad unrest [i.e. anxiety] | Which no life can lack' (p. 484).

Auden's prose comment at the end of 'The Seven Ages' re-establishes the mystical terms of the quartet's experience. The following Part Three, 'The Seven Stages' (p. 485, prefaced by Aida's moving words to her father Amonasro in Act III of *Aida*) represents their search 'as a single organism' for 'that state of prehistoric happiness which, by human beings, can be imagined only in terms of a landscape bearing a symbolic resemblance to the human body'. Thus the spiritual quest by the psyche in the process of overcoming its division into the four faculties can be represented or understood only in quite other terms, as intimate physiological allegory, for instance, or in fairy-tale images ('Grandmother's House' in Rosetta's speech on p. 484 refers us to *Red Riding Hood*, itself capable of a psycho-sexual interpretation). Auden was 'surprised people avoided saying anything about the Stages. It is, in a way, the most important part of the poem . . . And I put in that business about the landscape to make it easier' (to Ansen, 8 October 1947).

Auden revealed to Ansen that the physiological symbolism was derived from the Zohar, in the Sperling and Simon edition of 1931 ('Yes I used the 5 vol Zohar . . . just picked bits out'). He might also have had in mind J. M. Pryse's interpretation of the Seven Seals of Revelation in his *The Apocalypse Unsealed* (1910), a book which he would have known via D. H. Lawrence (cf. Lawrence's *Apocalypse*, chapter 10: 'the opening and conquest of the great psychic centres of the body'). The title of the section was supplied by Kierkegaard's *Stadier paa Livensveget*, translated in 1940 by Walter Lowrie as *Stages on Life's Way*. Lowrie confessed that the word stages 'does not so well express Kierkegaard's meaning as does the word "spheres" or "existence-spheres", words which are used more frequently in the *Stages*.' For Auden, however, the numerical symbolism from Dante and the Zohar (which was no doubt suggested by the seven days in which the soul goes to and fro between the house and the grave, mourning for the body, II.325) was crucial, and a multiple categorisation by sevens was the basis of the major work which he set about writing after the publication of *The Age of Anxiety*, 'Horae Canonicae' (see p. 457). Other patterns of seven in the Zohar are the seven ordeals (v.188) and the seven inferior grades of godhead (1.388). It was Auden's way of structuring the Jungian act of regenerative exploration that is at the heart of the section. The seven ordeals suggest a critical moment of spiritual judgement, at death: 'As the spirit makes its journey through the body and takes leave of each separate member and parts from it, that member immediately dies. When the spirit is about to depart, having thus taken leave of the whole body, the Shekinah stands over the body and the spirit straightway flies off' (Zohar, ed. Harry Sperling and Maurice Simon, 1931–4, v.187). Though the characters in *The Age of Anxiety* are not at the point of death, their quest is linked to the judgement of their souls on All Souls' Night.

Their 'urge to find water' (p. 485) probably represents their establishment of the Jungian collective unconscious as a field of exploration. At any rate, Auden only reluctantly agreed with Ansen's suggestion that Quant's 'salt lake' was the blood. It could have an amniotic significance, but the Zohar symbolism requires them to begin at the belly. This is Rosetta's 'sad plain . . . Rimmed with rushes and moss'. Malin's verses on p. 486 ('How still it is') were first printed as 'Noon' in *Silo*, Spring 1946. 'Lugalzaggisi, the loud | Tyrant of Erech [Babylon] and Umma' was a Sumerian monarch ruling between 2677 and 2653 BC, and may be found in Arnold Toynbee's *The Study of History*, I.109, although Auden may have remembered him from Gerald Heard, *The Ascent of Humanity* (1929), p. 105. The mountainous district into which they all, from their several starting-points, begin to advance is represented (as before in Auden) as man's first mammary objective, contrasted with Emble's 'inedible hills' in their fallen, war-torn landscape. Appropriately it is given to Rosetta to describe these 'twin confederate forms . . . white with lilies': the mother's breasts represent that solace 'Where the great go to forget themselves, | The beautiful and boon to die' (p. 487). 'Clouds' in this stanza is used in the Derbyshire dialectal sense of 'mountains'. Compare the refrain of Auden's 'Shepherd's Carol' (Novello, 1962): 'Love's all over the mountains, where the beautiful go to die.' It is here, as Quant's 'dream' suggests, that myth originates. The little monks ('really monks, Mother Church', according to Auden) are attempting to translate a 'vision' of innocence confronting sexuality into the language of the *Märchen* appropriate for an urban populace. And it is from the mother's breasts that there come the contrary motivations of the 'pilgrims' puffing 'Up the steep bank' (i.e. the religious impulse as a continual regret for the experience of weaning) and of Emble the sensualist running 'in the other direction, | Cheerful, unchaste' (p. 487). 'How still it is', 'Lights are moving' and 'Bending forward' were reprinted in the Penguin selection of 1958 and in the 1966 *Collected Shorter Poems* as 'Three Dreams'. Quant's bribes (as they struggle up the belly on p. 488) are inappropriately urban. 'A celluloid sandwich' is presumably photographic film, and 'silk eggs' the eggs of silkworms. Danish buttons were two-shell metal buttons of stamped steel introduced in the early nineteenth century (Auden was pleased to point out that their inventor, B. Sanders, had a Birmingham association).

The travellers then proceed to the heart ('the tumbledown Mariners Tavern . . . miles inland'), from which they see railroads and rivers running east and west (i.e. veins and arteries). Emble's stanza here (p. 489) sketches the general corporeal geography. They now split up (Rosetta with Emble to the left, Quant and Malin to the right) to reach 'the rival ports' (hands) and to complete the second stage of their journey (p. 403). Their lyrics during this stage are purely evocative of the self-confrontation which the landscape induces. Emble, in the metre used by Arnold in 'Heine's Grave' and 'Rugby Chapel', shows the individual at odds with the apparently settled world he moves through; Quant becomes aware of his earliest parental relationship; Rosetta contrasts her aristocratic illusions with the encroachment of 'plainer minds'; Malin is disturbed by the proximity of the heart.

In the third stage of their journey they move, from their contemplation of the ocean of the blood, inland again towards a common goal. Their shared poem, 'These ancient harbors are hailed by the morning', was first printed in *Inventario*, Autumn–Winter 1946–7, with the title 'Landfall'. In Quant's and Rosetta's train poem, a 'blowhard' (p. 494) is a braggart, and a 'pyknic' (p. 495) is a viscero-tonic type (from the typological classification that Auden picked up from Kretschmer). Their goal is the city (according to the Zohar symbolism, the nose and throat), where they are together again, though as Quant says: 'What mad oracle could have made us believe | The capital will be kind when the country is not' (p. 495). In other words, they cannot, as they approach the head, expect rational solutions to human anxiety. Their new location provides experience of the tongue's 'facetious culture' (Malin's speech on p. 496 was first printed in *Commonweal*, 20 December 1946, with the title 'Metropolis'). Civilisation demands a Niebuhrian emphasis on sin ('How are these people punished?') and finds the supreme ironical expression of man's independence of will in the likely self-destruction of the recently exploded atomic bomb ('the artful | Obliterating bang'). Auden admitted that the city he had in mind as a model was Brussels.

From here they travel on in the fourth stage of their journey, to the big house (i.e. the brain). Quant's speech on p. 498 describes the house, with allusions to the brain's geography. Rosetta runs inside. Her speech on p. 499 ('Opera glasses on the ormolu table') was first printed in the *New Yorker*, 28 September 1946, with the title 'Spinster's Song'. For Kibroth-Hattaavah, see Numbers XI.34 ('there they buried the people that lusted'). It is mentioned in Robert Graves's *The White Goddess*, p. 328n, though it is likely that Auden remembered it from Dean Farrar, *Eric, or Little by Little*, chapter ix: 'Kibroth-Hattaavah. Many and many a young Englishman has perished there!' Auden included this passage as an example of purple prose in *A Certain World*, p. 311. Rosetta eagerly looks out through the eyes, but all she sees is the isolation and selfishness of created things, 'a World that is fallen, | The mating and malice of men and beasts, | The corporate greed of quiet vegetation, |•And the homesick little obstinate sobs | Of things thrown into being' (p. 500). This concept is Heidegger's *Geworfensein*, being 'thrown' into existence. When Rosetta says 'let us go quickly', Auden may be thinking of the flight of Being from the shock of its thrownness (see Martin Heidegger, *Being and Time*, trans. J. Macquarrie and E. Robinson, 1962, 276).

In reaction to this disappointment, they race on to the fifth stage, the end of which is marked by a 'forgotten graveyard'. This in the Zohar scheme is the forehead complex. Auden had in mind the treatment of the whale's head in *Moby-Dick* according to Ansen. The verses which Emble reads

(p. 501) begin with the epitaphic vocative formula 'Stranger, . . .' already familiar in Auden, for the skull is only a 'still museum' exhibiting 'the results of life', and the characters may not enter '*Without a Subject*'. The next part of their journey is heralded by a fresh pairing, Rosetta with Quant (subjective faculties), and Emble with Malin (objective faculties). In this way, their erotic objectives (Quant's for a 'daughter-wife', Malin's for a 'son', Emble and Rosetta for each other) are prepared for as they arrive at the sixth stage.

This stage is completed by their arrival (p. 504) at the 'hermetic gardens' (in the Zohar scheme, the ears, through which one receives spiritual direction). This is presented (in 'How tempting to trespass in these Italian gardens,' first printed in *Changing World*, Summer 1947, with the title 'Baroque') as the Earthly Paradise where man's fallen nature may temporarily be redeemed: 'The ruined rebel is recreated | And chooses a chosen self.' Love is seen as conferring Being upon Becoming, a means for the timeless to meet with time: 'the sudden instant | Touches his time at last' (p. 505). The imagery, 'cypresses and cisterns' and the wicket gate from *The Pilgrim's Progress*, recalls the temenos of 'New Year Letter', lines 860 ff, a passage which stressed the dangers of man imagining that these glimpses of the timeless (visions of Agape) could in any sense be permanent. Here 'the extraordinary charm of these gardens begins to work on them also. It seems an accusation.' Their joy turns to an uneasy awareness of their defects, Quant's of the imagination which makes him dissatisfied with what he has; Emble's of his Don Juanism; Rosetta's of her snobbery; and Malin's of his intellectual narcissism. They turn away one by one into a labyrinthine forest of guilt (the hair) where fragments of their sorrowful songs are heard (p. 507). 'The Limping One' referred to by Quant on p. 508 is probably the Button-Moulder from *Peer Gynt*.

The whole process of the seventh stage here re-enacts the Fall, since their defects are all forms of pride, the archetypal sin. This leads them into the Desert, the place of trial (in the Zohar symbolism, the back). Here their doubts assail them: Malin describes the deceptions of the desert (the roasted rats borrowed from *Letters from Iceland*, p. 144) and says that he would have no reason to believe 'the wrinkled | Reports of explorers' (i.e. saints) who claim that 'this desert is dotted with | Oases where acrobats dwell | Who make unbelievable leaps' (cf. Kierkegaard). Thus the religious solution does not present itself, the hero takes up his 'defiance of fate', and the 'gentle majority' assume a Bosch-like placidity (p. 510). This speech of Emble's retraces the autobiographical passage about the exceptional child for whom a deep 'Urmutterfurcht' provides the drive towards 'knowledge' from 'New Year Letter', lines 1087–152. But this drive is itself an evasion, a hope for a 'last landscape' where 'a number is unknown', and is to be disappointed, for while since Freud we may believe our dreams to be purposive (and Auden in 1966 was glad to recognise that they are) they are not, as Rosetta begins by asking (p. 511), indicative.

The real world 'from which their journey has been one long flight rises up before them now as if the whole time it had been hiding in ambush'. This intrusion of reality scatters the quartet 'to the four coigns', or corner stones, of the Jungian *t'ai chi t'u*: they are again divided, and the phantasmagoric journey ends as themes of war and chaos accompany their ascent into consciousness. (Long Ada in Rosetta's penultimate speech seems to be modelled on Long Meg and the Sterne Circle at Keswick, which was left to Barbara Hepworth in 'Last Will and Testament' in *Letters from Iceland*.) It is now closing-time, and the bartender is turning off the lights. Only a faint memory of their experience in the hermetic gardens remains for Emble and Rosetta; she invites them all back to her apartment, hoping that Malin and Quant will refuse (but they don't).

Part Four, 'The Dirge' (p. 515), was in the Texas notebook originally the mock dirge which Emble composed immediately after the row with his father (p. 469). In this draft the dirge was followed immediately by the fourth Age, and the third Age followed the Fourth. As a generalised lament for the passing of the secular lawgivers who are the heroes of the City, it retains its air of mockery, since the authentic 'great one who, long or lately, has always died or disappeared' must really be Christ, certainly not Franklin D. Roosevelt (d. April 1945) who appears to be the immediate model. President Roosevelt was the executive of the modern paternalist state in the US in the pre-war years of the New Deal (the biblical 'seven years' of stanza 2, i.e. between 1933 and 1940) when he 'reformed the weeds | Into civil cereals and sobered the bulls'. Roosevelt thus becomes ironically representative of a substitute God, a 'semi-divine stranger with superhuman powers, some Gilgamesh or Napoleon, some Solon or Sherlock Holmes', and yet again we are reminded of *The Orators* (e.g. the second part of Book I). The passing of such a liberal humanist hero symbolises the merely ephemeral sanctions of the secular point of view, a recurrent aspect of Auden's religious theme. Some of the allusions in the first stanza alert us to the mock tone. The first two lines owe something to Housman's west-country yokels ('Oh, 'tis jesting, dancing, drinking | Spins the heavy world around', *A Shropshire Lad*, XLIX) and the last two borrow further from the broadsheet

used as an epigraph to Part Four ('Greatest sorrow England ever had |
When death took away our dear dad', 'The death of King Edward VII', lines
9–10) and which Auden had already included in his *Oxford Book of Light
Verse*, p. 520. The wailing washerwomen clearly come from *Finnegans Wake*,
and 'Tall Agrippa' is a character in *Struwwelpeter*. When the Dirge was
reprinted in *Horizon*, March 1948, it was entitled 'Lament for a Lawgiver'.

Part Five, 'The Masque' (p. 517) takes up the pastoral mode of the work
more deliberately. The characters are now trying to make something
exciting happen, when all they really want is to go home to bed. Thus the
growing attraction between Rosetta and Emble seems to them of great
importance, for in this way they may all try to recapture the vision of the
hermetic gardens. Viewed as an internal negotiation of the faculties, of
course, this section of the work becomes a touching adieu to any notion of
sexual love ennabling a religious enlightenment, something that had
seemed almost possible to Auden a few years earlier. Rosetta turns on the
radio and Emble asks her to dance. The 'brutal bands' providing popular
music in the small hours (p. 518) can mostly be found in Arnold Toynbee's
Study of History, since they are in fact Russian and Middle Eastern tribes
(Quaromanlics, II.151; Arsocids, III.449; Alonites, II.56–7; Ghuzz, II.442;
Guptas, I.85; Krimchaks, II.405; Timurids, II.144; Torguts, III.449). Malin
and Quant, representing the cerebral and imaginative aspects of Auden's
psyche, can do little but contribute some vicarious bawdy and whimsy.
Quant's prospector's ballad (p. 518) plays on the erotic *doubles entendres* of
the jargon of lead-mining: 'Laura' is a seam of ore, and her apparently nude
posture merely a description of its accessibility to mining. See Thomas
Sopwith, *An Account of the Mining Districts of Alston Moor* (1833), pp. 139,
140: 'improving prospects of the *grove*' and 'the throw of the strata is
attributed, as it were, to an *act* of the vein, – "*she throws* the north cheek
up".' Ledger = lying horizontally; cheek = side of a vein; plight = fold; grove
= mining shaft; random = direction of a vein; rise = working on the up side
of a shaft. Rosetta and Emble sing together a dróttkvaett ('Hushed is the
lake of hawks', p. 519). This is a complex courtly verse form used in Old
Norse poetry, which Auden mentions in *The Dyer's Hand*, p. 47, and
describes in detail in *Secondary Worlds*, pp. 67–8, and which he probably first
came across in Lee M. Hollander, *The Skalds* (1945). Its first four kennings
represent the four elements, air, earth, water and fire. 'Banners of
meaning' and 'host of days' are consciousness and history.

Then Malin (p. 519) invokes Venus with a little altar of sandwiches
borrowed from Ronald Firbank's *Vainglory*, chapter II ('The Masque' itself

is presided over by an epigraph from *The Flower beneath the Foot* which seems to confine its action to the aesthetic and ethical spheres from which Rosetta at the close reaches towards the religious. Auden confided to Theodore Spencer: 'Reluctantly . . . the Firbank epigraph must go.' But it didn't.). Rosetta and Emble's prayers and vows have a touching innocence which is none the less belied by their illusions and experience as revealed in the poem. Looking through the forelegs of mares in Emble's speech on p. 520 seems to be a superstition (cf. 'Look not at sky through the forelegs of mares' in 'A Happy New Year', Part I, stanza 5). The illogical 'If'/'When' formula of the vows on p. 521 may owe something to Rabelais, *Pantagruel*, Book IV, chapter xxxii. Malin's blessings (p. 522) similarly increase the air of self-delusion that the Earthly Paradise is at hand. His injunction to Emble to 'dance, a wild deer, in her dark thickets' recalls the celebrated double meaning of Shakespeare's *Venus and Adonis*, lines 229–40. But hate and suffering, as Auden clearly indicates in his prose comment, cannot be dispelled merely by 'alcohol, lust, fatigue, and the longing to be good'. This Rosetta begins to realise in the long speech (p. 527) which she makes after Quant and Malin have been seen to the elevator and she finds Emble has passed out on her bed.

She stresses their cultural and racial differences ('You'll build here, be | Satisfied soon, while I sit waiting | On my light luggage to leave if called | For some new exile') and alludes to Naaman's conversion in 2 Kings v when she says that if they married he would continue to feel gentile when he joined in 'the rowdy cries at Rimmon's party', even if, like Naaman, he had asked for the Lord's forgiveness in advance (p. 528). To see WASP society as an Assyrian god is a measure of the imaginative sympathy which Auden projects here into Rosetta's Jewish position. Auden was seriously enough involved with Rhoda Jaffe for a rumour of their impending marriage to appear in a Winchell column, which is why within a month or so, talking to Ansen, he could state 'I may not be a Roman Catholic, but I'm near enough to tell' (30 April 1947) and could also speculate on what would happen if he were converted to Judaism (March 1947). He is probably also remembering Kipling's poem 'Rimmon'.

The speech contains a good many Joycean puns and allusions, as indeed does the whole work ('mind your poise | And take up your cues, attract Who's-Who, | Ignore What's-Not. Niceness is all and | The rest bores'), but its extended intent is one of a most poignant seriousness, for not only does it show up Rosetta's illusions about her father and all she made him stand for, but it predicates the Jewish God whose omnipresence is a precondition of the Christian solution which Auden demands. The faith of the persecuted recognises the will of God even in the most unbelievable adversity (p. 529: 'our bodies are chucked | Like cracked crocks on to kitchen middens'; Auschwitz was liberated in January 1945), and Rosetta's acceptance of her real origins ('the semi-detached | Brick villa in Laburnum Crescent') and her real father ('How appalling was your taste in ties') is a paradigm of this. Her speech ends with the Hebrew prayer which translates as 'Hear, O Israel, the Lord our God, the Lord is one.'

Part Six, 'Epilogue' (p. 531), demonstrates that although Rosetta's recognition of a paternal deity may reflect an emotional need for God, it is left to Malin (and therefore to the intellect) to make the Christian choice. As Malin and Quant part, their counterpointed lyrics probe the illusory nature of human progress, though only Malin is sharply aware of the need for change and man's avoidance of it: 'We would rather die in our dread | Than climb the cross of the moment | And let our illusions die' (p. 533). This choice is not easy because it is 'too obvious and near to notice', and because man's double nature continually demands allegiance to the primitive forces which are the only ones really recognised by 'the poor muddled maddened mundane animal | Who is hostess to us all' (p. 534).

Quant's continued 'impromptu ballad' relates to the way in which liberal democracy copes in a war against evil, and in its relations with recalcitrant Nature by adjusting its ideology (e.g. p. 532: 'The Laurentian Landshield was ruthlessly gerrymandered', i.e. through efforts to accommodate the implications of the oldest rock-formations, in the basin of the St Lawrence river in Canada, to a pre-Darwinian understanding of the history of the earth). The initial point of reference appears to be the scene in Hardy's *The Dynasts* (1.1.iii) where Churchill's part is presaged by Pitt, Hitler's by Napoleon. The 'shiners' and the 'husky spectres' would then be the Spirits of the Pities and the Years, and the two Recording Angels. Auden commented to Theodore Spencer on this Malin/Quant counterpoint: 'Quant . . . cannot be himself; he must dramatise, his defence against the contemporary scene is to make it frivolous where Malin tries to see it sub specie aeternitate.' It appears that Spencer's criticisms resulted in some moderation in the tone of Quant's ballad.

Malin is the scientist, the intellectual, and as such is liable to resort to philosophical jargonising, but even so, his long last speech (pp. 534–5: the final seventeen lines revised and expanded from 'Bless ye the Lord: We elude Him, lie to Him, yet His love observes' in *Litany and Anthem for S. Matthew's Day*, September 1946) does clearly reflect the central concern of the work, the conditional reasons for man's anxiety and the actual preconditions of prayer and assent. Some details: '*Clarté*' is the spirit of the French Enlightenment, a term much used by Rosenstock-Huessy. 'The Great Boyg' is from *Peer Gynt*, 'Baal-Peor' from Numbers XXV.3–5. 'Their own disorder as their own punishment' is from St Augustine's *Confessions*. For 'concluding His children | In their mad unbelief', cf. Romans XI.32: 'For God hath concluded them all in unbelief, that he might have mercy upon all.'

Perhaps Auden, in bestowing beliefs upon fictional characters who are also personified faculties, is avoiding direct commitment here. The final words of prose comment indicate that the created soul is reprieved but not redeemed (for 'adoption . . . postponed', cf. Romans VIII.23: 'the adoption, to wit, the redemption of our body'). Certainly, however, the baroque style, with its paradoxical remoteness from, and direct grasp of, the here-and-now, presents a solution to the condition of anxiety as defined by Niebuhr. As in 'The Sea and the Mirror', it is the richness and candour of art which by implication continually absolves men from solving their insoluble predicament. Malin's last words stress the irresponsible childishness of human beings, but Auden's poem is such a subtle and generous effort of understanding that this speech, with its appeal to the traditional Judaeo-Christian God, paternal and inscrutable, seems like a historical position suited to the years of Auschwitz and Hiroshima; it is itself a poetical performance less artistically moving than that 'noble despair of the poets' which Malin condescendingly mentions (p. 533). Actually, *The Age of Anxiety* is rich not only in noble despair, but in a kind of inner glee and inventive response to the conditions of life which is the mark of great literature.

Poems first published in the Collected Poetry (1945)

Auden's first major collected edition was originally due for publication in April 1944. In the event its appearance was delayed by a year, allowing the two long poems of *For the Time Being* to be included. Naturally, in addition to the presentation of all the work that the poet at that time wished to preserve, there were new and uncollected poems which found their place in the volume. *The Collected Poetry* (1945) therefore contains most of the shorter poems which Auden had written between assembling the collection *Another Time* (1940) and February 1944. It also contains 'For what as easy', dating from 1931, but previously uncollected. For commentary on this poem, see p. 178. For commentary on the poems extracted from *The Dark Valley* and *Paul Bunyan*, see my sections on those works.

The volume was dedicated to Christopher Isherwood and Chester Kallman as if to the presiding midwives of his poetry, at the moment when that role had passed decisively from Isherwood to Kallman. Both were also, of course, major collaborators with Auden. The dedicatory quatrain (reprinted in CSP, p. 8, where it is retained as a dedicatory poem, and CSP66, p. 188) stresses both the universality and the individual uniqueness of Truth, somewhat in the spirit of the first of the fragments of Heraclitus which Eliot prefixed to *Four Quartets* (Diels, *Die Fragmente der Vorsokratiker*, I.77, fragment 2). A good example of 'knowledge that conflicts with itself' would be the Sermon from *The Chase* and *The Dog Beneath the Skin*, extracted into the volume as illustrating 'the fatal ease with which . . . the voice of God is replaced by . . . the Super-Ego'. Auden's readers in 1945 would have found it hard to realise that this heresy (the apparent subject of the sermon) was originally exemplified by its insane speaker, attacking communism. At its best, poetry can be defined as 'the clear expression of mixed feelings' (note to 'New Year Letter', line 829).

Abruptly mounting her ramshackle wheel

June 1942; 'In War Time', *Title* (Bryn Mawr College), May 1944; CP, p. 3; CSP, p. 19; EA, p. 460.

Auden wrote this poem while staying in the new Pennsylvania home of Caroline Newton, his patron, to whom the poem is dedicated (for Newton, see Carpenter, p. 311). Its rhyme scheme (abb caa dcc, etc.) results in a form of *terza rima* whereby, apart from the second stanza, the enclosed rhyme is shifted to the first line of the stanza. The effect borrows something of the assertive insistence of tercets. But what exactly Auden was asserting is not clear, except that the reasons for choosing war may, in spiritual terms, be the wrong ones and yet may still have a spiritual outcome. The core of the argument appears to be in stanza 8, where 'A pride of earthly cities premising | The Inner Life as socially the thing' has a distinctly satirical edge, as perhaps does the opening image of Fortune's wheel as a bicycle (compare, however, *The Age of Anxiety*, CP p. 534, where it is a Ferris wheel). The abruptness of Fortune's desertion alludes, of course, to the shock of Pearl Harbor (7 December 1941), the event that precipitated the US into direct conflict with the axis powers. Auden's title thus refers specifically to the involvement in the war (after endless debate about isolationism and intervention) of his adopted country. The 'Either/Or' that Auden glosses as a 'right to fall that is worth dying for' is Kierkegaardian. The poem seems to owe something to William Empson's poem about armaments, 'Reflection from Rochester'.

Around them boomed the rhetoric of time

?early 1941; 'Kairos and Logos', *Southern Review*, Spring 1941; CP45, p. 11; CSP, p. 25; CP, p. 305.

The terms of the title are related concepts in Protestant theology. The Logos is the all-creating Word of John i.1, and by extension the incarnated Christ ('And the Word was made flesh', John i.14). Kairos is a significant moment of time such as that incarnation represents. The latter concept was fully treated in Paul Tillich's *Kairos, zur Geisteslage und Geisteswendung* (1926), and developed in his *The Interpretation of History* (1936), Part Two, chapter II, where Auden probably read of it first, since it seems to affect his argument in 'Spain 1937'. Tillich writes:

> While time remains insignificant in that static type of thinking in terms of
> form, and even history presents only the unfolding of the possibilities and
> laws of the Gestalt 'Man', in this dynamic thinking in terms of creation,
> time is all-decisive, not empty time, pure expiration; not the mere
> duration either, but rather qualitatively fulfilled time, the moment that is
> creation and fate. We call this fulfilled moment, the moment of time
> approaching us as fate and decision, *Kairos*.
>
> (*The Interpretation of History*, p. 128)

The idea is also present in Rosenstock-Huessy's discussion of timeliness
revealed by the science of revolutions (*Out of Revolution*, 1939, p. 14).

Auden's four sestinas, then, chart different historical aspects of the
revelation of truth and man's incompetent handling of it. No. I is about the
early Christians in the Roman Empire (the last line is a version of a
quotation made by E. M. Forster from Jacopone da Todi: cf. the note to
'New Year Letter', line 56). No. II is a history of Christianity conducted in
the typically Rilkean images of unicorn (Logos), child (belief), roses
(truth), forest (history), dolls (humanity), etc. No. III treats the relationship
between language and truth in terms of Rilke's *Dinge*. No. IV presents the
result of human history: the sense of a missed opportunity, and of the
absconded God. Parallel ideas about the early Christians and the 'Now or
Never' may be found in *The Prolific and the Devourer*, pp. 45ff.

The form of the sestinas is unusual: each stanza uses the preceding
stanza's end-words in the order 315264 instead of the traditional 615243,
probably to avoid the effect of repetition at the beginning of each stanza,
wearisome in a set of four. (The departure from the traditional order in
Sebastian's sestina in 'The Sea and the Mirror' has an entirely different
explanation. See p. 362.)

Being set on the idea

January 1941; 'Atlantis', CP45, p. 20; CSP, p. 37; SP58, p. 86; CSP66, p. 202; CP,
p. 315.

Atlantis is the mythical island off the Straits of Gibraltar which Plato writes
about in the *Timaeus*, associated with Elysium, or the Isles of the Blest. The
Ship of Fools is an allusion to Sebastian Brandt's *Narrenschiff* (1494) in
which fools are shipped off to the Land of Fools. The first stanza thus
suggests that the quest for spiritual truth requires a recognition that one is
not exceptional (cf. 'The Quest', written the previous summer). The reader

assumes that all this is a generalised didactic account of a spiritual quest addressed to him. In fact, as the final stanza shows, the poem is addressed to a 'friend' ('my dear', even, in the first printing) and thus its admonitions acquire a particularised concern which give the poem a certain charm.

The Mediterranean metaphor is supported by describing humanistic rationalism as Ionia, religious enthusiasm as Thrace (i.e. the cult of Dionysus) and hedonism as Corinth or Carthage (cf. Augustine's *Confessions*). In stanza 3, the Thracian 'conch and dissonant gong' are borrowed from a translation that Auden had made of Goethe's 'Schach Sedschan und Seinesgleichen' ('Durch allen Schall und Klang') from 'Buch der Betrachtungen' in the *West-Östlicher Divan*. Auden had translated the poem (which Thomas Mann uses as the epigraph to *Lotte in Weimar*) at the request of Caroline Newton (see the *Saturday Review of Literature*, xxii, 21, 14 September 1940, p. 9). The 'four dwarf Kabiri' in the final stanza also come from Goethe (*Faust*, II, ii.iii.1075 and 1179). See also Schelling, *Die Gottheiten von Samothrace* (1815), p. 25. The Cabiri (Axieros, Axiokersa, Axiokersos and Kadmilos) are thought to be Phrygian deities who protected sailors and promoted fertility. It is not clear why Auden makes them 'dwarf'. Perhaps he confused the Kabiri in Goethe with the 'dwarf' Homunculus who achieves organic life through Proteus in this scene of *Faust*. The various pitfalls encountered on the quest may, the penultimate stanza suggests, be turned to advantage, even if the result is only a 'peep at Atlantis | In a poetic vision', for which one should 'Give thanks and lie down in peace' (a sentiment like that of Simeon in Luke ii.29, which links the poem with other works of the period concerned with the Incarnation). The poem might be regarded as a kind of Christian palinode to Cavafy's poem 'Ithaca', where keeping Ithaca (wisdom) fixed in the mind yields a rather different sort of secular homecoming, a sense of having after all lived your life.

Dear, all benevolence of fingering lips

?Autumn 1940; 'In Sickness and in Health', CP45, p. 29; CSP, p. 45; CSP66, p. 204; CP, p. 317.

This poem written in large-gestured, somewhat Yeatsian octaves is clearly in the nature of an epithalamium, as its title, drawn from the Anglican marriage vows, indicates. It was written for Auden's own 'marriage' with Kallman: the public dedication to Gwen and Maurice Mandelbaum (who taught philosophy at Swarthmore) was attached two years later at Mrs

Mandelbaum's request. The reference in the penultimate stanza to 'this round O of faithfulness we swear' alludes to Auden and Kallman's exchange of rings. It is an epithalamium with a difference. It begins by demanding humility and forgiveness in love, particularly in a 'murderous year', the first of the War, when the need for physical contact can so easily cheapen 'Sorrow' (again a complex use of the word, with the primary suggestion of human concern and Heideggerian anxiety). The self which is offered should be acknowledged as the desert it is, 'where dwell | Our howling appetites' (there is a probable allusion in the second stanza to Isherwood's travel book, *The Condor and the Cows*). Love is destructive and demanding, and creates the 'syllogistic nightmare' of the false alternatives of Tristan and Don Giovanni, lovers that seek to escape the demands of time and the body either by rejecting them or by destroying them, and in their double failure produce the sublimation of Eros into political violence (stanza 7: 'reject | The disobedient phallus for the sword'). Both types in this poem suggest a homosexual scenario: on the one hand the 'great friends' who 'make passion out of passion's obstacles', and on the other the 'unhappy spook' who 'haunts the urinals'. Auden would have first found the Tristan and Don Juan myths linked together in the work of Denis de Rougemont (translated as *Love in the Western World*, 1940). He expounds the polarity in 1948 in 'The Greeks and Us' (*Forewords and Afterwords*, pp. 23–5). Brangaene is Isolde's maid, who gave the lovers the love potion in the first place.

In stanza 8, Auden introduces into the chaos of 'our stupid lives' (Kierkegaard's 'Before God we are always in the wrong', quoted in a letter to Spender of this year) the idea of the 'absurd' redemption of Christ: 'Yet through their tohu-bohu comes a voice | Which utters an absurd command – Rejoice.' Not only do these lines seem to allude to Yeats's 'The Gyres' ('What matter? Out of cavern comes a voice, | And all it knows is that one word 'Rejoice'), but they turn the idea to a specifically religious acceptance of the world by using the Hebrew *tohu-bohu*, which is the very word used in Genesis i.2 (translated as 'without form and void') to describe the chaos out of which God created the world. The word may be a direct borrowing from Rimbaud's 'Le Bateau Ivre', although Browning uses it in 'Jochanon Hakkadosh', and Auden would have found commentary on it in the Zohar (II.398).

The italicised stanza which follows elaborates the creativity of God, and the poem continues by praising the real form of love, which is the love of God, and through him of the individual ('you and I, | Exist by grace of the Absurd'). The original stanza 11 ('The scarves, consoles, and fauteuils of the mind') was omitted in 1966. New stanzas 11 and 12 recapitulate the Tristan/Don Juan polarity in twin prayers to the 'Essence of creation' and to Love to guard the lovers from the extremes of 'sublimation' or 'animal bliss', and to 'permit | Temptations always to endanger' their love so that they may 'love soberly', preserved 'from presumption and delay'. The paradox here (treating sex as a sort of church ritual, but at the same time still wanting to be as integrated and quiescent as lichens) is somewhat reminiscent of the second stanza of 'Lay your sleeping head, my love'. Although the poem's conclusions (owing much to Kierkegaard) are argued out in religious terms, this remains essentially, like many of the poems of the early 1940s, a love poem. The context of Auden's spiritual need is frequently, in the most humane sense, erotic: fate is addressed as 'O Felix Osculum' (the 'happy kiss' of Christian celebration), and the implied God of Genesis, who '*showed the whirlwind how to be an arm*', also '*gardened from the wilderness of space | The sensual properties of one dear face.*'

Each lover has some theory of his own

?early 1941; *Harper's Bazaar*, 15 March 1941; 'Are You There?', CP45, p. 35; 'Alone', CSP, p. 50; CSP66, p. 199; CP, p. 312.

This pseudo-villanelle (only the rhyme words of lines 1 and 3 are repeated) is in effect a series of jottings on the demands and objectives of Eros. The rhymes build upon the ambiguity of 'own' (i.e. both 'self' and 'possess') and the paradox of a lover actually feeling more 'alone': the poem thus explores the nature of love as a relationship. The core of the poem is the third stanza, where these senses of 'own', hinting at possession as an absorption into the self (i.e. in an identity with the loved one), once again give us the myth of Narcissus (for the Freudian significance of this, see my discussion of '1929', p. 60). In stanza 4 Auden varies the traditional four elements of air, water, fire and earth and replaces air with 'the child', as a significant example of the pre-erotic, unable to imagine rejection by the Not-self (in the case of the waterfall, compare the 'forthright catadoup' in the later poem 'Serenade'). Without their exactly repeated lines, the enclosed stanzas of the villanelle seem possibly even more gnomic than usual, because the lyric element of the form's artifice has been removed. Marianne Moore thought that the procedure of the poem, with two lines in each stanza enjambed, ended up sounding like Ogden Nash (*Predilections*, 1955, p. 85).

Generally, reading palms or handwriting or faces

?Summer 1942; 'To the Model', *Dodo* (Swarthmore College), February 1943, and
Harper's Bazaar, April 1945; 'The Model', CP45, p. 45; CSP, p. 61; SP58, p. 85;
CSP66, p. 216.

This poem is generally reminiscent of Marianne Moore's manner when
meditating about artefacts. If 'the body of this old lady exactly indicates her
mind', is it really clear that speculation about her past is quite irrelevant
(stanza 3)? The essential human element which her body provides cannot
be divorced from the experiences which that body has undergone and
which have contributed to physical habit, stance, expression, and so on. Yet
Auden wishes to show that what is essentially human ('She survived
whatever happened; she forgave; she became') lies beyond measurable
experience, and certainly beyond the investigations of the psychologists
(Rorschach's blots, or the IQ test pioneered by Binet). And he is making
the point in the context of graphic art, which must rely upon the physical
presence to evoke the human nature beyond it.

Johnny, since today is

February 1942; 'Many Happy Returns', CP45, p. 68; CSP, p. 84; CSP66, p. 208; CP,
p. 320.

This birthday poem was written for the seven-year-old John Rettger, son of
Esther and James Rettger (an English instructor at the University of
Michigan, at Ann Arbor, where Auden was also teaching). Auden describes
himself as a 'doubtful Fish' because though just a Piscean (born on 21
February) and not an Aquarian like his subject, he is sceptical about the
value of horoscopes. He wishes for Johnny a path between extremes (stanza
14: 'Tao is a tightrope', Tao being the path of virtuous conduct in
Confucianism; at this time Auden was reading Arthur Waley's *The Way and
its Power*, a translation of the quietist Tao tê Ching; 'Socratic Sign', see Plato
Apology of Socrates, 31D for the oracle or *daimon* which from childhood had
deterred Socrates from certain actions). The tone of the poem shares
something of the occasional impromptu soliloquising of 'Heavy Date',
whose form it adopts, taking it much nearer to the jagged precipitation of
syllabics. Although Auden wishes for the boy a 'sense of theatre', he is well
aware that such self-consciousness (which in a good sense can lead to self-
understanding) is also the occasion for human pride, the feeling that one

can control one's destiny. With a comfortable avuncular twist in the argument (there is a lot of half-apologetic sermonising in this poem) Auden allows such pride its small holidays (like 'birthdays and the arts'), because by playing at being gods we are admitting that we are human. Auden runs through the qualities which will instil spiritual alertness with a pleasant enough air of improvisation. Stanza 9 concludes with a Shakespearean allusion also used in 'The Sea and the Mirror' (see p. 359). 'Negative Prehension' in stanza 11: A. N. Whitehead believed that civilisation advances by extending the number of important operations which we can perform without thinking about them. The *via media* is tied up finally with an existentialist ribbon ('Follow your own nose', perhaps alluding to another Johnny, Keats's 'Song of Myself'). It is hard to see the poem as part of 'the published record of l'affaire C', although the cautious philosophical air fits well enough with the facts of Auden's crisis and its aftermath, and Kallman had just celebrated his own twenty-first birthday in January.

Kicking his mother until she let go of his soul

?August 1942; 'Mundus et Infans', *Commonweal*, 30 October 1942; CP45, p. 72; CSP, p. 89; SP58, p. 91 (title italicised); CSP66, p. 211; CP, p. 324.

With its title borrowed from an early sixteenth-century play and its fine comic distinctions and tea-table syntax from Marianne Moore, this poem disguises with charm a serious qualification about human nature: we have unlearned the technique of existing without shame that we had as babies, so that now only a saint is comparable with a baby as 'someone who does not lie' (stanza 4). The natural processes are praised (stanza 3: 'his seasons are Dry and Wet') with a certain wry air of conscious unfastidiousness; these finally become an image of our own needs that we are so reserved about, since 'we had never learned to distinguish | Between hunger and love.' There is a pleasant vein of tenderness in much of the poem, natural since its infant subject was Wystan Auden Stevens, son of Angelyn and Albert Stevens of the University of Michigan at Ann Arbor where Auden was teaching (he had cured Mrs Stevens of an allergy to feathers and virtually enabled her to consider having the child at all). Interestingly, despite all this and much hospitality from the Stevens, Albert's name was misrepresented as 'Arthur' in the poem's dedication in the *Collected Poetry* of 1945.

The first time that I dreamed, we were in flight

October 1942; 'The Lesson', CP45, p. 116; CSP, p. 128; SP58, p. 93; CSP66, p. 214;
CP, p. 326.

The poem describes three dreams, which Auden himself interprets at the
end. All Auden's dream poems carry conviction (in *Letters from Iceland* he
revealed his habit of noting them down in the middle of the night), and
these three, despite literary echoes of Kafka, Owen ('The Show') and
Through the Looking Glass, have the right kind of emotional coherence to be
half-genuine. They present occasions of willed or wish-fulfilled love, in all of
which the lovers are indulging in a self-sufficient idyll or adventure, at the
centre of the stage. Lip-service is paid to Agape (literally: 'Our lips met,
wishing universal good'), but the dreams modulate into states of anxiety:
rejection, sterility, self-consciousness. The conclusion returns to a paradox
of the will familiar in Auden's work. The will to love cannot be, because Eros
is a gift, requiring grace.

The journals give the quantities of wrong

December 1940; 'Poem', *Decision*, February 1941 and *Horizon*, April 1941;
'Christmas 1940', CP45, p. 118; CSP, p. 130; EA, p. 458.

This poem is somewhat in Auden's 'woozy' rhetorico-didactic manner, and
for that reason did not last long in his favour. As a reaction to the first year
of the war it is (like the slightly later, and infinitely superior 'At the Grave of
Henry James') an interesting piece of evidence of that detachment which
his friends observed in him in the aftermath of his conversion. And if the
opening stanzas have anything like the Blitz in mind, then the note struck of
grandiloquent incomprehension, though fully understandable, is to be
regretted in a poem which at the same time offers to understand the
religious significance of the purely geological epochs of the world (stanza
4) and which draws conclusions in terms of the sort of Either–Or (stanza 8)
of which elsewhere he had been sceptical: that 'we serve the Unconditional'
or accept a Hitlerian model of evil. In life, of course, Auden accepted a very
practical third alternative ('The defeat of Hitler is an immediate necessity
about which there can be no discussion', *Decision*, January 1941). The Great
Boyg (stanza 3) is borrowed from *Peer Gynt*. The Dioscuri (stanza 7) are the
Heavenly Twins, Castor and Pollux, sometimes confused with the Cabiri
(whom Auden invokes in 'Atlantis'). The sequence 'beggar, bigwig,

mugwump' (stanza 9) seems to be intended to comprehend all social classes who claim to stand outside political issues (and therefore are receptive to a 'vision of that holy centre where | All time's occasions are refreshed'). A real beggar, however, would surely have had as great an 'interest' in the issue of intervention as argued by Roosevelt as he had had in the New Deal, whatever his actual views as a voter. Unless one can keep in mind the urgency of Auden's heavily philosophised faith, the joke about such a beggar not having to divide the Substance of Christ's sacramental body seems beside the point.

The sense of danger must not disappear

December 1940; 'Poem', *Decision*, April 1941; 'Leap Before You Look', CP45, p. 123; CSP, p. 135; CSP66, p. 200; CP, p. 313.

This poem uses alternate key words at the end of each stanza in a way which gives it the air of a pseudo-villanelle like 'Each lover has some theory of his own'. It manages ingeniously to ring all possible changes on the quatrain arrangement of two rhymes (nine of each in the whole poem). Such technical shadow-boxing seems neither as bland nor as menacing as a poet like William Empson could make it, but the sense of circumspection nicely underlines the 'danger' which is the subject of the poem, i.e. the risk involved in making the existential choice of life, more specifically the suggestion that Kallman might follow him in becoming a Christian (the Kierkegaardian 'ten thousand fathoms' was to crop up again at the end of Prospero's speech in 'The Sea and the Mirror').

The snow, less intransigeant than their marble

?Spring 1941; 'At the Grave of Henry James', *Horizon*, June 1941, and *Partisan Review*, July/August 1941; CP45, p. 126; CSP, p. 137; CSP66, p. 197; CP, p. 310.

This poem, once considered for inclusion in *The Double Man*, contains a plea to the novelist for a spiritual as well as an aesthetic discipline ('there are many whose works | Are in better taste than their lives') and Auden claimed that it owed a good deal to Reinhold Niebuhr. The visit to the Master's grave prompted twenty-eight stanzas of stock-taking in the *Horizon* version, reduced to twenty-four in 1945, and to ten in 1966. Much that was personal and local was to be lost. Auden's final version emphasised the need for spiritual and artistic exclusiveness: James's heart, 'fastidious as | A delicate nun' remained true to his art, and ignored the 'Resentful muttering Mass, | Whose ruminant hatred of all that cannot | Be simplified or stolen is yet at large' (stanzas 17 and 18: my references will be to the 1945 version, available in the 1979 *Selected Poems*, p. 119).

One of the poem's most interesting words occurs in the first line. By opposing the whiteness of the tombs to the now-melting landscape, Auden is making a point about human efforts to establish and maintain a conceptual integrity with which the natural environment in its mutability has no real concern. To say that marble is more 'intransigeant' than snow, however, is not only to symbolise and to oppose History and Nature in this way, but, because he has used the much rarer spelling of the word as if to draw attention to the fact that its original reference was to extremist Spanish Republicans (he used the commoner spelling in, for example, 'As it is, plenty'), also to suggest, as he does at the very end of 'Spain 1937', that it is death that is History's truly last word. That the earlier poem was in his mind is confirmed by stanza 10, where a version of 'Spain''s History offers a similar verdict: 'One after another we are | Fired into life to seek that unseen target where all | Our equivocal judgements are judged and resolved in | One whole Alas or Hurrah.' The setting in the first and second stanzas establishes, therefore, that while nature goes on and seasons change, resistance to death is our cultural priority, even though human life is reductively described as a 'series of errors' occurring within 'singular spaces'. (The reference in stanza 4 to 'distant clocks' which interfered with 'the heart's instantaneous reading of time' may be intended to refer to the unnamed household object manufactured by the Newsomes in James's *The Ambassadors*.)

In stanzas 6 and 7, in a striking triad of triads, Auden establishes the relation of man to his 'solar fabric': (1) the regulation of moral, economic and physical disorder by which humanity acknowledges its environment ('gendarmes, banks, | And aspirin'); (2) the triangular schema of the artistic process, made familiar by I. A. Richards, by which humanity recognises ('a-ha') that environment ('the beautiful . . . the master and the rose'); and (3) the requirements of the will, of death and of sex, within which humanity establishes its societies ('Our theatre, scaffold, and erotic city'). Stanzas 8 to 11 continue the invocation to James himself, begun in stanza 5, on the grounds that only the ironies of art can help us to redeem the failures of the will (the 'actor' who is 'never there when his really important | Acts happen'). As already suggested above, the scenario of 'Spain 1937' ('Yesterday . . . But today . . . Tomorrow', etc.) is remembered in a challenging definition of the unique present moment of the individual when his will is put to the test ('no one about but the dead . . . only the unborn', etc.). That this decisive moment is necessarily always a 'disaster' is underlined at the end of stanza 11 by a reference to James's story *The Beast in the Jungle*. The particular disaster of Nazism is developed in stanzas 12 to 15: the 'torches and snare-drum' which excite 'the squat women of the saurian brain' seem to belong to Dionysus as well as to the Nuremberg Rally (cf. the 'torches . . . and dissonant gong' of Thrace in 'Atlantis', and the 'bacchic fury' in 'Canzone', stanza 3). It is not entirely clear what women Auden is alluding to (though they are at one level culture-destroying Bacchae). 'Saurian' refers loosely to prehistoric lizards. There is a 'saurian aunt' in a detective story of 1940 which Auden could have read (G. Mitchell, *Brazen Tongue*, p. 67). The landscape of stanza 12 is pure Bosch. The whole of the passage from stanzas 7 to 15 was omitted in Auden's final text, and with it much of the justification for a prayer for intercession from a great novelist in wartime.

More of the allusions to James's own work occur in stanzas 15 and 16. 'The Great Good Place' was a short story of 1900, while 'the Real Distinguished Thing' alludes to James's description of his own impending death. '*Bon*' was James's term for the guardian angel of his inspiration, used in his notebooks, while 'overwhelming reasons pleading | All beautifully in Its breast' is a direct quotation from a notebook entry about *The Ivory Tower*, 4 January 1910 (*Complete Notebooks of Henry James*, ed. Leon Edel and Lyall H. Powers, 1987, p. 261). The phrase was also used of Mrs Brookenham's ingratiations in *The Awkward Age*, chapter 14.

There is not a little foretaste of Caliban in the tone adopted for this poem, allusions and mild Jamesian pastiche aside: it comes out in the feeling that there is something unmanageable about life, and that therefore the writer should avoid any temptation to manage it (e.g. the reference in stanza 23 to Julien Benda's attack on intellectuals, *La Trahison des clercs*). Real temptations are a different matter, of course: when in stanza 21 Auden refers to tribulations leaping with 'their long-lost brothers at last' he may have temptations in mind (see *The Double Man*, pp. 132–3, where he notes the desirability of tribulations becoming temptations, so that one can overcome them). In its heavily cut version, Auden seems to be trying out a case (perhaps for Ariel v. Prospero; cf. *The Dyer's Hand*, pp. 337ff) rather than defining a felt position; but the ingenious and articulate figurative movement of the poem still comes across with great power.

They're nice – one would never dream of going over

?February 1944; 'A Healthy Spot', CP45, p. 134; CSP, p. 144; CSP66, p. 215; CP, p. 328.

This poem was originally in typescript entitled 'Swarthmore' (the liberal arts college near Philadelphia, where Auden taught between 1942 and 1945: as he wrote to Caroline Newton, 'Everyone is very nice, but not very lively'). This 'niceness' in the poem is mysteriously linked with personal unhappiness and happy marriages, perhaps because Auden believed, with the failure of his own 'marriage' to Kallman, that wedded happiness required a lesser form of love than Eros (see *Forewords and Afterwords*, p. 64, for Philia as the securest foundation for a happy marriage). It seems that these kindly rational liberals refuse to acknowledge their 'hunger | For eternal life', or their own fallen natures. Since the pay-off lines of the poem involved a doubtful theory about the real nature of the 'smoking-room story' as a symbol of spiritual need, and since the symbolic unicorn of 'New Year Letter' and 'Kairos and Logos' could never be dead, the reader somewhat loses interest in the argument. There is something a little too comfortable about its exposure of cultured bourgeois timidity.

Time will say nothing but I told you so

December 1940; 'Villanelle', *Vice Versa*, January–February 1941; 'But I Can't', CP45, p. 135; CSP, p. 146; 'If I Could Tell You', SP58, p. 84; CSP66, p. 201; CP, p. 314.

Like 'Leap Before You Look' and some other work of this period, this villanelle, another encouragement to Kallman, is haunted by the flat manner of Empson. It is, however, fully lyrical (like Miranda's villanelle in 'The Sea and the Mirror') and successfully simplifies its sentiments in the manner of a popular song. The lions, brooks and soldiers might conceivably be a memory of *Through the Looking Glass*, chapters III and VII.

Whenever you are thought, the mind

February 1944; 'Few and Simple', CP45, p. 161; CSP, p. 169; CSP66, p. 213; CP, p. 326.

'Few and Simple' plays with the idea that we can never achieve independence of the mental and physical facts which make up our erotic memories, whether they are real or imagined, potential or actual. The context is Kallman's unfaithfulness, and Auden's consequently unsatisfactory sexual life. Thus thoughts of a passion no longer requited are as natural, familiar and intimate as if it had not been withdrawn; while the body is punctually obedient to desire even if there is no loved object available. The mind and the flesh are therefore the raw material of our subjective experience, 'enough | To make the most ingenious love | Think twice of trying to escape them.'

When shall we learn, what should be clear as day

September 1942; 'Canzone', *Partisan Review*, September–October 1943, and the *Bulletin of the New York Public Library*, November 1943; CP45, p. 161; CSP, p. 169; CP, p. 330.

Auden modelled his canzone on Dante's 'Amor, tu vedi ben che questa dovra', one of the Pietra group. The canzone has sixty-five lines, but only five end words (here 'day', 'love', 'know', 'will', 'world'). Such formalism (see also 'Kairos and Logos') was always a natural interest of Auden's, but Dante was an enthusiasm at this time, when he contemplated writing a Vita Nuova, with Kallman as Beatrice. The canzone seems to be trying to come to terms with the violence of his feelings about Kallman and Kallman's unfaithfulness, and to relate such feelings to the state of the world at large. The premise of the opening lines is the same as the conclusion of another poem about Kallman, 'The Lesson'.

In a garden shady this holy lady

July 1940; 'Three Songs for St Cecilia's Day', *Harper's Bazaar*, December 1941, and privately reprinted in pamphlet form by Caroline Newton, 1941; 'Song for St Cecilia's Day', CP45, p. 203; CSP, p. 233; 'Anthem for St Cecilia's Day', CSP66, p. 173; CP, p. 280.

Auden's revival of the Augustan tradition of the St Cecilia's Day Ode makes use of the Renaissance theory of the divine power of musical harmony, not to redeem humanity, but to remind it of its lost innocence: before the Fall we could hear the music of the spheres. Music does not 'translate', it is 'pure contraption' ('The Composer'), and is therefore not able to make moral statements about the world. Its power is to draw forth the emotions, not to represent them.

The poem is appropriately dedicated to Benjamin Britten, whose birthday fell on St Cecilia's Day (22 November). Britten set the poem in 1942 as 'Hymn to St Cecilia' for 'a small chorus of about fifty voices', and dedicated it to Elizabeth Mayer. The first performance was broadcast by the BBC Singers, conducted by Leslie Woodgate, on St Cecilia's Day 1942. The italicised stanza in Part I is repeated at the very end of the setting, and the italicised lines in Part III are sung by a soprano solo (Cecilia).

Auden's first draft Part III (with two additional stanzas, 'Dear daughter of our double misery' and 'Descend into your night of tribulation') was intended to serve as Part I, and the original Part III ('Open your gates, discover us, Daughter of Song: O, comprehend our defeat') was abandoned. According to Miller, pp. 60–1, 'Shepherd's Carol' ('O lift your little pinkie') was originally one of these songs. It was certainly at one stage part of 'For the Time Being', and it seems unlikely, in view of the drafts which do survive, that Miller can be right here. Full details of Auden's original text are given by Edward Mendelson in *On Mahler and Britten*, ed. Philip Reed, p. 186.

Part I begins with an Edith Sitwell touch, and continues with curious hints of bawdy, Auden told Spears that this was the same Anglo-Irish metre that he was to use in the brothel chorus in *The Rake's Progress*, I.ii: an example of it is 'The Groves of Blarney', which Auden had included in the *Oxford Book of Light Verse*. Dryden's 'Alexander's Feast' had shown the power of the different modes to evoke different emotions in the listener. Aphrodite is appropriate here because Cecilia's vows of celibacy ('like a black swan') suggest that the kind of music she was known for (as supposed inventor of the organ, she was proclaimed the patroness of church music in 1584) is a sublimation of the erotic. In Auden's draft of the new Part I (15 July 1940), in stanza 2 it is 'athletic Apollo in his rocky hollow' who responds, not the angels. But this must have seemed a shade too vulgar. The phrase 'eased their pain' is an echo of Dryden (Chloe does so for Amyntas in the 'Rondelay' from *Examen Poeticum*, in *The Poems of John Dryden*, ed. James Kinsley, 1958, II.844).

After the invocation to Cecilia, Part II introduces the voice of music itself – terse, immediate, riddling, whispering – which, in the first two stanzas, contrasts its nature with that of man, and, in the following two, says that it is a product of human life at the point where emotion has exhausted any possibility of action. Thus (as Part III goes on to show) it is able to fix and transform the emotions into something like their pure state, whereas in real life man is pathetically unconcerned about the civilisation he is destroying ('ruined languages') because that civilisation is a bizarre and irresponsible product of his fallen nature. It is like something thrown up by biological freak, a reasoning animal ('Impetuous child with the tremendous brain'). Cecilia's words, however, show great tenderness for the mortals who pray to her. They are like children who, with charm, gaiety and resilience, can learn to defy causal necessity by learning to love ('O wear your tribulation like a rose'). The last stanza creates a complex dialogue of soloist and chorus in a passage imitative, in Dryden's fashion, of various musical instruments. These instruments, in turn, symbolise the determined transformation of the emotions of Sorrow, Hope and Dread that were introduced at the beginning of the section.

Jumbled in the common box

January 1941; 'Song', *Nation*, 29 March 1941; CP45, p. 206; CSP, p. 235; 'Doomsday Song', SP58, p. 89; CSP66, p. 161; 'Domesday Song', SP68, p. 43; CP, p. 269.

This apocalyptic 'Domesday Song' hinges in its opening stanza upon one of the riddling triads that Auden was fond of (there are well-known examples in 'A Misunderstanding' and 'At the Grave of Henry James', for example). 'Orchid, swan and Caesar' are possibly intended to represent the realms of love, art and politics. 'Orchid' derives from Greek ορχις, a testicle (perhaps Auden remembered Pound's *Hugh Selwyn Mauberley*, 'Mauberley', II, where it is glossed as 'mandate | of Eros'). In draft, these lines were originally 'At the bottom of winter | Soil and swan and Caesar lie.' Whatever the intended categorisation, the meaning seems to be that human life in all its temporal individuation cannot escape from the chaos that lies outside time. There will be no order, only a debasement of thought and language and a reassertion of the crudely instinctual. The poem creates a sinister calm before a pointless disorder represented by the final tongue-twister. A mechanical virtuoso rhyming accentuates the blankness of this poem.

My second thoughts condemn

September 1942; CP45, p. 215; CSP, p. 245; CSP66, p. 163; CP, p. 271.

This lyric (which has never been given a title) juggles with the demands of desire and the claims of romantic love. The notion in the first stanza ('What right have I to swear | Even at one a.m. | To love you till I die?') is the germ of the more developed idea in 'Dichtung und Wahrheit' (' "I will love You for ever", swears the poet. I find this easy to swear too. *I will love You at 4.15 p.m. next Tuesday:* is that still as easy?'). The point here is that such an extravagant gesture belongs very much to the world of time in which it may be forgiven for being *Dichtung* (poetry) and not *Wahrheit* (truth), but that outside time the Truth sits in continual judgement ('All flesh is grass, and all the goodliness thereof is as the flower of the field . . . but the word of our God shall stand for ever', Isaiah xl) and no one 'on earth' (literally) can really measure the consequences.

Though determined Nature can

July 1941; CP45, p. 231; CSP, p. 260; CSP66, p. 162; CP, p. 270.

This lyric, written in the middle of Auden's 'crisis', when Kallman was asserting his sexual independence and Auden felt murderous (see Carpenter, Part II, chapter 3), objectifies the selfishness of Eros into the Accuser, the One whose name is Legion, the Devil. 'The Accuser' appears in the Zohar (IV.63), and is the Devil in his role as tempter (see also *The Age of Anxiety*, CP, p. 480). The repeated qualifications of the poem ('Though . . .') make this summoning involuntary, but it is none the less real, and reflects the dual and vulnerably betraying nature of passion.

Nones

Auden's first post-war collection of shorter poems was published in 1951 in the US, and in the following year in England. It was appropriately dedicated to Reinhold and Ursula Niebuhr, for it was to Mrs Niebuhr that he had first applied for information about the canonical hours, which he wished to make the framework of a sequence of poems, two of which are included in the collection and one of which gives it its title. She was the recipient of much comment from Auden about the problems of Christianity and writing, and the dedication (reprinted in CSP66, p. 318 and CP, p. 621) similarly looks at the relationship between poetry and truth. Auden seems to use the word 'glory' here to indicate an authentic vision or revelation (cf. ' "The Truest Poetry Is the Most Feigning" ', line 67). The phrase 'tears reserve' is verb + noun, not noun + verb, and the glory is 'left' in order to make poetry of it. Auden complains, however, that the language has been debased and that 'the grand old manner' will no longer do. Now the only civil style to have survived is 'the wry, the sotto-voce, | Ironic and monochrome'. A possible source of the final lines of the dedication is E. M. Forster's essay on T. S. Eliot in *Abinger Harvest* (1936), p. 88 ('For what, in that world of gigantic horror, was tolerable except the slighter gestures of dissent?'). The implied apologia here explains much in Auden's later conversational manner, even though 'the old grand manner' is not always abandoned. Auden put his feelings plainly in the *Kenyon Review*, Winter 1964: 'In so much "serious" poetry, poetry, that is to say, which is neither pure playful song nor comic, I find an element of "theatre", of exaggerated gesture and fuss, of indifference to the naked truth, which, as I get older, increasingly revolts me. This element is mercifully absent from what is conventionally called good prose.' (The point is put in Christian terms in the epigraph to Part II of *Homage to Clio*.)

Simultaneously, as soundlessly

'Prime' was reprinted in its eventual place in the sequence 'Horae Canonicae' in *The Shield of Achilles*, and is discussed on p. 458.

If it form the one landscape that we the inconstant ones

May 1948; 'In Praise of Limestone', *Horizon*, July 1948; N, p. 11; SP58, p. 129; CSP66, p. 238; CP, p. 540.

'In Praise of Limestone' was the first poem that Auden wrote in Italy. He had returned to the family cottage in the Lake District in April, and then in the following month visited Italy for the first time. In his Freud Lecture of 1971 he introduced it as one of a series of poems about the lead-mining world of his childhood:

> The lead-mines, of course, could not come in, because there aren't any in Florence, but the limestone landscape was useful to me as a connecting link between two utterly different cultures, the northern protestant guilt culture I grew up in, and the shame culture of the Mediterranean countries, which I was now experiencing for the first time.

The poem relies to an extent upon this contrast, and upon others, but they are not clearly systematised. The 'we' / 'they' of the poem may, then, be successively (a) human beings v. animals (i.e. 'the inconstant ones' versus the 'beasts who repeat themselves'); (b) artists v. non-artists (i.e. the child v. his rival brothers, in Auden's theory of art this rivalry being a wish to please the *Urmutter*); (c) English v. Italians (with their different conceptions of God); (d) valley-dwellers v. mountain-dwellers and nomads; (d) the lovers (Auden and Kallman) v. the seekers of 'immoderate soils'; and (e) human beings v. statues.

Thus the poem's power comes from the suggestive and shifting variety of its propositions. It is not merely a Horatian tribute to an Italian landscape which embodies Auden's particular Eden, where an expeditious control of stone and water has so naturally developed into the creation of statues and fountains. It is a statement of spiritual temptations, and of the eternal opposition between those who recognise the demanding reality of sin and death, and those who feel that virtue and human happiness are within man's reach.

It is also a poem which ultimately addresses Kallman and makes him an implied centre of attention. In lines 12–13 of the *Nones* version, 'the nude young male . . . lounges | Against a rock displaying his dildo', making him appositely both a notably sexual object (a dildo is a false penis in permanent erection) and a successful agent of art (since the dildo is a surrogate, as the fountains and statues are, and the *Urmutter* is to be charmed not by sex, but by art). The dildo is a symbol of the Freudian sublimation of sex into art: just as the obscene object itself turns into part of the babbled refrain of amorous Renaissance poetry, so the image of the nude young male 'is' not only Kallman but one of the innocent athletes (in fact a statue) which the poem sublimates at its conclusion when they are seen as being like the blessed, 'having nothing to hide'. (In the 1966 text this figure has become a 'flirtatious male who lounges . . . in the sunlight', more like an Ischian rent-boy than the model of a faultless love. For further discussion of the poem and of the sexual significance of the limestone landscape, see my 1992 Kenneth Allott Memorial Lecture, 'Pleasing Ma: The poetry of W. H. Auden.)

At the heart of the poem is praise of moderation. Writing to Elizabeth Mayer on 8 May 1948, Auden claimed that the poem's theme 'is that rock creates the only truly human landscape, i.e. when politics, art etc. remain on a modest ungrandiose scale. What awful ideas have been suggested to the human mind by huge plains and gigantic mountains!' The poet is homesick for the limestone landscape because it suggests exactly what can no longer be really believed in: the benign immediacy of nature and the self-sufficiency of a people who can control their environment and relate their appetites to their ultimate well-being. In the Berg draft, 'the band of rivals' at line 21 was originally 'their rivalry', linking the Italians more closely with the competitive siblings of the previous lines: the Florentine landscape is a natural paradigm of art. The MS draft also helps to explain the odd 'nomad's comb' at line 35, since it contrasts the 'male nude at rest, the temple on the promontory' with 'the portable objects of migrants, bracelets, seals, combs | infinity through a lattice'. (Compare 'Look not at sky through the forelegs of mares' in 'A Happy New Year', Part I, stanza 5. This seems to be a superstition, and the fact that Auden had recently reused it, as one of Emble's dangerous charms to bring Rosetta's spirit into his power, in *The Age of Anxiety*, CP, p. 520, gives it some force as a similar 'unsafe' perspective.) The artefacts of the nomad are, Auden implies in these and the following lines 39–43, simply of a different order even to bad art, which only 'the best and worst of us' (the absolutists) are free of the temptation to produce.

It is to these that Auden now turns his attention at lines 43 to 59, a celebrated passage of *paysage moralisé* which describes these exiles in terms of temptations other than those of art. The granite wastes lure putative saints; clays and gravels lure the seekers of power (an allusion here to Goebbels: 'If we are defeated, we shall slam the doors of history behind us'); the sea lures the nihilists. There was a serious demographic theory behind these metaphors. André Siegfried, in his *Tableau politique de l'ouest de France* (1913), analysed French voters according to types of soil. In particular, Siegfried contrasted the independent and democratic limestone plains with the feudal granite Bocage and the isolation, conservatism and priestly vocation that such rocky soil engenders: 'Calcaire ou granit, voilá la grande distinction à faire' (p. 10). Auden would have at least come across such ideas in books like Morris Bishop's *Pascal,* e.g.: 'The French like to ascribe the traditional character of the Auvergnats, shrewd, obstinate, miserly, fanatical, to the volcanic granite of their home . . . They burn with the inward flame of martyrs' (p. 2). The paradox in Auden's passage here is that although these voices cumulatively represent the forces of arrogant spiritual absolutism, they do also represent the alternative urge in man to face the unknown and to face death.

And in the difficult passage from line 60 onwards, Auden acknowledges that the Italian limestone is 'not the sweet home that it looks', even though as a 'backward and dilapidated' haven of art it can still mount a challenge to the absolutists, represented here by the modern poet and scientist. When Auden says 'it disturbs our rights', he presumably means that rights belong to the world of philosophical calculation rather than to the natural order. The sexual teasing of the scientist is one reminder of what more immediately concerns us in nature than astrophysics (Robert Craft, *Stravinsky: Chronicle of a friendship 1948–1971,* 1972, p. 25, has an anecdote of Auden himself pursued in Naples by a gang of *gamins*) and the poet is disturbed by the statues because pantheism actively links the world and the human mind in the way that his 'earnest habit' does not. This secular poet who calls 'the sun the sun, his mind Puzzle' is, although the poem does not say so, Wallace Stevens, about whom Auden had written a poem variously called 'Art History' or 'Miss God on Mr Stevens' from which the phrase is drawn: 'Dear, O dear. More heresy to muzzle. | No sooner have we buried in peace | The flightier divinities of Greece, | Than up there pops the barbarian with | An antimythological myth, | Calling the sun, the sun, | His mind "Puzzle" '. This text is from a letter to Ursula Niebuhr, 10 July 1947. Auden also wrote out a version in a copy of Stevens's *Transport to Summer.*

See 'Notes towards a Supreme Fiction' in that volume: 'The sun I Must bear no name, gold flourisher, but he I In the difficulty of what it is to be.' Stevens himself called 'The Comedian as the Letter C' an antimythological poem (*Letters*, ed. Holly Stevens, p. 778).

Thus it is that the landscape reminds us of the 'worldly duty' of the common life in which art and belief are, as Auden believed they must be, joined. Even in a context of sin and death and their hoped-for conquest ('a faultless love I Or the life to come') this worldly duty remains as a simple token of the innocence that attracted Auden in the first place. The poem develops on a number of levels. Even the streams themselves, at first chuckling through 'a secret system' of 'caves and conduits' (another phrase quarried from Anthony Collett, *The Changing Face of England*, p. 138) as though they were hiding from the visitor their real intention, become by the end 'the murmur I Of underground streams', as though that secret had been won and they shared with Kallman the poet's endearments ('My dear', 'dear'). It begins to take its place not as an ode, after all, but as a kind of love poem: the lovers explore a habitat conducive to their attempt to transcend time. The poet has shared his fear of losing time (lines 77ff) and it is this that gives the relevant lines their convincing personal tone as a domestic version of Common Prayer. Transcendence is assisted by music, which unlike sex 'can be made anywhere, is invisible, I And does not smell'. And resurrection itself is mysteriously premissed by the limestone, the maternal landscape become holy and perfected.

Sometimes we see astonishingly clearly

April 1949; 'One Circumlocution', *Third Hour*, 1951; N, p. 14; SP58, p. 132; CSP66, p. 322; CP, p. 626.

Since not only the subject of this poem is circumlocution, but its technique also, it is difficult in the manner of some other poems of Auden's like 'The Song' and 'Objects' (adjacent in later collections, but written at least half a dozen years later). The poems share a concern with definitions, and with linguistic problems, and the influence of Empson is apparent (not least in use of flat expository tercets with enclosed rhymes). There is a kind of careless oddity and cramped awkwardness of style which seems intended to match the puzzle of defining. In 'One Circumlocution' the problem appears to be that the lucid perception of a truth simply cannot be expressed with equal lucidity, since the result will seem simply 'blank'. The argued abstraction of language in the first three stanzas is itself an example of periphrasis, and the process of circumlocution can be seen in the Berg drafts. For example, in line 2 'out-there-when' (later 'out-there-now') was originally 'times out there' and in line 3 'here-for' was originally 'after'. The 'once-for-all' in line 9 is borrowed from Rosenstock-Huessy and is the Christian conception of eternity in the moment. Unlike the pagan world of valueless cyclical change, Christianity has shown 'how man can be eternal in the moment, how he can act *once for all*' (Rosenstock and Wittig, *Das Alter der Kirche*, 1927, I, 108, quoted in *The Christian Future*, 1947, p. 72). The 'compromise' of line 6 is the difficult accommodation of our sensed uniqueness (as Christian souls) with the knowledge that human experiences are shared (the pagan view). The stanzas appear to protest that language can never thus be fully true to feeling-states. In the next two stanzas the poet's role ('Tell . . .'; 'Speak well . . .') easily brings 'power' and 'wonder', but avoids the truth by fable and evasion in dealing with love in terms of resurrection or ghosts. The example in the final two stanzas is the more usual one of poetic ways of dressing up what would otherwise be the least illuminating of claims: 'I love you.' Some of these problems were later to be addressed in 'Dichtung und Wahrheit'.

As I listened from a beach-chair in the shade

?June 1950; 'Their Lonely Betters', N, p. 15; SP58, p. 133; CSP66, p. 280; CP, p. 583.

The generalisations here about man and nature are subdued and quasi-Frostian (and see the allusion in the final line to the antepenultimate line of Frost's 'Stopping by Woods on a Snowy Evening': human language has given us a moral responsibility beyond the immediacies and obliviousness of either bird-song or dark woods). The poem contains a personal rebuke: speech provides us with an awareness of time and with the possibility of lying, so that love (which is so instinctive and helpless in the case of the robin or the flowers) is often a matter of deceit and frustration. Thus the longing for letters implies a particular promise in the final stanza. The feeling is beautifully and stoically understated.

On and on and on

June 1947; 'Serenade', *Atlantic*, November 1947, and in *Phoenix Quarterly*, 1948; N, p. 16; CSP66, p. 164; CP, p. 272.

This poem was sent to Rhoda Jaffe, with whom Auden had an affair between 1945 and 1947. It exonerates the unashamed demands of the libido with a pleasantly weighted humility (compare Farnan, p. 119: 'Wystan suggested to Rhoda they have an affair. It was presented just like that: "I think we ought to have an affair" '). The 'shouts' or 'salute' of the first stanza (the aggression of the waterfall, the comic Dogberry nature of man) give place to the 'asks neighbourhood' of the final stanza. Since the poem is more or less a sexual invitation ('my embodied love'), the poetic sleight of hand in the culminating gentleness has a sly metaphysical conviction. In draft, the line was originally 'Assigns myself to you' (much more demanding, of course). Katherine Bucknell has pointed to a possible borrowing from Wordsworth's 'To a Highland Girl', lines 56–8: 'I would have | Some claim upon thee, if I could, | Though but of common neighbourhood.' For the 'mischief' of waterfalls, compare 'Alone' (discussed on p. 392).

Deftly, admiral, cast your fly

June 1948; 'Song', *Horizon*, November 1948, and *Voices*, Spring 1949; N, p. 17; SP58, p. 134; CSP66, p. 271; CP, p. 573.

This is a finely anecdotal song about the sins of the fathers visited on the children, using some of the properties of Auden's Roman analogy. The admiral and ambassador, retired functionaries of the Empire, are powerless to stop the unwanted love-affair between their offspring, just as they have been powerless to prevent the destruction of the fleets or the invasion of the Chateaux by 'unshaven horsemen'. In a draft, 'between your properties' was originally 'outside your memories': the change turns mere inculpability into a more precisely healing relationship (suggesting an exoneration of both belligerence and appeasement?) which will all the more devastatingly be put to the attentions of the avenging Erinyes. The 'slow deep hover' is borrowed from Anthony Collett, *The Changing Face of England*, p. 87.

In an upper room at midnight

May 1948; 'The Love Feast', N, p. 18; CSP66, p. 310; CP, p. 613.

This poem, concerned with the erotic possibilities of a late-night party, has disturbed some critics with its final flat, unrecalcitrant use of St Augustine's 'Make me chaste, Lord, but not yet' (*Confessions*, viii, 16). In fact, the religious imagery pervades the poem (especially in the opening reference to the 'upper room' of Mark XIV.15, in the notion of the new arrivals as catechumens, or candidates for baptism, in the allusion in stanza 4 to Dante's 'L'amor che move il sole e l'altre stelle', appropriate in a poem written in Florence, and a further quotation from Augustine in stanza 6) and seems plainly intended by Auden as an assertion of the validity of Eros. The poem went under other titles in draft ('Saturday Night', and 'Was it Gay?'). The published title is significantly an allusion to the *agape* or love-feast of the early Christians, which Auden had picked up from Gerald Heard (*The Social Substance of Religion*, 1931, chapter ix). In *Theology*, November 1950, p. 412, Auden complained: 'In some circles recently there has been a tendency to see the notion of love as eros or desire for getting and the notion of love as agape or free-giving as incompatible opposites and to identify them with Paganism and Christianity respectively. Such a view seems to me a revival of the Manichean heresy which denies the goodness of the natural order.'

Let out where two fears intersect, a point selected

1950; 'Air Port', N, p. 19; 'In Transit', CSP, p. 237; CP, p. 539.

With its gentle Horatian tone and lulling internal rhyming, this is one of the least tense of Auden's poems about border or limbos. Having before the war made a significant symbolic use of flying in his poetry, yet having mostly travelled even great distances by sea, now the actuality of air-travel prompts a rather different perspective. This poem shows man as only a wishful fugitive from his environment in place or time. The two fears may be both the two flights that the airport connects, and the common concern for safety of the general staffs and engineers: in both cases the uneasiness of post-war travel is economically sketched in. With the unreality of the airport waiting-room, more of a Purgatory than a community ('some class of souls', stanza 5), Auden contrasts the reality of those places that have meaning because life is lived there, and that are, as it were, under the protection of a *deus loci*; places also where the choices and revelations of life are unquestionably present (an allusion in stanza 4 to Goethe's Italian journey). Again airborne, the poet sees spring's processes of renewal, and in a familiar image (the literal débâcle of a river, the breaking up of the spiritually constricting ice) forecasts the hope which real possession of even a congested surface can bring. This is the renewal of the will to live, pardon for 'the maculate cities'.

There is a time to admit how much the sword decides

June 1948; 'Ischia', *Botteghe Oscure*, Autumn 1948, and *Nation*, April 1950; N, p. 21; CSP66, p. 241; CP, p. 543.

This tribute to the Italian island where from 1948 Auden rented a house in which to spend each summer was written in response to an accusation from Brian Howard that he had no visual sense (Carpenter, p. 358). Its syllabic form (13/12/7/8) is adapted from the form of the Freud elegy and the 'Epilogue' to *The Double Man*, and seems particularly appropriate to the kind of local descriptive-meditative poem that this is. The change of heart for which one should be grateful (apart from St Francis) is the fact that the era of Mussolini is over (seen with rich irony in the first stanza as the Leader of Eliot's 'Triumphal March'). Stanza 5: Parthenopea: Parthenope was the siren who threw herself into the sea for love of Ulysses and was cast up in the bay of Naples. Stanza 8: Epomeo is Ischia's highest mountain, an extinct volcano. Stanza 16: Restituta (d. AD 284) is the patron saint of Ischia's Lake Ameno. The poem expresses the *otium* of Auden's Mediterranean period with an agreeably relaxed humour, the only darkening of the scene being a donkey who 'breaks out into a choking wail | Of utter protest at what is the case' (i.e. the entire world, see Wittgenstein's *Tractatus*).

What there is as a surround to our figures

1948; 'Pleasure Island', *Commentary*, May 1949; N, p. 24; CSP66, p. 229; CP, p. 343.

'Pleasure Island' is more Cherry Grove than Ischia, though like 'Ischia' it owes something to Brian Howard (at Cherry Grove on Fire Island, part of Long Island, was a summer shack owned jointly by Auden and James and Tania Stern from the mid-1940s). During the leisurely course of the poem the amoral holiday island ('where nothing is wicked | But to be sorry or sick') distracts and saps the energy of visiting writers and becomes 'this | place of a skull', i.e. Golgotha, the place of crucifixion. Nemesis arrives with appropriate insidiousness as a kind of Mephistophelean highwayman confronting 'Miss Lovely' and asking for 'her money *and* her life' (my emphasis). ('We must love one another or die' indeed, but love cannot be bought.) 'Miss Lovely' is surely a relative of Howard's 'Mr Pleasure' in his poem 'Gone to Report' (*Horizon*, 1940; see also Auden's later poem 'Amor Loci').

Having finished the Blue-plate Special

July 1947; 'In Schrafft's', *New Yorker*, 12 February 1949; N, p. 27; CSP66, p. 220; CP, p. 334.

The 'globular furore' which the eupeptic smile of the anonymous lady in the restaurant is blandly ignoring might well be said to be about food, the international haves and have-nots. But this is not a foretaste of Auden's Brechtian tag 'Grub first, then ethics', for in a mysterious way the lady's smile is explicitly beatific: this is a poem about innocence, an apotheosis of the mundane, like Salinger's fat woman who is Jesus Christ. It also perhaps glances at the epicure's assurance in Sydney Smith's 'Recipe for a Salad' ('Fate cannot harm me, – I have dined today'). Auden used to claim that he was too much of the Thinking Type and too short-sighted to write topographical poems in Betjeman's manner. In his introduction to Betjeman's *Slick but not Streamlined* (1947) is a long list of such poems that he would like to write if he could, including one on 'Schrafft's Blue Plate Special'. The Berg draft has a cancelled penultimate stanza which unnecessarily disposes of the obvious reasons for her 'rapt unsocial look' ('To be planning a splendid wedding | Or thinking of writing a book | Hardly fitted that face').

The piers are pummelled by the waves

January 1947; 'The Fall of Rome', *Horizon*, April 1947, and *Nation*, 14 June 1947; N. p. 28; SP58, p. 138; CSP66, p. 218; CP, p. 332.

'The Fall of Rome' was supposedly produced in response to a challenge from its dedicatee, Cyril Connolly, to write a poem that would make him cry (see *The Sunday Times*, 2 March 1952, p. 3). Connolly (editor of *Horizon*, where the poem first appeared) was himself a great prophet of doom, and also elaborated the notion of the 'imaginary friend' (stanza 3) in *Enemies of Promise*. The comic world of surrealistic decadence and bureaucracy is familiar from earlier Auden, but the analogy between the Fall of Rome and the decline of modern civilisation was to become characteristic of his post-war period, and here the strange blend of classical and contemporary detail in the unlikely stanza of *In Memoriam* (Auden was editing Tennyson) carries extraordinary conviction, a memorable nursery rhyme for historians.

The first two stanzas recall the 'Journal of an Airman' in *The Orators*. The outlaws in stanza 1 seem to be the only reference to persecuted Christians (the seven sleepers of Ephesus resorted to a cave). The pursuit of the Fisc in stanza 2 may have been suggested by Charles Cochrane, *Christianity and Classical Culture* (1944 edn, p. 182). Stanza 4: Auden was inclined to prefer the endomorphic type to either the ectomorphic ('Cerebrotonic Cato') or the mesomorphic ('muscle-bound Marines'). The typology is from W. H. Sheldon. The 'Little birds' in stanza 6 recall Lewis Carroll's 'Little birds' in *Sylvie and Bruno Concluded* (included by Auden in his *Oxford Book of Light Verse*, p. 458).The beautiful final stanza lifts the poem out of its atmosphere of absurd apocalypse to suggest the mysterious inevitability of natural processes which take no account of human power. There is some question about historical cause and effect here. W. P. Nicolet (*Explicator*, November 1972) said that Auden confirmed that the reindeer were on the move 'because of the shifting migration patterns of the northern peoples' which will bring Rome into conflict with Germanic tribes. This does not quite fit with Auden's earlier remarks on the subject in his 1966 article 'The Fall of Rome': 'The decline of the Roman Empire has been attributed to many causes: defects in the economy, a falling birth-rate, the dessication of the grasslands in Asia which set the barbarians in motion, Christianity, etc.' (*Auden Studies* 3, p. 126). The common cause of the movement of both barbarians and reindeer was this dessication. The absolute phrase 'altogether elsewhere' means therefore not only 'far from the Roman Empire', but 'in the realm of Nature rather than that of History'. The Germanic threat goes unmentioned in the poem, so that the reindeer take on an almost epiphanic presence.

The Emperor's favourite concubine

May 1948; 'Music Ho', N, p. 29; CSP66, p. 271; CP, p. 574.

The theme of the Fall of Rome is continued in this poem about Christianity as it appears to the Romans. The doom of the Empire (palace intrigue, mutiny in the provinces and apocalyptic signs) seems to its inhabitants merely boring: it is a story they have heard before. In the 'Transformation Scene' (i.e. the Incarnation: the metaphor is of a pantomime) the sense of life as a second-rate performance continues; the point is parallel to that of Caliban's description of our imperfect vision of the perfect life as being like 'the greatest grandest opera rendered by a very provincial touring company indeed' ('The Sea and the Mirror', CP, p. 443). The Roman understanding of a Christian dispensation in which God commands us to love one another reduces it simply to a crude command to 'enemies to screw'.

Their learned kings bent down to chat with frogs

January 1947; 'Nursery Rhyme', *Mademoiselle*, October 1947; N, p. 30; CSP66, p. 219; CP, p. 333.

'Nursery Rhyme' is simply an exercise in cheerfully sinister nonsense, elaborately linked by rhyme, phrase and refrain. Auden found out about its Portuguese form from Theodore Spencer. It is called a *cantiga*, and is based upon two sets of rhyme vowels, structured as follows:

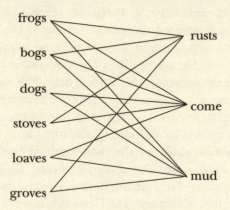

Its particular kind of suggestiveness would seem to owe something to Graves, but its nonsensical lineaments are apparent from the drafts (where, for example, line 3 was originally: 'The suburbs are shaken by the pilot's cry' and line 9 'Orphans are making soldiers/witches out of mud') and explication is relatively pointless.

In the bad old days it was not so bad

June 1948; 'The Managers', *Horizon*, November 1948 and *Reporter*, 10 May 1949; SP58, p. 139; CSP66, p. 300; CP, p. 603.

'The Managers' contrasts with the rulers of the past the grey faceless rulers of the present, who inhabit offices rather than palaces and whose decisions involve calculated risk rather than arbitrary authority. They are children of Apollo (cf. 'Under Which Lyre') to whom the exercise of power is a compulsion like a game, which is its own reward. Thus they are not to be pitied. The poem drifts forward on its Skaldic rhyming with an extemporising air which none the less accumulates an analytical concern.

The eyes of the crow and the eye of the camera open

June 1949; 'Memorial for the City', *Horizon*, November 1949; N, p. 34; Part III reprinted as 'Barbed Wire' in SP58, p. 142; CSP66, p. 289; CP, p. 591.

A dedication to the memory of Charles Williams was added to the text in the 1966 *Collected Shorter Poems*. Williams, who had died in April 1945, a month before the collapse of Nazi Germany, was a significant influence on Auden, and the source of some of the ideas and techniques in the poem. However, the influence is equally strong of Eugen Rosenstock-Huessy's *Out of Revolution: Autobiography of Western Man* (1939), an unusual and now forgotten effort to make *weltgeschichtisch* sense of revolutionary moments in history, and also to an extent his *The Christian Future or the Modern Mind Outrun* (1947).

The City is both the Christian community and Europe: Auden maintains a multiple focus throughout the poem. His Memorial is consciously written in the years after Auschwitz, but his concern is also to trace the history of Christendom and its significance to the Christian believer. This significance, inevitably based on the redemption of the soul through suffering, enforces an acceptance of the idea of both body and community. The epigraph from Dame Julian of Norwich underlines this by showing that the kingdom of God is not something wholly removed from the real world: '*In the self-same point that our soul is made sensual, in the self-same point is the City of God ordained to him from without beginning.*' This quotation, immensely useful to a Christian poet who was always suspicious of the Manichaean heresy, had already been used by Williams in *The Descent of the Dove* (p. 224), with the comment that natural justice is a necessary preliminary to all charity. When justice has completely broken down, as in war, then despair seems inevitable.

Part I argues against such despair, even though its perspectives are insistently governed by the remorseless objectivity of the observing crow and camera (the text in the 1966 *Collected Shorter Poems* emphasises this structure by introducing a white line before the third appearance of the pair at line 24). In the first section, the natural world observed by crow and camera is described as Homer's world, a bleak place where the activities of human beings, and even of the gods, remain marginal to the large unconcerned processes of Nature ('She'). In the second section, the incidents of war have no normative significance to the crow or camera. If Auden's crow has a touch of 'The Twa Corbies', his view of photography (rather different from the view he held before the war in poems such as 'Letter to William Coldstream') has been influenced by Rosenstock-Huessy, who explicitly discussed films of wartime events which, he claimed, 'do not reveal their whole significance to the camera. We supply the moral evaluation' (*The Christian Future*, p. 55). In a kind of parody of the scenario of 'Spain 1937', History, as 'a whistling messenger', simply takes these meaningless moments and disappears with them into a defile. In the third section, crow and camera are as steady and candid as they can be, but are limited by their temporal viewpoint. 'The crime of life is not time' returns to the insisted contrast throughout Part I that the Christian world is different from the classical world in respect of its attitudes to time: 'Homer's world' (line 12), 'the post-Vergilian City' (line 27) and 'our grief is not Greek' (line 30) all underline the Huessyan idea that pagan histories begin *within* time, so picturing life as a decline, or as a cycle. Hellenism postulated two distinct types of human excellence, the heroic and the civic: 'the problem, indeed, was to reconcile the two' (Charles Cochrane, *Christianity and Classical Culture*, 1944 edn, p. 86). Also from Cochrane comes the discussion of the Pax Augusta (pp. 27ff) and of the new starting-point after Athanasius when history became an account of human freedom (pp. 376–8) that helped Auden to define the limitations of the Vergilian City. In this way, in the very shadow of the crematorium, Auden insists that 'our hurt is not a desertion', for it is felt in the 'self-same point' in which the City of God had been ordained to us, at the intersection of the sensual and the eternal.

In Part II of the poem (where there is a much greater use of the internal rhyming borrowed from Williams) Auden provides an adroit potted history of Christendom based to an extent on the revolutions expounded by Rosenstock-Huessy in *Out of Revolution*. He begins by describing the Papal Revolution of 1075 and the consequential precarious equilibrium of power between Pope Gregory VII and the Holy Roman Emperor, each, according to medieval theory, one half of the indivisible God. Thus is introduced the principle of dualism into the political world (Auden's 'yes and no' is an allusion to Abelard's *Sic et Non*, the treatise which inaugurated the dialectical methods of Scholasticism). Behind the simple unifying power of a secular and temporal authority ('Fear of the stranger was lost on the way to the shrine') lies the blueprint of a Christian policy intended to prevent the rise of purely secular empires. Auden would have understood from Rosenstock-Huessy the seminal importance of the Gregorian revolution against the Emperor (for 'Pope Gregory whispered his name' see his discussion of the 'Dictatus Papae' and Gregory's claim '*unicum nomen est papae*' in *Out of Revolution*, pp. 537ff). More important is the comfortable symbolism of medieval life in matters of religion: the 'double meaning' that divided authority represented becomes in the second stanza a natural habit in daily life in the sense that the spiritual life more and more came to be embodied in the secular and the representational ('limbs became hymns' as tangible images of the supposed miraculous cure; aggression was worked out in the crusading spirit; and astrology expressed the fatalism of an anthropocentric universe).

In the third stanza this is developed into a description of the praiseworthy attempts to establish 'the Sane City', where a supranational network of letters and travel ('Scribes and innkeepers') combined with the co-operation required for the Crusades and with the rationalisation of dogma (a reference in lines 3–4 to the Nicaean Council) are aspects of that urge for order which may be found in the treatment of landscape in religious painting after 1300 (see Rosenstock-Huessy, p. 583: 'The Madonna, the fixed visual centre of the divine service in the church, is framed by the political vision of the new city-state: the Landscape'). But this kind of control of the 'dry rocks' is seen in the following stanza as producing the reaction of the Reformation (Rosenstock-Huessy's Lutheran Revolution of 1517); the dry rocks, like Luther's 'sandy province', clearly represent the human sense of sin, which is not ultimately appeased by 'the machine that so smoothly forgave and saved | If paid'. The mechanical indulgence could not bridge the 'grinning gap' between man and God which Luther perceived. The Sane City had become the Sinful City, and 'her conclusions were to include all doubt' (all this Auden had expounded in greater detail in 'New Year Letter'; for the 'grinning gap' of Hell, see 'New Year Letter', line 1671).

The fifth stanza (where the internal rhyming steps up significantly) describes the ascendancy of art in the Renaissance; the sixth, the growth of science ('Nature was put to the Question') and a polite culture. This is Rosenstock-Huessy's Industrial Revolution of 1776. In the seventh stanza, secularism is taken to its extreme in the ideals of the 'Rational City', with its egalitarianism and utilitarianism. This is the French Revolution of 1789. The shift to Romanticism is cleverly done here, as 'her pallid affected heroes | Began their hectic question for the prelapsarian man' (a reference to the idealistic Godwinism of Shelley). The remainder of Part II describes the religious exploration of the Romantic tradition in terms of the sea-voyage and its disasters, a device familiar in Auden's thinking (cf. stanza 6 of 'Paysage Moralisé'). It is clear that he had in mind the ideas that he was expounding in his Page-Barbour Lectures (given at the University of Virginia in 1949, and published as *The Enchafèd Flood*).

Part III returns to the present, to the bombed landscape of the 'Abolished City'. Auden's descriptions owe something to his experiences as a Research Analyst in the US Strategic Bombing Survey in Germany between May and August 1945. The omnipresent barbed wire is the human pride and will which destroys the community. The ultimate image of man ('behind the wire | Which is behind the mirror') is an expendable automaton, a creature of the flesh responsible for the wire and the ruins, reducible to a number and owing no allegiance to the weeping soul. The human clay is seen finally, despite Dame Julian, as still awaiting the City of God.

Part IV describes, in riddling terms, man's redeeming qualities of innocence and humility, ironically introduced at the end of the previous section as '*Our Weakness*'. Some of the definitions from myth and literature are difficult to explain, but the key is perhaps in line 8: Jesus's Fifth Word from the cross was 'I thirst' (John xix.28). This expression of bodily need, stressing Christ's humanity and suffering, is both a fulfilment of prophecy (Psalm lxix.21) and a confession of weakness. The riddle's answer is therefore 'the body', the common humanity that through confession, like the utterance of the riddle itself, may defy corruption, not merely endure it ('a stumbling-block to the stoics') because it recognises the claims of the spirit that are otherwise strange to it. Don Quixote proved that he was not enchanted in his cage by admitting (1.xlvii) his desire to relieve himself. The model of Christ finally provides a certain hope that the materialist City, now 'Metropolis', will be judged. The form of this section is based closely on Welsh riddling poems such as *Cerdd am Veib Llyr*, or the *Hanes Taliesin* riddle in Lady Charlotte Guest's translation. Its eighteen lines represent the thirteen consonants and five vowels of the Ogham alphabet. Auden would have found the inspiration for this structure in Robert Graves's *The White Goddess* (1946) where it is extensively discussed (see particularly pp. 59 and 81). This model underlines the role of language in the solution to the riddle:

it is not only our Weakness but our Weakness understanding and speaking Adam's cry of '*O Felix Culpa*' (his understanding of the Fortunate Fall) and being therefore quite unimpressed by the 'speeches' of Metropolis.

Yes, these are the dog-days, Fortunatus

1949; 'Under Sirius', *Horizon*, October 1949; N, p. 39; SP58, p. 143; CSP66, p. 243; CP, p. 545.

'Under Sirius' deals with a theme that Auden returned to again and again in this period: the cultural parallel between the decadence of the later Roman Empire and of the post-war western world. Here the traditional reign of madness under Sirius, the dog-star, is represented as a decline in the art of poetry: 'the Sibyl utters | A gush of table-chat.' The stream of inspiration is drying up, 'the baltering torrent | Shrunk to a soodling thread'. (Incidentally, 'soodling' has taken some hard knocks as an instance of Auden's nonce-words, though – *pace* G. S. Fraser – it is not one, having been used by John Clare. It is marvellously appropriate in context, with suggestions of 'doodling', 'soothing' and 'footling', all the marginal qualities of the kind of minor verse which Auden wishes to evoke.)

It is plain that Auden is in some sense talking about his own development here, as typifying the general cultural scene. The poem's address to 'Fortunatus' is reminiscent of the devices of Cavafy. Venantius Fortunatus (*c.* AD 530–600) was the last Latin poet of Gaul, a charming *bon viveur* and writer of occasional verses, who took holy orders in later life and became Bishop of Poitiers. His Hymn to the Holy Cross provided the epigraph to 'Horae Canonicae' (see p. 458). It therefore seems that Auden's spiritual interrogation is in some sense a self-interrogation, however good-humoured the tone. It is a qualification of the parallels in the later poem 'The Epigoni' and uses the comfortable diction and tone which its questions undermine in order to set up a tension between a Fortunatus making the most of his limitations and a Fortunatus whose glimpses of divine Grace make him fear divine Judgement. The 'pantocratic riddle' is the question which, like the Almighty (the Pantocrator of Byzantine art), lies behind everything: 'Who are you and why?' In many of Auden's poems of this decade it becomes a kind of Christian touchstone against which the Horace-Auden or the Fortunatus-Auden may set the classical virtues. Here Auden plainly condemns those who refuse their chance, but it seems that under Sirius (as in the desert of 'For the Time Being') the chances are not easy to see.

There were lead-mines here before the Romans

1949; 'Not in Baedeker', N, p. 41; CSP66, p. 249; CP, p. 551.

'Not in Baedeker' fills in the mining details omitted from the Italian landscape in 'In Praise of Limestone'. It begins with a beautiful if questionable expression of inevitability ('Is there a once that is not already?'), as Auden indulges in a travel-book excursion into his dream Eden (cf. *The Dyer's Hand*, p. 6). The topographical quotation is probably a cento. For the second sentence see Thomas Sopwith, *An Account of the Mining Districts of Alston Moor* (1833), p. 15 ('the wild and lofty rocks and hilly banks form a subject fit for the pencil of Salvator Rosa'). Oddly enough, 'worthy of . . . Salvator Rosa' occurs in James, *The American Scene*, p. 32. Some details (the cathedral roofs, for example) look back to 'Lead's the Best' (*Juvenilia*, p. 127) though the two poems are worlds apart, and nowhere so much as in the note in the later poem of 'the accidental' seen as a species of the historical: the imitation of a clergyman with a cleft palate becomes a curious symbol of a poet's genius wasted on triviality. One would guess that the Larkin of 'Church Going' had read this poem.

Sirocco brings the minor devils

1949; 'Cattivo Tempo', *Horizon*, October 1949; N, p. 43; CSP66, p. 245; CP, p. 547.

'Cattivo Tempo' dramatises the mental and moral depression brought by the Sirocco, a subject that had also been described by Graves in 'Sirocco at Deyá'. Auden found the names of the minor devils Nibbar and Tubervillus in Maximilian Rudwin, *The Devil in Legend and Literature* (1931), mistranscribing them (with thirteen other names) into a 1945–61 notebook (Berg). Thus Nibbar should really be 'Nybbas ('the great parodist' according to Johannes Wierus, see Rudwin, p. 80) and Tubervillus should be 'Tutevillus', the demon of church gossip (see Rudwin, pp. 84–5). Auden makes Nibbar and Tubervillus correspond to the twin aspect of the Sirocco. If the wind blows over sea, it is hot and moist and brings 'ga-ga and bêtise', the element of parody, or perhaps here self-parody (Rudwin, p. 81, says that to Nybbas is given 'management of dreams and visions on earth', appropriate to the poet). If the wind blows over land, it is desiccating and dusty and brings 'gossip and spite'. These become particular pitfalls for Auden, since either his poetry or his table-talk will suffer, and mere silence is no remedy. The light, successful touch of such a moral exercise seems itself a good enough remedy for the enervating wind and its insolent demons. See also 'The Cave of Making' for these 'lip-smacking | imps of mawk and hooey'. Auden made later use of Rudwin in the poem 'Merax & Mullin'.

Absence of heart – as in public buildings

?Spring 1950, 'The Chimeras', N, p. 45; CSP66, p.311; 'The Chimaeras', CP, p. 614.

The chimeras who mauled the troubled Romantics in Part II of 'Memorial for the City' now receive a poem of their own. The classical chimaera was a monster with a goat's body, a lion's head and a dragon's tail; in modern usage it is any wild fancy or unfounded idea. In the poem, Auden uses the term for any of those illusions that we have about life which ignore in particular the truth of the individual and the individual's needs, turning him or her into the notion of 'the public' (see stanza 1). This is closely linked in Auden's mind with the notion of 'the crowd' (cf. *The Dyer's Hand*, p. 63). In the grip of such illusions, Auden implies, individuals become literal nonentities. They are not alive. In an interesting discussion of the poem in *Quaderni d'Italianistica*, V, 1, 1984, pp. 97–109, James Weldon relates these non-beings to those of Dante's *Inferno*, Canto III. He suggests that Auden's final three stanzas contain an expanded translation of line 51 of the Dante ('let us not speak of them; but look, and pass' in the Carlyle–Okey–Wicksteed translation).

That we are always glad

1949; 'Secrets', *Ladies Home Journal*, August 1950; N, p. 46; CSP66, p. 318; CP, p. 622.

In 'Secrets', Auden exposes a love of secrets as a love either of the excitement of dramatic irony (stanza 1) or of social power (stanza 2). In either category, and in all the cases that Auden so entertainingly elaborates the categories with, the motive is unworthy: 'our commonest fault' is the Professor's own short-sightedness translated to the moral sphere, i.e. our lack of pity, pity being conquered by our desire for superiority. Ironically Auden goes on to define love in terms of sharing a secret, albeit, in the Christian context which the last lines rather disappointingly introduce, one which is as irrelevant to God as it is to the animals 'who . . . have nothing to hide'.

The Kingdom of Number is all boundaries

June 1950; 'Numbers and Faces', N, p. 47; SP58, p. 145; CSP66, p. 319; CP, p. 623.

'Numbers and Faces' begins with a sexual caveat (compare 'To ask if it is big or small proclaims one | The sort of lover who should stick to faces' with the equation of big pricks, big money and big bangs in 'Marginalia'). Lovers of big numbers are mild eccentrics: both concentrate on the inhuman. Love demands concern for a different kind of number, i.e. one which 'is always real' (the individual). None could be called good except Infinity (God), which is not really a number at all because boundless. The ideas in the poem owe something to Rudolf Kassner's *Zahl und Gesicht* (1919), which Auden had been reading at the time (see his introduction to *The Living Thoughts of Kierkegaard*, 1952). Rather fine cancelled passages in draft reveal the poem to have originally been addressed to a child (he did not, however, first meet his nieces until March 1951):

> Child, could you feel at home in a place
> Which is all boundary, at a time
> Which is always any o'clock. If so
> You are one of the lucky few to whom
> The Kingdom of Numbers belongs. Go there to live.

> Count on your fingers with eyes wide open[:]
> Small numbers end when you lose count.
> Count to yourself with eyes tight shut[:]
> Large numbers begin when you have to take breath.

What we know to be not possible

'Nones', the title poem, was reprinted in its eventual place in the sequence 'Horae Canonicae' in *The Shield of Achilles*, and is discussed on p. 460.

When, to disarm suspicious minds at lunch

1948; 'A Household', N, p. 52; SP58, p. 146; CSP66, p. 314; CP, p. 618.

Auden revealed to Monroe Spears in a letter of 11 May 1963 that this poem is a self-portrait (compare his 'Port and Nuts with the Eliots', *New Yorker*, xxv, 9, 23 April 1949, p. 85: 'Like most important writers, Mr T. S. Eliot is not a single figure but a household. This household has, I think, at least three permanent residents.' These residents Auden amusingly categorises as 'the archdeacon', 'a violent and passionate old peasant grandmother', and 'a young boy who likes to play slightly malicious practical jokes'). The poem 'A Household', composed along similar lines, was not the first such allegorical dramatisation he had made of his own personality: compare 'The month was April', where the elements are rather more complex, though more openly allegorical, than in the 'trinitarian analysis' of 1948. Here, unlike the earlier poem, the appetitive senses are for Auden more character-istically female (the mother whom he pretends is saintly but is in reality a slattern) while the poetic gift is male (the son he pretends is brave but is in reality a coward). Moreover, they are in league: the 'gift' betrays the 'senses' into self-indulgence and the senses betray the gift into hypocrisy. The third element of the trinity, the 'he' of the poem, is disguised as an executive (playing golf, signing mergers) and thus represents the will, who should be able to control the other members of the household but cannot. Despite the exaggeration appropriate to a guarded confession, and despite touching on two evidently sensitive issues of his middle years, authenticity and bohemianism, this poem is oddly less revealing than the earlier one.

All winter long the huge sad lady

1947; 'The Duet', *Kenyon Review*, Autumn 1947; N, p. 54, *Changing World*, May–July 1948, and the *Listener*, 24 November 1949; CSP66, p. 228; CP, p. 342.

This poem, with its contrasting outlook on love of the lady with her grand piano and the beggar with his barrel-organ, seems to make a point about the vulnerability of romantic idealism compared with the resilience of the erotic appetite (the beggar's 'one glass eye and one hickory leg' have a distinctly phallic air). It appears, in the riddling baroque manner of *The Age of Anxiety*, to propose that time can be redeemed only by full acceptance of all that it brings, and contrasts the lady's cloistered and melodramatic *lacrimae rerum* with the exposed and deprived beggar's joyful acceptance of all life's opportunities. But the point is not quite so simple as it appears, particularly if we take it as a poem in part reflecting on Auden's own heart-injury at the hands of Kallman. The beggar's song, indeed, relates to an unpublished contemporary poem 'The Picture' ('How many times between my latest sin') which precisely questions the sort of consolations he proposes. It shares two lines with the last stanza of 'The Picture' ('Why are we forced to fib, to cry: – "Oh good! | this is the life our daily life intends: | Light Industry is humming in the wood, | We know the time and where to find our friends" ') and while celebrating something not so clearly felt to be a lie, does so in the terms of distanced hopelessness found in Auden's earlier song about the six beggared cripples ('O for doors to be open'). That his optimism is as self-indulgent as the lady's pessimism is underlined by those blue birds in the penultimate line which look as though they have flown in from 'Zip-A-Dee-Doo-Dah' sung by James Boskett in Disney's *Song of the South*, and voted Best Song of 1947.

1 Behold the manly mesomorph
2 Give me a doctor partridge-plump

?June 1950; 'Footnotes to Dr Sheldon', N, p. 56; CSP66, p. 269; CP, p. 570.

Auden was happy to make use of W. H. Sheldon's work on human physiological types (*Varieties of Human Physique*, 1940), and had already expressed his own preference for the endomorphic type rather than the ectomorphic or (here particularly) mesomorphic types (see 'The Fall of Rome', stanza 4) and was still expressing it in 1962 (see *The Dyer's Hand*, p. 345). However, he came to have mixed feelings about the value of such work. He thought that Sheldon's case histories in the later work *Varieties of Delinquent Youth* (1949) showed 'a rather nice and intuitive man' but that 'the theoretical part is a classic case of pseudo-sciensy rubbish' (letter to Geoffrey Gorer, 23 May 1950). According to Miller (p. 162) the endomorphic doctor of Part 2 was Auden's own physician, David Protetch.

Ares at last has quit the field

1946; 'Under Which Lyre: A Reactionary Tract for the Times', *Harvard Alumni Bulletin*, 15 June 1946, and *Harper's Magazine*, June 1947; N, p. 57; CSP66, p. 221; CP, p. 335.

'Under Which Lyre' was written for the Harvard Chapter of the fraternity Phi Beta Kappa. The title alludes to Pistol's words to Shallow in 2 *Henry* IV, I.iii after the death of Henry IV: 'Under which King, Bezonian?' (Shakespeare uses 'Bezonian' here to mean 'rascal', but it also had the sense of 'a raw recruit', which Auden takes up in stanza 2; there is another reference to the play in stanza 11). In the post-war world, when Ares, the Greek god of war 'at last has quit the field', the perennial conflict between two of the other gods becomes once more of primary concern. The *Hymnus Homericus ad Mercuriam* is the source for Hermes' invention of the lyre on the first day of his life, and for his conflict with Apollo, his elder brother. Horace uses the phrase 'Mercuriales viri' as a term for *literati* in the Odes (II, 17. 29–30), though Hermes as the messenger of the gods is more usually associated with dreams and the underworld. Apollo was traditionally associated with codes of law and the inculcation of high moral and religious principles: Auden sees his 'lyre', therefore, as only an authoritarian simulacrum of the genuine Hermetic one (stanza 13), and his art as consequently official and factitious. The distinction is similar to that between Apollonian and Dionysiac poetry developed by followers of Graves in the 1950s; Auden, however, does not limit his ingenious categorising to the sphere of the literary, but uses it to express his personal advocacy of the generous, disorganised, instinctive life as against the humourless pedantry and authority of the self-important. There are many good academic jokes, appropriate to the poem's occasion, but it survives, with a sympathetic insistence, its witty after-dinner tone (on the actual 10 a.m. dullness of its audience, see Harry Levin, *Memories of the Moderns*, 1981, p. 152). It is a serious protest against bureaucracy, against the 'managers' of life, whether they be dictators or diet-faddists, and in its final stanzas suitably borrows from Byron's decalogue in *Don Juan*, 1.204–6 and from Sydney Smith ('Take short views, hope for the best, and trust in God', *Lady Holland's Memoir*, chapter 4).

When things began to happen to our favourite spot

May 1948; 'For T. S. Eliot', *T. S. Eliot: A symposium*, ed. R. March and M. J. Tambimuttu, 1948; 'To T. S. Eliot On His Sixtieth Birthday (1948)', N, p. 63; CSP66, p. 275; CP, p. 577.

Auden's need to pay tribute to the poet who wrote *The Waste Land* and *The Hollow Men* prompts him to allusions ('unheard-of drought' . . . 'the right | Language for thirst and fear') which do not sit easily in a short poem with his central metaphor drawn from the detective story, where the 'crime' is original sin. The poem may be compared with 'Detective Story' in *Letters from Iceland*, with the ideas in Auden's essay 'The Guilty Vicarage' in *The Dyer's Hand*: 'The interest in the detective story is the dialectic of innocence and guilt' (p. 147), and with 'New Year Letter' (lines 233ff). The subservience of even a great detective to the ultimate processes of the Law would seem to imply the inferiority of poetic activity to the divine truth, underlined by the reference to Hamlet's awareness of the universality of human failings (II.ii.561).

Orchestras have so long been speaking

May 1947; 'Music is International', *American Scholar*, Autumn 1947, and *Horizon*, October 1947; N, p. 64; CSP66, p. 226; CP, p. 340.

'Music is International' was written for the Columbia chapter of the fraternity Phi Beta Kappa. It seems that it was only on 23 May that Auden heard from Jacques Barzun at a publisher's lunch that he was booked to deliver the Phi Beta Kappa poem on 2 June. 'I was furious but professional conceit wouldn't let me refuse lest it be thought that I couldn't compose a poem in a week. *I worked like a beaver*' (to Ursula Niebuhr, 10 June 1947). The result demonstrates the ornate conversational style which Auden began to adopt in the 1940s at its most exhibitionist, appropriately perhaps for a poem commissioned by the honorary fraternity of the American academic élite. One factitious element in the style (its use of obscure words) may also owe something to the challenge, since this is the first poem of his for which there appears to be clear evidence that he used a pre-existing list of words culled from the OED or elsewhere and managed to work them all in ('slot, mornes, motted, mammelons, sottering, frescade, halcyon, hideola, mansion, prosopon').

Auden has treated music more respectfully, many readers will feel (e.g. in 'The Composer' or 'Anthem for St Cecilia's Day'), and here gives undue emphasis to music's role as a wish-fulfilling drug ('the mornes and motted mammelons' – i.e. the small hills and wooded hummocks – give the bourgeois Eden a Gothicly erotic air, for example). When Auden wishes at lines 47–8 to strike a more serious note in the demands which music makes of us, he is a victim of his own procedure and risks an astonishing shift of register (the lines to a late stage, as the Buffalo notebook makes clear, were merely: 'To return, though, | To the performance itself. How much can we learn | From this noise . . .'). The Elohim are according to Rosenstock-Huessy 'the divine powers in creation' (*Out of Revolution*, p. 727) and this is probably the sense that Auden has in mind, for he talks in the following line about the difficulty of forgiveness (compare the final line of 'The Composer'). However, although it is true that in the Zohar (which Auden had used as a source for *The Age of Anxiety*) the word is a generic name for all the seven grades, or degrees of creative power, of Jahweh, it is much more commonly used as the name of the Jewish deity in his role as Judge. Speculations of this kind are not particularly useful to the poem, and indeed, Auden's examples of valuable behaviour to which music ought to yield in importance are so apparently trivial ('feeding strays or looking pleased when caught | By a bore or a hideola') that the moral argument almost founders as it pursues its dubious Wordsworthian conclusion ('We may some day need very much to | Remember when we were happy', etc.). There have been several explanations of the origin of 'hideola', but Dorothy Farnan's is the most reliable: coined by Kallman, a portmanteau of the 'hideous' town of Mineola (Farnan, p. 79). Despite all this, the poem is a buoyant display of quick-thinking, well served by the pace of the syllabic form and the Skaldic rhyming (also used in 'The Duet' and 'Pleasure Island').

Be patient, solemn nose

May 1950; 'Precious Five', *Harper's Magazine*, October 1950; N, p. 67; CSP66, p. 285; CP, p. 587.

Auden here enjoins the five senses ('Be patient . . . Be modest . . . Be civil . . . look straight . . . Praise . . . the Earthly Muse . . . Be happy') to serve the natural law, and in so doing to concur in the divine law, whose singular command is '*Bless what there is for being*'. The drafts (Texas 1950 notebook, fols 28ff) show that the negative formulations at the end of each stanza were an original part of the tabulated schematic concept of the poem, reminding the sensual body of the absolutes ('The way', 'The life', 'The beauty', 'The good', 'The truth') which elude it.

The nose is seen as the organ which is aware of time (perhaps as a tribute to Proust?). It is asked, in terms of the landscape of quest, to persist 'Up the storm-beaten slope | From memory to hope' even though the 'calm enchanted wood' of childhood has gone.

The ears are the poet's 'ear' for poetry, 'spoiled darlings', he modestly proclaims, in an 'undisciplined' age. There is a pointed criticism of his public when he says that 'It cannot take pure fiction, | And what it wants from you | Are rumours partly true', and he concludes the stanza by admitting the need for inspiration. His ears must go back to school and drudge, but even then poetic success is a 'luck' which the ears celebrate but cannot predict.

Hands are the instruments of action and power, but in a funny contrast between 'hairy wrists | And leg-of-mutton fists' and 'A tight arthritic claw | Or aldermanic paw' Auden appeals to hands to be exploratory and generous, not merely to evoke the authority of the past.

Eyes are instruments of intelligence (beware of mirrors: no self-deception is possible) and in 'living men' complement the heart (seat of feeling) on a 'mutual undeceiving'. 'True seeing' is not merely a matter of 'sight'.

The tongue is the instrument of praise of 'the Earthly Muse', praise for just that daily quality of life enjoyed by the tongue's 'old self' as instrument of taste, and of its twin, the penis. The tone of quiet meditative acceptance which brings the faculties under control is maintained in the final stanza, where any 'anger and despair | At what is going on' is shown to be useless: the theological position is one of Leibnizian optimism. The trimeters (as usual in Auden) have a pace and gravity that link the poem with some of the philosophical lyrics of the 1930s.

A cloudless night like this

August 1948; 'A Walk After Dark', *Commonweal*, 11 March 1949; N, p. 71; CSP66, p. 231; CP, p. 345.

In 'A Walk After Dark', the poet, stock-taking in middle-age, praises the 'clockwork spectacle' of a starry night for keeping pace with his age and moods. Now the galaxy may be seen as middle-aged too, because astronomy has discovered that the red light emitted by the furthest stars that are going away from us at great speeds can be used as an indication of their age, and that they are often so far away and so old that they may not even exist any longer. Yet despite these thoughts, 'only the young and the rich | Have the nerve or the figure to strike | The *lacrimae rerum* note' (cf. 'The Duet'). The poet, on the other hand, stresses his responsibilities towards the truth, which involves not only the 'wronged' and their political disasters being ignored (there were more details in the originally drafted stanza 6: 'A boy is whipped in a cell, | An old woman is bundled out | Of the home she loved so well'), but also the possibility of miraculous interference in the natural law (stanza 7) heralding a second coming which will deliver judgement on 'My person, all my friends, | and these United States'. The poem is a fitting farewell to the America of the 1940s.

Uncollected Poems 1940–48

There's wine on the table, and friends and relations

?January 1940; 'To Chester Kallman, b. Jan. 7, 1921', printed in Farnan, p. 25.

This nineteenth birthday poem for Chester Kallman is a hastily written piece in anapaestic quatrains. Auden uses the Jungian analysis of psychological types to warn Kallman of the needs and dangers of Thought and Sensation (he considered Kallman a Thinking–Sensation type, and himself a Thinking–Intuitive type). For the Lame Shadow, see my discussion of its use in *Paul Bunyan* on p. 314.

Because it is in you, a Jew . . .

December 1941; bowdlerised text printed in Farnan, p. 65.

This Christmas Day verse letter to Kallman was presumably sent or given to him (it is addressed 'Dearest Chester'). In it, the events and persons of the Nativity all find outrageous counterparts in their relationship in ways which movingly underline the humanity, shame, hope and regrets which Auden had come to feel about his love and about his jealousy of July 1941, which made him wish to commit murder (see Carpenter, pp. 311ff). The poem therefore casts light on personal interpretations of Joseph in 'For the Time Being', although some other details (especially the comparison of '*les morceaux de commerce*', i.e. pieces of rough trade, to the shepherds) seem extravagant. The most interesting stanza is the fifth, relating Kallman to the Holy Family. What Auden calls the 'serious relation' of a child to its parents in providing some kind of pattern in its later choice of a love-object is, of course, a formula that covers many crucial psychological stages, including the Freudian transference that induces the son to adopt the role of his mother and to become homosexual in the first place (see Freud, *Group Psychology and the Analysis of the Ego*, 1922, p. 66). This transference is not fully implied here, while the interrelatedness of the mother-role and the father-role emotionally and physically can lead to unresolvable speculations. In readings of *The Ascent of F6*, Auden took the part of Ransom and Kallman took the part of Ransom's mother. Auden's cheerful acceptance of his sexuality led to some strange transformations and impersonations. 'It is Ma who has the penis' he once noted (Berg 1964–5 notebook), thinking not so much of his own hen-pecked father as of the roles generally played by oral homosexuals. Sex was for him a kind of symbolic magic, and playing 'Son-and/or-Mother' in bed illuminated a real human relationship (*Forewords and Afterwords*, p. 453). The stanza omitted in Farnan (the ninth) referred to Kallman's curvature of the spine and Auden's 'resentment against being small'.

I'm sure the good fairy

March 1942; 'Happy Birthday', printed in Miller, p. 80.

This brief poem was written for the tenth birthday of Grace Stevens (sister of the subject of 'Mundus et Infans' and daughter of one of Auden's colleagues at the University of Michigan). Grace had once said on hearing that she was the living picture of her grandmother: 'I wish I was only the picture of myself!' Auden's charming tribute restores her to her own identity.

O lift your little pinkie

?1942; 'A Shepherd's Carol', *Musical Times*, October 1962, as a Novello song-sheet of the same date (collected in *Sing Nowell* [nd], p. 12), and also on a sheet accompanying a recording of Britten's *Part Songs* (Argo RG 424, 1964); *As I Walked Out One Evening*, p. 92.

'A Shepherd's Carol' is included, as section V.2, in an early transcript of 'For the Time Being' made by Angelyn Stevens. Miller, p. 60, even suggests that it was already part of 'Songs for Saint Cecelia [sic]', although this seems unlikely (see p. 402). The setting by Britten dates from 1944, when it was broadcast by the BBC in a programme called 'A Poet's Christmas'. The early printed texts derive from this setting and therefore contain some of Britten's misreadings: the line 'If I were a Valentine and Fortune were abroad' should read 'If I were a Valentino and Fortune were a broad'. The line cannot now be musically redeemed. The full and corrected version appears in *As I Walked Out One Evening*. A 'horse-opera' is a Western, 'the velvet' means winnings, 'pinkie' means finger (Miller reports Auden as being interested in whether the word could possibly have sexual connotations). A 'solid sender' is an enthralling jazz musician.

Has Hitler died? Is coffee to be had?

December 1942; 'The Queen's Masque', *Libretti*, Appendix II, p. 422.

Auden took time off from writing 'The Sea and the Mirror' to compose this brief masque for Chester Kallman's twenty-third birthday in which Kallman is invoked as Anastasia, a Queen of sexual misrule. It is hard to know which is more lamentable, the level of the camp jokes or the relegation of Sibelius, Shostakovich and Brahms to the realm of the Queen of Dullness (who naturally prays to the Great Boyg from *Peer Gynt*). Mendelson explains the still-explicable topical references in his edition. Wonne = joy, strich = a hustler. The most interesting material, the songs for the three ghosts, was sent as an afterthought. Auden uses the relative privacy of foreign languages to issue covert rebukes to Kallman. The first 'Blues' (half-Lenya, half-Dietrich in style) may be roughly translated as follows:

In days of spring when winter colds still settle damply in handkerchiefs and noisy pricks grow in trousers, Lady Love's little boy is calling on me. How are you doing, you old bugger? Is there anything new, a love affair, for example, without worry or recrimination? Does the world know what is up, or are they already saying again 'There's nothing in it, and that's a fact'? He has something, that fleshy gay Cupid, no? Although he's a bit crazy. Well yes, he was bathed too hot as a little child. You cheeky beggar, what are you doing there now? Look, man, that's my heart you're eating. That's out of the question: it doesn't taste good. Anastasia has poisoned it. It is manifold, and never goes away, the harm she does me.

The second 'Blues' may be translated as follows:

The queen of beautiful thighs, Anastasia, has made me many promises in that bed down there; truly, she's a good sort, but she doesn't keep them. Anastasia has promised the body that she'll show it those beautiful angels again which, you know, are like that: the slut has forgotten; the little ones don't come. Anastasia has promised the heart that she will give it a call at seven o'clock on Sunday. Midnight's gone: the stomach waits for her 'hullo', but she doesn't telephone. For Anastasia I've lost my heart, she's killed me. I've licked madame's bottom, alas, alas. I'd like to say to her Shit, Shit, but I can't.

The third 'song' is a parody of the monks' chanting from *The Ascent of F6*, and is capable of some decoding: 'Bojo' (i.e. the author of the masque) has been made 'gaga' by Anastasia (i.e. Kallman). Contra the *Libretti* text, the second line should read 'Gigli homo che Aphasia', which suggests that Auden thought the great singer insensitive to the words he sang. In the last line, Ransom from the play is interpolated into words which conflate a hairy tribe with the enchantress Acrasia from Spenser's Bower of Blisse. Auden took the part of Ransom in readings of the play with Kallman; Kallman took the part of Mrs Ransom.

Let the whole creation give out another sweetness

1944; 'Anthem for S. Matthew's Day', folded sheet, 21 September 1946; 'Anthem' (first line 'Let us praise our Maker, with true passion extol him'), EG, p. 59; CP, p. 332.

There were two sections of the Anthem which Auden produced for the Dedication and Patronal festival of the Church of St Matthew, Northampton in 1946. The second section, headed 'Bless ye the Lord' was later revised and used as the ending of Malin's last speech in *The Age of Anxiety* ('We elude Him, lie to Him, yet His love observes'). The first section is the present poem, headed 'Praise ye the Lord', and is the cancelled ending for *The Age of Anxiety*. It was reprinted in *Epistle to a Godson*, with a new first line: 'Let us praise our Maker, with true passion extol Him.' Auden had two stipulations about his St Matthew's fee: '(a) It shall be a bit more than you can afford. (b) You shall donate it to any fund for the relief of distress in Europe which does not intentionally exclude the Germans.'

It was a Spring day, a day for a lay, when the air

Autumn 1948; 'The Platonic Blow', *Fuck You*, March 1965; 'A Gobble Poem', *Fuck books unlimited*, 1967, and other unauthorised printings.

A full account of the pirated and underground publication of this poem is given in *Bibliography*, Appendix II. It is not the only pornographic poem that Auden wrote. In 1949 he was, according to Ansen, at work on a girl's monologue: 'I've done the last half, the brutal part. Now I have to do the first half, the tender part. They both end in tears.' The style of 'The Platonic

Blow' is modelled, incongruously, on that of Charles Williams (compare Part II of 'Memorial for the City'), but the inspiration was Catullan ('You simply could not get a line [like] Paedicabo vos atque irrumabo printed today. I'd like to write some poems like that', he said to Ansen on 12 April 1947).The odd sense of 'Platonic' in the title is, presumably, because it is Plato's view of love as Eros, not the Christian view of love as Agape, 'a stream of *gettings*', as Auden once put it, as opposed to givings (see also his Introduction to Baudelaire, *Intimate Journals*, 1947, p. 26). There is a typescript of the poem (which includes the misplacement of the fifth stanza as described in the *Bibliography*) typed partly on the versos of a typescript of 'Mimesis and Allegory', dated 'Autumn 1948', and ascribed to 'Miss Oral', as though for pseudonymous circulation, if restricted. There is some evidence, however, that the poem as known is not complete. Auden still wrote of it as being in the process of composition in mid-December (Farnan, p. 184). The most interesting phrase occurs in stanza 11, where Bud's penis is described in terms usually reserved for divinity: 'ineffably solemn and wise'. This is presumably the solemnity of a ritual occasion. The penis, knowing more than it can say, can only perform.

The Rake's Progress

In May 1947 Igor Stravinsky saw the Hogarth engravings of 'The Rake's Progress' at the Art Institute of Chicago, and thereafter planned an operatic moral fable on the subject in the manner of Mozart. It was Aldous Huxley who suggested Auden as a librettist, and Stravinsky, who had recently seen and admired *Night Mail*, was happy to proceed. The details of the relationship are revealed in their correspondence, which appears in *Stravinsky: Selected correspondence* (1982), ed. Robert Craft, I.299–324.

Auden was flattered by the association. Under Kallman's guidance he had become much more knowledgeable about opera than when writing *Paul Bunyan* with Britten. He had begun to understand the subaltern relationship of librettist to composer, for example; he knew more about dramatic structure, and about the characterisation of operatic archetypes. His celebrated view of a libretto as not being addressed to the public but acting as 'a private letter to the composer' and then being 'as expendable as infantry to a Chinese general' (*The Dyer's Hand*, p. 473) is a somewhat overstated version of an unexceptionable belief in the supremacy of the musical share of operatic collaboration. And the kind of inaudibility he finds in the words of opera is again probably exaggerated (one word in seven is usually heard according to 'The World of Opera', *Secondary Worlds*, p. 90). However, this view partly accounts for the fact that the libretti written in collaboration with Chester Kallman are in their details of limited poetical interest, whatever the authenticity of their themes. In the case of *The Rake's Progress*, the action was worked out scene by scene, and the musical numbers plotted, by Stravinsky and Auden together from October 1947. Kallman was soon brought in by Auden (who broke the news to Stravinsky in January 1948 when sending him Act I). Some essential changes of plotting resulted from this (the three wishes, the bearded lady) and there is no doubt that Kallman's contribution was crucial. Act III was ready by 9 February 1948. Stravinsky completed the setting on 7 April 1951, and the first performance was given in Venice in September 1951. The libretto and score were published in August 1951.

In 1951 Auden had some reservations about the pastiche element in the score, in particular worrying that musical echoes of Handel and Mozart would somehow make the opera seem old-fashioned (Robert Craft, *Stravinsky: Chronicle of a friendship*, 1972, p. 26) but the Kallman view that 'it is a tribute to opera in much the same way that *Apollon Musagète* is a tribute to the dance' (note in libretto booklet included in the 1964 Columbia recording) no doubt soon prevailed. Kallman's participation also enabled the important theme of Anne Trulove's fidelity to the unfaithful Tom Rakewell to be artistically controlled: Auden largely wrote Rakewell's lines and Kallman largely wrote Anne's, reversing their own emotional relationship, which the opera indirectly represents. The division of labour between Auden and Kallman was explained in detail to Robert Craft thus:

> *Act I.* Scene 1. Down to the end of Tom's aria . . . 'This beggar shall ride.' W. H. A. from there to the end of the scene. C. K. Scene 2. W. H. A. Scene 3. C. K. *Act II.* Scene 1. Down to the end of Tom's aria . . . 'in my heart the dark.' C. K. from there to the end of scene. W. H. A. Scene 2. C. K. Scene 3. W. H. A. *Act III.* Scene 1. C. K. (except for lyrics sung off-stage by Tom and Shadow). Scene 2. [Shadow's] verses at beginning and end of scene. W. H. A. middle (card-guessing game). C. K. Scene 3 and Epilogue. W. H. A.

For a view of the relative quality of Kallman's contributions, see Robert Craft's review of the *Libretti* in the *New York Review of Books*, 3 November 1994, p. 52.

Auden and Kallman seized upon the opportunity afforded by the opera's eighteenth-century pastiche to write about a religious predicament in terms of the rationalisation of appetite with which that century was obsessed. Their hero, Rakewell, is a manic-depressive because Auden considered it a characteristic of the manic-depressive to be excited by the anticipation of experience and inevitably disappointed by its realisation. Rakewell is a gloomy and Byronic exemplar of the human will struggling to be free of necessity. Even his pleasures disgust him. Only the memory of an ennobling love haunts his ruinous career, and finally saves him. The libretto uses a variety of myths to suggest that Rakewell is an archetypal hero. Like the quest-hero, he has three wishes. The first ('I wish I had money', p. 51) is answered by news of a fortune which whisks him away from the opening pastoral idyll with Anne (the uncle's estate may have been suggested by Isherwood's uncle leaving his estate to Isherwood in the summer of 1940). The second ('I wish I were happy', p. 61) is answered by a proposal from his Mephisthophelean servant, Nick Shadow, that he should deny both reason and desire, and marry a bearded lady from St Giles's Fair. And the third (of a magical dream: 'I wish it were true', p. 71) is answered by Shadow's unveiling of the bread-making machine which is to bring about his final bankruptcy and ruin. All these wishes represent false illusions of life, manifestations of Rakewell's (or Everyman's) fallible nature. The third may even be intended as a bizarre version of one of the temptations of Christ, here applied to the delusions of material progress affecting capitalist society.

The use of the Faustian myth may have been suggested by Jung, by whom Auden was particularly influenced at the time. There are many examples in his work of the Jungian 'shadow', usually called by him the 'lame shadow'. This form of the alter ego represents all a character's inferior qualities manifested in his or her uncontrolled emotions: 'I have called the inferior and less commendable part of a person the *shadow*. We have met with the figure in literature; for instance, Faust and his shadow Mephistopheles' (Jung, *The Integration of the Personality*, 1940, p. 20). If Nick Shadow is the Jungian 'shadow', then Anne may well be the Jungian 'anima' (the inner aspect of the personality, corresponding to the 'persona' or outer aspect: *Paul Bunyan* significantly contains a scene of 'Lame Shadows and Animas', p. 29, and Auden said that the blue ox Babe was intended to be Bunyan's anima). In this case the morality play aspect of the story is more pronounced: the characters are Tom's bad and good angels respectively, and the libretto is something of a psychic allegory like *Paid on Both Sides, The Ascent of F6* and *The Age of Anxiety*.

Although Rakewell is thus motivated by his own unspoken desires, he is aware of a deeper desire to be free of them. To an extent he is also an example of the type of the dandy, whose one ambition is 'to become subjectively conscious of being uniquely himself' (Auden's Introduction to Baudelaire's *Intimate Journals*, 1949, p. xviii). This is a less socially conditioned motive than that of Slim, Johnny and Hel in *Paul Bunyan*, and it is not uniquely the problem of the parasitic artist of *Elegy for Young Lovers*, but it does establish a link between these three operas. Auden's Baudelaire Introduction continues:

[The Dandy] is, in fact, the religious hero turned upside down – that is, Lucifer, the rebel, the defiant one who asserts his freedom by disobeying *all* commands, whether given by God, society, or his own nature. The truly dandyish act is the *acte gratuite*, because only an act which is quite unnecessary, unmotivated by any given requiredness, can be an absolutely freely self-chosen individual act.

Rakewell's marriage to Baba the Turk is certainly an *acte gratuit*, but only perhaps in the Gidean sense of 'un crime immotivé', like Lafcadio's in *Les Caves du Vatican*. As Sartre was keen to point out, the freedom and choice of human existentialism belong always to a total situation, and not to mere caprice (*L'Existentialisme est un Humanisme*, 1954, p. 74). Rakewell's absurd marriage is only a grotesque parody of the true Christian choice. This choice is symbolised later in the opera when, on the suspended stroke of midnight after the year and the day allowed him by Shadow, he irrationally chooses the Queen of Hearts for a second time as a gesture towards Anne's love which still haunts him. Baba threatens, in her wisdom and good nature, to upset the balance of the fable. She is the exemplar of Audenesque aperçus (e.g. p. 92: 'all they say or do is theatre', modelled on Hazlitt, cf. *Faber Book of Aphorisms*, p. 4), has a touching fidelity to her career (pp. 69, 80–81), and is magnanimous to Anne (p. 80). Unlike Rakewell, she is a symbol of the artist, and the beard represents her genius (Auden's BBC talk on 28 August 1953). When Rakewell says at the end of Act II, echoing *Othello*, v.ii.100: 'I have no wife' (p. 74), this denial almost seems more outrageous than his initial marriage to her.

Shadow is cheated of his human soul by the sublimated power of love, although in revenge he makes Rakewell mad. The rest of the opera elaborates the symbolism of Bedlam. (Ingeniously, even the front-of-curtain so-called 'limericks' at the close of the opera are in fact versions of the traditional Renaissance 'mad-song', cf. D'Urfey's 'I'll sail upon the dog-star'). Bedlam is a purgatory in which transfigured love (Anne as Venus) has power to redeem the human soul from torment (Rakewell as Adonis) in a scene which ironically relates to the opening idyll (also presided over by 'the Cyprean Queen'). A Christian significance of Innocence and Experience is implicit here, and Anne's last barcarolle seems nearer to the Shelley of *Prometheus Unbound* than to the Neo-classicism whose terms the opera's language has so closely followed (in his BBC talk, Auden called it 'a rather bare-faced crib from *Peer Gynt*'). In a sense, the work is pulled in two directions here, for its symbolism is essentially Romantic in colouring. Ever deflationary, Auden and Kallman wrote an extra scene in September 1951 for their own amusement, where Trulove and Mother Goose go off together at the end.

Delia

After completing the libretto for *The Rake's Progress*, Auden and Kallman drew up a scenario for another opera libretto in 1949, *On The Way*, which they hoped might interest Stravinsky, but this was never written. The characters included Giorgio Sbuffone, 40, a liar; Lord Tantalus, a chief of police; three bards modelled on nineteenth-century composers: Vergile Mousson, 25 [Berlioz], Gregor Schöngeist, 18 [Mendelssohn], and Giocondo Pollicini, 40 [Rossini]; Gisella Saltimbocca, 30, alias Lady Tantalus, a cook; and the Muse, represented by Stella, Maria and Laura. The scenario has been printed in the *Libretti*, p. 479. The precise implications of the farcical episodes described are not fully clear, but among the themes exposed are the fatuousness of supposing that poets are always revolutionaries, and the old Flaubertian imperative of working alone and pursuing only your muse. The authors presumably intended an exposure of the romantic personality in art as an experimental process open to comic error. The strange title may have been intended in this sense (with a suggestion of the German 'unterwegs', both the process of direction or destination, and the place where things are left behind in the process of direction, perhaps with a memory of Heidegger).

According to Robert Craft (*A Tribute*, p. 154) this idea did not get beyond the talking stage. Nor, despite encouraging it, did Stravinsky set Auden and Kallman's next libretto, *Delia*, a piece 'suggested by' Peele's *The Old Wives' Tale*, and completed in 1952. Stravinsky had talked with Auden about a one-act opera capable of performance by amateurs, and had given the impression that he wanted something like a Jonsonian masque. Auden suggested as a subject the marriage of Art and Science performed by the Goddess of Wisdom, and letters were exchanged during the libretto's composition, concluding with Stravinsky's telegram 'Happy hear you completed libretto for project, which I hope will not be stillborn' (ironically sent on 1 April). The libretto was published in *Botteghe Oscure* in 1953. It appears in *Libretti*, p. 95.

The story of the magus Sacrapant and of the rescue of the captive Delia by Eumenides (a knight, not the Greek Erinyes) is elaborated by Peele with a rustic framework and comic sub-plots in an affectionate parody of Tudor romantic drama. The framework and the telling of the tale disappear in *Delia*, and so do Eumenides' comic servant Jack, and Delia's two brothers who come searching for her. Lampriscus goes, and Erestus (changed by Sacrapant into a bear) is conflated with the friar who serves Delia and is given the name of Bungay from Greene's play *Friar Bacon and Friar Bungay* (often printed together with Peele's in collections of Elizabethan plays such as that of the World's Classics, ed. A. K. McIlwraith, 1934). Zantippa, the shrewish daughter of Lampriscus, becomes Bungay's wife in the librettists' new sub-plot, while the conflict of Orlando (Eumenides) and Sacrapant is foregrounded as a conflict like that of Tamino and Sarastro in *The Magic Flute*, with many additional elements from fairy-tales and from Shakespeare. There are echoes in Orlando of Orlando seeking Rosalind in *As You Like It*, of Ferdinand confronting Prospero in *The Tempest*, and of the prophecy-defying Macduff in *Macbeth*. He is the lucky third son of fairy-tales, assisted by a crone who turns out to be both a Queen of the Night, as in *The Magic Flute*, and Dame Nature. There is a radical difference here, in period, style and subject, if not in genre, from what Stravinsky was expecting.

The texture of the libretto is something of a Tudor hodge-podge (mock hexameters, echo-effects, parody of the mass, and so on), unified by the blandness and pastiche of librettese. There are some details of poetic interest. The framing choruses (pp. 99 and 125) are both in the form of the Spanish *cossante* (for details, see p. 462). In the first, the ring-dance of the animals contrasts with the previous scene of Orlando at the crossroads in a manner suggestive of the opera's theme, the attainment of the ideal only in nature and in love. It was a juxtaposition to be used a few years later in the sonnet 'Words' in *Homage to Clio*, where it signified the uncertain truth-function of language. When Sacrapant opens the rock (p. 106) there is an acrostic on Stravinsky's first name; when Sacrapant is defeated and the rock again splits open (p. 124), there is an acrostic on the first name of Stravinsky's wife, Vera. Delia's vision of childhood (p. 107) is a version of Baudelaire's 'vert paradis' which so appealed to Auden: the 'green more live' is the soul's volition which will lead irrevocably from innocence to experience when she chooses Orlando after and despite the pageant of Time. The following banquet and the round sung by three owls (pp. 107–8) is Elizabethan pastoral as mediated charmingly by a Christina Rossetti or a Walter de la Mare. There was, of course, a round already in Peele's *The Old Wives' Tale*, and it was the most celebrated passage in the play ('Whenas the rye reach to the chin'). It does not appear in *Delia* perhaps because Auden had already used it in Act II, scene 4, of his adaptation of *The Duchess of Malfi* in 1946 (it had also been used, along with Auden's 'A Summer Night', in Britten's *Spring Symphony* of 1949). The pageant itself (p. 115) uses rhyme royal in Skelton's grand allegorical manner (there are rougher Skeltonics at pp. 102–3). The final Chorus (p. 125) with its blessing both of 'the Queen' (i.e. the Queen of the Night) and of the 'green world temporal' (i.e. the world of fallen nature in which the quest is conducted) was adapted as the poem 'Lauds' in 'Horae Canonicae' (see p. 461).

It is evident that the librettists intended the use of fairy-story material to express 'universal and profound human experiences' (Preface to Auden and Kallman's translation of *The Magic Flute*, 1957, p. 9; *Libretti*, p. 129). Their translation of Schikaneder is in many respects parallel to *Delia*, and they were confident enough in their understanding of such symbolic material to rearrange the scenes in Act II of their version of *The Magic Flute* in order to make better sense of Pamina's trials (*Libretti*, p. 131). Their translation (dedicated to Anne and Irving Weiss, see p. 489) also contains a 'Proem' (*Libretti*, p. 135) which sets out the argument and background of the opera, a 'Metalogue' (*Libretti*, p. 152; for commentary, see p. 476) and a 'Postscript' (*Libretti*, p. 182) in which the Queen of the Night engages Auden and Kallman on their limitations both as translators and as modern men. Representing the Dionysian principle in perpetual conflict with the Apollonian light of Sarastro, she claims to be identical with a number of symbols that Auden has used before, including Goethe's 'Mothers' and Wagner's Erda, the embodiment of *Urmutterfurcht* (see 'New Year Letter', lines 1092, 94). The Queen of the Night in *Delia* (who kisses and restores Sacrapant's lamp in the last scene so that their wars may be rebegun) also represents such a principle, although she is benign, unlike Astrafiammante in Mozart. In many respects, *Delia* represents a moral framework closer to *The Magic Flute*'s source in Wieland's *Lulu*, with a good fairy and a wicked magician, rather than the other way round.

The Shield of Achilles

The Shield of Achilles was the second of the three post-war collections of shorter poems which contributed to the 1948–1957 section of the 1966 *Collected Shorter Poems* and the 1976 *Collected Poems* which began with 'In Transit' and ended with 'Good-Bye to the Mezzogiorno'. It is thus central to his 'Mediterranean' period, and is notable for the inclusion of the two important sequences 'Bucolics' and 'Horae Canonicae'. Both American and English editions appeared in 1955, the first in February, the second in November. The dedicatory poem to Lincoln and Fidelma Kirstein (reprinted in the 1958 *Selected Poems* and the 1966 *Collected Shorter Poems*) seems to reveal Auden's awareness of a drying-up of poetic inspiration and the corresponding value of the lucky truth at a time of sterility (compare the dedicatory poem of *Homage to Clio*). For Auden, however, the 'wrong time' of the final line was in theory a distinctly challenging circumstance, for he was now acutely conscious of the danger of literary inauthenticity due to writing something too early or too late. It was from Rosenstock-Huessy's science of revolutions that he derived this idea of 'timeliness' (*Out of Revolution*, p. 14).

The sequence 'Bucolics' was recorded by Auden on 12 December 1953 (Caedmon TC-1019). According to Auden's 'Note' on the record sleeve, the common theme of the poems is 'the relation of man as a history-making person to nature'. Each topographical phenomenon is invested with a serious moral identity as a *genius loci* which assists or detracts from his notion of the Good Life, and the sequence appears, with the epigraph 'Fair is Middle-Earth nor changes, though to Age' in SA, p. 13; without the epigraph in CSP66, p. 255 (it is transferred to a section of shorts in this and later collections); without the epigraph, in SP58, p. 161; CP, p. 556. 'Middle-Earth' is the traditional term for the earth as it exists in medieval cosmology between Heaven and Hell, although it had recently been popularised in J. R. R. Tolkien's *Lord of the Rings* (Auden had reviewed the first volume in 1954). The sacramental image suggests that it is only the individual human body which changes, and that the spirit (of which the body, like the bread and wine, is a sign) does not. The poems will be treated individually below, and their publication details given separately.

Deep below our violences

September 1953; 'Winds', *London Magazine*, November 1954; SA, p. 15, dedicated to Alexis Leger (i.e. St Jean Perse, who had himself written a poem 'Vents').

'Winds', though the first poem of the sequence, was written last of all, at first only as a kind of invocation to the series but later extended. It is important as establishing a religious setting for the sequence which otherwise might be obscured. The winds recall the 'Pliocene Friday' of the birth of *homo sapiens* (Friday was the day on which God made man; Pliocene the geological era in which human remains were first found), and therefore symbolise the 'holy insufflation' of God the Creator breathing into human nostrils the breath of life. Metropolis is the Fallen City, the product of man's asserted will. Human institutions regulate ('law-court and temple') the hidden passions and motivations of each individual ('First Dad' is both First Cause and Our Father; the 'watch' and 'many little maids' possibly two ways of explaining divine purpose, i.e. Paley's analogy of finding a watch and the nymphs of pantheism). 'I am loved, therefore I am' is taken not in the sense of God's love being a necessary condition for well-being, but as a pseudo-Cartesian argument for self-sufficiency (cf. Diaghilev in 'September 1, 1939'). Thus the lion is not lying down with the kid (Isaiah xi.6) because of the 'bubble-brained creature' God chose: an extinct fish, an insect or a crab or whatever, might have made a better job of it. The 'bubbles' in the brain of man's ancestor are the cerebral hemispheres (see Loren Eiseley, *The Immense Journey*, 1958, pp. 52ff).

Such theological and evolutionary musing is lightly replaced by the wind as weather, and how concern for the weather can be 'an image | For our Authentic City' (as opposed to the Fallen Metropolis of the first stanza).The 'brigs of dread' come from 'A Lyke-Wake Dirge': the Brig o'Dread is the narrow bridge to Purgatory from which the wicked fall into Hell (see also 'For the Time Being', CP, p. 368). All this merely acts as a bridge passage to the longest and final stanza, the poet's invocation to 'Goddess of winds and wisdom', i.e. the Muse, to bring him inspiration, save him from writing nonsense and remind him of the purity of the subjects he celebrates: 'Earth, Sky, a few dear names'. 'Arthur O'Bower' refers to a riddle for the wind ('Bower' = Scottish 'bowder', a squall of wind) quoted by Beatrix Potter in

Squirrel Nutkin. 'Anamnesis' is the Platonic theory of the 'unforgetting', i.e. recollection of memories of, a prior existence.

Sylvan meant savage in those primal woods

August 1952; 'Woods', *Listener*, 11 December 1952, and *New Poems by American Poets*, ed. R. Humphries (1953); SA, p. 18, dedicated to Nicholas Nabokov, the composer who later set Auden and Kallman's version of *Love's Labour Lost.*

In 'Woods', Auden turns to a rhymed iambic formality (the Venus and Adonis stanza seems appropriate) as if to comment ironically on society's decorum which has treated woods as the residue of the primitive and dangerously numinous ('Crown and Mitre warned their silly flocks | The pasture's humdrum rhythms to approve | And to abhor the licence of the grove'). Auden would have remembered Piero di Cosimo's painting of a forest fire in the Ashmolean Museum, Oxford, and may have been reading Panofsky's *Studies in Iconology* (1939) with its distinctions about different kinds of primitivism in Renaissance painting. Stanza 3 refers indirectly to the rape of Philomela, turned by the gods into a nightingale. Stanza 6 refers to 'Pan's green father', i.e. the woodpecker (an odd understanding of Robert Graves's argument in *The White Goddess*, p. 355, that 'Dryope', Pan's mother, means a woodpecker). The rhythms of the poem itself are far from humdrum, and in the final stanza take on a rib-prodding Empsonian menace. The argument is that woods constitute, not merely a location for bizarre rites or easy seduction, but a concentrated expression of man's basic condition (some brilliant descriptions here of sounds, as woodpeckers, cuckoos, doves, fruit and leaf enact their symbolism of generation and death), and that a society's attitude towards its trees is a good sign of its health.

I know a retired dentist who only paints mountains

July 1952; 'Mountains', Ariel Poem (Faber and Faber, 1954); SA, p. 20, dedicated to Hedwig Petzold, in whose house in Kitzbühel in the Tyrol Auden had stayed during the summer of 1925.

Despite the nostalgic tribute to local trains in stanza 3, 'Mountains' tends to take an oddly jaundiced view of its subject. The fastidious tone supports the investigated notion of safety and comfort running through the whole sequence, the difficulty of managing 'the Flesh, | When angels of ice and

stone | Stand over her day and night who make it so plain | They detest any
kind of growth'. Mountains have always represented some kind of challenge
in Auden's poetry, but in this poem response to the challenge breeds
fanatics and hermits (there is an unusually sharp vignette of mountaineers),
and it is suggested that, despite their value as a refuge (stanza 5 remembers
'O what is that sound that so thrills the ear'), mountains are best
appreciated from a distance. The retired dentist of the opening is Edward
Kallman, father of Chester. The final line may be an allusion to Leslie
Stephen's 'A Bad Five Minutes on a Mountain'.

A lake allows an average father, walking slowly

?September 1952; 'Lakes', *New Poems by American Poets*, ed. R. Humphries (1953); SA,
p. 23, dedicated to the philosopher Isaiah Berlin.

The lakes that Auden is concerned with are charmingly described in family-
sized terms. Anything larger, though still drinkable, is, he says, an
'estranging sea', borrowing the phrase, via Arnold's 'To Marguerite', from
the Horatian 'oceano dissociabile' (*Odes*, I, 3), The 'lacustrine atmosphere'
breeds good manners. The first ecumenical council of the churches, at
which Constantine made Arianism heretical and therefore established
trinitarianism (stanza 3), was held on 'the Ascanian Lake' at Nicaea in
Bithynia. For this reason, Auden claims, lakes are ideal places to hold peace
talks ('Widdershins' means anti-clockwise, 'deasil' clockwise). The modest
scale of a lake is even flattering to a drowning man's sense of fatalism, and
so the examples continue in Auden's best essay-manner (the Webster
reference is from *The Duchess of Malfi*, V.V.52) culminating, in the
penultimate stanza, with an acknowledgement that one is likely to defend
one's ideal landscape aggressively (as Wordsworth resented the growing
popularity of the Lake District) because it represents a Paradisal retreat
which no appeal to common humanity ('amniotic mere' = womb) can make
one wish to share. It is this wrily critical point which governs the final
stanza's conscious whimsy about one's daydreams. The list is one of Auden's
favourite devices, and this one might just not know when to stop if it were
not kept in some sort of abbreviated tether by its alexandrine (the closest
prosodic analogy is Milton's 'Rocks, caves, lakes, fens, bogs, dens and shades
of death', to which 'Moraine, pot, oxbow, glint, sink, crater, piedmont,
dimple' becomes a kind of moral opposite). Needless to say, quite missing
the deliberate irony in Auden's tone in the final line ('Just reeling off their

names is ever so comfy'), critics have seized upon this 'comfy' and read it, as they read much of Auden, as unconsciously twee. This is a notorious example, and has been picked on by Nemerov, Larkin, Dodsworth and others, and by Jarrell, who exclaimed: 'Comfy, that's it! Just reading the poems is ever so comfy.' But Auden is adjusting, as he always does, the tone and diction to suit the meaning, and the meaning here is that such Paradisal retreats are a dangerous illusion (that Nature is benign, that they can be defended by savage dogs and man-traps, and so on) and therefore that contemplation of owning one is not only a *comfortable* activity, but, with all the limiting social overtones of the phrase, like the petit-bourgeois colonisation of Windermere, *ever so comfy.*

Old saints on millstones float with cats

?August 1953; 'Islands', SA, p. 25, dedicated first to Giocondo Sacchetti, his Ischian servant, and then in CSP66 to Giovanni Maresca, the local barber: for the quarrel with Sacchetti, see Farnan, p. 211.

'Islands', by being in short quatrains, seems more evidently a catalogue-poem than the others, pointing out that on islands are to be found saints, pirates, convicts, natives (despite Hobbes, innocent natural man ousted by civilised man), tyrants, poets and sunbathers. Elba, Lesbos, Capri and Ischia are linked as examples of the Ego's habitat. The saints and their cats were no doubt suggested by the anonymous Irish poem 'The Monk and his Pet Cat', which Auden liked well enough to include in *A Certain World*, p. 53.

I can imagine quite easily ending up

?July 1953; 'Plains', *London Magazine,* April 1954; SA, p. 27, dedicated to Wendell Johnson, a young friend of Auden's and subsequently an English professor at the City University of New York.

'Plains' provides a landscape without form or direction. Plain-dwellers are without choice in love: they are at the mercy of the primeval mother-goddess of the anthropologists (stanza 4), and of the strong who 'chamber with Clio' (stanza 6, i.e. make history, history being, as Auden remarked elsewhere, the 'realm of man's freedom and of his sin', *Theology,* November 1950). Thus plains are a nightmare landscape of victimisation for the poet, who is not a man of power (though he would like to own a cave with two exits: isn't the human body, i.e. the self that is even more frightening than

plains, a kind of cave with two exits?). Plains are a reminder of the
extensiveness of evil. Not even in poetry is anything 'lovely', and poetry is
not even real ('the case', i.e. the world, an allusion to Wittgenstein already
used in 'Ischia').

Dear water, clear water, playful in all your streams

July 1953; 'Streams', *Encounter*, June 1954; SA, p. 30, dedicated to Elizabeth Drew,
the critic.

In contrast to the nightmare of 'Plains' is the idyllic love-vision of 'Streams',
whose stanza was, as he explained to Wendell Johnson in a letter of 30 July
1953, a hybrid obtained by crossing the classical Alcaic with the Welsh
Englyn Cyrch. He marked stanza 2 as follows:

Air is <u>boast</u>ful at times, earth slovenly, fire rude,

a

But you in your bearing are always immac<u>ul</u>ate,

b

The <u>most</u> well-spoken of all the <u>old</u>er

a   c

Servants in the house<u>hold</u> of Mrs. <u>Nature</u>'

c   b

In this scheme c_1 and b_2 are disyllabic Skaldic rhymes. The water of the
streams is (as in 'In Praise of Limestone' or 'Ode to Gaea') 'pure being', an
eternally innocent presence unrelated to size ('unchristened brooks' as
much as the Brahmaputra, the great river of north-east India). Water may
provide national barriers (stanza 5) and ridicule the human motivation that
makes use of them (stanza 7), and in this role it is beyond human power to
spoil. But as a sacramental blessing upon his nobler ideals it prompts the
dream of the croquet match and procession of Eros in stanzas 12–17 which
is almost a sign of grace. In stanza 11, the reference to the philologist
Gaston Paris, who lectured on the *Chanson de Roland* during the siege of
Paris in 1870, calling the scientific pursuit of the truth a 'grande patrie'
beyond wars, may have been prompted by Rosenstock-Huessy, *Out of
Revolution* (1939), p. 231. Auden was staying at Keld, in Yorkshire, and on
22 June 1953 wrote to a friend from Kisdon Beck ('Am spending two nights
in one of my Holy Places without letting a soul know where I am. I am
writing this after tea on a grass bank beside a waterfall in a limestone gorge,

with buttercups and clover in front of my nose. What a spot to hold hands and swear an eternal tie'). Auden was worried that the dream might sound too queer. To Mrs Hawthorne in a letter of 19 August 1965 he wrote that it was 'meant to be a kind of modernised Petrarchan *Trionfo d'Amore*'.

Guard, Civility, with guns

Epigraph to Section II: 'In Sunshine and in Shade', SA, p. 33; CSP66, p. 270.

The mathematician and engineer Archimedes was killed by Marcus Claudius Marcellus, 'the Sword of Rome', at the sack of Syracuse in 212 BC. In the period of the McCarthyite witch-hunts, Auden's injunction has a certain nobility, since only a concern for the verbal exactness of the truth could counter political persecution by louts. The preservation of personal ideals in the face of the taunts of the Crowd is further suggested by the probable source of the title of Part II of the volume in the final paragraph of Charles Dickens's *Little Dorrit*: 'They went quietly down into the roaring streets, inseparable and blessed; and as they passed along in sunshine and in shade, the noisy and the eager, and the arrogant and the froward and the vain, fretted and chafed, and made their usual uproar.' Dickens for his part probably found the phrase in Wordsworth's *The Excursion*, 1.700.

She looked over his shoulder

1952; 'The Shield of Achilles', *Poetry*, October 1952; SA, p. 35; SP58, p. 152; CSP66, p. 294; CP, p. 596.

The title poem of the collection puts the post-war scene into just the kind of oblique and dramatically archetypal context that brings out both its full horror and its religious meaning. Thetis looks for the classical virtues on her son's shield (*Iliad* XVIII). She looks for order and good government but finds only its negative image, a spiritless totalitarianism; she looks for religion, but finds only a military execution parodying the crucifixion; she looks for art, and finds only an aimless violence. Auden was aware that the function of descriptions of shield-decoration in classical epics could be to represent life as it generally and eternally is, both in war and in peace (see, for example, ' "Aeneid" for our time', *Nation*, 10 March 1951): his poem is claiming that the distinction between the two had become in his era almost meaningless. (For the Homeric view, see Oliver Taplin, 'The Shield of Achilles within the *Iliad*', *Greece and Rome*, XXVII, 1, April 1980, pp. 1–21).

The quiet pace and feeling in this poem, and its conscious simplicity of diction, give it a moving conviction and grandeur. The passages in rhyme royal are closer in manner to the sonnets of 'In Time of War' than to Auden's earlier, generally satirical use of the stanza. Thetis' dismay is counterbalanced by the fated shortness of Achilles' life (*Iliad*, IX, 410 ff), so that Hephaestos' provision of such a shield seems significantly like the Christian God's provision of human free-will, as though the landscape of evil were a necessary condition for redemption. Any optimism in the thought of the death of the 'Iron-hearted man-slaying Achilles' is beautifully and ironically understated in the conclusion of the poem (for the epithets, see *Iliad*, XXII, 357; XVIII, 317 and Taplin, p. 19) so that the reader is left in effect lamenting what has replaced the Homeric. Taplin also implicitly demonstrates that the great scene between Achilles and Priam at XXIV, 503ff, is very much about someone weeping 'because another wept'. Just as the cause of war has become something to be argued by statistics and not discussed, and just as heroic combat has been replaced by execution, so Achilles has been 'replaced' by a ragged urchin who exists in a moral vacuum. It is an elaboration of the translation of Marcellus, in the epigraph to this section of *The Shield of Achilles*, into a 'lout'.

The sailors come ashore

1951; 'Fleet Visit', *Listener*, 3 January 1952; SA, p. 38; SP58, p. 154; CSP66, p. 247; CP, p. 549.

'Fleet Visit' seems somewhat to qualify a contemporary statement of Auden's in *The Enchafèd Flood* that 'the sailor on shore is symbolically the innocent god from the sea who is not bound by the law of the land and can therefore do anything without guilt' (p. 122). For here the 'natives pass with laws | And futures of their own', while the sailors (who have come out of their hollow ships, not as masterful intruders out of the Wooden Horse, but as ordinary conscripts in possession of a middle-brow bourgeois culture) are uncertain of their role. The ships themselves, however, are 'far from looking lost': Auden's teasing defence of their presence, on the purely aesthetic grounds that they look beautiful, is an interesting by-product of the Pax Americana, as though the purpose of NATO could really be disregarded for a second in 1952, however striking the 'pattern and line' of the ships in the Mediterranean harbour.

A shot: from crag to crag

1952; 'Hunting Season', *Third Hour*, 1954; SA, p. 40; CSP66, p. 247; CP, p. 548.

'Hunting Season' elaborates the proposition that the wooing of lovers is analogous to the hunting instinct. The first two stanzas achieve this with typical Audenesque drama and economy (the genital symbolism of oven and rifle, for example, and the transferred epithet 'startled'). The third stanza, however, can do little more than add a comic flourish: if all ideals conceal conflicting instincts of both pride and appetite, then even the poem must stop while the poet eats.

A starling and a willow-wren

1953; 'The Willow-wren and the Stare', *Encounter*, November 1953; SA, p. 41; SP58, p. 155; CSP66, p. 272.

This ballad in something of Auden's older manner offers a delicate and touching scepticism about human motivation in love. Behind it lie the dualities invoked in medieval debate poems (compare, in that genre, Auden's own 'Out of sight assuredly, not out of mind', *Juvenilia*, pp. 194ff). When the 'laughter-loving spirits' are replaced by 'their kinder partners' (i.e. their animal roles, as in 'the act of kind') the fire of Joy and of gratification is a place of silence. The intention is to civilise and to make sacred a passion that the poet suspects is grounded in greed and fear: the comments of the birds range from the admonitory to the humorously resigned, and lend a philosophical distance to the age-old argument. When the starling says 'God only knows', we may be able to take this literally as well, a reminder of Auden's belief that 'agape is the fulfilment and correction of eros, not its contradiction' (*Theology*, November 1950, p. 412).

'When rites and melodies begin'

August 1953; 'The Trial', *Times Literary Supplement*, 17 September 1954, and *Harper's Bazaar*, December 1954; 'The Proof', SA, p. 43; SP58, p. 157; CSP66, p. 273; CP, p. 576.

This formally balanced lyric was, according to Auden, an experiment in the manner of Campion in contrasting iambs and anapaests, and in trisyllabic substitution. It is about the trials of Tamino and Pamina in *The Magic Flute*,

II.v. Their love is seen by Auden as a type of Grace, won only by Tamino's perseverance and Pamina's faithfulness. In the opera it is the flute, given to Tamino by Astrafiammante (representing the instinctual life opposed to Sarastro's rule of reason) which tames the elements (the 'fermatas' here are musical pauses). There are hints that Auden sees their love as a symbol of the regaining of Paradise. 'Innocent? Yes. Ignorant? No' glances at C. S. Lewis's comment on Milton's prelapsarian Adam and Eve (*Preface to Paradise Lost*). Diana Dodge Lewars has notes on Auden's 1943 Swarthmore course: 'Temptation of Pamina and Tamino (silence, i.e. to grant each other individual identity. Not to try merging like Tristan–Isolde)'. But if Pamina and Tamino are seen allegorically as 'Anima – the unconscious with selfhood' and 'Ego', as the notes suggest, then their union, if not their merging, is an older theme in his work.

By all means sing of love but, if you do

?September 1953; ' "The Truest Poetry is the most Feigning" ', *New Yorker*, 13 November 1954; SA, p. 44, CSP66, p. 315; CP, p. 619.

The title is from Touchstone's remark to Audrey in *As You Like It*, III.iii, a kind of inverted syllogism naively betraying his own doubtful motives in wooing her: poetry is the language of lovers, and what lovers swear in poetry they feign, thus poetry is most typical ('truest' in that sense) when it is most feigning. Auden plays with Touchstone's meaning in his elaboration of the poet's 'ingenious fibs' about his feelings. Drafts show that it was 'poor Dante' who, when Beatrice asked 'Do you love me?', knew well 'The Thomist answer is cosi-cosi' (Texas). Line 10 borrows from the Countess Morphy: 'Plain cooking cannot be entrusted to plain cooks' (see *Faber Book of Aphorisms*, p. 369). Auden's examples culminate in the splendid all-purpose encomium hastily adapted (with the modification of epithets like 'lily-breasted' into 'lion-chested') to praise a Franco. This idea about all-purpose political verse may have been prompted by Cavafy's poem 'In a Township of Asia Minor' (see Auden's Introduction to *The Complete Poems of C. P. Cavafy*, tr. Rae Dalven, 1961, p. xii). The 'Goddess of wrynecks and wrens' is the Moon-Goddess (see Graves, *The White Goddess*, p. 173). The 'Great Reticulator of the Fens' was actually Saigon, King of Natrium, used by Auden in a poetry lecture as an example of identity in a more or less static world (Howard Griffin's notes in 1941). See also W. J. Perry, *Origins of Magic and Religion* (1923), p. 30, for the great benefit of Egyptian kings initiating irrigation systems. Auden had been a serious reader of Perry twenty years earlier.

Ultimately Auden takes the sense of 'truest' to imply 'conveying the truth', as we might expect, by showing that it is poetry's very trickery that reveals its awareness of the fact that the truth is unknowable. This is even so in the case of the love poem pure and simple ('No metaphor, remember, can express I A real historical unhappiness') and is doubly so in the case of 'truth in any serious sense', which, 'like orthodoxy, is a reticence'. For this latter unidentified *bon mot*, a great favourite of Auden's, see *The Dyer's Hand*, p. 21, and *The Faber Book of Aphorisms*, p. 77, which give contradictory hints as to its source. In *Forewords and Afterwords*, pp. 71 and 276, it is ascribed to an Anglican bishop.

O where would those choleric boys

September 1953: 'A Sanguine Thought', SA, p. 47; CSP66, p. 269; CP, p. 570.

This slight anapaestic epigram about political language was reprinted as a 'Short' in the 1966 *Collected Shorter Poems* and in the *Collected Poems*. It shares with the epigraph to its section of the book a concern for linguistic truth as a counter to political incitement, or more particularly for the ways in which rhetoric governs the political will.

Self-drivers may curse their luck

1954; 'A Permanent Way', SA, p. 48; SP58, p. 158; CSP66, p. 282; CP, p. 585.

'Self-drivers' are those who hire cars, not only those who drive themselves as opposed to being driven. If this poem is as particular about 'a love and a livelihood' as it appears to be, then the metaphor of travel is about adventure and its cost. There is something, too, of the protestant/catholic opposition in the metaphor: there is comfort in the 'dogma' of the train's rails, as there is comfort in imagining a possible choice without having to make it. The poem defends a settled love and a settled way of life, having once and for all 'chosen and paid'. Inevitably the attachment to Kallman comes to mind, and distinction made in his earlier poetry between 'straight' and 'crooked' love (e.g. in 'A Bride in the 30's').

Gently, little boat

1948; reprinted, with revisions, from *The Rake's Progress*, 'Barcarolle', SA, p. 49.

See the commentary on *The Rake's Progress*, p. 439.

Appearing unannounced, the moon

?1951; 'A Face in the Moon', *Botteghe Oscure*, 1951; 'The Moon Like x', *Third Hour*, 1954; 'Nocturne I', SA, p. 50; 'Nocturne', CSP66, p. 283; CP, p. 586.

In the first of the two nocturnes the mind admits to the heart that 'both are worshippers of force'. Thus the moon, mockingly invoked as a supernatural talisman, a love goddess, is seen to be only a myth or a machine, since Eros is an appetite with its own unaffected compulsions. The lover is real, though, and his moon-substitute on a purely practical plane might be any other real person belonging to the world of natural appetite (merely 'x', an algebraic representation of human possibility) who can, as he thought the moon could, 'make | Or break you'. This element of fortuitous influence in a real, as opposed to mythological or mechanical, world is seen wryly as a counterbalance to a dangerous solipsism: 'My world, the private motor-car | And all the engines of the State'. In effect, it is a tribute to the purely human, somewhere between myth and machine. Accepting the human in the algebraic terms of the poem is potentially saint-like: the 'x' is anyone who happens to need you (cf. 'The Virgin and the Dynamo', *The Dyer's Hand*, p. 63), though Auden's examples are designed to be comic and exasperating enough to absolve him from claiming sainthood, even if he is unhappy at merely being 'a small functionary'. The terms were borrowed from Henry Adams, and used by Auden as early as 'New Year Letter', line 1466 and note.

Make this night loveable

October 1953; 'Nocturne II', SA, p. 52; 'Nocturne', SP58, p. 159; CSP66, p. 274; CP, p. 577.

The second nocturne deals with its difficult dreams with more emotional directness. The address to the moon itself is not deconstructed: it involves the satellite in its role as a symbol of the imagination, able to make absent friends accessible in dreams. The shift from 'friends' in stanza 1 to 'love' in the final stanza has an element of calculated dramatic shock: the poem suddenly turns into a charm against jealousy. Auden explained to Wendell Johnson that the hidden three-foot norm of lines 1, 2 and 4 was trochaic, and of lines 3 and 5 iambic. The poem is difficult to scan in this way.

At peace under this mandarin sleep, Lucina

October 1953; 'In Memoriam L.K.A. 1950–1952', SA, p. 53; SP58, p. 160; CSP66, p. 268; CP, p. 570.

This epitaph for one of the Kallman–Auden cats (her initials were properly hyphenated in later texts) is an englyn. Auden pointed out to Wendell Johnson its pattern of rhyme and assonance as follows (obligatory rhymes in capitals, 'extra decorations' in lower-case):

c		d	e		f	A	g	B
g	B	c		g		d	h	A
		g	d	g		I	e	A
		e	d	j	j	I	h	A

Lucina was a minor Roman deity, one of the midwifely attributes of Juno, enabling babies to see the light of day; and also a character in Ariosto and Boiardo. Epomeo is Ischia's highest mountain.

To save your world you asked this man to die

October 1953; 'Epitaph for the Unknown Soldier', SA, p. 54; CSP66, p. 268; CP, p. 570.

Like Auden's Unknown Citizen, his Unknown Soldier has made no complaint, but the powers which have used him cannot make his world free or happy. The epitaph is distinctly a poem of the Cold War.

From this new culture of the air we finally see

August 1954; 'Ode to Gaea', broadcast in BBC programme 'New Verse', October 1954, and printed in the *Listener*, 15 December 1954; SA, p. 55; CSP66, p. 251; CP, p. 553.

There had been glimpses of 'this new culture of the air' in 'In Transit', written four years earlier. Here, with the widest perspectives, it prompts a meditation of great virtuosity. Like 'Ischia' it is in a 13/12/7/8 syllabic stanza, though rhymed, with a manner of procedure reminiscent of the Horatian ode. The aeroplane allows a view of spring, season of love, as an annual movement of natural masses, a 'vernal plunge' in which 'her desolations' are 'glamorously carpeted | with . . . delicious spreads of nourishment', and where on land, with Auden's talent for descriptive riddling at its best, the mating of creatures begins. The view of Gaea (the earth) that science provides is in contrast with the unknown monsters beyond the boundaries of the cartographer's Christendom and seems even more mysterious, because less concerned with the human than with the inanimate, such as water, sketched in a brilliant phrase: 'she joins girl's-ear lakes | to bird's-foot deltas with lead-blue squiggles.' The sneering words in stanza 9 were borrowed from a debate on homosexuality in the House of Lords in May 1954 (see Jenkins, *Auden Studies* 3, p. 87).

In response to this neglect, man must first cultivate his sense of order and good manners (stanzas 10 onwards). In Stanza 16, the tipsy poet is Anacreon, and the baby he cursed male. Auden shows that it is natural to invent a wilful Olympian deity who may tire of the Greeks and become interested in the Scythians (the Hippemolgoi, or mare-milkers), and whose destructions, therefore, are unpredictable and inevitable. Thus it is that 'manners' may be preferable to a 'kantian conscience' (i.e. believing that your behaviour is good only when it is consciously obeying the moral law), and thus it is that the last stand in the passes may be made by admirers of Praed, Rossini and Carême. This unlikely prospect was to be elaborated with less challenging mock-effeteness in the later poem, 'Grub First, Then Ethics', which culminates in a similar stand of gourmets at Thermopylae. The failure of Athens at Syracuse in 413 BC is brought in as evidence (from Thucydides' acccount of the Sicilian Expedition, included in Auden's *Portable Greek Reader*, 1948) that we cannot control the world but merely imagine better ones. Gaea remains unapproachable, and finds human ideals irrelevant. Only Amphion (who drew stones after him with his magic lyre) has ever moved her (and that is a joke).

The sequence 'Horae Canonicae', which concludes *The Shield of Achilles*, was long in the making. Auden spoke of his plan 'for a series of secular poems based on the Office' to Ursula Niebuhr in 1946, and in the following year borrowed from her a book on the subject. These Offices, the canonical hours, are based upon the events of the Crucifixion and are the Church's set times for prayer and meditation every three hours of the day, thus dividing the twenty-four-hour period into eight. The natural sequence therefore runs: Prime (6 a.m.), Tierce (9 a.m.), Sext (noon), Nones (3 p.m.), Vespers (6 p.m.), Compline (9 p.m.), Matins (midnight) and Lauds (3 a.m.). Auden omits Matins (which are in any case in practice often said immediately before Lauds). This change, reducing the offices to seven, allowed him to accommodate Hugo de St Victor's eight Orders of the Sacraments (perceived by Rosenstock-Huessy to correspond exactly to his conception of the ideologies of Revolutions) with the more suggestive symbolism of sevens which Rosenstock-Huessy himself developed (see *Out of Revolution*, pp. 547ff: the missing eighth here appears to be the Creator himself) and which is corroborated in certain respects by Robert Graves in *The White Goddess*, which Auden was also reading at the time (see especially chapter 15, 'The Seven Pillars').

To assist him conceptually in the writing of the poem, Auden drafted many tables of septenary categories (e.g. in pages from a notebook owned by Robert Wilson, Berg; in the 1950–54 notebook at Texas; and in the 1947–64 notebook in the British Library). These categories go far beyond even the arcane historical, theological and anthropological connections posited by Rosenstock-Huessy and Graves. They include, for example, social categories, physiological categories and even personal categories (the latter taking Auden himself from the age of seven and a half to the age of fifty-two and a half, i.e. six years into the future, beyond the completion of the sequence). Auden also attempted in his drafts to subsume them into a tripartite grouping of 'one household . . . one world . . . one God' based on Rosenstock-Huessy's concept of 'una sancta', that there are many sects but only one world-wide economic society (*Out of Revolution*, p. 495). It is clear that whatever the significance of such symbolism in his sources, for Auden the tables were little more than a suggestive aid to the writing of the poems. The framework as it survives in the sequence itself is simply the barest reminder of the devotional. It leaves the individual poems free to range widely in their attempt to define that continual awareness of the guilt and sacrifice which is the foundation of Christianity and of the Christian's efforts to re-establish a temporal community (see, for example, the significantly chance rhymes of *will* and *kill* in 'Nones').

The sequence is therefore about the nature of such a community, glimpsed through the daily recreation of the events of Good Friday. Later, Auden was to write: 'Christmas and Easter can be subjects for poetry, but Good Friday, like Auschwitz, cannot . . . Poems about Good Friday have, of course, been written, but none of them will do' (*A Certain World*, pp. 168–9). Auden had probably never ceased to be affected by the Crucifixion. A letter to William McElwee of Good Friday 1928 is headed 'Jesus died today', and at that time Auden was in the habit of writing Easter Sunday poems. The sequence appears, with the epigraph ' "Immolatus vicerit" ' ('having been sacrificed, the victory will have been his'), in SA, p. 59; SP58, p. 177, CSP66, p. 323; SP68, p. 101; CP, p. 627. The epigraph comes from the opening stanza of Venantius Fortunatus' Hymn to the Holy Cross (see *Oxford Book of Mediaeval Latin Verse*, ed. F. J. E. Raby, 1959, p. 74: 'Pange, lingua, gloriosi proelium certaminis | et super crucis tropaeo dic triumphum nobilem, | qualiter redemptor orbis immolatus vicerit.' The hymn is sung in the Roman Church on Maundy Thursday. For Auden's poem about Fortunatus, 'Under Sirius', see p. 421.

The poems will be treated individually below, and their publication details given separately.

Simultaneously, as soundlessly

August 1949; 'Prime', first appeared on the recording *Pleasure Dome*, Columbia ML 4259, 1949; N, p. 9; SA, p. 61.

Auden used the first poem in the sequence as a major exemplum in a Swarthmore lecture of 9 March 1950 on 'Nature, History and Poetry', and distributed a leaflet to the audience which contained both the poem and early manuscript readings. Some of this material is reproduced in Spears, pp. 317–8, as an illustration of the discipline of the syllabic form chosen (lines of nine and seven) and of the effects of internal rhyming. In the draft tables, Prime is associated with the Fall, with the individual and with the French Revolution (which perhaps explains the phrase 'rebellious fronde' in the first stanza). The body wakes at 6 a.m. dispelling the dreams of the active subconscious and thus symbolising the creation of Adam, 'without a name or history'. A variety of sources feed into this treatment of the cognitive and the volitional ego and their daily-renewed relationship with the world in which the individual finds himself (e.g. the 'I-and-the-world-about-me' of Husserl, *Ideas*, tr. Gibson, 1931, and Valéry, as quoted in the epigraph to part II of 'Balaam and His Ass' in *The Dyer's Hand*, p. 109). As soon as the will comes into play (moving an arm, breathing), human nature is assumed and the Fall is re-enacted ('Paradise | Lost of course and myself owing a death') with all the human responsibility for history which that implies.

After shaking paws with his dog

October 1953; 'Terce', *Catholic Worker*, January 1954; SA, p. 63.

'Terce' (more properly, perhaps, 'Tierce') finds at 9 a.m. that the anonymous individual of 'Prime' has become the specific hangman, judge or poet who will, unknowingly, participate in the coming crucifixion (in the draft tables, Terce is associated with the sentencing of Christ and with 'The law abiding'). The daily prayer of the working man is ironically answered: 'not one of us will slip up', and 'by sundown | We shall have had a good Friday.' The unconcern of the numerous deities leaves responsibility firmly with man, even though the Christian paradox of God's omnipotence and man's free-will is briefly raised in parenthesis. The whole sequence is concerned with the contribution which the individual is asked to make to the scheme of guilt and redemption.

You need not see what someone is doing

Spring 1954; 'Sext', SA, p. 65.

'Sext' treats in three parts the social organisms necessary for the sacrifice (noon is the hour of the Crucifixion, associated in the draft tables with the sacrifice of Abraham and with the English Revolution of 1649). These are agents, authority and the crowd. These are also the constituent elements of civilisations: first, the idea of a vocation which leads men to ignore 'the appetitive goddesses' (Aphrodite, Artemis) and yields the 'notion of a city'; second (contrasting with this, as does Apollo with Hermes in 'Under Which Lyre', or the tyrants with the true 'makers of history' in the poem of that title), the executives, representatives of the will, without which the courtesies of the city could not exist; third, the crowd, the negative witnessing crowd ('its existence is chimerical', *The Dyer's Hand*, p. 63). Without the last of these, man would ironically be no better than the 'social exoskeletons', the ants and termites, whose society can never develop into a community because it has no idea of Satan ('The Prince of this world').

What we know to be not possible

July 1950; 'Nones', N, p. 48; SA, p. 70.

By 3 p.m. the deed is done, and in the terrible siesta time which follows, the individual tries to come to terms with his responsibility. He cannot blame the crowd, which has dispersed. The averted presence of the Madonna symbolises man's betrayal of his potentiality: the building of the city is only half-finished, and it seems impossible that it should ever be completed by men who themselves feel like discarded artifacts. The fourth stanza suggests, in notably Eliotic terms, that the betrayal is the betrayal of Eros: 'We shall always now . . . under | The mock chase and the mock capture, | The racing and tussling and splashing, | The panting and the laughter, | Be listening for the cry and stillness | To follow after.' Auden yoked love and violence together in several poems at this period (e.g. in 'Nocturne I', line 12, or 'Memorial for the City', line 18). The guilt is a dilemma of man's nature, though the will may dream of evading its responsibility (stanza 6 is a splendidly atmospheric nightmare, culminating in an image perhaps drawn from James's story 'The Private Life') and the flesh may be technically 'wronged' (stanza 7), just as awed by the betrayal as the watching animals (Auden introduces such details like a Renaissance painter).

If the hill overlooking our city . . .

June 1954; 'Vespers', *Encounter*, February 1955; SA, p. 74.

'Vespers' returns, at 6 p.m., to the urge to build the Just City, whose beginnings were defined in 'Sext'. In the draft tables Vespers is associated with Rosenstock-Huessy's Papal Revolution of 1075 (cf. 'Memorial for the City' II), which may have something to do with the division between spiritual and temporal authority implicit in the duality of the Arcadian and the Utopian. This duality is in effect a parallel contrast between his own ideal Eden and the materialist's New Jerusalem, in terms reminiscent of the Hermetic–Apollonian categories of 'Under Which Lyre' and possibly, too, of the distinction between a community and a society in *The Enchafèd Flood*, p. 36. He has defined his distinction elsewhere: 'In their relation to the actual fallen world, the difference between Eden and New Jerusalem is a temporal one. Eden is a past world in which the contradictions of the present world have not yet arisen; New Jerusalem is a future world in which they have at last been resolved' (*The Dyer's Hand*, p. 409). The distinctions in

'Vespers' wear an air of lightness. Auden's Eden, in particular, with its miners playing medieval musical instruments in a landscape not unlike that of West Oxford, is deliberately more bizarre even than his Eden in *The Dyer's Hand*, pp. 6–7, but the distinctions do act as a reminder to each idealist of the peculiar paradox that the Christian *felix culpa* embodies ('but for him I could forget the blood, but for me he could forget the innocence'). They are, indeed, *doppelgängers*.

Now, as desire and the things desired

Spring 1954; 'Compline', SA, p. 78.

At 9 p.m. 'Compline' returns us to sleep, as an image of death ('the end, for me as for cities, | Is total absence'), and as a state in which the heart's motion, like that of the stars, merely obeys necessity. The draft tables associate Compline with the Last Judgement and with the unnamed revolution of 998, which is the date of the introduction of the liturgy invented by Odilo of Cluny to celebrate All Souls (see my commentary on *The Age of Anxiety*, p. 370). This penitential context allows the sequence which has begun with unwilled matter in the realm of nature to return to a consciousness of history within the realm of time, i.e. to remember (as the poem insists for its first three stanzas, like a refrain, that it does not) what happened between noon and three, the hours during which Christ hung on the cross. In the last stanza, where this is indeed remembered, Auden shifts the sequence into its role as prayer by quoting the mass and asking for forgiveness for himself and Kallman ('dear C') and for them to be spared 'in the youngest day' (which may be both the Last Day and the ever-present Now in which consciousness of guilt must arrive). The final image is of 'the dance' of the Trinity ('perichoresis', or circumincession, was a standard term of scholastic theology describing the mysterious interrelation of the Father with the Son, and of both with the Holy Ghost).

Among the leaves the small birds sing

1952; as final chorus of the libretto 'Delia', *Botteghe Oscure*, 1953; revised as 'Lauds', SA, p. 80.

After such a visionary moment in 'Compline', the final poem in the sequence shows humanity waking not to guilt but to worship. This musical representation of the mass-bell, the commanding imperative of Christian communion, is achieved in the form of the Spanish *cossante* which Auden had found described in Gerald Brenan's *The Literature of the Spanish People* (1951), p. 54. In the Texas 1950–54 notebook (fol. 101) Auden's mnemonic plan for the repeated lines also shows the original rhyme scheme of the *cossante* which he abandoned:

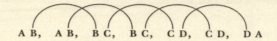

A B,   A B,   B C,   B C,   C D,   C D,   D A

The rhythm of the lines suggests that it was this poem that Auden was referring to when he mentioned the influence of Wyatt's 'Wherewith Love to the harts forest he fleeth' on 'certain lines' of his own (*The Dyer's Hand*, p. 46). Such a model was metrically appropriate for the original use of the poem as the final chorus in 'Delia', adapted from Peele's sixteenth-century play *The Old Wives' Tale*. The most significant change that Auden made to this chorus when adapting it for 'Horae Canonicae' was to replace the refrain (*'Day breaks for joy and sorrow'*) with a new one that describes the individual sinners that make up the church congregation: '*In solitude, for company*'. In making the change it seems likely that the image of the revived mill-wheel in stanza 5 put him in mind of Edward Thomas's 'The Mill-Water', and its similar line 17: 'Solitude, company'. 'Lauds' was set by Lennox Berkeley as the first of his *Five Poems* (Chester, 1960).

Homage to Clio

Auden's third post-war collection of shorter poems was published in April 1960 in the US and in July 1960 in England. It includes half a dozen poems that had appeared in the 1956 pamphlet *The Old Man's Road*. In October 1956 he took up his duties as Professor of Poetry at Oxford, and in October 1957 he bought his house at Kirchstetten; from 1958 he was speaking German during his summers. The change was celebrated in the poem 'Good-Bye to the Mezzogiorno' and eventually in the terminal dates '1948–1957' with which he described his Mediterranean period in the 1966 *Collected Shorter Poems*. *Homage to Clio* includes the 'unwritten poem' 'Dichtung und Wahrheit' of 1959 and another half dozen poems which were written after he left Ischia, but essentially it marks the end of a distinct phase of his writing.

Bullroarers cannot keep up the annual rain

1959; HC, p. 7; CSP66, p. 270; CP, p. 572.

The volume is dedicated to Professor E. R. Dodds and his wife. Auden had been introduced to Dodds by his father at a meeting of the Staff Social Club at Birmingham University while still an undergraduate, and they had remained friends ever since. The dedicatory quatrain is, like that of *The Shield of Achilles*, consciously apologetic for a drying-up of inspiration. The bull-roarer is a device of wood and string whirled round the head to make a noise in certain rain-inducing religious ceremonies of the Australian aborigines. It seems a pointed symbol for the pretentious rituals of certain kinds of meaningless poetry. Auden favourably contrasts methods of dry farming, which elsewhere he was to describe as the only technical advance made by the Romans in agriculture (in an article, 'The Fall of Rome', written for a *Life* series in 1966, see *Auden Studies* 3, p. 120).

Between those happenings that prefigure it

?1959; HC, p. 13; CP, p. 716.

The epigraph to Part I is a paradox about the Incarnation: 'anamnesis' is the unforgetting of the soul's prior existence, or the process of learning by recognition, in Plato's theory, so that the quatrain is also in a sense about the mysterious and significant 'event' in each human life that is its redemption.

Our hill has made its submission and the green

June 1955; 'Homage to Clio', *Encounter*, November 1955; *The Old Man's Road*, 1956; HC, p. 15; CSP66, p. 307.

In the title poem of the collection, Auden puts himself into a context of nature in the season of spring: his uncertain belonging is not so much because he is no creature's prey and emits no satisfactory pheromone, but because of the mental and silent world of language (stanzas 1 to 5). Callan (p. 224) has pointed out the resemblance of the opening to Horace's ode 'Diffugere nives . . .'. The initial reflection is upon the differences between the human world and the natural world ruled by the twin urges of sex ('Provocative Aphrodite') and hunting ('Virago Artemis'). Robert Graves's *The White Goddess* (1946), chapter 22, is perhaps the source of many of Auden's ideas about these goddesses. The point about humanity is that it is aware of itself as a multitude of individual consciousnesses whose desires are historically conditioned. If life were merely a matter of instinct (like the cock in stanza 9 'pronouncing himself himself | Though all his sons had been castrated and eaten'), we would be like other species, making our 'tribal outcry' at the proper season. We would prefer to be unique (Auden refers again in stanza 10 to our strange disbelief in our parents' sexual begetting of us; compare his analysis of Pascal in *The Profile and the Devourer*, 11).

Our individual awareness is presided over by Clio, the Muse of History who creatively intervenes between us and the 'magical centre' (stanza 8) of the absolutely natural instinctual life which the animals enjoy, symbolised in the poem by noise. Clio, described as the Muse of Time and the Madonna of Silences, is, in effect, the Virgin Mary. The mother of Christ gave the timeless and the bodiless an existence, and brought silence to decisive sound. On Corpus Christi Day 1956, Auden wrote to Ursula Niebuhr, sending the poem:

you were so much in my mind while I was writing it, as the only person I know who will understand my Anglican problem: – Can one write a hymn to the Blessed Virgin Mary without being 'pi'? The Prots don't like her and the Romans want bleeding hearts and sobbing tenors. So here is my attempt which I submit to your severe, theological and feminine eye.

Artemis and Aphrodite are powers whose rule we must obey, but birth and death for us are also unique historical fact (stanza 17). Auden's argument at this point establishes those who defy Clio as secular tyrants, thus, like the children of Artemis, victims of time. In stanza 19, the 'Short, The Bald, The Pious, The Stammerer' are nicknames of medieval kings. The Duke of Cumberland was originally the Duke of York in drafts (cf. the nursery rhyme 'O, the grand old Duke of York', who in a version by Robert Graves, *Less Familiar Nursery Rhymes*, 1926, is actually the Duke of Cumberland). The Laxey Wheel is in the Isle of Man (Auden left it to Sean Day-Lewis in 'Last Will and Testament', *Letters from Iceland*, p. 254). In drafts, Auden worked long and elaborately at the implications of distinct secular and temporal 'motion' and 'story' being embodied comprehensively in the images of the Duke and the Wheel (Texas 1950–54 notebook).

Within a shadowland of trees

1957; 'Reflections in a Forest', first printed as a broadside by DePauw University, reprinted in *DePauw Alumnus*, December 1957, and *Listener*, 23 July 1959; HC, p. 18; CP, p. 669.

'Reflections in a Forest' follows the familiar Auden procedure of contrasting humanity with nature (in this case, trees) and underlining the paradoxical advantages of duplicity. Quarrelling, lies, bluff and so on, depend entirely upon a human conception of what is not the case, which trees do not have. But it is our very awareness of such distinctions (e.g. between the naked and the nude, the first a sacred symbol that actively expresses what it is, the second passively expressed and profaned) which ultimately helps us to discover the truth about our destiny.

We don't need a face in the picture to know

1959; 'Hands', HC, p. 20; CP, p. 670.

'Hands' is a physiological essay with a light and inventive touch: these are our distinctive feature, whose language is international and whose characteristics (fingerprints, handwriting) are individual and exact. The contrast here is with the human mind which does not acknowledge limitations, praying not to the finite god of purpose, but to the *Deus Absconditus*, the hidden god (see Isaiah, xlv.15), and aware of absence and time.

Waking on the Seventh Day of Creation

July 1959; 'The Sabbath', *Observer*, 6 September 1959; HC, p. 22; SP68, p. 81; CP, p. 672.

'The Sabbath' shows that only man among the creatures shares in the divine purpose: the poem is engagingly offhand about human persistence, and contrasts our late appearance in terms of the geological time-scale with our importance as biblical lords of creation.

There is one devil in the lexicon

1955; 'Merax & Mullin', *Semi-colon*, 1956; *The Old Man's Road*, 1956; HC, p. 23; CSP66, p. 312; CP, p. 615.

The lexicon that Auden actually used was Maximilian Rudwin, *The Devil in Legend and Literature* (1931), where Mullin (p. 80) is described as 'principal *valet de chambre* to his Satanic Majesty' and Morax (p. 79) as 'a great earl and president'. Auden noted these names down in haste in a notebook, and as with Tutevillus and Nybbas (see the poem 'Cattivo Tempo', which calls them Tubervillus and Nybbar) was not wholly accurate in doing so. These devils are illusions about Eros which lie in wait for those who, as it were, want to escape from the realm of Clio to the realm of Aphrodite (compare 'who would unwish themselves' with the 'mere commanders' of 'Makers of History': 'What did they do but wish?'). 'Wishing' is thus to assert one's freedom and one's propensity to sin; it becomes a characteristic of jealousy and impotence (and of the satirist) to deny this in oneself and yet to ascribe its perversions to others, just as in a war (very much the activity of those who 'wish') a world of unobliging objects is comically assumed to be sexually aberrant. Almost as a footnote to this is described a 'nastier, more deadly' devil, who urges 'laodicean' (i.e. indifferent) lovers to 'swear | Undying love'. The dangers of such a delusion were elaborated by Auden in 'Dichtung und Wahrheit' in the same volume.

Should the shade of Plato

This poem found its proper place in the sequence 'Thanksgiving for a Habitat', in *About the House* and is treated on p. 491.

All that which lies outside our sort of why

1956; 'Objects', *Encounter*, January 1957; HC, p. 27; CSP66, p. 320; CP, p. 624.

'Objects' is the first of three sonnets in *Homage to Clio* which share a certain air of extemporised 1950s flatness, almost suggesting in places a deliberate pastiche (i.e. the offhand Empsonian opening to the sestet here: 'There is less grief than wonder on the whole'). The sonnet proposes that animals' acceptance of death does not make their lives any the less rich: their self-sufficiency is some guarantee of Life's value. Indeed, our loss, as human beings, is concerned only with 'our bestial substance', which, with the soul, makes up the 'person': our mourning is in fact for a division unknown to animals.

A sentence uttered makes a world appear

?1956; 'Words', HC, p. 28; CSP66, p. 320; CP, p. 624.

'Words' uncovers the twofold nature of the relationship between language and truth. First, language is true in itself, as being an enclosed system ('Words have no word for words that are not true': evidently Auden had been reading Wittgenstein). Second, it is true as being the natural form that the truth takes, a fact that explains the urge to gossip and the chance symbolising of 'our fate' in words. But behind Auden's examples here is an insinuation that words ultimately cannot explain the truth. The most significant 'Arcadian tale' presumably is the story of the Fall of Man in Eden. As a hard-luck story it becomes a prevaricating excuse with extenuating circumstances, as though the language itself in which the tale has to be told carries all the guilty weight of Adam's partial understanding.

Similarly, the lonely quest parodied by rustics in a ring-dance, while as thematically attractive as the double-plot of drama (and actually created as a dramatic contrast by Auden in the transition from the first scene to the first chorus in *Delia*), hardly allows 'verbal chance' the opportunity to express a truth faithfully. Indeed, Auden's familiar choice of symbol in his final line in itself underlines the impossibility of really knowing the truth one is seeking. If the Knight (the soul) does not know, how can the rustics (language)?

So large a morning so itself to lean

1956; 'The Song', *Truth*, 12 October 1956; HC, p. 29; CSP66, p. 321; CP, p. 625.

'The Song', which is about the purity of song, itself attempts an unusual purity of verbal effect. It consists of two sentences, which are less syntactically obscure than they first appear (eleven marks of punctuation in the TS prepared for the printer were deleted by Auden, and instructions were given to include only the stops at the end of the octave and sestet). In a harmonious dawn landscape, a bird is racing with its own reflection in a lake. Its double is quite as daring, but the bird's rebellious will compels a struggle which is gratuitous, since natural beauty is effortless, and leaves 'care' behind. The morning 'can cope with' the bird, because it has no need to be concerned: when the bird (representing the poet) climbs to song (art here as compensation), it 'lacks all picture of reproach', presumably reproach to the lover who has caused the 'care' and the sullying of whiteness ('drab' as a verb having a sexual meaning). The sense is curiously close to that in the final stanza of the early poem 'Taller today, we remember similar evenings', where dawn in a valley also brings a 'peace | No bird can contradict'. Nature is always generously greater than individual human unhappiness. Thus its beauty transcends the moral significance of the motive to song ('what it started up to say') and the bird finally merely sings in harmony with dawn and with nature.

Serious historians care for coins and weapons

1955; 'Makers of History', *London Magazine*, September 1955; *The Old Man's Road*, 1956; HC, p. 30; CSP66, p. 297; CP, p. 600.

This poem is the plainest assertion of one of Auden's major historical themes in his work of these years, that serious historians care less for the powerful rulers, who so often have become legendary, than for the craftsmen and artists who are responsible for the tangible remains of their civilisations, without which even the legend could not be understood. The theme is implicit in Auden's earlier use of Blake's opposition of the Prolific and the Devourer, but here it carries a fresh paradox due to Auden's conception in the volume's title-poem that Clio is a muse of silence. The rulers may be mere commanders, but by 'wishing' (stanza 6) they actually enter the world of myth, becoming legendary and composite. Auden distinguished between 'to wish' and 'to will' in some MS notes on Freedom and Choice in the 1947–8 notebook (Berg): 'Freedom of wish is infinite, though not really freedom. To wish = to wish that what is, should not be. Which is impossible. To will is to choose a possible future based on the existing present.' The rulers' 'immortality' is akin to nature's (stanza 5), while true achievement is anonymous and therefore in Clio's terms silent.

Begot like other children, he

1959; 'T the Great', HC, p. 32; CSP66, p. 299; CP, p. 601.

'T the Great' is a ruler of the kind described in 'Makers of History' who has passed into legend. Auden's anagrammatic riddle underlines the fact that a tyrant's name, by being itself legendary, becomes a mere cipher. A bogey such as Tamburlaine is perpetually replaceable. He is eventually succeeded by 'N' (Napoleon), who in turn is succeeded by 'S' (Stalin). Despite the light tone of the disyllabic and trisyllabic rhyming couplets, this is another serious poem about what is historically important (Clio's cup) and is an attempt after Stalin's death in 1953 to put his terrors into historical perspective.

No, Virgil, no

1959; 'Secondary Epic', *Mid-Century*, December 1959; HC, p. 34; CSP66, p. 296; CP, p. 598.

It is interesting to compare 'Secondary Epic' with 'The Shield of Achilles' in his previous collection: the move to the shield of Aeneas (made by Vulcan, i.e. Hephaestos, *Aeneid*, VII.675ff) represents a shift of interest generally noticeable in *Homage to Clio*, from the moral to the historical. Here Auden is interested in the fact that prophetic scenes on the shield could naturally not extend further into the future than 31 BC (the latest reference in the poem, the date of the victory of Octavius at Actium). The idea probably came from

Charles Cochrane, *Christianity and Classical Culture*, 1939, pp. 27ff, where he discusses the true significance for Virgil of the *Pax Augusta*, and Virgil's own importance in consolidating the Augustan vision, Auden imagines some 'refugee rhetorician' adding a later gloss about the Fall of Rome to the barbarians (this is wittily exemplified in a minor eighteenth-century blank verse like that of, say, Dyer), and at the end of the poem he exposes the prophecies of Anchises in Book VI for mentioning Romulus and Augustus, but not disclosing 'the names predestined for the Catholic boy | Whom Arian Odovacer will depose'. This refers to the barbarian ruler Odovacer, or Odoacer, who in AD 476 deposed the ironically named Romulus Augustus, last Emperor of the West, forcibly retiring him to a villa in Ravenna. There is a fine scornful passage about the unworthy 'Momyllus Augustulus' in Gibbon, chapter 36. Auden referred again to Romulus Augustulus ('a boy who bore the names of the founder of the Republic and the founder of the Empire'), and to Turnus being avenged by these events, in his 1966 article 'The Fall of Rome' (see *Auden Studies* 3). His former teacher, Frank McEachran, had written about Romulus Augustulus in his book *The Destiny of Europe* (1932), p. 51.

No use invoking Apollo in a case like theirs

1955; 'The Epigoni', *Poetry London–New York*, March–April 1956, and *Nimbus*, Summer 1956; *The Old Man's Road*, 1956; HC, p. 36; CSP66, p. 302; CP, p. 605.

'The Epigoni' examines literary Alexandrianism. The epigoni (a succeeding and less distinguished generation, so called after the sons of the Seven against Thebes) are here the Latin poets of the declining Empire, involved in just that cultural predicament which Auden had already likened to our own: an impotent expectation of barbarianism, and the poetic choice of 'dramatizing their doom' or 'expiring in preposterous mechanical tricks'. They sensibly chose the latter, 'epanaleptics, rhopalics, anacyclic acrostics', forms which 'can safely be spanked in a scholar's footnote' but which have in the circumstances a kind of nobility. If we call them shallow, it is because our generation would not conform to Auden's touchstone for critics (see *The Dyer's Hand*, p. 470).

The watch upon my wrist

?; 'Parable', HC, p. 37; CP, p. 716.

This is either a trite exposition of Paleyan natural theology or a wry Kafkaesque pill for religious despair. In the printer's TS of *Homage to Clio*, it is annotated (not in Auden's hand) 'To Margaret Gardiner WHA'.

Looking up at the stars, I know quite well

?September 1957; 'The More Loving One', *Esquire*, April 1958; HC, p. 38; CSP66, p. 282; CP, p. 584.

'The More Loving One' seems merely to be an extravagant way of coming to terms with an unreciprocated love: how much worse it is to be the loved one who cannot return the affection. The absence of all 'stars' may be contemplated, like the absence of desire, with only a precarious equanimity.

Expecting your arrival tomorrow . . .

1959; 'Dichtung und Wahrheit (An Unwritten Poem)', HC, p. 39; CP, p. 647.

The notion of an unwritten poem, published as such in the poet's lifetime, is not of course new. Some, but not all, of the sections of Coleridge's 'The Blossoming of the Solitary Date Tree', for example, are versified. The fifty sections of 'Dichtung und Wahrheit' do not, however, make any attempt at versification. Nor is much of the material conceived or arranged in a way which begins to seem poetical (the italicised portions, prefaced by 'I should like to say', are an exception). The subtitle is a ruse, in fact, for 'Dichtung und Wahrheit' is not so much an unwritten poem, but an essay on the impossibility of such a poem's subject, that of knowing what one means when one thinks 'I love You'. Auden's manner in writing it is largely the manner of his most economical and aphoristic prose, from *The Prolific and the Devourer* to the essays on 'Reading' and 'Writing' in *The Dyer's Hand*, the manner of his 'pensées'.

The title is borrowed from Goethe's autobiography, *Poetry and Truth*, and it summarises the central concern of the poem (for I shall consider it such) that a good poem need not conform to the biographical circumstances of the writer's life. Does Auden argue this as an evasion? The donnée of the poem is the imminent arrival of the loved one, a new passion. The thing that makes it so different from a poem like 'Calypso', also about such a situation, is that the state of being in love is subjected to lengthy metaphysical questioning (the contrast of poetry with music and painting, the contrast of erotic with epic subjects, the necessary involvement of loving in the past and loving in the future, the irrelevance of sex, the possibility of Romantic Hate, and so on, are the topics of disquisition). Behind this questioning is the partly submerged secondary theme, which necessarily arises from the difficulty of knowing what one means when one says 'I love You': does one love out of some arbitrary and ultimately unjustifiable and inexplicable exposure to the unique individual that 'You' happens to be (in this case; the 'You' who is shortly to arrive)? Another work by Goethe explored the issues raised by this conundrum. In his novella *Die Wahlverwandschaften* the meaning that Auden is attempting to express would be accounted for by the notion of affinity. Counter to affinity is the more expedient notion of juxtaposition. Auden explores the latter in place and in time. The absolutes of affinity are undermined by the awkward practical questions of juxtaposition in possibly the best-remembered section of the poem, XLVIII: ' "I will love You for ever," swears the poet. I find this easy to swear too. *I will love You at 4.15 p.m. next Tuesday*: is that still as easy?' This proviso rewrites the admonitions of Time in 'As I Walked Out One Evening' of 1937 ('Time will have his fancy | Tomorrow or today') in a decidedly more devastating way. It is possibly no coincidence that Frédéric's assignation with Madame Arnoux is for a Tuesday afternoon, and that his panic sets in after four o'clock (Flaubert, *L'Education sentimentale*, II, vi). It is because the fateful reasons for love's failure are similarly unpredictable (her little boy was taken ill) that Auden's largely general example of the fallibility of juxtaposition is all the better for this ghost of a 'source'.

Although you be, as I am, one of those

HC, p. 53; CSP66, p. [7]; CP, p. xxxi.

The epigraph to Part II of *Homage to Clio* was annotated in the printer's TS 'For Chris'. It reappeared as the general dedication to the 1966 *Collected Shorter Poems*, and to the *Collected Poems*, in which Isherwood's name is joined with Kallman's. In the *Kenyon Review*, Winter 1964, Auden made its point in more general terms of decorum: 'In so much "serious" poetry, poetry, that is to say, which is neither pure playful song nor comic, I find an element of "theatre", of exaggerated gesture and fuss, of indifference to the naked truth, which, as I get older, increasingly revolts me. This element is mercifully absent from what is conventionally called good prose'. 'Gentile' is used here in the sense of 'heathen'.

Steatopygous, sow-dugged

1959; 'Dame Kind', *Encounter*, May 1960; HC, p. 55; CP, p. 667.

'Dame Kind' is one of a trio, including Aphrodite and Frau Minne, introduced in 'Dichtung und Wahrheit', section XV, to lend an ironic dignity to the act of love which Auden's argument needed to marginalise in that context. The poem itself is a quirky colloquial rampage, intended to be 'slightly unpleasant perhaps' in a reaction against the problem of writing the truth about love (see 'Dichtung und Wahrheit', section L), a delicate verbal qualification of the sentiments of homage, in which 'the *Chi-Rho*' (the Christian fish symbol) is a signal for academic retreat, and Petrarchan love is a 'hypochondriac | Blue-Stocking'. The language of the poem has, appropriately enough, more than its share of the demotic in those parts where it is critical of a prissiness towards the primal urge she represents; the delicacy is reserved for an implicit respect for her age-old pandering rituals. Auden's suspicion of Manichaeanism is evident here in his criticism of the 'mim look | and gnostic chirrup': the body must be accepted.

Woken, I lay in the arms of my own warmth and listened

Summer 1956; 'First Things First', *New Yorker*, 9 March 1957; HC, p. 58; CSP66, p. 281; SP68, p. 82; CP, p. 583.

On 9 March 1957, Auden wrote to Lincoln Kirstein: 'Have a new little heart flutter: 17. From California. Plays the viola di gamba, my dear. Am trying to get him into Christ Church as an organ scholar. You will presently see a poem in the *New Yorker* which refers, both to the flutter, and to my new neurotic worry which is water.' It is a moving love poem, contrasting inarticulate nature with the human urge to make linguistic sense of the universe, to translate the storm's 'interjectory uproar' into the name of the loved one. It is a poem, too, of touching and dignified loneliness: the storm *has* power to evoke the sacred image, but in the cold light of morning it is seen that all it has really done is to fill the cistern. 'Thousands have lived without love, not one without water' is a line that Auden was delighted to learn from Dorothy Day that a New York hooker had quoted when only allowed a shower once a week in prison (*Poets at Work*, p. 295).

This graveyard with its umbrella pines

?1956; 'Island Cemetery', *Gemini*, Autumn 1957; 'An Island Cemetery', HC, p. 59; CSP66, p. 248; CP, p. 550.

This poem offers an interesting parallel to Housman's 'The Immortal Part', as Spears has pointed out (p. 325). Probably an allusion to Valéry is intended, too. The tone is light, approving the clinical impersonality of the skeleton, being rather offhand about the afterlife, toying with the idea of burial as a kind of agriculture, and refusing to play Hamlet to the Ischian gravediggers.

Hail, future friend, whose present I

1955; 'C. 500 A.D.', *The Old Man's Road*, 1956; 'Bathtub Thoughts (*c.* 500–*c.*1950)', HC, p. 61; CSP66, p. 303; CP, p. 606.

In 'Bathtub Thoughts' Auden presents more specifically the parallel implicit in several post-war poems between his own situation and that of a cultured inhabitant of the late Roman Empire (the final lines were at one time in draft in the Berg 1945–61 notebook: 'The last bilingual senator | Takes the last hot bath on earth'). The bond is expressed here as a mathematical relationship between two numbers in a sequence whose length 'chance only knows', since the words which Auden imagines the Romano-Briton addressing to him are also the words which Auden is addressing to an unknown 'further friend': the civilisation which is symbolised here by plenty of hot water may be destroyed more than once.

Across the Great Schism, through our whole landscape

1955; 'The Old Man's Road', *Perspectives*, Winter 1956; *The Old Man's Road*, 1956; *Listen*, Summer–Autumn 1957; HC, p. 62; CSP66, p. 304; SP68, p. 83; CP, p. 607.

'The Old Man's Road' is the road of spiritual self-discovery which ignores all the established positions of religious orthodoxy, but it is also very much the common man's sense of how things may be done, and how life may be lived. 'The Old Man' himself is more particularly 't' Owd Man' of the Pennine lead miners, their reverential term for both the miners of the past and the old workings which were memorials to their skills and traditions. The phrase was current in the Alston Moor district in Auden's youth (see W. R. Mitchell, *Pennine Lead-Miner: Eric Richardson, of Nenthead,*

1979, p. 7). 'Old Man' is also Elliot Smith's 'Palæoanthropic' man of the Stone Age (see W. J. Perry, *The Growth of Civilization*, Pelican edn, 1937, p. 22). Those who follow his road have freed themselves from the bonds of history even though they are 'assuming a freedom its Powers deny', because for Auden history is, in fact, the realm of human freedom and of sin. The old man's road, therefore, belongs very much to the world of nature, the realm of necessity and of obedience to God's creation: in other words, the Quest that the road represents is the quest for innocence or authenticity of being.

I choose the road from here to there

?1958; 'Walks', HC, p. 64; CP, p. 673.

'Walks' takes the circular stroll as a symbol for larger experience (there is no need to decide when to turn back). The last three stanzas consist, however, of a kind of coda which parallels the neighbourly examples in the first stanza, taking neighbourliness a little further into love. Whatever the metaphysical shape and therefore purpose of the walk on a public road, the presence of the private linking path (making the T or Q) is a guarantee of a particular social purpose.

In that ago when being was believing

?1958; 'In that Ago', *Observer*, 29 March 1959; 'The History of Truth', HC, p. 66; CSP66, p. 306; CP, p. 610.

'The History of Truth' proposes that the truth in a pre-scientific era was a given fact, a reality which its artifacts could mirror simply by existing, since 'being was believing'. Our ephemeral products barely exist (either in time, like paper dishes, or space, like kilowatts) and therefore imply an anti-model, an 'untruth anyone can give the lie to'.

All fables of adventure stress

1955; 'The History of Science', *New Statesman*, 9 June 1956; *The Old Man's Road*, 1956; HC, p. 67; CSP66, p. 305; CP, p. 608.

'The History of Science' uses the myth of the lucky Third Brother in fairy-tales to postulate a Fourth Brother, milder even than the third, who ignores the offered advice, choosing the heroic 'North', and yet discovers 'a wonderful instead' which is as satisfactory as the original object of his quest. The point is that science proceeds as much by chance and error as by enlightened direction.

A Young Person came out of the mists

Autumn 1950; 'History of the Boudoir', HC, p. 69; CSP66, p. 270; CP, p. 571.

Auden was a compulsive writer of limericks, and not all of them by any means (including the best) were printed. 'History of the Boudoir' survives well enough as the third of the series of 'History of' poems in *Homage to Clio* by virtue of appropriate form and double bluff (the sense of disappointment in the limerick's avoiding the directly sexual reference is now one possible function of the form) but loses some of its point out of this context. Love, like truth and science, like all human exploits, has its illusory aspects. In one sense, the limerick is about language.

Relax, Maestro, put your baton down

1955; 'Metalogue to *The Magic Flute*', *Harper's Bazaar*, January 1956, and *Listener*, 26 January 1956; *The Magic Flute*, English version by Auden and Kallman, 1956, p. 57; HC, p. 70; CSP66, p. 276; CP, p. 441; *Libretti*, p. 152.

The Metalogue was spoken by the singer playing Sarastro between the two acts of *The Magic Flute* in the American television production in 1956 (the Mozart bicentenary) for which Auden and Kallman had transformed the libretto. It serves as a constructive deflation in the manner of an Augustan epilogue. The jokes outweigh the tribute, but they are good, and the whole piece forms an elegant pastiche of Dryden. The translation of the characters to an academic background for speculations on their modern significance (lines 68–85) is a brilliant stroke. 'Cancrizans' (line 26) is a canon's theme inverted in the second part. John Cage (line 54) wrote music for prepared piano. Macaulay (line 57) expected 'every schoolboy' to know 'who imprisoned Montezuma, and who strangled Atahualpa'. Walter Mitty (line 63) is the character created by James Thurber in *The Secret Life of Walter Mitty*.

As the poets have mournfully sung

Autumn 1950; 'The Aesthetic Point of View', HC, p. 74; CSP66, p. 270; CP, p. 572.

Like the earlier limerick in *Homage to Clio,* 'History of the Boudoir', this one uses the form to retail a sly truth about human aspirations, here defeated indiscriminately by death. The camp tone of the limericks was not well taken by critics in the context of the volume, and Auden might have been better served by printing a larger selection, including the conventionally dirty ones (see p. 554).

The tribes of Limbo, travellers report

1957; 'Limbo Culture', *Atlantic,* November 1957; HC, p. 75; CSP66, p. 312; CP, p. 616.

The comic definition of Limbo culture (no words for *yes* or *no,* no pronouns distinguishing between persons, and so on) looks like a covert needling of a prevaricating lover, the eternal maybe. This addiction to inexactness seems to indicate only a self-love ('For that, we know, cannot be done exactly'), and here, perhaps, the religious parallel suggested by the name 'Limbo' asserts itself: exactness, and unselfish love, would suggest the state of grace that only 'baptism' could bring (cf. *Inferno,* iv). In drafts the original title was 'Suppose' (Berg 1945–61 notebook).

Though mild clear weather

1956; 'There Will Be No Peace', *Time and Tide,* 1 December 1956; HC, p. 76; CSP66, p. 313; CP, p. 617.

Auden described 'There Will Be No Peace' as 'one of the most purely personal poems I have ever written. It was an attempt to describe a very unpleasant dark-night-of-the-soul sort of experience which for several months in 1956 attacked me.' The sense of motiveless persecution which characterises paranoid delusions is carefully evoked through the quiet and insistent elaboration, in a self-addressed second person, of how the poet feels. Though many years separate them, in the 1966 *Collected Shorter Poems* this poem was significantly placed next to 'A Household'.

He told us we were free to choose

?1958; 'Friday's Child', *Listener*, 25 December 1958; HC, p. 77; SP68, p. 85; CP, p. 675.

The poem is dedicated to the memory of Dietrich Bonhoeffer, hanged by the Nazis on 9 April 1945. 'Friday's Child' is here the martyred Christ of Good Friday, although it is the nursery rhyme 'Monday's child is fair of face' which suggests a tacit answer to the weighed anger or compassion of stanza 3: 'loving and giving' must be the key to the Christian justice of the Judgement day that even 'conscious unbelievers' (stanza 10) feel sure of. Here on earth he 'leaves | The bigger bangs to us': this is a freedom of choice that we have never quite understood. Our science has made us capable of making bombs that could destroy the planet. Auden's God in this poem is absolved from capriciousness precisely by that refusal to save appearances which led to the Incarnation and the Redemption: the theology is thus somewhat circular in argument.

The metaphor of 'saving appearances' is borrowed from astronomy: in this sense it is the devising of hypothetical patterns of movement to account for the apparent movement of heavenly bodies in the received Ptolemaic system, and therefore accommodates true spiritual knowledge with empirical knowledge according to the principles of Plato. The Copernican revolution consisted in seeing that a hypothesis may not only 'save the appearances', but also be physically true. Auden got these ideas from Owen Barfield, *Saving the Appearances: A study in idolatry* (1957), especially chapter VII. Barfield's brilliant study of conceptual language in the scientific age provided other ideas which get into the poem, such as Auden's 'self-observed observing Mind' in stanza 6 (see Barfield's 'alpha-thinking' and 'beta-thinking' on p. 25). Barfield believed that being 'free to choose' (as Auden puts it at the beginning of the poem) was tantamount to the option of 'belief', and equivalent to our consciousness in organising the particles of the universe into representations. It is science's way of freeing us for a final participation in the world about us, extra-sensory and non-empirical.

Out of a gothic North, the pallid children

September 1958; 'Good-Bye to the Mezzogiorno', *Encounter*, November 1958; published as a pamphlet, with translation by Carlo Izzo, December 1958; HC, p. 79; CSP66, p. 338; CP, p. 642.

In 'Good-Bye to the Mezzogiorno' (dedicated to Carlo Izzo, who had published a translation of a selection of his poems in 1952) Auden marked the end of a phase in his poetic career, and took the opportunity in leaving the land of the siesta of once more examining the difference between North and South that for him validated his own unwavering 'Northernness'. One primary distinction had been made, for example, in an article for *Vogue* (15 May 1954, p. 62): 'One must have a proper moral sense about the points of the compass: North must seem the "good" direction, the way towards heroic adventures, South the way to ignoble ease and decadence.' In the poem Auden brings to his contrast between the 'gothic North' and the 'sunburnt otherwhere' just that contrast which readers have felt between the New York and the Mediterranean poetry, between 'those who mean by life a | *Bildungsroman* and those to whom living | Means to-be-visible-now', between (predominantly) anxiety and happiness. We Northerners are eager to learn, but have nothing to teach in our encounter with the South (like Goethe in his fifth Roman Elegy taking time out of an erotic encounter to compose hexameters: Helena is the presiding spirit of the ideal in Goethe's *Faust*, Part II, appearing as Queen in III.i after the Walpurgisnacht of II.iii). The happiness is no doubt the happiness of 'ease', and of emotional liberation, but it must be moderate ('one little scream at *A piacere* [the musical instruction 'ad lib'], | Not two'. The mood of thankfulness even extends to 'a certain *Monte*', the landlord who would not sell him his Ischian house (details of this episode are given in Izzo's article in *Shenandoah*, Winter 1967, p. 81).

Henry Adams

For this and the other thirty-one clerihews printed in the 'Addendum' to *Homage to Clio*, under the heading 'Academic Graffiti', see p. 527.

Let both our Common Rooms combine to cheer

1957; 'Lines addressed to Dr Claude Jenkins . . .', HC, p. 91; CSP66, p. 279; CP, p. 582.

Claude Jenkins was a Canon of Christ Church and had been Regius Professor of Ecclesiastical History since 1934. This Common Room tribute from the then Oxford Professor of Poetry contains genuine warmth. '*Mercury*' is the pond in Tom Quad named for its central statue. '*Little*' is Cyril Little, then the Senior Common Room Butler.

Elegy for Young Lovers

The twenty-five-year-old Hans Werner Henze first met Auden and Kallman in Ischia in 1951. He wanted Auden to write the text of a monodrama for him, but nothing came of the proposal, presumably because the librettists, working on *Delia*, still had hopes of continuing their collaboration with Stravinsky. Henze met them again in Ischia in 1953, but seems to have been intimidated. He tried again in 1958, with plans for an intimate chamber opera. A rough draft of the scenario for *Elegy for Young Lovers* was made at Kirchstetten in the summer of 1959, with the characters and story being evolved from Henze's musical requirements. The opera was completed in 1960 and first performed and published in 1961. Auden and Kallman added a short postscript, 'Genesis of a Libretto', to the published libretto, and Auden described and commented on the opera in *Secondary Worlds*, pp. 101–9. Much additional material relating to the composition of the opera appears, of course, in *Libretti*. Details of Auden's probable contributions are given (roughly: Act One, scenes II, III and V; Act Two, scenes I, II, III, V, VII (possibly also IV and VI), and the dialogue between Hilda and Elizabeth in IX; Act Three, scenes VI, VII and VIII). Auden claimed that Kallman wrote about 75 per cent of the libretto.

Unlike *Paul Bunyan*, *The Rakes's Progress* and *Delia*, this opera relies greatly upon the perfectly reasonable and inventive, but primarily melodramatic, characterisation of a play like *On the Frontier*. No doubt this is eminently suited to the artifice of opera; the methods of construction as recounted in the postscript seem ideally to reflect Auden's notions about characters in opera ('persons who insist on their fate, however tragically dreadful or comically absurd', *Secondary Worlds*, p. 94). The key to the conception of the opera, however, the poet Mittenhofer, was seen by the librettists as embodying a crucially necessary myth. In this case, the myth is that of the artist-genius of the nineteenth and early twentieth century, and it ties in understandably with some of the concerns of the unwritten *On the Way* (which also was to take place in an Alpine inn).

Mittenhofer is required to be a 'great' poet. Auden described him to Lincoln Kirstein as 'a cross between W. B. Yeats and Stefan George', and to

Elizabeth Mayer, with whom he was translating Goethe's *Italienische Reise* at
the time, as 'rather a good portrait of G'. The postscript, after explaining
Mittenhofer's connection with Vienna, claims that 'the only things about
him which were suggested to us by historical incidents were drawn from the
life of a poet – no matter whom – who wrote in English.' The occasion and
indeed tense would seem to forbid self-reference, but see Mendelson
(*Libretti*, p. xxvii–xxviii). The librettists' intention seems to underline the
Yeats sources (Mittenhofer maintains his sexual potency by frequent
injections, and his poetry is largely inspired by the transcribed visions of a
madwoman). The self-confessed theme also derives most obviously from
Yeats ('The intellect of man is forced to choose | Perfection of the life or of
the work'). Mittenhofer chooses the latter, and thus needs to be pampered
and humoured like a baby. All the other characters are made to serve his
needs, even the unfortunate young lovers, whose 'illusory but rhymable
love' is the substance of Mittenhofer's latest poem, which, since it is to be an
elegy, must demand their actual destruction. To Toni he is an 'old sorcerer'
(perhaps like Sacrapant in *Delia*). To himself, he is a Prospero who cannot
release Ariel. Auden's Prospero could not envisage suffering without saying
something ironic or funny about it (CP, p. 409); Mittenhofer cannot feel
anything without wondering how he can make poetry out of it (*Libretti*, p.
218). The character of Mittenhofer (and the whole paradox of the
ostensible theme, the paradox of the artist-genius) is treated with a lightness
and humour very reminiscent of the plays of the 1930s.

   More ambitious is the symbolism of love's illusions. This is managed by a
curious juxtapositioning at the end of Act One of the discovery of Hilda
Mack's dead bridegroom, lost for forty years in a glacier, and the coming
together of Toni and Elizabeth. This symbolism is maintained at the climax
of the opera, when the couple, dying on the mountain, imagine they have
been married for forty years, and discover that their love has little effective
meaning as they 'say farewell to a real world' and unlearn their lies alone as
they prepare to face God (the scene was cut for the Glyndebourne
performance which Geoffrey Gorer heard; Auden wrote to him on 4
August 1961: 'You're right, of course, about the need for a final scene
between the young. After the Schwetzingen performance we realized that it
would have to be rewritten and recomposed and also placed before the
orchestral storm, but felt that, until it was, cutting was the lesser of two
evils'). The symbols and images of this theme are insistently sacrificial:
Hilda Mack prophesies the couple's death as an offering to the Immortal,
their 'Mortal heart neither | Simple nor wicked' (*Libretti*, p. 199). The

Havisham-like Hilda's bridegroom is some kind of sacramental victim, too. The point seems to be that human love must be subservient to divine love, and yet be an image of it, particularly of Christ's. It is at this point that both themes meet, in Mittenhofer's arrogation of the Christian role of blessing the pair in his poem (see his words in Act Two, scene x, *Libretti*, p. 226) which to him is like reclaiming Eden, but which actually requires their death (see Bucknell, *Auden Studies* 3, pp. 159–61, for allusions here to Andersen's 'The Snow Queen'). Eden is also the illusion of his patron Carolina, whose own death is his service. Thus his great poem, performed in the final scene by the wordless voices of his entourage, has an entirely ambiguous status: it appears to be built on the motto 'In death they were not divided' even though Auden's (cut) scene VII leaves them as isolated souls.

About the House

The collection *About the House* (published in the US in July 1965, and in the UK in January 1966) was the first that Auden produced from the house in Austria which he bought with the proceeds of the Feltrinelli Prize in 1959 (the house itself cost $12,000 of the $30,000 of the prize). The title may well be consciously drawn from the 1934 sonnet 'A shilling life will give you all the facts', as suggested by Edward Callan (p. 250). It is certainly appropriate to the settled maturity of the figure described in the sestet of that sonnet that Auden wrote to Howard Griffin (31 December 1966) that in this volume 'For the first time I felt old enough to speak in the First Person.' The dedicatory poem to Edmund and Elena Wilson ('A moon profaned by') was written in the light of US and Soviet competition to reach the moon, and rehearses a theme common in later Auden, of the threats of irresponsible science to a world where only language can make human beings known to each other, and the 'here and now' is the locus of the common life largely celebrated in the volume. Its form is the Japanese *tanka* (thirty-one syllables, the first and third lines of five syllables, the rest of seven).

The first part of the collection is the sequence 'Thanksgiving for a Habitat', a sequence about the rooms of his Kirchstetten house familiarly referred to by Auden as his 'Hausgedichte' (letter to Gorer of 13 September 1963). The first notes for a sequence of this kind date from 1959. The sequence is prefaced by a quotation from the Vulgate (Psalms xvi, translating as: 'The lines are fallen unto me in pleasant places; Yea, I have a goodly heritage'). Gratitude for this heritage bubbles over wittily as Auden takes us round his study, the cellar, the attic, the lavatory, the bathroom, the kitchen, the guest-room, the dining-room, the bedroom and the living-room. He is well aware of the dangers of a public celebration of the domestic virtues, and thus the poise and humour of the sequence pleasurably steer a tasteful course between intimacy and sermonising. Auden told Gorer that the subject was 'what worldiness really means'. A favourable sense of this worldly heritage in such mundane terms is rather new in Auden's work. One can see a similar concern in earlier poems taking a generalised symbolic form (as, for instance, in 'Bucolics'), but here for the first time the daily circumstances of the individual's life are seen not only to be symbolic of that individual's existential nature, but to have meaning in themselves, in particular as an assertion of the values of the body against the Manichees (followers of the third-century Persian Manichaeus's heretical beliefs, in which Satan is represented as coeval with God and the body a source of evil). The sequence is reprinted in the 1968 *Selected Poems*, p. 117 (without the Postscripts) and the *Collected Poems*, p. 688.

From gallery-grave and the hunt of a wren-king

?Spring 1962; 'Prologue: The Birth of Architecture', AH, p. 13. The dedication is to John Bayley (the architect John B. Bayley, not Professor John Bayley).

The symbolic suggestiveness and allusive range of the later style is abundantly in evidence here. In the opening we are taken from the earliest profound anthropological human ceremonies to a modern world of debased ritual and holiday without holiness in 'hardly a tick by the carbon clock' (compare Sir James Jeans, *The Stars in their Courses*, 1931, p. 153: 'The human race, whose intelligence dates back only a single tick of the astronomical clock, could hardly hope to understand so soon what it all means'). The gallery-grave is actually an early example of indigenous architecture (see Hetty Pegler's Tump in the following poem) while 'the hunt of a wren-king' is explained in Frazer's *Golden Bough* as the folk-custom of hunting the Gold Crest Wren (known in Greece and Rome as 'the little king') with birch rods on Christmas Eve (cf. 'The Cutty Wren', included by Auden in *The Oxford Book of Light Verse*). The 'Old Man' is the lead-miners' authority for the way things have always been done (see the commentary on 'The Old Man's Road' p. 474). Time in the poem is measured in two ways by its three italicised words: the linear time of *After* and *Once*, which ties humanity to its historic present, and the hypothetical time of *If*, which brings conceptual release. This is why man as an architect is governed not only by technology ('concrete or grapefruit') but by potentiality, and why nature ('that Immortal Commonwealth') 'won't quite do'. Nature has 'masons and carpenters' (termites, bees, wasps, and so on) but neither architects or heretics. This subtly introduced notion of an effortless truth in nature is a common theme of the sequence. It is left to a humorous 'Postscript' to imply that the 'second nature of tomb and temple' (i.e. both a surrogate nature, and a human instinct) is in fact the religious impulse of humanity, our awareness of identity and morality, and that what we are essentially building is a symbol of our own soul's fortress, wary of fraternisation.

Nobody I know would like to be buried

August 1962; 'Thanksgiving for a Habitat', *New Yorker*, 17 August 1963; AH, p. 15. Dedicated to Geoffrey Gorer.

The poem is in memory of a conversation which Auden had with Gorer when the latter visited Kirchstetten. As Auden acknowledged, when sending a revision of it to Elizabeth Mayer on 8 September 1962: 'To keep the diction and rhythm within a hairsbreadth of being prose without becoming it is a task I find very difficult.' The poem examines the nature of the creature who is to inhabit the habitat, now acknowledging that rituals must change. We are at the mercy of 'the flesh | Mum formulated' and of our social circumstances, too. Our houses are surrogate bodies. We cannot, as William Randolph Hearst tried to do when he built his palace at San Simeon (stanza 2), recreate a nobler past. 'Adulterine castles' (stanza 3) are those built without licence from the Crown; Auden dignifies teenage violence in order to reduce its significance to a pose as empty as Hearst's. 'Schönbrunn' (stanza 4) is the Imperial Palace in Vienna, Hetty Pegler's Tump a transeptal gallery four miles south-west of Stroud in Gloucestershire (cf. the 'gallery-grave' of 'The Birth of Architecture').

Auden justifies his asserted privacy (as a kind of modest Hearst, shuddering at, but tolerant of, 'the race of spiders') by an ornithological analogy (stanza 13) and a developing comic tone in the poem. The humour of this (and other poems in the volume) lies in the hideous possibilities that are envisaged: of, for instance, being destroyed in a thousand millionth of a second 'at the nod | of some jittery commander' (stanza 17). Assuming the submissive posture to wolves (stanza 18) was what Peter Pan did (looking at them between his legs). A toft-and-croft (stanza 19) is a homestead with arable land attached. The ending of the poem ('a place | I may go both in and out of') is taken directly from George Macdonald's *Lilith*: 'There are places you can go into, and places you can go out of; but the one place if you do but find it, where you may go out and in both, is home.' This was quoted by Auden in his essay on George Macdonald in *Forewords and Afterwords* (p. 273), it was included in his *Faber Book of Aphorisms* (p. 365) and in *A Certain World* (p. 184). What the quotation does not say, but which

Auden may well have had in mind (significantly in the context of a poem about certain death and illusory Edens) is that the one place that you only come out of is the womb, and the one place you only go into is the tomb.

For this and for all enclosures like it the archetype

July 1964; 'The Cave of Making', *Listener*, 1 October 1964; AH, p. 18. In memoriam Louis MacNeice.

The model for the poet's study is Weland's Stithy, or forge (Weland is Wayland the Smith, the Volundr of the Elder Edda). Wayland was one of those commemorated in the elegiac Old English poem, 'The Complaint of Deor', which Auden had imitated before and may be in his mind here, thinking of the misfortunes of minstrels (MacNeice had died unexpectedly in 1963). The fate that made them neighbours was MacNeice's going up to Merton in 1926 when Auden had already been a year at Christ Church; later they became friends when MacNeice became an Assistant Lecturer in Classics under Professor E. R. Dodds at Birmingham University in 1930. Later they collaborated on *Letters from Iceland*. The fellow-feeling expressed in the poem is one of class and generation as much as vocation: their fathers knew how to use handkerchiefs but neither were patrician (porphyry-born, i.e. to wear the purple toga), and they both were little boys before the First World War, a time when the world decisively changed. Despite the sense of the lost world that they have shared, the poem works its way to a central assertion that 'More than ever | life-out-there is goodly, miraculous, lovable'. The assertion is accompanied by a reminder that for Auden the failure of humanism and consequent underlining of the truth of original sin was due to the triumph of totalitarianism in the 1930s: 'we shan't, not since Stalin and Hitler, | trust ourselves ever again: we know that, subjectively, | all is possible.' Auden's Swarthmore course, 'Romanticism from Rousseau to Hitler', emphasised the danger of Romantic possibility that the Horatian virtues celebrated in the sequence emphatically repudiate.

To the dead MacNiece, however, nothing is now possible. He has 'slipped out of Granusion' into the Country of Unconcern. Granusion is the region of the lower atmosphere into which Nature and Urania descend in Bernardus Silvestris' twelfth-century *Cosmographia*:

Granusion is located in a secluded and remote spot at the eastern limit of the earth. Having received, through the tender ministry of the sun in its freshest youth, a most happy evenness of climate, it is lush with grass and burgeoning with rich growth. The name of the place is Granusion because it is continually bringing plants of all sorts to maturity.

(Part Two, chapter 9, in Winthrop Wetherbee's translation, 1973, pp. 110–11)

The Greekless Bernardus had misunderstood a phrase in his source, Chalcidius, who described the breathable air as a moist substance, called by the Greeks 'hygran usian'. Auden found this arcane misunderstanding in C. S. Lewis, *The Discarded Image* (1964), pp. 59–60, a book much concerned with the 'Cosmic Model' which Auden had a few lines earlier deemed to have become German (Einstein, presumably). Granusion, though recondite, is a touching and ironic image of the moist, fertile and breathable earth that MacNeice had quitted, for he died of viral pneumonia after recording underground sound effects in the Settle caves for a radio play and then getting soaked on the Yorkshire moors. The affection with which he is welcomed at any time in Auden's ubity ('whereabouts') is in pleasant contrast to the threatened stranger of the 'Postscript' to 'Prologue: The Birth of Architecture'.

'The Cave of Making' restates poetry's doubtful relation to the truth (Goethe believing, unlike the *symbolistes*, that poetry cannot be, but can only bear witness to, the truth), its manipulation by 'lip-smacking | imps of mawk and hooey' (for these personal demons, see the commentary on 'Cattivo Tempo', p. 422), and its status as the only art which demands either serious attention or to be ignored. There is a comment by Auden on the lines about Goethe in a letter to David Luke of 4 October 1965: 'Goethe's insistence on Nature being schön (and his dislike of the Cross) was, as you know, a defence mechanism. Few people have had such a horror of illness and death as he had, so he had to pretend they weren't there.' Auden's wish to be 'a minor Atlantic Goethe' became one of his most repeated mots. In an interview in *Isis* 8 November 1967, he added 'in a Rolls Royce with chauffeur'.

Material which didn't quite get into the poem is arranged in the 'Postscript', an interesting clue to Auden's methods of composition, for many longish poems have the air of being compiled from similar aphorisms arranged according to theme. In this 'Postscript', Auden introduces the *haiku*, used extensively in the book as a whole, to investigate some of the paradoxes of poetry's relationship with truth. He then takes up the notion of the poet as a necessarily good man (cf. Marianne Moore quoted in *The Dyer's Hand*, p. 305: 'rectitude *has* a ring that is implicative, I would say'), and we are given the doubtfully appalling vision of God reducing him to tears on Judgement day by reciting by heart the poems he would have written had his life really been good. At the same time, however, Auden is clear that vice has been inspiring, that he knows 'what imagination I can owe temptation I yielded to, I that many a fine I expressive line I would not have existed, I had you resisted.' The moral ambiguity is an interesting one, and none the less serious for being capriciously expressed.

A cellar underneath the house, though not lived in

July 1963; 'Down There', *John Crowe Ransom, a Tribute*, 1964; AH, p. 24. Dedicated to Irving Weiss.

Irving Weiss had been at university with Kallman, and he and his wife Anne (and later their four children – two daughters and then two sons, the younger Auden's godson – who have generalised roles in this poem and the following one, dedicated to Anne) became very friendly with Auden in Ischia in the early 1950s, and later in New York (see Farnan, pp. 168–74). The libretto to Auden and Kallman's translation of *The Magic Flute* is dedicated to them. This cellar poem brings the notional 'cave' of the study and bedroom poems closer to fact, for it is actually underground ('key-cold', as Henry VI's daughter-in-law chillingly describes his corpse in *Richard III*, I.ii.5). The cellar is the deep area of our resources, our 'safe-anchor' ('A father sends the younger boys to fetch something I For Mother from down there'). We are close to the topic of *Urmutterfurcht* (see 'New Year Letter', line 1,095) but the journey here suggests less the familiar psychological quest into the maternal water-scooped limestone than a piece of controlled spiritual husbandry.

Men would never have come to need an attic

July 1963; 'Up There', *John Crowe Ransom, a Tribute*, 1964; AH, p. 25. Dedicated to Anne Weiss.

If the cellar is a place of storage for the future, the attic is a place for storage of the past. In 'Down There' the boys were sent as a test of male courage to fetch something for Mother: in 'Up There', the sisters escape from Mother's rage. But both places are under feminine control, the first with providence (the mewed commons, the hidden provisions) and the second with nostalgia (the disorganised detritus of the past). 'Up there' is also a mode of biblical reference to God discussed by John Robinson in *Honest to*

God (1963), pp. 11ff, and Auden may have chosen the title for this ironical reason (i.e. that God can only be said spiritually and metaphysically to be 'out there', not 'up'). Auden may also have been struck by the 'three-storeyed' universe that Bishop Robinson talks about in these pages. The poem is written in Catullan hendecasyllabics.

Seated after breakfast

July 1964; 'The Geography of the House', AH, p. 26. Dedicated to Christopher Isherwood.

Auden returned to the stanza-form of 'Heavy Date' for a poem which distinctly benefits from its cogitatory movement. The poem blends some familiar observations about the psychological role of excretion with some ingenious double-meanings that lend it a comic lightness of touch. It was Shakespeare who first described sex as 'a joy proposed' (Sonnet 129). For the Manichees (stanza 9) see p. 485. The dedication to Isherwood may be a wicked memory of his unforgettable Mortmere story, 'The Horror in the Tower', about the coprophile Lord Wranvers and the unforgettable 'geography' of his family seat.

It is odd that the English

April 1962; 'Encomium Balnei', *Encounter*, August 1962; AH, p. 29. Dedicated to Neil Little, a painter friend living on Ischia.

'Encomium Balnei' ('in praise of the bathroom'), itself formally resembling the 'mallarmesque | syllabic fog' it refers to, takes up where 'Bathtub Thoughts' in *Homage to Clio* left off in its allusions to 'the caracallan acreage', i.e. the public baths in Rome, built by Caracalla (Marcus Aurelius the second). Here, the point is less the threat to the civilisation that hot water represents than a celebration of it. The kind of escapism that the bathroom provides combines a classical comfort with the sacrosanct political right of withdrawal and privacy derived (Auden elaborately proposes) from the desert saints, who didn't actually believe in washing. To take a bath is to feel good, to feel at one with the body. Auden explained (to Peter Salus) that 'hoggers and lumpers' are 'shorthand for whole-hoggers and those who lump everything together, i.e. religious or political bigots'. See *Letters from Baron Friedrich Von Hügel to a Niece*, ed. Gwendolen Greene, 1928, p. 41: Von Hügel is writing about the discrimination necessary for appreciating Tertullian ('How weary I am of the *lumpers*, the *whole-hoggers!*') and later gives an example of 'lumping', when he so refers to Socrates' doctrine of opposites (p. 160).

Should the shade of Plato

1958; 'On Installing an American Kitchen in Lower Austria', *New Yorker*, 7 March 1959; HC, p. 24; 'Grub First, Then Ethics (Brecht)', AH, p. 33. Dedicated to Margaret Gardiner, whom he had first met in Berlin in 1929, through John Layard.

'Grub First, Then Ethics' has the Brecht epigraph from *Homage to Clio* translated and promoted as the new title. The 'American' kitchen of the earlier title was the term for a fitted kitchen when they first arrived in Austria (see Stella Musulin, *Auden Studies* 3, p. 218). There is a distinction to be made here between the good-naturedly epicurean solidarity of Auden, and the Marxist accusations of Brecht. The psychological truism in stanza 4 (needing to get your calories before considering love or chess) leads Auden to a number of bright, characteristic generalisations ('a cook [can be] a pure artist', 'in murder mysteries | one can be sure the gourmet didn't do it') in his most fluent and conversationally occasional manner. However, the altered title forces us to remember the real context of the Act II finale of *The Threepenny Opera*, with all the desperate but exultant relentlessness of Weill's setting:

> Ihr, die ihr euren Wanst und unsre Bravheit liebt
> Das eine wisset ein für allemal:
> Wie ihr es immer drecht und wie ihr's immer schiebt
> Erst kommt das Fressen, dann kommt die Moral.
> Est muss es möglich sein auch armen Leuten,
> Vom grossen Brotlaib sich ihr Teil zu schneiden.

> (You who love your own belly and our honesty,
> Once and for all learn this single thing:
> However you twist it and however you get round it,
> Feeding comes first and then comes morality.
> First it must be possible for poor people, too,
> To cut their share of the big loaf.)

Brecht is showing how the exploitation of the poor by the rich is accompanied by just the kind of moral preaching to them that keeps them subservient. The irony is that when the poor do get their slice of cake, then society will be able to see what morality is really about. A religious analogy is worked up in the poem: Auden claims that his kitchen is numinous (stanza 3), and later identifies an omelette with the Eucharist. The poetic achievement here, incidentally, should not be underestimated: at one time Auden could not see himself writing an ode to a kitchen refrigerator. The citizens of the Just Society admit to being a minority, and the poem ends by showing how likely it is that they will be called upon to fight off the hordes at 'her Thermopylae' (perhaps an echo here of Cavafy's 'Thermopylae'). 'Her vagabond forum | is any space where two of us happen to meet | who can spot a citizen | without papers': perhaps a necessary qualification to all the talk of territory and status that lies behind the sequence. The mock *ubi sunt* passage in stanza 1 that would have surprised Plato deliberately involves the relatively obscure: Thomas Telford (1757–1834) was the engineer whose career began as surveyor of public works for Shropshire, and he built both the Caledonian canal and 1,200 bridges; John Muir (1838–1914) described riding out a storm at the top of a Douglas Spruce, while exploring one of the tributary valleys of the Yuba river, in *The Mountains of California* (1894), pp. 248–57; 'Mr Vynyan Board' is Sir A. Vyvyan Board, a director of the Hector Whaling Company who experimented with a humane electric harpoon in the late 1940s.

Ours yet not ours, being set apart

June 1964; 'For Friends Only', AH, p. 37. Dedicated to John and Teckla [sc. Thekla] Clark.

Auden had proposed to Thekla Pelletti in Ischia in the early 1950s, before she met John Clark, by all accounts having come round to the feeling that a marriage of convenience for a homosexual was quite in order. Since his wife Erika was still alive, however, it is not clear what the status of the offer really was. The Clarks, who moved to Florence, remained good friends with Auden. The poem is a visitors' book compliment in reverse, conveying a few dogmas of the household gods, and written in an unusual form of alternating lines of seven and five words, based upon the principles of Chinese poetry. 'Tum-Tum' (stanza 7) was a nickname of Edward VII, so Auden's memory of biscuits in the family guest-room is that of a three-year-old. On Auden's misspelling of 'Thekla' see Thekla Clark, *Wystan and Chester* (1995), p. 104. Mrs Clark prints an earlier version of the poem on pp. 105–6 (the sixth stanza was entirely rewritten).

The life of plants

?Spring 1963; 'Tonight at Seven-thirty', AH, p. 39. Dedicated to M. F. K. Fisher.

The sacramental implications of eating are resumed in 'Tonight at Seven-thirty'. The references to divine dining are oddly reductive: there are no obvious allusions to the sacramental aspect of the *agape* in 'Christ's cenacle' (stanza 3) or the saints chewing 'pickled Leviathan' (stanza 2, a reference to Psalm lxxiv.14: 'Thou brakest the heads of leviathan in pieces, and gavest him to be meat to the people inhabiting the wilderness'). It is one of the most verbally baroque poems of the sequence, where table-talk is seen as a way of life ('a laugh is less | heartless than tears'), and even as a reverent acknowledgement of an order other than human, since speech can paradoxically re-present 'the true olamic silence' (i.e. to bring to mind the silence of eternity, which, in the sense of the Hebrew 'olam' as the unity of the cosmos in time, is to take the diner out of herself). There are notes in a 1945–61 notebook (Berg) for a poem on eating in which 'silence' is a key end-word. The last three stanzas of 'Tonight at Seven-thirty' contain a partial précis and elaboration of M. F. K. Fisher's prescription for gastronomical perfection quoted in *A Certain World*, p. 135.

Don Juan needs no bed, being far too impatient to undress

June 1963; 'The Cave of Nakedness', *Encounter*, December 1963; AH, p. 42. Dedicated to Louis and Emmie Kronenberger. Auden had edited *The Viking Book of Aphorisms* with Kronenberger in 1962.

'The Cave of Nakedness' returns, in a more informal manner, to the concern of the individual, to the habitat as body (it was a poem which at one time he thought of dedicating to John Layard). With a stoical glance at sex, privacy and celibacy, Auden moves to the more central function of the bedroom, where sleep is a replenishment of human purpose. He can both entrust his future to the Gospel Makers (compare the white paternoster in 'A Summer Night') and take pills to ward off insomnia's 'Vision of Hell'. He sees a night of sleep as a symbol of rebirth, with an emphasis that takes the argument of the whole poem (from 'Don Juan' to the 'County of Consideration') on a significant journey from Eros to Agape, the fulfilment of Eros. The second short of the 'Postscript' is based on the aphorism of Eugen Rosenstock-Huessy: 'Sexuality throws no light upon love, but only through love can we learn to understand sexuality.' The third was also quoted by Auden when writing about Trollope (*Forewords and Afterwords*, p. 266). The fourth throws light on 'Our bond, friend, is a third party' in *The Orators* (EA, p. 64).

A living room the catholic area you

?July 1963; 'The Common Life', *New York Review of Books*, 16 December 1963, and *London Magazine*, January 1964; *The Common Life*, 1964, with translation by Dieter Leisergang; AH, p. 46. Dedicated to Chester Kallman.

'The Common Life' takes up the 'reneighbouring' idea from 'The Cave of Nakedness' in its celebration of the living-room as the place where Auden's long-platonic relationship with Kallman was most fruitful. The religious metaphor for these individuals in their living-space is established in stanzas 1 and 4 ('catholic area'; 'protestant being') in a way that reminds the reader of the definition of the distinction often quoted by Auden, that the truth is catholic but the search for it protestant. The distinction is paradoxical, for though the visitor is aware on entering of the dogmas of the household, it is privately a place where two individuals are aware of each other not as a *We*, but as '*Thou* and *I*', the primary encounter of all actual life, as described by Martin Buber (*I and Thou*, Part I). They also create a mysterious common world between them, like the relationships between the symbols of algebra (those 'impossible yet useful numbers' developed by Rafael Bombelli, *L'Algebra*, 1572). The poem pays tribute to a style of living and a friendship of twenty-four years (to describe as 'cater-cousins' a relationship that the poet, and many observers, still regarded as marriage shows a moving delicacy and reserve; for the poem to rank love and truth as it does in the final stanza may indicate a similar delicacy with respect to sacrifices made).

We've covered ground since that awkward day

?1964; epigraph to 'In and Out', the second part of AH, p. 49; CP, p. 717.

The title 'In and Out' to the section of miscellaneous poems in the volume is presumably taken from the final line of 'Thanksgiving for a Habitat', representing the negotiations that poetry makes with the world outside (and inside) the new home. In terms of the personality, it also alludes to the differences felt between the self and the name, the private being and the public reputation, that is the subject of the first poem in the section. The section itself takes up the theme of man's uncertain respect for the present world in which he finds himself. Humanity ought to be as grateful for this larger habitat as the poet is for his personal bailiwick, but though 'even melancholics | Raise a cheer to Mrs | Nature for the primal | Pleasures she bestows' ('The Geography of the House'), the larger responsibilities seem to have been mismanaged. The epigraph is built upon paradox: that evolution proceeds in stages that may be positive or negative (forward/astray; building/crime) and that this is not so much a matter of biological will (patience, impatience) as of natural geophysical forces that govern biological conditions (sunlight, salt, time).

Corns, heartburn, sinus headaches, such minor ailments

September 1961; 'A Change of Air', *Encounter*, January 1962, and *Kenyon Review*, Winter 1964; AH, p. 51; CP, p. 721.

Soon after Auden had completed his translation of Goethe's *Italienische Reise* with Elizabeth Mayer he sent her this poem, explaining that although Goethe was not the subject, he prompted it. It is reminiscent of earlier poems of Auden's about spiritual quest and enlightenment and the way in which other people regard it as having made little difference to one's daily appearance (cf. Sonnet XVI in 'The Quest': one of the themes of *The Double Man* is that only God can really tell the saintly from the suburban). In Auden's reply to the symposium of critics who discussed the poem in the *Kenyon Review*, Winter 1964, he stated: '*You*'s age, sex, social status, profession, and persona-ego problem are those of whoever happens to be reading the poem.' This is perhaps disingenuous, since the impersonal second-person in which the poem's propositions are conducted is essentially the same as in the poem 'There Will be No Peace', which Auden acknowledged as personal. The minor ailments of the first stanza are the psychosomatic symptoms of the 'estrangement between your name and you' which signals this persona-ego problem, this conflict between a person's inner and outer biography. In the *Encounter* text, the going 'Elsewhere' (which seems a rather Eliotic process of withdrawing 'from movement') was expressed in lower case. The change was the result of Spender's puzzling in the symposium. By 'Elsewhere', as Auden's notes for the poem make clear (Berg 1945–61 notebook), he meant 'life so internal as to be inaccessible to inspection. As like here as possible except that it makes no demands, gives no advice. Ignores you'. He contrasted it with 'Here' ('Where one ought to be.'), 'Nowhere' ('Chaos. No demands or needs are certain') and 'Somewhere' ('A stage. The I leaves the plot to name him [*illegible*] to a biographical subject or an experimental object').

Opposed, then, to going 'Elsewhere' are real and exotic acts of change which are mere 'mollycoddling'. The familiar example of Rimbaud is suggested, making this a version of the Truly Strong Man argument over again, and the visit to Hammerfest of May 1961, which may also in a sense be part of this poem, another Cape Wrath (see 'From scars where kestrels hover'). Incidents from Goethe's life appear in the final stanza. It was the Grand Duke of Weimar who complained (not to his cousin) that Goethe was more aloof after his Italian journey. The Grand Duke here stands in for 'Society, Literary Critics, etc.', which makes it clear that Auden has literary fame in mind in the poem. His notes identify the sense of 'name' as being based on past work. Among the notes is also this telling observation: 'You have sought a home before you were ready for it. i.e. a shelter from yourself.'

Really, must you

September 1960; 'You', *Badger*, Autumn 1960, and *Saturday Evening Post*, 3 March 1962; AH, p. 53; CP, p. 722.

'You' is the Mind's address to the Body, governed by the scientific observation that the two are split through having developed at different rates. Even so, this does not explain why it is Mind which feels guilt (corollary to the celebration of the corporeal life elsewhere in the volume), or why human anxiety belongs wholly to the spiritual life.

Who, now, seeing Her so

?May 1964; 'Et in Arcadia Ego', *New York Review of Books*, 3 June 1965; AH, p. 55; CP, p. 724.

The simple style in this poem contrasts strikingly with the rococo conversationalism of some of the longer-lined pieces in the style Auden acquired in the 1950s. Using the *haiku* stanza, it has a different kind of abbreviated purity of style which however does not reject lexical deliberation. This is a fine poem, whose imagery co-ordinates without fuss a truth about the nature of evil and superstition with a truth about the holiness of settled nature in terms of modern Austria, where the rural environment confronts technocracy and recent genocide. The familiar words of the title are actually spoken by Death.

For over forty years I'd paid it atlas homage

May 1961; 'Hammerfest', *London Magazine*, March 1962; AH, p. 57; CP, p. 725.

Auden wrote to Hedwig Petzold on 31 May 1961: 'Have always longed to see this place and now I have. Beautiful landscape, no architecture and too much Salvation Army.' Whether the Norwegian town Hammerfest was still 'the northernmost township on earth' might have been in doubt, with rival candidates in Canada and Siberia, but it was true that it had long been a lodestone for Auden (to Ansen in 1947 he said: 'I might have ended up in Hammerfest'). Auden does not disguise its obvious dreariness, evident in its produce (beer and deep-frozen fish-sticks) and its geology and flora (stanza 3), but the skill with which he develops his argument that its lack of echoes is a sign of innocence is masterly: the poem is a chilling reminder of the most basic forms of human futility and self-deception, and Hammerfest's 'holiness' is of an admonitory kind.

Unwashed, unshat

April 1964; 'Iceland Revisited', *Lesbók Morgunbladsins*, 31 May 1964, and *Encounter*, July 1964; AH, p. 59; CP, p. 727. Dedicated to Basil and Susan Boothby.

Basil Boothby was ambassador in Iceland at the time of Auden's 1964 visit (of which he gives an account in *A Tribute*, pp. 95ff). The poem is in fact a series of *haikus*, mostly single ones, although there is one pair and one trio. Auden pays tribute to Iceland as a place where 'all men are equal | But not vulgar – not yet.' The occasion, though, is one for feeling middle-aged and missing the comforts of civilisation. The significance of place is not approached with the power and relevance of the earlier poem which most comes to mind, 'Journey to Iceland'. Travel now for Auden was less an exploration than a tour of fame that reminded him of his deficiencies. Boothby recounts his rescue in an air-taxi. The three who 'slept well' are Auden, MacNeice and Michael Yates, on their earlier visit. A bondí is a farmer. Hekla is a mountain in southern Iceland.

Among Pelagian travellers

June 1963; 'On the Circuit', *New Yorker*, 4 July 1964; AH, p. 61; CP, p. 729.

Pelagian travellers believe that they can reach their destination without God's grace. The poetry-reading circuit (Columbia-Giesen-Management were Auden's agents) provides a comic background to the Audenesque genre, the aeroplane poem, although here the poet's eye is not on the world below him so much as on his suitcase. If the state he is visiting is dry, the only alcohol he will get will be from his own bottle after the reading. The memorable word he coins for this situation is 'grahamgreeneish'. Despite such feared deprivations, the poem ends (with deficient irony, one feels) with blessings for the USA, 'so large | So friendly, and so rich', a Drydenesque formula, as John Whitehead has pointed out (see Dryden's 'Epilogue to the University of Oxford, 1674': 'Till our return we must despair to find | Judges so just, so knowing, and so kind').

What on earth does one say at a Gaudy

?1958; 'A Toast', AH, p. 64; CP, p. 751.

Auden's Gaudy toast, in the manner of Praed, must have served well enough after a college dinner (it appears that it was composed two years early, perhaps for a Gaudy that he could not attend). The Strauss opera in stanza 1 is *Intermezzo*. In stanza 6, 'D' is Robert Hamilton Dundas, Tutor in Greek history from 1909 to 1955, then an Emeritus Student of Christ Church; 'Roy' is Roy Harrod, Student of Christ Church since 1925, Auden's former tutor and currently Curator of the SCR; 'Hooky' is Lieut.-Col. Denys Hill, Student and Steward of Christ Church since 1946; 'Little' is Cyril Little, the Christ Church SCR butler. They are all four of them (including Auden, making his speech) linked in their responsibility for the entertainment of the Gaudy.

Necessity knows no Speech. Not even

?April 1961; 'A Short Ode to a Philologist', *English and Mediaeval Studies*, ed. N. Davis and C. L. Wrenn, 1962; AH, p. 66; CP, p. 753.

Here Auden pays tribute to J. R. R. Tolkien, the Old English scholar, by elaborating comment on the proposition that the health of a society depends upon the health of its language, since language is the prime instrument of free-will. Kraus's aphorism ('Language is the mother, not the handmaid, of thought') was quoted in *A Certain World*, p. 260. For 'Frisch's bees' in stanza 1, see Karl von Frisch, *Tanzsprache und Orientierung der Bienen* (Berlin, 1965). Auden told Tolkien on 18 January 1963 that he had actually heard the term 'integrity-ridden' (stanza 3) in a radio commercial for an investment agency. He makes reference to it in *Secondary Worlds*, p. 127. 'Dame Philology' in stanza 4, the foundation of language, is borrowed from Skelton's 'Speke Parott', line 43, and in introducing her Auden takes an opportunity to salute again the fourteen-volume *Oxford English Dictionary* in his admirably devious route to his intended encomium.

Why *then*, why *there*

February 1964; 'Elegy for J. F. K.', *Sunday Times*, 22 November 1964, *Washington Post*, 22 November 1964, *Evening Standard*, 23 November 1964; setting by Stravinsky, 1964; AH, p. 67; CP, p. 754.

The elegy for President Kennedy was written, in the *haiku* stanza, to be set by Stravinsky (see Igor Stravinsky and Robert Craft, *Themes and Episodes*, 1966, pp. 56–9). Auden told Stravinsky that the final stanza was flexible, and could be used anywhere or as a refrain. The setting opens with it. The words commemorate the anniversary of the assassination with curiously little reference to its subject (unfortunate if we remember the confessed strategies of ' "The Truest Poetry is the Most Feigning" '). The opening stanza ('Why *then*, why *there*, | Why *thus*, we cry, did he die?') seems to conduct an invisible argument with Eugen Rosenstock-Huessy, quoted in *A Certain World*, p. 262 ('The primary questions for an adult are not *why* or *how*, but *when* and *where*').

Withdrawn from the Object-World

1964; 'Lines for Elizabeth Mayer', AH, p. 68; CP, p. 755.

Elizabeth Mayer (the recipient of 'New Year Letter') was eighty on 6 April 1964. Auden's tribute, in the *haiku* stanza, has great charm, not least by virtue of the playful sense of ephemerality and conflation of epochs that the opening stanzas establish. It was the Grand Duke of Weimar's 'glass coach' that gave Goethe the Cinderella-like opportunity in November 1775 of a life at Court (see Auden and Elizabeth Mayer's Introduction to Goethe's *Italian Journey*, 1962, p. xviii), but we note that Elizabeth Mayer's own father had been Chaplain to the Grand Duke of Mecklenburgh (Carpenter, p. 211) so that the sand-clock was perhaps an object she had known. It was presumably a governess of Elizabeth Mayer's who played Chopin's Scherzo in B flat minor. The noble gases are helium, neon, argon, krypton, xenon and radon (the last two 'seduced', in the sense that they were thought to be chemically inert until the compounds xenon hexafluoroplatinate (v) and radon difluoride were produced in 1962).

Deep in earth's opaque mirror

?1963–4; 'Symmetries & Asymmetries', AH, p. 70; CP, p. 731.

'Symmetries & Asymmetries' contains more notebook material that never quite became poems. The discovery of the *haiku* as a repository for this sort of material was clearly liberating for Auden (only three of the forty-three are not in the *haiku* stanza), and a similar collection, *Marginalia*, was published in 1966. The epigrams are discrete but related: they gnomically confirm Auden's preoccupation with the comic spectacle of mankind sulking or dreaming in a world puzzled by 'Dame Kind's thoroughbred lunatic', and chronicle the ironies of our narcissism, pretentiousness and violence. The range of observations, and range of disciplines from which they are drawn, are wide, but nearly all are governed by rueful paradox.

Unmarried, nearsighted, rather deaf

?1961; 'The Maker', *Poetry in Crystal*, 1963, *New York Times*, 28 April 1963, and *Of Books and Humankind*, 1964; AH, p. 82; CP, p. 737.

'The Maker' is a footnote to the craftsmen of 'Makers of History' in *Homage to Clio*, who similarly in their extra-historical role teach 'the Quality . . . that charm is useless, | A threat fatal'. In this context, the maker is not a musician because his hammer has its own rhythm ('labouring demes' in stanza 3 are working localities, like a factory tuned in to 'Music While you Work'). The Quality exert their power against the flux of history in vain; the allusion in the final stanza to the story in *Struwwelpeter* of the thumbsucker and the Scissor Man implies a psychological determinism behind the supposed authority of the will which only art (the sculptor, here) can understand and redeem.

Unrhymed, unrhythmical, the chatter goes

?1963; 'At the Party', AH, p. 84; CP, p. 738.

Though 'At the Party' can be read as a party poem (like 'The Love Feast'), considering the extensive metaphors of reading and song, and the opening accusation of tunelessness (which would be odd if a literal party were the only subject), it can be seen to have another dimension of meaning as a symbol of the selfish egotism of confessional poetry and its 'howl for recognition'.

Lost on a fogbound spit of sand

?Summer 1964; 'Lost', AH, p. 85; CP, p. 718.

This quatrain, the merest trace of a dream, carries an authentic though understated fear in its premonition of death. Auden suffered from corns, which was why he so often wore slippers in public. Since the poem is contemporary with 'The Cave of Making', it may owe something to a memory of MacNeice's poem 'Charon'. According to Nevill Coghill, Auden sent the quatrain to him and 'dared the mild, endearing boast that it was "as good as Landor"' (letter to Kallman, 30 September 1973).

A sweet tooth taught us to admire

?July 1964; 'Bestiaries are Out', AH, p. 86; CP, p. 739.

'Bestiaries are Out' returns to an idea from 'Prologue: The Birth of Architecture', where similar insects are shown to be builders but not architects, in the sense that it is only human beings who self-consciously create a habitat for their immortal souls. Bees provided behavioural analogies for human society in the eighteenth century ('Philosopher and Christian Preacher' are Bernard Mandeville and Isaac Watts), but today we see how different they really are, how indeed the only political model they provide is mechanical and totalitarian.

If all a top physicist knows

1961; 'After Reading a Child's Guide to Modern Physics', *New Yorker*, 17 November 1962; AH, p. 88; CP, p. 740.

This poem (a result of reading G. Gamow's *Mr Tompkins in Wonderland*, 1940, and *Mr Tompkins Explores the Atom*, 1945) is healthily irreverent about science by asking what we want the knowledge *for* (there are echoes here of ideas at the end of Part One of *The Age of Anxiety*). True enough, but perhaps as a sentiment slightly upstaged by the portentous theological nudge in the final stanza. For stanza 2, see Gamow, chapter 10, 'The Gay

Tribe of Electrons'. The idea in stanza 3 about being partly somewhere else is explained in chapter 7, 'Quantum Billiards', and the notion of 'saddle' space in chapter 4, 'The Professor's Lecture on Curved Space, Gravity and the Universe' (in the combined reprint of 1965, *Mr Tompkins in Paperback*).

From leaf to leaf in silence

May 1964; 'Ascension Day, 1964', *London Magazine*, August 1964; *The Common Life*, 1964, with translation by Dieter Leisergang; AH, p. 90; CP, p. 742.

'Ascension Day, 1964', written in the *haiku* stanza, treats the Holy Thursday ritual of the risen Christ in terms of a lover's parting, caused, as it were, by the 'glum Kundry' in us all which sets out to impede the spiritual quest that Christ provides (Kundry is the enchantress in Wagner's *Parsifal*, who becomes a symbol of the penitent sinner).

Komm Schöpfer Geist I bellow as Herr Beer

July 1962; 'Whitsunday in Kirchstetten', *Reporter*, 6 December 1962, *Wort und Wahrheit*, May 1963, and *Listener*, 7 November 1963; AH, p. 92; CP, p. 743.

The final poem in the collection is dedicated to Father H. A. Reinhold, a Catholic liturgist whom Auden had first met at Swarthmore in exile from Germany. It somewhat reverses the quotation from Karl Kraus which Auden had used as an epigraph to 'A Short Ode to a Philologist': 'Language is the mother, not the handmaid, of thought' doesn't seem to hold for the ecumenical point that lies at the heart of the poem. It is much concerned with linguistic boundaries, and with geographical boundaries, too, since the fact that the Episcopal Auden is attending a Roman Mass implies a decline in the secular influence of the churches which is elaborated in the second part of the poem, and the early observation about which side of the Iron Curtain Niederösterreich happens to be on is taken up at the end of the meditations upon the Russians' Cold War threats. See Stella Musulin, *Austria: People and landscape* (1971), p. 182, on Lower Austria's position on the line between East and West: 'Essentially, it was still the marchland of the Dukes of Babenberg, the original Ostarrichi, the Eastern Realm.' A Russian conquest of the West is felt to be unlikely (a comfort encouraged by the general ecumenical goodwill in the poem). But what about the Chinese? What, indeed, about the Africans? Retreating wryness here does not dispel the real nervousness in the glum laugh about paying the price for an

Imperialist heritage (rather less than goodly, in this case). 'Gemütlichkeit' is cordiality; 'menalty' is the middle classes; 'papabile' is qualified to be elected Pope; 'magnalia' are great works. The Emperor Franz Joseph (1830–1916) was called 'the Unfortunate' because his wife was a suicide and his brothers executed in Mexico and assassinated at Sarajevo. In 1914 it was his ultimatum to Serbia that led Austria and Germany into the First World War.

The Bassarids

The proposal to Hans Werner Henze to create an opera based on Euripides' play *The Bacchae* came from Auden in 1961, during rehearsals of their *Elegy for Young Lovers* for its English première at Glyndebourne, when Henze had asked Auden if they might work together again. Henze read the play in 1962, and Auden and Kallman's libretto was completed in September 1963. As Henze later explained, the project was a powerful challenge to him:

> One morning I received a huge unregistered parcel, just through the normal mail; it had burst half open so that leaves of paper were almost dropping out. That was the original manuscript of 'The Bassarids'. I read it in bed that morning and I stayed in bed for three days, completely knocked out. I thought it was terribly involved, terribly difficult, and I was paralysed by the idea that I should have to create music for so many ideas and such – how do you say it? – highly charged emotions. I felt it was too much of a challenge. It took me a long time to understand it.
>
> (*Observer Magazine*, 6 October 1974, p. 57)

Auden and Kallman made Henze listen to *Götterdämmerung* before composing the music, but his antipathy to Wagner made him turn instead to Mahler as a model. The opera is composed in the form of a four-movement Mahlerian symphony. It was given its first performance at the Salzburg Festival in August 1966 (in German: the first performance in the librettists' own words was at the Santa Fe Opera in 1968).

Kallman wrote more than half of the libretto (Auden to Dodds, 8 October 1963; over thirty pages of the sixty-seven page Schott text exist in Kallman's hand in a Texas notebook). Full details are given of the collaboration in *Libretti*, pp. 683–4. The Intermezzo is almost certainly Auden's work. The text of the libretto issued by Schott in 1966 uses square brackets to indicate those parts not set by Henze. Page references here are to the text in *Libretti*.

The Bassarids is a free adaptation of Euripides, but the title is taken from a lost play by Aeschylus, *Bassarides*. The word is rare in English (it was not in the OED) but had been used by Robert Graves in *The White Goddess* and in his poem 'The Destroyed' (*Collected Poems*, p. 265). It refers to both male and female followers of Dionysus, and lends a greater universality to the theme.

In Euripides, Dionysus takes revenge upon Agave and Pentheus for denying his divinity. The librettists are less concerned with Dionysus as a type of religious force, though much play is made with his power to reveal unconscious motivation. His manipulation of Agave and Pentheus actually tells us more about the strange maternal relationship at the centre of the opera than his portrayal as a Regency dandy might suggest. Myth has the power, Auden believed, to explain to us forces beyond our control. If in this case it has lied (according to the epigraph from Gottfried Benn, who in 'Verlorenes Ich' claimed that the Ego is lost in a modern world which cannot recognise the truth of Christianity), it must be because of the psychological ambiguity in what is revealed to Pentheus: as so often in Auden, repression creates the terms of its perception of its own possibility of liberation.

The parallels of Dionysus/Christ are not taken up. Dionysus is a catalyst, a presence by which the other characters can assert their religious positions. To Agave he provides a meaning in life which she has lost, an identification with nature (see her aria on p. 275). To Pentheus, a stoic-humanist, he represents the instinctual life which he has repressed in his rational pursuit of 'the True Good'. The other characters in their various ways relate to the Dionysiac cult as to a religious choice (Cadmus is unwilling to commit himself, Tiresias is merely being fashionable, and so on), but in the case of Pentheus, the sexual challenge is significantly present ('Here you may do, | Do, do, | Do the forbidden | Shameless thing', p. 270).

In allegorical terms, this would imply that Pentheus' puritanical suppression of the cult represents the familiar ascendency of the Ego over the Id (represented by the stage's division in depth into Thebes and Mount Kithairon), and that the final implacable triumph of Dionysus represents the dangers of not allowing the instinctual life its expression – in the Euripidean formula which only occurs in Kallman's later 'Prologue': 'DO NOT IMPRISON THE GOD!' (*Libretti*, p. 715). Auden discusses the damaging results of repression in *Secondary Worlds*, and compares Pentheus with Sarastro in *The Magic Flute*: 'Suppose, we cannot help wondering, there had been no Tamino and Pamina to provide a tidy and happy conclusion, would Sarastro have enjoyed his happy triumph for long?' (p. 110). Auden reminds us that today we again understand how it is possible for whole communities to be demonically possessed, and in the Epilogue to *The Bassarids* is embodied the Dionysiac triumph in a vision of two enormous fertility idols on Semele's tomb in the ruins of Thebes, with the Bassarids in adoration. The child with the doll that says 'mama' smashes it in glee, repeating, in conscious worship, the unconscious murder of Pentheus by his mother.

The implication is clear. Pentheus had wished for knowledge of his mother's sexual nature, and his repression had stemmed from this hidden wish. When he is given her mirror by Dionysus, what he 'sees' is the comic Intermezzo, a piece of pastoral whimsy in which the Olympian appetites are portrayed in Neo-classical terms, alternately rakish, coy and vulgar. Agave plays for the handsome Captain, a Dionysus-surrogate and, significantly, an administrator who has already stood in for Pentheus in his political role and here would seem to represent Pentheus' own desires (in a letter to Dodds of 12 September 1963, Auden, significantly for the contemporary application of the opera's psycho-political message, described him as an 'Eichman'). Pentheus is disappointed at the vision, and wishes he could have 'Seen the raw deed plainly' (p. 293). Sadly, the Intermezzo was cut in the 1992 edition of the full score.

From this point Pentheus is caught, and determines to observe the Bassarids at their supposed orgies by visiting Mount Kithairon himself. In this ensuing voyage into his real subconscious he is, like Ransom in *The Ascent of F6*, symbolically destroyed by his repressed instincts, here again embodied in the aggressive mother. The scene (p. 301) in which he struggles with his Dionysus-nature, and comes to some understanding of his psychic identity, is rather obscure, as many of the key moments of the opera are, but is evidently intended as a revelation of lust which destroys him effectively even before he is actually dismembered by his mother.

The setting of the opera is a deliberate farrago: the Bassarids are hippies, Tiresias an Anglican archdeacon, and so on. In this the librettists felt that they were realising certain suggestions of Dodds in his edition of *The Bacchae* (1944). Although they felt that Henze had overscored the Intermezzo, they were in no doubt that he had written a masterpiece.

Various suggestions for a further collaboration with Henze came to nothing. Auden became interested in the possibilities of *Love's Labour's Lost* as an opera in the mid-1960s, and eventually in 1969 produced an adaptation with Kallman which was set by Nicolas Nabokov and premièred by the Deutsche Oper at the Théâtre de la Monnaie in Brussels on 7 February 1973. Although using few of Shakespeare's words apart from the opening and closing arias (Kallman said that they 'stamped Shakespeare to bits and then put it together again', *New York Times*, 8 August 1971), the adaptation contributes less original Auden-and-Kallman than we find in their versions of Peele or Euripides. Holofernes and Sir Nathaniel disappear and the reduced scenario is made yet again into a vehicle for the mythical resolution of Reason and Passion. The text is printed in *Libretti*, p. 315.

City Without Walls

The collection *City Without Walls* was first published in England in September 1969, and in the US in January 1970. It contained poems written while Auden was artist-in-residence in Berlin for six months in 1964–5, funded by the Ford Foundation, and while later during 1965 and 1967 he was rereading and revising his entire canon for subsequent publication in the 1966 *Collected Shorter Poems* and the 1968 *Collected Longer Poems.* The geographical and temporal detachment that these circumstances afforded may have been responsible for the volume being better received than its predecessor. It was dedicated to the *Observer* music critic Peter Heyworth (who was also in Berlin on the Ford programme) with a dedicatory verse ('At Twenty we find our friends for ourselves, but it takes Heaven') that shows the poet conscious of his age, a note that the volume returns to at its close, with the poem 'Prologue at Sixty'.

. . . Those fantastic forms, fang-sharp

1967; 'City Without Walls', *New Yorker*, 27 April 1968; CWW, p. 11; CP, p. 748.

The title poem of the collection denounces Megalopolis, that state of urban culture resulting from excessive technology which deprives the city of any human size or identity. It has become a mechanised desert where natural man is reborn ('Asphalt Lands', like Huston's film *The Asphalt Jungle*, are lawless). In this environment a new primitive man develops, with a new form of tribal warfare (stanzas 5–6) and even a new Adam and Eve, for whom the Sabbath is a sterile blank (stanzas 7–9). The diction reminds us that the focus of Auden's Jeremiad is a spiritual lack: we are all hermits now, but like 'idiorhythmic' monks with their own permitted life-style, we have no agreed community of worship (stanza 8) and no sense of our own importance or identity (stanzas 10 ff). A possible consequence of this 'Gadgeted Age' is the nuclear disaster and its aftermath described in stanzas 17–20, a hideous picture, but hideously funny, the point perhaps at which the Auden-Juvenal takes over from Auden-Jeremiah. The poet's realisation of his own excess, and of the consequent dismissive framing device, lower the tension. The argument here is somewhat distant from the felt realities of the diatribe: is someone who takes pleasure in suffering (*Schadenfreude*) quite the same as someone who is indifferent (pococurante)? However, we are left uneasy. Isn't the bored third voice in reality our own voice, the voice of real indifference that permits the spread of Megalopolis?

Reaching my gate, a narrow

February 1965; 'Joseph Weinheber (1892–1945)', *London Magazine,* July 1965; CWW, p. 17; 'Josef Weinheber (*1892–1945*)', CP, p. 756.

Josef Weinheber was one of the most important Viennese poets of the twentieth century, an enthusiastic Nazi at the time of the Anschluss, though later disillusioned. He committed suicide in 1945. He was an inhabitant of Kirchstetten, and is saluted as neighbour in space if not in time by Auden, who first saw Kirchstetten in 1956 and bought the house next to Weinheber's house in the following year. The Austrian poet might have been good to talk to about verse over a glass of white wine, but his role in the poem is principally as a locus of reaction to the peripatetic 'Shadow' of evil. In stanza 3, when Goebbels asks him what can be done for the arts and culture of the Ausmarck, he replies in the Viennese dialect: 'in Ruah lossen' ('leave 'em alone'). A different version of this story can be found in Nadler's biography of Weinheber (p. 350).

Auden found his information about the Austrian peasant Jägerstätter, beheaded for pacifism, in Zahn's book *In Solitary Witness* (1964), which he was reading in July 1964. The other German phrases in the poem are both quotations from Weinheber's poems. In stanza 5: 'All this is dreadful, here only silence is appropriate' (from the poem 'Auf des Unabwendbare', 'To the Inevitable'); and in the last stanza, his commitment as a poet is 'to give a name to the Abyss' (from the poem 'Kammermusik', 'Chamber Music'). The latter quotation comes from the passage where the viola speaks to the violins (compare 'viols' in Auden): 'Mein grauer Scheibel macht es mir zur Pflicht, | Den Abgrund euch zu nennen. Wie ihr beide | Verschwistert hingeht, kindliche, besticht | Selbst noch der Streit um nichts. Ich aber leide' ('My grey hair makes it my duty to name the abyss for you. As you two childlike spirits skim along, even the quarrel about nothing becomes attractive. But I suffer', Patrick Bridgewater's translation). The complete translation appears in *A Certain World*, p. 58. Weinheber has learned the art of celebrating the human in the most demoralising way. At the centre of the poem (stanzas 6–7) is the hinge which links the Nazi regime with the idea of the more permanently shifted cosmos which runs through the poem: 1956 was the year in which it was discovered that not all physical reactions are symmetrical (Yang's demonstration of a left-spinning bias in radioactive particles). This gives a double edge to the 'kidnapped physicists' of stanza 7, and an extended double focus for the moral and political anxiety in the poem; it even seems to account for nuclear weapons in stanza 9. The poem is written in alternate lines of seven and five syllables. In stanza 3 'damage | and malengine' (power to damage, and evil intention) are both words used by Malory. 'Unplace' (stanza 8) is an invented word by analogy with German *unmensch*. In stanza 12 'impaled' means simply 'fenced in'.

All folk-tales mean by ending

April 1965; 'An Epithalamium for Peter Mudford and Rita Auden', *New Yorker*, 31 July 1965; 'Epithalamium (*for Peter Mudford and Rita Auden, May 15th, 1965*)', cww, p. 21; cp, p. 760.

Also written in alternate lines of seven and five syllables (though with the final pair in each stanza reversed), the poem celebrates the marriage of the younger of Auden's nieces. The poem is a verse counterpart of the standard uncle's wedding-speech, full of back-handed compliments, baleful praise of the body, and hints about the pitfalls of marriage. The poem burrows into and through biology to finds ways of celebrating human uniqueness. Stanza 5 reminds us of the recent interest in DNA, stanza 6 that the human body is appropriate for its purposes ('ciliates' are lower organisms that move by oscillating their tiny hairs), stanza 7 that our supremacy is an inheritance from dead reptiles (that became extinct during the Permian age, 248 million years ago, the uppermost geological layers of the Palaeozoic strata, when up to 90 per cent of all marine species died). In the final stanzas of the poem, the original father ('Ur-Papa') of humanity is portrayed as a vagrant ('gangrel') pseudo-rat, as if further to marvel at our willingness to choose the bodily life at all and still be able to 'thank | Mrs Nature for doing | . . . the handsome by us' (stanza 5). Finally, whereas genealogy may acknowledge such an unlikely physical ancestor ('Seth-Smith' is Peter's, 'Bonnergee' Rita's, mother's maiden name, thus invoking a series of such backward perspectives on the 'distaff' side) as the creatures of God (with

Adam as the true Ur-Papa) we all have our absolutely unique names, owing nothing to biological origin, as every particle does. Auden's understanding of the role of names here is illuminated by the lecture 'Words and the Word' in *Secondary Worlds*, pp. 119–44. The paradox of marriage in God's eyes (which here almost seems to bypass biology) is that despite the uniqueness ('nonesuch being') the couple are like crystalline complementary forms ('enantiomorphs') which match if placed against each other ('super-posable'), a sexual joke that almost disappears in the complexity of the argument. Auden told Peter Heyworth that the medical and geological references were put in because his brother John was a geologist and Rita a medical student at the time.

In our beginning

July 1965; 'To Professor Nevill Coghill upon his Retirement in A.D. 1966', *To Nevill Coghill from Friends*, 1966; 'Eulogy', CWW, p. 23; CP, p. 762.

Again Auden uses a pattern of alternating five- and seven-syllabled lines for this tribute to Nevill Coghill. Auden was an Exhibitioner in Natural Sciences at Christ Church, Oxford, but changed to English in his first year. He was sent out for tuition to Nevill Coghill, then a young Fellow of Exeter College. For Coghill's view of his pupil, see *T. S. Eliot: A symposium*, ed. R. March and Tambimuttu (1948) and *For W. H. Auden, February 21, 1972*, ed. P. H. Salus and P. B. Taylor (1972). Auden now sees the period between childhood and the 'Age of Care' as a period of innocence and simplicity ('columbine', literally dove-like) whose lucky irresponsibility is a matter for fond gratitude. The generalised argument, comparable in some respects to Eliot's 'Animula', is abandoned after five stanzas and replaced by the specific tribute to Coghill as a tutor concerned more with his pupils' development than with his own image, and by the concluding wishes for his retirement. An insight into Auden's lexical procedures is afforded by a list in a 1965 notebook of odd words to use, all beginning with 'p', including 'potamic' (stanza 5, Oxford's river-threaded meadows) and 'a plump of tutors' (stanza 7, 'a don distinct | from the common plump'). 'Pococurante' from this list gets into 'City Without Walls'.

Liebe Frau Emma

June 1968; 'In Memoriam Emma Eiermann', *London Magazine*, August 1968; 'Elegy In Memoriam Emma Eiermann (*ob. Nov 4th, 1967*)', CWW, p. 27; CP, p. 766.

Charles Miller reports that Auden knew that his housekeeper and her brother were incestuous lovers: ' "Charlie, they are the earthiest creatures imaginable, and Chester knew at once that they are sibling lovers! They have lived together since childhood, they survived war and expatriation, they are so inseparable that they sleep together!" Wystan looked at me keenly, chuckling' (Miller, p. 122). The poem begins and ends tenderly in German ('Dear Frau Emma, now then, what have you done now? . . . You good woman, sleep in peace') and evokes her pride in the garden or her suspicion of Kallman's young Greek friends with enough humour to allow his suspicion a place in the poem (stanza 13). The furious reaction to fruit-picking is supported by Basil Boothby (*A Tribute*, p. 97). The poem uses a stanza of five- and seven-syllabled lines.

The concluded gardens of personal liking

August 1967; 'A Mosaic for Marianne Moore (*on the occasion of her eightieth birthday, Nov. 15th, 1967*), *New York Review of Books*, 9 November 1967, and *Wilson Library Bulletin*, March 1969; CWW, p. 30; CP, p. 768.

Most of the images in this tribute to Marianne Moore are from her poems, and many of these were given as examples in Auden's essay on her in *The Dyer's Hand*, pp. 296–305. It is, then, a 'mosaic' as it claims to be, and as her own poems tend to be. Referring to the worlds of the imagination as 'concluded gardens' (i.e. the *hortus conclusus*, or enclosed garden) Auden takes us at once into a theory of art (he was simultaneously with this poem preparing the University of Kent lectures that became *Secondary Worlds*) and into the work of Marianne Moore, for whom poetry was 'an imaginary garden with real toads in it'. For man as an unelephantine creature, see 'Insignificant Elephants'. The amusing account of the invitation by the Ford Motor Company to name their new model had appeared in the *New Yorker*, 13 April 1957: 'Edsel' was *not* Marianne Moore's choice.

Into what fictive realms can imagination

April 1968; 'The Horatians', *New Yorker*, 24 May 1969; CWW, p. 33; CP, p. 771.

When Auden sent 'The Horatians' and 'Ode to Terminus' to E. R. Dodds on 22 June 1968, he remarked: 'Have lately been obsessed with Horace and enclose two results of this. I imagine one has to be elderly to appreciate him.' In this poem the Horatian decencies are celebrated with a similar slight defensiveness against the absolute commitments in politics or love of 'Enthusiastic Youth' (stanza 13), and with an unusual emphasis on the character of English followers of Horace (and a Welsh one: the Radnorshire village in stanza 5 may be Clyro, curacy of diarist Francis Kilvert). The magnificent opening definition of opera both grand and comic leaves the reader slightly uncertain about what the opera-loving Auden really thinks of a Horace who cannot be imagined in operatic terms. Only in the concluding stanzas do Auden's views of the limiting role of poetry really ring true, as in 'The Quest', no. XII, which similarly proposes an ironic role when faced with the suffering of martyrs the poet cannot emulate (for Marcus Atilius Regulus, the consul defeated and tortured by the Carthaginians, see Horace's *Carm.* 3.5; for the artist's way of looking at the world 'with a happy eye', see Wittgenstein in *The Faber Book of Aphorisms*, p. 268).

He thanks God daily

?1965–6; 'Precious Me', *Quest*, Winter 1965–6; 'Profile', CWW, p. 36; CP, p. 774, with 'Addenda' written in 1973.

Apparently a more intimate garnering from the same store of *haikus* and *tankas* as 'Marginalia', 'Profile' rehearses the admissable quirks and reassurances of the irreducible Ego (which in the *tanka* that provided its original titles uses the royal 'we' to address the fallible body that he regards with distant fondness, amusement or exasperation).

On a mid-December day

January 1965; 'Since', *Encounter*, May 1965; CWW, p. 39; CP, p. 777.

This poem of nostalgia defies its nostalgia uncertainly, for we feel that the consolatory friendliness of the poet's Kirchstetten neighbours is directed not least at the obese and famous public man: the private man who will not admit to feeling lonely is still frying sausages only for himself. The remembered meal is, by contrast, a model of relished simplicity and hostly good cheer, like something out of Horace ('In a flagged kitchen I we were served broiled trout I and a rank cheese'), fitting sacrament to the magical human contact it prefigures, equally simple (even, in a way which made some readers uncomfortable, impersonalised), but of a power to bring tranquillity ('halcyoned'). The abruptness of the memory, the apparently continental setting (the memory is probably of Poprad in Czechoslovakia, which Auden visited in the summer of 1934 with Michael Yates and Peter Roger: see 'In Search of Dracula', reprinted in *Auden Studies* 2, p. 19, and stanza 16 of 'Prologue at Sixty'), the familiar sound of water in the dark (from the gorges of a nearby tributary of the Vistula), all give the poem the power and inevitability of a dream. Of all Auden's love poems it is one of the most moving, personal and direct. Like many of the poems in the volume it is written in lines of seven and five syllables.

I could draw its map by heart

July 1965; 'Amor Loci', *New Measure*, Autumn 1965; CWW, p. 41; CP, p. 779.

The 'real focus of desolation' in the last stanza of this poem centres on the analogy which Auden had used before between the love of a landscape and the love of a person (compare especially 'The Prophets'). It seems clear that the human betrayal of love is a covert rebuke to Kallman, since the impersonality of 'a frivolous worldling' is surely too imprecisely directed either at the poet himself or the race in general, even if this is the paraphrasable intention. Similarly, the heroic postures of the Alston Moor lead-miners, celebrated in much of his earliest work, play no part in the craving for bodily sensation which 'Mr Pleasure' demands: industry wants cheap power, and the man wants cheap pleasure. 'Mr Pleasure' comes from a poem of Brian Howard's which Auden admired, 'Gone to Report' (reprinted in *The Golden Horizon*, ed. Cyril Connolly, 1953, pp. 14–15).

The slow extraction of the dwindling lead ore (a frequent theme in early Auden: see 'Lead's the Best' in *Juvenilia*) becomes, in terms of the central analogy, an act of true love. The Jew Limestone is the ninth carboniferous layer, 24 feet thick, beneath which it was believed that it was not worth mining. But this belief was myth, since several of the most profitable lead deposits had been worked in strata lower than the Jew limestone (see the *County History of Cumberland*, 1905, I.6). Auden had referred to 'the Jew bottom limestone' in the opening chorus of *The Chase* (*Plays*, p. 111). Auden's geological point must be that love is driving a hard bargain, but that one must persevere. He wouldn't, naturally, have forgotten Kallman's Jewishness, since this is not the only occasion on which he celebrated it in a shocking metaphor.

Auden's Christian jokes about Jews are always deeply serious. See, for example, his dislike of the doctrine of the Immaculate Conception, which he felt embodied 'a not very savory wish to make the Mother of God an Honorary Gentile. As if we didn't all know perfectly well that the Holy Ghost and Our Lady both speak British English, He with an Oxford, She with a Yiddish, accent' (*A Certain World*, p. 71). Kallman was celebrated for his 'yiddisher momma' impersonations, and Auden, despite his short 'a's, retained his own Oxford accent. The most challenging poem about Kallman's Jewishness is the Christmas poem of 1941 (a version of which is printed in Farnan, p. 65). 'Amor Loci' appears to be saying that if you go deep enough the ore can, after all, be found. The shallower demands of 'Mr Pleasure' (and the impatient 'frivolous worldling') will never find it. 'Amor Loci' is so graced that it becomes 'Locus Amori', and there is of course a sense in which the unexpected ore is also the revelation of Christ, who himself went beyond the Jewish religious tradition (Auden significantly dignifies 'Love' in the final stanza with a capital letter). For the significance of Eden and New Jerusalem, see 'Vespers' in 'Horae Canonicae'.

Nose, I am free

1966; 'Metaphor', *Quest*, Spring 1967; CWW, p. 43; CP, p. 719.

This little observation may be intended to be a serious reflection on the duty of loving our neighbour as ourselves: the metaphor would suggest that the price to be paid is related to the deficiency, i.e. that being 'free' to love gives us the option to 'pay' by not being loved ourselves. It is thus a secular quid pro quo contrast with the 'Love' in 'Amor Loci' which 'however often smeared, I shrugged at, abandoned I . . . does not abandon'.

Trying to understand the words

May 1967; 'Bird Language', CWW, p. 44; 'Bird-Language', CP, p. 780.

Auden probably knew very well the functions of bird-song in areas such as mating and territory; he uses the fiction that it is emotionally expressive to indicate, through human recognition, the emotions that would, if they existed, seem appropriate. He described the poem as 'a piece of trivia' in a letter to Elizabeth Mayer of 19 May 1967. An earlier poem, 'Their Lonely Betters', provides a realistic and direct answer to the speculations of this one.

Little fellow, you're amusing
Ever since observation taught me temptation

?December 1963; I. 'Songs of the Ogres'; II. 'Song of the Devil', *Isis*, 25 October 1967; *Two Songs*, 1968; no. I reprinted in *New Statesman*, 1 August 1969; CWW, p. 47; CP, p. 781.

See my commentary, p. 555, on the versions included in *Libretti*, p. 509 ('Lyrics for "Man of La Mancha"').

Except where blast-furnaces and generating-stations

1968; 'Forty Years On', *New York Review of Books*, 26 September 1968; CWW, p. 50; CP, p. 783.

Auden begins by comparing the present technological landscape of Austria with the Austria he first encountered in the 1930s (probably his visit to the Tyrol before going up to Oxford) but soon merges his own voice with that of the vagabond ballad-maker Autolycus in *The Winter's Tale* (from which Prince Florizel, the coast of Bohemia – actually a coastless part of the Austrian Empire – the bear that killed Antigonus, and the Kingdom of Sicily are also drawn in lines 1–9). As a rootless 'Bohemian', Auden celebrates his adaptability in a democratic age ('shop' is shop-talk, 'Bonzen' are big-wigs, '*Sitz-Fleisch*' is perseverance) and shows how the spirit of the rogue similarly responds to the challenge of the technological age: Autolycus becomes a fixer. The Shakespearean landscape of redemptive wooing amidst the sheep-shearing has been replaced by 'a plain run smoothly by Jaguar farmers'. In the final dream of death, the marriage of Autolycus' voice with the poet's own is more satisfying, for Auden has never been at ease with the purely dramatic monologue (it is clear from drafts that Auden had already begun the poem when he had the dream, which is first written in prose: the final question appears as 'When has Autolycus ever stood on his dignity?'). Sixteen lines from the end, 'boggle' was corrected in the *Collected Poems* to 'oggle' (shudder).

Fate succumbs

1965–8; compiled from short poems previously gathered as follows: 'Precious Me', *Quest*, Winter 1965–6; 'Marginalia', *New York Review of Books*, 3 February 1966; 'Filler', *New York Review of Books*, 12 May 1966; 'Dear Diary', *Harvard Advocate*, Fall 1966; in *Marginalia*, 1966; 'Marginalia', CWW, p. 55; CP, p. 785.

These *haiku* and *tanka* (and one limerick) may be roughly classified as followed: Section I, social anthropology (with some material taken from the American psychoanalyst Erik Erikson's *Insight and Responsibility*, 1964); Section II, authority; Sections III and IV, ironies of political and religious myth (with some material taken from the eleventh-century theologian Michael Psellus, the twentieth-century historians Ilsa Barea and Friedrich Heer, and the nineteenth-century ornithologist Charles Waterton); Section V, personal loneliness (beginning with an observation that he had made at Huertenbade Strasse in a notebook on 23 October 1964 when beginning his six months in Berlin for the Ford Foundation). In the same section, the third *haiku* was prompted by a notebook thought from Idris Parry ('Sanity is perhaps the ability to punctuate'). Among the unacknowledged sources, '*I travelled alone | to Bonn with a boring maid*' derives from Margot Asquith ('I went to Dresden alone with a stupid maid', *The Autobiography of Margot Asquith*, ed. Mark Bonham-Carter, 1962, p. 57). In Section III '*Anopheles*' is the malaria-carrying mosquito. In Section IV, a 'metacismus' is the metrical fault of pronouncing a final 'm' that should be elided in front of a vowel. The general model for this collection of epigrams is probably Goethe and Schiller's *Xenienalmanach* (1796), which contained satirical distichs on contemporary writers, but he had been writing similar squibs since the late 1920s. The wit and penetration of these are remarkable. Compare II.4 with 'what is not forbidden is compulsory' in 'Talking to Myself', stanza 1.

Spring-time, Summer and Fall: days to behold a world

August 1968; 'In Due Season', *Confrontation*, Spring 1969; CWW, p. 87; CP, p. 801.

Sending the poem to E. R. Dodds on 5 September 1968, Auden remarked: 'I am . . . rather proud of *In Due Season*, an attempt to write accentual Asclepiadeans' (this is the metre of Horace, *Carm.* 1.1, spondee, choriamb, choriamb, iamb). The attempt is itself referred to in stanza 3, which in a way gives an account of the writing of 'In Due Season' itself. In the poem, natural objects are indeed in a sense lured into 'man's plot to become divine', as the final stanza claims, through being lent individuality which in nature only the human recognises, all else being automatically pro- grammed to its seasonal behaviour. The 'intelligence' we desire is both our distinctive quality of understanding and the information that reaches us from God: nature is merely the undifferentiated mediator of 'sacramental signs'. (Auden had proposed in a radio talk, 'Nowness and Permanence', printed in the *Listener*, 17 March 1966, that 'It is even possible that we may recover a sense of phenomena as sacramental signs.')

On High Feast-Days they were given a public airing

1968; 'Rois Fainéants', cww, p. 88; cp, p. 802.

The 'rois fainéants' were the 'idle kings' of the later Merovingian Empire, little more than puppets, enthroned and deposed by powerful mayors of the palace. The last of them was Childeric III, deposed in 750 by Pepin III the Short, the first Carolingian. Grimoald was mayor of the palace in Neustria (died 714). Davenport-Hines (p. 322) makes the ingenious and credible point that Auden intends an analogy with the manipulated impotent authority of the modern popular singer, and by further extension, poet.

Unbiased at least he was when he arrived on his mission

May 1966; 'Partition', *Atlantic*, December 1966; cww, p. 89; cp, p. 803.

Auden's earlier poems about briefed agents nearly always contained a psychoanalytical resonance, or were evidently allegorical. This one, written at a time of fresh conflict between India and Pakistan (India had invaded West Pakistan on 6 September 1965) looks back specifically at the partition of the Indian subcontinent in 1947 along Muslim and Hindu divisions. To divide personnel, assets and liabilities of the Indian Empire in the seventy-two days before the transfer of power, a partition Council was set up in June 1947. The lawyer in the poem is Sir Cyril Radcliffe upon whose recommendations the partition was made. Radcliffe's role, like that of all bureaucrats in Auden's poetry, is presented as calculating, self-exonerating and insensitively low-keyed (compare Herod in 'For the Time Being'). Radcliffe was the British Chairman of the two Boundary Commissions set up to define the exact boundaries of the new provinces of West and East Punjab and of West and East Bengal. The Muslim and non-Muslim members were deadlocked, and it was Radcliffe who made the decisions.

The tone of the couplets is close to that of 'The Unknown Citizen', with its ironical self-satisfaction at shallow materialist solutions to deep and insoluble human problems. However, it has to be said that Radcliffe had an uphill battle. For example, when he proposed to protect the irrigation system of the Punjab, Jinnah said that he would prefer a desert to any lands rendered fertile because the Hindus allowed them to be irrigated, while Nehru declared: 'What India will do with her rivers is India's business.' The arbitration of 9 August did not prevent chaos, and the death of half a million Muslims.

The Ogre does what ogres can

September 1968; 'August, 1968', *Observer*, 8 September 1968; cww, p. 90; cp, p. 804.

'August, 1968' was 'my reaction to the invasion of Czechoslovakia' as he told Dodds (5 September 1968), and it bears a title in the earlier manner of Auden's political poetry: a month and a year. The Ogre has been familiar in Auden's poetry since 'Letter to Lord Byron', Part II; here, the excuses for the Russian invasion are seen as monstrous examples of the art of political lying.

Thumping old tunes give a voice to its whereabouts

June 1966; 'Fairground', *New Yorker*, 20 August 1966; cww, p. 91; cp, p. 804.

In this poem written in syllabic sapphics, the ordered life of age, with its shortened perspectives, is contrasted with the escapism of youth, for whom the fairground provides a model of ecstasy (stanzas 3–4) or ordeal (stanzas 5) which turns the participant momentarily into saint or hero, through 'jeopardy, | panic, shock . . . dispensed in measured doses | by fool-proof engines'. The irony of this poem lies perhaps in its proposition that the fairground's 'disarray' is as precisely controlled as the bourgeois exploits of the old, and indeed is part of them, for the human body infinitely repeats (stanza 6) the commands of the life force (compare 'Venus Will Now Say a few Words').

Out of a bellicose fore-time, thundering

July 1966; 'River Profile', *New York Review of Books*, 22 September 1966, *Poetry Book Society Supplement*, ed. Eric W. White, 1966, and as a broadside; CWW, p. 93; CP, p. 806.

The idea for 'River Profile' might well have come from Coleridge's plans for 'The Brook' (*Biographia Literaria*, chapter X). The epigraph from Novalis (the Romantic poet and novelist, Friedrich Leopold von Hardenberg, 1772–1801) underlines the biological analogy of the poem. Since organisms originated in salt-water, the cycle of the primal 'spherical dew-drop of life' from rain ('head-on collisions of cloud and rock', stanza 1) to sea ('a huge amorphous aggregate', stanza 11) does double duty as a history of human organisation and as the profile of a river. Each stanza represents a moment identifiable, in Auden's view, with a degenerating stage of culture (the 'country' of each third line, brilliantly sketched with encapsulating epithets before it collapses via the short fourth line of the sapphic stanza into the succeeding stage). Since the river is a cycle, we must believe that history is a cycle, too, and this is why the 'country' that man has created can finally be redeemed, like the unlovely monster of a fairy-tale. The 'fore-time' of the opening line may be borrowed from David Jones, *The Anathemata* (in the first section, 'Rite and Fore-Time', it is the age during which man's distinctive creativity is formed).

Talented creatures, on the defensive because

May 1966; 'Insignificant Elephants', *Encounter*, September 1966; CWW, p. 95; CP, p. 807.

This oxymoronic poem (in lines of twelve and seven syllables) questions the miracles and martyrdoms of the saints as tending to be compensations in myth for the absolutely natural lives (and deaths) which members of our species ought to be able to lead, because 'Virtue' has no viable publicity (stanza 1: 'Talented'; stanza 2: 'story-tellers'; stanza 3: 'reporters, news'; stanza 5: 'snapshot'). Auden was clearly taken with the notion from the *Bestiary* that the uniquely rare and large exotic animal, the elephant, has its significant degrees of insignificance. This theme is central in Auden: the saintly are indistinguishable from the suburban. Here, however, sainthood is given a sometimes sceptical airing. In stanza 3, Hugh of Lincoln (?1246–55) was a child supposedly tortured and murdered by a Jew (the subject of

Chaucer's *Prioress's Tale*), and Peter Claver (1581–1654) was a Jesuit ministering in Cartagena, the chief slave market of South America. From the 'nudge to invent', Auden then moves to 'bosh' in stanzas 7 and 8. For Catherine, see Cardinal Schuster, *The Sacramentary* (1930), v. 302, where he writes that the story of St Catherine 'is unfortunately unsupported by any authority.' Barbara is 'in the category of pure romance' (*Butler's Lives of the Saints*, rev. 1956, iv. 488), while Uncumber's 'story is a curiosity of hagiology and is hardly worth including in a collection of lives of the saints but for the fact that it has the unenviable distinction of being one of the most obviously false and preposterous of the pseudo-pious romances by which simple Christians have been deceived or regaled' (*Butler*, iii. 151).

Auden had been reading the *Penguin Book of Saints* (as he admitted to Anne Fremantle in a letter of 8 May 1966). He had also reviewed E. R. Dodds's book *Pagan and Christian in an Age of Anxiety* (1965) in the *New York Review of Books*, 17 February 1966. It is Dodds, pp. 47–53, who writes about the dreams of St Perpetua, martyred at Carthage in 202 or 203. The dream in stanza 10 is about a shepherd at the top of a ladder who offers Perpetua curds milked directly from his sheep. It clearly has a latent sexual meaning, as Dodds notes (p. 51). Auden's review mentions Dodd's account of Perpetua's dreams with approval: 'Since Freud we are all again agreed that "dreams are purposive".'

The High Priests of telescopes and cyclotrons

May 1968; 'Ode to Terminus', *New York Review of Books*, 11 July 1968; CWW, p. 97; CP, p. 809.

The Horatian preoccupation (described in his letter to Dodds of 22 June 1968, see p. 513) allows Auden to praise the Roman god of boundaries in the same spirit as he once invoked the Lords of Limit or the dwarf Kabiri (see 'A Happy New Year' and 'Atlantis'). These are forces which make life possible by setting limits: boundary-marks are numinous because they define the essential nature of things. They are also, the poem perhaps paradoxically suggests, a supremely human requirement when science destroys the boundaries of the large and small (stanzas 1–4: the telescopes observe unlimited receding galaxies and the cyclotrons accelerate the unstable subatomic particles). Praise of Terminus merges, then, with gratitude for the proper scale of the 'placid tump . . . that heavenly freak', the Earth, where man is required as Lord of Creation to recognise and 'manage' what his ordinary senses reveal to him. It is terminus who controls the shape of things by providing structural goals. Auden draws into the poem at this point all his concerns, from the blessing of metrical rules to the grace of the *agape* (stanzas 13–14). This late Auden, as ever suspicious of science, wanting things to be recognisably themselves, is a natural development of the early Auden, for whom the household gods of limit were a symbol of duality. If it is a reductive contemplation of the truth, it is so in the Horatian spirit of the concluding stanzas, where both the aesthetics of science and the hypotheses of art are greeted with a *nil admirari*.

Excellence is a gift: among mankind

May 1962; narration for Donald Owen's film *Runner* (National Film Board of Canada, 1962); 'Runner', CWW, p. 103; CP, p. 811; *Libretti*, p. 411.

Auden's narration for this film celebrating the seventeen-year-old long distance runner, Bruce Kidd, was written to a rough-cut sent to him by the National Film Board. (According to the producer, Tom Daly, the second and third speeches of the Announcer were not by Auden.) Inevitably, in celebrating the prowess of a runner, a poet's mind will look to Greek models. While engaged on his commission, Auden wrote to Ursula Niebuhr on 11 May: 'I want to find a modern equivalent to Pindar.' He had previously used Pindar in the Odes of *The Orators*, especially in the second, which celebrated a victory of the Sedbergh Rugby Team (see pp. 114ff). Pindar celebrated the Thessalian boy athlete Hippokleas, winner of a long-distance foot-race, in his tenth Pythian ode. The antiphonal effect of the two speakers (matching *areté* with ring-dance, and picking up moral aphorisms the one from the other in heroic alliterative measure was not achieved in the film. Auden commented: 'Unfortunately it required two speakers and only had one; it wasn't very well spoken either. I should have been there to direct it' (Elizabeth Sussex, *The Rise and Fall of British Documentary*, 1975, p. 79). It is the second, and implicitly Christian speaker, who uses slight echoes of Yeats and Eliot ('Byzantium' and 'Burnt Norton') in the final speech to bring the commentary to a revelation of 'Grace and Surprise'. An earlier poem which related the camera's eye to the limitations of the Greek ideal was 'Memorial for the City', Part 1. There the camera's eye did lie, but the point in fact was similar: 'Fate is Freedom' . . . 'We are not to despair.'

Without arms or charm of culture

January 1965; William Walton, *The Twelve: An anthem for the feast of any apostle*, 1966; CWW, p. 108; CP, p. 815.

Auden knew Walton on Ischia, where in 1953 he made suggestions, at Walton's request, for the final quintet of *Troilus and Cressida* (see *Libretti*, pp. 503–6). Walton's *The Twelve*, for mixed voices and organ, was given its first performance on 16 May 1965 by the choir of Christ Church, Oxford, directed by Sydney Watson. Cuthbert Simpson, its dedicatee, was Dean of Christ Church, both Walton's and Auden's college (and Watson had been a contemporary of Auden's there). Auden's account of the mission of the apostles to spread the gospel is sketched in short phrases with heavy internal rhyming for which Walton responded, after the bass solo, with antiphonal writing for the choir. The central mezzo-soprano solo is based on Bach's Passion chorale, 'If I should e'er forsake thee' and the Twenty-third Psalm, ending with God's words to Moses. In the final section, Auden shows how the apostles made the old superstitions harmless. This regularisation of the salvific frame of things leads to the conceit of the twelve apostles as analogous to the twelve winds and twelve months, a governing spiritual order parallel to theirs in space and time. Their glorification is treated by Walton as a large-scale fugue, *a tempo vivo*. Auden wrote to Ursula Niebuhr: 'It is frightfully difficult to be contemporary without becoming South-Banky.' It is possible that the equation of the apostles and the winds 'in an oval glory' was suggested in part by the end-paper map in Rosenstock-Huessy's *Out of Revolution*, a book much admired and recommended by Auden. This map, 'The World Adjudicated to the Twelve Apostles', is in oval shape, a reproduction of one drawn by a Spanish monk Beatus in 776, with the heads of the apostles distributed according to their missionary districts.

In the First Age the frogs dwelt

1967; 'Moralities', *London Magazine*, February 1968; text issued with the recording of 1968 (DGG SLPM 139 374); Hans Werner Henze, *Moralities: Three scenic plays by W. H. Auden from fables by Esop*, 1969 (two-piano score); CWW, p. 110; CP, p. 816.

'Moralities' was commissioned, with music by Henze, by the Cincinnati Musical Festival Association and first performed on 18 May 1969. Despite the description on the title-page of the 1969 score, the work was not intended to be staged. The Aesopian sources are (numbers from the edition of Emile Chambry, Paris, 1927): I (no. 66: you are better off with a harmless ruler than with a tyrant); II (no. 136: kites neigh and forget how to sing); III (no. 308: do not be pleased by good fortune – it can change). Much of the text falls back on the feminine-rhymed couplets that Auden came to adopt for his later satirical work, but it is also notable in I for an early use of the double-dactyls invented by John Hollander and Anthony Hecht (see *Jiggery-Pokery: A compendium of double dactyls*, 1967, dedicated to Auden), and in III for the lively skipping-game quatrains of the passengers guilty of the Pelagian sin of self-worship. The quatrain 'Kiss her once, kiss her twice' was written in 1952 (in the 1950–4 notebook at Texas, fol. 157).

Mr Dean, Canons and Students of Christ Church . . .

1968; 'A Reminder', Christ Church *son et lumière* programme, June 1968; CWW, p. 118; CP, P. 823.

Auden's 'reminder', serving as prologue to the Summer 1968 *son et lumière* programme at Christ Church, is that together with language, algebra is the joint heir ('co-parcener') of human wisdom, absolute where language is relative.

Dark-green upon distant heights

April 1967; 'Prologue at Sixty', *New York Review of Books*, 18 May 1967; CWW, p. 121; CP, p. 828.

'Prologue at Sixty' is dedicated to Friedrich Heer, author of *The Intellectual History of Europe*, which Auden recommended to David Luke in September 1966. The poem is called a 'Prologue' because, as stanza 8 points out, the spirit develops out of and away from bodily death. Material things, like the Austrian forest of the opening stanzas, can 'live well by the Law of their Flesh', but for humanity the flesh is not enough. At sixty he is beginning to 'listen, beyond hope' to the impossible claims of the soul (compare Prospero in part I of 'The Sea and the Mirror'). Created in God's image, he awaits a consummation of his being in a dimension of time beyond created life (the awaited Eighth day of the final stanza). The evidence of this hope lies in language, one of the human characteristics that distinguishes the race from other created things like forests.

Language, so often celebrated by Auden, here runs as a ground-bass beneath the largely descriptive structure of the poem – his tribute to Austria and its admission to his private map of sacred places (stanzas 15 to 17). The Solihull gas-works are also mentioned in 'Letter to Lord Byron' (IV.10), Auden's favourite place when as a small boy he lived in Solihull ('a village then'); the Blue John Mine is in the Derbyshire Peak District: Auden visited it as a boy while staying in nearby Bradwell; he saw the Ffestiniog Railway (which brought slate from Blaenau Ffestiniog down to Porthmadog in Merioneth) in the Easter holidays of 1914; he visited the three dams that fed Birmingham with water from Rhayader in August 1913 (see Carpenter, plate 2b); Cross Fell is the highest point of the Pennines, and visible from Alston Moor, the site of Auden's favourite lead-mining district; Keld in Yorkshire is the town from which one may (and in June 1953 Auden did) visit Kisdon Beck (see the commentary on 'Streams' p. 448); Cauldron Snout is another Pennine sacred place, mentioned in 'New Year Letter', line 1,121; Fürbringerstrasse and Friedrichstrasse were in the working-class district of Hallesches Tor in Berlin: Auden moved to 8 Fürbringerstrasse in January 1929 from the middle-class suburb of Nikolassee; Auden visited Isafjördur in north-western Iceland in 1936 (see *Letters from Iceland*, chapter XV); Epomeo is the highest mountain in Ischia, visible from Auden's first house on the island in the Piazza Santa Lucia, Monterone; Auden stayed for two days in Poprad, in eastern Czechoslovakia, in August 1934, in company with Michael Yates and Peter Roger (see the commentary on 'Since', p. 513); Basel, in Switzerland, and Bar-le-Duc in Meuse, France, were reached nine days later on the same journey; Auden lived at 7 Middagh Street in Brooklyn from October 1940 (from which he could see the Con-Ed stacks, the chimneys of the electricity generator of the Consolidated Edison Power Corporation). The buttons in stanza 21 were a particular *bête noire* of Auden's. In a letter to James Stern of 20 April 1967 he transcribed some of their slogans ('Help Stamp Out Reality', 'Save Water: take showers together', 'Dracula Sucks', 'Marcel Proust is a Yenta').

The general emphasis is on the paradoxical internationality of language, in both space and time. In an architectural metaphor, the poet understands the Christian message in German (stanza 7) just as he expects to be understood by the protesting generation of 1960s youth (stanza 21), for the core of what is human is instantly translatable, as at Pentecost, the speaking in tongues (compare 'to hear is to translate' in 'A Reminder'). The idea of translation develops easily from its simpler physical meaning: trees cannot move (stanza 3) though men can be 'dislodged' (stanza 5) as the poet has been, first from his Icelandic origins, and later from the country of his birth. He has been 'translated', as it were, into that Christian community which acknowledges a Pentecostal internationalism. Nations are dismissed in the poem as rapacious and interfering (stanzas 6 and 13) and wedded to an aggravating technology (stanzas 18–20). Auden is not Icelandic, English, American, Austrian, or whatever. He is a cosmopolitan citizen of the spirit whose members can only be memorialised in a newspaper obituary, i.e. in language.

Academic Graffiti

Of the sixty clerihews printed in *Academic Graffiti* (1971), thirty-two had appeared in *Homage to Clio* (and a few of these were reprinted from the *New Yorker*, 4 April 1953). In his Forenote Auden paid a generous tribute to the illustrations of Filippo Sanjust, who does manage, with an air of extemporisation, to achieve good likenesses and ingenious interpretations of Auden's sometimes whimsical points. Sanjust had been responsible for the sets and costumes of *The Bassarids*.

The essence of the clerihew is the fine line to be drawn between the apposite and the absurd, and between the public and the private life. Sometimes here one can test this by supposing a clerihew's gist transferred (even as a minor detail) to a serious biographical or critical poem. In cases where Auden had already treated his subjects in this way (Goethe, James, Lear, Nietzsche) one may therefore make a useful distinction: James and Nietzsche are more authentic clerihews than Goethe or Lear, because, although too silly to survive such a notional transference, they nonetheless make a substantive, even a considerable, interpretative point. The clerihew should, of course, include as much purely incidental silliness as possible (often deriving from the rhyme, or from the bathos of the metric) without abandoning such substance. A good example is the Thackeray/daiquiri rhyme, an irrelevant necessity immediately redeemed by the point about his sensitivity about his readers.

Auden supplied footnotes of his own, and jokes suffer from explanation. However, a few notes follow. (no. 1) Henry Adams (1838–1918), author of *The Education of Henry Adams*, presents a notable case of a traditional morality confronting the chaos of the modern industrialised world. (3) *Fach*: profession; *kluge*: clever. (6) They were the same person (William Cecil, secretary to Elizabeth 1, became Lord Burghley in 1571). (7) Blake was hostile to experimental science. (8) Bridges's long poem *The Testament of Beauty* influenced Auden in his youth (see p. 54). (10) Martin Buber's *Ich und Du* (1923) was an important theological influence on Auden (God is the 'Thou' who enables human I–Thou relations with other beings, though not between men and vegetables). (15). Hugo De Vries (1848–1935) was a

Dutch botanist who established a theory of evolution by discontinuous steps, or mutations. *Xylem* and *Phloem* are respectively the harder and softer kinds of plant tissue. (18) Fulke Greville (1554–1628), English poet. (19) Experimenting with a prism in 1790, the poet Goethe became convinced that Newton was wrong and that a new chromatics was needed. *Geheimrat*: privy councillor. (20) Haggard's popular romance *She* was published in 1887. (21) Handel used the common form of his name after taking naturalisation as a British subject in 1726. (28) Kant's categorical imperative (the necessity of acting within the moral law) was distinguished from the hypothetical imperative (the necessity of acting to achieve a particular result). (33) Joseph Lister (1827–1912) was the founder of antiseptic medicine, using carbolic acid effectively in surgery from 1865. (50) Count Mosca is the Chief Minister at the Court of Parma in Stendhal's *La Chartreuse de Parme* (1839). (51) Auden also wrote about Stifter in his poem 'Pseudo-questions' (see p. 534). (53) Thomas of Erceldoune, fl. ?1220–?97, traditionally foretold the accession of James I. (54) Thomas Traherne (1637–74) was a poet who wrote nostalgically of the felicity of childhood. (58) 'Bosie' was the nickname of Lord Alfred Douglas.

Epistle to a Godson

Both the American and the British editions of Auden's penultimate collection of poems were published in 1972. The volume is dedicated to Orlan Fox, whom Auden had first met as an undergraduate at Columbia University in 1959. Fox is taken to be the addressee of 'Dichtung und Wahrheit', but the relationship later became more complex and largely avuncular (see Fox's memoir 'Friday Nights' in *A Tribute*, pp. 173–81). In the dedicatory poem to Fox, a stanza of the syllabic sapphics used in nine poems in the volume, 'vex' and 'bother' are both associated with asking awkward questions, and have similar overtones of the dismissed and trivial ('how vexing', 'I can't be bothered') that stress Auden's view himself here as sprightly irritant.

DEAR PHILIP: 'Thank God for boozy godfathers'

April 1969; 'Epistle to a Godson', *New York Review of Books*, 5 June 1969; EG, p. 9; CP, p. 832.

Auden takes on his role as godfather to Philip Spender uncertain about the continuity of past and future: change renders advice outdated, and the prospect of a polluted or desolated world leaves paternal wishes fraught with a tender shrug of hopelessness. 'To be responsible for the happiness | of the Universe is not a sinecure' (stanza 15) but it is daunting as a serious role for the inheriting generation. In the following stanza 'good grief!' is the perennial exclamation of the hapless Candy in Terry Southern and Mason Hoffenberg's spoof erotic novel: the implication is that chastity is absurdly impossible. As a quester, Spender will need, Auden finally concludes, only that Horatian poetry which celebrates the quotidian (but mindful of the Christian apocalypse, with its promise of regeneration). The final piece of advice is borrowed directly from the Red Queen in *Through the Looking Glass*, chapter 11. Frank Kermode remarked apropos of Auden's lexical borrowing: 'sometimes you find two learned freaks together, in such a way that it looks as if the poet has only that morning been browsing:

eutrophy [stanza 10], eucatastrophe [stanza 20]' (Haffenden, p. 471). Although Kermode's remark is true of Auden's general notebook practice, the second of these words could not have been found by browsing in Auden's favourite OED, and may well be his invention (a version of the Christian *felix culpa*, good coming out of disaster) contrasting deliberately with 'eutrophy', the more specific condition, increasingly found in lakes in the 1960s, of sterilisation through over-fertilisation. In stanza 7, 'ochlocracy' is rule by the mob, and 'ochlocratic media' are therefore tabloid newspapers. In stanza 8, 'gallow' as a verb meaning to frighten was used in *King Lear* but is now obsolete. 'Concinnity' (stanza 19) is beauty. Georg Cantor (stanza 21) was a nineteenth-century mathematician who developed the theory of transfinite numbers.

Most patients believe

May 1969; 'The Art of Healing: In Memoriam David Protetch M.D.', *New Yorker*, 27 September 1969; EG, p. 13; CP, p. 835.

David Protetch, who had been Auden's New York doctor for many years (the poet had known him as a student at Ann Arbor), died of cancer of the pituitary in May 1969. The tribute proposes that human illness is an individual matter which requires intuitive understanding to heal, a lesson learned, as Auden says, from his father (and supported by the theories of the post-Freudians that Auden had studied in his youth). In a notebook Auden also wrote: 'He was one of the very few doctors I have met who understood what Sir William Osler meant when he said "care for the individual patient more than for the particular disease from which he is suffering".' Auden quoted Osler's aphorism in *A Certain World*, p. 256, saying that he learned it from his father; he also quoted the Novalis. A 'nisus' (stanza 11) is an impulse or endeavour.

When you first arrived in Kirchstetten, trains had

September 1970; 'Lines to Dr Walter Birk on his Retiring from general Practice', *New York Review of Books*, 11 February 1971; EG, p. 16; CP, p. 769.

The second of the pair of elegies for doctors presents illness as a special kind of language originating in the uniqueness of the human contrasting with the seasonal regularity of animal health (compare 'for nothing can happen to birds that has not I happened before' with 'You may kiss what you like: it has often been kissed before' of *The Dog Beneath the Skin* chorus, *Plays*, p. 219: sex is what we share with animals). '*Schlamperei*' is slovenliness. Joseph Weinheber has also written a poem for this Kirchstetten doctor.

On this day tradition allots

May 1969; 'A New Year Greeting', *Scientific American*, December 1969, and published separately for use as a Christmas card by the editors of *Scientific American*; EG, p. 18; CP, p. 837.

The dedicatee of this poem, Vassily Yanowsky, was a Russian *émigré* doctor and writer whom Auden had met at The Third Hour, a theological discussion group. He seems an appropriate recipient of this speculation about the poet's body as a bacteriological microcosmos and the poet as an indifferent god to the denizens of his skin. Many of the details, as acknowledged (the squames of keratin, like rafts; the tropical forest of the armpit; the pool of the sweat gland duct; the woods of the scalp; etc.), are drawn from an article by Mary J. Marples in *Scientific American*, January 1969.

The nose and palate never doubt

May 1969; 'Smelt and Tasted', *Poet* (Madras), June 1969; *Windless Orchard*, February 1970; EG, p. 20; CP, p. 839.

This poem and the following one form a pair which in an uncommonly low-key style direct their unexceptionable physiological comments on four of the five senses towards a subtle parallelism and contrast. In each poem the first stanza suggests a variability or indifference in the message of the senses (changing taste, ephemeral sounds), the second a means of transcending physical limitations (the *agape*, continuity of the visible world). Whatever the fallibilities of these faculties we share with animals, they are for us, he suggests, a means of strengthening love and defying time.

Events reported by the ear

May 1969; 'Heard and Seen', *Poet* (Madras), June 1969; *Windless Orchard*, February 1970; EG, p. 21; CP, p. 840.

For comment, see previous poem.

To call our sight Vision

?1962; 'I Am Not a Camera', EG, p. 22; CP, p. 840.

These nine observations on photography partly derive from notes on p. 276 of the 1947–64 notebook that show Auden keen to gather evidence of the art's lack of subjectivity. Compare 'Close-ups, angle shots. The impersonal perspective, Texture-shape of things' with no. 4, and 'Remember/flash. The past without the present that remembers' with no. 7. Auden's interest in peering through lenses at 'the remote or the small' (no. 5) is of long standing. Compare ' "Sweet is it", say the doomed . . . ', lines 67ff. Auden's suspicion of photography as a necessarily choiceless amoral disposition of fact was much influenced by Rosenstock-Huessy's ideas in *The Christian Future* (1947). See the discussion of 'Memorial for the City', p. 418.

In his dream zealous

June 1969; 'A Bad Night', *Armadillo*, 1970; *Isis*, 6 June 1971; EG, p. 24; CP, p. 842.

There was bound to be some point at which Auden would attempt to exorcise his growing habit of taking his words from the obscurer corners of the OED or transferring their grammatical roles: the diction in this lexical exercise may all be traced to that dictionary, though as usual with late Auden most of the dialectal or archaic forms are perfectly clear in their context. In fact, there is a purpose to this excess, which matches the nightmare mood and is itself a homely example of the second stanza's despairing protest – that poetry even by 'bards of sentence' can fail to console or avert depression, seeming 'fribble or fop' to the victim (contrast William Blake's 'Savages are Fops and Fribbles more than any other Men', *Complete Writings of William Blake*, ed. Geoffrey Keynes, 1966, p. 468). Another depression, that of John Philips in *The Splendid Shilling* is evoked by line 24. Auden may have remembered 'hirpling' from Wilfred Gibson's play *Krindlesyke* (1922), a possible influence on *Paid on Both Sides*.

It's natural the Boys should whoop it up for

August 1969; 'Moon Landing', *New Yorker*, 6 September 1969; reprinted and revised in *Wort und Wahrheit*, November–December 1969 and *London Magazine*, January 1970; EG, p. 26; CP, p. 843.

Auden sees the moon landing as an overwhelming interference with a numinous object, although the 'Old Man, made of grit not protein' (stanza 8) is merely a comforting presence, a symbol, proverbially not made of green cheese. For Auden irreverence is 'a greater oaf' than superstition, and he sees space travel as a natural consequence of the male aggressiveness that flaked the first flint, an idea made much of in Stanley Kubrick's film *2001: A Space Odyssey*, released in 1968. Werner von Braun developed missiles for the Nazis during World War Two before working on the US Space Program. He put in an ironic appearance in the *Faber Book of Aphorisms* (p. 222) for saying: 'Basic research is when I'm doing what I don't know I'm doing'. The first two lines of stanza 6 are derived from Samuel Johnson's remarks about the Giant's Causeway: 'BOSWELL. "Is not the Giant's-Causeway worth seeing?" JOHNSON. "Worth seeing, yes; but not worth going to see".' (Boswell's *Life*, for Tuesday 12 October 1779). Auden quotes it in the *Faber Book of Aphorisms*, p. 378. His brilliant inversion of Johnson pays ironical tribute to an aimless technology ('what I don't know I'm doing'). 'Apparatnik' (stanza 10) is a version of 'apparatchik' (member of the Communist Party machine) with the Russian/Yiddish suffix -nik that was frequently attached to words in the age of the sputnik.

Martini-time: time to draw the curtains and

May 1969; 'The Garrison', *Third Hour*, 1970; *Shenandoah*, Spring 1970; *Badger*, Autumn 1970; EG, p. 28; CP, p. 844.

Auden and Kallman again turn out in defence of the City (compare 'Grub First, Then Ethics') fortified by the mystical celebration of food and drink, and the fellowship of the dead through recorded music and language. The tortoise-like Nemesis ('brachypod' is short-footed) that opposes the City is essentially the same as the 'trivial | thrust of the Present', that slow but inexorable progress of destructive time which will obliterate humanity, but which the human community, fortified by cultural fellowship with the dead can 'wend', or turn in a different direction. The poem is another attempt to express the paradox of Becoming and Being: the final three lines ('to serve as a paradigm | now of what a plausible Future might be | is what we're here for') offer a means of enlarging the Present's trivial thrust into an image of Heaven.

Who could possibly approve of Metternich

June 1969; 'Pseudo-questions', *Vanderbilt Poetry Review*, Spring–Summer 1972; *Atlantic*, September 1972; EG, p. 29; CP, p. 845.

Auden's view that the artist's genius survives his opinions or social circumstances (cf. 'In Memory of W. B. Yeats') is here put forward with uncompromising directness. Stifter (1805–68) actually tutored Metternich's son for a time. Auden's friend David Luke had recently translated three novellas by Stifter (mentioned by Auden in *Forewords and Afterwords*, p. 404). Stifter has his clerihew in *Academic Graffiti*. The background to Auden's view of Wagner's double-dealing over his copyrights, and of his anti-Semitism, may be found in his review 'The Greatest of the Monsters' (January 1969), collected in *Forewords and Afterwords*. Auden also reviewed the first work of Stifter's to appear in English, *Rock Crystal*, in the *New York Times Book Review*, 18 November 1945. The title of the poem may allude to I. A. Richards's distinction between 'pseudo-statements' and 'statements' (i.e. between literature and other forms of language). 'Pseudo-questions' would therefore be the illusory issues about literature which occur to 'critics with credos'. But see OED 'pseudo-', sense 1a ('false') and 2 ('something not corresponding to reality'). The pseudo-questions are false because they attempt to compare two orders of reality (cf. the Historian and the Poet in *Secondary Worlds*, p. 50). For 'pseudo-persons', see Auden's 'Nature, History and Poetry' (*Thought*, September 1950).

I'm no photophil who burns

October 1971; 'Stark bewölkt', *Atlantic*, September 1972; EG, p. 30; CP, p. 846.

This poem in Auden's version of the Welsh *cywydd* (for details of the form, see p. 541) is a straightforward complaint to the 'weather-god' about the immovable cloud-cover of the title. It doesn't venture, as it might have done if written a few years later, beyond the meteorological into issues of pollution or global warming. An overcast summer is simply bad for human behaviour. Auden's pigmentation certainly made him no lover of light (line 1). 'Phyllomania' is an abnormal development of leaves. '*Beamterei*' are public officials. The poem is dedicated to the Baroness Musulin, a neighbour of Auden's, author of *Austria: People and landscape* (1971), for which Auden wrote a foreword.

Every created thing has ways of pronouncing its ownhood

June 1969; 'Natural Linguistics', *Harper's*, October 1969; *Candelabrum*, April 1970; broadside, 1971; EG, p. 33; CP, p. 848.

This exercise in classical elegiacs is dedicated to the Old Norse scholar Peter Salus, who collaborated on the translations that Auden made with Paul B. Taylor. Auden was attempting, as he explained in a letter to Elizabeth Mayer of 24 June 1969, 'something in the manner and metre of [Goethe's] *Die Metamorphosen der Pflanzen*'. To Dodds in September he feared that the elegiacs were 'somewhat licentious'.

'Natural linguistics' is a conceit that not only animal behaviour but even states of inert being are a form of language without any of the hesitations, ambiguities or misrepresentations of human language. The '*koine* [absorption of ancient dialects into a common language] of visual appearance' applied, say, to a pebble removes the discussion at once from communicable language into a realm of metaphysics, albeit with much wit. A 'releaser' (line 21) is a translation of Konrad Lorenz's *Auslöser*, a sign stimulus governing behaviour in an animal species. In the final couplet of the poem, to be 'rhetorized *at* [rather] than *about*' establishes the Forsterian primacy of personal above conceptual relations.

Wide though the interrupt be that divides us, runers and counters,

May 1970; 'The Aliens', *New Yorker*, 21 November 1970; EG, p. 35; CP, p. 849.

Auden was clearly proud of 'writing a poem in hexameters about insects' (*A Tribute*, p. 176) and his pride may well have been in the unusual view taken as much as in the form (which was one he was to turn to increasingly in his last years). Most writers have taken the organisation of the bee or the ant as an instructive model of human society, but Auden finds nests or hives 'unamiable towns', and their inhabitants no more than 'animate tool-kits'. The amusing theological scenario which he invents to account for the sense of threat that insects convey to men depends upon their having, as it were, successfully eaten of the Tree of Knowledge. There are verbal echoes of Milton in the poem as if to enforce the Christian account of the Fall which he is replacing. The opening ('Wide though the interrupt . . . ') derives from *Paradise Lost* III.83–4 ('nor yet the main Abyss | Wide interrupt can hold'), where 'interrupt' has a participial form and the Latin meaning 'broken open'. For 'collateral love' (line 20), see *Paradise Lost* VIII.426. An Archon (line 40) was in Gnosticism a maleficent demon deriving originally from the Babylonian planetary gods, called Keepers of the Seven Gates. The idea in Gnosticism is that God couldn't possibly have invented such a terrible place as the sensible world. The Gnostic scenario defeats itself, however, for insects can only be accommodated into creation as an alternative life-form biding its evolutionary time: Auden ends the poem with a shrug.

Our earth in 1969

May 1969; 'Doggerel by a Senior Citizen', *Poetry*, December 1969; EG, p. 37; CP, p. 851.

The dismissive title is perhaps justified here, for Auden's couplets seem nervous of achieving the force and clarity of those in such contemporary poems as 'Smelt and Tasted' or 'Heard and Seen'. Auden fudges the distinction between characteristics of the modern world to which he has reasonable objections and those about which he is merely prejudiced or which in some obscure sense challenge his nostalgia. On the whole, the world he feels he has lost was governed by sane rules of conduct since abandoned. Without wishing to argue the moral point, the reader may well feel that steam transport and compulsory Greek are not necessarily to be associated with these rules. The hellish liturgical reforms Auden refers to in stanza 7 were essentially the work of the Archbishops' Liturgical Commission set up in 1955, which produced the *Second Series Liturgy* in 1967 ('the familiar feel of Cranmer normally only occurs in options which can be avoided', Colin Buchanan, *Modern Anglican Liturgies*, 1968, p. 122). For Auden's views on liturgical reform, see also *A Certain World*, pp. 225–6. The point about not doubting one's parents' values even when rebelling against them was also made in his interview with Daniel Halpern, *Antaeus*, Spring 1972.

A poet's hope: to be

1969–1970; 'Shorts I', EG, p. 39; 'Shorts II', CP, p. 853.

This set of twenty-seven *haiku* and *tanka* aphorisms (with one in syllabic sapphics) is as usual largely miscellaneous, although there is a subtext which rehearses the human adventure among the purposes of nature and which contrasts man's own sense of volition, identity and moral responsibility with the mechanical world in which he finds himself. Some familiar themes of this subtext are duality (no. 13), suspicion of Manichaeanism (nos 3, 4, 12, 15, 24), hostility to the claims of science (nos 6, 7), attacks on the Managers (nos 2, 21), and the unique claims of the spirit (no. 23). 'Oncers' (no. 19) are those who prefer one-night stands to a longer relationship.

Listen, good people, and you shall hear

December 1968; 'The Ballad of Barnaby', *New York Review of Books*, 18 December 1969; published with the score, 1970; EG, p. 43; CP, p. 824.

The music for this cantata was composed by pupils at the Wykeham Rise School, Washington, Connecticut, where the first performance was given on 23 May 1969 (see Harry Gilroy, 'Auden writes opera narrative for a girls' school', *New York Times*, 7 May 1969). The form is suitably simple, a rough-metred ballad stanza previously used for 'Sue', and rather unlike anything that Auden had published before. The guitar accompaniment is reminiscent of the narrative interludes in *Paul Bunyan*. The legend is that of 'Le jongleur de Notre Dame', which Auden may have found anywhere, though the serious purpose of the story makes it possible that he took it directly from Wallace Stevens, who applied it significantly to the energies of his own imaginative life ('And a jig – and a jiggety-jiggety-jig. There is *my* juggling, my dear', letter to Elsie Moll, 8 December 1908, *Letters of Wallace Stevens*, ed. Holly Stevens, 1966, p. 114).

How many ravishing things whose innocent beauty astounds us

1970–71; 16 in *New York Quarterly* (Winter 1970); 'Shorts II', EG, p. 47; CP, p. 856.

This set of aphorisms in elegiacs consists of thirteen on literature and sixteen on science and sociology (with a number that refer to a customary topic in these years, his critique of the forms of youthful protest, cf. 'Circe'). The ideas of literary timeliness in nos 6 and 7 were elaborated many times by Auden, e.g. in the interview with Daniel Halpern in *Antaeus*, Spring 1972.

All are limitory, but each has her own

April 1970; 'Old People's Home', *New York Review of Books*, 23 June 1970; revised in *10 Poets 10 Poems*, 1971; EG, p. 51; CP, p. 860.

Auden's friend Elizabeth Mayer, dedicatee of 'New Year Letter', suffered a stroke in her eighties and was in an old people's home. Auden visited her regularly, but found the experience depressing (see Carpenter, pp. 431–2). Auden's prayer for a speedy exit from life became a frequent topic of conversation, and reappeared urgently in the last lines of *Epistle to a Godson* (see 'Talking to Myself'). 'Limitory' should probably be 'limitary' (existing on a boundary or leading a limited existence).

Her Telepathic-Station transmits thought-waves

May 1969; 'Circe', *London Magazine*, September 1969; EG, p. 52; CP, p. 861.

'Circe' is a belated rebuke to the flower children of the 1960s, for whom in the popular mind drugs, peace and sex became talismans of unconcern. The poet's opening attempt to involve us all in the possibility of this modern Lotus-eating has been abandoned by the time that we reach the final two stanzas where he is openly admonitory, having argued that libertarian sloganising and a contempt for Conscience and Knowledge can issue, as it were, in a mass-murderer like Charles Manson.

No one now imagines you answer idle questions

June 1971; 'Short One for the Cuckoo', *Atlantic*, August 1972; 'Short Ode to the Cuckoo', EG, p. 54; CP, p. 862.

The magic of the cuckoo's song surpasses its shocking nesting habits ('cuckolding' its host, and so alarming husbands). Auden's annual diary entry in the final stanza is therefore 'of a holy moment' (i.e. significance) because of its pretence at being perennial in the face of 'the death of friends'. This is as close as he can come to the immortality of Shelley's skylark or Keats's nightingale. The 'shout' of the cuckoo is borrowed from Housman (*Last Poems*, XL).

Chaucer, Langland, Douglas, Dunbar with all your

June 1971; 'Ode to the Medieval Poets', *Poetry*, November 1971; EG, p. 55; CP, p. 863.

A poem to celebrate the beginning of summer is dashed by the thought that the poets of Christendom would have done it better, despite a supposed disadvantage in lacking the comforts of our technological age. The sort of modern poet Auden has in mind in stanzas 2–4 is probably Robert Lowell, of whom he morally disapproved.

The Year: 452. The Place: the southern

July 1970; 'An Encounter', *New Statesman*, 15 January 1971; EG, p. 56; CP, p. 864.

Attila was in Northern Gaul in 451. He took Metz and Orleans, and then in 452 took Aquileia, Concordia, Altinum, Vicentia, Verona, Brescia, Bergamo, Milan and Pavia. Pope Leo excused himself from the Council of Chaledon on the grounds of Attila's imminence. He appeared in the barbarian's camp with two distinguished senators, Avienus and Trigetius. After their meeting, Attila recrossed the Julian Alps and died in the following year when preparing an expedition against Constantinople. The reasons for the retreat include factors irrelevant to Auden's speculation (plague, superstition, the offer of tribute, dissension among Attila's heirs) but nor does Auden mention the tradition that St Peter and St Paul appeared to Attila, threatening him with instant death if, as Gibbon put it, 'he rejected the prayer of their successor' (*Decline and Fall of the Roman Empire*, chapter xxxv). This scene, painted by Raphael, would have undermined in its specificity the more intriguing mystery in Auden's poem of 'What can Leo have | actually said?'

Housman was perfectly right

September 1971; 'A Shock', *New Yorker*, 18 March 1972; EG, p. 58; CP, p. 865.

Returning to Kirchstetten, Auden is frisked for weapons at Vienna's airport. The poem does not acknowledge that in the era of aeroplane piracy this is a reasonable precaution, and that a frisking is only 'horrid | or silly' if self-esteem allows you to forget that a hijacking is worse.

Let us praise our Maker, with true passion extol Him

1944; 'Anthem for S. Matthew's Day', folded sheet, 21 September 1946; 'Anthem' (first line added), EG, p. 59; CP, p. 332.

For comment, see p. 434.

Eagerly, Musician

March 1971; 'Hymn to the United Nations', programme of the UN Day concert, 24 October 1971; reprinted in *New York Times* and *Times*, 25 October 1971; published in score, 1972; 'United Nations Hymn', EG, p. 60; CP, p. 827.

As Auden generally acknowledges, lines 32–8 and 41–2 are borrowed from the final nine lines of 'Runner', written in May 1962 and published in *City Without Walls*. Lines 33–4 ('Begotten notes | New notes beget') seem to be a reminiscence of Yeats's 'Byzantium' ('blood-begotten spirits . . . Those images that yet | Fresh images beget') appropriate to Auden's idea of music as a holy and circular locus of transfiguration.

How wonderfully your songs begin

May 1969; 'To Goethe: A Complaint', EG, p. 62; CP, p. 718.

This brief complaint is probably fair enough, since Auden himself never confused nature in his poems with the individual beloved (compare 'Dichtung und Wahrheit' on numinous encounters in the human and in the non-human contexts).

The Road of Excess

1971; 'Contra Blake', EG, p. 62; CP, p. 718.

Compare 'Circe': Blake's Palace of Wisdom (from the Proverbs of Hell in *The Marriage of Heaven and Hell*) is, in Auden's view, no more than her 'secret citadel' of dangerous permissiveness. This is another warning shot fired at a generation who admired Blake for the wrong reasons. Compare Auden's remarks in the Foreword to the *Faber Book of Aphorisms*: '*The road of excess leads to the palace of wisdom* is . . . a valid aphorism if one can safely assume that every reader knows the importance of self-control; one cannot help feeling that, were Blake our contemporary, he would have written *sometimes leads'* (p. vii). The Slough of Despond is from Bunyan's *The Pilgrim's Progress.*

As *quid pro quo* for your enchanting verses,

September 1971; 'A Toast to Professor William Empson on the occasion of his retirement in 1971', EG, p. 63; CP, p. 771.

William Empson retired from his Chair of English at the University of Sheffield at the end of the academic year 1970–71. Empson's poem 'Just a Smack at Auden' had appeared first in *The Year's Poetry 1938* (ed. D. K. Roberts and G. Grigson) and was collected in *The Gathering Storm* (1940): Auden defuses its deliberately needling quality by contrasting verses which 'enchant' with verses which simply 'occur' (or do not occur). He also contrasts Cambridge poetry with Oxford poetry (stanza 3), although his emphasis (stanza 4) is finally on the poets' historical twinning (Empson was just under five months older than Auden) in 'an open-hearthed, nannied, un-T-V'd world, where I cars looked peculiar'. In this respect, the sentiment may be compared with Auden's review of Waugh and Ackerley, 'As It Seemed to Us' (*Forewords and Afterwords*, p. 492).

Gate-crashing ghost, aggressive

August 1971; 'Loneliness', *Atlantic*, September 1972; EG, p. 64; CP, p. 866.

Auden claimed that this poem is formally 'an imitation of a Welsh medieval metre called *cywdd* [sic]' (letter to Nevill Coghill, August 1971). It is not, however, rhymed as it should be, but is instead 'laced with alliterations'. See Joseph P. Clancy, *Medieval Welsh Lyrics* (1965), p. 10: many *cywyddau* are made up almost entirely of descriptive and metaphoric images, with a spiralling or radical structure, rather than a progressive one. The *cywydd deuair hirion* uses a seven-syllable line and a couplet rhyming an unstressed with a stressed syllable, but Clancy claims that normal English rhyme destroys the rhythms of the *cywydd* couplet, and in his translations he uses only the contrast of the stressed and unstressed final syllables. Similarly he retreats from *cynghanedd* as technically impossible, substituting a full use of alliteration and internal rhyme to give some equivalent flavour of the originals. The ebullience of this poem is in deliberate contrast to its theme, or is, rather, an exorcism of it.

From us, of course, you want gristly bones

July 1970; 'Talking to Dogs', *Harper's*, March 1971; *London Magazine*, April–May 1971; EG, p. 66; CP, p. 867.

The poem is written in memory of Auden's Kirchstetten housekeeper's Alsatian (*Poets at Work*, p. 305), but it is as much about dog-owners as dogs (in a letter to E. R. Dodds of 17 July 1970 he said 'I kept thinking of you both as I was writing this'). The poem falls into a series of aphoristic observations, in which it is the quality of objectivity or lack of self-conscious selfhood that makes dogs appeal to humans. The false use of dogs turns them into agents of *our* self-regard.

Plural the verdicts we cast on the creatures we have to shake hands with!

May 1971; 'Talking to Mice', *New York Review of Books*, 2 September 1971; *Poems for Shakespeare* (1972); EG, p. 68; CP, p. 868.

This charming poem of regret and apology for putting down mousetraps plays on the paradox that if the mice were able to understand the poem they could have been educated into social habits that would have saved them. The hexameters lend a slightly jaunty tone to what is in effect a speech of self-exoneration, of domestic *Realpolitik*. To live 'fit-sides' (line 28) is to be on the same footing. To 'obtemper' (line 18) is to restrain. The latter appears in a list of words beginning with 'o' ready culled for use from the OED in the Einschreibbuch notebook of 1965–73 (the immediately following items are 'the ochlocratic media', used in 'Epistle to a Godson', and 'to osse', used in 'Moon Landing'). There are many such lists in late Auden.

Spring this year in Austria started off benign

April 1971; 'Talking to Myself', *New Yorker*, 24 June 1972; EG, p. 70; CP, p. 870.

It was this benign spring of 1971 that turned into the overcast summer of 'Stark bewölkt', but for the moment it provides an environment ('the about') healthy enough ('sane') for Auden to appraise his physical self with some elaboration and equanimity. In stanza 1, 'what is not forbidden is compulsory' is from T. H. White's *The Once and Future King*, chapter xiii (see the *New York Review of Books*, 18 October 1973). The *haiku* of 'Marginalia',

11.4 ('The tyrant's device: | *Whatever Is Possible* | *Is Necessary.*') is a human version of this mineral absolutism. Auden argues for individuation as a form of miracle (stanza 5). He was later to extend this argument in his criticism of the scientific view of the chance origins of human life in 'Unpredictable but Providential' (see p. 546). 'Random my bottom!' is a formula borrowed from the conversation of Brian Howard. The architecture unimposing in profile of stanza 6 is probably phallic rather than facial (see the poem to Kallman of Christmas Day 1941, stanza 9, and 'In Praise of Limestone': 'The blessed will not care what angle they are regarded from'). Abuse of the body, and the body's revenges make up most of the rest of the poem (with some incidental speculation about the body as a political metaphor). The tone is one of respectful acknowledgment of the only partly understood Other, and of the psychosomatic negotiations familiar from Auden's early theories. One is reminded that Auden always believed that the body would win if allowed to present its own case (see 'Balaam and his Ass' in *The Dyer's Hand*, p. 132).

Thank You, Fog

Auden's final volume was posthumously published in 1974. Short in substance at the time of Auden's death, it was filled out with the anti-masque 'The Entertainment of the Senses', written with Kallman, and unlikely according to the poet's usual practice to have been included in a collection of shorter poems. The *haiku* dedication to Michael and Marny Yates confronts forty years of unaging friendship ('None of us are as young'; CP, p. 883). Yates had been in his final year at the Downs School when Auden arrived as a teacher in 1932, and shared the Iceland visit. Auden's 'last poem' is printed by Mendelson in his introductory Note to the volume ('He still loves life'). Two of its exclamations are hypermetrical if it is to be a *haiku*, and, as exclamations, should be 'Oh' not the vocative 'O', of which the sequence of four inevitably recalls Eliot's 'Shakespeherian rag' (*The Waste Land*, ll.128).

Grown used to New York weather

May 1973; 'Thank You, Fog'; *TLS*, 27 July 1973; *Vogue*, October 1974; TYF, p. 13; CP, p. 886.

The title poem of the posthumous collection is grateful for a feature of the English weather which for one week at Christmas kept strangers away. The fellow guests are James and Tania Stern (see p. 357), the hostess Sonia Orwell, the magic number four clearly reminding Auden of the enchanted ring of colleagues in 'A Summer Night' of forty years earlier. Beyond this 'glad circle', however, is not the possible revolution, but simply 'the world of work and money.' Some of Auden's late verbal habits perhaps hinder one's reading of this poem. 'Merle' and 'mavis', for example, are poetic words for blackbird and thrush, but their modern use as girls' names is an impediment to imagining their having been singing their song since Elizabethan times and earlier. In fact, despite the musical and percussive diction, Auden is describing the birds as *not* singing, and there is a momentary and unhelpful ambiguity in the word 'refrain'. A 'sapid' supper would have been good to eat, but the overtones of 'insipid' and 'vapid' suggest otherwise. 'Festination' and 'volant' are key words in Oliver Sacks's *Awakenings*, shown to Auden in proof in February (*A Tribute*, p. 195).

Beckoned anew to a World

August 1972; 'Aubade', *Four Quarters*, Spring 1973; *Oxford Poetry Magazine*, March 1973; *Atlantic*, July 1973; TYF, p. 15; CP, p. 881.

This poem subtitled 'In Memoriam Eugen Rosenstock-Huessy' was originally 'after' this writer first read by Auden in 1939 (Rosenstock-Huessy died in 1973). The poem contrasts the dimension of Place, defined by relationships, and the dimension of Time, defined by choices. It owes much to Rosenstock-Huessy's ideas in his *Speech and Reality* (1970), in which humanity is shown to be formed and made aware of itself by four kinds of speech, orienting us to the past, to the future, to our inner self and to the world outside (see 'Aubade', stanza 1). Society sustains itself in its time and space axes, and it is by human speech that space and time are created. Stanza 2 can be better understood in relation to Rosenstock-Huessy's 'Cross of Reality' as it is known (human self-awareness in four grammatical stages: 'Thou' addresses and creates the future; 'I' is discovered in response; 'We' makes history, returning the gift of having been addressed; 'He' is man as known in the outside world; the idea is summarised by Clinton C. Gardner in his Introduction to *Speech and Reality*, p. 6). For 'there is no Neuter Gender' etc., see *Judaism Despite Christianity*, ed. Rosenstock-Huessy (1969), p. 15 (inanimate objects were addressed as 'thou' in the mythopoeic tribal mentality of the ancient Near East). In stanza 3, Auden's culminating definition of the City as a temporal entity governed by the imperative of listening is also influenced by Rosenstock-Huessy. See *Speech and Reality*, p. 24: '*Audi, ne moriamur*. Listen, lest we die; or: listen and we shall survive is an a priori that presupposes a power in man to establish relations with his neighbour that transcend their private interests.'

Auden's conclusion is not only a version of this *Audi, ne moriamur*, but less obviously a reworking of the troublesome line 'We must love one another or die' from 'September 1, 1939' that triumphantly reasserts human immortality as the condition of being listened to by future generations. Auden must have been grateful for a theory in which the Holy Spirit is so closely identified with the 'speech of mankind'. The reference to Augustine in lines 7–9 is from the *Confessions*, XIII.xi ('sum enim et scio et volo: sum sciens et volens, et scio esse me et velle, et volo esse et scire': 'For I both am, and know, and will: I am knowing and willing; and I know myself to be and to will; and I would both be and know', Loeb edn), a passage providing an analogy for understanding the Trinity.

Spring with its thrusting leaves and jargling birds
is here again

June 1972; 'Unpredictable but Providential', TLS, 2 February 1973; *New Yorker*, 14 April 1973; TYF, p. 17; CP, p. 876.

Auden sent this poem to E. R. Dodds on 15 June 1972, remarking: 'This is rather prosy, I fear, but I wanted to see if I could manage a "Lucretian" sort of poem. My private title is *Contra Monod*.' Jacques Monod (1910–76) was a biochemist, author of *Le Hasard et la nécessité* (1970, translated 1971). Writing to Anne Fremantle about the paradox of believing in both immortality and eternity he complained about the similar paradox of B. F. Skinner thinking that thought is conditioned and went on:

> It's the same with Jacques Monod. Monod is wrong, because the moment you introduce the word random, you can't be objective in stating the theory that you weren't meant to be – except in the case of autistic children. In fact, if everything is random, you cannot possibly be objective about something that is random. I prefer to believe that the invention of photosynthesis is not random but just luck. And I'm sure that Monod must just once in his life have believed, when he heard a voice saying to him 'Thou shalt serve science'.
>
> (*A Tribute*, p. 91)

The poet (like Lucretius in *De Rerum Natura* though with greater brevity) finds himself accommodating the scientist's account of creation with the Christian's. It isn't clear why 'some Original Substance' being given 'a sporting chance' to become 'a Self' (i.e. luck rather than randomness) isn't just as much of a challenge to providence as Monod's theory, and indeed Auden does not avoid describing it as a 'genuine Accident'. From this point on, everything is in the hands of evolution, and Auden keeps the tone light (his geological 'ballet' evokes Disney's *Fantasia*). Gondwana is the hypothetical supercontinent thought to have broken up in Mesozoic or late Palaeozoic times to form most of the present land-masses in the southern hemisphere: Auden's description in lines 15–16 is therefore of the creation of the peninsula of India. (See also my comments on 'Talking to Myself', p. 542.)

For us who, from the moment

June 1973; 'Address to the Beasts', *New Yorker*, 8 October 1973; *London Magazine*, August–September 1974; TYF, p. 19; CP, p. 889.

The first draft version of 'Address to the Beasts' was written in prose paragraphs, and indeed most of its substance is unexceptionally asserted through having been better argued or dramatised elsewhere (e.g. the last stanzas are the starting-point of the Act II, scene iii Chorus of *The Dog Beneath the Skin*, *Plays*, p. 240).

The archeologist's spade

August 1973; 'Archeology', *London Magazine*, August–September 1974; *New York Review of Books*, 12 December 1974; TYF, p. 22; CP, p. 894.

An earlier poem proposed that true history is an account of craftsmen rather than tyrants ('Makers of History', see p. 468). This one goes further in its suggestion that true history is invisible, for our essential being seeks its embodiment out of time altogether. We guess at the disasters that beset our ancestors just as we guess at their myths and rites, but we cannot reconstruct their effect on individuals except by way of understanding the general function of myths and rites as a means of escaping from our temporal individuality ('Only in rites | can we renounce our oddities | and be truly entired').

Sessile, unseeing,

?July 1972; 'Progress?', TYF, p. 25; CP, p. 878.

This short *haiku* series takes creation (plant, beast, man) through the dimensions of their speculative existence. The apparently enlarging horizon is only questionably progressive because man's anxiety is a direct result of the conflict between the spiritual apprehension he possesses as man and the spatial/temporal apprehension he possesses as animal, focused by language, and involving perhaps an ambiguous confusion about the world that his language picture ('the Absent | and Non-Existent') in which the Absconded God can be rationally denied.

Dark was that day when Diesel

July 1972; 'A Curse', *Daily Telegraph Magazine*, 20 October 1972; *Harper's*, April 1973;
TYF, p. 26; CP, p. 882.

Auden's cursing of Rudolf Diesel (1858–1913), inventor of the internal
combustion engine, appeared appropriately enough in the Motor Show
number of the *Daily Telegraph Magazine*. About a dozen years later a version
of the 'odorless and noiseless | staid little brougham' was produced in the
unsuccessful shape of Sir Clive Sinclair's C5. Auden has been proved to be
wrong about passive smoking in line 13. Austin Dobson's 'Little Blue-
Ribbons' was a 'staid little' woman.

How *can* you be quite so uncouth? After sharing

July 1972; 'Ode to the Diencephalon', *New Statesman*, 20 October 1972; *New York
Review of Books*, 30 November 1972; TYF, p. 27; CP, p. 878.

The diencephalon is the middle brain, the most significant part of the brain
stem, where animal instincts are translated into physiological activity. Its
relationship with the cortex (the surface layer of nerve cells in the cerebral
hemispheres which screens information) is a subject which had long
interested Auden (see, for example, his informed criticism in 1930 of
George Dibblee's *Instinct and Intuition: a study in mental duality*, EA, p. 301).
The poem similarly discusses the relative roles of diencephalic instinct and
cortical censorship (see A. T. W. Simeons, *Man's Presumptuous Brain*, 1960,
chapter 2, discussing reactions to danger; Simeons's book is an evolutionary
interpretation of psychosomatic disease).

Pascal should have been soothed, not scared by
his infinite spaces

1972–3; 'Shorts', TYF, p. 28; CP, p. 883.

Inescapably, many of these shorts are observations that have not been
absorbed into longer poems about the relationship of man to animals, or
the ethics of the *polis*. For example, no. 6 contains a point about
stammering very similar to one made in 'Natural Linguistics'. No. 1 refers
to Pascal's pensée 91. No. 2 was sent to Lincoln Kirstein on 10 July 1972
with the title 'The Elements'.

In the Hungry Thirties

February 1965; 'Economics', TYF, p. 31; CP, p. 717.

The paradox of relative need: a 'public' statement to be compared with a private one written in the following month (see 'Glad', the first of the 'Three Posthumous Poems').

It's rather sad we can only meet people

August 1973; 'Posthumous Letter to Gilbert White', *New York Review of Books*, 18 October 1973; *London Magazine*, August–September, 1974; TYF, p. 32; CP, p. 893.

This light poem is a kind of avoidance of the genre of Imaginary Conversation either between White (1720–93) and Henry Thoreau (1817–62), or between Auden himself and White. There is, finally, a double emphasis on the value of reading: it is our substitute for meeting people and avoids all the embarrassments latent in meeting, and it allows us to make fruitful comparisons. It is, therefore, a poem not so much about nature (Auden is dismissive of his expertise here) as about language. Auden quoted White on echoes (Letter XXXVIII, 12 February 1778) in *A Certain World*, p. 143. His other observations in this poem are also found in *The Natural History of Selborne*: the 'joyless stupor' of the tortoise (Letter L, 21 April 1780); the modesty, or rather immodesty, of frogs (Letter XVII, 18 June 1768); in his poem on the subject, the rainbow's 'federal arch' (White acknowledges Genesis ix.12–17); and the musical pitch of owls (Letter X, 1 August 1771).

How broad-minded were Nature and My Parents

July 1973; 'A Contrast', *TLS*, 4 October 1974; TYF, p. 34; CP, p. 892.

The contrast is between the repressive Censor and the aggressive Public Prosecutor of Auden's Personal City, i.e. between suppressed anxiety about the past and haunting anxiety about the future. Auden's conclusion ('Well, well, I | must grin and bear it') is appropriate, of course, because the 'prosecutions', once survived, will become in time the forgotten cases of the Censor.

All of us believe

August 1973; 'The Question', TYF, p. 35; CP, p. 894.

Auden often returned to this question of being unable to imagine one's parents having sex. It is a concept that strangely runs counter to the pure quest of the mental hero (compare 'the deed that has made all the saints' in 'Pascal', stanza 11, or the Whale that maims Ahab as a symbol of the parents-in-bed in *The Enchafèd Flood*, p. 115). It is, in a sense, the donnée of the Intermezzo of *The Bassarids*. Compare Augustine's strange tribute to his parents in the *Confessions*, IX.xiii ('per quorum cernem introduxisti me in hanc vitam, quemadmodum nescio': 'by whose bodies thou broughtest me into this life, though how I know not', Loeb edn). Christ's 'extra' chromosome (the Y chromosome that provides male characteristics) could only have come from male sperm: a parthenogenetic clone of the mother would have had to be female.

I can't imagine

May 1973; 'No, Plato, No', *A Keepsake from the new library at the School of Oriental and African Studies*, 1973; *New York Review of Books*, 1 November 1973; TYF, p. 36; CP, p. 888.

Having thoughts of death, Auden here sees the body as a servant to be dismissed. The duality is familiar in Auden (providing his poetry with many of its significant tensions and temptations). The early aphorism from the 1929 journal (EA, p. 297) states it plainly: 'Body and Soul (Not-Me and Me) can have no independent existence, yet they are distinct, and an attempt to make one into the other destroys.' The poem's vigorous anti-Platonism is defused by the trick of making the body female, perhaps a sign that what has been lost in parting from the mother can in some way be regained. The poet's body is 'Her' not only because it is homosexual, but because it is the greatest gift from the mother, and now belongs with female nature. However, despite Auden's extensive association of nature with the feminine, being restored to Mother Earth is in fact a release from whatever responsibility the female principle carries in organic life ('she' is a servant like Ariel to the poet's Prospero) and can lead only to an undifferentiated material existence (like the mineral world that Auden fictionally inhabits in James Merrill's *The Changing Light at Sandover*). The Arielesque irresponsibility is contrasted with the poet's ludic sense of 'fun' in stanza 1, an Adamic or perhaps Aristotelian existence of naming.

Do squamous and squiggling fish,

July 1972; 'Nocturne', *Journal of Hellenic Studies*, 1973; broadside, 21 February 1974; TYF, p. 37; CP, p. 879.

This night-piece reviews the natural world, 'where *can* and *ought* are the same' (compare 'where what is not forbidden is compulsory' in 'Talking to Myself'). It contrasts the innocence of sharing in that world, and its attendant superstitions, with the ignorance we have inherited along with aeroplanes and telescopes. The form of the poem is the Welsh *cywydd* (see my commentary on 'Loneliness', p. 541).

When pre-pubescent I felt

?May 1973; 'A Thanksgiving', *New York Review of Books*, 12 December 1974; TYF, p. 39; CP, p. 891.

This tribute to his mentors is modelled metrically on Goethe's *Gegenwort* (as Auden admitted to David Luke in a letter of 21 September 1973). The relationship between literary models and life-events is biographically unexceptionable, although the emphases are occasionally odd (Eliot not mentioned; Brecht instructive not in his appeals to social justice but in response to a collapsing economy). It is not clear why 'beeking' is preferable to 'basking', its virtual synonym.

The din of work is subdued

April 1972; 'A Lullaby', *A Tribute to W. H. Auden*, 1973; *New Yorker*, 6 August 1973; TYF, 41; CP, p. 875.

The sexless peace of the age of sixty-five is celebrated in terms familiar from earlier writing (the daring parallel '*Madonna* and *Bambino*' is prefigured in *The Dyer's Hand*, p. 196, where the fat man withdraws from sexual competition 'by combining mother and child in his own person, to become emotionally self-sufficient'; Narcissus as an oldie is prefigured by Narcissus the hunchback and Narcissus the drunk in *The Dyer's Hand*, p. 94). '*Frettolosamente*' means 'hurriedly'. In 'No, Plato, No', the poet's body was female; here it is a baby, to be sung asleep. Auden wrote to E. R. Dodds on 18 May 1972: 'The second stanza of *A Lullaby* is, of course, a bit satiric. The phantasy of being "*sinless and all-sufficient*" is certainly not "rational": I know quite well I am neither.'

The poets tell us of an age of unalloyed felicity
Ladies and gentlemen, you have made most remarkable

1963–4; 'Two *Don Quixote* Lyrics' ('The Golden Age' and 'Recitative by Death'),
TYF, p. 43; CP, p. 719; *Libretti*, pp. 513, 518.

See my commentary on p. 555.

Ladies and gents

September 1973; 'The Entertainment of the Senses', TYF, p. 47; *Libretti*, p. 359.

The anti-masque 'The Entertainment of the Senses', written with Chester
Kallman, was commissioned by the composer John Gardner to be included
in a performance of John Shirley's masque *Cupid and Death* (1653,
performed 1659), planned by the Redcliffe Society. Cost prevented a
staging of the masque, but 'The Entertainment of the Senses' was
performed by itself in a concert version at the Queen Elizabeth Hall on 2
February 1974. In Shirley's masque, Cupid and Death lodge at an inn
where the Chamberlain exchanges their arrows, causing the young to die
and the old to fall in love. He himself is shot by Death, whereupon he falls in
love with the pair of dancing apes that he has been showing at fairs. Auden
asked for the two apes to be replaced by five, who would then represent the
five senses in the anti-masque. Details of authorship are given in *Libretti*, p.
739, but in broad terms Kallman was responsible for the Second and Third
Apes and for the refrain. '*Mild und Leise*' ('Kind and gentle') is the opening
of Isolde's *Liebestod* in *Tristan und Isolde*, although Auden naughtily referred
Gardner to Chabrier's *Souvenirs de Munich* as a musical model.
   The anti-masque attacks the mechanical debasement of modern life,
particularly in the sphere of the erotic. The audience is reminded of the
dismal quality of sensual enjoyments now available: genuine simulated
sealskin briefs, deodorised skin, battery chickens, transistor radios, and so
on. Hardly in the vanguard of satire, the attack is dissipated by the jaunty
anapaestic prosody associated with the genre (compare the acolytes'
masque in *Volpone*). The ultimate point of the piece is that it is hardly even
worth it to be an honest sensualist, since Death awaits everyone, but this
message is obscured by a repeated illogicality in the apes' refrain which
contains a perverse double negative ('You'd be wiser | Not to be
defenceless') running counter to their injunction to be 'with-it, with-it,
with-it till you're dead'. The lines about Elizabeth David and Jane Grigson

were omitted in the setting for reasons of ephemerality (Gardner to Kallman, 3 February 1974). The joke about Isolde discovering that 'We must love one another *and* die!' is both belated and trivialising, since there was never a moment's danger in 'September 1, 1939' of a confusion between Eros and Agape (see p. 292).

Uncollected Poems 1949–73

A friend, who is not an ascetic

Autumn 1950; of the eight limericks published in *As I Walked Out One Evening*, nos 1, 'A friend, who is not an ascetic' and 3, 'After vainly invoking the Muse', were published with variations in Farnan, pp. 205–6; no. 2, 'A Young Person came out of the mists', in HC, p. 69; and nos 5, 'T. S. Eliot is quite at a loss', and 7, 'To get the Last Poems of Yeats', in HC.

In no. 1 the smallest of the elves is of course a phallic joke (Auden was at times concerned about the size of his penis; see also my comments on 'Talking to Myself', p. 543). There is another version of no. 6 in circulation in which the Bishop-Elect is given an internally rhyming 'dong'.

How serene and jolly it is to sit here

September 1953; 'Il Bar Internazionale', Callan, p. 225; *W. H. Auden a Forio* (1984), p. 23.

Written for Maria Senese, proprietor of the Bar Internazionale in the main square of Forio, Ischia, these sapphics form a graceful visitors book compliment. By 'the third sex' Auden clearly means homosexuals, although the traditional meaning, as in Byron's *Don Juan*, v.xxvi, is 'neuters', particularly clergymen.

Out of a dream of ease and indolence

November–December 1963; 'Lyrics for *Man of La Mancha*', *Antaeus*, Winter–Spring 1981, contains: (1) 'Highway to Glory Song: Out of a dream of ease and indolence'; (2) 'Don Quixote's Credo: A true Knight, worthy of the name'; (3) 'Song of the Barber: There's some magic influential'; (4) 'Song of the Enchanters: Little Knight, you are amusing' ('Song of the Ogres', *Two Songs*, 1968; *New Statesman*, 1 August 1969; CW, p. 47); (5) 'The Golden Age: The poets tell us of an age of unalloyed felicity' (TYF, p. 44); (6) 'Sancho Panza's Dream: I dreamed of an island where I was a Governor' ('Highway to Glory: Sancho's Version', TS); (7) 'Song of the Quest: Once the voice has quietly spoken, every Knight must ride alone'; (8) 'Song of

Dejection: There's a buzz in my ears crying: "Is there a point in these" '; (9) 'Let's get together, folks!' ('Song of Folly', TS; 'Song of the Clown', Wasserman TS); (10) 'The progress you have made is very remarkable' ('Recitative by Death', TYF, p. 46); (11) 'In my game of winning'; (12) 'Since Social Psychology replaced Theology' ('Song of the Devil: Ever since observation taught me temptation', CW, p. 48); (13) 'We must go now'; (14) 'Song of the Knight of the Mirrors: Look! Unlearn your bookish lore'; (15) 'Don Quixote's Farewell: Humor me no longer, Sancho; faithful Squire, all that is past'; (16) 'Finale: Good-bye, now, and good luck! Enjoy your liberty!'; *Libretti*, p. 507.

Auden and Kallman were commissioned by Dale Wasserman in 1963 to write the songs for a musical version of his television play *I, Don Quixote*. The existing songs (all by Auden) were not considered suitable, and *Man of La Mancha* was premièred in 1965 with lyrics by Joe Darion. It is clear from Wasserman's account of the collaboration in the *Los Angeles Times*, 5 March 1978, that it was Auden's traditional view of Quixote as a victim of comic delusions who has to repent of his folly that caused his work to be dropped. Wasserman took the view that Quixote's 'impossible dream' is 'a madness we happen to need'. However, it is also clear from Auden's distinction between Quixotic Madness and Tragic or Comic Madness in *The Dyer's Hand*, p. 451, or his treatment of it as holy madness (*The Dyer's Hand*, p. 136), that the Don's delusions are at the heart of his interpretation of Cervantes's novel as a celebration of the ironic Christian hero. Wasserman's romantic version would simply sentimentalise this critical position.

(1) introduces the theme of a quest for 'our heart's desire' (references at the head of some of the songs are to act and page number of the Wasserman play). (2) sets out Quixote's belief in the virtues and responsibilities of the Knight Errant. (3) simply recounts the modern role of the chameleon-like talkative barber. (4) was revised for *City Without Walls*, the 'Enchanters' (i.e. human agents like Don Ferdinand and his companions in *Don Quixote*, 1.46) becoming 'Ogres'. Readers who happened to remember 'Letter to Lord Byron', II, might have thought the song written thirty years earlier, with its version of the Burns stanza and the resurrection in Gus of the earlier version of the average man that he found in the work of Disney or Strube ('Little fellow', substituted for 'Little Knight', was a common term for Chaplin's tramp). The difference is that in 1936 the average man was content with his role as 'the ogre's private secretary', since he subconsciously needed the ogre to support his vain dreams of heroism. Quixote acts as well as dreams. (5) is the Don's view of the 'Enchanters' and is a version of the Fall (Quixote's speech about the

Golden Age when eating acorns with the goatherds in chapter 11 is the obvious model for this trisyllabically-rhymed lyric). (6) concerns Sancho's dream of his long-promised island governorship, which by virtue of a practical joke arranged by the Duke and Duchess is actually given to him in II.42. Sancho's speech of resignation as he mounts his donkey Dapple once more is in II.53. Interestingly, there is an early Auden reference to this whole episode in Po's speech in *Paid on Both Sides* (*Plays*, p. 23), and see *The Dyer's Hand*, p. 137, for Auden's view of Sancho as a 'holy' realist in this matter. (7) is Quixote's view of the difficulties and uncertainties of the Quest. As an ironic Quest hero he does not quite conform to any of the types presented in 'The Quest' in *The Double Man*. The song borrows the 'Bridge of Dread' from 'For the Time Being' (CP, p. 368, itself borrowed from the 'Lyke-Wake Dirge'). (8) is a further reprise of the opening song, at a moment of self-doubt. (9) to (13) occur in the Interlude of Folly, Death and Sin, each of these allegorical personages singing in turn. Their promptings give evidence of Auden's hatred of noise, drugs and speed at this time, and the tone of the verse looks forward to the largely unsuccessful demotic of 'The Entertainment of the Senses'. Sin's song was given a new first stanza for its appearance as 'Song of the Devil' in *City Without Walls*. Formally, it embodies one of the weaknesses of most of the songs: as a series of choruses without a refrain, it makes few concessions to the structural demands of popular music. Many of the ideas in the song (on Social Psychology replacing Theology, for example, or on Free-Will) may be traced back to 'New Year Letter', though Sin's principal weapon here, his Market Research view of morality, seems to be new. (14) refers to the episode of the 'Knight of the Mirrors', i.e. Sampson Carrasco attempting to trick the Don into returning home, in *Don Quixote*, II.12–13. (15) is Don Quixote's farewell (*Don Quixote*, II.74) and (16) a choric Finale, a further reprise of the opening song.

At break of dawn

July 1964; 'Aubade' ('Three Posthumous Poems' II), CP76, p. 562; CP, p. 747.

The aubade is a dawn love-song: this example is deliberately and crudely direct in its *carpe diem* theme, with the poet's sexual tastes providing the key to the metaphor (a widow because of the death of available erections seems to be the idea). This is the earliest of three poems on sexual subjects which Auden, calling them 'posthumous poems' in letters to friends, did not rule out for such eventual publication. Together with one of the addenda to 'Profile' (and with his poems in German and the openly self-indulgent 'The Platonic Blow') they share the distinction of being poems that directly recognise the poet's own homosexuality.

Hugerl, for a decade now

March 1965; 'Glad' ('Three Posthumous Poems' I), CP76, p. 561; CP, p. 746.

The 'posthumous' sexual poems have a melancholy air of erotic self-consolation in the context of the abandoned physical relationship with Kallman. This poem (called, on one TS, 'H. K. 1965') is the most considerable of them, because the relationship is the most complex, Auden learning (stanza 4) to treat Hugerl as something more than a hustler ('*Strich*'; a '*Freier*' is a client; '*es ist mir Wurscht*' means 'it is all one to me') after being burgled by him. The background to the relationship may be found in Carpenter (pp. 396 and 403): Hugerl was working-class, and he married Christa. Auden claims to be happy with this arrangement, and the final words are defiant, though significantly (and unusually) ambiguous. The plain meaning of them would seem to be 'if prudish people purse their lips, it's all one to me', but the sense of 'mump' = 'to sponge' refuses, in Hugerl's presence, to go away.

When one is lonely (and You,

?1967; 'Minnelied' ('Three Posthumous Poems' III), CP76, p. 562; CP, p. 747.

The *Minnelied* was a medieval German love-song. Kallman knows why Auden is lonely and is presumably meant to feel sorry that only the hired gratification of a call-boy can prevent him from envying the audible sexual activity of cats. Behind the rebuke somewhere one senses an intention to feel tender toward Bert (compare 'Glad') but the intention has been lost. Bert fulfils a function comparable to that of memory in 'Since', and the reader may be interested to compare these poems.

Index of Titles and First Lines

Figures in **bold** refer to main entries.

General Index